MAGILL'S
LITERARY ANNUAL
1996

MAGILL'S LITERARY ANNUAL 1996

*Essay-Reviews of 200 Outstanding Books
Published in the United States during 1995*

With an Annotated Categories List

Volume Two
Na-Z

Edited by
FRANK N. MAGILL

SALEM PRESS
Pasadena, California   Englewood Cliffs, New Jersey

LIBRARY OF CONGRESS CATALOG CARD NO. 77-99209
ISBN 0-89356-296-3

FIRST PRINTING

PRINTED IN THE UNITED STATES OF AMERICA

MAGILL'S
LITERARY ANNUAL
1996

NATIVE SPEAKER

Author: Chang-Rae Lee (1948-   )
Publisher: Riverhead Books (New York). 324 pp. $22.95
Type of work: Novel
Time: The late twentieth century
Locale: El Paso, Texas, and New York City and suburbs

A Korean American man grapples with the personal difficulties of marriage, family bonds, and parenthood while discovering the public difficulties of politics in a multicultural society

> *Principal characters:*
> HENRY PARK, a Korean American working as a cultural spy
> LELIA, his wife, a white American and a speech therapist
> DENNIS HOAGLAND, the founder of the spying firm
> JACK KALANTZAKOS, another operative, Henry's friend
> EMILE LUZAN, a Filipino psychoanalyst
> JOHN KWANG, a Korean American politician in New York City

In this first novel, Chang-Rae Lee, who teaches writing, discovers provocative strategies to describe what seems to be an inarticulate sense of unease permeating the psyche of the narrator and protagonist, Henry Park, the son of Korean immigrants. One theme, captured simply and eloquently by the title, has to do with differences in the way language is used. Another much more disturbing and original metaphor is that of spying.

The nonlinear narrative of the novel begins on an intimate, personal note, as Lelia, married to Henry for several years, is leaving him. In a muted parody of a list of goals and achievements to strive for, she leaves Henry instead with a list of his characteristics, most of them flaws, that she has compiled over the previous year. The list, it turns out, represents an intersection of the personal and professional in his life, including such descriptions as "emotional alien," "Yellow peril: neo-American," "stranger/follower/traitor/spy." Later, he discovers another scrap of paper with the phrase "False speaker of language."

Since none of these terms makes much sense in the first five pages, they serve as a wonderful hook to pull the reader in, searching for their meanings. The story of the Parks' marriage starts in El Paso, Texas, at a party, where Henry's extreme self-consciousness and anxious behavior attract Lelia. She drives a pickup truck delivering canned food and clothes for a relief agency; she gives English lessons to the many Mexicans and Asians on her route, for in that town everyone wants to learn English. Lelia and Henry are conscious of each other as speakers. Henry is attracted to her because she can really speak; he finds himself listening closely to her and pictures her "executing the language" word by word, every letter with a border. Lelia, in turn, tells him that he looks like someone listening to himself, very careful, attentive—not, she guesses, a native speaker.

The theme of the incredible challenge and power of language is handled with deft skill throughout the novel. Lelia becomes a speech therapist, making it her life's work to help children learn to speak English and thereby participate in the culture. The Parks' marriage is rocked by at least one obvious tragedy, the accidental death of their only child, Mitt, but flounders because of Henry's inability to articulate his devastation in a way that Lelia can understand. He, meanwhile, struggles with the cultural and generational difficulties of language use.

The portrayal of Henry's parents, particularly his father, blends into what might be described as the sociological coloring of this novel. His father, a highly educated Korean, comes to the United States, joins a Korean money club, opens a fruit and vegetable stand, works long and hard hours, uses his family to help him, prospers and expands, and provides generously for his family's comfort. Yet he must be watchful and suspicious of members of other ethnic groups who come to his stores, and the more he prospers, the fewer close friends he has.

Oddly, this father and Henry's love-hate feelings toward him sound like literary clichés even before there is enough fiction about Korean American families to allow for any portrayal to be a cliché. In part, such familiarity is a tribute to the universality of the father-son theme, the immigrant-making-good theme, and, more unhappily, the unfavorable media attention focused on the conflict between Korean American and African American communities.

Ironically, the father himself recognizes the extent to which his account of his personal story may simply pander to or reiterate the public narrative: "Knowing what every native loves to hear, he would have offered the classic immigrant story, casting himself as the heroic newcomer, self-sufficient, resourceful." Within the family, language is used to conceal and lie, with the deadliest affection. The mother's liver cancer and treatments are covered with various stories as the disease progresses, with talk of regular Saturday meetings and finally of an incurable Korean fever, to protect their son from the tragic knowledge.

The degree to which speaking and silence can be viewed so differently as a cultural and gender issue crystallizes in the depiction of the father's relationship with the poor Korean woman who comes to run the household after Henry's mother dies. She does not speak English; indeed, she hardly speaks at all and is even nameless. Henry refers to her as Ahjuhma, a form of address to an unrelated woman, and knows her by no other name. Lelia finds it utterly appalling that the two men can be so cavalier about the identity of the woman who serves them for twenty years. Henry cannot explain it to her, understanding only that it is an appalling situation for Americans who live on a first-name basis. In the regimented and rigorous Korean language, he thinks, there are no moments when the woman's name would come out naturally; even his parents addressed each other by titles, not personal names.

Apart from these specific cultural differences in the ways language is used, Henry acknowledges changes required by context. Koreans, he recognizes, "depend too often on the faulty honor of silence, use it too liberally and for gaining advantage." He himself, not unnaturally, has inherited the facility to use language to meet the expectations of others. It seems almost inevitable that he drifts into working for an espionage firm with the name Glimmer and Company. He is recruited by the founder,

Dennis Hoagland, who claims to have recognized a growth industry when he saw one in the mid-seventies: The new wave of immigrants at the time created a need for a firm specializing in "ethnic coverage." The firm handles requests for information about immigrants in the United States from multinational corporations, foreign governments, and interested individuals. Henry becomes a skillful operative, "contriving intricate and open-ended emotional conspiracies" with selected subjects and writing extensive reports analyzing their background and psychological profiles and providing sundry bits of information.

The theme of the use—as well as misuse, abuse, and withholding—of language is thus seen to spiral outward into the communal, political arena. The metaphor of espionage is striking, strongly evoking the sense of paranoia, cynicism, betrayal, alienation, and loneliness so familiar in twentieth century life and literature and perhaps even more endemic among those transplanted into an alien culture.

The artistic skill Lee demonstrates in integrating the notion of the "native speaker," with all that it evokes of belonging in the language one speaks, with the larger communal and political action of spying is both wonderfully creative and puzzling. The inevitable question arises, what motivates this basically kind and well-intentioned man to make a living sidling up to strangers, befriending them only to betray them?

Henry's insights result from failure. The major job described in the novel, the culminating act of Henry's career, is his infiltration into the political organization of John Kwang, a Korean American preparing to run for mayor of New York City. Before that, however, Henry dwells much on a failure that haunts him: his investigation of Emile Luzan, a Filipino psychoanalyst who ultimately dies in what is termed an accident, after Henry's reports have been presented. His "failure" as a professional is that he allows himself to get too close to his prey. Though the operatives are encouraged to create personas close to their own lives, they cannot afford to cross the thin line between using the details of their lives for a job and living those details.

Getting too close to Luzan, revealing intimacies of his troubled relationships, forgetting, in short, that he is acting as a patient of the psychoanalyst and instead *becoming* a patient—this is the cardinal professional sin Henry commits. Dennis and his friend Jack watch over him vigilantly thereafter to prevent any more "breakdowns." In Henry's investigation of "his own kind" there is a strange echo of Henry's father's success, and the success of other immigrants who exploit fellow immigrants.

An eerie connection between "native," "speaker," and "spy" begins to emerge. The last job Henry can stand to do is to report on John Kwang, a charismatic leader, whose initials, J.K., and political fortunes mirror (though less successfully) the political vicissitudes of an illustrious, longer-established Irish American family. Henry joins the band of dedicated young people who have committed their political energies to Kwang. With its multiethnic makeup, this group of supporters is an accurate microcosm of the kind of coalition needed to elect him. Struggling to refute the limiting label of "special interest" candidate, Kwang also must "tell the story" of the grocers and small businessmen, many Korean, who send in the small contributions that add up to pay his campaign expenses. The connection between Kwang's experiences as a politician in a major multiethnic American city and Henry's father as a newly arrived immigrant grocer is obvious. Yet Kwang must transcend the story to appeal to other groups if he is to survive politically.

This particular story fails. Perhaps Kwang is not the "native speaker" he needs to be, not tuned in enough to political customs and ways of doing business. His political downfall comes from both his own weakness and the weaknesses of cultural systems in competition. Driving drunk with a young woman, an illegal alien, in the passenger seat, he is involved in an accident. The scandal grows with the suggestion that the contributions to his campaign, functioning very much like the *ggeh* or money club that enabled Henry's father and many other Koreans to succeed, are a matter of concern to both the Internal Revenue Service, because of tax issues, and the Immigration and Naturalization Services (INS), because the contributions help identify unregistered aliens. An INS sweep effectively kills Kwang's career, for it is the ultimate betrayal in his community.

Father figure though he may be, Kwang also serves as a doppelgänger, or double, for Henry. Adroitly using the "they-all-look-alike" stereotype, the author suggests the spiritual connection between the two men. Henry finds himself mistaken for Kwang when he scouts neighborhoods prior to a campaign effort. Like the other campaign workers, Henry is mesmerized by Kwang, perhaps enchanted by this revelation of how a Korean American male can function in American society. For the narrator/ protagonist of *Native Speaker*, the aspect of the double in John Kwang is ultimately therapeutic. Though seemingly in shock at the tragic reverberations brought about by his reports, Henry benefits by letting go of his job as a cultural spy. He leaves the firm and, momentarily adrift, joins Lelia in her work as a speech therapist for young children who are not native speakers. He becomes the Speech Monster, a job he likes. As the novel ends, Henry seems to be on the way to working through his demons, the cultural in the personal.

Henry and Lelia's story ends on a somber note. The classic immigrant tale his father told to please the "natives" does not work right now, if it ever wholly did. Henry and Lelia's story proceeds differently because it is not about making money, not about becoming prosperous or making it at all costs. In a way, it is the aftermath of the first story, about what it means to be a "native," about belonging—to oneself, one's love, family, friends, community.

The city, embodying the larger community, has hired Lelia to teach English as a second language, but Lelia has too many children in her class to be able to make a difference in their speech. All she can do is show them something that Henry needed to learn growing up, that language is fun and it is perfectly fine to "mess it all up." For these newcomer children, the native-born Henry is a wonder. To them, he perceives, his voice moves in time with his mouth, truly belonging to his face. In the last phrase of the novel, "I hear her speaking a dozen lovely and native languages, calling all the difficult names of who we are," Henry may be passing along an epiphany about the varieties of "native" and of "speech."

Shakuntala Jayaswal

Sources for Further Study

Booklist. XCI, February 15, 1995, p. 1059.
Boston Globe. April 16, 1995, p. 27.
The Chronicle of Higher Education. XLI, April 7, 1995, p. A6.
Library Journal. CXX, February 1, 1995, p. 98.
Los Angeles Times Book Review. March 19, 1995, p. 3.
New Statesman and Society. VIII, August 25, 1995, p. 32.
The New York Times Book Review. C, April 9, 1995, p. 24.
The New Yorker. LXXI, July 10, 1995, p. 76.
Publishers Weekly. CCXLII, January 9, 1995, p. 54.
The Times Literary Supplement. October 27, 1995, p. 23.
USA Today. May 12, 1995, p. D5.

NEW AND SELECTED POEMS

Author: Gary Soto (1952-   )
Publisher: Chronicle Books (San Francisco). 177 pp. $22.95; paperback $12.95
Type of work: Poetry

A superb selection of Soto's poems published during the course of nearly twenty years

In this collection, which includes twenty-three poems gathered here for the first time, Gary Soto records the textures and meanings of his life and those of friends and strangers with whom he shares the San Joaquin Valley and Fresno, California, and trips to Mexico as a tourist. He seeks and finds evocations of meaning in the details of those lives, those places, those avatars of the quotidian, exploring themes of childhood awareness; of place—fields, lots, streets, houses, and nature in mostly quite small segments—and its impact on people; of work, particularly the hard physical hoeing and picking work of the Mexican field hand, often in contrast with the hard mental labor of the poet; of the consequences of that work on the people and the community; of nature expressed in rain, insects, clouds, heat; of the life of poverty; of eating and feeding; of religion and belief, the manifestations of something beyond the physical. In its close and attentive observation of the details of nature both urban and rural, Soto's poetry is full of such images as "a windowsill of flies," "the leaves of cotton plants/ Like small hands waving good-bye," "an unstrung necklace/ Of dead flies," and ants, many ants, "a leash of ants," "the scurry of red ants at my feet," "words like the march of ants," and statements such as "A scurry of ants searched for a living." Taken together, it seems clear that the insect images, especially those of the ants, suggest the Mexican-Chicano workers themselves and the complex of meanings that they have as a result of society's particular construction of them and their construction of themselves.

Another recurring image is embodied in the verb "unravel." In "The First," an elegy offering tribute to Native Americans, descendants of the first human inhabitants of the land, Soto images

> The beaver curling
> Into handbags;
> Their lakes bruised
> Gray with smoke
> That unraveled from cities.

The coming-apart force is both active and passive in its destructiveness. In another poem, "Chuy" (Chicano) sits,

> Spoon in hand,
> Striking the ants
> That unraveled
> From spools of dark
> Holes.

In "Mission Tire Factory, 1969," the contrasts between the affluent and the working class are figured ironically, with images from television shows such as *Ozzie and Harriet* and *The Donna Reed Show* contrasting with the gut-busting work the laborers do in the tire factory:

> And today the world
> Still plots, unravels with
> Piano lessons for this child,
> Braces for that one.

The tire factory worker, the field worker, the packing-plant worker grow old, as in "The Seventieth Year." "We hear you want to die," the speaker says to "Grandpa," an old man who has been without work since Sun-Maid closed. The speaker assures him, ironically, that life goes on, that "ants unravel/ From their dark holes in the trees." Yet even the poet in the poem "Old Prof with Both Hands on the Rail" sees that "now, at this age, burst veins unravel/ On my nose."

Another quality of Soto's verse is a strong narrative line. An excellent example is the dramatic monologue "The Tale of Sunlight," from his book by the same name. The narrator tells a memory to his nephew, a story of his personal encounter with the supernatural. The poem opens with a natural, direct injunction:

> Listen, nephew.
> When I opened the cantina
> At noon
> A triangle of sunlight
> Was stretched out
> On the floor
> Like a rug
> Like a tired cat.

The light was no ordinary light, and as the speaker tells the story, he opened the shutters, but the "pyramid/ Of whiteness/ Was simply brighter." Astonished, he did not open the cantina for business but sat down at a table to watch the light silently as it crossed the floor to hang on the wall. A fly settled on it and disappeared in a puff of smoke. The man tapped it with a broom and spat on it; "the broom vanished./ The spit sizzled." He avows the truth of this encounter to his nephew and as testament offers his finger:

> This pink stump
> Entered the sunlight,
> Snapped off
> With a dry sneeze,
> And fell to the floor
> As a gift to the ants
> Who know me
> For what I gave.

The power of this poem lies partly in the spare simplicity of the narration and partly in the clarity of the images of the spiritual force, evoking at once ecstatic visions of the Godhead as pure light and the sacrifices of the curious faithful as they seek, as all people seek, to understand the "blank eye" of God toward the suffering of the Mexican field worker whom the ants know "for what I gave."

The spirit world is explored elsewhere in Soto's early poems, in other sorts of visitations—for example, the troubled revenant in "Spirit," his father's ghost, making his presence known with "cemetery grass" and moved furniture, the grandmother who responded by dropping to her knees, kissing the rosary, and repeating prayers "until a white paste/ Gathered in the corners/ Of her mouth"; the old beliefs in ghosts and in the power of ritual to assuage them is fully enacted in this poem. In "Braly Street," which appeared first in *The Elements of San Joaquin* (1973), the narrator visits the dying neighborhood where he had lived during his early childhood with his parents, a neighborhood bulldozed to make room for redevelopment after his uncle and his father died in 1957 and 1958. The loss is of place, life, faith, but there is a gain too—of pain, of memory, love, family. One will not find a religion or religious life unfolded here in terms of church and priest. It is first and finally at immediate, experiential levels that Soto's religious life finds expression and is most convincing.

Through a series of recurring images and themes, Soto suggests his ethos. As noted, the recurring image of "unraveling" appears in poems across the full spectrum of his work. In "Chuy," a long "portrait" poem—one of a number selected from *Where Sparrows Work Hard* (1981)—Chuy's purposeless activity contrasts severely with that of the ants, who do not, it would seem, feel the despair that is a daily presence in the lives of Mexican workers. That "Chuy" is a portrait of despair is argued in each of the scenes describing his activities as he wanders in the shadows of his world, having bottled a number of odd objects including a leaf, a thread, and a lock of his hair, labeled the bottle with his name, and buried it,

> So when the sun
> Is a monocle
> Pocked gray
> And earth is lost
> To shadow, an explorer
> Far from the stars
> Would know where he steps
> Stepped Chuy, stooping
> Among the ruins.

One would like to think that the ending of this poem somehow suggests a kind of final affirmation for Chuy, that even his life makes a mark that will be seen and pondered. Yet for now, the dominant idea is that society, the context in which Chuy and his fellow Chicanos operate, is a culture in ruins, his life one transported

> By telephone,
> By rumor,

> By the shoe
> That grinned ratlike
> All the way
> To death.

What Soto does well and consistently is to transform gritty, closely observed reality into something informing, something meaningful, something made sacramental by the power of the poet's vision. Another contemporary Latino poet, Victor Hernandez Cruz, has argued in the PBS television series *The Language of Life*, narrated by Bill Moyers, that the power of language can stop politicians and knock down walls. Soto's poetic language may not stop politicians or knock down walls, but it certainly can evoke with an aching intensity particular days and particular events in one's life—an equally useful result. For example, in "Finding a Lucky Number," another dramatic mono-logue, this one from *Black Hair* (1985), the poet narrates to a twelve-year-old some events in his life when he himself was twelve, the specific sensory detail of rolling

> chocolate
>
> In my mouth. . . .
> And a dog was staring into a paint bucket
> And a Mexicano was raking
> Spilled garbage into a box.

Thus Soto creates a texture of that day when he encountered a group of Italian men "clicking dominoes/ At a picnic table" and is told by one that twelve is a lucky number. There is nothing cataclysmic here, only Soto's remarkable capacity to evoke a scene.

In "Old House in My Fortieth Year," in the "New Poems" section, Soto returns to the theme of transience and mutability that periodically attracts his attention in such poems as "Small Town with One Road," "Apple," and "A Better View"—a fear, it would seem, of making merely one slip and thus returning to his origins, to the field, to marching again along "a long row of cotton/ Or beets," or being homeless: "I'm the man pushing a cart." Such fears are not unique to Soto. Anyone who has moved out of his or her "class" or "traditional occupation," whether farming or being a laborer, knows moments of fear when it is apparent just how thin a line separates the homeless person from oneself. Hoeing cotton or writing poetry, picking fruit or teaching classes at the university, one must ask from time to time just what it is that separates one activity from the other. With the academic recession of the late 1980's and the decade of the 1990's—especially severe in California, a state that once led the nation in education at all levels—any academic has to reflect with Soto on the tenuousness of his or her position.

Yet something deeper is hinted at in "Old House in My Fortieth Year." "By fortune, I'm now at home in this body": such a line brings up memories of the wheel of fortune, turning one now up, now down. Civilization is never far, Soto reminds us, from the plague, the horde of advancing barbarians, their upraised swords gleaming in the morning sun. Security depends on the "heart down to business/ And slapping blood through its swinging door."

The next poems, "Waterwheel," "Afternoon Memory," and "A Better View," all iterate a theme of Heraclitean flux, the unpredictability of life, and some of the strategies one uses to cope with its half-realized presence. Blood drips from a gash in the finger inflicted when a ten-year-old climbs on a roof to see the world from a better vantage point. Blood, the stuff of life, the surety of the heart's working, drips because "all you wanted was a better view—/ Glimpse of the water tower and tall factory,/ The kind of beauty that shimmers on a pool in summer." Yet seeing "too much/ Of a world truant with disease" makes a youngster grow up too fast and write wonderful, fact-filled, image-packed, closely observed, gritty poems of and by and out of that diseased world, makes the forty-year-old worry about security and change and think back on times of simple lust in a barn or on a sofa, or of the simple joy of eating the flesh of a sweet orange. Soto makes his poems celebrate and mourn the world, as both paean and elegy to it and to one—to all—who pass through it.

New and Selected Poems articulates Soto's vision compellingly. This volume should be read both for its retrospective quality and for the power of its vision and music.

Theodore C. Humphrey

Sources for Further Study

Library Journal. CXX, May 1, 1995, p. 100.
Los Angeles Times Book Review. May 21, 1995, p. 10.
Ploughshares. XXI, Spring, 1995, p. 188.
Poetry. CLXVII, December, 1995, p. 156.
Publishers Weekly. CCXLII, March 27, 1995, p. 79.
San Francisco Chronicle. November 19, 1995, p. B11.
Voice of Youth Advocates. XVIII, October, 1995, p. 260.

THE NEXT AMERICAN NATION
The New Nationalism and the Fourth American Revolution

Author: Michael Lind (1962-   )
Publisher: Free Press (New York). 436 pp. $25.00
Type of work: History; current affairs

A scathing critique of multicultural America in the context of a revisionist reading of the American past and a vision of what might be the American future

For those who live, actually or spiritually, inside the Beltway of Washington, D.C., a political change of heart becomes the stuff of high drama, even when the protagonist is hardly known beyond the limits of the federal district. Thus it was, not too long ago, with Michael Lind. Still in his early thirties, Lind had risen to a position of some eminence within conservative circles, especially among conservative Washington insiders—circles within a circle, one might say—assuming the role of executive editor of *The National Interest*, a conservative journal highly influential among the sorts of people likely to be influenced by a journal.

Then, in the winter, 1995, issue of *Dissent* (apply here the description previously given of *The National Interest*, substituting "liberal" for "conservative"), Lind's article "The Death of Intellectual Conservatism" announced to a small but excruciatingly attentive world the author's denunciation of conservatism and many of its works. Conservatism, said Lind, is intellectually bankrupt. Within weeks Lind was enjoying a celebrity that promised to extend beyond the Beltway. Readers unlikely to encounter him in *The National Interest* or *Dissent* found Lind the object of excited attention in *The New Republic*, *The New York Review of Books*, *Harper's*, *The New Yorker*—indeed, even *The Village Voice*.

That Lind seemed to be moving left when the elections of 1994 suggested to many that the country was moving right added piquancy to the story. Moreover, Lind proved an engagingly articulate defector. Not satisfied merely to abandon his conservative allegiances, he quickly went to work developing, more or less in public, a liberal alternative. *The Next American Nation: The New Nationalism and the Fourth American Revolution* is the culmination of that process, even if it is not the end of its author's ideological odyssey.

Responses to the book from left, right, and center often treat it as a chapter in the story outlined above. *The Washington Post* calls Lind the apostate avenger. A headnote to a favorable review in the *Boston Globe* salutes the vision of a convert to liberalism. The conservative monthly *Commentary* assigns to a negative review the title "About Face." Some express uncertainty as to the exact terms of Lind's turnabout. For Ellen Willis, in the left-oriented *The Nation*, Lind remains an unreconstructed neoconservative. If readers are confused on this point, it is because neoconservatism as a movement has deconstructed; people have forgotten what a neoconservative formerly sounded like. Is it a symptom of clarity or of confusion that one reviewer hailed Lind as spokesman of the radical center? This emphasis may no doubt be justified, but it would be a pity if it blinded readers to the importance of the book as a valuable, if by no means flawless, contribution to America's ever-evolving public philosophy.

The book makes a number of controversial claims, some of them regarding divisive issues of the time, but it is possible that none is more controversial than the hardly explosive assertion that America is indeed a nation, a concrete historical community whose members share a common language, common folkways, and a common vernacular culture. In making this claim, Lind opposes the multiculturalists, for whom there is no single American culture, and the democratic universalists, for whom America is the embodiment of an ideal. Both these positions, by the way, are more than adequately represented among Lind's reviewers.

Lind further distinguishes his position, which he calls liberal nationalism, from nativism, which requires some sort of racial or religious test for membership in the nation. He establishes historical roots for his position in the strong-state nationalism of George Washington, Alexander Hamilton, Daniel Webster, Abraham Lincoln, and Theodore Roosevelt, in the New Deal liberalism of Franklin Roosevelt, Harry Truman, and Lyndon Johnson, and in the color-blind racial integrationism of Frederick Douglass and Martin Luther King, Jr. Liberal nationalism, he argues, offers a new understanding of the American past, based on a realistic analysis of the three republics that have shaped American history.

The first of these, Anglo-America, was in existence before 1789 and lasted until 1861. In this America, the national community was identified with the Anglo-Saxon or Anglo-German element of the population. This America had its civic religion, Protestant Christianity, and its political creed, federal republicanism.

After the Civil War, a second republic, Euro-America, was born. In this republic the national community expanded to include all Americans of European descent, thus enabling the absorption of the waves of immigration late in the nineteenth century. This republic, too, had its civic religion, a Christianity no longer specifically Protestant. The political creed of this more inclusive America was federal democracy.

The third republic, arising out of the civil rights revolution following World War II, is the multicultural America of the present hour. This America has abandoned the idea of a national community, along with the defining principle of the Civil Rights movement—the ideal of a color-blind society. In place of national community, Americans recognize five communities, defined by race: White, Black, Hispanic, Asian and Pacific Islander, Native American. Lind would argue that these communities have not been merely recognized; they have been created. They are part of the legacy of Richard Nixon, brought into being in 1973 by Statistical Directive 15 of the Office of Management and Budget, drawn up to establish consistent rules of racial categories in order to fulfill racial quotas. Whether this America has a civic religion is questionable, but it has a secular philosophy that lays great overt stress on authenticity while in fact encouraging conformity to the values and patterns of conduct attributed to the group—racial, sexual, religious—to which one belongs. The point is to be authentically black, or authentically a woman, or authentically gay (or white, a man, straight, though these are less often commended) rather than to be authentically oneself.

The political creed of multicultural America is a centralized multicultural democracy. While this Washington-centered racial federalism refutes white supremacy, it does so in favor not of color-blind liberalism but of an elaborate system of racial preferences for citizens officially designated nonwhite. Initially justified as reparation for past injustice, this system is increasingly championed as promoting diversity, which, it seems, needs no further justification. Thus the benefits of the system become available to recent immigrants who can make no credible claim to a history of oppression in the United States.

Clearly, in his discussion of multicultural America, Lind moves from historical analysis to polemic. That what angers him may result from policies cherished by many liberals might make one question just how liberal Lind's liberal nationalism is. Yet Lind can point to the origin of much that is most debatable about contemporary affirmative action policies in the machinations of the liberals' favorite demon, Nixon. Affirmative action as it has come to be known begins to look suspiciously like a move in Nixon's southern strategy, the deliberate attempt to divide America along racial lines as a way of ensuring lasting Republican majorities.

For Lind, multiculturalism is little more than a rationalization for tokenism. It is how the white overclass maintains its dominance. The white overclass, Lind argues, is a genuine social class, "a group of families, united by intermarriage and a common subculture, whose members tend to predominate in certain professions and political offices, generation after generation." This class perpetuates itself by its dominance in such institutions as the elite university, exploiting the practice of maintaining lower standards for the children of alumni than for interlopers from outside the overclass, and, overall, in the process of defining and distributing credentials, those tickets to social dominance. For the overclass, multiculturalism functions as an alternative to the radical reform or dismantling of the class system. Affirmative action policies whose principal beneficiaries continue to be white, middle-class women represent no real threat to the interests of the overclass.

The threat to society arising from all this is what Lind calls Brazilianization: "Like a Latin American oligarchy, the rich and well-connected members of the overclass can flourish in a decadent America with Third World levels of inequality and crime." The upsurge of gated communities in the America of the 1990's provides a foretaste of what may come.

Lind places his hope in the emergence of a fourth America, "Trans-America," as he calls it. This fourth America will be characterized by a color-blind, gender-neutral regime of individual rights, combined with government activism promoting social and economic equality. It will put into practice a cultural and economic nationalism, incorporating limits to immigration and a social tariff in the interests of a transracial middle class. Needless to say, there will be no room in Trans-America for affirmative action or for such other offshoots of multiculturalism as racial gerrymandering. By this term Lind refers to the creation of congressional districts designed to guarantee black majorities. Not only is such gerrymandering a violation of the principles of color-blind liberalism, he says, but it has already led to a weakening of the influence of black voters. This helps to explain why racial gerrymandering had the full support of George Bush, as splendid a white, affluent, well-descended, Yale-educated, Republican example of the overclass as one could hope to find.

There will be in this next America no campaign financing of a sort favorable to corporations and the rich—among other things, no paid political advertising on television. The dominant economic system will remain capitalism, but a capitalism friendly to the middle class, with excessive and unproductive inequalities checked and reversed by government intervention in the marketplace. As for the cultural tensions, particularly between races, that continue to plague America, they will give way to cultural fusion resulting from racial amalgamation, as the ever-accelerating tendency to marry outside one's racial or ethnic group inevitably dissolves the significance of group identity as such.

Lind's vulnerabilities are clear enough. The proposals and prophecies that constitute his account of the next America will seem abhorrent to those for whom government activism or racial amalgamation or both is a blueprint for dystopia. Some liberals and conservatives will unite, perhaps for different reasons, in rejecting Lind's anti-immigration arguments. Certain of his proposals, such as proportional election of Congress, seem unlikely to become reality anytime soon, even if they are attractive in the abstract. Parts of his diagnosis of America's national ailment can be questioned. Is multiculturalism as strong as he suggests? Is his portrait of the overclass entirely free of distortion?

Although one tends to think of realism as a good thing, critics from both left and right have argued that Lind underestimates the real importance of idealism in American history and culture. He is accused of undervaluing the ethical commitments generating programs such as affirmative action; he was, after all, a conservative until very recently. Can nationalism be seen in as benign a light as Lind seems to suppose, or is it an ultimately divisive force in a world already sufficiently divided?

It is an significant virtue of this important book that it convinces the reader of the urgency of such questions. It is a book that provides rich historical contexts for issues that are often understood, or misunderstood, in narrowly contemporary terms. It also offers a number of incidental provocations, including Lind's iconoclastic analysis of the Jeffersonian heritage and his reaffirmation of an alternate heritage descending from Hamilton.

Some conservative critics have condescendingly suggested that Lind's enthusiasm for active government exposes him as out of touch with the American people who, in the elections of November, 1994, expressed clearly enough their rejection of government as a solution to anything. Writing early in 1995, these critics could hardly foresee that the elections of the following November would at least raise questions as to the clarity of the message that conservative pundits and politicians claimed to be receiving. At any rate, *The Next American Nation* is a book for readers who understand that the public philosophy is not bound to follow the election returns.

W. P. Kenney

Sources for Further Study

Business Week. August 7, 1995, p. 12.
Commentary. C, July, 1995, p. 62.
Foreign Affairs. LXXIV, July, 1995, p. 140.
The Nation. CCLXI, August 28, 1995, p. 211.
National Review. XLVII, September 11, 1995, p. 60.
The New Leader. LXXVIII, June 5, 1995, p. 7.
The New York Review of Books. XLII, October 5, 1995, p. 30.
The New York Times Book Review. C, June 25, 1995, p. 7.
Publishers Weekly. CCXLII, May 29, 1995, p. 73.
The Wall Street Journal. June 23, 1995, p. A12.
The Wilson Quarterly. XIX, Summer, 1995, p. 80.

NOTES OF A WHITE BLACK WOMAN
Race, Color, Community

Author: Judy Scales-Trent
Publisher: Pennsylvania State University Press (University Park). 198 pp. $19.50
Type of work: Current affairs

A light-skinned African American law professor contemplates racial divisions in the United States, multicultural pedagogy, and how assumptions about color have shaped her own identity

Judy Scales-Trent draws on various genre techniques, including excerpts from a diary, anecdotes about private experiences, family history, pedagogical description, and commentary on social relations, to weave together a narrative that intertwines her explorations of self with the larger social context of race and identity. In her choice of title, as well as in her text, she attacks ideas of black-white dualism that are at the heart of racial prejudice against African Americans and have structured the patterns of historical discrimination against black citizens from slavery through emancipation and its aftermath. In doing so, she lends her voice to a long tradition in African American writing, both in using the technique of personal narrative as a means of sorting out identity and critiquing society at large and in dealing with the theme of color as caste and its role in shaping a community of consciousness among black people, drawing lines of difference between blacks and whites, creating hierarchy between blacks of different skin tones, and to a great extent predetermining an individual's ability to move between the socially constructed borders of black and white communities. In approach and theme Scales-Trent's contemporary work is thus linked with such historical, and now canonical, works as Frederick Douglass' *Narrative of the Life of Frederick Douglass* (1845) and James Weldon Johnson's *Autobiography of an Ex-Colored Man* (1927). As the work of an African American woman exploring issues of status and color awareness, it is also part of the tradition of established black women fiction writers such as Frances E. W. Harper, whose *Iola Leroy* (1893), dealt with mixed-race heritage and the rise of a black professional class in the years after the Civil War, or the many treatments of the pain of passing for white, including Nella Larsen's novels *Quicksand* (1928) and *Passing* (1929).

Although Scales-Trent is highly cognizant of the fact that racial divisions are directly related to the control and distribution of tangible and intangible resources— income, medical care, occupations, residential opportunities, education, civil rights— it is primarily the social and cultural ramifications of ideas of racial difference, rather than issues of political economy, with which her book is concerned. As a lawyer and teacher, she uses the pages of her memoir to educate her readers and critique pedagogical practices. Her introduction sets her autobiographical musings in the context of the way that the law has historically been used to codify racial differences and discrimination, including the racial purity or antimiscegenation laws that were passed in many American states during the decades of slavery, increased in the Jim Crow era following Reconstruction, were challenged during the Civil Rights movement, and continue to influence the way that people of various colors are officially defined. She returns to a legal framework in the appendix, where she discusses the ways she has taught classes and introduced issues of race and social justice into the law school curriculum.

At the heart of Scales-Trent's analysis is the fact that much racial identity and prejudice is generally assumed (that is, almost subconscious or implicit in nature), and racial categorization is ultimately not a matter of legal definition or of biology, but of long-standing and mostly unexamined social practice. She explains,

> Because I am a black American who is often mistaken for white, my very existence demonstrates that there is slippage between the seemingly discrete categories "black" and "white." This slippage is important and can be helpful to us, for it makes the enterprise of categorizing by race a more visible—hence, a more conscious—task.

In place of rigid categories, Scales-Trent ultimately advocates a concept of multi- or biculturalism: emphasizing the interplay of influences between black and white throughout American history and across the African diaspora and the extent to which many people of color are not either-or but *both* black and white. At the same time that she addresses the social pervasiveness of white racism against black people, she notes the pain produced within black communities because of differences in color and the factionalization and internal ostracisms that such differences can produce.

Her own identity, despite her pale appearance, is strongly that of an African American, and many of the tales she tells in the memoir sections of her book explore the difficult consequences of being one thing internally while appearing externally to be another. One of the most poignant of these recollections is the identification she feels with a small black girl she sees dressed in a pink organdy dress, reminding her strongly of her own young self when she was growing up in North Carolina. The child, however, feels no similar identification with Scales-Trent and indeed is afraid of her, because what she sees is a white woman. Such contradiction between internal and external reality is revisited in many forms and exists as a constant conundrum in Scales-Trent's personal choices. In loving a dark man who became her husband, she in effect endangered him in some social settings where strangers would interpret their relationship as interracial. In professional settings, white colleagues would often assume her likeness to themselves. This would present her with the ethical and personal dilemma of seeming, if she took a passive or private approach, to be passing as white and thus feeling that she was denying her blackness, or of demanding, if she took an active and militant approach, an explicit statement about her racial heritage, whereupon she would suffer the repercussions from changes in some people's reactions to her.

In facing these hard choices and experiencing the ways other people categorize her, she writes of the benefits of understanding such matters of assigning identity in cultural terms and of the strength she has garnered through the ability to recognize analogy in others. She finds sisters in other women of color, in Asian American, Hispanic American, and Native American experiences. She finds similarities in the experiences faced by lesbians, who, like her, must sometimes make decisions about coming "out" with explicit self-definitions in the face of other people's assumptions. In recognizing these connections, Scales-Trent overcomes her personal sense of isolation—as a woman caught between black and white worlds whose own desire and loyalties place her in the black one—and builds her case for a bicultural or multicultural ideal.

This ideal is carried into her teaching. She makes innovations in curriculum to impress on students their own commonalities with people whom they may have thought quite different from themselves. In doing so she breaks down assumed barriers not only of racial definition but of linear and dualistic thinking and academic disciplines. Her approach to teaching in the law school includes team-teaching with professors from humanities and social science departments, assigning reading from literature or films with cultural and justice themes, and requiring hands-on community fieldwork or observations. Direct involvement helps her students change the way they think about other people with whom they share a city or a state and consider their own identity in more complicated ways.

In describing this ideal and the ways she seeks to implement it in the classroom, Scales-Trent shifts from an autobiographical emphasis on the angst produced by being continually defined as an aberration or anomaly—perpetually different in either of the two dominant racial worlds—to emphasizing the positive aspects of her "twoness." She likens the options for connection that result from her doubled identity to a kind of bilingualism. Again looking at society, around her, she sees others whose experience parallels her own: the blond Jew, the person in a wheelchair, and others for whom daily life means being placed on the outside or being compelled to make occasional corrective proclamations of self.

Despite Scales-Trent's message of multiplicity and call for her audience to embrace contradiction and avoid the easy categorizations that lead to separatism and unequal practices, one of the strongest subthemes that emerge from her book is a nationalistic pride in blackness. For Scales-Trent, ease of mind and personal fulfillment are ultimately connected to her concept of home. Home is where one is from, what one is, where one started, in the sense of both geography and cultural roots—food, hair styling, religion, the family matters that are forever associated with the home place. She remembers a feeling of belonging to all the black adults on the Jim Crow train as she traveled to North Carolina to visit her extended family as a young girl; she recalls the safety of her all-black childhood world. Making a psychological "home" of self-worth within oneself is likened to that feeling of steadiness, unshaken by outward definitions. The opposite—the occasional self-hatred she feels, the loneliness she experiences in the disjunction between the southern black and northern white communities of her youth and adulthood—she describes as a kind of homelessness, a condition of being the perpetual stranger. She compares this feeling to that of Native Americans who have left the reservation where they grew up but maintain an internal Native American cultural identity while living in a white-defined world.

Home is also family, and part of the story told here is the coming to terms with the white element of the Scales-Trent family and also noticing, by examining family photographs, what has become of it. Near the turn of the century, there was the interracial marriage of white grandfather and black grandmother Tate, followed by a family of sisters, including Aunt Midge, with blue eyes and porcelain skin, and then, two generations later, a group of lovely brown grandchildren born of siblings who each married someone darker than themselves, weeding out the whiteness, affirming the beauty of the blackness, protecting their children from the danger incurred in being too dark or the alienation of being too light.

"Home" means not only biological family but family away from home: the family of all black people—including white-looking black people—who share "white folks sure can be a fool" stories making white people the Other and confirming the kinship among blacks, or who look at Scales-Trent and recognize Africa in her hair, or who talk with the sound of North Carolina in their voices, even in New York or Washington, D.C., confirming a commonality behind the question "Where're you from?" The belonging that exudes from the passages on family is a remedy to the alienation and doubt often expressed in Scales-Trent's ruminations on herself alone.

Notes of a White Black Woman: Race, Color Community is a provocative book written from the center of the politics of identity and multiculturalism, the focus of important intellectual debates on progressive university campuses in the 1990's. Written out of first-person experience, it is testimony to the watchword of the women's movement that grew out of the Civil Rights movement of the 1960's and 1970's: The personal is political. At the same time that her study reflects current affairs, Scales-Trent reaches back through a long tradition of African American women's writing to reexamine, in a new social context, the dilemmas and choices for commitment that face the black woman whose skin is light.

Barbara Bair

Sources for Further Study

Booklist. XCI, March 1, 1995, p. 1165.
The Chronicle of Higher Education. XLI, January 27, 1995, p. A17.
Contemporary Sociology. XXIV, September, 1995, p. 599.
Hecate. XXI, May, 1995, p. 74.
Publishers Weekly. CCXLII, March 20, 1995, p. 51.
The Washington Post. May 19, 1995, p. D2.
Women's Review of Books. XIII, October, 1995, p. 18.

OF LOVE AND OTHER DEMONS

Author: Gabriel García Márquez (1928-   )
First published: Del amor y otros demonios, 1994, in Spain
Translated from the Spanish by Edith Grossman
Publisher: Alfred A. Knopf (New York). 147 pp. $21.00
Type of work: Novel
Time: The second half of the eighteenth century
Locale: The New Kingdom of Granada

A young girl undergoes the horrors of exorcism when a possible rabies infection is treated as demonic possession by the Holy Office of the Catholic Church

Principal characters:
> SIERVA MARÍA DE TODOS LOS ÁNGELES, a mercurial daughter of Creole nobility
> DON YGNACIO DE ALFARO Y DUEÑAS, the withdrawn second Marquis de Casalduero
> BERNARDA CABRERA, his disenchanted wife
> DON TORIBIO DE CÁCERES Y VIRTUDES, the diocesan bishop, resigned to his faith
> FATHER CAYETANO DELAURA, an aspiring Vatican librarian, battling personal demons
> ABBESS JOSEFA MIRANDA, the head of the Convent of Santa Clara

For Sierva María de Todos los Ángeles, existence is precarious from the very beginning. The only child of the funereal second Marquis de Casalduero, Don Ygnacio de Alfaro y Dueñas, and his drug-dependent wife, Bernarda Cabrera, Sierva María is so puny at her premature birth that the African slave to whom she is later entrusted promises the Virgin Mary that if God permits her to live, the girl's hair will not be cut until she marries. Abandoned thereafter to a half-savage upbringing while the listless marquis withdraws further from society, and his commoner wife finds solace in her fermented honey, cacao, and many lovers, Sierva María grows up a phantasmal and enigmatic creature, illiterate and prone to lying. On the fateful eve of her twelfth birthday, she is one of four people bitten by a dog later discovered to be rabid.

As terrible suffering and two deaths ensue among the other victims and news of his daughter's possible infection reaches his ears, Don Ygnacio undergoes a change of heart, regretting his inexcusable neglect of Sierva María. He retrieves her to live in their decayed ancestral mansion and sets out to investigate optimal treatments for her. Returning horrified from the Amor de Dios Hospital, where a sufferer of the dog bite lies half-paralyzed and dying, Don Ygnacio encounters the blasphemous licentiate Abrenuncio de Sa Pereira Cao, a doctor infamous for his unconventional ideas and remedies, whom he convinces to examine Sierva María. Abrenuncio's prognosis is far from alarming: The girl is unlikely to contract rabies and should be made as happy as possible in her new home.

For a while, all goes well as father and daughter gradually forge a relationship and discover a shared interest in music. Eventually, however, Sierva María comes down with a strange fever and is subjected to the torturous medical remedies of her day. Abrenuncio counsels the marquis on the uncertainties inherent in science as well as faith, and the situation appears resolved until the bishop of the diocese, Don Toribio de Cáceres y Virtudes, troubled by reports of the girl's odd behavior, summons Don Ygnacio to his palace for a religious consultation.

Sierva María may be possessed by demons, the bishop affirms, and in spite of her father's doubts ought to be transferred to the Convent of Santa Clara for immediate spiritual attention. At the convent, the silent, long-haired girl is at first ignored or treated as an oddity by the nuns and novices under the direction of the embittered Abbess Josefa Miranda, whose long-standing grudge against the Holy Office predisposes her to dislike to Sierva María. The girl's virtual imprisonment coincides with more violent, inexplicable behavior, and when rumors of peculiar occurrences at the convent reach the bishop, he appoints Father Cayetano Delaura to exorcise Sierva María of demonic possession. Delaura, an aspirant to the post of Vatican librarian, declares his reluctance to undertake a task for which he considers himself unqualified. The bishop, however, insists on his participation and dispatches him to the convent.

An avid reader of books both ecclesiastical and forbidden, Delaura is skeptical about the Holy Office's conclusions concerning demonic possession. In treating the captivating Sierva María, he relies principally on smuggled pastries, consoling blandishments, and quotations from the Spanish Renaissance sonnet writer Garcilaso de la Vega. The young priest is moved to see her strapped down inhumanly in her own filth; with the help of Martina Laborde, her cellblock companion, he slowly manages to win her confidence. The arrival of a new viceroy, Don Rodrigo de Buen Lozano, who declares an era of renovation, prompts a more gentle handling of the supposedly possessed girl, whose beauty affects him as much as it has Delaura.

When the bishop finally orders Delaura to carry out the exorcism, the wavering priest, fighting his own demons, pays a surreptitious visit to the apostate Abrenuncio to confer on his crisis of conscience. Later in her cell, Delaura informs Sierva María that her father wishes to see her; she reacts frantically, spitting repeatedly in his face. This so excites Delaura sexually that the bishop discovers his acolyte flagellating himself to be rid of his own "possession."

Despite being condemned to serving at the Amor de Dios Hospital for lepers as penance for his temptations, Delaura secretly visits Sierva María nightly in her convent cell, sneaking through a hidden sewer entrance left from the days of the convent's battle with the Holy Office. Martina Laborde's untimely escape, however, leads to the discovery and closing of this breach and thus to the cessation of the marriage-minded couple's nocturnal encounters of poetry and cakes. The bishop's hastened attempt at exorcism ends inconclusively in a sudden asthma attack; a second attempt by the priest of the town's slave neighborhood, Father Tomás de Aquino de Narváez, ends equally suspiciously in his unexplained drowning. Finally, emaciated and weakened after five sessions with the bishop and shorn of the flowing hair that had been consecrated to the Virgin Mary, Sierva María dies of love, dreaming of snow and once again sprouting the enthralling locks that symbolized her elfin volatility.

Gabriel García Márquez's deft ability to suggest, but never to insist exclusively upon, supernatural causality behind the observable events of *Of Love and Other Demons* reaffirms his position as the leading practitioner of the Magical Realism he popularized with *Cien años de soledad* (1967; *One Hundred Years of Solitude*, 1970) and later with such notable short stories as "Un señor muy viejo con unas alas enormes" (1968; "A Very Old Man with Enormous Wings," 1972) and "La increíble y triste historia de la cándida Eréndira y de su abuela desalmada" (1972; "The Incredible and Sad Tale of Innocent Eréndira and Her Heartless Grandmother," 1978). In Edith Grossman's stellar translation from the Spanish, the novel's atmosphere pulsates with otherworldly uncertainty and ambiguity, which perfectly complements the work's central, unresolvable tension between religious and empirical explanations of the natural world as embodied in the baffling case of the ill-starred Sierva María.

Delaura's realization that love, and not demonic possession, may be the foulest fiend of all not only displays one of the novel's abiding conceits but also demonstrates García Márquez's specialized, figurative use of language, which from the title forward heralds the work's sustained ambivalences and ultimately renders impossible an absolute, unified interpretation. Many of the novel's metaphysical elements, for example, are introduced through the rhetorical tropes of simile and metaphor, as when the bishop compares ideas to angels or Delaura comes into view with the speed of a genie emerging from a bottle. The frequent use of the verbs "seem" and "appear" also permits *Of Love and Other Demons* to straddle the line between the knowable and the imperceptible, while still other strange occurrences may be imputed to exaggeration, as in Delaura's memory of a possessed woman in Burgos who defecated continually until her cell overflowed with excrement.

More uncanny phenomena may be attributed to the stylized narrative technique of limited or biased point of view. That the mad former object of Don Ygnacio's affections, Dulce Olivia, spreads rumors of Sierva María's bearing Delaura's two-headed child can reasonably be put down to her jealousy as a woman scorned. Bernarda's belief that Sierva María can suddenly appear without a sound similarly has tangible roots in the mother's fear and loathing of her only child. While quite a few sisters at the convent, too, claim that Sierva María can make herself invisible, it is far more likely that they simply negligently overlook her. At one point, the abbess goes so far as to complain to the bishop that since the girl's arrival, pigs have spoken and a goat has given birth to triplets. Abrenuncio's near brush with the stake for having purportedly resurrected a dead man is similarly motivated by calumnious tongues: Only his patient's claim before an Inquisition tribunal that he never lost consciousness, even while in his shroud, saves this Portuguese Jew from death for heresy.

The reader must be willing to accept a fair amount of coincidence, too, to ward off the easy lure of supernatural explanations that lurk behind the improbability of the novel's unaccountable happenings. While Father Tomás de Aquino's unresolved drowning, for example, has an earlier analogue in Bernarda's finding Sierva María's doll floating in a water jar "murdered," no evidence exists to substantiate Satanic involvement in either event. Yet what rational explanation exists for the sudden, simultaneous deaths of all the convent's macaws during Sierva María's stay? *Of Love and Other Demons* presents such conundrums on page after page, urging the reader to incorporate events that range from an ill-omened eclipse that partially blinds Delaura, to rabid mountain monkeys' assault on a cathedral, to the changing color of holy water into a coherent totality that resists a complete favoring of the methods of either reason or faith. The death by lightning of Don Ygnacio's first wife, Doña Olalla de Mendoza, admits at least three possible explanations and is yet another instance of the work's persistent ambiguity.

To cloud even further the process of determining fact from fiction within its narrative world, *Of Love and Other Demons* introduces alternative realms of being—the landscape of dreams and the canvas of portraiture—where conventions of the irrational and the subconscious color all attempts at exposition. Is it pure coincidence that Sierva María and Delaura both dream of her eating grapes while watching snow fall outside a window, or are the would-be lovers so inextricably linked in their passion that they share mental processes? On a similar note, should the girl's assertion that a painting depicting her subduing demons is an absolute likeness be read as the product of a literal, perverse, or possessed mind?

These obfuscating shifts over planes of existence continue with the eerie mingling of art and life that, on still another level, threatens to undermine the stability of any one textual interpretation. Besides the novel's use of the actual sonnets of Garcilaso de la Vega, of whom Delaura claims his father is a direct descendant, the reader learns that Doña Olalla was once a music student of Scarlatti Domenico, whose name is a playful transposition of the name of the famous eighteenth century composer.

It is the short italicized preface to the novel, however, that best displays this blending of competing narrative worlds that serves as an apt counterpoint to the collision of empiricism and religious dogma that runs throughout explanations of the action of the work. In this brief account of how he purportedly came to write *Of Love and Other Demons*, García Márquez describes his early days as a journalist and an assignment he received to cover the disinterment of the crypts beneath the same Convent of Santa Clara that appears in the novel. There, he noted some surprising irregularities: The convent provided the final resting place for the bodies of the bishop and abbess. Don Ygnacio was missing from his tomb, presumably because his remains were discovered, as chapter five recounts, two years after he was eaten by turkey buzzards on an isolated road where he died after a final conversation with Bernarda.

The most peculiar find of all, though, spilled forth from one of the crypts on the high altar: twenty-two meters of coppery hair connected to the skull of a young girl, which had apparently continued to grow after her death. The sight of her bones prompts García Márquez to recall his grandmother's recounting of the legend of a twelve-year-old marquise who had died of rabies but whom the people of the Caribbean continued to venerate for her miracles. Thus, the close of *Of Love and Other Demons* brings the reader full circle to its beginning, but without offering a less puzzling or enigmatic account of the novel's transcendental world.

Gregary J. Racz

Sources for Further Study

Americas. XLVII, January, 1995, p. 63.
The Economist. CCCXXXVI, July 8, 1995, p. 85.
Los Angeles Times Book Review. May 14, 1995, p. 3.
The Nation. CCLX, June 12, 1995, p. 836.
The New York Times Book Review. C, May 28, 1995, p. 8.
Publishers Weekly. CCXLII, March 27, 1995, p. 72.
Time. CXLV, May 22, 1995, p. 73.
The Times Literary Supplement. July 7, 1995, p. 23.
The Washington Post Book World. XXV, May 14, 1995, p. 3.
World Press Review. XLI, July, 1994, p. 48.

ON GOLD MOUNTAIN
The One-Hundred-Year Odyssey of a Chinese-American Family

Author: Lisa See (1945-   )
Publisher: St. Martin's Press (New York). 394 pp. $24.95
Type of work: History; biography
Time: 1867-1994
Locale: Principally Sacramento and Los Angeles, California; Dimtao and Fatsun (Foshan), China

Journalist Lisa See documents the tenacious pursuit of the American Dream by her ambitious great-grandfather Fong See and the establishment of two extended families against the turbulent backdrop of the continuously intersecting histories of the United States and China

Principal personages:
FONG DUN SHUNG, a village herbalist transported to California in 1867
FONG SEE, the fourth son of Fong Dun Shung, sent to California in 1871 at the age of fourteen to find his father
LETTICIE (TICIE) PRUETT SEE, a redheaded teenage orphan employed by Fong See who later becomes his wife
EDDY (MING QUAN) SEE, the youngest of five children born to Fong See and Ticie, manager of a famous Depression-era restaurant in Los Angeles
STELLA COPELAND SEE, Eddy's wife, another redheaded Caucasian woman
SISSEE (JUN OY) SEE, the only daughter of Ticie and Fong See, at once a devoted Chinese daughter and a shrewd businesswoman
RICHARD SEE, the only son of Stella and Eddy, a roustabout turned anthropologist
CAROLYN LAWS, an accomplished writer, the third Caucasian female to join the See family through a short-lived marriage to Richard
LISA SEE, the redheaded daughter of Carolyn and Richard, a journalist

Lisa See's history of her Chinese-American ancestry revolves around the powerful personality of her entrepreneurial great-grandfather Fong See, whose arrival in California in 1871 led to the founding of numerous successful businesses that ultimately enriched not only the offspring of the two families he established in the United States but also the peasants of his native Chinese village. In the process of illuminating Fong See's life, the author sketches in the social and political histories of the two nations between which Fong See repeatedly traveled in the course of his nearly one hundred years of life.

The family's initial foray onto "Gold Mountain," as the Chinese termed America, began with the hiring of the herbalist Fong Dun Shung to minister to the needs of the nearly thirteen thousand Chinese laborers at work building the transcontinental railroad. Accompanied by two of his four sons, he prolonged his stay to establish a business dispensing his much-valued medical expertise. This irresponsible decision reduced his wife and youngest son to desperate straits at home, and so an offer by a wealthy patron to finance the youngest boy's trip to America was eagerly accepted.

Building upon his father's herbalist enterprise in Sacramento, Fong See soon proved the wisdom of abandoning traditional birth-order seniority for more modern practices of rewarding the most talented with the greatest authority. Under his leadership, the three brothers transformed their father's business to meet a lucrative if unusual market demand for crotchless lingerie among the prostitutes of 1870's California. Fong See demonstrated a keen desire to remake himself along Western lines, yet his hunger to be accepted among white Americans was met with a steadily growing bigotry. Caucasians ignored the contributions of these "Chinamen" in opening up the West by rail and changing the Sacramento Valley into fertile farmland, instead casting them as illegitimate competitors for jobs and resources. Fong See's financial successes were all the more remarkable given laws and practices forbidding Chinese ownership of land, marriage to whites, and equitable access to immigration. The Exclusion Act of 1882 was mirrored by equally virulent state legislation that See explicitly compares to contemporary political campaigns against so-called illegal aliens.

In depicting the verve with which "Gold Mountain See" pursued his vision of a familial dynasty expressive of the possibilities inherent in his new home, Lisa See makes clear the parallel pioneering spirit of her great-grandmother Letticie (or "Ticie"), the sole daughter of a hard-luck family that traveled west on the Oregon Trail in 1875. Resisting the prospect of servitude among unloving relatives in unpromising farm country, Ticie daringly made her way at age eighteen to Sacramento, where she insinuated herself into the employ of Fong See. Initially baffled by her persistence, he eventually saw the wisdom in her suggestions for improving customer relations and hence sales. She became his clerk, then his bookkeeper and adviser concerning expansion of his product line. Ticie urged him to begin dealing in imported curios, which would begin to make his real fortune; similarly, her increasingly educated eye for beauty led the company into the Asian antique business, which would become the family's lasting economic and cultural legacy.

If Fong See stands at the narrative center of this parable about the American Dream, Ticie's story constitutes its emotional core. Ever the rebel, she allowed devotion to her employer, nineteen years her senior, to spill over into a love officially outlawed in a state that forbade miscegenation. Convinced of Fong See's sincere desire to create a Western family with a wife who would be partner and soulmate rather than Old World servant, she entered into the nearest approximation of a legal marriage available to her: They signed a formal contract recognizing their alliance. This union produced four sons and a daughter and was blessed by expanding economic prosperity.

In 1897, aware of a newly rising wave of anti-Asian sentiment, Ticie prompted Fong See to move the family and its enterprises to Los Angeles, reputedly the most tolerant city on the West Coast. The Sees, as they became known through a classic bureaucratic error, were thus in a strategic position to benefit from Southern California's dynamic growth throughout the century.

The rewards of her tightly knit Eurasian family were many for Ticie, allowing her to escape the stultifying division between workplace and home known as male and female "separate spheres." The continuity between the family and its businesses meant that every member was part of the daily routine in both realms, and Ticie continued to play an important role in the family's financial ventures. Yet most Caucasian women shunned her socially, as did her birth family. Ticie sought to learn about conducting herself in "proper" Chinese fashion even as she insisted on sending her children to public schools and celebrating holidays of both cultures. Her determination to allow their offspring typical American pastimes offended her illiterate husband's impatience with time-wasting activities (including homework) and challenged the absolute authority he increasingly came to regard as his due as the family patriarch.

Ironically, the hunger for Westernization that had freed Fong See to seize opportunities for himself on Gold Mountain began to give way to a yearning for China as he found that his success failed to secure for him the stature and position among Americans that he had anticipated. A trip to China following World War I, when Fong See was at the height of his entrepreneurial achievement, laid bare his grievances against his adopted country and the woman who embodied it. Fêted as a hero in his native village, Dimtao, he dispensed largesse like a mandarin and nurtured a swelling resentment at his mistreatment in California. When Ticie rejected his plan to leave their youngest son, Eddy, in China to oversee his properties and care for his aged mother, Fong See angrily remained behind himself and before long took another wife, a sixteen-year-old, with whom he began a new family. Ticie's hopes for a reconciliation were dashed, and their contractual "marriage" was legally dissolved.

The schism in the 1920's between Fong See and Ticie marks the book's narrative climax, and the account that follows is necessarily less unified, since Lisa See must describe not only the subsequent histories of the Sees, headed by Ticie, but also those of the Fongs, as the second family is named (a unit that ultimately included seven children, the youngest fathered when Fong See was in his eighties). Because the author descends from the former group, she concentrates her attention there, explaining the roles the five See children assumed as they both delighted in freedom from the patriarch's iron control and suffered from his cold abandonment. Ming, the eldest, became the family's primary business agent. Ray, always the most hostile to his Chinese legacy and his father's perceived tyrannies, chafed under Ming's privileged status and eventually formed an alliance with Bennie, the third son, to open a furniture factory that he could manage. Sissee, the conciliator, became her grief-stricken mother's tireless companion. Eddy, youngest brother and nominal cause of the family breakup, floated from job to job within the family nexus, briefly translated his enthusiasms into a successful Depression-era restaurant called Dragon's Den, and eventually found himself excluded from a reorganization of family assets years after their mother's death.

Within this generation, it is the fate of the author's grandfather Eddy that most obviously concerns her. His inability to settle comfortably into the family business after the closing of Dragon's Den put him in marked contrast to both of his enterprising parents, yet his dedication to the family ideal marked him as his mother's son and provided the most sustained bridge back to Fong See. The author identifies another cross-generational pattern among the women from whom she is descended, for Eddy married Stella Copeland, a waiflike redheaded girl of steely will who, like Ticie, saw in the Sees' concept of family a stability lacking in her own disordered upbringing. Nevertheless, betrayal stalked these lovers, too, with Eddy proving as unfaithful to his wife as Ming and Ray were to theirs. Only one healthy child blessed the union of Stella and Eddy; a second pregnancy ended in abortion on the heels of Eddy's adultery, and a third resulted in a hydrocephalic child dead within days of its birth. Yet Stella and Eddy managed to salvage their marriage, with Ticie's descent into alcoholism perhaps ample evidence of the price of dissolving heart-binding ties.

These events unfold against the backdrop of the tumultuous 1920's, 1930's, and 1940's, with dramatic swings from economic boom to bust followed by World War II's transformative impact on the social landscape of California. The rise of Hollywood was felt in Chinatown as well as elsewhere in Los Angeles, and both family businesses traded with set designers of the major studios. The virulence directed against Japanese Americans during the war had contradictory effects upon the Chinese in the region. When postwar consumer appetites sought a "modern" look to reflect a new generation's confidence, Ray designed a blend of Californian and Asian motifs that he called "Calinese"—and became thereby the true heir to his entrepreneurial father.

Finally, as emblems of the 1950's nonconformist challenge to bourgeois complacency, the author offers her own parents: Richard, the exotically handsome son of Eddy and Stella, and Carolyn Laws, yet another fair-haired woman sprung from a severely troubled Caucasian family. After a quirky courtship, they married under the cloud of an assumed pregnancy that failed to materialize, only to rectify the situation rather quickly with the real thing. Lisa was born in Paris in 1955, to intellectually ambitious but alcoholic young parents who soon divorced. Fong See himself died in 1957, ending an era just as the final block of old Chinatown was torn down to make way for new Los Angeles.

Lisa See's method in telling her story is at times as provocative as the strong personalities she depicts. She repeatedly concedes the problems she faces in culling fact from the myriad competing family legends dealing with Fong See. Faced with such impenetrable knots of "history," she adopts novelistic techniques to render her personages dramatically immediate. She regularly enters into the psyches of her "characters" to provide glimpses into their subjective lives.

The balance of historical narrative and family saga is generally well managed in *On Gold Mountain*, although there are numerous examples of flat or uninspired prose where cliché creeps into the phrasing. The author's divisions of the text to juxtapose Ticie's or Stella's experiences growing up to those of each woman's male counterpart prove awkward at points, although more so in the case of Stella. Lisa See's visit to China—the final chapter—promises more emotional resolution than it delivers, a failing reflective of most efforts to recover a familial trail in stubbornly alien territory. Still, well researched and filled with human variety and drama, this is a rich text rewarding the careful attention readers must pay to it.

Barbara Kitt Seidman

Sources for Further Study

Booklist. XCI, August, 1995, p. 1927.
Library Journal. CXX, August, 1995, p. 84.
Los Angeles Times Book Review. July 23, 1995, p. 4.
The New York Times Book Review. C, August 27, 1995, p. 20.
The Oregonian. August 6, 1995, p. C6.
Publishers Weekly. CCXLII, June 5, 1995, p. 43.
San Francisco Chronicle. August 13, 1995, p. REV2.
The Washington Post Book World. XXV, August 20, 1995, p. 1.

ON THE ORIGINS OF WAR AND THE PRESERVATION OF PEACE

Author: Donald Kagan (1932-   )
Publisher: Doubleday (New York). Illustrated. 606 pages. $30.00
Type of work: History
Time: The fifth century B.C. to twentieth century A.D.
Locale: Primarily Western Europe

In five case studies, which range from the Peloponnesian War to the Cuban Missile Crisis,
Donald Kagan analyzes the events which led to either war or peace

> *Principal personages:*
> THUCYDIDES, the ancient Athenian historian
> PERICLES, the Athenian leader who fails to deter Sparta from attacking
>   Athens
> HANNIBAL, the leader of Carthage who launched a war of vengeance on
>   Rome
> KAISER WILHELM II, the German emperor during World War I
> SIR EDWARD GREY, Britain's foreign secretary during World War I
> ADOLF HITLER, the chancellor of Germany during World War II
> SIR NEVILLE CHAMBERLAIN, the prime minister of Great Britain,
>   1937-1940
> NIKITA KHRUSHCHEV, the Soviet leader during the Cuban Missile Crisis
> JOHN F. KENNEDY, the thirty-fifth president of the United States,
>   1961-1963

On the Origins of War and the Preservation of Peace presents readers with a
wide-ranging analysis of the question of how a major political crisis can lead to war.
To find his answers, historian Donald Kagan discusses five such crises, which range
from the ancient Peloponnesian War to the Cuban Missile Crisis. All together, Kagan's
conflicts span the course of nearly 2,500 years of human history.

Throughout his detailed narrative of each conflict, Donald Kagan presents the latest
scholarship on the issues and visits rich primary source material. Especially interesting
is Kagan's method of exploring possible alternatives to the historical actions taken.
His book often interrupts the description of actual events by posing the question of
what historical leaders may have done in order to preserve a peace which eluded them
in all but the last example. Kagan's concluding thoughts on each conflict similarly
stimulate the thoughts of the reader. For example, was there a possibility of stopping
Hitler's quest for Nazi domination of Europe, or was the world condemned to suffer
World War II?

Kagan's choice of the five crises reflects, to some degree, his own research interests
in the classical antiquity and the twentieth century. Thus, all examples come from these
two epochs; he discusses the Peloponnesian War between ancient Athens and Sparta,
the Second Punic War between Rome and Carthage, the two world wars, and finally
the Cuban Missile Crisis.

While this selection leaves out much, it nevertheless constitutes a productive choice.
Most noticeably, Kagan's selection enables him to compare two different kinds of
conflict in both the ancient and the contemporary world. Thus, while both the Pelo-

ponnesian War and World War I were started by complex situations that suddenly got out of hand, both the Second Punic War and World War II were triggered by one leader's unbending will to war. The Cuban Missile Crisis, finally, offers a ray of hope. This is true even though, as Kagan shows convincingly by backing up his claims with documentary sources newly made available, the Kennedy Administration emerges less than spotless and is made to share blame for the onset of the crisis.

Kagan's work is thankfully free of much abstract scholarly jargon and complicated, scientific-looking mathematical academic models of the kind which never last for very long before becoming outdated and rejected. Instead, Donald Kagan has looked for his theoretical ideas to the ancient Greek military historian Thucydides, an eyewitness of the Peloponnesian War from 431 to 404 B.C. Kagan argues well for the timeless wisdom of Thucydides' observations on the origins for war, which Kagan presents to readers in the introduction of his book.

Thucydides held that nations go to war over issues of "honor, fear, and interest," and Kagan believes this to be one of the first, and most profound, analyses of the causes of war. National prestige may lead a nation such as the Germany of Kaiser Wilhelm II to pursue a disastrous foreign policy guaranteed to alienate almost all of its European neighbors. Fear that Sparta may gain too powerful an ally motivated Athenian intervention in a crisis among Greek city-states, just as the specter of a new world war led Great Britain to try to appease Hitler.

Embracing what his fellow historians would call a moderate neorealist position, Kagan plausibly argues that states will continue to act to protect their national interests. Just as the Western Allies could not allow Hitler to have Poland, the United States could not tolerate the placement of nuclear missiles in Cuba. In both cases, preparing for war became the only solution to prevent the creation of unacceptable alternatives.

Perhaps most strongly, Kagan identifies ambiguous, mixed political messages as one of the prime factors contributing to the outbreak of war. Kagan often faults leaders for a failure to pursue a straightforward policy; he argues in favor of unambiguous messages that take into account military realities and are strong on deterrence. A warning that is backed up by military readiness and prowess, Kagan argues, might have prevented many a war from occurring.

To prove his ideas, Kagan begins by dissecting the origins of the Peloponnesian War. Kagan's own previous studies of this conflict make it an ideal starting point for his ambitious project, and turn his discussion into a fascinating account of political brinkmanship. As Kagan shows, the political situation in Greece in the second half of the fifth century B.C. somewhat uncannily resembled that of the Cold War. The two major powers, Sparta and Athens, tried to coexist in an uneasy peace. In this atmosphere of mutual distrust, a third state, Corinth, tried to further its own interests by seeking to attack the city of Corcyra, whose inhabitants asked Athens for help. Since Corinth was allied with Sparta, a global Greek conflict loomed.

Faced with a potential loss of prestige and power if Corinth were to get away with her attack, Pericles of Athens decided to embark on a series of dangerous half measures which neither mollified, nor deterred the Spartans. Angered by Pericles' relative intransigence, yet unconvinced that Athens could really hurt Sparta in a war, they decided to attack, and the peace was lost.

Here as elsewhere, Kagan's narrative of each conflict is lucid, and his arguments are well taken. As he does further on in the book, Kagan concludes his discussion of each specific conflict with a summary of the causes of the war. What is missing in these summaries, however, is a larger discussion of how the mechanics and events of each specific conflict could fit into an overall pattern.

For the Peloponnesian War, for example, Kagan might have drawn useful comparisons with similar conflicts. The Korean War and even the Vietnam conflict come to mind. Both conflicts occurred in a global situation similar to that of ancient Greece, when two or more superpowers were in danger of being drawn into direct conflict with each other because of the actions of a third state. Yet Kagan's work remains relatively reticent as regards larger analogies drawn from conflicts not studied in detail here.

What is missing in regard to an expanded global perspective, however, is made up for by the rich detail of each of Kagan's five case studies. His discussion of the events leading up to World War I is particularly interesting because of Kagan's inclusion of the prewar conflicts, such as the numerous Balkan crises, which did not cause a global war. Here, then, readers can observe success and limits of late nineteenth and early twentieth century power politics, and diplomacy.

Finally, for Kagan, it was Kaiser Wilhelm II's unreasonable pursuit of a naval building program that pushed the European nations into an atmosphere of distrust and conflict. Germany appeared opposed to friendly coexistence. Kagan cites strong documentary evidence to support his point that the Germans pushed the Austrians into declaring war on Serbia as a retaliation for the assassination of their archduke by a Serb. Once Russia made it clear that it would not tolerate this, events quickly spun out of control. By toying too long with the idea of neutrality and refusing to build a strong military, Britain also complicated the issue in Kagan's eyes. Like the ancient Spartans, the Germans in 1914 did not believe their English enemy would fight or be a serious threat, and thus remained undeterred.

Turning back to the ancient past, Kagan argues that the Second Punic War was essentially the result of Roman political failure. Faced with Hannibal's preparations for war, Kagan writes, "the Romans pursued a policy that was both too hard and too soft, unclear, self-deceptive, and, therefore, dangerous." Instead of maintaining peace on their terms, they found themselves in a long war which they nearly lost.

To prevent World War II, Kagan proposes, the Allies would have had to keep Germany down after their victory in World War I. If the Allies had continued to enforce their Treaty of Versailles, which severely constricted Germany's military capabilities, Hitler could not have won the early campaigns of his war. As late as 1936, Kagan writes, the French could have reoccupied Germany's Rhineland at little cost to them, and put paid to Nazi dreams of world power. The Allies' failure to react efficiently to the threat of a rearmed, vengeful Germany led to Hitler's insatiable attacks on Europe and gave him an early lead that nearly proved fatal to the Allies. Sir Neville Chamberlain's politics of appeasement is singled out for its shortsightedness.

While Kagan's military analysis is correct, it is hard to imagine that the Western democracies really could have reacted with this political ruthlessness. Many Europeans desired peace after the bloodletting of World War I, and only realized too late that Hitler was not going to stop without a new war.

On the Origins of War and the Preservation of Peace concludes with a case study where peace prevailed. Somewhat surprisingly, however, Kagan severely blames President John F. Kennedy for having failed to stand up to Soviet leader Nikita Khrushchev. Having allowed Fidel Castro to crush the anti-Communist invasion at the Bay of Pigs, Kagan argues, convinced Khrushchev that Kennedy was "soft" and would not really stand up to Communist aggression elsewhere.

Kagan convincingly argues against the lingering popular perception that the new missiles in Cuba did not alter the nuclear balance of power. Prior to acquiring these new bases, the Soviet threat to America was much smaller than generally imagined. Here, Kagan blames the Kennedy Administration for not dispelling the myth that the Soviets were America's nuclear equals and that the Cuban missiles hardly mattered. Had the public realized how much ahead America really was of the Soviets, Kagan argues, there would have been more room for negotiation during the crisis.

Citing freshly released formerly secret American documents, Kagan is sure to shock some readers by documenting John F. Kennedy's initial position, which dangerously hovered on an acceptance of the new missiles. Public protest forced him to abandon this idea. As Kagan shows, however, the Americans traded the removal of the Soviet missiles on Cuba for that of American missiles in Turkey, in spite of official assertions that there was no such linkage.

Kagan's work ends by warning of the pitfalls of wishful thinking. There will be people who, like Hitler or Hannibal, will challenge the peace. It is only the strong who can dissuade the evil of launching a war they believe they might win. Thus, Kagan's conclusion that the maintenance of peace remains an important, and costly burden for the strong nations represents a sobering voice at the end of a millennium that has seen much war, and never stopped of dreaming about peace. As Kagan would argue, peace has been dreamed of too often, and work to accomplish it has often been neglected.

R. C. Lutz

Sources for Further Study

The Christian Science Monitor. January 26, 1995, p. B1.
Foreign Affairs. LXXIV, March, 1995, p. 148.
Los Angeles Times Book Review. January 22, 1995, p. 1.
National Review. XLVII, March 6, 1995, p. 65.
The New Republic. CCXII, June 19, 1995, p. 43.
The New York Review of Books. XLII, April 20, 1995, p. 6.
The New York Times Book Review. C, January 22, 1995, p. 8.
The Wall Street Journal. February 13, 1995, p. A12.
The Washington Post Book World. XXV, January 29, 1995, p. 1.

ONE BY ONE FROM THE INSIDE OUT
Essays and Reviews on Race and Responsibility in America

Author: Glenn C. Loury (1948-   )
Publisher: Free Press (New York). 332 pp. $25.00
Type of work: Current affairs; essays

A collection of previously published articles and book reviews by a foremost African American conservative

In the United States, African Americans are "representative persons." That is, their behavior is not perceived as springing solely from internal sources. Rather, it represents something; it serves to assist majority culture to measure the decline or progress of the race itself. Successful blacks reap individual benefits but also function as demonstrations of "what a black person is really capable of." "Failures" cannot experience the simple misery of their lot, for, however dimly, they know that they have provided material for those who want to say, "There, I told you so!" They have failed to be "a credit to the race."

Most members of other minority groups in the United States also function as representative persons. Yet their burden is immeasurably lighter. For example, Koreans never served as slaves and so are exempt from the infinitely complex psychology of guilt and innocence that bedevils black-white relations. Of Koreans one could never say, as Orlando Patterson says of his people, "The black population, for two thirds of its history in the United States—248 of 377 years or .6578 of its history, to be exact—was an enslaved group, physically, economically, socially, legally, sexually, morally, and psychologically, subjected not only to the exploitative whim of individual white owners but at the violent mercy of all whites."

As Shelby Steele has vividly pointed out, white Americans desperately wish to construct a defense of their own innocence in relation to this history. Few do so by exculpating the institution of slavery. Most proclaim their noninvolvement, the contemporary irrelevance of the question, and their fervent best wishes for "black improvement." What is seldom noticed is that all such defenses leave blacks with something to prove—that the racists are wrong, that advocates of color-blind policies are right, that the suspicion of racial inferiority that hangs in the American air can gradually be dispelled, or that this is indeed Babylon.

The profoundest argument that America remains a deeply racist nation lies exactly in this domain. If a group of people "have something to prove"—if the actions of one of their number are quickly generalized to the whole (more than thirty million persons, in this case)—they are not unique selves but representative persons. As such, they are excluded from the quintessential American experience: to be considered purely as individuals—unencumbered by ancient ties, archaic histories, outlived traditions, ancestral and tribal enmities. When a young white male is sent to prison, no one says, "He has shamed the white race." Caucasians enjoy the status of true individuals; blacks meanwhile still remain "race men."

Such is the context within which the remarkable saga of Glenn Loury is playing itself out. Loury's career as a black intellectual has been predicated on the audacious theory that American individualism is vibrant enough to be the political philosophy of African Americans. He has long held that blacks have been too reluctant to make use of the opportunities that America affords, opportunities that realistically exist despite racism's undeniable grip. In the prologue to *One By One from the Inside Out*, he makes his credo very clear:

> Thus, ironically, to the extent that we individual blacks see ourselves primarily through a racial lens, we sacrifice possibilities for the kind of personal development that would ultimately further our collective racial interests. We cannot be truly free men and women while laboring under a definition of self derived from the perceptual view of our oppressor, confined to the contingent facts of our oppression. . . . It seems to me that a search for some mythic authentic blackness too often works . . . to hold back young black souls from flight into the open skies of American society.

Such a point of view must impose multiple burdens on any African American who holds it, and it is clear that Loury has found them occasionally unendurable. While he has refused to view himself "primarily through a racial lens," others have insisted upon it. A product of the Chicago's South Side, Loury grew up in the charged racial environment of the 1960's. Having majored in mathematics with an interest in both social issues and abstract modeling problems, Loury completed a Ph.D. in economics at the Massachusetts Institute of Technology (MIT) in the mid-1970's. He eventually became a tenured faculty member at Harvard University and, in the words of Robert S. Boynton, "an intellectual hero of the Reagan right." Loury was instrumental in acquainting Americans with what seemed like a new species: the black conservative intellectual. With Clarence Thomas, Shelby Steele, Stanley Crouch, Stephen Carter, Julius Lester, and Patricia Williams, Loury has opened entirely new perspectives on the debates over affirmative action, civil rights, crime, welfare, and urban decay.

This volume is a collection of Loury's writings from the preceding eleven years. The most substantial pieces appeared first in such publications as *First Things*, *The Public Interest*, *Moment*, and the *Harvard Journal of African American Public Policy*. Readers would, however, be well advised to begin with the newly composed epilogue ("New Life: A Professor and Veritas"), for here the dimensions of the burden Loury has carried become clear. He confesses that his extraordinary success as an academic and public intellectual left him spiritually dead and emotionally wasted. He acknowledges "slavery to drugs and alcohol," persistent marital infidelity, severe depression, and overwhelming egocentrism.

With a frankness about spiritual and personal matters rarely found in academic books, Loury recounts his conversion to Christianity. It began at an Easter service in 1988; he had been invited by a minister while he was a patient in a substance-abuse program at a psychiatric hospital. After that, he began to read the Bible and experience an erosion of his resistance to the reality of the spiritual: "I began to make more room within my heart for the message of the Gospel. Things in my life began to change."

In his teaching of ethics at Harvard's Kennedy School of Government, he spoke candidly about his new sense of God's mercy and grace. Charles Colson's *Born Again* (1977) was a text that he used with students to show that "ultimately, personal morality must be the bedrock of professional ethics, and religious conviction can play a central role in empowering a person to adhere to such a personal moral code." Since then, Loury has been reunited with his extended family and his adult children from a prior marriage. His present wife has borne him two children, and the book is dedicated to this beloved trio.

Loury's epilogue helps account for the theological references and perspectives that occasionally appear in the essays and reviews published in the 1990's. Yet on the whole, the ideas presented here seem rather consistent. By this point in his career, a settled constellation of "Louryan" views exists. These are most fully presented in "Black Dignity and the Common Good," "Two Paths to Black Progress," and "Economic Discrimination." Some of the book's most interesting material appears in the book reviews, where he evaluates works by conservatives such as Charles Murray and Shelby Steele as well as those by such liberals as Andrew Hacker, Derrick Bell, and Cornel West. A notable feature of the collection is Loury's attention to the present strained relations between Jews and African Americans.

What then are Loury's key positions? At least four present themselves. The first is his insistence that the American public exists in a "post-Civil Rights" era but that important segments of black America have failed to come to terms with that fact. Throughout, Loury evinces the greatest respect for Martin Luther King, Jr., and the achievements of "the Movement." Indeed, its successes constitute the premise of many of Loury's arguments. He insists, however, that to carry into present realities the strategies, rhetoric, and mental habits of the civil rights era is thoroughly counterproductive. Those strategies focused rightly on extracting fundamental citizenship rights from government—voting, access to public accommodations, fair employment practices, school desegregation. To continue to rely on such approaches is misguided, however, for it deepens the already unhealthy reliance on government-initiated solutions that exists in the black community and underestimates the amount of opportunity the system affords.

Loury's second major theme follows from the first: True freedom of thought is in short supply in African American intellectual circles. Old stalwarts of the Civil Rights movement, invoking the militancy of W. E. B. Du Bois or Thurgood Marshall or those to the left of King, have imposed an "orthodoxy" on their followers. The urban underclass, black youth unemployment, welfare dependency, academic underperformance, black incarceration rates—these problems are persistently traced to "structural injustice" and fundamental racial bias. For Loury, the power of this orthodoxy was vividly demonstrated in the Clarence Thomas Supreme Court appointment drama, in which Thomas' conservative views disqualified him a priori in the eyes of "the Civil Rights establishment."

Third, when their leaders persist in finding in racism the source of all problems, black Americans are deprived of an important experience of democracy. Here Loury is at his most provocative, arguing that blacks are being taught simply to dismiss white fears and criticisms. Yet "attending to the sensibilities of whites is directly in the interests of blacks. Because we live in a democracy, we bear the burden of persuading our fellows of the worth of our claims upon them." This requires that African Americans return to the spirit of the philosophy of Booker T. Washington, which stressed self-improvement and the virtues of "thrift, industry, cleanliness, chastity and orderliness." Loury rejects Washington's aversion to politics, but he is prepared to say that a "profound pathology" now exists in some areas of black culture. Such a pathology cannot be cured through the interventions of whites and is not best healed by political means.

Yet is it not naïve to ask of a people with radically unequal resources and staggering social and historical liabilities to cure their own "pathologies" by engaging in self-help? In dealing with this issue, Loury's fourth major theme surfaces—the need for very discriminating "supply-side" interventions. While he distrusts the central state and favors the strengthening of "mediating institutions" (churches, voluntary organizations, neighborhoods, work-related affiliations), he is not prepared to rely on benign neglect or laissez-faire. Rather, "government intervention aimed specifically at counteracting the effects of historic disadvantage, and taking as given existing patterns of affiliation, will be required." Practically, this would mean "less of an emphasis on desegregation, and more stress on targeted efforts to improve the schools, neighborhoods, and families where poor black children are concentrated." The disparity between "the social capital" (skills, opportunities, knowledge, property, "connections") owned by whites and that owned by blacks is so great that a "color-blind" public policy will not suffice.

Loury's analysis of affirmative action reflects the measured and discriminating constructive position that he wants to promote. Affirmative action is subject to "reputational externalities," he argues; that is, it produces unintended economic and psychological consequences that vitiate its impact. Affirmative action, Loury believes, encourages whites to discount black achievement and sows self-doubt in the hearts of black achievers. The far better course is for government to focus on the "supply side" of black development—producing better students and workers through assiduously applied interventions. Thus, Loury qua economist sounds themes that are decidedly nonconservative. In calling for "a targeted effort at performance enhancement among black employees or students," he remarks that government dare not act in a "color-blind" way. Such polities presume "a direct concern about racial inequality" and involve "allocating benefits to people on the basis of race."

Glenn Loury remains a man on the move, an evolving thinker. This is good, because deep strains appear in his work. His concrete policy prescriptions often seem far more centrist and even liberal than his overarching political philosophy. The "open skies" of American society do not seem quite so open to struggling black entrepreneurs and job seekers. What motivation will black youths have to seize on targeted programs in schools and job training if they suspect that they will excluded from the good jobs anyhow? The warm welcome Loury has received in conservative ranks has been chilled by the poisonous new "facts" of racial inferiority introduced by his former Harvard colleagues Charles Murray and Richard J. Herrnstein in *The Bell Curve: Intelligence and Class Structure in American Life* (1994). Does their call for a return to "individualism" mean at all the same thing as Loury's? Finally, one wonders how much his breakdown was brought on by the desire of conservatives to use his talents to further their cause—in other words, to turn Glenn Loury into another "representative person."

Leslie E. Gerber

Sources for Further Study

Booklist. XCI, April 15, 1995, p. 1458.
Essence. XXVI, November, 1995, p. 68.
Kirkus Reviews. LXIII, March 1, 1995, p. 301.
The Nation. CCLX, April 24, 1995, p. 567.
National Review. XLVII, June 26, 1995, p. 56.
The New York Times Book Review. C, May 21, 1995, p. 3.
Publishers Weekly. CCXLII, March 20, 1995, p. 49.
Reason. XXVII, May, 1995, p. 60.
The Wall Street Journal. May 19, 1995, p. A12.
The Wilson Quarterly. XIX, Summer, 1995, p. 77.

ONE NATION UNDER A GROOVE
Motown and American Culture

Author: Gerald Early (1952-   )
Publisher: Ecco Press (Hopewell, New Jersey). 135 pp. $17.00
Type of work: Essays

The acclaimed Motown Music Corporation is considered as an intersection for themes of race, class, youth culture, and the transformations of American society in the 1960's and 1970's

The accent in the title of Gerald Early's book should fall on the phrase "and American Culture," for this essay, expanded into book length from an original appearance in *The New Republic*, is neither another history of the Motown Music Corporation of Berry Gordy, Jr., nor critical analysis of the "Motown sound." Instead, *One Nation Under a Groove: Motown and American Culture* is an intelligently argued reflection on the Motown phenomenon as a major cultural episode in recent American history, one that has everything to do with the history of civil rights and race relations, youth culture, the aspirations of the black middle class, and the rapid growth of the popular music industry.

Perhaps another accent should fall on the phrase that begins the title: "One Nation." Arguably the most significant achievement of Motown music was its eradication of the boundaries that had separated rhythm and blues (known early in the 1950's as "race music") from so-called pop music, which had meant "white" until at least the late 1950's. Motown music was the self-proclaimed "sound of young America" during the 1960's, the decade that elevated "young America" into iconic cultural status. The music transcended racial lines at precisely the time American law refused the logic of segregation—though Early reminds readers, in carefully reasoned passages, that black audiences experienced the music in significantly different ways from whites.

Early, director of African American studies at Washington University in St. Louis, is the author of essays on a variety of topics concerning race and popular culture, including *Tuxedo Junction: Essays on American Culture* (1989) and *The Culture of Bruising: Essays on Prizefighting, Literature, and Modern American Culture* (1994). The latter study is echoed in several passages in the present book, as Early is wont to use Joe Louis and Muhammad Ali as figures who represent black pride and dignity. In his introduction, Early reveals a wary attitude toward popular culture as a realm of expertise, a scholarly identification he wishes to refuse. He is quick to refer the reader to such acknowledged experts on black music as the prolific critic Nelson George.

However much he admires and enjoys Motown music, Early is after the larger subject of black popular culture as American popular culture, exemplified by the "crossover" success of Motown music. Crossings, crossings-over, and crossing boundaries are the privileged metaphors of *One Nation Under a Groove*: southern blacks crossing the Mason-Dixon Line on the way north earlier in the century, crossing the line between the music of the black church to secular music, and crossing the line between the rhythm and blues and pop music charts. This last crossing prefigured, in part, the crossing of the "legal" boundaries that had separated black and white America.

In the mid-1990's, one reads Early's graceful essay with a mounting sense of loss and sadness, given the resurgence of racism and racial antagonism on all fronts in American political culture, certainly reflected in the marketing of popular music. Rare indeed is the modern record store where "rock" or "pop" does not mean "white," while "rap" is ghettoized along with "rhythm and blues." The implication is that the record-buying public will never cross such lines as these, a cultural assumption reinforced by the disturbing films of Spike Lee and John Singleton.

The details of Berry Gordy's life are well known from other sources: how he left a career as a prizefighter to open a record store in Detroit and then to become a songwriter and promoter (writing or cowriting some of singer Jackie Wilson's earliest hits) in the early 1950's; how he established Motown Records in 1961; how in the first years his entire family, including his parents, were involved; how the company, under one roof, housed writers, recording engineers, producers, and performers (with more than one role being filled by many, most famously Smokey Robinson), in what Martha Reeves (of Martha and the Vandellas) and many others have described as an extended family atmosphere.

Early bears down forcefully on the theme of family, demonstrating that Motown won the hearts of middle-class blacks because it conformed to the cherished myth of the black family, a myth that began to be nurtured in the face of slavery's cruel disregard of actual families. Families are where young people are trained in correct comportment, and Gordy's company was famous for insisting on the grooming, posture, and behavior that would give the lie to racist assumptions about minority slovenliness or excessively casual demeanor, even employing an etiquette expert to prepare young performers for the scrutiny they would endure on long tours, extending to the Jim Crow South.

Here and there, Early comments on a particular Motown hit such as the anthemic "Dancing in the Street" by Martha and the Vandellas, which the author argues was heard differently by blacks and whites. For black audiences, it seemed a clarion call for activism, while to whites it was simply good-time, carefree music. Readers learn occasional bits of trivia relating to a hugely successful record, such as the revelation that "I Was Made to Love Her" narrowly rescued Stevie Wonder's career with Motown—Gordy had been about to drop him because his voice had changed (no more "Little Stevie").

For the most part, however, Early is in search of themes applicable to the broadest outlines of the African American cultural experience, as his four chapter titles make evident. "Family Happiness" is the title of the first chapter, with a few interesting twists on the theme (from memoirs written by Reeves, Robinson, and others) of the "family" atmosphere Gordy instilled in the Motown headquarters at 2648 West Grand Boulevard in Detroit, emblazoned with the sign "Hitsville U.S.A." Early compares the fervent black advocacy of "family" with the sentimental Italian American take on it, just as he treats Gordy's earliest attempts to launch the career of Jackie Wilson as efforts to emulate an Italian "crooner" such as Frank Sinatra.

Early calls part 2 "A Usable Black Present or the Lessons of Booker T. Washington and Joe Louis." Gordy the former prizefighter harks back to Louis, the dominant symbol of black masculine pride and dignity in the early decades of the twentieth century. At the same time, in his persevering entrepreneurship he exemplifies the "by your own bootstraps" message of Booker T. Washington. The fact that Gordy's successful career unfolded in the Midwest is of major significance to this Midwestern author. Early explains that the Midwestern states have played an important role in the history of black migration and the modern black urban culture that, by the early 1950's, saw several prominent independent record companies specializing in what was coming to be called "rhythm 'n' blues."

One such label, one of the most important black-owned companies before Motown Records, was Chicago's Vee-Jay Records, which featured such artists as Jimmy Reed, John Lee Hooker, Dee Clark, Gene Chandler, and Betty Everett, as well as a number of jazz artists whose style fell somewhere between the "jump" sound of Kansas City of the late 1940's and the bebop-influenced "cool" jazz of the 1950's. Performers in Midwestern centers such as Chicago, St. Louis, and Kansas City had pioneered the evolution away from the big band sound (prohibitively expensive by the early 1950's) toward the smaller combos that made up for their size with a louder, often amplified sound—the sound that became rhythm and blues and then early rock 'n' roll.

The Detroit version of this sound, especially as captured by early Motown recordings, was notable for its secular character. It has become a commonplace to describe "Motown" as gospel influenced, but it is noteworthy that none of the vocal groups associated with "Hitsville U.S.A."—such as Martha and the Vandellas, the Marvelettes, the Miracles, the Supremes, the Four Tops, or the Temptations—originated in churches. Gordy was after his own version of a completely "pop" sound, and even though his company became known for the collective sound and style of its many groups, he was always intent on finding the one "star" whose career would soar beyond all previously reached heights. For a time Diana Ross became that star.

Ross took her cues from Gordy, whose most extravagant spotlighting of her talents was certainly the often-criticized 1972 film *Lady Sings the Blues*. The resentment felt by the many female Motown singers (especially Reeves and the two other members of the Supremes) who were eclipsed by the overexposure of Ross has been well documented. Ross may have been content to let Gordy direct her career, but arguably more talented artists such as Stevie Wonder and Marvin Gaye began to chafe under the overly regimented, paternalistic corporate style. By the end of the 1960's, they had each won exclusive artistic control of their performances and recordings, announced most dramatically by Gaye's visionary 1971 album *What's Goin' On?*

This is the subject, in part, of Early's final chapter, "The Shrine and the Seer," which spells the end of Motown in the Motor City. The same year that Gordy rather reluctantly released Gaye's groundbreaking album, he pulled up stakes to join the burgeoning music industry of Hollywood. In the Roger Weisberg documentary film *Road Scholar* (1992), about poet Andrei Codrescu's automotive journey in quest of

America, Codrescu visits all that remains of Motown in Detroit, the building on West Grand Boulevard that still bears the "Hitsville U.S.A." sign. It is a somber occasion, emphasizing the irreparable sense of loss Detroit citizens feel over Motown's abandonment of the city.

The sense that Motown's success was the result of far more than one determined entrepreneur's hard work is reinforced by the stories of disc jockeys whose cooperation and enthusiasm were crucial in guaranteeing the making of a hit record. The "seer" of the chapter is the late Gaye, whose artistic vision increasingly broke free of the Motown formula. Early comments on what a tortured, conflicted man Gaye was. Yet however much he may sympathize with the singers, Early does not detract from Gordy's own achievements and their implications for the upwardly mobile aspirations of the black bourgeoisie.

One of the most lasting of these achievements was certainly that of breaking once and for all with the tiresome practice in early rock 'n' roll of "cover versions" of songs by black artists. Throughout the 1950's, a rhythm and blues or doo-wop act would cut its record for the black audience, but then the songs would be rerecorded in a sanitized cover version by a white group (for example, "Sh-boom" by the Chords, later covered by the Crew-Cuts). Gordy made sure that, under one roof, black musicians recorded songs written and arranged by in-house songwriters, making records that would make their own way up the pop charts. One of the most significant marks of this achievement, Early argues, was surely the 1967 Motown release *The Supremes Sing Holland/ Dozier/Holland*, a tribute to the label's brilliant songwriting team.

Finally, however oppressive Gordy's corporate paternalism may have been for some Motown artists, the affirmation of the larger sense of "family" is a quality Early persists in admiring. He sees this as an important mark of racial difference: that blacks and whites view the relationship between individuality and community in starkly opposing terms. He asserts that whites regard "the individual's empowerment as a safeguard against the community's tyranny; blacks see the community's empowerment as the safeguard of the individual's dignity and fate."

At such points, *One Nation Under a Groove* becomes much more than a book dealing with pop music. It provides reminders of what white Americans can gain from the distinctive contributions of their black fellow citizens, if only they will listen. For a brief few years, long enough to help make Motown Records an enormous success, they appeared to do so.

James A. Winders

Sources for Further Study

Emerge. VI, September, 1995, p. 72.
Essence. XXVI, July, 1995, p. 56.
The Nation. CCLXI, July 3, 1995, p. 26.
San Francisco Review of Books. XX, May, 1995, p. 4.

THE ORIGIN OF SATAN

Author: Elaine Pagels (1943-   )
Publisher: Random House (New York). 214 pp. $23.00
Type of work: Sociology of religion

The social consequences of the concept of Satan, especially as it developed in early Christianity

Elaine Pagels, a professor of religion at Princeton University, gained attention beyond the academy with the publication in 1979 of *The Gnostic Gospels.* An analysis of the Nag Hammadi Library, which was discovered in 1945 in the Egyptian town for which it is named, the book argued for a reconsideration of the early history of Christianity. Pagels, through her study of dozens of previously unknown documents found at Nag Hammadi, concluded that the standard account of the early Christian church did not take sufficient account of the diversities of Christian belief in the first and second centuries before the canon of Scripture had been settled, orthodox doctrine codified, and the institutional form of church hierarchy established.

More specifically, various so-called Gnostic groups circulated their own "gospels" and other writings that departed from the emerging doctrinal orthodoxy. In fact, Pagels claims, the leadership in the early Christian communities rejected or suppressed certain Gnostic Christian documents for social and political reasons, so as not to hinder the institutional development of the church.

Basic to much of Gnosticism was the belief that the spirit, through special knowledge (*gnosis* in the Greek means, Pagels says, "insight" or "wisdom"), could somehow participate in the cosmic redemption initiated by Jesus Christ. At issue was the question of authority. Orthodox Christians insisted on the literal resurrection of Christ, Pagels speculates, because only the apostles could witness to that singular event, and only those to whom the apostles chose to pass their testimony to could in turn authoritatively pass it to those who came after. The Gnostic Valentinus, by contrast, emphasized an authority based on *gnosis*, a kind of personal knowledge of the deep truths of Scripture not given to "ordinary" Christians but potentially available to anyone. Orthodox bishop Irenaeus, writing against the Valentinians, saw such spiritual pursuits as divisive of the Christian community—both its organization and its morality.

The Gnostic perspective forms the coda of *The Origin of Satan.* One of the Nag Hammadi documents, the Valentinian *Gospel of Philip*, refuses to divide the world into cosmic opposites of moral and immoral. The question for *Philip*, as Pagels puts it, is "how to reconcile the freedom *gnosis* conveys with the Christian's responsibility to love others. . . . When *gnosis* harmonizes with love, the Christian will be free to partake or to decline, according to his or her own heart's desire."

Contrary to the charges of the Gnostics' accusers that they taught that they had gone "beyond good and evil," Pagels contends that at least some of the Gnostic cults had a keen awareness of the struggle against evil. Yet instead of characterizing evil as Satan, the outside invader, as did orthodox Christians, the author of *Philip*, at least, asks his readers to "know" the "root of evil" within. Coming to this inner awareness is an individual quest, subject to no outside standard of morality. The very recognition of this root of evil serves to eradicate it, for when one sees through the self-deception that one is acting for a just cause, the energy for further evil pursuits simply dwindles. Such teachings are only for mature Christians, those who understand the spiritual (as opposed to the literal) meaning of Scripture. For others, the church's ecclesiastical hierarchy might well be necessary, at least until those others come to *gnosis.*

Though Pagels does not simple-mindedly endorse the Valentinian position, it is evident in *The Origin of Satan* that it is considered a salutary contrast to the beliefs of orthodox Christians. The central thesis of the book is not merely that one group of people has on occasion "dehumanized" another group of people, but that in the

> Western Christian tradition . . . the use of Satan to represent one's enemies lends to conflict a specific kind of moral and religious interpretation, in which "we" are God's people and "they" are God's enemies, and ours as well. . . . Such moral interpretation of conflict has proven extraordinarily effective throughout Western history in consolidating the identity of Christian groups; the same history also shows that it can justify hatred, even mass slaughter.

Pagels writes a social history of Satan, or rather the Satanic impulse—what she says is the "belief that [Christians'] enemies are evil and beyond redemption." Such an assumption has been challenged by Christian leaders such as Francis of Assisi and Martin Luther King, Jr., but Pagels mentions them only in passing. Her attention is focused on what she considers the dominant Christian tradition.

Pagels finds in the four canonical gospels, Mark, Matthew, Luke, and John (composed, she says, in that order), something of a sinister development in the history of "demonizing" the Other. The Gospel of Mark (written, says Pagels, around the year 70, at the end of the Jewish revolt in Palestine and some thirty-five years after the death of Jesus) describes the conflict between Jesus and other Jews, framed in cosmic moral terms as a conflict within the Jewish community. Ten or twenty years later, when the Gospel of Matthew was composed, the enemies of Jesus had become primarily the Jewish leaders known as Pharisees. The Gospel of Luke, traditionally thought to have been penned by a Gentile and written roughly the same time as Matthew, portrays Christianity as representing "true Israel." Finally, sometime before the end of the first century, the Gospel of John depicts Christians as alienated from the Jewish community for having preached Jesus as the Messiah. Pagels notes that John's bitterness against those he calls "the Jews" is palpable.

As the Christian movement gradually became a Gentile movement, between the years 70 and 100, a new enemy emerged. "As earlier generations of Christians had claimed to see Satan among their fellow Jews," Pagels writes, "now converts facing Roman persecution claimed to see Satan and his demonic allies at work among *other Gentiles.*" In the following decades, however, as church leaders endeavored to make the content of the faith plain for Gentile converts, the focus turned inward once again, to those called heretics. The five-volume attack on deviant Christians written around the year 180 by the church bishop Irenaeus characterized heretics as greedy, lustful, even mad, teaching the doctrines of Satan.

This leads to the contrast of orthodox Christianity's demonization of false teachers with Pagels' portrayal of the teachings of the Gnostics about recognizing the evil within as far gentler.

Though studded with footnotes, the material in *The Origin of Satan*, reworked from separate articles published in scholarly journals, is intended for a general audience. Pagels does not mean to provide the reader with a balanced assessment of current historical and biblical research; her purpose is polemical, and as she presses for her interpretation of the sociology of Satan, she frequently ignores any alternative renderings of the implications of current research. One telling example is her claim that the Gospel of John does not merely demonize certain Jewish groups, such as the Pharisees, but broadly characterizes "the Jews" themselves as incarnations of Satan. Yet as at least one reviewer has pointed out, since the gospel frequently explains for the reader various Jewish customs, it is likely that the intended audience was unfamiliar with details of the various Jewish groups arrayed against Jesus; reference to "the Jews" could be a simplified categorization and not an ethnic demonization. Further, Pagels' thesis rests in part on the notion of some kind of Satanic incarnation (parallel to the orthodox Christian belief in the incarnation of Christ) because Pagels wants to make the case that the demonized person is beyond the pale, in a sense no longer human. Certainly it may fit the purpose of a group to dehumanize its perceived enemy (without and within), but orthodox Christian doctrine speaks not of Satan being incarnated but rather of Satan "entering into"—influencing—someone, or of groups of people (enemies of Christ) as followers of Satan. Human moral choices have cosmic implications, but it does not follow that those doing Satan's work are no longer human.

One can detect in the book the vague outline of Pagels' own spiritual quest. She was moved to explore the shape of the invisible world after her husband of twenty years, the physicist Heinz Pagels, was killed in a hiking accident in 1988. (A year earlier, the couple's six-and-a-half-year-old son, Mark, had died.) Her studies showed her that among certain Jews and Christians the universe was seen as morally ordered and human beings were part of a spiritual battleground with the stakes immensely high. Pagels told historian David Remnick in an interview,

> I began to see . . . the extent to which I perceive things through this idea of a universe of good and evil. It didn't matter that I was not a believer in the traditional sense. These stories, whether you believe them literally or not, are shadow images, the mental architecture we live in, and they are pervasive. . . . For people more religious [facing tragedy]—well, some might get angry at God, but that made no sense to me. In the ancient Church, they got mad at Satan. That seemed to make more sense. And so I had to ask, What is Satan? What's the Devil?"

In a chapter titled "The Social History of Satan: From the Hebrew Bible to the Gospels," Pagels traces the development of the figure of Satan in ancient Jewish tradition. Most peoples have divided the world into binary opposites, such as "we-they," and Pagels notes that God's covenant with Abraham, found in Genesis, is expressed in terms of blessing (whoever blesses Abraham and his offspring) and cursing (whoever curses Abraham and his offspring). Pagels contends that in this pronouncement establishing a new nation, God "defines and constitutes its enemies as inferior and potentially accursed." Yet if it is the case that the enemies of the new nation are potentially accursed, they are also potentially blessed, and whether the Genesis account implies inferiority, as Pagels insists, is debatable. The author needs the notion of inferiority, however, so she can characterize the development of the concept of Satan as a dehumanizing force.

Satan also came increasingly to be characterized not as the enemy from outside but "the intimate enemy—one's trusted colleague, close associate, brother." Satan is the intimate of God, who turned against him. Satan divides Israel against itself (the Hebrew prophet Zechariah blames Satan for factionalizing a nation beset by exile), as he was later to divide Christian against Christian.

Central to the development of the concept of Satan was the Essene community, a Jewish sect that grew during the Roman occupation of Palestine. "Had Satan not already existed in Jewish tradition," Pagels writes, "the Essenes would have invented him." Ethnic identity was no "true Israel." Instead, the exclusivist group emphasized "moral over ethnic identification" in its ritual demands. The Essenes picture the moral battle in cosmic terms, as the Prince of Light's struggle against the Prince of Darkness. It is but a short distance from the Essenes to the canonical Christian gospels, Pagels notes, which in various ways characterize the battle in moral, not ethnic terms, and which employ the "intimate enemy" motif to demonize first other Jews and then, as Christianity became a Gentile movement, heretical Gentiles.

Pagels' thesis is intriguing, but there are faults, chiefly the mischaracterization of orthodox Christian doctrine, the concentration on the canonical gospels with the corresponding slighting of the accounts of Satan in the New Testament letters of Paul and the Book of Revelation, and the rosy portrayal of Gnostic spirituality. This suggests that the story told in *The Origin of Satan* says more about an author who finds a view of the universe cast in cosmic moral terms distasteful, than about how evil on a massive scale could have entered human experience.

Dan Barnett

Sources for Further Study

The Christian Science Monitor. August 1, 1995, p. 14.
Commentary. C, September, 1995, p. 54.
The Nation. CCLX, June 26, 1995, p. 931.
The New Republic. CCXIII, July 10, 1995, p. 30.
The New York Review of Books. XLII, September 21, 1995, p. 18.
The New York Times Book Review. C, June 18, 1995, p. 9.
The New Yorker. LXXI, April 3, 1995, p. 54.
The Virginia Quarterly Review. LXXI, Autumn, 1995, p. 124.
The Wall Street Journal. June 21, 1995, p. A16.

ORIGINAL SIN

Author: P. D. James (1920-   )
Publisher: Alfred A. Knopf (New York). 416 pp. $24.00
Type of work: Novel
Time: The 1990's
Locale: London

When malicious tricks and bizarre deaths occur at a venerable London publishing house, Scotland Yard Commander Adam Dalgliesh and his young aides confront a puzzle whose solution lies in the past

Principal characters:
ADAM DALGLIESH, a commander at London's Scotland Yard
DANIEL AARON, an inspector at Scotland Yard
KATE MISKIN, a detective inspector at Scotland Yard
GERARD ETIENNE, the new managing director and chairman of Peverell Press
CLAUDIA ETIENNE, his sister, also a director of the firm
FRANCES PEVERELL, another partner, the last of the Peverells
JAMES DE WITT, a senior editor and a partner of the firm
GABRIEL DAUNTSEY, a partner and editor in charge of poetry

P. D. James's detective novels are longer than those of most other authors in the genre, not because the crimes are unusually complex and take more time to unravel but because solving a mystery is not her only interest. Indeed, Baroness James of Holland Park (she was honored with the title in 1991) always has tested the generally accepted limits of detective fiction, leisurely presenting characters and milieus in order to delineate themes as well as to provide the wherewithal for crime solving. James is more than merely a genre writer. *Innocent Blood* (1980) and *The Children of Men* (1993) are standard novels, and *Original Sin*, like its Adam Dalgliesh and Cordelia Gray predecessors, is at the same time a richly textured and thematically complex book and a traditional whodunit.

James uses the Thames, across which characters travel to work and in which one of them dies, for symbolic as well as utilitarian purposes. By evoking the river's links with British history, she signals early in the novel that the crimes have a historical context. A cloth snake intended to block drafts ends up coiled around a murder victim's neck and its head stuffed into his mouth. Not simply a killer's grotesque finishing touch, this is also a clear symbol of original sin behind the crime.

Familiar mystery-genre traits also are present: One murder begets others; suspects belong to the same social or professional group; everyone has an opportunity to commit the crimes; family conflicts, financial problems, and threats to one's professional position are apparent motives; and the provocation for the initial murder is embedded in the past. Scotland Yard Commander Adam Dalgliesh and his assistants go through a predictable routine of examining crime scenes, interviewing principals, reconstructing sequences of events, determining the reliability of alibis, consulting with forensic experts, and familiarizing themselves with past and present relationships.

The basic pattern of detective fiction is familiar, but the mystery is only a starting point for James's expansive narrative, which revolves about the partners and staff of a venerable London publisher.

Peverell Press, founded in 1792, is headquartered at Innocent House, an imposing Thames-side Georgian structure to which most staff members come to work via a launch from across the river. Inexplicable acts of seemingly wanton mischief, including altering proofs and stealing artwork, afflict the staid firm during a crucial transition period in which one long-time partner, Jean-Philippe Etienne, retires and gives his shares to his son Gerard, and the other partner, Henry Peverell, dies and wills his holdings equally to Frances, his daughter, and Gerard, now managing director. Newly installed Gerard, worried that Peverell Press will go bankrupt unless it changes its old-fashioned ways, plans to fire staff, move from the imperial headquarters, and cut unprofitable authors. This determination to drag the firm belatedly into the twentieth century disrupts the superficial tranquillity of Innocent House, resurrecting old personality conflicts and begetting new ones.

The first major crisis is the suicide of Sonia Clements, a long-time senior editor to whom Gerard had given notice. She is found asphyxiated in an aerie where Gabriel Dauntsey, as part of Gerard's housecleaning, has been reviewing the publishing company's archives. In this same venue Gerard's body later is discovered in bizarre circumstances that bring Dalgliesh and his young team—Detective Inspector Kate Miskin and Inspector Daniel Aaron—to Innocent House.

Sonia Clements, Dalgliesh learns, was Henry Peverell's mistress for eight years, so her death is easily explained as the act of a grieving, lonely woman confronted with the additional trauma of losing her job. The suicide is relevant to the plot because Gerard's killer uses Clements' modus operandi and almost succeeds in masking the murder but for the need to justify the act to Gerard, which complicates the scheme and leads Dalgliesh to rule out suicide. The suspects are close at hand in Innocent House—four partners, the accountant, the receptionist, Gerard's secretary, a disaffected author—and everyone has a motive.

For example, Gerard's sister Claudia, like the other partners, does not support his plan to forsake Innocent House, and she must approve before the move can take place; nevertheless, when she pleads for a large sum of money so her lover can buy an antique business, Gerard refuses. Claudia is her brother's heir, but he is engaged, so she may see her financial prospects diminishing if he marries. Frances Peverell, the last of her family and Gerard's former lover, is affronted not only by his plan to destroy Peverell Press traditions but also by his intent to wed a noblewoman. Senior editor James de Witt, with the firm since he left Oxford University and in love with Frances Peverell, believes that Gerard led a promising young author to contract acquired immunodeficiency syndrome (AIDS). Gabriel Dauntsey, also a partner and now in his seventies, for years has been responsible for the Peverell Press poetry list. Once a promising poet but now forgotten, he sees not only his poetry domain in jeopardy under Gerard's regime but also his home, for he lives in a company flat next to Innocent House.

These and others have secrets and sometimes lie to establish or support others' alibis. Dalgliesh has come across such a crowd before and is very much the leader of his team, but in *Original Sin* he has more substantive assistance than in earlier cases. His young associates may be relegated to doing legwork, but Miskin and Aaron make major contributions, and the latter—a new member of Dalgliesh's Special Squad—not only discovers the revelatory evidence but also tracks down the murderer. Daniel Aaron is a major player in the novel, and James devotes considerable time to him, making much of the fact that he is Jewish, largely indifferent to this heritage, and at odds with his family, who are ashamed of his job. The second and less favored son, he joined the police as an act of defiance against his parents, whereas his older brother had gone to university, read law, and been called to the bar. Aaron wants to apologize for rejecting his faith and is haunted by visions of naked people—young, middle-aged, elderly—moving en masse into World War II gas chambers.

For much of the book, James's portrait of this alienated young man seems peripheral, an interesting digression of questionable relevance. Because Dalgliesh thinks that the answer to Gerard's murder lies in the past and that vital evidence could be something in writing, Aaron embarks upon the task of checking documents in the archives room, searching for an unknown clue but motivated by an intense desire to prove himself. His search uncovers an unsigned manuscript, a proposal for a novel provisionally titled "Original Sin." Set in Vichy France between 1940 and 1944, the book is to deal with a Jewish mother and her twins, who are hidden by friends and given false papers but then betrayed and sent to Auschwitz, where they are murdered. The writer proposes to "explore the effect of this betrayal—one small family among thousands of the victims—on the woman's husband, on the betrayed and on the betrayers," and the unsigned manuscript incorporates the author's extensive research, such as testimony from survivors. The documentation reveals that Jean-Philippe Etienne, a community Resistance leader, betrayed Sophie Dauntsey and her four-year-old twins Martin and Ruth, a photograph of whom also is in the file. Etienne admitted his action at the time but claimed that it had been necessary for a greater purpose: to maintain the Germans' goodwill while working underground against them.

Having found evidence against Gabriel Dauntsey which confirms Dalgliesh's suspicions, Aaron keeps quiet about his discovery and decides to confront the man. This leads him on a car chase as Dauntsey, having just killed Claudia and abducted Frances, heads toward Etienne's retirement home, where he asks Etienne to acknowledge the betrayal. The old man, asking how he could be expected to remember specific names, responds, "I did what was necessary at the time. A great number of French lives depended on me. It was important that the Germans continued to trust me if I were to get my allocation of paper, ink and resources for the underground press."

When Dauntsey justifies his own actions by saying he killed a son and daughter to avenge the killing of a son and daughter, Etienne taunts him: "Justice should be speedy as well as effective. Justice doesn't wait for fifty years." Dauntsey counters: "Time takes away our strength, our talent, our memories, our joys, even our capacity to grieve. Why should we let it take away the imperative of justice?"

Finally, Etienne asks why Dauntsey tried to purge guilt by murdering innocent people and then devastates his accuser with startling information:

If you want to act like God, Gabriel, you should first ensure that you have the wisdom and knowledge of God. I have never had a child. . . . I am totally infertile. My wife needed a son and a daughter and to satisfy her maternal obsession I agreed to provide them. Gerard and Claudia were adopted in Canada and brought back with us to England. They are not related by blood to each other or to me.

Throughout this climactic scene, Aaron is an observer "isolated in a moral quarantine"; he does prevent Dauntsey from walking off to kill himself. When Dalgliesh arrives, he asks, "You let him go deliberately? He didn't break free?" Aaron responds, "No, sir. He didn't break free. . . . But he's free now."

He admits to Kate Miskin: "I couldn't bear to see him handcuffed, in the dock, in prison. I wanted to give him the chance to take his own path home." Whereas she laments that he has ruined his career, he focuses on Etienne's indifference to the Dauntseys' fate, his lack of remorse, and his belief that they were expendable. When she asks about the innocent author whom Dauntsey killed, Aaron counters: "You're so confident, aren't you, Kate. So certain you know what's right. It must be comforting, never having to face a moral dilemma. The criminal law and police regulations: they provide all you need, don't they?" He then returns to the house to retrieve, for himself, the old photograph of Dauntsey's family.

Daniel Aaron, then, is at the thematic center of *Original Sin*, an outsider who confronts the awesome ambiguity of issues that James develops. Others in the novel are confident about their moral stances, but Aaron appreciates the complexity of these matters, and this awareness disturbs him. His Jewishness heightens his sensibility in this instance, but long before he knows where the case is heading, he comes across as introspective and acutely concerned with matters of morality and the difficulty of reaching definitive moral conclusions. Unlike most detectives, Aaron cannot always allow evidence, exhibits, and trials to take precedence. In this novel of original sins—betrayal of the marriage vow and in the Holocaust—Daniel Aaron stands as a touchstone by which everyone else should be judged.

Gerald H. Strauss

Sources for Further Study

The Christian Science Monitor. February 23, 1995, p. B3.
The Economist. CCCXXXIV, February 4, 1995, p. 81.
London Review of Books. XVI, December 22, 1994, p. 20.
Los Angeles Times Book Review. April 9, 1995, p. 13.
New Statesman and Society. VII, November 11, 1994, p. 37.
The New York Times Book Review. C, April 2, 1995, p. 11.
The New Yorker. LXXI, March 6, 1995, p. 126.
The Times Literary Supplement. October 21, 1994, p. 20.
The Wall Street Journal. February 24, 1995, p. A8.

OSWALD'S TALE
An American Mystery

Author: Norman Mailer (1923-   )
Publisher: Random House (New York). 791 pp. $30.00
Type of work: Biography
Time: The early 1960's and early 1990's
Locale: Minsk, Byelorussia; Dallas; New Orleans

A masterful late addition to Mailer's huge and seamless oeuvre and a timely reminder that the implications of the Kennedy assassination remain ever with the American people

Principal personages:
> LEE HARVEY OSWALD, the man widely believed to have assassinated
> President John F. Kennedy on November 22, 1963
> MARINA OSWALD, his Russian wife
> MARGUERITE OSWALD, his talkative, eccentric mother
> RUTH PAINE, a friend of Marina Oswald

The April 19, 1995, bombing of the federal building in Oklahoma City activated in many Americans the same habits of mind as did the 1963 assassination of President John Kennedy. As Norman Mailer puts it in his superb biographical study of the young man who either acted alone or was a patsy in the Kennedy killing:

> Many Americans moved into the wild with no more than the strength of their imaginations. When the frontier was finally closed, imagination inevitably turned into paranoia (which can be described, after all, as the enforced enclosure of imagination—its artistic form is a scenario) and, lo, there where the westward expansion stopped on the shores of the Pacific grew Hollywood. . . . By the late Fifties and early Sixties, a good many of these scenarios had chosen anti-Communism for their theme—the American imagination saw a Red menace under every bed including Marina Oswald's.

Oswald's Tale: An American Mystery is first a not-so-tacit rebuke to the Warren Commission, whose a priori task Mailer rightly claims was to decide that Oswald acted alone, since to entertain any other possibility would be to open a Pandora's box of dirty laundry in the U.S. intelligence services and government. The mere fact that after thirty-two years a writer of Mailer's stature published yet another book on the assassination constitutes the final nail in the coffin of the Warren Commission Report, published by Bantam Books less than a year after the fact and whose back cover proclaims it to be "THE TRUTH BEHIND THE MOST SHOCKING CRIME OF THE CENTURY!"

In "The Real Meaning of the Right Wing in America," an essay collected in *The Presidential Papers* (1964), many of whose themes and topics *Oswald's Tale* revisits, Mailer wrote: "Indeed, so long as there is a cold war, there are no politics of consequence in America. It matters less each year which party holds the power." By the early 1990's, the Cold War had ended, the American penchant for paranoid scenarios was casting about for new themes, and politics of consequence were reemerging as hostile partisans of ever more deeply entrenched political positions sought new villains-cum-scapegoats. The loose assortment of private paramilitary groups that quickly became notorious in April, 1995, as "the militias" seemed to believe that the federal government and the United Nations were conspiring to deny them their inalienable rights. Many other Americans decried "the militias" as the latest menace to society—accusing them, most disingenuously, of paranoia. Worth bearing in mind is Mailer's claim (in *The Presidential Papers*) that "the crucial characteristic of modern totalitarianism is that it is a moral disease which divorces us from guilt."

As *Oswald's Tale* illustrates brilliantly, mere factual truth is an irrelevance, and one denies this only when opting for existential timidity over an acceptance of the pervasive ambiguity that is inherent in the world. No amount of ridicule or reassurance ever will change the mind of a conspiracy theorist, nor on the other hand will Americans ever know beyond doubt who in addition to or other than Oswald may have conspired to assassinate Kennedy. "It is worth remembering that in life, as in other mysteries, there are no answers, only questions, but part of the pleasure of intellection is to refine the question, or discover a new one," Mailer reminds readers. "It is analogous to the fact that there are no facts—only the mode of our approach to what we call facts."

Mailer brings to his study the hard-won wisdom of a mature and near-great novelist, and his approach demonstrates that crucial to any piece of writing is what the writer himself brings to his task: his personal background, political or factual assumptions, prose style, and decisions on what to include and omit. As elsewhere in his writings, Mailer shows himself to be a prodigious reader as well as a bold and subtle thinker and a narrative artist of the first order. With masterful self-assurance, he realigns extracts from several earlier books on the assassination, combining them with his own research and speculation to arrive at his goal: a narrative that touches, though scarcely solves, the mystery of Oswald's identity and motivations. One must admire the sheer audacity, so characteristic of Mailer; yet again he demonstrates that the biggest writers are the ones who choose and master the biggest topics. Although he very carefully is not writing fiction here, Mailer as usual possesses the courage necessary to pursue the implications of his own earlier statement, in *Cannibals and Christians* (1966), that "there's no clear boundary between experience and imagination."

Mailer organizes his tale into two "volumes" titled "Oswald in Minsk with Marina"—Minsk is the capital of Belarus, the former Soviet Republic of Byelorussia, where Oswald lived from 1959 to 1962—and "Oswald in America." The Minsk material was prompted by the KGB's *glasnost*-inspired offer to show Mailer some of its files on Oswald—an offer Mailer calls a writer's equivalent of "an Oklahoma land-grab." Nearly fifty pages pass at the beginning with no mention of Oswald, as Mailer obeys his sense of the importance of sketching in the background of Marina's early life (which he does via a series of tangentially connected vignettes). Then follows an unfolding of their early married life, by way of original interviews with Oswald and Marina's Russian friends. Mindful that most modern readers are younger than he (he was born in 1923), he takes care to recapture the Cold War atmosphere of the time, to which end the Minsk sections of the book contribute nicely; how many Americans in 1961 had the remotest clue what day-to-day life really was like in the Soviet Union?

"Oswald in America" relies heavily on paragraph-length extracts from earlier books on the assassination, a daring tactic that succeeds by virtue of the intellect at work on the task of realigning them. A good example of Mailer's achievement is the section on Jack Ruby near the end, titled "The Amateur Hit Man," which was excerpted in *The New York Review of Books* (May 11, 1995).

One reason the assassination still matters is that—regardless of who pulled the trigger—it remains the most vivid parable of the fact that the United States is in large measure, behind the veneer of democracy and liberty, a police state. Kent State, Watergate, the Iran-Contra scandal, the Gulf War—all these only confirmed what Americans began, to their horror, to discover in 1963.

> Given [FBI Director J. Edgar] Hoover's conclusion in the first twenty-four hours after JFK's assassination that Oswald did it all by himself, the word passed down the line quickly: FBI men would prosper best by arriving at pre-ordained results. The process was guaranteed to produce flattening of evidence, destruction of evidence and, if it came to it, creation of evidence. . . . Hoover's one-day solution of the murder was probably reflexive: There was enough awful stuff under enough official rugs—FBI and CIA both!—to dictate the avoidance of anything resembling an all-out investigation. The next best thing, therefore, was accomplished—the appearance of a thorough investigation.

Mailer reminds readers that there existed inside the FBI an undercover Counter-Intelligence Program (COINTELPRO). He quotes from *The American Police State: The Government Against the People* (1976) by David Wise: "In case after case, it was disclosed that many an FBI informant was playing the role of *agent provocateur*, often teaching activist groups how to use explosives, and urging that the members commit specific crimes." Who will ever be able to say who is working on behalf of whom?

Oswald's Tale should be recognized above all as an installment in Mailer's huge and seamless oeuvre; the author's persona is strongly present as ever, and his usual obsessions are in evidence. Mailer fumed as long ago as *The Naked and the Dead* (1948) against "the mores of the weekly slick-paper magazines," and in *Cannibals and Christians* he remarked casually, as only a true intellectual guerrilla would, that "there is that Godawful *Time* Magazine world out there, and one can make raids on it. . . . One can even succeed now and again in blowing holes in the line of the world's communications."

Mailer expresses his ethos of literary composition well in his incisive critique of Robert Penn Warren's famous novel *All the King's Men* (1947), which, like *Oswald's Tale*, explores a real-life American political mystery (the career and assassination of Louisiana governor Huey Long), successfully enough though less brilliantly. "Warren might have written a major novel if he hadn't had just that little extra bit of craft to get him out of all the trouble in *All the King's Men*," suggests Mailer in *Cannibals and Christians*.

> If Penn Warren hadn't known anything about Elizabethan literature, the true Elizabethan in him might have emerged. I mean, he might have written a fantastic novel. As it was, he knew enough about craft to [use it as an escape hatch]. And his plot degenerated into a slam-bang of exits and entrances, confrontations, tragedies, quick wits and woe.

The significance of the Kennedy assassination, like that of the Vietnam War, lingers. "The reaction in Dallas to the capture of Oswald could aptly be described as having been Pavlovian," writes Anthony Summers in *Conspiracy: Who Killed President Kennedy?* (1980), an excellent book that is among those from which Mailer quotes. "The moment local officials realized their prisoner had been in Russia, and discovered armfuls of Communist propaganda amongst his belongings, they began babbling about an 'international Communist conspiracy' to kill the President." (It must not be forgotten that in 1995 the Pavlovian first response of many was to assume that "Middle Eastern terrorists" had done the deed in Oklahoma City.) Summers continues, "After the assassination the public was burdened with no quandary. Wherever the guilt lay, the man identified as killing President Kennedy was stamped as a disciple of the extreme left. Rightly or wrongly, the political left was implicitly convicted along with Oswald."

Mailer does not know the world yet and possesses the courage to say so—to say and show that neither he nor anyone ever will know the full truth about the Kennedy assassination, but that it still, most emphatically, is worth writing about. There are no answers, only questions. *Oswald's Tale* is the most artful and salutary possible demonstration that the past *is* the present; hence the obvious implications of the Kennedy assassination are and will remain every bit as relevant as they were in 1963, quite regardless of whether Oswald acted alone or was a patsy.

Ethan Casey

Sources for Further Study

The Economist. CCCXXXV, June 10, 1995, p. 77.
Los Angeles Times Book Review. June 4, 1995, p. 2.
The New Republic. CCXIII, July 17, 1995, p. 46.
The New York Review of Books. XLII, June 22, 1995, p. 7.
The New York Times Book Review. C, April 30, 1995, p. 1.
Newsweek. CXXV, April 24, 1995, p. 60.
Publishers Weekly. CCXLII, March 20, 1995, p. 48.
Time. CXLV, May 1, 1995, p. 94.
The Wall Street Journal. May 17, 1995, p. A18.
The Washington Post Book World. XXV, April 30, 1995, p. 1.

OUR GAME

Author: John le Carré (David Cornwell, 1931-   )
Publisher: Alfred A. Knopf (New York). 302 pp. $24.00
Type of work: Novel
Time: The mid-1990's
Locale: England and the Caucasus

Retired British agent Tim Cranmer searches for a friend and fellow spy whose disappearance is connected to the fight for independence in a small Russian republic

Principal characters:
> TIM CRANMER, a longtime British spy forced into retirement by the end of the Cold War
> LARRY PETTIFER, his friend and a former double agent, a man of divided loyalties
> EMMA MANZINI, his young mistress
> KONSTANTIN CHECHEYEV, Pettifer's Soviet contact during his years as a double agent
> MARJORIE PEW, a British agent investigating Pettifer's disappearance

With the 1963 publication of his third book, the phenomenally successful *The Spy Who Came In from the Cold*, British author John le Carré established himself as one of the spy genre's finest contributors. In the years that followed, le Carré continued to chronicle the cat-and-mouse games of Cold War espionage in such novels as *The Little Drummer Girl* (1983), *A Perfect Spy*, (1986), and the three books that make up his acclaimed Karla Trilogy, *Tinker, Tailor, Soldier, Spy* (1974), *The Honourable Schoolboy* (1977), and *Smiley's People* (1980).

History, however, has overtaken le Carré's fictional world and rendered it obsolete, with *glasnost* and later the collapse of the former Soviet Union bringing the Cold War to a close. Le Carré has responded to the changing political landscape by successfully adapting his familiar themes to the times, exploring the new world of thawing relations with the Soviet Union in his 1989 novel *The Russia House* and the sometimes troubling memories of longtime agents in *The Secret Pilgrim* (1991).

With *Our Game*, le Carré turns his attention to the plight of Cold War spies cast adrift by their former employers in the wake of the Soviet Union's dissolution. For Tim Cranmer, the end of the Cold War has meant his forced retirement from the British Secret Service, where company policy has decided that old cold warriors may be ill-equipped to deal with the new world order. Cranmer retreats to his country home and turns his attentions to the family vineyard, determined to build a new life for himself with his beautiful young mistress, Emma Manzini.

For Tim's friend Larry Pettifer, however, the transition from spy to ordinary citizen is an uneasy one. Tim had recruited Larry for the service early in his career and, in agents' parlance, had "run" him, supervising him throughout his life as a double agent and acting as mentor, companion, and confidant. Larry is a charming adventurer and accomplished liar by nature—a far more daring and impulsive spirit than Tim, who has in many ways lived vicariously through his friend's escapades in the field. Forced now to resign himself to the life of a university professor, Larry is clearly ill-suited to the change.

Shortly after Larry's first meeting with Emma, Tim begins to suspect that his friend and his mistress are having an affair. When the two disappear, Tim is summoned to London and questioned at length by the service about Larry, their friendship, and Larry's role as a double agent. He learns that Larry has remained in contact with his onetime Soviet supervisor, Konstantin Checheyev, and that the two men have stolen a fortune from the Russian government. Checheyev is a Muslim from the province of Ingushetia, a region in the Caucasus seeking independence from Russia, and it has become apparent to the service that the former Russian spy is now acting on behalf of his small homeland—perhaps with Larry's help.

Unknown to the service, Tim is harboring two secrets: He has not divulged the news of Larry and Emma's affair, and he fears that he may have killed Larry during a fight over Emma. Under suspicion himself, he cautiously begins his own investigation and turns up evidence that Larry is indeed alive and that he and Emma are involved with an arms dealer and are shipping weapons to Ingushetia. Following their trail, he finds that the dealer has been murdered by the Russian mafia, and he fears that Larry and Emma have also fallen victim to its violence.

Tim pursues the trail to Paris, where he finds Emma awaiting Larry's summons to join him in the Caucasus. Traveling under a false passport, Tim reaches Russia and is soon taken prisoner by a group of Ingush rebels, only to learn that Larry has in all likelihood been killed in a recent battle. As suspicions that Tim is acting on behalf of the British government fade, he finds himself treated more as a guest of the rebels than as their prisoner and realizes that he is slipping gradually into Larry's role. Checheyev arrives to join the group, and the rebels fly to a remote village, where, as the book ends, Tim has left his old life behind and has embraced the people and the cause for which his friend gave his life.

With *Our Game* le Carré acknowledges the end of the sort of international intrigue that served as his fictional milieu for three decades. A former British intelligence agent himself, he created a world for his characters that, while imaginary, contained enough truth within its borders to offer his readers a unique glimpse into the shadowy world of espionage. So recognized a master of the spy novel is he that real spies are said to have adopted as their own the slang he invented for his fictional agents.

Yet the format of the spy novel has always been only a serviceable framework within which le Carré could explore the human issues that have fascinated him. Love, betrayal, deception, and human frailty have been the underlying themes of his work and not the plot mechanics that drive most entries in the genre. What interests le Carré—and what raises his novels above the level of mere thrillers—is the wild card that human nature will inevitably provide in even the most carefully thought-out areas of endeavor. It is clear from *Our Game* that this theme is as viable in a post-Cold War novel as it was throughout his earlier career.

At the heart of *Our Game* is the complex relationship that has existed for many years between Tim Cranmer and Larry Pettifer. Tim is the steadier, more predictable of the two, while Larry is capable of a passion and very personal idealism that his friend both envies and exploits. Larry's success as a double agent is made possible not only by his skills at deception but also by his ability to embrace on some level the ideology of the role he is playing. Although his overriding loyalty is to the British government, Larry is capable of submerging himself almost completely in his identity as a Russian agent—a quality that at times causes a potentially volatile schism in his psychological makeup.

Tim recognized this quality early in his friendship with Larry and exploited it when he recruited him for the service. As Larry's handler within the service, Tim plays on his understanding of his friend's strengths and weaknesses, creating a brilliant double agent who at the same time has been rendered incapable of any other sort of life. When Larry seduces Emma, recruiting her to his cause much as Tim had recruited him, it is his way of taking revenge—a fact he articulates during their fight, saying, *"You stole my life. I stole your woman. Simple as that."* It is his devastating countermove in the "game" of the book's title.

Larry has long teased Tim by maintaining that Tim has persuaded him to lead the life that Tim himself has never dared to take on—a situation that has in reality led to an unspoken resentment in both men. Now, Larry and Emma's disappearance forces Tim into an active role fraught with the same dangers that Larry has faced throughout his career. His pursuit of his friend and his mistress—the only two people in his life about whom Tim truly cares—takes him deeper and deeper into the realm of deception and role-playing in which he has long watched Larry move. The immersion becomes so complete that at the book's close he has come at last into full possession of the life that he had forced his friend to live in his stead.

For Larry's part, the life of a double agent has been both his salvation and his despair. The role has called upon all of his talents and intelligence, while at the same time splintering his sense of his own identity. When the service forces him into retirement, he is left with nothing, and his unhappiness and sense of abandonment leave him ripe for a passionate attachment to a new cause. He finds it through Checheyev, his old Soviet intelligence contact, whom he has long regarded with genuine admiration and friendship. The plight of Checheyev's people becomes for Larry the cause he has sought throughout his life, and there is an almost religious fervor in his embrace of the Ingush rebels and their struggle. Although he loses his life through his actions, as Tim notes, "if Larry had led the wrong life, he had at least found the right death."

The theme of loyalty and betrayal that shapes Larry and Tim's relationship is present in every aspect of the book's plots and subplots. They are the qualities that form the basis for the world of espionage and that each agent must deal with in his or her own way. This has also been true for Tim and Larry's Soviet counterparts. Checheyev has for years abandoned his own people and served the state, but the end of the Cold War and the struggle for independence among the republics reawakens his sense of loyalty and purpose, and it is this that he communicates so successfully to Larry. To further the rebels' cause, Checheyev has betrayed the government he once served and, like Larry, recovered his own sense of identity in the process. Loyalty and betrayal in their oldest form are also present in Larry and Emma's betrayal of Tim, and in Tim's refusal to place Emma in danger by informing the Service of her role in Larry's plan. For all of the book's characters, long-held loyalties are superseded by more recent ties that have affected them on a level unmatched by anything in their previous experience, causing them to rethink the rules that had previously governed their lives.

For John le Carré, "our game" is a term that encompasses both the world of espionage in which his characters have spent their lives and the more personal playing out of Larry and Tim's complex relationship. With this novel, le Carré skillfully acknowledges that the former "game" as he knew it has come to a close. The latter, however, remains impervious to shifts in the geopolitical landscape; it lies within the realm of human nature and will be there for him to draw on in books to come.

Janet Lorenz

Sources for Further Study

The Christian Science Monitor. March 16, 1995, p. 12.
Los Angeles Times Book Review. March 26, 1995, p. 2.
The New York Review of Books. XLII, April 20, 1995, p. 4.
The New York Times Book Review. C, March 26, 1995, p. 13.
The New Yorker. LXXI, March 20, 1995, p. 102.
Newsweek. CXXV, March 6, 1995, p. 67.
Publishers Weekly. CCXLII, February 6, 1995, p. 76.
Time. CXLV, March 20, 1995, p. 76.
The Times Literary Supplement. May 12, 1995, p. 19.
The Wall Street Journal. March 3, 1995, p. A8.
The Washington Post Book World. XXV, February 26, 1995, p. 1.

OUR VAMPIRES, OURSELVES

Author: Nina Auerbach (1943-   )
Publisher: University of Chicago Press (Chicago). 231 pp. $22.00
Type of work: Literary history
Time: 1816 to the 1990's
Locale: Primarily Great Britain and the United States

In her exploration of Western culture's fascination with the vampire, Nina Auerbach has found a novel and revealing metaphor for society's metamorphoses over some 180 years

Principal characters:
> DRACULA, the eponymous protagonist of Bram Stoker's 1897 novel, who serves as the locus around which subsequent vampires and discussions of vampires revolve
> VARNEY, the protean vampire hero of a popular mid-Victorian English serial, *Varney, the Vampire: Or, The Feast of Blood* (1845-1847), by James Malcolm Rymer
> CARMILLA, the female vampire heroine of Joseph Sheridan Le Fanu's 1872 homoerotic novel of the same name
> LESTAT, the vampire hero of Anne Rice's Vampire Chronicles, which commenced with publication of *Interview with the Vampire* in 1976

While Nina Auerbach admits the significance of vampires in universal folk tales from time immemorial, her interest in "our vampires, ourselves"—as indicated by her title, with its witty allusion to another modern work of self-conscious sociology, the Boston Women's Health Book Collective's *Our Bodies, Ourselves* (1973)—lies in tracing the evolution of the vampire myth in modern Western society. She begins with the English Romantics, locating the origins of Anne Rice's appealing contemporary vampire, Lestat, in George Gordon, Lord Byron. Byron's "Fragment of a Novel," published in 1816, is a vampire tale that grew out of a journey through Brussels to Geneva that he took that year with his physician, Dr. John Polidori. En route, the two had a falling-out, and Polidori took his own revenge, amplifying Byron's narrative of travel with a sinister companion into *The Vampyre* (1819), which features a vampire named Lord Ruthven who is modeled on Lord Byron.

Polidori's creature, like Byron himself, was surrounded by an atmosphere of homoeroticism. As Auerbach notes, "Out of a hating, needing companionship between men came not only Romantic poetry, but the Romantic vampire." Rice's gorgeous and aristocratic late twentieth century creations, the vampire lovers Louis and Lestat of *Interview with the Vampire* (1976), are direct descendants of this Byronic forebear, but before the lineage reached them, it took a number of fascinating detours.

There are, as Auerbach observes, vampires and vampires, and the first of these to be able, by drinking his victims' blood, to turn them into his progeny was Varney, the protagonist of James Malcolm Rymer's mid-Victorian best-seller *Varney, the Vampire: Or, The Feast of Blood* (1845-1847). Varney's dual identity—he is both the urbane Sir Francis Varney and a subhuman monster—is reminiscent of another classic of Victorian English literature, Robert Louis Stevenson's *The Strange Case of Dr. Jekyll and*

Mr. Hyde (1886). Indeed, as Auerbach notes, Varney is all too typical of an outwardly polite society that was becoming increasingly predatory, a transformation Karl Marx described thus in *Das Kapital* (1867): "Capital is dead labour which, vampire-like, lives only by sucking living labour, and lives the more, the more labour it sucks."

In Joseph Sheridan Le Fanu's *Carmilla* (1872), the vampire's involvement with society becomes an intense entanglement with a specific individual. Carmilla, whom Auerbach calls "one of the few self-accepting homosexuals in Victorian or any literature," makes explicit the desire inherent in Byron's and Polidori's Romantic explorations of vampiric friendship between sympathetic, same-sex intimates. Carmilla, who feeds only on women, falls in love with Laura, a distant relative who shares Carmilla's patrician background and whose life Carmilla longs to share. "I live in your warm life and you shall die—die, sweetly die—into mine. . . . You and I are one forever," she seductively declares to Laura—and indeed, the two identities meld in death.

Auerbach's exploration of vampire evolution comes into its own with her discussion of Bram Stoker's *Dracula* (1897), of which she says: "I suspect that Dracula's primary progenitor is not Lord Ruthven, Varney, or Carmilla, but Oscar Wilde in the dock." Wilde, the scandalous dandy of his day, was convicted for homosexual offenses under the Labouchere Amendment of 1885 and was imprisoned in 1895, the year Stoker began to write his *Dracula*.

The lineaments of Stoker's vampire were drawn from the author's friend Henry Irving's stage portrayal of Mephistopheles. Irving, whose patriotic take on English theater earned for him a knighthood the very day Wilde was convicted, was hailed after his death as the person who had saved England from the decadent cult of Oscar Wilde. Auerbach makes out a convincing case that Stoker created Dracula out of devotion to Irving, whom Stoker continued to champion even after the former fell out of public favor, and in reaction against Wilde, one of whose former love interests ultimately became Stoker's wife.

The Labouchere Amendment not only outlawed homosexual acts but also lent same-sex sentiment or orientation, particularly between men, opprobrium. Whereas earlier vampires had freely loved mortals of their own sex, in the wake of Wilde's conviction, Auerbach argues, Stoker made his vampire into an isolate. Unlike Wilde, she declares, Dracula is careful; as with Irving, the vampire's greatness is subsumed by institutional regulation. The result, she believes, was at least a temporary impoverishment of the vampire tradition—but one that mirrored changes in the larger society: "Dracula's disjunction from earlier, friendlier vampires makes him less a specter of an undead past than a harbinger of a world to come, a world that is our own."

As Dracula, the vampire became recognizable by his "fruity accents, eccentric clothes," an alien whose world is circumscribed by rules: He must sleep in his coffin to retain his vitality; when he travels, he must take with him some of his native earth; he must avoid garlic, mirrors, crucifixes, and—above all—daylight. The oddities of the Transylvanian count became, in the hands of filmmaker Tod Browning and his star, Bela Lugosi, even more pronounced in the 1931 film version of *Dracula*.

Auerbach wryly notes: "[Lugosi as Dracula] wears his tuxedo, cape, and medals not only indoors, but in his coffin." He speaks, she says, as if reading his lines phonetically, with little understanding of their meaning. Unlike the other male characters in the film, he wears lipstick and eye makeup. Clearly, he is perverse, in every sense of the word. In short, he is Oscar Wilde, who has returned from being buried alive in Reading Gaol a creature solitary, suspicious—and sinister.

Stoker's Dracula and Lugosi's later embodiment of him are inarguably the vampire gold standard in modern Western culture. Yet as Auerbach repeatedly demonstrates, vampires are infinitely adaptable; they are capable not only of shape-shifting, a quality first bestowed by Stoker, but indeed of completely making themselves over in order to reflect the differing times they inhabit. During the Edwardian age they came into their own as psychic vampires, who sustain themselves not so much on the blood of their victims as on these individuals' energy, emotions, and creativity. This variant of vampire continues into the late twentieth century, appearing in Karl Edward Wagner's story "The Slug" (1991) as a "friend" who so imposes on the protagonist-writer's time as to rob the latter of his career. Lugosi's dramatic Dracula, Auerbach argues, gave rise to the garish but still civilized Christopher Lee Dracula variations produced by England's Hammer Studios between 1958 and 1970.

In the 1970's, vampires experienced a profound revival. The upsurge of the feminist movement gave rise to a newly sensitized but still romanticized Dracula in the 1973 television version of *Bram Stoker's Dracula*, starring Jack Palance, and to a Byronic vampire savior in the 1979 *Dracula* film starring Frank Langella. The homoeroticism of the Romantic originals resurfaced, too, in Anne Rice's Vampire Chronicles, begun in 1976 with *Interview with the Vampire*. When the political assassinations of the 1960's—the deaths of John F. Kennedy and Robert Kennedy, Martin Luther King and Malcolm X—robbed America of its leaders, vampires filled the void.

Standing head and shoulders above all others, perhaps, was the "real" Dracula, the cruel but efficient fifteenth century Romanian king known as Vlad the Impaler. Vlad Tepes, or Dracula (the word, meaning "devil," is more a title than a name), came to prominence—was resurrected, as it were—with the publication in 1972 of Raymond McNally and Radu Florescu's historical work *In Search of Dracula*. One could hardly have found a more authoritarian figure than this Dracula, who publicly impaled his enemies on stakes but managed at the same time to prevent his people from being swallowed up by the expanding Ottoman Empire. Vlad Tepes' legend actually played little part in the creation of Stoker's Dracula, but it seems to have had quite an effect on the vampires of the 1970's. As Bela Lugosi's Dracula and Boris Karloff's Franken-stein's monster did during the Great Depression, later revelations about the real Dracula "buttressed Americans' commitment to the devils they knew."

For Auerbach, however, the signal vampires of the era were the leaderless killers of Stephen King's *'Salem's Lot* (1975), which she connects with the Watergate scandal. Auerbach explains in her introduction that "vampires and American presidents be-gan to converge in my imagination, not because I think all presidents are equally vampiric . . . but because both are personifications of their age." Her book, which was conceived during the presidency of George Bush, "when impalpable fears afflicted America," and which was originally titled (in tribute to Franklin D. Roosevelt) "Fear Itself," goes a long way toward fulfilling her aim of connecting individual fears with the wider political and ideological climate they inhabit. Auerbach makes an insightful connection, for example, between the comforting patriarchal atmosphere engendered by the Reagan years and the discovery of a "cure" for vampirism—the infusion of a father's blood—in Katherine Bigelow's 1987 film *Near Dark*. At the same time, she makes a case for Rice's eternally youthful and beautiful vampire males, bored with immortality, as the ultimate fantasy of young men suddenly grown fearful of their own mortality because of the advent of acquired immunodeficiency syndrome (AIDS).

For the most part, however, Auerbach finds that toward the end of the twentieth century vampires had become segregated from society, even marginalized. In a 1991 AIDS-inspired vampire novel, *Dracula Unbound*, Brian Aldiss posits a race of mindless, unsympathetic vampires bent on destroying humanity. Bram Stoker, revived as a character in the novel, syphilitic and exhibiting a new brand of homophobia, refers to these creatures as "a disease." Louis and Lestat in the Vampire Chronicles are also pictured in opposition to human society, obsessed only with discovering their own origins and interacting with their own kind. The female, female-oriented vampire of Le Fanu's *Carmilla* makes a reappearance as Jewelle Gomez's black lesbian vampire in *The Gilda Stories* (1991), but this time she is given only vampire companions and is robbed of her predatory potency.

Vampires are, as Whitley Strieber described them in his novel *The Hunger* (1981), "another species, living right here all along. An identical twin." In more recent times, however, the gulf between us and them has become unprecedentedly wide. Auerbach believes that our vampires need a "long restorative sleep" to revivify them now that they—and we—have muddled through the amorphous, ill-defined period of the Bush and Clinton administrations. Only then, she implies, will they waken to engage and entertain us once again.

Lisa Paddock

Sources for Further Study

The Chronicle of Higher Education. XLII, November 24, 1995, p. A11.
The Nation. CCLXI, November 20, 1995, p. 608.
The New York Times Book Review. C, October 29, 1995, p. 33.
The Times Literary Supplement. November 17, 1995, p. 8.
The Washington Post. November 17, 1995, p. F2.

PALIMPSEST
A Memoir

Author: Gore Vidal (1925-   )
Publisher: Random House (New York). Illustrated. 435 pp. $27.50
Type of work: Memoir
Time: 1925-1964
Locale: The United States, Guatemala, Italy, France, and Great Britain

An eminent man of letters recalls his early career in politics, literature, and the Hollywood film industry

> *Principal personages:*
> GORE VIDAL, novelist and essayist
> THOMAS PRYOR GORE, his grandfather
> JACQUELINE BOUVIER KENNEDY, the wife of President John F. Kennedy

Literary critics have not looked upon Gore Vidal as a southern writer, despite his argument that they should. "I am southern," Vidal said in an interview in 1995, and *Palimpsest*, Vidal's memoir of his first thirty-nine years, provides evidence that his southern background indeed shaped his writing and politics.

Vidal grew up in the 1920's and 1930's in what he has described as "the then southern city of Washington, D.C." He spent most of his childhood in the home of his maternal grandfather, Senator Thomas Pryor Gore, whom Vidal called "Dah." Thomas Pryor Gore, born in Mississippi in 1870, came from a family involved in politics. His father, a Confederate veteran, was clerk of Walthall County, Mississippi. Father and son became members of the Populist Party, but the younger Gore switched to the Democrats in 1896, supporting William Jennings Bryan in that year's presidential election. The younger Gore had ambitions to run for the United States Senate, but in Mississippi entrenched incumbents occupied both seats, so he migrated to Texas, then to Indian Territory, which he helped organize into the state of Oklahoma. In 1907, he was elected Oklahoma's first U.S. senator. Vidal's maternal grandmother, Nina Gore, was also southern, a member of the Kay family, slaveholders from South Carolina who moved to Texas after the Civil War.

As Vidal puts it, "the blood of generations of honor-minded crazed southerners" flowed through his veins, and he developed a strong, traditional southern belief in honor himself. When he was young his hero was Billy the Kid, whose story Vidal would later dramatize in two films. Vidal admired Billy's code: "Kill my friend and I will kill you." As Vidal got older, his sense of honor changed. "Now," he writes, "honor is to try to tell the truth."

An effort to tell the truth characterizes Vidal's writing. He refuses to evade issues. In *Palimpsest*, for example, he is open about his sexuality. He describes in a straightforward way his affairs with men as well as women: his first sex with a girl, at age twelve or thirteen; his affair with Jimmie Trimble, a classmate at St. Albans, from whose death as a marine scout on Iwo Jima in World War II Vidal has never recovered;

a one-night stand with Beat novelist Jack Kerouac; affairs with writer Anaïs Nin and actress Diana Lynn; couplings with hundreds of anonymous men. Vidal also refuses to distort his true thought. Often his candor takes the form of unexpected, wicked comments about the famous. In *Palimpsest* he writes that the Duchess of Windsor had her brain scrambled by anesthetic given in her "fourth or fifth face-lift." "Orville and Wilbur Wright," Vidal tells us, "were lifelong bachelors, as *Time* magazine used to write when eager to suggest uranism."

Southern literature emphasizes family history and a sense of the past. Historian Joel Williamson in *William Faulkner and Southern History* (1993), for example, argues that Faulkner drew on the history of both his maternal and paternal ancestors in creating his novels about the fictional Yoknapatawpha County, Mississippi. *Palimpsest* shows that Vidal used the same technique in writing his American Chronicle novels, beginning with *Washington, D.C.* (1967) and going through *Hollywood* (1990). Vidal says that the idea for *Washington, D.C.* came to him while he watched the guests at the wedding reception of his half-sister Nina Auchincloss. It is possible to recognize in *Palimpsest* family members who became characters in the novels: Vidal's grand-father Thomas Pryor Gore became James Burden Day, Vidal's mother Nina Vidal became Enid Sanford, John F. Kennedy provided the model for Clay Overbury (Hugh D. Auchincloss, Vidal's stepfather, was also Jackie Kennedy's stepfather). A character based on Vidal's great-grandfather, the Confederate veteran from Missis-sippi, appears in the novels in dreams and visions. This character serves in the novels as a reminder of the past, a symbol of the lost ideals of the original American republic.

In *Palimpsest*, Vidal traces the history of the Vidal family to its origins in fourteenth century Austria. The Vidals were related by marriage to the Traxlers, a Swiss family that Vidal family legend claimed had been creditors of the French king. Vidal used this material, too, in the American Chronicle novels. The Traxlers appear as characters in *1876* (1976). Vidal's father, Eugene Vidal, appears briefly in *Hollywood* as an army flier and former West Point football star.

If the South influenced Vidal's writing, the South also shaped Vidal's politics. Vidal writes in *Palimpsest* that in the 1950's, when he moved to New York and began to contribute essays to *The Nation* and *Partisan Review*, he found himself different from the New York intellectuals who wrote for those journals. The New York intellectuals engaged in political debates over Marxist theory, debates between Trotskyites and Stalinists that had been going on for twenty years. Vidal's politics had not been shaped by discussions of Marxist theory but by conversation around the family dinner table, where he had imbibed the radical southern populism of his grandfather.

As a southern populist, Senator Gore "represented the ruined farmers of the Civil War, who would later be victimized by eastern financiers, playing casino with the price of cotton," Vidal writes. Historian C. Vann Woodward in *The Burden of Southern History* (1960) contended that the unique history of southerners—defeat in the Civil War, the poverty that followed—made them less likely than other Americans to believe victory in war inevitable, made them better able to understand the risk that war entails. Senator Gore embodied the southern mentality Woodward described (a fact that Vidal seems to have acknowledged by naming the fictional character based on Senator Gore "Burden Day"). Gore was an isolationist who opposed American entry into World War I. Vidal explains, "For someone brought up in the wreckage of the Civil War, any *foreign* war seemed like perfect folly. For someone who detested the country's ruling class, the idea of a war that would be profitable only to the Rockefellers and to the Morgans was insupportable."

Vidal affirms that "the radical populist base of the Gores had made me an instinctive noninterventionist." In his political essays, Vidal has argued that in the post-1945 era the business elite that dominated America concluded that industries that became rich during World War II would continue to prosper if the country were kept on a wartime footing. This elite, then, Vidal has contended, perpetuated the Cold War and created a national security state that has gradually destroyed the traditional freedoms of the original American republic. Vidal's ideas closely resemble Thomas Pryor Gore's southern populist views.

Woodward has suggested that because southerners have had a different historical experience than other Americans, southerners may see American history from a different perspective, may view cherished national myths with some degree of detachment, and may regard idealistic American political rhetoric with a degree of skeptical realism. Senator Gore displayed that kind of skeptical realism. Vidal records, for example, his grandfather's reaction to Abraham Lincoln's Gettysburg Address:

> "Was there ever a fraud greater than this government of, by, and for the people?" He threw back his head, the voice rose: "*What* people, *which* people? When he made that speech, almost half the American people had said the government of the North was not of, by, or for *them*. So then Lincoln, after making a bloody war against the South, has the effrontery to say that this precious principle, which he would not extend to the southern people, was the one for which the war had been fought."

Vidal learned to regard American history and American politics with the same skeptical realism his grandfather did. He asserts, "If I got anything from Dah, it was the ability to detect the false notes in those arias that our shepherds lull their sheep with."

In *Palimpsest*, Vidal puts that skeptical realism to use in his portrayal of the Kennedys, to whom he sarcastically refers as "the Holy Family." Because of his relation to Jacqueline Bouvier Kennedy, in the late 1950's and early 1960's Vidal was a Kennedy family insider, a guest at the White House during John F. Kennedy's presidency and a visitor at the Kennedy home in Hyannis, Massachusetts. Vidal presents the Kennedys in an unflattering light. There is gossip in *Palimpsest* about the Kennedys' sex lives, not only about John Kennedy's promiscuity but also about Jackie Kennedy's sexual adventures (including affairs with actor William Holden and President Kennedy's brother Robert). More important is Vidal's critique of John Kennedy's presidency. According to Vidal, Kennedy believed that U.S. presidents achieve greatness only by leading the country in wartime. Vidal argues that Kennedy wanted that kind of greatness for himself. Not content simply to perpetuate the Cold War, Kennedy tried to win it. The result, Vidal contends, was that Kennedy deliberately took the country from one foreign-policy crisis to another—in Cuba, Berlin, Laos, Vietnam—risking American lives for the sake of his personal ambition.

Vidal ends his memoir with the year 1964, a turning point in his life. Inspired by his grandfather, Vidal had always held political ambitions. In 1960, Vidal ran as Democratic candidate for Congress from the Twenty-ninth District in New York. Though he did not win, he did well enough that in 1962 he was offered the Democratic nomination for U.S. senator from New York, an offer he turned down. In 1964, however, Vidal openly campaigned for Kenneth Keating, Republican candidate for senator from New York, who was running against Robert Kennedy. That campaign resulted in a final break between Vidal and the Kennedys and ended Vidal's political career in New York.

The year 1964 became a turning point in Vidal's life for another reason as well. In the late 1940's he had achieved success as a novelist, but in the early 1950's, needing money, he had turned away from the novel to write film and television scripts. By 1964 he had made enough money to live without working for the rest of his life. He decided to leave Hollywood and politics behind to return to novel writing, and he moved to Rome, which became his principal residence for the next thirty years.

Vidal stated in a 1995 interview that his southern background had made him feel like "an odd man out" in America. In Rome he found a more congenial life. After 1964 he also became, he writes, "more intensely political that I was in my conventional youth." In Rome over the next thirty years he would write the essays and novels in which he would develop his critique of America—writings that would give him the reputation of being a radical. Conservative radio commentator Rush Limbaugh remarked after the Republican victory in the 1994 congressional elections, "The age of Lenin and Gore Vidal is over." Limbaugh did not understand Gore Vidal. Vidal's radicalism had nothing to do with Vladimir Lenin. Vidal's radicalism, as *Palimpsest* makes clear, derived from the tradition of Thomas Jefferson and of the Populists—the southern tradition.

Donald M. Whaley

Sources for Further Study

Chicago Tribune. October 15, 1995, XIV, p. 3.
London Review of Books. XVII, October 19, 1995, p. 8.
Los Angeles Times Book Review. October 1, 1995, p. 2.
New Statesman and Society . VIII, October 27, 1995, p. 44.
The New York Times Book Review. C, October 8, 1995, p. 7.
Newsweek. CCXXVI, October 9, 1995, p. 82.
San Francisco Chronicle. October 8, 1995, p. REV1.
Time. CXLVI, October 9, 1995, p. 76.
Vanity Fair. November, 1995, p. 60.
The Washington Post Book World. XXV, October 8, 1995, p. 3.

THE PAPERBOY

Author: Pete Dexter (1943-   )
Publisher: Random House (New York). 307 pp. $23.00
Type of work: Novel
Time: The 1960's
Locale: Rural northern Florida, Daytona Beach, and Miami

The story of a father and two brothers, all in the newspaper business, and of a murder investigation that has profound effects on their lives

> Principal characters:
> JACK JAMES, the narrator, driver of a newspaper truck, formerly a
>   member of the University of Florida swim team
> WILLIAM WARD (W. W.) JAMES, his father, publisher of a small-town
>   newspaper
> WARD JAMES, Jack's older brother, star investigative reporter for a
>   Miami newspaper
> HILLARY VAN WETTER, a convicted murderer
> CHARLOTTE BLESS, the woman who loves Van Wetter
> YARDLEY ACHEMAN, Ward's flashy, unscrupulous partner

Pete Dexter's novel *Paris Trout* (1988) won a well-deserved National Book Award for its portrait of a villainous store owner and of the small Georgia town that turned a blind eye to his misdeeds. *The Paperboy*, which also has a small-town southern setting, is no less violent and no less preoccupied with evil than the earlier book. This time, however, Dexter's focus is on the damage that well-intentioned people can do and, more specifically, the harm that can result from the journalistic pursuit of truth.

Like *Paris Trout*, *The Paperboy* has its murderous racist, Thurmond Call, the long-time sheriff of northern Florida's Moat County. Yet *The Paperboy* actually begins four years after Sheriff Call's death. Although over the years the community had tolerated his habit of killing black suspects and fugitives and was not particularly troubled when he stomped to death a drunk and quarrelsome white man, Jerome Van Wetter, the victim's family was incensed. Unfortunately for Sheriff Call, the Van Wetters were a particularly lawless and malevolent lot. No one was surprised when, not long after Jerome Van Wetter's demise, the sheriff's disemboweled body was found on a Moat County highway. It was obvious that a Van Wetter had come out of the swamps to take revenge.

The chief suspect in the crime was a cousin of Jerome, Hillary Van Wetter, who was already famous for cutting off a policeman's thumb after a routine traffic stop. Hillary was arrested, tried, and convicted, and as the novel begins, he is soon to be executed. At this point, a love-struck woman and two newspapermen from a liberal Miami paper become involved in the case.

The woman is motivated by an obsessive love. Charlotte Bless, formerly a postal worker, has made a habit of corresponding with jailed killers. Yet she had never become as infatuated with any of the others as she now is with Hillary. Quitting her job in New Orleans, she has brought her voluminous files and records to Florida, with the intention of procuring help for Hillary, getting him freed, and marrying him.

The two newspapermen do not have Charlotte's blind faith. They have been sent to Moat County simply to look into the case, and like the good investigative reporters they are, both of them begin with open minds as to whether Hillary killed the sheriff. Although superficially they might seem alike, Yardley Acheman and Ward James do not have the same values, and it is this difference that in large part determines the course of the story and ultimately causes two deaths.

Yardley is totally motivated by self-interest. Journalism to him is a convenient route to fame and fortune—convenient because he is indeed a fine writer. Recognizing his talent, his newspaper routinely assigns Yardley to do the actual writing of any story on which he is working. Supposedly Yardley also helps with the investigation, but usually he just lazes about, sleeping with any attractive women whom he can manage to impress, until the information that someone else has collected is presented to him. Then he goes to work, weaving that raw material into polished, publishable copy. Yardley does not care very much about facts or truth. He is interested only in the words he writes and in what they can get him.

Yardley's partner Ward James is quite different. Ward is uncompromisingly idealistic, convinced that the sole purpose of any newspaper is the pursuit of truth. So strong is his belief in his vocation that Ward will not only work hard to find the facts he needs but will even risk his life, not merely for a story but for one that is accurate and complete. Ward had once walked through a downed airliner, which might have exploded at any moment, in order to understand what the doomed passengers had experienced. Now Ward insists on venturing into the swamps to talk to the Van Wetter family, even though it has been made clear that if he bothers them, he may not come out alive.

If Dexter shows these two attitudes toward the profession of journalism as polar opposites, he also emphasizes the fact that they are not the only possible stances. Ward's publisher father, too, has a compelling sense of duty. In a conservative, even backward area, he has systematically expressed his liberal views. Perhaps the reason people remain loyal to his newspaper is that they know how devoted W. W. James is to his community. That dedication to the general welfare explains W. W.'s uneasiness about any new investigation into the Call-Van Wetter case. Certain that the county is better off without both men, W. W. is inclined to let matters rest. It is significant that he tries to explain his feelings to his sons long before the story is published. When it does appear under Ward's byline, however, W. W. is blamed, and he is punished for his son's betrayal of the community with the loss of friends and of advertising revenue.

Himself a former journalist, Dexter clearly respects people like Ward and his father who, though differing on practical matters, are marked by principle and by courage. Nevertheless, in *The Paperboy* he shows how a lofty profession can be misused for selfish purposes. Thus a journalist such as Yardley Acheman can influence legal action and win a Pulitzer Prize with a story built on his own fictions, and a journalist such as Ellen Guthrie can acquire a newspaper, with its profits and its power, by pretending to care about the aging publisher. Even more dangerous, however, are the self-deceived, such as Helen Drew, who tricks Jack into exposing his brother. Helen does not need to admit, even to herself, that she is really out to get revenge against Yardley, when she can justify the most immoral action as the duty of a good reporter, hot on the trail of truth.

Such issues of journalistic ethics and the power of the press are closely related to another major theme in *The Paperboy*, the difficulty of admitting one's own identity. Like the Van Wetters, who barricade themselves in their swamp, several of the other characters in the novel live out their lives in hiding. Their situation may not be as obvious as that of Helen Drew, who stays in a swimming pool as long as possible rather than emerging, wet clothes clinging, to expose her fat, unlovely body to the ridicule of her fellow workers.

Unlike Helen, W. W. and Ward do not appear to have anything to conceal. Evidently because of a fear of intimacy, however, W. W. systematically conceals his feelings from his sons, relying on what Dexter calls a kind of verbal "shorthand" to keep from actually saying anything to them. Unfortunately, by thus distancing himself from his sons, W. W. makes it easy for the predatory Ellen Guthrie to oust them from his house and, she hopes, from his life. W. W. remains an ostrich until the end. As Jack points out, he will never talk about Ward's death, but spends his final years retelling old stories from the distant past.

Temperamentally, Ward is much like his father, but he has an even clearer reason for maintaining his distance from others. In the 1960's, an admission of homosexuality not only would result in social ostracism but also would almost certainly cost a journalist his career. Ward pays a high price, however, for failing to confide even in his own brother. Because Jack has no idea that Ward might need to be protected, he is almost too late to save him from a group of sailors who attack him. Ward's hospitalization enables Yardley to invent his lies, and thanks to Helen, the end result for Ward is humiliation, the loss of his sense of achievement and his self-respect, and, finally, a decision to kill himself.

Whether in the form of the ocean, a swimming pool, or the swamp, water is used throughout *The Paperboy* as a symbol of isolation and retreat. The Van Wetters, or at least the males in the clan, own the swamp. As long as they remain there, they feel safe. They realize, however, that while they can eliminate occasional intruders, they cannot repel an invasion in force. This explains their reluctance to help Hillary get out of prison and, later, their decision to surrender him to the authorities. The Van Wetters are not unlike the other residents of Moat County, who tolerated Sheriff Call as a matter of expedience, or members of the top echelon at the fictional *Miami Times*, who decide that it is more practical to ignore the evidence than to jeopardize their reputation. Thus the swamp can be seen as a symbol of retreat, not only from society but also from moral principle.

To Jack, the swimming pool at the University of Florida symbolizes another form of retreat. During his hours of practice, Jack finds himself losing a sense of personal identity. This living death so terrifies him that he has to quit the swim team. Gradually, however, Jack becomes more secure about who he is, and the ocean becomes a source of renewal for him, enabling him to face problems on shore. Thus though Ward makes a final retreat by drowning himself, Jack returns to Moat County, wrests control of the newspaper from Ellen, and begins to lead a life that is purposeful—or, more precisely, made endurable by hard work.

Nevertheless, Jack must live with the results of the journalistic investigation in which he was involved, if only as a minor figure. He has seen the elderly lawyer who had represented Hillary, if inadequately, deprived of a reputation earned through a productive lifetime. He has seen his own father suffer as the community to which he had devoted his life blamed him for events over which he had no control. Worst of all, he knows that if the newsmen had never come to Moat County, Charlotte would still be alive. Admittedly, Charlotte herself was determined to get Hillary out of prison and to become his wife; however, she could never have accomplished her goal without the intervention of the Miami newspaper, which had the funds to mount a full-scale inquiry into the case and the circulation and influence to strike fear into the hearts of politicians.

Clearly, Dexter respects journalists who operate on the basis of principle and despises those who are motivated by self-interest. Nevertheless, one cannot ignore the probability that even if Hillary Van Wetter had been released on the basis of newly discovered truths, rather than Yardley's lies, innocent people would still have suffered. *The Paperboy* is not a cynical novel, but it does remind readers that life is more complex than it might seem. Even the pursuit of truth has inherent dangers.

Rosemary M. Canfield Reisman

Sources for Further Study

AJR: American Journalism Review. XVII, April, 1995, p. 56.
The Christian Science Monitor. February 16, 1995, p. 12.
London Review of Books. XVII, October 5, 1995, p. 23.
Los Angeles Times Book Review. January 1, 1995, p. 3.
New Statesman and Society. VIII, June 30, 1995, p. 38.
The New York Times Book Review. C, January 22, 1995, p. 7.
Publishers Weekly. CCXLI, November 7, 1994, p. 62.
Southern Living. XXX, March, 1995, p. 142.
Time. CXLV, January 23, 1995, p. 58.
The Times Literary Supplement. May 19, 1995, p. 19.
The Washington Post. January 17, 1995, p. C2.

PASSING THROUGH
The Later Poems, New and Selected

Author: Stanley Kunitz (1905-   )
Publisher: W. W. Norton (New York). 175 pp. $18.95
Type of work: Poetry

Without hiding from life's terrors, Stanley Kunitz has sung a song of affirmation for more than sixty years

Slowly but surely, Stanley Kunitz has become a major voice, an eminence, almost the presiding spirit, of American poetry in the twentieth century. When his first book appeared (*Intellectual Things*, 1930), writers such as T. S. Eliot, William Carlos Williams, and Ezra Pound were in early middle age. Although he claims that such writers had little standing when he was an apprentice poet, it was in part through their works that Kunitz absorbed the early modernist spirit. Perhaps through Eliot, or perhaps from his own reading during his bachelor's and master's programs at Harvard University, Kunitz had become enamored with the metaphysical poets. The play of intellect characteristic of the metaphysicals found its way into his work and, one might argue, informs the title of that first volume. Yet Kunitz rejected what he considered Eliot's emotional sterility and championed a more personal and passionate art. No doubt this stance explains his preference for William Butler Yeats. While the impact of his reading marks Kunitz's early, somewhat difficult, ornamented style—a style refined in his second volume, *Passport to the War* (1944)—the poems of Kunitz's maturity have a plainer finish. They are less showy, but more truly profound.

In his earlier work Kunitz is a traditional versifier, somewhat akin to the poets of the pre-Eliot generation—Edwin Arlington Robinson (1869-1935), for example. Like his good friend and contemporary Theodore Roethke, Kunitz makes an important transition from traditional to free verse, but he seems more comfortable as a free-verse poet than Roethke ever did.

That transition took place between Kunitz's Pulitzer Prize-winning third volume, *Selected Poems, 1928-1958* (1959), and his next collection, *The Testing-Tree* (1971). By this time truly an elder, Kunitz remade himself into a contemporary of much younger poets. The new style of Stanley Kunitz is accurately described by Marie Hénault (in her *Stanley Kunitz*, 1980): "free meters; syntactic relaxation; at times elimination of punctuation; the dropping of conventional line capitalization; and often the lack of stanzaic structure and rhyme." Moreover, the later Kunitz employs a tougher, less poetic diction.

Early or late, Kunitz is hard to pin down. He has been a father figure to other poets since *Selected Poems*, and this image was enhanced by his reputation as a scholar that derived from his editorship of various literary reference tomes, such as *Twentieth Century Authors* (1942). Furthermore, Kunitz served for many years as editor of the Yale Series of Younger Poets, putting himself in the position of sanctioning young writers. Kunitz's prefaces to these collections (most of them prepared in the early

1970's) were usually the first and often the best short appreciations of poets (such as Robert Hass and Peter Klappert) who went on to further acclaim. As consultant in poetry to the Library of Congress (1974-1976), Kunitz was a perfect fit for cultural leadership. An active mentor to aspiring poets in workshops at Columbia University and elsewhere, he has founded no school or tradition. His gift as a critic and teacher has been to recognize diversity and the individual voice.

Selections from *The Testing-Tree* make up more than a third of the present volume. Other sections include poems written after *The Testing-Tree* and first brought together in *The Poems of Stanley Kunitz, 1928-1978* (1979), poems from *Next-to-Last Things* (1985), and nine new poems not previously collected. *Passing Through: The Later Poems, New and Selected*, then, may be thought of as balancing *Selected Poems* by presenting the best (or at least the author's favorite) poems written since that prize-winning collection. It is the definitive "later" Kunitz.

An important part of Kunitz's career during the mid-1970's included bringing the work of European writers, primarily Russian writers, to English audiences. His translations of Anna Akhmatova, Andrei Voznesensky, and Ivan Drach each resulted in a book. *Passing Through* contains two translations of Osip Mandelstam, three of Akhmatova, and one each from Aba Stolzenberg and Giuseppe Ungaretti. To Kunitz, it would seem, such translations hold a value equivalent to that of his original work, and thus he includes them among his own poems. In his essay "On Translating Akhmatova" (found in *A Kind of Order, a Kind of Folly: Essays and Conversations*, 1975), Kunitz argues that though "translation is usually regarded as a secondary act of creation," the major translation efforts (such as George Chapman's *Homer*, 1598-1611, and Edward FitzGerald's *Rubáiyát of Omar Khayyám*, 1859) "demonstrate the fallacy of this view."

For Kunitz, moreover, translation is an act of self-renewal, "of entering the skin and adventuring through the body of another's imagination." In a long career, Kunitz' translations at the entrance to old age helped energize his art for another two decades.

Kunitz has no shortage of recurrent themes in his later work. Nature and human-kind's place in it (see especially "Raccoon Journal" and "The Wellfleet Whale"), relationships, various kinds of human frailty and resilience, memory, and place figure prominently in this late harvest. Kunitz's persona is always vulnerable but never subdued. All seasons after middle age are a testing time.

Readers can trace the toll of time on body and spirit yet find Kunitz's life-affirming and transformative impulse everywhere. "The Layers" concludes with the speaker remarking, "I am not done with my changes." In "The Round," Kunitz describes the beauties of the morning ("light flowed in rivulets/ over the humps of the honeybees") and the "curious gladness" that led him to his desk to write. He concludes: "I can scarcely wait till tomorrow/ when a new life begins for me,/ as it does each day,/ as it does each day." The title poem, written on the occasion of Kunitz's seventy-ninth birthday, announces, "The way I look/ at it, I'm passing through a phase:/ gradually I'm changing to a word." In this collection's final poem, "Touch Me," Kunitz still finds that "the longing for the dance/ stirs in the buried life."

Kunitz identifies with the life force that he witnesses all around him. He knows of and warns against humans' civilizing tendency to subdue that force. In "The Knot," he recalls trying to seal a knot in the door lintel, to keep it smooth and flush with the rest of the wood surface. Yet the knot bleeds through "with a rush of resin/ out of the trauma/ of its lopping-off." This "obstinate bud,/ sticky with life," is an emblem of Kunitz's own being. He imagines it revitalized as limb and tree until "I shake my wings/ and fly into its boughs."

The imaginative transformation at the end of "The Knot" is another hallmark of Kunitz' art. Reminiscent of John Keats's "Ode to a Nightingale" (Kunitz edited *The Poems of John Keats*, 1965), it nevertheless underscores how fully Kunitz is rooted in this world. His flight is not into abstraction or eternity, like that of Keats's world-weary speaker, but into another form of life. His appetites are earthly, like the speaker in the late poem "Hornworm: Summer Reverie," who identifies with the caterpillar "stretched out on a leaf,/ pale green on my bed of green,/ munching, munching."

Kunitz's later poems are an outstanding representation of memory's call. Because Kunitz has been able to remain active as a poet far past the age when most writers dry up, the accumulation of poems about memory or spurred by memory has mounted in significance. Moreover, because few writers have accomplished so much in old age, few have left such a record of time's advances and the constant pressure of mortality. The first poem in the final, "New Poems" section of *Passing Through* is "My Mother's Pears." A wonderful tribute to Kunitz's mother, this poem is also a tribute to memory and to the poet's ability to bring the past into the present. A gift of Worcester pears brings back memories of their source, trees planted by the mother when Kunitz was a child "beyond the last trolley-stop/ when the century was young." In memory, Kunitz sees himself and his sisters working to bring life out of death. The planting is a marker for the mother's decision to remarry (the father has committed suicide). The young boy struggles "to set the pear tree in the ground,/ unwinding its burlap shroud." The mother cries, "'Make room for the roots! . . . Dig the hole deeper.'" The act is at once a burial and an offering for the future.

Such reverberating images and tones that braid life and death are frequent in Kunitz' art, as is the theme of the lost father, suggested above. The early loss of Kunitz's father and the later loss of his stepfather (when Kunitz was in his early teens) are reflected in several fine poems, among them "The Portrait" and—less obviously—"Halley's Comet" with its quasi-religious yearning:

> Look for me, Father, on the roof
> of the red brick building
> at the foot of Green Street—
> that's where we live, you know, on the top floor.
> I'm the boy in the white flannel gown
>
> sprawled on this coarse gravel bed
> searching the starry sky,
> waiting for the world to end.

The state of fatherlessness is a state of partial paralysis, a waiting that perhaps has no end. In his moving "Journal for My Daughter," Kunitz stands in place of his vanished father: "You say you had a father once:/ his name was absence./ He left, but did not let you go." (An alternative reading would make "you" Kunitz and the speaker his daughter.) Kunitz's quest for identity is troubled by the absent father, and it may very well be that he has built much of his long life, his career, around the role of symbolic fatherhood to others because of this sense of absence and incompleteness in his own life.

The creative process is a version of Kunitz' fathering, and he pays it much attention as a subject of his poems. Since for Kunitz both life and art are nourished by and in turn become the nourishers of change, it is fitting that a major poem of his later period is "Proteus," an invocation of the sea god with his "famous repertoire of shifting forms" and known also for his prophetic vision. Kunitz honors Proteus in a return to the traditionally measured line, a departure from the irregular three-stress medium that became his prosodic signature with *The Testing-Tree*.

The chorus of praise for the achievement of Stanley Kunitz will undoubtedly, and deservedly, continue to swell. He was honored by election to the American Academy of Arts and Letters in 1974, and President Bill Clinton awarded him a National Medal of Arts in 1993. Among his fellow poets, he has long been an exemplar of commitment and patient achievement. His poetry is marked by wisdom that is never glib and visionary moments that always seem honest. His verse is sturdy, well made, and at its best truly stunning. He has told readers the story of the twentieth century in the West as well as anyone. He also has captured human dreams and fears, as in these lines from "The Abduction":

> Our lives are spinning out
> from world to world;
> the shapes of things
> are shifting in the wind.
> What do we know
> beyond the rapture and the dread?

That Stanley Kunitz has lived to know and to offer such a well-ripened gift is both his treasure and our own.

Philip K. Jason

Sources for Further Study

Boston Globe. December 7, 1995, p. 65.
Chicago Tribune. December 31, 1995, XIV, p. 4.
Library Journal. CXX, October 15, 1995, p. 65.
The New Leader. LXXVIII, October 9, 1995, p. 14.
The New York Times. November 30, 1995, p. C13.

THE PATH TO POWER

Author: Margaret Thatcher (1925-   )
Publisher: HarperCollins (New York). Illustrated. 656 pp. $30.00
Type of work: Memoir
Time: 1925-1979
Locale: Grantham and London, England

A memoir of Margaret Thatcher's political career up to the point at which she became prime minister of Great Britain

Principal personages:
> MARGARET THATCHER, the prime minister of Great Britain, 1979-1990
> DENIS THATCHER, her husband
> JAMES CALLAGHAN, the prime minister of Great Britain, 1976-1979
> EDWARD HEATH, the prime minister of Great Britain, 1970-1974
> SIR KEITH JOSEPH, a Conservative member of Parliament who was
> Thatcher's closest political ally
> ENOCH POWELL, a right-wing Conservative member of Parliament who
> influenced Thatcher's political beliefs

The Path to Power is the second volume of Margaret Thatcher's memoirs, even though it covers the early years of her life from her birth until she became prime minister of Great Britain in 1979. Although it contains considerably more information about her private life than the first volume did, it is primarily an account of how she entered politics and became a successful politician.

Thatcher's career has drawn much comment because she overcame two important barriers to rise to the top of British politics: She was female and she was of humble origin. Her father, Alfred Roberts, owned a small grocery store in Grantham, England, and Margaret and her sister grew up in the rooms above the shop. Thatcher claims that the economic ideas for which she became famous later in her life were learned as a child as she watched her father conduct his business. Thatcher was deeply influenced by her father, a local politician who eventually became mayor of Grantham. Thatcher stresses the poverty of her home life but acknowledges that the family had a maid and that her father had sufficient money to finance her education at a private girls' secondary school and at the University of Oxford.

Perhaps the first important turning point in her career came in 1943, when Thatcher became a student at Oxford. The significance of her time at Oxford did not involve academic achievement: She had not been offered a scholarship, and she was graduated with a second-class degree in chemistry. Much more important was her involvement in student political life. Although she had been reared as a Liberal, she joined the Oxford University Conservative Association. Thatcher became its president during her final year, even though she was denied the experience of debating in the Oxford Union because women were not permitted to become members. Being active in the Conservative Association enabled her to meet many top Conservative politicians and to form friendships with people who would later help advance her political career.

Thatcher gives credit to her husband, Denis, for important assistance in her rise to the top of British politics. They met in 1949 when she was a parliamentary candidate, but it was not love at first sight. It was difficult for them to date because his Saturdays were committed to rugby football and hers to political meetings. Yet he became an asset to her political career in several respects. Thatcher states that when they married in 1952, Denis knew as much about politics as she did and much more about economics. Perhaps even more important, he was a wealthy man; marriage to him meant that Thatcher could focus her energy on her political career. It also meant that she could combine motherhood with a political life, because she could afford a nanny for the children and a servant to help with housework.

Much of the interest in Thatcher's life has stemmed from the fact that she was the first woman prime minister in Great Britain. This was a considerable accomplishment, not least because the Conservative Party and the House of Commons were both very masculine institutions. Thatcher says little about the gender stereotypes and male prejudice she had to overcome. Surprisingly, she is much more candid about how she benefited from being female. She admits that when she was first adopted as a Conservative Party candidate in 1949, it was partly because she was a woman and the party expected to receive favorable publicity from selecting a female candidate. After being elected to the House of Commons in 1959, Thatcher rose rapidly to high office; she acknowledges that being female was an important reason for her unusually quick advancement. She had been in the House of Commons for only a year when she was appointed parliamentary secretary to the ministry of pensions. Thatcher states that she was appointed because the post had previously been held by a woman and it was the convention that women should occupy a certain proportion of government positions. The same factor contributed to her later promotions to the shadow cabinet and then to the cabinet in 1970.

Thatcher was never a member of the women's movement and had little interest in women's groups. She has little to say about the efforts by feminists to make it possible for women to have opportunities to be active in public life. When she does mention feminism, it is usually in a critical way, as when she claims that feminists were responsible for diminishing the common courtesies that were formerly shown toward women. Given her lack of interest in the problems of other women, Thatcher admits that it was curious that her fellow ministers should look to her to identify the women's point of view on issues discussed by the cabinet.

The image of Thatcher as a spokeswoman on women's issues was especially questionable in light of her opposition to many of the reforms advocated by feminists. Feminists urged tax allowances for child care to make it financially more attractive for married women to work, but Thatcher opposed such allowances. Feminists also campaigned for liberalization of the divorce law and for legalized abortion. Although she voted for these bills, Thatcher claims that she did so for nonfeminist reasons and later regretted having supported them.

In light of her later attacks on the welfare state, it is ironic that Thatcher's first government position was in the ministry of pensions, where she was involved in administering an important sector of the welfare state. Although it is generally assumed that she had nothing but disdain for the Beveridge Report, the basis for the postwar welfare state, Thatcher praises William Henry Beveridge for the conservative principles he introduced into the British welfare system.

Thatcher's first cabinet appointment was as secretary of state for education from 1970 to 1974. This was a crucial period in her career prior to 1979, as it was the only cabinet position she held before becoming prime minister. The Conservative Party election platform had included opposition to the conversion of schools to comprehensive schools and a desire to protect the grammar schools from closure. Thatcher portrays herself as a strong and successful proponent of these policies during her tenure as education secretary. She does not mention that more grammar schools were closed between 1970 and 1974 than in any other comparable period nor that the shift to comprehensive schools actually accelerated while she was in charge of education. "Thatcherism" later came to imply adherence to principles even when they came into conflict with public opinion, but at this stage in her career Thatcher had not yet become a Thatcherite.

As prime minister, Thatcher was such a vocal advocate of cutting social programs that this became a central principle of Thatcherism. As education secretary, however, Thatcher was not a Thatcherite; she was a forceful proponent of greater spending on education and developed plans that called for a 50 percent increase in spending on education over the following decade. Thatcher had several successes as education secretary: She was able to save the Open University from closure, she obtained approval for a major increase in construction of school buildings, and she gained cabinet acceptance for the provision of nursery-school education for up to 90 percent of all four-year-olds. Although she admits that the intense public criticism for having ended the free milk-in-schools program was "deeply wounding," the publicity diverted attention from the substantial spending increases for which she was responsible.

Thatcher was a cabinet member in Edward Heath's 1970 government, which became famous for its abrupt reversal in economic policy. After having been elected on a platform of reduced government spending, rejection of controls on prices and incomes, and an end to the Labour policy of providing subsidies to bankrupt firms to prevent them from collapsing, Heath's government took a U-turn and began to follow these policies. Thatcher later condemned Heath for this policy reversal, claiming that Heath, in contrast to herself, lacked the courage of his convictions. Yet as a cabinet minister Thatcher participated in the policy shift. She admits that if she was opposed to it as a matter of principle, she should have resigned, but she claims that she had not yet fully worked out an alternative at the time.

When did Thatcher become a Thatcherite? Thatcher admits that although she read F. A. Hayek's *The Road to Serfdom* when it was published in 1944, she did not fully grasp its implications. It was not until the mid-1970's, under the influence of Sir Keith Joseph, that she was converted to the ideological position that became known as Thatcherism. The combination of high unemployment and extremely high inflation between 1973 and 1976 undermined support for the Keynesian policy of deficit spending. Encouraged by Joseph, Thatcher became convinced that monetarist economic policy provided the theoretical justification for what she wished to do: shift the focus of economic policy from promoting growth to controlling inflation and reduce the role of the state in the economy.

Thatcherism has come to mean a radical change in economic and social policy, but until the 1970's there was little hint that Thatcher would fundamentally alter the Conservative program. The first and only occasion on which she voted against the Conservative Party line occurred in 1961, when she advocated corporal punishment for young violent offenders. Once she became convinced in the 1970's that consensus politics was wrong, however, she led the reshaping of Conservative positions on incomes policy, trade unions, and government spending, which involved a repudiation of what Conservative governments had supported since 1951.

Although Thatcher was extremely hardworking and a capable politician, luck was a factor in her unexpected rise to the top of British political life. Keith Joseph's decision not to run against Ted Heath in the 1975 Conservative Party leadership contest was an important example. Joseph's refusal gave Thatcher the opportunity to run as the candidate of the party's right wing. Thatcher also admits that it was lucky that Prime Minister James Callaghan did not call a general election in 1978. A Conservative victory would have been much less likely that year than in 1979, when the election was held. Almost certainly a defeat in 1978 would have resulted in the Conservative Party's replacing Thatcher with someone else as its leader.

Since Thatcher has remained active in British politics, her memoir is very much a defense of the choices she made in advancing her political career. Yet while shaped to present the image of herself that she would like to leave to posterity, it does contain far more revealing glimpses of her inner self than her first volume of memoirs. Although *The Path to Power* will not be the final word on Margaret Thatcher, it is essential reading for those interested in her life or in women in British politics since 1945.

Harold L. Smith

Sources for Further Study

Contemporary Review. CCLXVII, August, 1995, p. 105.
The Economist. CCCXXXV, June 24, 1995, p. 82.
London Review of Books. XVII, July 6, 1995, p. 7.
New Statesman and Society. VIII, June 23, 1995, p. 45.
The New York Times Book Review. C, July 9, 1995, p. 5.
The Observer. June 11, 1995, p. 13.
The Spectator. CCLXXIV, June 17, 1995, p. 39.
The Times Literary Supplement. July 14, 1995, p. 27.
The Wall Street Journal. July 6, 1995, p. A6.
The Washington Post Book World. XXV, July 23, 1995, p. 1.

PAUL CELAN
Poet, Survivor, Jew

Author: John Felstiner (1936-   )
Publisher: Yale University Press (New Haven, Connecticut). 344 pp. $30.00
Type of work: Literary biography
Time: 1920-1970
Locale: Romania, Germany, Vienna, and Paris

A richly integrated analysis of the poetry and life of the greatest poet writing in German since World War II

> *Principal personage:*
> PAUL CELAN, a Romanian-born poet of Jewish descent

The story of Paul Celan, born Ancel (Celan is an anagram), is not unlike that of many creative survivors of the Holocaust. Primo Levi, the brilliant Italian memoirist and essayist, recorded his suffering at and liberation from Auschwitz with a searing honesty that earned for him the awe and admiration of thousands of readers. Nevertheless, he finally took his own life many years after World War II. So did Jean Amery, and so did Paul Celan. All three wrote about the Holocaust and seemed to rise above their ordeal through the power of their literary art, but finally some irresistible force called them back to the suffering of their fellows in the darkest hour of Jewish experience. They were able to make art out of memory, but memory could not be purged. As has been said of Celan, he achieved "radiance without consolation."

John Felstiner has labored hard and long to map Celan's tragic quest. Felstiner gets readers to believe in the terrible earnestness of Celan's desperate attempt to memorialize the suffering of his people not by belaboring the sadness and despair and even madness that plagued Celan the man but by looking closely and intently at Celan the poet. His mother's murder by the Nazis haunted Celan all his life. She was shot at a labor camp when she proved too sick to work; his father died at the same camp. Celan's mother had brought him up to love the German language and its literature; in Czernowitz, at the eastern border of the old Hapsburg empire, where Celan was born, Jews with cultural aspirations strongly identified with the German language. It was Celan's fate, as a poet, to be locked into the same language that was used for the slogan "Arbeit Macht Frei" (work will make you free) over the gates of Auschwitz. In a strange way, this paradox committed him to a purification of the German language, which had been contaminated by Nazi jargon and racist thinking. It is a supreme irony that this Romanian Jew, a survivor of the Holocaust who lived in Paris, should have become the outstanding German poet of the later twentieth century.

In Felstiner's book, readers learn how Celan escaped from a labor camp and after the war made his way to Vienna and finally Paris; how he married a French artist whose parents were Catholic reactionaries; how Celan dealt with the German philosopher Martin Heidegger, whose Nazi past revolted him but whose philosophy of being proved vital to the development of his own ideas; how Celan and Nelly Sachs, another great German Jewish poet, came to a mutual understanding of their mission as survivor-poets; how Martin Buber, the great German Jewish philosopher, fell short of Celan's expectations—primarily because Buber seemed almost facile in his willingness to make "peace" with Germany; how in the last decade of his life Celan submitted to electric shock therapy; how he finally had to live apart from his wife and child because of acute depression; and how, late in April of 1970, Celan, a strong swimmer, jumped into the Seine. His body was discovered a week later by a fisherman seven miles downstream.

Readers learn all these things in Felstiner's narrative, but they are never allowed to drift very far from the poetry. Felstiner makes clear that from the very beginning of Celan's life as a poet after World War II, he was totally committed to revealing the essence of what the Jews had suffered. This meant questioning and exposing the Christian values of hope and redemption, which, ironically, many Gentiles believed to be at the heart of his work. Celan used Christian metaphors in a kind of reverse typology; instead of prefiguring Christian salvation, which is the traditional way that Christians interpret the Old Testament, Celan's Christian metaphors—particularly the crucifixion itself—refer back to Jewish suffering and become tropes for the bloodletting that Jews suffered at the hands of a Christian world, a form of persecution that reached its satanic apotheosis in the "final solution" of the German extermination of the Jews:

> It was blood, it was
> what you shed, Lord.
>
> It shined
>
> It cast your image into our eyes, Lord.

All of this becomes very important because of the way in which Celan's poetry has been used by Germans to overcome the legacy of guilt associated with the Holocaust. Educators and critics in Germany have translated Celan's infinitely subtle and often devastatingly ironic poems into visions of reassuring Christian transcendence. The poem "Tenebrae," from which the above lines are taken, has been read by German readers in ways that favor traditional Christian interpretation. One German critic writes "that when the body and blood of men, not of Christ, are sacrificed in Celan's poem, this 'extends the meaning' of the Eucharist." The philosopher Hans-Georg Gadamer, who sees a Christian existentialism in Celan's poem, speaks of the "commonality between Jesus and us" as the poet's central theme. Here is Felstiner's judgment on such a reading:

Yet the subversions in "Tenebrae" do not support an idea of commonality; nor does the poem's "we" migrate into Gadamer's "us." "Eli, Eli lama sabachthani?" we hear in the Gospel account of Jesus' final hour, "My God, my God, why hast Thou forsaken me?" (Matt. 27:46). That that cry sounded originally in Psalms or that the Lamentations of Jeremiah form part of the Tenebrae service does not signify a continuity, as far as Jewish history is concerned.

Celan's most famous poem is "Todesfuge" ("Death Fugue"), which he wrote shortly after the war ended and which eventually became an icon in Germany for dealing with the Holocaust, an icon that encouraged confrontation of the truth at the same time that it distanced it through aestheticization. The poem is famous for its stark imagery and incantatory repetition:

> Black milk of daybreak we drink it at evening
> We drink it at midday and morning we drink it at night
> We drink and we drink
> We shovel a grave in the air . . .

German schoolchildren recited this poem; it was put to music and sung in choirs; it has been recited at important occasions of state in the German parliament. Despite the sincerity and contrition that underlie the German embrace of "Todesfuge," the way it has been ritualized in music and politics tends to distance the reader from the poem. For example, much has been made of the musical fugue as a clue to the poem's structure, and high school students have been guided through formalistic readings in which Celan is closely compared with Johann Sebastian Bach. This kind of analysis softens the force of Celan's dark irony: The Nazis made prisoner-musicians play orchestral music as victims marched to murderous hard labor or their deaths in the gas chambers: "we drink you at midday Death is a master from Germany." Felstiner notes Celan's pun on "master" (*Meister* in German) as conflating artist and dancing master with tyrant. The Nazis were artists at murder.

In the early 1950's, Celan's powerful imagery attracted readers and earned him a considerable reputation not only in Germany but also among poets and critics worldwide. He earned several prestigious prizes in Germany. He was very sensitive, however, to hostile criticism and chafed angrily at the notion that he was more of a technical virtuoso than a poet with a subject. The truth is that he was increasingly drawn to an inspired silence, a crafted silence, as the only way to do full justice to the unspeakable nature of his subject—the Holocaust and its moral and psychological burden. This crafted silence took the form of an increasingly abstracted, gnomic, abbreviated diction and syntax. The luxuriant imagery and rhythmic cadences of the early verse yielded gradually to the stripped and bare, often teasingly truncated lines of his last poems. The curious thing is that these poems, desiccated and stark, often evoked erotic and life-affirming impulses. Here are some lines from a poem written in celebration of Celan's one trip to Israel—only one year before his suicide:

> There stood
> a splinter of fig on your lip
>
> There stood
> Jerusalem around us. . . .
>
> I stood
> in you.

Peter Brier

Sources for Further Study

Choice. XXXIII, November, 1995, p. 469.
Journal of the History of Ideas. LVI, July, 1995, p. 524.
Los Angeles Times Book Review. June 11, 1995, p. 3.
The New Republic. CCXIII, October 30, 1995, p. 35.
New Statesman and Society . VIII, July 21, 1995, p. 38.
The New Yorker. LXXI, September 18, 1995, p. 106.
The Observer. July 9, 1995, p. 14.
The Times Literary Supplement. June 2, 1995, p. 3.
The Village Voice Literary Supplement. June, 1995, p. 29.
The Washington Post Book World. XXV, August 6, 1995, p. 5.

THE PHILOSOPHER'S DEMISE
Learning French

Author: Richard Watson (1931-   )
Publisher: University of Missouri Press (Columbia). 133 pp. $22.50
Type of work: Memoir
Time: December, 1986, through September, 1987
Locale: St. Louis, Missouri, and Paris, France

Richard Watson, a notable American scholar of the French philosopher René Descartes, relates his frustrating attempts at learning to speak the language of his French colleagues and peers

Principal personages:
> RICHARD WATSON, an aging Cartesian scholar and college professor from St. Louis
> MAYA RYBALKA, the wife of his friend and colleague, and a native Frenchwoman who agrees to a six-month stint as Watson's French tutor
> MADAME GENEVIEVE RODIS-LEWIS, a highly distinguished French Cartesian scholar with whom Watson dreams of having a scholarly conversation in impeccable French
> CLAIRE AND THE PROFESSOR, two of Watson's five French instructors at the Alliance Française in Paris

Richard Watson is a professor of philosophy at Washington University in St. Louis, Missouri. He is also highly regarded in the United States as a scholar of the French philosopher René Descartes. He has immersed himself in the language, culture, and ideology of French academic society for an impressive twenty-five years and has received awards, accolades, and the respect of his peers for his efforts. The one thing keeping him from fully enjoying his academic success was his perceived failure to be included by the French Cartesians in their very close social and scholarly circle.

Watson's chance at this inclusion finally arrived in December of 1986, when he was invited to present a paper the following June at the Centre National de la Recherche Scientifique in Paris at a conference celebrating the 350th anniversary of the publication of Descartes' *Discours de la méthode* (1637; *Discourse on Method*, 1649). The feat of reading his paper and fielding questions from his peers—aloud, in spontaneous French—was to be both his opportunity and his trial.

For as long as he had been steeped in the French language—reading it, writing it, even translating highly technical texts from French to English and back again—Watson had never learned to speak the language of his scholarly subject spontaneously. To learn to speak French like a Frenchman, so as to be accepted into the virtually impenetrable world of French Cartesian scholars, became the passion and driving force for the next nine months of Watson's existence. This singularity of purpose, and the tenacity with which he grasped it, sets the tone that permeates this autobiographical tale of learning to speak a foreign language once one has reached late middle age.

Realizing that a semester of French at the university or even a quite rigorous language course would not be sufficient for his rather specific needs, Watson sought the counsel of a close friend and fellow professor, Michael Rybalka. The advice given was to seek private tutoring from his wife, Maya Rybalka, a native of France who taught French at the Alliance Française in St. Louis. Being a Basque, Maya apparently did not share the ultra-pretentious disdain that Parisians are said to feel for American-imbued French. Nevertheless, she corrected, scolded, and sometimes mocked Watson through six months of daily intensive instruction, thinking all the while that he would surely give up his vain attempt.

Watson did not give up, but neither did he succeed. He was unceremoniously rebuffed at the conference by nearly all the native French scholars, not because of a lack of depth, insight, or clarity in his presentation but because of his inability to show a command of the language that even neared fluency from a native French speaker's perspective. Most painful for Watson in this situation was the cold shoulder given him by Madame Genevieve Rodis-Lewis, the second oldest and perhaps most distinguished of all Cartesian scholars in both Europe and North America. Yet her brush-off only added fuel to his desire to learn to speak French and be accepted. Thus he enrolled at the Alliance Française for the last three months of a four-month intensive introductory course. The final examination of this course was viewed as either a validation or revocation of one's passport into the French mystique, depending on whether one passed or failed.

Focusing particularly on two of his five instructors in the course, Watson relates anecdotes regarding language in general and French as a foreign language specifically. The pretensions of the French people, the rigidity of their allegiance to the purity of their language and culture, and his own resistance to giving up his native language in favor of another are all subjects touched upon as he frets about being a student again.

His first instructor at the Alliance Française, referred to only as Claire, was a young, vivacious Frenchwoman who coquettishly coddled, then playfully pushed Watson and his fellow male students to adopt her teachings. Spanning over forty pages, nearly a third of the entire book, Watson's discussion of Claire and the antics in her classroom serves little more than to illuminate the sexual ambience of the class and his own need to reassure himself that he has not become too much of an old fogy to be a part of it. Perhaps as an attempt to affirm his charisma, Watson spends far too much time describing the varying traits of beauty and sensuality exuding from the ethnically diverse collection of women in his class and how they all flirted with him in one way or another. Given his self-characterization as a happily married man, his report of how he toyed with the idea of a tryst with a very young fellow student is a rather pathetic and false attempt at titillation.

The narration of his interactions with the Professor, his instructor for the third portion of the class, is far more relevant to what appears to be the author's desired intent in writing *Learning French*. That is, here Watson offers a provocative yet wryly humorous discussion of the role that language plays in regard to self and cultural definition, patriotic allegiance, and foreign assimilation. A tall, angular, English-looking Frenchwoman of a certain age, the Professor was no-nonsense and stony, inspiring both respect and fear in her students as she drilled them relentlessly. In the fast-paced, impartial environment the Professor created, Watson was stripped of his scholarly credentials, his wisdom of age, and his superiority in being American, and left feeling like a young, relatively slow-minded schoolboy struggling to avoid humiliation in front of his peers. The stress of the conviction that he was failing, that he did not want to fail, and that he had to see the course to its end regardless frightened Watson out of his narcissistic musings, freeing him to ponder his fervent need to learn French in a more focused manner.

Watson successfully conveys his almost perverse need to learn to speak French. Citing one of four Cartesian maxims provided as a guide to life, he identifies with the tenacious adherence to a single path decided upon by a traveler lost in a forest. Having made such a choice, the traveler at least can make some progress, as opposed to expending all of his energy walking in circles. The mocking tone that Watson adopts in his account of this maxim leads the reader to suspect that such single-mindedness is of dubious merit at best, if not completely imbecilic. One hopes that the author intends this ironic self-parody.

Watson then brings into play the Napoleonic Code, which essentially says that those in power set the rules, that it is up to the rule-setters to decide whether a rule has been broken, that even a minor deviation from any rule constitutes a violation, and that the accused is guilty of breaking that rule unless he or she can provide a means for vindication. Watson relates this code and its strict methodology to the instruction at the Alliance Française, thus providing yet another justification for the difficulties he encountered there. Such a code, he says, is in direct opposition to the foundation of American society in that it denies one the rights to individual expression without punishment and to be viewed as an equal under the law of the land. As an apology for the low mark he received on a paper in which he did not follow the instructions precisely, Watson provides quite a dramatic and compelling sociopolitical statement.

Watson then decides that real men do not speak French. As evidence, he makes fun of the effeminate facial contortions required for pronouncing many French words— *l'oiseau* (the bird) is given as a primary example. He denounces French poetry, the inadequacies of French soldiers, the pretentiousness of the French, and the rigidity that they manifest in guarding the purity of their language. The one exception he makes in his string of disparagements is in regard to French cave explorers, whom he reveres as both graceful and manly. Watson, coincidentally, is himself an avid explorer of caves and has been accepted by the great explorers—French and otherwise—in that field.

At one point, Claire informed Watson that he spoke English using French words and that he must not coin his own French phrases and metaphors, especially since he was not even a Frenchman, much less a famous national poet. These criticisms brought to a head Watson's conflict between wanting to learn French so as to be accepted by his French colleagues and wanting to protect his sense of American righteousness, allegiance, and individuality. French, it would seem, threatened to undermine his very existence and singular personality.

Although he makes the concession that if one cannot speak, think, or write in one's native language without interference from outside sources, then the extinction of one's indigenous culture is at risk, Watson still leaves the impression that integration and assimilation constitute the higher moral ground. He decides that the invention of language and especially the frequent academic requirement that one learn a foreign language are some sort of conspiratorial technique devised to control human behavior. One must follow unquestioningly all manner of illogical and inconsistent rules in order to adopt a new language even superficially. As with the blind loyalty exhibited by many modern workers at assembly or clerical, thought-numbing jobs, having a willingness to be disciplined by and adhere to the terms of another language is essentially pledging one's allegiance to an alien power. Watson realizes, or rather hopes, that it is only his commitment to his personal freedom of expression that has kept him from learning French.

Stylistically, Watson employs a rather forced lightness that does not always flow evenly. The passage from beginning to middle to end in what apparently strives to be a linear story is composed of digressive anecdotes. The reader frequently needs to go back in order to discover the appropriate reference frame and time line. Also, the intended humor is often undermined by the stilted prose of an ivory-tower academic.

Thematically, the only consistent message of the book has to do with the difficulties entailed in trying to fit in with an insular group. The facts that Watson's experience is with the French in Paris and that the subject is philosophy within an elitist academic structure seem irrelevant. In a five-page diatribe against the problem-solving strategies of the French, in which Watson describes a game he has invented called French Engineering, he is entirely caustic regarding cultural differences and ideological preferences.

Although some interesting distinctions are made between French and American culture, these seem secondary to the author's underlying motive in telling his story, which is fundamentally a rationalization for his failure to pass the four-month intensive introductory French course at the Alliance Française in Paris. While it is sometimes eloquent and wryly witty, *The Philosopher's Demise: Learning French* often seems little more than arrogant, self-indulgent fluff.

Leslie Maile Pendleton

Sources for Further Study

Booklist. XCI, March 15, 1995, p. 1302.
Kirkus Reviews. LXIII, February 1, 1995, p. 153.
Los Angeles Times Book Review. April 30, 1995, p. 6.

A PLACE IN SPACE
Ethics, Aesthetics, and Watersheds

Author: Gary Snyder (1930-   )
Publisher: Counterpoint (Washington, D.C.). 263 pp. $25.00
Type of work: Essays

New and old essays give expression to Gary Snyder's interests in Asian and Native American cultures and perspectives, call for increased awareness of environmental concerns, and propose solutions to global problems

In *A Place in Space: Ethics, Aesthetics, and Watersheds*, poet, translator, educator, and environmental spokesman Gary Snyder pulls together new and previously uncollected essays, book forewords, and speeches that did not fit in his earlier essay collections, notably the well-received *Earth House Hold* (1969), *Gary Snyder: The Real Work* (1980), and *The Practice of the Wild* (1990). Most of these twenty-nine short pieces, thirteen of which he wrote after *The Practice of the Wild*, reveal little new about Snyder's views but make many of his miscellaneous, historic opinions and credos more readily accessible for a new audience. *A Place in Space* provides a valuable service as an introduction for the general reader first encountering Snyder's contributions to awareness regarding the shared natural habitat, particularly his advocacy of all cultures' taking responsibility to preserve our environment. *A Place in Space* is also a clearly written demonstration of Snyder's knowledge on a wide variety of subjects from linguistics to literature, from natural science to anthropology, from Native American myth to Asian history.

On one level, readers familiar with Snyder's previous work may find much of this material reworkings of themes present in his earliest poetry in *Riprap* (1959) and *Myths and Texts* (1960), as well as his later 1974 Pulitzer Prize-winning poetry collection *Turtle Island*. Even new readers may find his ideas repetitive throughout this volume and may find themselves primarily interested in either specific sections or essays focused on particular topics, especially in the latter sections that address current issues. Still, for readers familiar with Snyder's previous works, the latter pieces in this volume will reveal the depth of an important poet's growth from the ideas he has developed into lifelong themes. Most important, his purpose is both to instruct and to persuade; in both content and style, he is largely successful in achieving his objectives.

In roughly chronological sequence, with new passages updating earlier publications, Snyder organizes these essays into three categories: ethics, aesthetics, and watersheds (the latter two categories overlap in content and meaning). Each section is centered in Snyder's spiritual and physical home, the Northwest of the American continent that he calls Turtle Island, a term he took from his studies of Native American myths. This point of reference gives an otherwise potentially disparate collection a true organic unity linking time and space. Snyder becomes a focal point fusing cultures, history, and a thought-provoking base from which to envision the future.

For example, "Ethics," largely a compilation of short political tracts, begins with writings from the 1950's about the "San Francisco Renaissance" and the Beat poetry movements in which Snyder was a major participant. He recalls his first meetings with fellow Buddhist poets Jack Kerouac, Philip Whalen, and Allen Ginsberg, reviewing their first publications in the context of the then-important shifts in the American poetry scene. These once prophetic observations foreshadow his calls for changes in culture at the end of *A Place in Space*, which complete the cycle that frames this book. "A Virus Runs Through It," his review of William Burroughs' postmodern novel *The Ticket That Exploded*, is particularly helpful in explaining this complex, difficult book and is a surprising and unusual commentary by one former Beat on another—a literary task that Snyder has seldom undertaken elsewhere.

Snyder restates, in lists and pamphlet form, his well-known social positions on population control, pollution, and protection of the environment in "Energy Is Eternal Delight," "Nets of Beasts, Webs of Cells," and "A Village Council of Beings." Throughout these essays, Snyder emphasizes his Buddhist belief in human beings' interconnectedness with and interdependency on the natural environment. Speaking from the perspective of a modern, pragmatic Buddhist, Snyder stresses cooperation between Eastern and Western cultures and advocates respect for Native American practices, which he believes add depth to human understanding of life as a whole. He has long made all of these concerns central themes in his prose and verse. Snyder believes that such a expansionist, inclusive awareness among human beings will literally save the planet. His tone alternates between direct calls for political activism, as in his 1970 Earth Day speech, and gentle reflections on life and art, as in "The Yogin and the Philosopher," that illustrate the deeply spiritual context in which his social doctrines are rooted.

It is the "Aesthetics" and "Watersheds" sections, however, that best illustrate Snyder's wide range of knowledge and interests, providing detailed insights into his poetic philosophy, his background in natural science, and his deep understanding of Asian and Native American cultures. In the longer, amply detailed essays grouped under the "Aesthetics" heading, particularly "Walked into Existence," "What Poetry Did in China," and "Language Goes Two Ways," Snyder explains his poetic sensibilities. He discusses the importance of Chinese and Japanese influences on his thought, especially the spiritual precepts outlined in "Goddess of Mountains and Rivers." He traces the historical evolution of images in Chinese poems, especially of women and nature, and praises the wisdom of the narrative Hindu epics, showing parallels between Eastern concerns and Native American oral traditions—for example, the terseness of Zen masters in one culture and the storytelling techniques of medicine men in pre-Colonial America. He is particularly instructive when providing insights into the forms and craft of Asian languages, a subject with which he is intimately familiar, having served as a translator of both Japanese and Chinese verse for more than forty years. Equally instructive are his explanations of Buddhist practices, particularly meditation in "A Single Breath," which clarifies for Western readers the context in which Chinese verse is composed.

Snyder's discussions of the essence of poetry once again reveal the importance of his cross-cultural studies as well as his well-documented following in the footsteps of the twentieth century poetic school of Imagism, notably the structures formulated by its leader, Ezra Pound. All these influences cumulatively helped to shape Snyder's creative doctrines. For Snyder, poetry floats between nonverbal states of mind, and following the Imagist notion that verse should be clean and precise, Snyder emphasizes that modern poetry should deal with the ordinary, the simple realities of everyday life. Going beyond Imagist precepts, Snyder believes that poetry has a cultural responsibility to preserve the power of the primitive or tribal voice; he argues for the value of tribal poetry for its own sake, not merely for anthropological study. He demonstrates this by retelling Native American myths in "The Incredible Survival of the Coyote."

In the "Aesthetics" section, Snyder's interest in nature is perhaps best expressed in "Unnatural Writing," where he says that consciousness, mind, imagination, and language are fundamentally wild, all products of a biodiversity full of information and richness. He questions the idea that art should impose order on the chaos of the natural world; instead, he argues that creativity draws from wildness. For Snyder, wildness is the actuality of things as they are, and he imagines future artists writing from the perspective of insects or from under the sea, outside human concerns, taking nature writing into realms beyond the human emphasis on the use and exploitation of what should not be considered merely "resources." Snyder predicts that human consciousness will evolve beyond cultural tastes for the pure, beyond the now-common distaste for blood and organisms. Such earthy things, he says, are more real than the unnatural thinking that separates human beings from the place that they occupy. Again, these points are not new—Snyder's essay "Poetry and the Primitive," for example, explored these issues in the 1970's. Yet his clarity and simple use of language here will introduce new readers to a perspective worthy of renewed and broader appreciation.

The final essays of the "Watersheds" grouping in *A Place in Space*, primarily first-time publications of addresses that Snyder delivered on various occasions, look to the future. In "Exhortations for Baby Tigers," Snyder urges the "post-Cold War, post-nature" Western civilization not to look to a "Pax Americana" of monolithic unification. In these prophetic visions, he stresses the importance of diversity and the need to rethink old socialist concerns beyond the context of workers' liberation. He restates his conviction that human consciousness must move beyond self-centeredness to correct problems such as global warming, racism, and sexism, which Snyder claims arise from a nervous, "prickly" culture intolerant of dissent. He believes that people must forge individual definitions of happiness rather than absorb mainstream notions of acceptability. Nevertheless, he finds hope in the idea that individuals can look to local communities as their places of identification rather than national identities; the problems of Africa, he says, continue to reflect artificial colonial boundaries that were unrelated to the continent's natural and cultural realities.

In these "Watersheds" essays Snyder addresses a number of issues not previously explored in earlier works, although his solutions echo familiar ideas. Now that he has become an acknowledged and important spokesman for the environment and for cross-cultural understanding, his calls to create decentralized "natural nations" based on ecosystems and biological communities instead of political boundaries take on new meaning in a worldwide climate portending great changes at the advent of a new century.

While associated primarily with the Beat generation concerns of the post-World War II generation, Snyder now speaks of using the Internet to encourage cooperation between governmental agencies and local communities—for example, to establish land-management databases to help make plans for future conservation and managed growth of the human population. Thus, while restating and underlining themes that have occupied his life, *A Place in Space* both brings his notions into a pragmatic present and then projects them into the future. His voice proves worthy of consideration as more than that of a visionary prophet: His writings are a conduit of ideas that point to hopeful solutions beyond the limits of normal political thinking. Snyder's push to rethink habitats in terms of cultural bioregionalism, with politics oriented to place rather than outmoded concerns of nationalism, may prove to be as important a philosophy as any proposed by a poet.

It is appropriate that Snyder ends *A Place in Space* by invoking Walt Whitman, one of his poetic mentors, who called for a new America in the mid-nineteenth century. On many levels, Snyder brings Whitman's inclusive, expansionist vision into a contemporary call for a new planetary vision built on Whitman's notions of mutual respect for cultural differences. It seems clear that Snyder's reputation will rest on both his poetry and the ideas expressed in his essays. He is a major American voice of the latter half of the twentieth century, best understood in the tradition of earlier Romantics such as Whitman and Ralph Waldo Emerson. If this volume prompts readers to explore the work of Gary Snyder further, it will more than serve its purpose. On its own, it is a volume that calls for profound individual and cultural changes, and the ultimate measure of its success must be in the lives and actions of readers who are inspired to demonstrate a new, deeper awareness of all aspects of life.

Wesley Britton

Sources for Further Study

Booklist. XCII, September 1, 1995, p. 32.
The Progressive. LIX, November, 1995, p. 28.
Publishers Weekly. CCXLII, July 31, 1995, p. 62.
San Francisco Chronicle. October 29, 1995, p. REV6.

THE POINT

Author: Charles D'Ambrosio
Publisher: Little, Brown (Boston). 243 pp. $19.95
Type of work: Short stories

A powerful debut collection of lyrically charged stories that bring into light those threshold moments when life suddenly takes a turn for the worse

Charles D'Ambrosio's first book of stories, *The Point*, is not merely another promising debut. Three of the stories from this collection—the title story, "Her Real Name," and "Open House"—stand as singular achievements in the form; each offers luminous moments that shed new light onto age-old themes, including sacrifice, salvation, forgiveness, grace. True, D'Ambrosio is working over familiar territory, an emotional landscape crossed by the likes of F. Scott Fitzgerald, John Cheever, and more recently Richard Ford; yet where other young writers are clearly derivative, their influences tattooed across their crease-beaten brows, D'Ambrosio breathes renewed narrative vibrancy and drive into mythologies worn thin, revising twice-told story lines and branding them with his own distinct vision, voice, and name.

"The Point," which Robert Stone cited as one of 1991's best short stories, tells of Kurt, a thirteen-year-old narrator who is wiser than his years, aware that "certain things in life can't be repaired." Such things include the loss of his father, a medic during the Vietnam War who saved lives but ended up, back home, ending his own life with a shotgun, "his head . . . blasted away."

Kurt lives with his party-throwing mother on the Point, an affluent beachside community whose inhabitants, the "crazed rumhounds" with whom young Kurt is best acquainted, have been beached by their own self-destructive, self-controlled tides. Kurt's home has been the site of countless drunken soirees,

> silver smoke swirling in the light and all the people suspended in it, hovering around as if they were angels in Heaven—-some kind of Heaven where the host serves highballs and the men smoke cigars and the women all smell like rotting fruit . . . the men laughing, the ice clinking, the women shrieking.

Kurt, ever since he was ten, has been assigned the task of escorting these inebriates to their homes. He considers himself "a hard-core veteran, treating each trip like a mission." The terrain that is crossed on these "missions" is an emotionally mined battlefield scarred by infidelity and divorce, numbed by Nembutal. If there is one thing that Kurt has learned about this world, it is that it is best "to stick as close as possible to the task at hand." His reasons are as follows:

> I've found if you stray too far from the simple goal of getting home and going to sleep you let yourself in for a lot of unnecessary hell. You start hearing about the whole miserable existence, and suddenly it's the most important thing in the world to fix it all up.

Yet as Kurt's father warned, "certain things can't be repaired." Kurt's father's death, for example, cannot be fixed. It is done and over, and nothing in Kurt's life, in his mother's life, will ever be the same. The same holds true for Mrs. Gurney, the liquored-up-on-vodka-and-tonic socialite Kurt is assigned, on the night of "The Point," to see safely home. On the way, after several detours and pit stops during which she half-strips off her clothes and foolhardily wonders whether Kurt considers her still beautiful, Mrs. Gurney, washed up before the age of forty, turns and says to Kurt: "'Do you know how suddenly life can turn?'"

Kurt knows that this question is bound to lead down a road best not taken. "We needed to get beyond this stage, this tricky stage of groveling in the sand and feeling depressed," he explains. Although he is sensitive and innocent enough to listen to all Mrs. Gurney's talk of self-pity and misery, nothing—and of this Kurt is fully aware—is so bad that it cannot be helped by a good night's sleep.

The characters in *The Point* are all struggling to patch things up, to fix things, to make things right. Each of the seven stories move toward and open up around moments when life, as Mrs. Gurney says, suddenly turns: most often *not* for better, but for worse, though for the most part D'Ambrosio's characters manage to see through to the other side of bad situations. They endure. They live. They cross over the threshold of darkness and step into the light of redemption and grace. Like John Cheever, who revealed to readers the untidy lives lived in houses that look immaculate on the outside, D'Ambrosio points out the dirty truth behind what cannot be seen: that, in fact, "the mess [is] all on the inside."

"The Point" is a story a young Fitzgerald might have written—one that Nick Carraway might have told—had he looked not toward Long Island's twin egg-shapes but rather to a place known as the Point, where shipwrecked lives wash in with the tidepools, off the coast of Washington State. Originally published in *The New Yorker,* it created quite a stir among readers of short fiction. The six stories that followed in the wake of "The Point"—the two strongest, "Her Real Name" and "Open House," appeared in *The Paris Review*—are testimony that D'Ambrosio has delivered on his initial promise.

"The Point" and "Open House," both told in the first person, are the bookend stories in this collection. Bobby, the narrator of "Open House," is a slightly older version of Kurt. Both are haunted by the suicides of crazed loved ones; both have been left behind to deal with the residual mess. In "The Point," Kurt's struggle to repair or replace the loss of his father seems almost pointless: No matter what Kurt does, his father is never coming back. In "Open House," however, the possibility for some sort of resolution between Bobby and his certifiably insane father is still within both reason and reach, if Bobby so chooses. The mess is on the inside, but it is on the outside too. It can be repaired, or else maybe cleaned.

D'Ambrosio's vision, which in "The Point" might be described as an innocence prematurely shattered, undergoes a transformation by the collection's closing story, "Open House." At the end, Bobby and his father have literally joined hands in a scene that reeks of poignancy: Father and son reverse roles as Bobby teaches his father, a man more at home holding a shotgun, how to cast a fly, "working the rod back and forth, the line flowing gently in watery curls, whispering over our heads." Father and son become one, shadows overlapping in the day's last light. The story ends with a moment of familial tenderness, an image that suggests forgiveness—and through forgiveness, grace: "I let the line fall and stood behind him, closing his hand around the cork, then closing my hand over his."

In this story the narrator airs out all of his family's dirty laundry, the skeletons in the closet, locked inside for years—a brother who blew off his head, another brother who is schizophrenic, a mother who is fanatically Catholic, and a father who, as Bobby explains in the story's first line, "behaved like one of those wolf-boys, those kids suckled and reared in the wild by animals." All these things, things rarely talked about, are released to roam the quiet suburban streets of a seemingly idyllic neighborhood where families such as "the Grands and Wooleys" can be frequently seen out on their chemically sprayed front lawns, "playing badminton in the lowering light." There is the hint of something dark and unsettling in this image of families at play. Darkness, D'Ambrosio seems to point out—"the lowering light"—is settling in, on the verge of swallowing the Grands and Wooleys. Something is moving in, like a sect of degenerates, a bad seed planted in the garden of Eden: a place where both Eve and evil exist side by side.

Nothing is ever what it seems. This is a theme recurring in the work of D'Ambrosio. In "The Point," the financially rich—pockets padded fat with cash, liquor cabinets stacked with malt scotch and vintage wines—are bankrupt in the spirit and heart. In the sweeping road narrative called "Her Real Name," a young woman dying of cancer, whose name is never unveiled, hides the scars of chemotherapy by wearing a wig. Though she is physically eaten away by disease and has very little to call her own in this world, she is spiritually alive, fueled by her Christian faith, the belief that miracles happen every day. When Jones, a drifter on discharge from the navy, picks her up from a gas station in southern Illinois, they point their beat-up car west, their destination unknown, perhaps not yet written, stopping along the way at roadside tourist traps, historical sites, mythical places, plots of dusty land where people have left their mark, "where battles had been fought and decided and down the streets of dirty, forgotten towns where once, long ago, something important had happened."

Something important and memorable happens in "Her Real Name": The dying young woman finds solace in the company of a stranger and, in turn, passes on to him a sense of sacramental absolution, a baptism by way of a burial at sea. Like other characters in *The Point*, Jones steps outside the limits of his character and performs an act that can be viewed as priestly. He is headed toward salvation, a man still drifting, though he has his destination well within his sight. The story winds to its lyrical and breathtaking resolution with these lines in a musically intensifying prose that is pure D'Ambrosio-brand ambrosia:

> Out beyond the breakwater the red and green running lights of a sailboat appeared, straggling into port. The wind lifted the voices of the sailors and carried them across the water like a song. One of the sailors shouted, "There it is." He stood on the foredeck and pointed toward the banner of flames rising in the sky.

Ideally, what most readers and critics look for in a first book of short fiction is a voice that is unmistakably and inimitably one's own. Unfortunately, only on rare occasions are such expectations met. Over the years, a few short-story writers such as Ernest Hemingway and Raymond Carver made their mark and built an initial reputation on the merit of a first collection. The jury is still out on whether Charles D'Ambrosio will be read in a hundred years. Still, *The Point* is a first book that is much more than simply promising. This is a book both sturdy and emotionally generous, with backbone and heart: a rare combination of gifts, a mixture of savvy and sentiment that cannot be taught. All of this from a young writer who is not afraid to point, to tell readers to listen, to look up.

Peter Markus

Sources for Further Study

Booklist. XCI, February 15, 1995, p. 1057.
Boston Globe. February 12, 1995, p. 60.
Houston Post. March 12, 1995, p. G11.
Kirkus Reviews. LXII, December 1, 1994, p. 1559.
Library Journal. CXX, February 1, 1995, p. 101.
The New York Times Book Review. C, February 26, 1995, p. 8.
Outside. XX, March, 1995, p. 149.
Publishers Weekly. CCXLII, January 2, 1995, p. 59.
The Washington Post Book World. XXV, April 16, 1995, p. 11.

THE POLISH OFFICER

Author: Alan Furst (1941-   )
Publisher: Random House (New York). 325 pp. $23.00
Type of work: Novel
Time: September 11, 1939-December 1, 1941
Locale: Europe, mainly Poland, France, and the Ukraine

This episodic but action-filled novel documents the experiences of a Polish spy/saboteur inside Nazi-occupied Europe during the early years of World War II

> *Principal characters:*
> CAPTAIN ALEXANDER DE MILJA, a spy/saboteur for the Polish resistance
> COLONEL ANTON VYBORG, his chief in Polish intelligence
> HELENA DE MILJA, his wife, who dies in a mental institution
> BORIS LEZHEV, an exiled Russian poet who dies in Paris
> GENYA BEILIS, a Parisian with whom de Milja falls in love
> FREDDI SCHOEN, a German naval officer friendly with de Milja
> GENERAL FEDIN, an exiled Russian who works with de Milja
> JANINA, a young radio operator caught by the Germans
> MADAME ROUBIER, de Milja's Paris mistress, part of his cover
> JEANNE-MARIE, a young Frenchwoman who works with de Milja
> RAZAKAVIA, the leader of a partisan band in the Ukraine
> SHURA, a Jewish woman whom de Milja saves

Alan Furst's *The Polish Officer* belongs to the genre of the spy novel, but it is a spy novel with depth. While providing the standard spy-novel action and characters, Furst avoids the James Bond comic-book effect and instead leans in the direction of such masters of the genre as Graham Greene and John le Carré. The depth in his work comes from the aura of a certain time and place that he creates. If the ability to create or evoke a world—say, Victorian or Edwardian England or Sigmund Freud's Vienna—is the mark of a true novelist, then Alan Furst has it.

The world Furst re-creates, here and in his previous novels of espionage—*Night Soldiers* (1988) and *Dark Star* (1991)—is Europe around the onset of World War II. With the lessons of World War I unlearned, Europe remains racked by ethnic stereotypes and old assumptions about cultural expansion by military might and conquest. One alarming development is that some hail Nazi conquest as a good thing, a means of achieving a united "New Europe," as though they are incapable of distinguishing the cure from the cause. New technology in weapons and communications—airplanes and radio signals that erase national borders—has continued to render the old assumptions obsolete. So Europe around the onset of World War II is a curious mix of the old and the new, of bolt-action rifles and Katyusha rockets, of horses and tanks, of Maginot line and Blitzkrieg, of *Wehrwille* and the dawn of mutually assured destruction.

Furst displays expertise in almost every aspect of Europe during these years, from military history to geography to culture. He certainly knows about guns and planes and acronyms. He seems to know the name of every town and village in Europe, not to mention railway lines, streams, and marshes. He describes the German technique for tracing and pinpointing radio signals, and he shrewdly identifies the low viscosity of German oil as an important factor on the eastern front. He also notes numerous other tidbits of information, such as a sign in Wilno gracing the Moscow road: One side (going) reads, "On 28 June, 1812, Napoleon Bonaparte passed this way with 450,000 men," while the other side (coming) reads, "On 9 December, 1812, Napoleon Bonaparte passed this way with 900 men." No subject appears to trip up Furst, except possibly agriculture. *The Polish Officer* ends in numbing winter cold, with the protagonist, Captain Alexander de Milja, and a Jewish woman escaping the Nazis by driving a heavy truck down a frozen river. Eventually they leave the river and reach the outskirts of Biala, where they park to await dawn: "Then," announces de Milja, "we can go into the open-air market with the produce trucks from the countryside." This seems like an uncharacteristic lapse, though "produce" here could refer to any kind of food, such as meat or stored-up root crops. Generally speaking, however, reading Furst is a painless way of improving one's education.

Furst's semidocumentary style also produces other benefits. In particular, it lends a layer of reality or credibility to the conventional features of a spy novel—plenty of exciting action, disguise, and intrigue, coupled with colorful but thinly drawn characters. Although *The Polish Officer* lacks a suspenseful plot, it has numerous episodes of gripping action. The novel's opening section, "The Pilava Local," contains such an episode: With Warsaw under attack, Captain de Milja is put in charge of a train carrying the national gold reserves to Romania—a harrowing journey beset by fleeing refugees, twisted rails, strafing planes, bandits, and bureaucracy. In later episodes, de Milja steals a German plane to drop leaflets over Warsaw, rides in a ship hold loaded with coal for Sweden, becomes cozy with German officers and their hangers-on in Paris, blows up a ship to light Calais Harbor for British bombers, lights up a field in Brittany for French paratroopers, and, fighting with partisans in the Ukraine, helps blow up a German troop train and raid a German prison. Along the way, de Milja assumes various disguises, most notably as Boris Lezhev, an exiled Russian poet, and as Anton Stein, an ethnic German from Czechoslovakia who deals in coal.

The episodic structure actually contributes to the novel's semidocumentary effect, without which some of the action might strain belief. Despite his inauspicious beginnings as a cartographer, a man who does not know any better than to grab a machine gun's hot barrel, Captain de Milja becomes a master of disguises with more lives than a cat. While others are falling all around him and he is repeatedly shot at, de Milja makes one narrow escape after another. The least believable instances occur, again, near the end, as if the author were growing tired. De Milja is with a band of partisans holed up at a farm when they are surrounded, outnumbered, and attacked. Jumped by two of the enemy, de Milja, in the process of falling backward, has the "foresight" to shoot "each one in the abdomen." Somehow, he and the Jewish woman break through the encircling enemy to a truck that, luckily, "de Milja had driven . . . a little way into the forest the night before." Then, somehow, they drive on the same tank of gasoline for days to make their escape.

Furst's semidocumentary style similarly cushions the captain's romantic involvements. Typical for spy heroes, de Milja has had an unhappy marriage and is separated from his wife, who resides in a "private clinic" withdrawn from the world. Perhaps this is reason enough to take up spying, since de Milja has become a man "not in love with life." In any event, his unhappy experience leaves the door open for encounters with other women, who seem only too willing to oblige. There are several of these in the novel, including Madame Kuester, who without a word spoken elevates her naked bottom for him; Madame Roubier, who burns a pink light in her boudoir; and even the Jewish partisan Shura, as they are parked together on the frozen river. None of these middle-aged women is exactly beautiful, which is possibly another concession to realism.

Yet the woman with whom de Milja falls in love, Genya Beilis, is beautiful, sexy, and smart and has many other admirable qualities. She even joins him in his spying. Yet he turns down her proposal that they run off together to Switzerland, so eventually she goes by herself and marries another man. There is something quaintly existential about de Milja's decision, even though he is no great philosopher. As he tells Shura at the end, with a proper shrug: "I have to keep fighting. . . . [In] a world of bad people and good people, a war that never seems to end, you have to take sides." His embrace of the partisan Shura symbolizes the choice he has made.

De Milja has a point, one that Furst underscores by setting his novel during the early years of World War II. It was a rather bleak time for civilization, with the Nazis triumphing, Great Britain standing alone, and the United States watching. As Winston Churchill was well aware, the outcome was far from certain. If anything, events pointed toward a Nazi victory, toward the "New Europe" hailed by French collaborationists. Furst's depictions of the Nazis—brutal, banal, but efficient—are a reminder of what that "New Europe" could have been. Furst also has a few words for the collaborationists, summed up by de Milja's comment that "France spread her legs."

In short, Furst seems to focus on this brief period because it was a time of crucial decisions for the world. For nations such as Britain and individuals like de Milja, the decision to "keep fighting"—with all the sacrifice it entailed and with the distinct possibility of losing—could not have been easy. In retrospect, one can complacently endorse their decision as right. Yet at the time, and in those circumstances, what would one have done?

The Polish Officer ends on December 1, 1941, with Captain de Milja parked on the hill outside Biala. With four more years of war to go, did he survive? Did he live on to fight the Russians and survive the Communists? Did he ever find happiness? Does he tell his stories today in a Warsaw nursing home? Such questions are more or less irrelevant. What matters most is that at a pivotal point in history, the heroic captain was capable of existential choice.

Harold Branam

Sources for Further Study

Booklist. XCI, December 19, 1994, p. 802.
Chicago Tribune. February 26, 1995, XIV, p. 5.
Houston Chronicle. April 2, 1995, p. Z19.
Kirkus Reviews. LXII, December 1, 1994, p. 1560.
Library Journal. CXX, January, 1995, p. 136.
The Observer. March 5, 1995, p. 21.
Publishers Weekly. CCXLI, December 19, 1994, p. 46.
St. Louis Post-Dispatch. April 2, 1995, p. C5.
San Francisco Chronicle. April 23, 1995, p. REV9.

THE PORTABLE JACK KEROUAC

Author: Jack Kerouac (1922-1969)
Edited, with an introduction, by Ann Charters
Publisher: Viking (New York). 626 pp. $27.95
Type of work: Essays, poetry, letters, and miscellaneous fiction

Ann Charters has edited the first one-volume collection of Jack Kerouac, including samples of his poetry, essays, and letters, but concentrating on "The Legend of Duluoz," which Kerouac conceived of as the "enormous comedy" constituted by his novels

Jack Kerouac is still the most famous fictionist of the Beat Generation of the 1950's, even more than a quarter-century after his death at forty-seven, and here Ann Charters has collected representative samples from his major works into one large "portable" volume. Unfortunately, and as with any collection such as this, the reader gets only a taste of Kerouac from all the fragmentary excerpts and will need to turn to one of the complete novels, probably *On the Road* (1957), in order to get a fuller sense of what makes Kerouac an important American writer.

In addition to a half-dozen introductions and appendices, the body of *The Portable Jack Kerouac* consists of seven sections, including selections of poetry and letters, essays on jazz and Buddhism, and theoretical pieces and applied examples of Kerouac's "spontaneous prose" writing method. Yet the bulk of the volume, and nearly three-quarters of its length, consists of eighteen short stories and excerpts from the major novels which form the "Duluoz Legend" master work, written between 1951 and 1967, and arranged in chronological order, from Kerouac's birth in 1922 (described in *Doctor Sax* in 1959) to an excerpt from *Big Sur* (1962), when Kerouac was visiting the California coast and fighting the alcoholic paranoia that followed on his fame.

In the introduction to *Big Sur*, Kerouac described the grand plan behind his fiction:

> My work comprises one vast book like Proust's except that my remembrances are written on the run instead of afterwards in a sick bed . . . just chapters in the whole work which I call *The Duluoz Legend*. . . . The whole thing forms one enormous comedy, seen through the eyes of poor Ti Jean (me), otherwise known as Jack Duluoz, the world of raging action and folly and also of gentle sweetness seen through the keyhole of his eye.

Charters allows readers for the first time to see this scheme unfold in one volume, and her arrangement of the different pieces reveals just how autobiographical all of Kerouac's prose essentially was. With little changed except the names, Kerouac writes of the trauma of the death of his older brother Gerard when Jack was four—Gerard will become a Christlike figure hovering over the later novels—of growing up in Lowell, Massachusetts, in a French-Canadian family, starring as a high school athlete, and going to Columbia University on a football scholarship. After a knee injury, Kerouac dropped out of college, joined the Merchant Marine during World War II, and landed in New York City right after the war—and into the middle of an explosion of the arts that Kerouac both participated in and helped to chronicle. At this point in the volume, sections from his best novel, *On the Road,* take readers across the country in Kerouac's descriptions of Sal Paradise and Dean Moriarty's explorations of what the author called "the holy road."

> It was drizzling and mysterious at the beginning of our journey. I could see that it was all going to be one big saga of the mist. "Whooee!" yelled Dean. "Here we go!" And he hunched over the wheel and gunned her; he was back in his element, everybody could see that. We were all delighted, we all realized we were leaving confusion and nonsense behind and performing our one and noble function of the time, *move*. And we moved!

From this fictional peak in 1957, the decline is swift, through fame, drugs, travel to Tangiers with William Burroughs ("Bull Lee"), and Kerouac's struggles with alcohol and loneliness. At the time of his death in 1969, he had been living with his mother in a trailer park in St. Petersburg, Florida.

Kerouac's prose was always a mix of fact and fiction, and the arrangement of the seventeen pieces here puts the chronology of his life, from his "confessional picaresque memoirs," together. Kerouac did not write his life story with such historical neatness, which is why Charters' method is useful in putting it into some order. It is also helpful because Charters can insert short stories (such as "Jazz of the Beat Generation," 1955) into the appropriate places in Kerouac's life story.

Charters is also right to emphasize the importance of the "spontaneous prose" method that Kerouac created and that aptly characterizes the style of his books. "He developed a literary style," she writes in her introduction,

> to enable him to write down his memories of what had happened in his past, shaped by the heightened emotional responses generated by the writing process itself . . . with a characteristic . . . spin of heightened emotion and headlong narrative energy.

Or, as Kerouac himself described his writing style in characteristic capitals, "UNINTERRUPTED AND UNREVISED FULL CONFESSIONS ABOUT WHAT ACTUALLY HAPPENED IN REAL LIFE." (Later a more systematic Kerouac would spell out the nine "Essentials of Spontaneous Prose," in a piece of that title included here.) Kerouac boasted that he wrote *On the Road* in three weeks in April of 1951 on a one-hundred-foot roll of paper. As Truman Capote would complain, what Kerouac was doing was "typing, not writing," but Charters demonstrates both the strengths and the weaknesses of this "spontaneous prose" method. At its best, Kerouac's style expressed an energy found not frequently enough in twentieth century American fiction; more often, unfortunately, it did not achieve those heights and ended up only as a kind of unpunctuated prose breathlessness:

> But the latest and perhaps really, next to Mexico and the jazz tea high I'll tell in a minute, best, vision, also on high, but under entirely different circumstances, was the vision I had of Cody as he showed me one drowsy afternoon in January, on the sidewalks of workaday San Francisco, just like workaday afternoon on Moody Street in Lowell when boyhood buddy funnguy G.J. and I played zombie piggybacks in mill employment offices and workmen's saloons.

This excerpt, from *Visions of Cody* (1973), rushes on for another six pages at the same dazzling speed. At his best, Kerouac captured the energy of the Beat rebellion against American conformity in the 1950's; often, however, he was merely another writing rebel flailing against what he considered the confining rules of English prose.

The *Portable Jack Kerouac* should remind readers of the influence of jazz on Kerouac's prose as well as on the other writers of the Beat Generation. (One section of five Kerouac essays here is titled "On Bop and the Beat Generation.") Coming to writing maturity in the late 1940's and early 1950's, Kerouac, Allen Ginsberg, William Burroughs, and their friends drew on the jazz experiments of the postwar period, of musicians such as Charley Parker, Miles Davis, and Thelonious Monk. As Charters describes this process,

> Trying to capture the emotional truth of his direct experience, Kerouac let the words pour out onto the page instead of editing them in the writing process. Listening to jazz, he learned to extend the line of his sentences and to follow the sounds of words, writing for the ear as much as for the printed page.

Kerouac's poetry, especially his blues poetic forms, show this influence. It is not very good, in retrospect, but it demonstrates the spontaneity, musicality, and other "cool" qualities of jazz forms.

What emerges from this fusion of jazz and poetry in Kerouac's novels is a remarkable prose energy, and it figures prominently in his portraits of some remarkable and unforgettable characters. Kerouac drew again and again on the adventures and exploits of a shifting group of people, mostly men, led often by the legendary Neal Cassady and consisting of Burroughs, Ginsberg, and later Gary Snyder, Philip Whalen, and other Beat writers. Some of the best passages in "The Legend of Duluoz" describe Kerouac's moments with these companions: running down a California mountain with Snyder ("Japhy Ryder" in excerpts from *The Dharma Bums*, 1958), for example, or traveling through Tangiers with Burroughs ("Bull Hubbard" here in *Desolation Angels*, 1965). (An "Identity Key" in the appendices will help readers identify Kerouac's friends under their various pseudonyms in the different novels.)

While the excerpts give readers a sample of Kerouac's prose style and subjects, they unfortunately fail to give a sense of any one work, to capture the experience that reading a whole Kerouac novel may bring. They are rather frustrating fragments that, one hopes, will send readers back to the whole works again.

Charters has included only seven letters from this prolific letter writer; while these are significant, more would have helped flesh out the portrait of the writer that emerges in this volume. (Fortunately, Charters edited a companion volume in 1995, also from Viking, titled *Jack Kerouac: Selected Letters 1940-1956*.) Similarly, she has chosen not to excerpt the novels that fall outside the "Legend of Duluoz" plan, and that omission also diminishes the larger picture of Kerouac.

Kerouac never actually finished reading the novels of Marcel Proust, to which he boastfully compared his own work. Like many American writers before him—Stephen Crane, Frank Norris, Jack London, F. Scott Fitzgerald—Jack Kerouac died before the full measure of his career could be taken. Still, he will continue to be a major twentieth century American writer, not only because of his connection with the Beat Generation—a term, meaning "beatific," that he coined in conversation in 1948 with John Clellon Holmes, to whom this volume is dedicated—-but also because he helped to free American literature from its constraints after World War II. It is significant that, like the American jazz from which he learned so much, he is held in much higher esteem in Europe than in his homeland.

Kerouac himself drew attention to the parallels between the Beats of the 1950's and the "Lost Generation" of Fitzgerald, Ernest Hemingway, Gertrude Stein, and other expatriate writers of the 1920's, in the essay *"Beatific:* The Origins of the Beat Generation," written in 1959 and collected here in the "On Bop and the Beat Generation" section. The parallels are striking, even down to the "automatic writing"—like Kerouac's "spontaneous prose"—with which Stein had experimented thirty years earlier. Like the Lost Generation in Paris in the 1920's, Kerouac and his crew in New York and San Francisco in the early 1950's were trying to carve out an aesthetic movement to overcome the anomie and alienation that war and the postwar boom were imposing on America. While the first "lost" generation wandered Europe in search of some elusive meaningfulness, Kerouac drove back and forth between coasts searching for some lost spiritual connection to life. A measure of the importance of Kerouac's generation is the freedom and flowering of American writing in the next half-century.

David Peck

Sources for Further Study

Booklist. XCI, February 15, 1995, p. 1054.
Choice. XXXII, January, 1995, p. 782.
Gentlemen's Quarterly. LXV, February 2, 1995, p. 70.
Library Journal. CXX, January, 1995, p. 101.
The New Republic. CCXII, April 24, 1995, p. 43.
The New York Times Book Review. C, April 9, 1995, p. 2.
The New Yorker. LXXI, March 27, 1995, p. 96.
Publishers Weekly. CCXLII, February 13, 1995, p. 64.
The Review of Contemporary Fiction. XV, Spring, 1995, p. 161.
San Francisco Chronicle. March 19, 1995, p. REV1.
Whole Earth Review. XV, Spring, 1995, p. 95.

THE PREACHER KING
Martin Luther King, Jr., and the Word That Moved America

Author: Richard Lischer (1943-   )
Publisher: Oxford University Press (New York). 344 pp. $25.00
Type of work: History
Time: The 1940's to the 1960's
Locale: The American South

Drawing extensively on Martin Luther King's unpublished speeches and sermons, Richard Lischer recaptures the true voice of King as an African American preacher

Principal personage:
DR. MARTIN LUTHER KING, JR. (1929-1968), a Baptist minister who became the primary leader of the Civil Rights movement

It is the voice that one remembers most: that rich, deep baritone, full of controlled intensity, reason, and passion combined, a voice that loved words and the sounds they made, and that for a few short years held the nation in thrall. Read some of the speeches of Dr. Martin Luther King, Jr., and they do not remain in the mind for long; hear them, and one can hardly forget them. It is likely that few people remember even a phrase from Louis Farrakhan's two-hour speech at the Million Man March in Washington, D.C., in October, 1995; yet King's fourteen-minute "I Have a Dream" speech, given in front of the Lincoln Memorial in August, 1963, lives on in memory as one of the most inspiring, and most quoted, speeches ever given by an American. In 1993, President Bill Clinton called it "the greatest speech in my lifetime."

Richard Lischer has performed an invaluable service for all those who were and still are enthralled by King's oratory. Much of *The Preacher King: Martin Luther King, Jr., and the Word That Moved America* is based on analyses of unedited audiotapes and transcripts of King's sermons and speeches, particularly those given in African American churches and at mass meetings. Some of these recordings were made by police surveillance units in Birmingham and Selma and have not been examined by biographers before. (Ironically, these taped testimonies of the power of King's oratory and the celebratory spirit of the mass meetings were found among the collected papers of the notorious Birmingham police commissioner, Eugene "Bull" Connor.) According to Lischer, it is these speeches that reveal King's true voice as a preacher, not the sanitized versions that King preached to white congregations or that appeared in print. The latter, published sermons such as those collected in *Strength to Love* (1963) were polished up in order to give them more general appeal, but the effect was to dilute them to the point that they seemed no more than a collection of liberal platitudes. In contrast, King preached a vibrant, distinctively African American gospel, rooted in the traditions of the black churches in which he grew up and in which he preached all of his adult life.

Lischer's approach to King is similar to that followed by King's biographer Taylor Branch in *Parting the Waters: America in the King Years, 1954-63* (1988) and by

Stephen Oates in his well-known biography *Let the Trumpet Sound: The Life of Martin Luther King, Jr.* (1982). It represents a step away from many earlier studies that overintellectualized King and placed too much emphasis on his debt to the liberal Protestant theological tradition—for example, his engagement with thinkers such as Walter Rauschenbusch, Reinhold Niebuhr, and Paul Tillich. Yet Lischer is careful to avoid a tilt to another unbalanced view of King. Unlike some critics, he does not claim that King's embrace of such mainstream theological positions was essentially a pretense, undertaken to align himself and his movement with white America. On the contrary, according to Lischer, in his graduate studies King genuinely assimilated those intellectual influences, and they shaped the religious activist aspect of his mission. Lischer further argues that it is in the interplay of two languages—the one King inherited from the black church and the one he acquired in theological school—that the key to his achievement lies.

The first part of *The Preacher King* explores King's formation in the African Baptist church, beginning in Ebenezer Baptist Church in Atlanta, where his father preached and he was the precocious "preacher's kid." Here King first absorbed the pattern of call and response between preacher and congregation, a reciprocal pattern by which the preacher draws energy from his audience and energizes them in return. He also absorbed the two main strands of black church tradition. These were, first, the Sustainers, who ministered to the needs of an oppressed people but did not try to alter social conditions, and second, the Reformers, who, like King's own grandfather, used the pulpit as a means to fight for racial freedom. Lischer examines the roles played by particular individuals in mediating this tradition to the young King. These included not only his father but also Benjamin Mays, president of Morehouse College, where King studied as an undergraduate; Gardner C. Taylor, the greatest black preacher of the day, who became King's model of an ideal preacher; and J. Pius Barbour, another Baptist preacher who influenced King while the latter was studying at Crozer Seminary.

Although King did not acknowledge in public the influence of this black tradition, it supplied him with a theological scheme in which sin was followed by suffering, which in turn led to redemption and reconciliation. He also learned to acquire the prophetic rage that is peculiar to those who embody the sufferings of an oppressed people and to nourish his fascination with language, since the black church took delight in verbal performance as a manifestation of the power of the spoken word.

King explored and developed his own gift for the spoken word in his courses in homiletics at Crozer. Unlike most white sermons, black preaching emphasized sound rather than form. A sermon was not an expository essay, one that could be read with no loss of effect. It depended for its effects on spoken elements, involving rhythm, timbre, and tonality, and resembled a musical drama that invited participation rather than merely intellectual assent. King learned to master this type of sermon at the same time that he learned the well-organized, rationally argued format that white homiletics advocated. His synthesis of the two styles was one of the secrets of his success on the national stage.

It was during his five-year pastorate at the Dexter Avenue Baptist Church in Montgomery that King established his canon of sermons. He used fewer than a hundred, and much of the material was borrowed. He relied on formulas, outlines, and titles that he inherited from other preachers, although he often adapted them for his own purposes. The formulas included many memorized set pieces, which he stored like an inventory of parts, ready to be inserted immediately at exactly the right moment in a sermon. The famous "I Have a Dream" is one such set piece. To carry off such a technique successfully, the preacher needed an excellent memory, good timing, and mental agility, all of which King possessed in abundance. Some critics have faulted King for a lack of originality, but Lischer points out in King's defense that prominent preachers borrowed one another's material all the time; like comedians, they were always looking for good material.

Perhaps the most fascinating chapter in this always engrossing book is titled "The Strategies of Style." Here Lischer analyzes King's rhetorical strategies in terms of the poetic techniques he habitually used. The way King spoke was just as important as what he said. Lischer helps the reader to see the poetic quality of King's speech by arranging some passages from his sermons in stanza form, such as the following set piece about America:

> Just look at what we've done
> We've built gargantuan bridges
>   to span the seas
> And gigantic buildings
>   to kiss the skies:
> Just look at what we've done.

Lischer comments on the density of poetic techniques in these few lines, involving alliteration, chiasmus (the reversal of initial consonants in lines 2 and 4), near rhyme (seas/skies), and metrical regularity. These were only a few of the techniques in King's repertoire. He seemed to speak almost constantly in images and metaphors, with the poet's gift of seeing beyond the immediate physical world to the workings of the unseen spiritual world. Some of his most explosive effects were achieved through the insistent building of repetitions, and these were of two kinds: anaphora, the repetition of the same word or group of words at the beginning of successive clauses, and epistrophe, in which the repeated phrase is at the end of the clauses. Each repetition would increase the intensity of the effect.

One of King's most powerful techniques was what Lischer calls "sacred association," in which King presented the struggle for civil rights in terms of biblical events. For his hearers, ordinary towns in the American South suddenly became transformed into dramatic theaters for the unfolding of God's justice and righteousness. This strategy of "elevation" was vital in investing King's humble foot soldiers with the belief that they were part of a noble cause that transcended their small individuality.

Equally fascinating is Lischer's analysis of the sound track of King's speeches and sermons. On King's voice, for example:

It is a beautiful voice with a breathtaking range. Within a few minutes his voice moves from husky reflection to the peaks of ecstasy, but he always manages to keep both his voice and the ecstasy under control. Like a good singer, he will open his mouth wide to hit the notes but will not reach or strain. His voice never breaks. Its power is such even in the emotional climax of the sermons, King is usually not letting it out but reining it in.

Following Jon Michael Spencer, Lischer likens King's speaking style to that of a jazz performer, making use of vocal inflections like the bending and lowering (blue notes) of pitch and sliding from tone to tone (glissando). An example of the latter is when King draws out words of one syllable into three or even four distinct notes: "Lord" becomes in one sermon "Law-ah-aw-awd," a tonal curve in which the last note returns to the first. King's voice also contained a natural vibrato, a kind of tremor or quaver that seemed to give to his speech an added dimension, suggesting depth of soul and of experience, as if he somehow incarnated all the suffering and hope of his race. It was this tremulous quality to that voice that, as Lischer points out, evoked a visceral response in the audience.

Lischer also traces the evolution of King's rhetorical strategies. In the first decade of his public career, he adopted a posture of identification. He sought to align the emerging Civil Rights movement with mainline Christianity and politically liberal white America. His style was inclusive. He would address white audiences as "we" and would speak the language they understood, peppering his speech with references to well-known Western poets and philosophers, the virtues of democracy, and the wisdom of the Declaration of Independence and the Constitution. His starting point was always the unity of the races.

By the last two years of his life, however, this strategy of identification had essentially been replaced by one of confrontation. King realized that the problem ran deeper than he had at first believed. Racism was not merely a blot that ran counter to the true spirit of America; it was a fundamental flaw that had been with the country since its birth. The nation was "born in genocide when it embraced the doctrine that the original American, the Indian, was an inferior race." King also took to pointing out that some of the authors of the American Constitution were men who owned slaves. In Montgomery in 1968, he even said that America was capable of putting blacks in concentration camps. In King's speeches from this period, the old metaphors are gone; transcendent images of hope are less frequent. The new language is of social and economic analysis. King now condemns the whole system, not only individual behavior, and in doing so he crosses the boundary from reform to revolution. This is an aspect of King that is not celebrated throughout the United States on Martin Luther King Day in January; the public memory of him is frozen at the identification stage of his strategy.

The Preacher King is an invaluable book because it recaptures King as what he fundamentally was—a Baptist preacher in the African American church. One can only hope that the audiotapes that formed the basis of Lischer's research, which are currently stored in various research collections, will one day be made more widely available so that that majestic voice may continue to ring out from the silent pages of history.

Bryan Aubrey

Sources for Further Study

American Heritage. XLVI, September, 1995, p. 90.
Black Scholar. XXV, Spring, 1995, p. 71.
Booklist. XCI, March 15, 1995, p. 1286.
Chicago Defender. January 17, 1995, p. 13.
Choice. XXXIII, October, 1995, p. 312.
Kirkus Reviews. LXIII, January 1, 1995, p. 59.
Library Journal. CXX, March 1, 1995, p. 92.
Publishers Weekly. CCXLII, January 23, 1995, p. 56.

THE PROMISE OF REST

Author: Reynolds Price (1933-   )
Publisher: Scribner (New York). 353 pages. $24.00
Type of work: Novel
Time: April through August, 1993
Locale: North Carolina and New York

The third novel in Reynolds Price's A Great Circle *trilogy,* The Promise of Rest *describes the reconciliation between Hutchins Mayfield, his estranged wife, and their AIDS-stricken son Wade, who returns to North Carolina*

> *Principal characters:*
> HUTCHINS MAYFIELD, a poet and professor at Duke University
> ANN GATLIN MAYFIELD, his estranged wife
> WADE MAYFIELD, their thirty-two-year-old son, a New York architect
>   who is dying from the effects of acquired immunodeficiency
>   syndrome (AIDS)
> GRAINGER WALTERS, Hutch's aging black cousin
> STRAWSON STUART, Hutch's friend and former student
> EMILY STUART, Strawson's wife
> WYATT BONDURANT, Wade's lover, who commits suicide after learning
>   that he has AIDS
> IVORY BONDURANT, Wyatt's sister
> RAVEN BONDURANT, her son by Wade
> MAITLAND MOSES, one of Hutch's creative writing students
> JIMMY BOAT, a black male nurse who cares for Wade and other AIDS
>   patients

The Promise of Rest, the third novel in Reynolds Price's trilogy of the Mayfield family, follows *The Surface of Earth* (1975) and *The Source of Light* (1981). The complete trilogy, *A Great Circle*, traces the odyssey of the Mayfield family through nine generations in the North Carolina and Virginia Piedmont. *The Promise of Rest* continues the story of Hutchins Mayfield, now an accomplished poet and professor at Duke University. Hutchins is estranged from his wife, Ann, who recently left after forty years of marriage to begin a life as a legal secretary, but he is still in touch with friends and relatives in his rural homestead, including his 101-year-old black cousin Grainger Walters, a patriarchal figure.

Besides Ann's departure, the other great loss in Hutchins' life has been his estrangement from his son Wade, an architect in New York. Wade's companion, Wyatt Bondurant, is a young African American book designer who is openly hostile to white southerners, especially Hutchins and Ann, and deeply possessive of Wade. Unfortunately, Wyatt contracted AIDS and shot himself after he discovered that he had infected Wade as well. For the past six months, Wade has been languishing in a New York apartment as his condition worsens—blind, unable to work, and cared for by Ivory Bondurant, Wyatt's sister. Wade has refused all communication with his parents and has not opened their letters. Fearing the worst, his parents are worried about his condition but cannot help him. Wyatt had made it clear to Wade that he would have to choose between him and his parents, and Wade has continued to shun his parents out of loyalty to his dead friend. Wyatt's spirit seems to hover over Wade, even on his deathbed, like Heathcliff haunting Catherine in *Wuthering Heights* (1847). The novel is divided into three sections—"Bound Home," "Home," and "Bound Away"—which recount Wade's return home to die.

One of the most emotionally compelling of Price's novels, *The Promise of Rest* explores the complex issue of AIDS and the enormous moral, medical, and psychological demands it places on friends and family. Hutch is forced to confront the pain of his estrangement from Wade at Grainger's birthday party, when Grainger hands him the telephone and invites him to speak with his son. Hutch has been unable to forgive Ann for leaving him, and their shared parental responsibility for Wade has sharpened their conflict.

When Wade's parents learn of his deteriorating condition, Hutch's old friend Strawson Stuart urges him to drive to New York and bring Wade home. There they meet Ivory Bondurant and Jimmy Boat, who have been caring for Wade. Boat, a short, wrinkled man of deep faith, is a particularly appealing character, an angel of mercy who has nursed twenty-three dying AIDS patients.

The Promise of Rest is Price's frankest treatment of homoerotic love, an issue hinted at in previous novels. He examines the moral and psychological pressures generated by AIDS within the gay community and the range of responses, from the *carpe diem* irresponsibility of young Maitland Moses to the generous care offered by Boat. The homoerotic theme is foreshadowed early in the novel with Hutch's seminar discussion of John Milton's pastoral elegy "Lycidas" (1638), dedicated to the poet's friend Edward King, who drowned at sea. Most important, Hutch is forced to confront the unresolved issue of his attraction to his friend and former student Strawson, whose affection Hutch could not fully reciprocate. It is suggested that Hutch's unresolved bisexual impulses have contributed to the failure of his marriage. In a bitter telephone exchange, Ann accuses Hutch of caring more for Strawson than for her but not having the courage to act on his feelings. She rebukes him for marrying her when he loved Strawson more.

Eros serves as the dominant force in the novel, and the characters' discussions of the varieties of love are reminiscent of Plato's *Symposium*. Here, as in his previous novels, Price makes extensive use of the epistolary form, with letters from each of the main characters used to fill in details of past relationships. The reader will also find here the clever, witty dialogue and repartee, the verbal sparring and posturing, that are typical of Price's style.

The impact of Wade's slow death at home from AIDS constitutes the moral and emotional focus of the novel. Hutch must restructure his life to provide the continuous nursing care that Wade requires, while he slowly tries to heal the estrangement from his son and wife. Hutch must try to accommodate Ann's desire to be with her son; she accuses him of trying to keep her away so that Hutch can care for Wade by himself—a not totally unjustified complaint.

The Promise of Rest raises important moral, ethical, and theological issues in regard to homosexuality. Price uses dialogue to dramatize controversial social attitudes toward homosexuality and AIDS. In a moment of anguish, as he is caring for the dying Wade, Boat asks Hutchins whether he believes that AIDS is a punishment for homosexuality or whether there is some redemption for the terrible suffering that Wade and other AIDS patients suffer as their disease progresses. Boat seeks reassurance that being gay is not morally wrong, regardless of social attitudes, even though he has surely earned his own redemption through his care for others.

Hutch is able to reassure Boat of his fundamental decency, but Hutch is less effective in counseling one of his students, Maitland Moses, to avoid the risks of homosexual promiscuity. Maitland's response to the threat of AIDS is a kind of fatalistic *carpe diem*, choosing to live for the moment and ignore the possible consequences of his risky behavior. Maitland rejects Hutch's cautionary advice with thinly concealed contempt and accuses him of forgetting what it is like to be young.

Meanwhile, in the face of their son's death, Hutch and Ann are trying to work toward reconciliation. Boat is forced to mediate between them to gratify Wade's desire to have both of his parents present, but he has seen these conflicts before:

> Through all his nursing, he'd run up against a hundred kinds of family trouble—parents who flatly refused to bring a sick son home, some who even refused phone contact; others who'd send no more than checks and only appear after their son died, just in time to confiscate his property, denying his loyal mate so much as recognition.

Wade's death forces Hutch to confront his guilt over his family's slave heritage and his estrangement from his wife and son. He recognizes that he has been cold and aloof, barren of love and poetry. For Hutch, creativity requires love, and he cannot complete the short lyric whose first line haunts him—"This child knows the last riddle and answer"—until after he has scattered Wade's ashes in a creek that Wade had loved as a boy. Part of Hutch's complex atonement for his guilt will lie in his accepting his obligation to Ivory and Raven and in his reconciliation with his wife.

Ann is bitter over the waste of Wade's good life and his death from AIDS. She craves a grandchild who would remind her of her son. Suspecting Hutch's bisexual attachment to Straw, she is jealous of their long friendship. Once Wade has been cremated, she is opposed to his desire to be interred with Wyatt in Sea Cliff, New York. What ultimately unites Hutch and Ann is the appearance of Ivory Bondurant's eight-year-old son Raven, who resembles Wade as a child and may actually be Wade's child. Hutch has unfairly kept from Ann the news of Raven's paternity, contained in a letter from Wade, but now he believes that he must share the information with her to offer her some consolation.

On the day of the interment, Hutch, Ann, Ivory, and Raven drive to Hutch's homestead in rural North Carolina. There they meet old Grainger, who gives Hutch his great-grandfather Rob Mayfield's wedding ring to place in Wade's burial urn; Hutch in turn gives it to Raven for safekeeping. Hutch then asks Raven to help him spread Wade's ashes in the creek bed and promises that they will stay in contact as Raven grows. Yet there is the sense of "a family's end, its story told."

Price is powerfully able to make the reader feel the emotional impact of AIDS, which he calls "the cruelest plague in six hundred years." He spares the reader none of the intimate details of this devastating illness nor the demands of care placed on friends and family members. Price's own struggle to recover from spinal cancer has no doubt made him more sympathetic to the plight of AIDS patients.

Wade shows great courage and determination to die as himself, not hiding or compromising his identity. One of the most moving episodes occurs when the gaunt, emaciated Wade appears before Hutch's narrative poetry class, which has come out to Hutch's home, and tells them the story of his illness. Price lingers over the details of Wade's death at home, allowing the reader to feel the power of the Mayfields' grief for their lost only son. The memorial service at Duke Chapel allows friends and family members to recollect the best moments in Wade's life, so that he grows in stature through his absence.

Perhaps a key to understanding the novel is the episode that opens the novel, in which Hutch explicates "Lycidas" for his seminar students. Milton's elegy establishes the tone for the novel and provides a subtle structural motif of the classical pastoral elegy, with its announcement of the death of the beloved friend, the procession of mourners, the expressions of grief and loss, the memorial for the dead, a consolation, and the final apotheosis of the spirit of the beloved dead. Hutch stresses the authenticity of this first of Milton's great lyric poems, a sincere expression of his grief and loss. Then a student challenges him with the question whether he has written any poems about his son, and Hutch is forced to admit that he has not written one word on the subject. AIDS is the contemporary equivalent of drowning at sea, and Hutch's grief for his son is genuine but unproductive of any great poetry. Despite Hutch's extravagant praise of Milton, the student wonders whether anyone in genuine grief could write a poem that would be read for centuries. The same question haunts Hutch as he looks back over his career as a poet and tries to select lyrics for a volume of collected poems. This is the aesthetic question posed by *The Promise of Rest*, in which Price dramatizes, through Wade Mayfield's pointless early death, the devastation wrought by AIDS.

Andrew J. Angyal

Sources for Further Study

Hungry Mind Review. XXXI, Summer, 1995, p. 22.
Library Journal. CXX, April 1, 1995, p. 125.
Los Angeles Times Book Review. July 16, 1995, p. 4.
New Republic. CCXII, April 24, 1995, p. 34.
The New York Times Book Review. C, May 14, 1995, p. 9.
San Francisco Review of Books. XX, July, 1995, p. 25.
Time. CXLV, May 22, 1995, p. 73.
The Washington Post Book World. XXV, July 16, 1995, p. 4.

PURSUED BY FURIES
A Life of Malcolm Lowry

Author: Gordon Bowker (1934-   )
First published: 1993, in Great Britain
Publisher: St. Martin's Press (New York). Illustrated. 672 pp. $29.95
Type of work: Literary biography
Time: 1909-1957
Locale: England, France, Spain, the United States, Mexico, Canada, Haiti, and Italy

An exhaustively researched account of the novelist's life, tracing his origins, his travels and dreams of becoming a writer, his triumphant production of Under the Volcano, *the unsuccessful struggles that followed, and his mysterious death at age forty-eight*

> *Principal personages:*
> (CLARENCE) MALCOLM LOWRY, an English novelist
> ARTHUR OSBORNE LOWRY, his father, a Liverpool cotton broker
> EVELYN BOWDEN LOWRY, his mother
> ARTHUR RUSSELL LOWRY, his older brother
> JAN VANDERHEIM GABRIAL, his first wife
> MARGERIE BONNER LOWRY, his second wife and collaborator
> CONRAD AIKEN, his mentor, an American poet and novelist
> NORDAHL GRIEG, a Norwegian novelist who influenced him

The brief, tragic life of novelist Malcolm Lowry had a strong legendary quality. In his own writing Lowry projected fictional versions of his experiences repeatedly into contexts redolent with famous precursors from myth and literature. His lifelong struggles with alcoholism, chronic guilt and self-doubt, spiritual exile, and despair have provided ample material for biographers. Douglas Day's award-winning *Malcolm Lowry: A Biography* (1973) and the highly acclaimed documentary film *Volcano: An Inquiry into the Life of Malcolm Lowry* (1977), written and directed by Donald Brittain and narrated by Richard Burton, helped to fix the popular image of Lowry as the paradigmatic doomed artist, a visionary drunkard possessed by inner demons that he managed as a writer to harness only once, in his 1947 masterpiece *Under the Volcano*. So entrenched is this image that the task of reinterpreting Lowry's life in light of recently discovered information is formidable.

Biographer Gordon Bowker has expended prodigious time and energy in accepting this challenge. Having edited two previous volumes devoted to reminiscences of Lowry and critical essays about *Under the Volcano*, Bowker has been on Lowry's trail for many years. He has traveled to all Lowry's familiar haunts, interviewed surviving relatives and friends, consulted school and medical records, and examined private papers and unpublished manuscripts. Such industry and care have produced a wealth of detail and event that greatly enriches the picture of Lowry's experiences. Yet as the main title of the book, *Pursued by Furies,* suggests, Bowker has not entirely demythologized Lowry. Rather, he has provided what amounts to a countermyth—grounded in exhaustive research—that will probably refocus perceptions of Lowry the man and writer for years to come.

Born July 28, 1909, in Liscard, Cheshire, Lowry was the youngest of four brothers. His father, Arthur O. Lowry, was a prosperous Liverpool cotton broker, a teetotaler, and a physical-fitness enthusiast. Evelyn Bowden Lowry, his mother, was distant and unaffectionate, content to allow her children to be reared by a succession of nannies. At fourteen Malcolm entered the Leys School in Cambridge, where he was active in sports and developed literary interests. He also became infatuated with jazz and took up playing blues on the "taropatch," or tenor ukulele. Surreptitiously, he began to drink heavily. Encouraged by one of his schoolmasters (the model for James Hilton's "Mr. Chips"), he wrote his first stories for the school's literary magazine.

Lowry dreamed of going to sea, sustained by his reading of Herman Melville, Joseph Conrad, Jack London, and the early Eugene O'Neill. In 1927, he left school to sail as a cabin boy on the S.S. *Pyrrhus*, bound for the Far East—a position arranged for him by his father. Lowry later attended the University of Cambridge and was graduated without distinction in 1932. He wrote his first novel, *Ultramarine* (1933), during college. Bowker's research sheds new light on the suicide of Lowry's classmate Paul Fitte, in which Lowry was implicated as an accomplice and for which he would feel guilty ever afterward. By early 1933, Lowry had decisively broken with his family, though remaining financially dependent on his father, and he began a wayward, rootless existence.

Lowry had already made pilgrimages to visit two contemporary writers whom he admired greatly: the American poet Conrad Aiken and Norwegian novelist Nordahl Grieg. Aiken's novel *Blue Voyage* (1927) and Grieg's *Skibet gaar videre* (1924, *The Ship Sails On*, 1927), were dominant influences on *Ultramarine*. A war correspondent during World War II, Grieg was killed when his airplane was shot down by the Nazis in 1943. To Lowry, Grieg exemplified the serious literary artist who was idealistic and socially responsible. In contrast to this "good angel," Aiken was ultimately a sinister influence, as Bowker presents him. This view represents an important reinterpretation of the complex Aiken-Lowry relationship, which would last for twenty-five years. Bowker's Aiken is a darkly self-absorbed, twisted manipulator, a confirmed misogynist whose motives were genuinely "evil." Bowker goes as far as to claim that "if there was a threatening monster lurking not far below the skin of Malcolm Lowry, Conrad Aiken must take responsibility for consciously, for his own lurid experimental purposes, having been its Frankenstein."

A few reviewers have challenged Bowker's attribution of willful malice to Aiken and implication that Lowry was a mere passive victim. The chronic alcoholism, the ruined marriages, the trunkful of unfinished (and perhaps bogus) literary projects, the rootlessness and instability—these all stemmed from Lowry's own character. Despite Bowker's presentation of copious facts that document Lowry's behavior, Bowker's dualistic good angel–bad angel analysis at times participates in Lowry's own myth-making and seems to cloud basic ethical issues.

Bowker breaks new ground in his treatment of Lowry's volatile and essentially unsatisfying relationships with women. Contributing to Lowry's problems with women were the emotional gulf between him and his mother, doubts about his sexual potency, the alcoholism, chronic melancholia, and great literary insecurities. His wives, Jan Gabrial and Margerie Bonner, were both Americans with interests in film acting and in writing. Margerie's crucial role as a nurturer of (and, not infrequently, a collaborator in) Lowry's writing—particularly during the fourteen-year period of relative sobriety spent together in a squatter's shack in Dollarton, British Columbia—is well known. Margerie was primarily responsible for the publication of his posthumous works: *Hear Us O Lord from Heaven Thy Dwelling Place* (1961), *Selected Letters of Malcolm Lowry* (1965), *Dark as the Grave Wherein My Friend Is Laid* (1968), *Lunar Caustic* (1968), *October Ferry to Gabriola* (1970), and *Psalms and Songs* (1975). She was also Day's principal source of information, and not surprisingly she appears in a generally favorable light in his biography. Bowker's Margerie is far different. Proud, theatrical, condescending, she is presented as fundamentally resenting Lowry's acclaim as an artist. Few of their friends seem to have been able to abide her sentimental fantasies, tantrums, and strongly proprietorial attitude toward Lowry. Margerie's willingness to consider shock treatments and even a lobotomy for treating Lowry's alcoholic depression in his final years, her contradictory accounts of his death (he died of asphyxia induced by an overdose of barbiturates combined with alcohol), and her readiness to publish heavily edited versions of his uncompleted writings after his death all receive broadly condemnatory treatment here.

Bowker's presentation of Jan Gabrial is far more generous than that of Day and others. Lowry met Jan in the spring of 1933 in Granada, Spain, where he was traveling with Aiken and his wife. Despite tensions between Aiken and Jan, she and Lowry quickly fell in love; they were married the following January in Paris. Jan soon went home to New York, and Lowry followed in September. They lived separately for a time in Greenwich Village until, for ten days in the summer of 1936, Lowry was confined to the psychiatric ward of Bellevue Hospital.

Reunited, Lowry and Jan moved to Mexico at the end of October, 1936, settling within a few weeks in Cuernavaca, where he began to write the early drafts of *Under the Volcano*. The following summer, they were visited by Aiken, who witnessed (and participated in) their marital woes, fueled by alcoholic binges. Aiken's autobiographical novel *Ushant: An Essay* (1952) is a primary source of the highly unsympathetic view of Jan that has prevailed until now. Aiken reported that Jan repeatedly deserted Lowry to be with other men, and by the following December she had left him for good, returning to Los Angeles. Meanwhile, Lowry drifted south to Oaxaca, where he spent several days in jail for public drunkenness and rowdiness. He was put on a train out of the country in July of 1938, by agents sent by his father. He and Jan were divorced in 1940; by this time Margerie Bonner had entered his life, and they had moved to Canada.

Where Day had been unable to locate Jan Gabrial, Bowker interviewed her several times and gained permission to quote from her journal as well as from Lowry's letters to her. The result, naturally enough, is a thoroughly fresh take on these crucial events on which Lowry drew in *Under the Volcano*. In Bowker's account, Jan emerges as a far more credible and interesting woman. Her family background, education (at

Radcliffe College and the New York Academy of Dramatic Arts), and professional ambitions as an actress and writer are for the first time set forth. She admits that she was in love with Lowry the brilliantly promising writer not the deeply flawed man, and was cognizant of his genius but wary of his self-destructive tendencies and his inordinate need for and resentment of a female caretaker. Denying that she had affairs with other men, she explains her separations from Lowry in terms of her basic need to survive and avoid being drawn into the abyss he felt destined to explore. Notwithstanding her need to save herself, Jan continued to care for Lowry and remained as concerned for his well-being as she was certain of his talent. In one of her last letters to him, she wrote:

> We were idyllic in Cuernavaca for three months. I became your mother, [but] now I am paying for it. You're a great writer, . . . the most gifted man I have ever known. You have it in you to become one of the century's greatest writers. But you need help, not band-aid. . . . You need professional help.

It is salutary to have a more sympathetic understanding of Lowry's first wife and the difficult choices that resulted in the dissolution of their marriage. Yet the copious information Bowker presents shows how both Jan and Margerie contributed much to Lowry's artistic development.

Although Bowker regards *Under the Volcano* as "the greatest modern novel about the struggle of mankind against the forces of evil"—Lowry claimed that he was "telling [us] something new about hell fire"—Bowker makes no real attempt to analyze the novel or other Lowry works. Day's critical biography, in contrast, offers a seminal interpretation of Lowry's masterpiece. On the other hand, Bowker presents a clearer account of Lowry's post-*Volcano* career. He traces Lowry's "tendency towards giantism," the ever-expanding scheme he gradually developed to contain his entire "bolus"—that is, all of his fiction. "The Voyage That Never Ends" was an ambitious metafictional structure that would involve multiple narrative frames, stories about writers writing about writers writing, and would embody the traditional epic theme of the heroic quest: initiation (*Ultramarine* and *Lunar Caustic*), death, descent into a Dantesque inferno (*Under the Volcano*), purgatorial wanderings (*Dark as the Grave* and *La Mordida*), and rebirth or reentry into Paradise (*October Ferry to Gabriola* and *Hear Us O Lord from Heaven Thy Dwelling Place*). He worked on this project by fits and starts throughout the next decade, moving between its components, but in fact never brought any of the post-*Volcano* works to completion before his death. Indeed, as Bowker maintains, the scheme was inherently unfinishable, especially given Lowry's idiosyncratic working habits, and one can even see it ungenerously as an elaborate hoax—a ruse for extending the advances he received from his publishers.

Eventually, however, Lowry's failure to deliver on his promises brought an end to the period of grace. His Random House editor, Albert Erskine, found the fragments of *October Ferry to Gabriola* to be inert and tedious, and their contract was terminated in 1954. It was a disastrous blow, coinciding with the Lowrys' final "eviction" from their beloved shack at Dollarton and their return to Europe. Their time of comparative stability, sobriety, and productivity was over. The three remaining years of Lowry's life consisted of more frequent alcoholic "fugues"; growing marital discord and remorse, tinged with violent resentment; largely abortive attempts to resume work on the epic "bolus"; melancholy and attempted suicide; futile attempts at psychiatric intervention; and the infamous "death by misadventure" in the village of Ripe, Sussex, on June 27, 1957.

Bowker's tendency to engage in a polarizing analysis, portraying Lowry's behavior as directly influenced for good or ill by other persons (Aiken/Grieg, Margerie/Jan) in effect reconstructs the legend of Malcolm Lowry as a doomed artist. Yet given the abundance of documented information he provides, others less inclined to adjudicate blame for Lowry's failings should be better able to find a solid factual basis for understanding this complex man and his works.

Ronald G. Walker

Sources for Further Study

Books in Canada. XXII, November, 1993, p. 31.
Canadian Forum. LXXIII, May, 1994, p. 39.
Contemporary Review. CCLXIV, April, 1994, p. 219.
The Economist. CCCXXIX, November 6, 1993, p. 123.
London Review of Books. XVI, January 27, 1994, p. 16.
Maclean's. CVI, November 22, 1993, p. 71.
The Nation. CCLXI, December 11, 1995, p. 755.
New Statesman and Society . VI, October 22, 1993, p. 37.
The New York Times Book Review. C, November 26, 1995, p. 21.
The New Yorker. LXXI, January 8, 1996, p. 80.
Notes and Queries. XLI, September, 1994, p. 415.
The Times Educational Supplement. October 15, 1993, p. 10.
The Times Literary Supplement. December 31, 1993, p. 6.
The Washington Post Book World. XXV, October 15, 1995, p. 5.

THE QUANTITY THEORY OF INSANITY
Together with Five Supporting Propositions

Author: Will Self (1961-   )
First published: 1991, in Great Britain
Publisher: Atlantic Monthly Press (New York). 211 pp. $21.00
Type of work: Short stories

Six stories by one of Great Britain's sharpest and most perversely imaginative satirists

American readers got their first taste of Will Self's genius for depicting the Ionesco-like absurdity of contemporary life in *Cock & Bull* (1993), a pair of complementary, comically obsessive novellas which, parodying Philip Roth's *The Breast* (1972; rev. ed., 1980) parodying Franz Kafka's "The Metamorphosis" (1915; English translation, 1936), take a weirdly angled look at sexual stereotypes and more. Appetites whetted for Self's brand of postmodern perversity, they got their second course in *My Idea of Fun: A Cautionary Tale* (1944), an explosively comic novel that combines Nietzschean will to power with the entrepreneurial spirit of postindustrial Britain to give new life to the old story of a left-leaning author looking aghast at what Margaret Thatcher has wrought. Together the two books prove that Self is, as *Granta* magazine proclaimed in 1993, "one of the best of the young British novelists." *The Quantity Theory of Insanity*, his first book, appearing tardily in the United States, along with a second collection, *Grey Area and Other Stories* (1996), published in the United Kingdom, demonstrate that Self is one of the finest and most wildly imaginative writers of short fiction from England or anywhere.

Self's Jewish background and his having read philosophy at Oxford University figure in his fiction far less noticeably than the years he spent as a heroin addict and his stint as cartoonist for *New Statesman and Society* and other magazines. The consummate satirist, Self is as intelligent as Jonathan Swift, as fantastic as Nikolai Gogol, and as nasty as Martin Amis, but the writers he resembles most are Nathanael West and Flannery O'Connor. The latter's guiding principle was "For the near blind you must write large," and this Self does. His cartoonish characters and narrative situations exist in the gray area between the seemingly realistic and the absurdly phantasmagoric, where researchers publish their findings in the ridiculous yet reputable-sounding *Journal of British Ephemera* while those less academically inclined try to satisfy their craving for something substantial by eating a bag of "the new poly-flavoured crisps: wiener schnitzel and red cabbage." A similar air of (im)plausibility surrounds the stories' self-generating logic: "There's a fat ham of a man down there who went mad one day and drank some bleach. They replaced his esophagus with a section cut from his intestine. On a quiet night you can hear him farting through his mouth."

As its full title suggests, *The Quantity Theory of Insanity: Together with Five Supporting Propositions* is a story cycle and as such bears a certain generic resemblance to works such as *Dubliners* (1914), *Winesburg, Ohio* (1919), and *The House-*

breaker of Shady Hill, but Self's North London has less in common with James Joyce's city, Sherwood Anderson's town, or John Cheever's suburb than with *Alice's Adventures in Wonderland* (1865). It is specific and familiar on the one hand, bizarre and hallucinatory on the other:

> Rosemount Avenue was one of those hilltop streets in suburban London where the camber of the road is viciously arced like the back of a macadamised whale. The houses are high-gabled Victorian, tiled in red with masonry that looks as if it was sculpted out of solid snot. Calling it an avenue was presumably a reference to the eight or so plane trees running down each side of the road. These had been so viciously pruned that they looked like nothing so much as upturned amputated legs.

Rosemount Avenue is where the narrator of the first "supporting proposition," "The North London Book of the Dead," finds his dead mother living. As she explains, "When you die, you move to another part of London, that's all there is to it." Actually, that is not all there is to it. The dead, he learns, exist alongside the living and have their own companies and support groups, even their own telephone directory, *The North London Book of the Dead*. (In *My Idea of Fun*, the same title refers to a rather different text, a kind of postindustrial *Tibetan Book of the Dead*, "a set of instructions for the dying" made up of the names of generic products chanted until voices merge "into one incantatory hum.") The son responds incongruously: Why, he wonders, is his previously snobbish mother living in unfashionable Crouch End? Why did she fail to call him to say that she was back? Why is she calling him now at work? "I'd never live down the ignominy of having a mother who phoned me at the office."

The insanity quotient increases in (and on) "Ward 9." The story concerns Misha Gurney, a new art therapist on the mental ward of a vast hospital. Patients and staff here are equally odd: Dr. Zack Busner, with his froglike appearance and "anomalous shoes"; senior registrar Jane Bowen, "who seemed to be all concavities"; the voluptuous nurse Mimi, who dispenses pills and quick sex in dark closets; patients such as Tom, Busner's son Adam, and Misha's predecessor (who happens to be Jane's brother)—the "meta-mad" whose psychoses are stylized parodies of the "real" thing.

Busner is one of Self's most recurrent characters and frequent targets, an R. D. Laing-like figure whose minor fame and fortune derive from having invented "The Riddle," a kind of psychotherapeutic Rubik's Cube. "Busner is the Hierophant. He oversees the auguries, decocts the potions, presides over rituals that piddle the everyday into a teastrainer reality." Misha sees in Busner "a world of complacency, of theory in the face of real distress." He is in effect merely a more up-to-date and slightly less mechanical version of the "corroded atrophied" microscopelike apparatus that Misha finds hidden away in the hospital's "secret underworld," directly across from the mysterious Mass Disaster Room. (In Self's fiction, the real disaster is not the one about to occur—the earthquake, the nuclear attack; it is the one going on right now, every day.)

Misha does not see that his days on the ward are numbered. Weighed and found wanting, art therapist is recycled as patient. As readers learn in "Inclusion," one of the *Grey Area* stories, Misha will take his own life and Busner will mourn his passing, not because Misha was a colleague, a patient, and the son of a friend, but because his death precludes his taking part in Busner's latest research project, testing a new drug made from "the refined crap of a bee mite" that cures depression by making users take interest in anything and everything, totally and indiscriminately.

Janner, in "Understanding the Ur-Bororo," is a variation on the Busner theme—less menacing, more comical.

> He was a driven young man whose wimpy physical appearance all too accurately complemented his obsessive nature. His body looked as if it had been constructed out of pipecleaners dunked repeatedly in flesh-coloured wax. All his features were eroded and soft except for his nose, which was the droplet of wax that hardens as it runs down the shaft of the candle. There was also something fungoid about Janner, it was somehow indefinable, but I always suspected that underneath his clothes Janner had athlete's foot—all over his entire body.

Janner's "book linking the observation of swirling laundry to traditional Buddhist meditation" becomes a hit, transforming the previously "unprepossessing" young man into The Anthropologist, a "pop academic" and "minor celebrity." First, though, Janner must study the decidedly unexotic Ur-Bororo, a South American (but otherwise very English-like) tribe. As Janner explains to the story's narrator, a former college classmate, now a teacher married to another teacher, the Ur-Bororo actually refer to themselves as "The People Who You Wouldn't Like to Be Cornered by at a Party." Everything about them is boring, their dreams, even their beverages: coya, "a luke-warm drink . . . [which] looks alarmingly like instant coffee, but the taste is a lot blander," and "the watery manioc beer" which produces "the kind of turgid flatulence which passes for high spirits among the Ur-Bororo."

The real target of Self's satire is not the nonexistent Ur-Bororo but those who turn to or churn out the various, invariably absurd theories that Self's dark comedies show to be ineffective at best, inhuman at worst (as inhuman as the marketing scam in "Mono-Cellular"), and always inane. "For a culture that was supposedly unaffected by the end of an era," one narrator points out, "we certainly showed a lot of interest in esoteric theories" ("Waiting"), and for much the same reason that the characters in *My Idea of Fun* turn to marketing, in order to offset "the painful nullity of their emotional lives." Consider the title-story narrator's progress as he explains the quantity theory's "human origins": "Sunday afternoon excursions [with his parents] to watch the construction of Heathrow airport"; an early interest, as a graduate student, in the nineteenth century phrenologist who held that "the 'shape' of the real, internal nose" was "the true indicator of hereditary disposition"; and his academic adviser Alkan's more recent but no less ludicrous "Implication Theory of Psychotherapy":

> instead of the analyst listening to the patient and then providing an interpretation, of whatever kind, Alkan would say what he *thought* the analysand would say. The analysand was then obliged to furnish the interpretation he thought Alkan would make. Alternatively, Alkan would give an interpretation and the analysand was required to give an account that adequately matched it.

When Alkan, already mad, disappears, the narrator tracks him down in paranoid Pynchonesque fashion. Gainful employment (or what passes for such in Thatcherite

England) follows: research psychologist with a cattle feed manufacturer, fellow at the "Institute of Job Reductivism," where he completes his thesis on "Some Aspects of Academic Grant Application in 1970's Britain" while his colleagues work on equally silly but even more reductive "reductivist studies," then off to "Concept House," where he tests the effectiveness—the *cost* effectiveness—of Busner's latest theory (this is after "Ward 9" but before "Inclusion") that in a therapeutic community, staff and patients should be free to adopt either role.

At this point, the narrator is only a doodle away from the insight that becomes the elegantly simple and simply absurd Quantity Theory of Insanity, according to which "there is only a fixed proportion of sanity available in any given society at any given time" and "any attempts to palliate manifestations of insanity in one sector can only result in the upsurge in some other area of society." Not surprisingly, the theory catches on, soon spinning out of the anal-retentive narrator's control. He is especially troubled when Adam Harley, named for the street where many London psychiatrists have their offices, recasts the quantity theory "as a therapeutic practice designed to palliate the idle sorrows of the moneyed" (a bit designed, one suspects, to remind readers what money can buy in the entrepreneurial 1980's and 1990's: justice, health care, body parts from India, the chance to dump toxic waste in West Africa, and so on).

Disheartened but not depleted, the narrator comes up with a few more theories to call his own. One takes the form of a perfectly tautological equation that actually measures the theorist's own mad state. The other, however, indicates that the story's mad theorist may be on to something after all: "The task now is to derive an equation which would make it possible to establish what I suspect is true. Namely that as more and more insanity is concentrated around educational institutions, so levels of mental illness in the rest of society. . . ."

Will Self is on to this and more: that the "rest of the world" is not doing any better. In the age of avarice, when, as *My Idea of Fun*'s Ian Wharton puts it, "people had begun to feel less ashamed about being greedy and wanting their fair share," theory is simply another commodity to be marketed like corn flakes or, as in the story "Mono-Cellular," babies, all one hundred gross of them, each in its own cardboard box and bubble wrap.

Robert A. Morace

Sources for Further Study

American Book Review. XVI, December, 1994-February, 1995, p. 8.
Boston Globe. February 15, 1995, p. 68.
Los Angeles Times Book Review. February 19, 1995, p. 6.
The New York Times Book Review. C, February 26, 1995, p. 11.
The Observer. October 23, 1994, p. 23.
The Review of Contemporary Fiction. XV, Summer, 1995, p. 216.
The Times Literary Supplement. December 20, 1991, p. 25.

THE REAL SHAKESPEARE
Retrieving the Early Years, 1564-1594

Author: Eric Sams (1926-   )
Publisher: Yale University Press (New Haven, Connecticut). 256 pp. $30.00
Type of work: Biography; literary criticism
Time: 1564-1594
Locale: Stratford, Lancashire, and London, England

*Through a careful study of contemporary documents and early references to Shakespeare,
Eric Sams seeks to shed light on the dramatist's early life and to expand the canon of his plays*

> *Principal personages:*
> WILLIAM SHAKESPEARE, the English poet and playwright
> JOHN SHAKESPEARE, his father
> ROBERT GREENE, an Elizabethan pamphleteer and dramatist
> THOMAS KYD, an Elizabethan tragedian
> SIR THOMAS LUCY, a rich Stratford landowner, justice of the peace, and
> Member of Parliament
> THOMAS NASHE, an Elizabethan author
> FERNANDO STANLEY, LORD STRANGE, the sponsor of a theatrical
> company

The documentary record of William Shakespeare's life to 1592 is sparse. Even his birthdate is uncertain. The Stratford-on-Avon parish register notes only the baptism of "Gulielmus filius Johannis Shakespeare" on April 26, 1564. About 1743, William Oldys first suggested April 23 as the date of birth, convenient since Shakespeare died on April 23, 1616. That is St. George's Day; the national poet and the patron saint of England thus could share the celebration.

The records of the Stratford grammar school for the 1570's do not survive. Presumably Shakespeare would have been sent to King's New School, though the first mention of his attendance appears in Nicholas Rowe's 1709 biographical preface to his edition of the plays. Rowe reports that John Shakespeare

> had bred [his son] for some time at a free-school, where 'tis probable he acquir'd that little Latin he
> was master of; but the narrowness of his circumstances, and the want of his assistance at home,
> forc'd his father to withdraw him from thence, and unhappily prevented his further proficiency in
> that language.

Documents testify to a decline in John Shakespeare's fortunes. In 1565 he was elected an alderman of Stratford, and in 1568 he became bailiff, equivalent to the city's mayor. As late as 1575 he was still adding to his properties, buying two houses in that year. Then in 1577 he stopped attending aldermanic meetings (though he remained an alderman until 1586) and began selling and mortgaging his lands. By 1590 his real estate holdings had been reduced to the one house on Henley Street where Shakespeare was born.

Even if Shakespeare had remained at the grammar school, by the age of fifteen he would have been apprenticed, probably to his father. From his birth to 1582, however, no documents trace his activity. On November 27, 1582, he was issued a special marriage license, and the next day a marriage license bond provided "that William Shagspere on thone partie, and Anne Hathwey of Stratford in the Dioces of Worcester maiden may lawfully solennize matrimony together." The special license argues haste; six months later, on May 26, 1583, Shakespeare's first child, Susannah, was christened, and on February 2, 1585, his other children, the twins Hamnet and Judith, were also.

In 1588 Shakespeare is named in a suit along with his parents in an unsuccessful effort to recover property from John Lambert, the future playwright's first cousin. Then in 1592 the mists clear. On March 3 of that year, Philip Henslowe, manager of the Rose Theatre, London, recorded a new play, "Harey the vj," acted by Lord Strange's Men. Thomas Nashe in *Pierce Pennilesse* (1592) wrote of the triumph of "braue Talbot" on the stage, a reference to Shakespeare's *1 Henry VI*, and Robert Greene attacked

an vpstart Crow, beautified with our feathers, that with his *Tygers hart wrapt in a Players hyde*, supposes he is as well able to bombast out a blanke verse as the best of you: and beeing an absolute *Johannes factotum*, is in his owne conceit that onely Shake-scene in a countrey.

The line that Greene italicized derives from *3 Henry VI*. By 1592, then, Shakespeare was in London writing popular plays; "Harey the vj" was performed fourteen times between March and June, when the theaters were closed first because of disorderly conduct and then because of plague.

The period between 1585 and 1592 is, however, a blank, commonly known as the "Lost Years," and this is the period that Eric Sams seeks to illuminate. His search takes him north of Stratford to Lancashire, where on August 3, 1581, Alexander Hoghton of Lea made a will that said in part, "And I most hertelye requyre the said Sir Thomas [Heskethe Knyghte] . . . to be ffrendlye vnto ffoke Gyllome & William Shakeshafte nowe dwellinge with me & eyther to take theym vnto his Servyce or els to help theym to some good master, as my tryste ys he wyll."

John Cottom is also mentioned in this will. Cottom, a Lancashire native, served as schoolmaster at Stratford from 1577 to 1581 or 1582. On May 13, 1582, Cottom's Jesuit brother Thomas was executed at Tyburn, and by that date Cottom had returned to Tarnacre, about ten miles from Lea. Sams argues that Cottom recognized Shakespeare's talents and recommended the young man as schoolmaster to Hoghton. John Aubrey in his *Brief Lives* (1681) reports that Shakespeare "understood Latine pretty well; for he had been in his younger years a scholmaster in the country." As Shakespeare indicates in *The Taming of the Shrew* (1593/1594), this role often entailed musical instruction, and the will suggests that it involved playacting.

According to Sams, Cottom was attracted to Shakespeare in part because of the youth's Catholicism. In 1580 a team of British Jesuits returned to England, and a renewed round of religious persecution erupted. The western part of Lancashire was heavily Catholic, so Shakespeare would be safer there than in his native Stratford, where Sir Thomas Lucy actively prosecuted recusants.

This theory, also accepted by Ernest Honigmann in *Shakespeare: The Lost Years* (1985), tantalizes, but was the teacher/actor William Shakeshafte the future dramatist William Shakespeare? Shakeshafte was a common Lancashire name. How reliable is Aubrey's account? Anthony Wood drew on Aubrey for information for *Atheniae Oxonienses* (1691-1692), a biographical dictionary of Oxonians. Wood described Aubrey as "exceedingly credulous" and claimed that Aubrey's reports contained "fooleries and misinformations which sometimes would guide him [Wood] into the paths of error." If Shakespeare was in Lancashire in late 1581, why did he return in 1582 to impregnate and then marry Anne Hathaway?

Was John Shakespeare, and hence his son, Catholic? Sams accepts as authentic John Shakespeare's "Spiritual Last Will and Testament," first reported in 1757. In 1790, Edmond Malone, the leading Shakespeare scholar of the age, published the document as genuine, but six years later he changed his mind: "In my conjecture concerning the writer of that paper, I certainly was mistaken; for I have since obtained documents that clearly prove it could not have been the composition of any of [Shakespeare's] family." Malone did not detail the documents he had obtained, and the "Spiritual Last Will" has vanished, so that its date and signature (or mark) cannot be authenticated. Against the argument of John Shakespeare's Catholicism is the fact that in 1559 he voted with the Protestant majority of the Stratford council to remove the Romanist curate Roger Dyos. William Shakespeare's baptism was Protestant, and to hold public office John Shakespeare would have had to take an oath of allegiance to the Church of England. In 1591, two reports noted John Shakespeare's absence from church services. Many listed in these documents were accused of Catholicism, but John Shakespeare's absence in both cases was attributed to fear of arrest for debt.

Sams accepts not only Aubrey's claim that Shakespeare was a schoolmaster but also the suggestion first put forward by Malone in 1790 that Shakespeare worked as a lawyer's clerk. Sams maintains that shortly after his marriage Shakespeare set out for London to escape prosecution for poaching Sir Thomas Lucy's deer. The deer-poaching episode was first reported at the end of the seventeenth century and de-rived from local gossip. In 1610, Sir Thomas Lucy III did bring a Star Chamber action over the poaching of deer, so this incident may have been the source of the reports. Yet in the 1602 quarto of *The Merry Wives of Windsor* (1600/1601), Justice Shallow, long regarded as based on Lucy, opens the play by declaring, "Nere talk to me, Ile make a star-chamber matter of it," the "it" being Sir John Falstaff's actions: "You have hurt my keeper,/ Kild my dogs, stolne my deere." The deer-poaching story has proved tenacious, but its authenticity remains suspect in the absence of documentary evidence.

In 1753, Robert Shiels recorded that the playwright William Davenant (aged ten when Shakespeare died) told the actor Thomas Betterton, who told Nicholas Rowe who told Alexander Pope who told Thomas Newton, that when Shakespeare first came to London the young man held horses outside the Theatre at Shoreditch. Sams accepts this story, as he does the other late seventeenth and early eighteenth century accounts of Shakespeare's early life, so that by 1589 the playwright had, according to Sams, been "a moneylender, a butcher, a schoolmaster, a law-clerk, a deer-poacher, an ostler, a call-boy, a translator and a pamphleteer." As Lady Bracknell would say, here is a life filled with incident.

Sams maintains that during this period Shakespeare was also writing plays. Orthodox dating of Shakespeare's works begins his career about 1590, but Sams, like Honigmann, wants him to start earlier, about 1586. Drawing on what he regards as allusions in pamphlets and the three "Parnassus" plays performed at Cambridge University (and that Sams says belong to the early 1590's rather than the conventional 1598, 1599, and 1601), he assigns to the 1580's *Titus Andronicus, Pericles,* and an early version of *Hamlet* as well as *Fair Em, Locrine, The Marriage of Wit and Wisdom, Dives and Lazarus, Edmund Ironside, Edward III, The Troublesome Reign of King John,* and *The Taming of a Shrew* (a different play from the canonical *The Taming of the Shrew).* In addition to revising the dating of the first three plays and adding the latter eight to the canon, Sams would place *King Lear* (1605/1606) and *The Famous Victories of Henry V* (1598/1599) in the list of Shakespeare's works. Sams also denies that the so-called bad quartos are inaccurate reconstructions of authentic plays; instead he sees them as early drafts.

The dating of plays and determining their authorship are not exact sciences, but Sams's arguments are not convincing. For example, he presents twelve reasons for assigning *The Taming of a Shrew* to Shakespeare and dating it around 1588. His first is that Shakespeare "was an originator, and *A Shrew* is the first modern comedy in English." The published version of *A Shrew* appeared in 1594 and claimed that the play had been acted by Pembroke's Men, a short-lived company that began in 1592 but in 1593 had to sell its costumes to pay its debts. A 1592 date for the play thus seems likely, and Shakespeare's connection remains unproved. The second argument is that Shakespeare was writing plays in the 1580's, but that is precisely the point under debate. Sams claims that "Shakespeare was no mere exploitative plagiarist" and so would not have cribbed from *A Shrew* for *The Shrew;* it is not at all clear, though, which play stole from which. Moreover, Greene accused Shakespeare of being "beautified with our feathers"—that is, plagiarizing; indeed, Shakespeare rarely invented a plot. Sams notes that "*A Shrew* quotes and parodies Marlowe," including *Dr. Faustus,* which Sams assigns to 1588 also. *Dr. Faustus* may, however, be as late as 1592 or 1593.

While Sams's arguments do not convince, he has performed a valuable service in calling for a reassessment of dating and canonicity. This process has already begun. In 1986 Gary Taylor, coeditor of the Oxford University Press Shakespeare, rejected *Edward III* as canonical, but in 1990 he and Stanley Wells accepted it. Thomas Merriam agreed, though in 1982 he had found only a small Shakespearean contribution. The 1608 quarto of *King Lear* had long been regarded as "bad," but many editors now grant that text equal status with the 1623 Folio, which they regard as an authorial revision of the earlier text. Sams has raised important issues that illustrate how scholars have still not plucked out the heart of Shakespeare's mystery.

Joseph Rosenblum

Sources for Further Study

Contemporary Review. CCLXVI, May, 1995, p. 277.
Library Journal. CXX, March 1, 1995, p. 72.
The Observer. March 5, 1995, p. 18.
The Times Literary Supplement. April 7, 1995, p. 21.

THE REDRESS OF POETRY

Author: Seamus Heaney (1939-   )
Publisher: Farrar Straus Giroux (New York). 212 pp. $22.00
Type of work: Literary criticism

Seamus Heaney attempts to provide a defense of the surprise and delight that poetry can provide for readers

The Redress of Poetry had its origin in fifteen lectures that Seamus Heaney delivered in his role as professor of poetry at the University of Oxford from 1989 to 1994. Ten of the lectures are reprinted in the book, which is both a defense of poetry and an analysis of poets ranging from Christopher Marlowe in the sixteenth century to Elizabeth Bishop in the twentieth century.

The introduction to the book gives a context for the various ways Heaney will discover that poetry provides a "redress" or relief to the reader. For example, he cites a late poem by Robert Frost called "Directive" to show that poetry is an "imaginative transformation of human life." Poetry does not dwell in the world of fact, represented by the painful events within the house Frost describes "in earnest," but in the imaginative world, suggested by the playhouse of the children. This imagined world can heal humans and make them "whole," by encompassing and transforming painful reality into pleasure.

The next chapter, "The Redress of Poetry," attempts to define some of the possible ways of seeing this "redress." Heaney begins with the more obvious definitions of the word as "reparation" or "compensation" of a wrong. Yet it can also mean to set right, to "restore" or "re-establish." These obsolete meanings suggest further ways that poetry may affect a reader. Furthermore, Heaney finds an even more obsolete defini- tion taken from hunting: "to bring back (the hounds or the deer) to the proper course."

The restorative power of poetry is, for Heaney, its most important function. Heaney is especially eager to defend the delight in poetry against those who would make it an instrument of political correctness and so serve some specific social or political purpose. He cites the example of the Irish rebel Thomas MacDonagh, who participated in and was executed after the 1916 Uprising. MacDonagh despised the British Empire and its refusal to give freedom to Ireland. As Heaney insists, however, MacDonagh did not reject the poetic tradition of Britain and even wrote a book on Thomas Campion's metrics. In the 1990's, that tradition, and the canon it represented, is being displaced by those who wish to replace it with literary works that are written by or for members of various groups that have been oppressed. Heaney wishes to preserve the "surprise" and joy that poetry provides in the face of such demands.

"Extending the Alphabet" deals with the style of Christopher Marlowe. Heaney speaks of how he was overwhelmed as a college student by hearing a skilled reader deliver Marlowe's mighty lines. In the essay, however, he discusses Marlowe's long unfinished poem "Hero and Leander." Some might find in that poem a defense of homosexuality or condemn it as being sexist, but Heaney insists that if read correctly, it yields a "fine excess" and a sheer pleasure in the power of language. Any attempt to use the poem for a partisan cause ignores what is most important in it; such a reading is self-serving, not a true response.

In an essay on John Clare's poetry, Heaney sorts out the permanent and important poems of Clare from the more ephemeral ones. He considers that the celebrated poems that Clare wrote in his madness and poverty do not represent him at his best or show the poet in his true poetic element. Instead, Heaney believes that the true poems of Clare are those on nature, such as "Mouse's Nest." Yet he singles out as Claire's most important and influential poems those written on the enclosure of the land in the nineteenth century, especially "Swordy Well." That model of protest still pays attention to poetic effects, as "effortless" as they may seem. Heaney cites, for example, the ballad stanza as a traditional form that "kept Clare on the right road poetically." At the end of the essay, Heaney sees Clare as a possible model for a postmodern poetry that can offer social protest yet still retain the imaginative demands of poetic language. He even claims that the best of recent British poetry is indebted to the style and practice of Clare.

The essay on Oscar Wilde's "The Ballad of Reading Gaol" is curious in the compromises Heaney seems to make in his demand for the primacy of poetic language over social content. He discusses Wilde's use of the ballad stanza in "The Ballad of Reading Gaol" as following the example of his mother. Wilde's mother wrote a number of propaganda poems for the cause of Ireland under the name Sperenza. The ballad stanza, however, was not appropriate for the content or the style of Wilde's poem. In addition, Wilde was too close to his subject and could not distinguish between the pain he suffered and the distance his art needed. Heaney claims, however, that the poem provides a "redress," since "Wilde the aesthete was stripped of his dandy's clothes to become Wilde the convict. . . . The master of the light touch came to submit to the heaviness of being and came, as a result, to leave his fingerprints on a great subject." This seems to contradict the earlier descriptions of what "redress" poetry might offer and to make a special claim for Wilde on nonaesthetic grounds. It is difficult to see how the change in Wilde's condition led to an increase in his art. Instead, it seems to have brought out unfortunate elements that had been hidden under the brilliant surface of Wilde's earlier writing.

The chapter on Hugh MacDiarmid looks at his poetry as a whole. Heaney discusses MacDiarmid's poetic conversion, when he changed his English poems into "synthetic Scots." Heaney praises some of the early poems, but he focuses on "A Drunk Man Looks at the Thistle." The thistle is, of course, the national emblem of Scotland. MacDiarmid treats it with typical irreverence as he creates a long list of Scottish heroes and declares, "Upon the thistle they're impaled"; so Scotland has from its early years rejected those who were most valuable to it. Heaney calls the poem a mixture of "passion and irreverence" and a "masterpiece," although he does not discuss its language or form in any detail. In contrast, Heaney believes that the later poems of MacDiarmid, which were written in English after his conversion to communism, are failures. The failure is attributable to MacDiarmid's losing touch with his roots and the language that had spurred his creativity. He replaced this dialect with a grand and universal political solution that hobbled his poetry.

The chapter on Dylan Thomas attempts to discover what part of Thomas' poetry has long-lasting value. Heaney claims that the earliest poems of Thomas are among his greatest achievements. Those poems have an exuberance in language that fits his descriptions of a union with nature and have a "pre-lapsarian wholeness." Yet when Thomas continued to use these stylistic mannerisms in his middle age, they became, according to Heaney, tiresome and unconvincing. He sees only one late poem that suggests a development in style and theme: the villanelle called "Do Not Go Gentle into That Good Night." There Thomas came to terms with death and age, themes that had been absent from his early and middle poems. Heaney suggests that Thomas' most famous poems, "Fern Hill" and "Poem in October," have the same sense of loss found in Wordsworth; however, Thomas did not, according to Heaney, grow beyond that loss into the "philosophic mind," as William Wordsworth did in "Ode: Intimations of Immortality." Heaney ends the essay by suggesting that a number of poems by Thomas will last and become permanent parts of the poetic tradition.

The chapter on Philip Larkin's "Aubade" is the most disturbing and controversial one in the book. Heaney compares Larkin's poem to "The Man and the Echo" by William Butler Yeats. He finds that Larkin's poem is depressing, even though it exhibits great poetic skill. Heaney quotes Czesław Miłosz's negative reaction to the poem in support of his own. He especially praises Yeats's ability to bring out opposite points of view on humanity's final fate and to keep the mind's "options" open. In contrast, Larkin takes a single-minded position: People die, and religion or friends are no consolation. Yet as Helen Vendler has said, "What is irremediable needs recognition too." Larkin's "Aubade" presents that grim point of view fully and powerfully. It is a great poem that is at least the equal of Yeats's, and one that speaks directly to the human condition at the end of the twentieth century. Heaney decides the case on his dislike of the uncompromising treatment of death in Larkin's poem and not its aesthetic value. This is, once more, a contradiction of his stated position on the primary values of poetry.

The chapter on Elizabeth Bishop's poetry is unusual in that it begins with a consideration of one of her short stories, "The Scream." The story is told from the perspective of a little girl. She is delighted to hear the sound of the blacksmith's anvil. In contrast, the scream of the title is of the girl's mother, who sinks into a permanent state of madness after the death of her husband. Heaney sees the "redress" that art can create in the ending of the story. The girl pleads for another sound: "Nate!/ Oh, beautiful sound, strike again." The sound on Nate's anvil is, for Heaney, an analogy to poetry. Moreover, Bishop's preoccupation with loss and finding ways of dealing with it can be seen in many of her poems. Heaney singles out her villanelle "One Art" as one of the finest examples of that practice. "There the scream was subsumed in the anvil note; here the disaster is absorbed when it meets its emotional and phonetic match in the word 'master.'" In this chapter, Heaney is sensitive to the details of the poem as well as the way redress can be achieved in poetry of a high order.

In the last chapter in the book, "Frontiers of Writing," Heaney discusses the political and literary situation in Ireland after the troubles in Northern Ireland and the renewal of bombing by the Irish Republican Army (IRA). His solution is to find a unity in the diversity of Ireland. He suggests that the form of a "quincunx" can bring together "five towers." The first tower is at the center of Ireland, in its "original insular dwelling." The others, which are arranged around it, are those of James Joyce, Edmund Spenser, Louis MacNeice, and William Butler Yeats. Such an Ireland is Protestant and Catholic, modern and ancient, and includes the aristocracy, the peasantry, and the urban dweller. It is an Ireland of the imagination, one that can overcome all sectarian divisions.

The defense of poetry is a genre that goes back at least as far as Aristotle. Its most common claim is that literature both teaches and delights. Heaney comes down squarely on the side of delight. That insistence on delight, however, does not exhaust the wide range of functions that poetry has in Heaney's formulation. For him, poetry must first of all delight; it then has some restorative power, suggested by the various meanings of "redress."

The breadth of Heaney's vision makes this one of the most useful and elegant statements on what poetry can do. In addition, his defense comes at a time when the delight to be found in poetry is little championed in criticism. Cultural and deconstructive criticism have ignored or distorted the formal elements of poetry that Heaney calls to our attention so eloquently.

James Sullivan

Sources for Further Study

Booklist. XCII, November 15, 1995, p. 530.
Boston Globe. November 16, 1995, p. 67.
The Guardian. September 15, 1995, p. 5.
Library Journal. CXX, November 1, 1995, p. 64.
The Nation. CCLXI, December 4, 1995, p. 716.
The New Yorker. LXXI, October 23, 1995, p. 84.
Publishers Weekly. CCXLII, October 30, 1995, p. 52.
The Spectator. CCLXXV, September 16, 1995, p. 39.
The Times Literary Supplement. October 20, 1995, p. 9.

THE REVOLT OF THE ELITES
And the Betrayal of Democracy

Author: Christopher Lasch (1932-1994)
Publisher: W. W. Norton (New York). 276 pp. $22.00
Type of work: History; current affairs

A historical analysis and self-styled populist critique of America's managerial elite, whose withdrawal from political affairs has produced, in the author's opinion, a "democratic malaise"

A century ago, urban reformer and muckraking journalist Jacob A. Riis warned that democracy was being undermined by the emergence of two Americas, separate and unequal, and that the key to fostering class harmony, civic responsibility, and a robust democracy was the strengthening of the primary group bonds of family, school, church, club, and neighborhood. Distinguished historian Christopher Lasch echoes these sentiments in this rather disappointingly disjointed collection of scholarly reviews and essays, published posthumously (supposedly Lasch completed the manuscript only weeks before he died of cancer). Versions of many of the chapters contained in *The Revolt of the Elites: And the Betrayal of Democracy* were previously published in such journals of opinion as *Salmagundi*, *Tikkun*, and *New Oxford Review*. In summation, the book is long on intellectual speculation and woefully short on original research. Nevertheless, Lasch's ideas are provocative, and his writing style is more readable than it has been in any of his recent books.

What most differentiates Lasch from humanitarian progressives such as Riis is the chillingly pessimistic tone of his social criticism, leveled against a new generation of irresponsible plutocrats. These vaguely defined "Elites," unlike the old aristocracy or the best of the robber barons, display little sense of noblesse oblige. According to Lasch, a political and spiritual crisis has been created by the civic behavior of this fluid jet-setting generation of corporate technocrats and information managers, who regard themselves as citizens of the world and look down on middle America as hopelessly ignorant and intolerant. Thus, just when world events seem to have signaled democracy's ascendancy, *The Revolt of the Elites* appears as a caustic critique of liberal capitalism in both its free-market apotheosis and its welfare-state apparition. Radical in his attack on economic privilege but conservative in his defense of fixed moral standards, the nuclear family, and such bourgeois values as hard work and ethical integrity, Lasch has written a virtual jeremiad against what he refers to as the contemporary therapeutic state, which exalts self-esteem but debases competence. Labeling himself a populist (part of a tradition that includes, in Lasch's opinion, both agrarian radicals and Southern Christian Leadership Conference freedom fighters), he argues that democracy must rest on individual responsibility rather than the veneer of misplaced compassion and victimization politics.

After an introductory essay titled "The Democratic Malaise," *The Revolt of the Elites* divides into three sections, "The Intensification of Social Divisions," "Democratic Discourse in Decline," and "The Dark Night of the Soul." Having produced no statistical data to buttress his central thesis—to wit, that America's privileged classes have become insular, global, migratory, and, in essence, unpatriotic—Lasch reprises arguments previously made in his *The Culture of Narcissism* (1978) and *The True and Only Heaven: Progress and Its Critics* (1991). Following in the pragmatic intellectual tradition of educator John Dewey and political scientist Herbert Croly (and writing disparagingly of elitist journalist Walter Lippmann), he is interested in the historical roots of ideas such as communitarianism and social mobility (which, in his opinion, has been bastardized into a bogus substitute for true opportunity). Lasch is less adept at articulating solutions than at pointing out America's shortcomings —and who could disagree with his outrage over the obscene economic disparities between the elite and the nonelite, the youthful nihilism of the urban underclass, the irrelevance of public education to student needs, and the widening chasm between the races and generations? His polemic on the declension of democracy is in the tradition of seventeenth century divine Cotton Mather and Gilded Age critic Henry Adams and, complete with quotations from eighteenth century theologian Jonathan Edwards, is intended to spark a moral revival, at least among its targeted audience, the intelligentsia.

The title *The Revolt of the Elites* is an ironic inversion of José Ortega y Gasset's classic *La rebelión de las masas* (1929; *The Revolt of the Masses*, 1932). Lasch is less interested in the industrial and financial professionals analyzed by Ortega y Gasset than in the informational elite who claim to speak for the United States yet, ironically, live isolated in cocoonlike, security-guarded enclaves atop the social hierarchy. Nostalgic for an imagined age when different classes came together as citizens outside the home and workplace, a time when folks reveled in freewheeling public debate on issues that actually had impact on their lives and were not alienated from or apathetic toward their political institutions, Lasch bemoans the diminution of standards, ideals, folkways, and frames of reference once the common property, so to speak, of the electorate. Particularly taken by Ray Oldenburg's *The Great Good Place: Cafés, Coffee Shops, Community Centers, Beauty Parlors, General Stores, Bars, Hangouts and How They Get You Through the Day* (1989), the author concludes that even though these "third places" were sometimes off limits to women and children, they promoted sociability and decency and deflated pretension and pomposity.

Other books that deeply influenced Lasch are Philip Rieff's *The Triumph of the Therapeutic* (1966), E. J. Dionne's *Why Americans Hate Politics* (1991), and Amitai Etzioni's *The Spirit of Community* (1993). Although not explicitly mentioned, perhaps because of the closeness of publication date, *The Revolt of the Elites* assesses the future of democracy in a manner that has much in common with Jean Bethke Elshtain's *Democracy on Trial* (1993). While critical of the Right's infatuation with free-market capitalism, by its very nature amoral, ethically neutral, and subservient to the cash nexus ("in our own time," Lasch declares, "money has come to be regarded as the only reliable measure of equality"), *The Revolt of the Elites* saves its greatest scorn for social engineers on the Left, who have ruined communities in the name of urban renewal and bused children out of their neighborhoods in a crazy, doomed attempt to achieve racial balance. In fact, rejected Supreme Court nominee Robert H. Bork, reviewing *The Revolt of the Elites* for *National Review*, marveled at how much in agreement he was with the book's conclusions. Infatuated with identity politics, elitist planners embrace self-esteem rather than self-reliance and self-respect, Lasch laments.

> The dominant brand of liberalism [is] obsessed with the rights of women and minorities, with gay rights and unlimited abortion rights, with the allegedly epidemic spread of child abuse and sexual harassment, with the need for regulations against offensive speech, and with curricular reforms designed to end the cultural hegemony of "dead white European males."

Even during the Progressive Era, moralists such as Jacob Riis were regarded by professional altruists as backward-looking for clinging to the premise that civic virtue rested on a shared morality. The cult of the expert was emerging. Lasch contends that by the time of Franklin D. Roosevelt, New Deal liberals were mistakenly operating from the premise that democracy could function independently from civic virtue, that enlightened self-interest was preferable to a society based on shame and guilt, and that institutions were more important than the character of the players. By the time postwar social scientists such as Daniel Bell and Talcott Parsons proclaimed an end to ideology, a whole range of symbolic, metaphorical, and emotionally charged strategies of communication had been discredited.

"God, not culture, is the only appropriate object of unconditional reverence and wonder," Lasch writes. Claiming that religion provides spiritual discipline against self-righteousness, he believes that its decline has left political culture in a sorry state. Liberal democracy, he asserts hyperbolically, thrived on the borrowed capital of theological traditions predating the rise of liberalism. Furthermore, religion's replacement by a deconstructionist sensibility has culminated into an all-out assault on ideals of every kind. In a chapter titled "The Soul of Man Under Secularism," first written as a centennial takeoff on Oscar Wilde's *The Soul of Man Under Socialism* (1891), Lasch declares that the postmodern mood is marked, on the one hand, by disillusionment with grand schemes (such as Marxism) and, on the other hand, by an illusion of personal freedom. Lasch believes that the central paradox of religious faith lies in discovering that the secret of happiness is renouncing the right to be happy. Religion's role, in his opinion, should be to challenge and confront rather than merely console. By refusing to acknowledge humankind's spiritual needs, relativists embrace an aesthetic as dissatisfying as metaphysical orthodoxy. Seen in that way, belief is a burden, a path to self-discovery, not a claim to some privileged moral status.

For democracy to have a future, Lasch believes, it must rest on self-governing communities, not on sanitized speech codes and other peripheral issues unrelated to redistributing wealth. Echoing nineteenth century reformer Orestes Brownson, who defined the "Laboring Classes" to include toilers of all sorts—everybody, in fact, save idlers and the leisure class—Lasch believes that democracy is incompatible with hereditary privilege. Luxury, he concludes, is morally repugnant and incompatible with democracy; individuals should not be able to claim unlimited accumulation far in excess of their needs.

Whereas Brownson feared that public schools would in time create an elite secular priesthood, the main philosophical fallacy among American educators (from Horace Mann on) is the delusion that a formal setting is necessarily the best environment for acquiring knowledge. Developing people should be left alone, Lasch believes, not showered with undeserved adulation or misplaced compassion. They need to take risks rather than be coddled. In their fear of fanaticism and racial warfare, the elite have promoted a social ethic of self-indulgence that has only intensified inequalities of wealth and opportunity.

In his carping, doomsday opposition to television and shopping malls, computers and feel-good psychologists, feminist careerists and multiculturalist academicians, abortion rights and affirmative action, Lasch seems hopelessly old-fashioned, almost antediluvian, and out of touch with the real world—especially for one who could chortle about President George Bush's surprise at a supermarket scanner and could ridicule Robert B. Reich, who became secretary of labor in the Clinton Administration, for his fawning obeisance to the "knowledge class" in *The Work of Nations* (1992). Willfully ignorant of information technologies, he underestimates their potential for forming communitarian networks and promoting democratic discourse. Since he never mentions any of the "Elite" by name, it is unclear how universally he means to carry his overreaching conclusions. Does he, for example, include the likes of cyberspace guru Bill Gates and film director Steven Spielberg on his list of those who lack civic virtue? Is an allegiance to a world order not as valid as a nationalist perspective?

Lasch too frequently sets up opposition straw men as objects of his scorn, such as director Spike Lee's supposed canonization of Malcolm X (in a film of that name) and attorney William Kunstler's alleged turning of New York politics into racial theater (in the Tawana Brawley case). Most tortured of all is his critique of academic "pseudo-radicals," whose poststructural conclusions to him have a numbing predictability and a moral bankruptcy. He excoriates a report published by the American Council of Learned Societies, *Speaking for the Humanities* (1989), for ignoring Foundationalism. He criticizes social historians for neglecting religion, borrowing concepts (such as stratification and status anxiety) too slavishly from social scientists, and concentrating too much on the close at hand, implying, misleadingly, that Clio, the muse of his chosen profession, has been stifled by an insidious new form of left-wing McCarthyism, with neo-Stalinist ideologues bent on imposing standards of "political correctness" on their colleagues.

Like his spiritual antecedents Jonathan Edwards and Henry Adams, Lasch was an original thinker: sui generis. He deserves to be remembered for his radical critique of the inequitable excesses of unregulated capitalism rather than for these grouchy ruminations. For believers and nonbelievers alike, however, his musings on ontological questions are quite powerful.

James B. Lane

Sources for Further Study

The Christian Science Monitor. February 10, 1995, p. 11.
Commonweal. CXXII, March 24, 1995, p. 19.
Hungry Mind Review. LXXXVII, Spring, 1995, p. 20.
London Review of Books. XVII, May 25, 1995, p. 13.
National Review. XLVII, January 23, 1995, p. 62.
New Statesman and Society. VIII, March 17, 1995, p. 39.
The New York Times Book Review. C, January 22, 1995, p. 1.
The New Yorker. LXX, January 30, 1995, p. 86.
Publishers Weekly. CCXLI, November 7, 1994, p. 56.
The Wall Street Journal. January 10, 1995, p. A18.
The Washington Post Book World. XXV, January 15, 1995, p. 1.

REVOLUTION OF THE MIND
The Life of André Breton

Author: Mark Polizzotti
Publisher: Farrar Straus Giroux (New York). 754 pp. $35.00
Type of work: Literary biography
Time: 1896-1966
Locale: Paris and New York

A comprehensive and compassionate life of the founding father of Surrealism

> *Principal personages:*
> ANDRÉ BRETON, the French poet and man of letters
> SIMONE, his first wife
> JACQUELINE, his second wife
> ELISE, his third wife
> AUBE, his daughter and only child
> LOUIS ARAGON, one of his closest friends, later an enemy after Aragon
>   repudiated Surrealism and championed Stalinism
> GUILLAUME APOLLINAIRE, the first poet to use the word "Surrealism"
>   and one of Breton's most important mentors
> PAUL ÉLUARD, the poet who replaced Aragon as Breton's confidant and
>   then was banished by Breton from the Surrealist movement
> BENJAMIN PERET, Breton's final Surrealist comrade, who never deserted
>   the cause

André Breton is not well known outside his native land, even though the example of his work and career inspired one of the most significant artistic movements of the twentieth century. Except for an unhappy exile in New York City during World War II and excursions to Canada, Mexico, the Caribbean, and Czechoslovakia, Breton spent nearly all of his life in Paris, arrogating to himself a circle that engendered and promoted Surrealism. Indeed, he was often designated the "pope" of Surrealism, because he zealously defended its aims, proclaimed its superiority to other movements, such as existentialism, and vigorously recruited converts and excommunicated apostates, holding court in the world of Parisian cafés.

It is a signal achievement of Mark Polizzotti's biography to show how Breton's background and personality perfectly meshed with his conception of Surrealism. Above all, Surrealism rejected the literary establishment; it attacked the Western bourgeois status quo; it undermined a faith in reason; it celebrated the imaginative as a subversive force for good, liberating human aspirations and recognizing originality. Surrealism accepted no authority except the creative urge; it sought spontaneity and innovation; it proclaimed itself the enemy of the European, classical tradition and of the religious beliefs and institutions that developed in the throes of the Roman Empire's decline.

These Surrealistic tenets derived from Breton's reactions against his conservative, provincial upbringing. He detested his mother Marguerite's rigid Catholicism and his father Louis' timid bourgeois values. The unfeeling Marguerite came to symbolize the societal authority that repressed the young André, who was quickly drawn to literature yet reluctantly pursued a medical career—doing it only as a means of retaining monetary support from his parents, who disapproved of his literary activities.

Breton sought surrogate fathers in the poets he admired—especially in Guillaume Apollinaire, whose resort to automatic writing, black humor, and exploration of dreams provided André with the basic elements that he would transform into what became Surrealism in the 1920's. Yet Apollinaire, like virtually all of Breton's masters, was eventually found wanting. Ultimately, Breton could not brook any authority other than himself. He seems to have been unconscious of just how closely his own authoritarianism resembled his mother's. Having rejected the Church and all conventional forms of authority, Breton set himself up as the sole arbiter of Surrealism, which (he thought) would be everything society was not, but which in his hands became a kind of renegade Church, a black mass that parodied rather than truly overturned society's structures.

Breton would have been outraged by such a characterization of his movement. Indeed, he would even have rejected the idea that it was a movement, for then Surrealism would be merely another artistic trend, living and then dying as it gave way to other artistic programs. For Breton, Surrealism was a sort of counterculture, a frame of mind that opposes the mainstream and refuses to be co-opted by institutions such as colleges, galleries, and publishing houses. Surrealists might give college lectures, publish, and show their work in galleries, but they should not be dependent on such institutions and, above all, should never be permanently employed by them. Only dire economic necessity forced Breton, for brief periods, to seek employment.

Polizzotti is sometimes so focused on documenting Breton's career that the outrageous fun of Surrealism and its absurdist elements become obscured. The biography really comes alive when characters such as Salvador Dali appear. Until he offended Breton, Dali was Breton's quintessential Surrealist. For example, Dali's invention of a dinner jacket studded with shot glasses full of milk captures the silly but subversive and inventive side of Surrealism. It was an art that depended on reversing expectations and deflating the conventional. For Dali, any aspect of society could be mocked; anything could be toyed with, deprived of its usual meaning, and reconstituted as a Surrealistic object. Yet Dali went too far for Breton and his followers when he adopted Adolf Hitler as a Surrealistic fetish. Dali was drawn to Hitler's magnetic force—a response that was not the same thing, the artist maintained, as becoming a fascist. On the contrary, Hitler became part of the artist's fantasies, and Dali did not see himself as magnifying the importance of Hitler's politics. Dali as a Surrealist did not consider that he could have a political position, since he believed that Surrealism by definition rejected politics.

It seems ironic as well as absurd that Breton should actually summon Dali to a trial designed to purge him from the Surrealist movement. Breton had rigged such tribunals before, and he would do so later as well. Breton could not see that his inquisitions simply parodied what governmental and religious establishments had always done to the recalcitrant. He was convinced that he was simply keeping his movement pure—

though he denied that it was a movement and that he was establishing himself as its head. Yet Dali was hardly vanquished at his hearing. He showed up swathed in several layers of clothing and with a thermometer in his mouth, complaining of a fever. As Breton tried to read the charges against the accused, Dali kept jumping up to defend himself, discarding clothing that made him too hot and then putting it back on again as he became chilled. His manic behavior reduced even his fiercest detractors to laughter, and though Breton had his way, the proceedings hardly humbled Dali or discouraged him from continuing in his own outrageous Surrealist style.

Breton had a decidedly thuggish personality. He carried a heavy cane and more than once used it to strike an opponent in a quarrel. His Surrealist comrades beat up critics who had offended their leader. Friend after friend found himself dismissed if he articulated any position that did not suit Breton. For all of his stress on Surrealism's unconventionality, Breton himself dressed the part of a patriarch, always attired in coat and tie and with manners that impressed several observers as virtually eighteenth century in their formality.

Breton was also Old World in his dealings with women, who were largely treated as love and dream objects. Few women penetrated the inner circle of Surrealism. Each of Breton's wives was treated as a muse, but once she failed to maintain her romantic aura, he sought her replacement in another, usually younger woman. His first wife, Simone, patiently put up with his infidelities for years, until she finally took her own lover and divorced him. His second wife, Jacqueline, tired of the part of his inspiration, also took a lover and developed her own career as a painter. His third wife, Elise, helped Breton settle into middle age and remained faithful to him in his declining years, perhaps winking at his largely platonic flirtations with younger women.

What is Breton's legacy? Polizzotti never directly answers the question. Is Breton only of historic importance, or will some of his writings survive? The biographer points out that by the 1960's most of Breton's work was being reprinted. More than a thousand people attended his funeral. Which books will last? Perhaps the biographer does not want to hazard a guess; perhaps he thinks that it is too soon to tell. Nevertheless, some estimation of their relative worth would seem in order.

But then Surrealism itself is a grand enough legacy for Breton—this the biography implicitly claims. For Breton, Surrealism was not merely works of art but a way of life. Everything was approached via the sensibility of a Surrealist. Unlike Dali, who saw Surrealism as a thing in itself, Breton believed in its social consequences. For example, he tried to make common cause with the communists. He reasoned that like Surrealists, communists wished to overturn bourgeois society and the Greco-Roman heritage. Breton wanted to form an alliance with the enemy of his enemy. The communists wished Surrealism to become subsumed in communism; there was no room among the Stalinists for individual variation or artistic temperament. Nevertheless, Breton tried valiantly to reconcile Surrealism and communism, arguing that a transformation of material conditions could not be accomplished without a transformation within the imagination.

When Breton realized that the Stalinists simply wanted to assimilate Surrealists into the Communist Party, he became a virulent anti-Stalinist—even traveling to Mexico to pay homage to Leon Trotsky. It is revealing that even in rejecting Stalinism, Breton had to seek a mentor; Trotsky became another of the many strong father figures Breton required—apparently as a replacement for his weak-willed father, who quietly took pride in his son's literary career even as Breton's mother pushed him away.

For Breton, the personal and the political were intertwined. When his best friend and fellow poet Louis Aragon became a Stalinist, Breton simply crossed him off his list and never spoke to him again. Aragon became the Judas, the Satan, of Surrealism—attacking Dali, for example, for those shot glasses full of milk. How many destitute children could have used that milk? Aragon asked. Yet Aragon, even in his humorless Stalinist phase, mourned the loss of his friendship with Breton, whereas Breton said more than once that he valued ideological good faith more than mere personal friendship. He was curiously blind to the party line he established even as he attacked everyone else's. It is sad, and it demeans Breton's stature somewhat, to learn that one of his few long-lasting friendships was with Benjamin Peret, who determined early that he would not contradict Breton on any matter of principle. The result was an almost infantile relationship, with Peret once stealing a chicken from a Breton meal, knowing that his master would scold him like an errant child but would also forgive him because the child would return to acknowledge his father's authority.

This biography presents Breton with all of his contradictions. Polizzotti neither defends nor condemns his subject, although he provides plenty of evidence that might be used for defending or attacking. The last chapter is quite moving as Breton faces his last years, realizing that he will soon die—as he had predicted, before the age of seventy. He carries on like an aged lion—an image that recurs in several chapters and in the photographs showing a large-headed man with swept-back waving hair, stocky and somber, though capable of the high jinks that Surrealists favored.

Breton was a contradiction in terms, since Surrealism, by definition, should not have had a pope. It would probably amaze him to discover that in this biography his life symbolizes both the authoritarianism that Surrealism resisted and the creative anarchy that it fostered.

Carl Rollyson

Sources for Further Study

Chicago Tribune. November 5, 1995, XIV, p. 4.
Los Angeles Times Book Review. August 27, 1995, p. 3.
The New Republic. CCXIII, December 18, 1995, p. 39.
New Statesman and Society . VIII, December 1, 1995, p. 39.
The New York Times Book Review. C, September 3, 1995, p. 5.
The Village Voice. October 10, 1995, p. SS19.
The Wall Street Journal. August 10, 1995, p. A7.

REWRITING THE SOUL
Multiple Personality and the Sciences of Memory

Author: Ian Hacking (1936-   )
Publisher: Princeton University Press (Princeton, New Jersey). 336 pp. $24.95
Type of work: Philosophy; science

A philosophical and historical analysis that links multiple personality disorder, memory, and the nature of the human soul

What does it mean to be a human being—both in a general sense and in the sense of being a specific individual? This is a fundamental and eternal question that has been asked by generations of philosophers. One widely held belief is that one's memory is one's identity. Yet what happens if one's memories are wrong, or were provided by someone else through hypnosis or psychiatric therapy? If certain memories make people unhappy, would they perhaps be better off having those memories deleted? If that were to happen, what would be the implications for identity? Ian Hacking, a philosopher of science, offers some thoughts about these questions. He also considers issues such as the practice and politics of mental illness, the history of psychology and mental illness, and the essence of memory.

Rewriting the Soul: Multiple Personality and the Sciences of Memory begins with an analysis of the history of multiple personality disorder since about 1970. Hacking then focuses on the history of certain types of mental illness during the years 1874-1886, when the prototype of a multiple personality was formulated by the French medical profession and, not coincidentally, the sciences of memory were established. Last, he introduces four theses that link his first two sections and enable him to ask and answer the questions that may have been the real purposes of writing this book. This is a case study to throw light on larger moral issues. The study of multiple personalities is only a means to an end.

When Hacking uses the word "soul," he is not referring to the immortal entity of theology. Instead, he wants to "invoke character, reflective choice, self-understanding, values that include honesty to others and oneself, and several types of freedom and responsibility." His soul is a collection of human emotions, not a single essence. It is memories and character. What he sees in the controversy over multiple personalities is an attempt to "scientize the soul through the study of memory."

Multiple personality disorder is a condition in which an individual has "two or more distinct identities or personalities or personality states. . . . At least two of these identities or personality states recurrently take control of the person's behavior." The victim appears to be suffering from amnesia, in that a particular identity will not remember what occurred when the individual was under control of a different identity. These multiple identities may vary in age, intellect, interests, physical skills, and even gender. Most sufferers are women—perhaps 90 percent—and most were apparently subject to abuse as children, especially sexual abuse.

One of the most interesting aspects of the disorder, at least for historians and philosophers, is the tremendous increase in reported cases in less than two decades. Before 1972, multiple personalities were thought to be extremely rare phenomena. A list could be compiled of all instances in the history of Western medicine. Perhaps there were one hundred acknowledged sufferers. Twenty years later, thousands of cases had been diagnosed in the United States alone. Hacking asks what caused this apparent epidemic. Have physicians finally been able to diagnose a condition that had always been common? Given the link to sexual abuse during childhood, was a precondition for the psychiatric community's recognition of the disorder the acknowledgement by society that such abuse was widespread? If society denied that child abuse was endemic, it could not accept the diagnosis of multiple personalities. Or is the apparent epidemic only that—an apparent epidemic created by a few well-meaning psychiatrists and fueled by sensational media coverage? Put succinctly, is multiple personality disorder a true disease? Psychiatrists do not agree.

Complicating the situation, particularly in the mind of the general public, is the issue of false memory. While undergoing therapy, patients have brought out memories of child abuse which their therapists claim had been repressed. Sufferers of multiple personality are easily hypnotized and very open to suggestion. Critics have asked whether these are true repressed memories or fantasies unconsciously introduced by therapists. To what extent do false memories challenge the validity of the diagnosis of multiple personalities?

On many of these questions, Hacking takes an agnostic position. He does not care whether multiple personality is "real," although like any good philosopher, he can spend paragraphs arguing what one means by "real." His concern is how "this configuration of ideas," as he terms multiple personalities, influences individual humans and society at large. He demonstrates the political, economic, social, and personal stakes involved in the answers. He also proves how political, economic, and social issues affect what might be thought to be a purely scientific issue—the diagnosis of mental illness.

Hacking spends only one chapter on the century between the concern for multiplicities in France in the late nineteenth century (the first multiple personality was documented by the French medical profession in 1885) and their apparently massive rediscovery in the late twentieth. In this chapter, however, he supplies the answer for the question why there were few multiple personalities during this century—sufferers were diagnosed as having schizophrenia. Symptoms or behaviors that would commonly result in a diagnosis of schizophrenia in 1939, for example, could be attributed to multiple personality disorder in 1995.

Then Hacking steps back to the years 1874-1886. "That was when a wave of multiplicity swept over France, when the sciences of memory firmed up, and when the idea of trauma, previously used only for a bodily wound or lesion, came also to apply to psychic hurt." At that time, psychologists were concerned with hypnosis, sleepwalking, and hysteria. Medical case histories were becoming commonplace.

The second section of the book is a series of thematic, episodic presentations rather than a historical narrative. It reaffirms a point that Hacking made earlier in the book:

Intellectual and social context play a large role in diagnostics; illness has been and is historically formed. For example, Hacking argues that multiple personality is a condition of the industrial West and is not diagnosed in more traditional cultures. Individuals manifesting similar symptoms exist in these other cultures, but, Hacking suggests, they have been categorized by Western anthropologists as being in trance states. Another example is the case of Félida X. In 1860, she was described as having spontaneously entered into something that resembled a hypnotic trance. Sixteen years later, in the context of the newly emerging sciences of memory, she was a woman with two personalities.

All of Hacking's historical discussions are, however, only background, providing evidence and context for his four theses. The first is that the sciences of memory appeared in the late nineteenth century. Before 1875, memory was not "an object of scientific knowledge." It was an art, a skill to be developed, a necessary tool for those who were part of high culture. Subsequent to that year, three sciences of memory appeared: neurological investigations of the location of types of memory, studies of recall, and memory in relation to psychological processes and forces. (The twentieth century has added transmission at the cellular level and modeling of memory in artificial intelligence.) Simultaneously with the development of the sciences of memory came a downward revision of its social status. Good memory became identified with lower social status. It was no longer the possession of the elite, who presumably were now more valued for their analytical skills.

The second thesis is that memory became "a scientific key to the soul." By this, Hacking means that the sciences of memory were thought to provide knowledge that would bring the soul, as he defines it—which hitherto had been central to Western culture but outside science—within the scientific sphere. There may not be any way to develop objective knowledge about the soul, but there were sciences that investigated memory. Memory could serve as a surrogate for the soul.

Hacking's third thesis is that the scientific investigation of memory produces "a surface knowledge; beneath [these facts] is the depth knowledge, that there are facts about memory to be found out." "Surface knowledge" is Hacking's technical term for what the word "knowledge" means in everyday conversation—"particular items counted as true, or as false." "Depth knowledge," however, is more ambiguous. It is a form of knowledge that consists of generally held assumptions about the existence, or at least potential existence, of surface knowledge. Depth knowledge "involves the kinds of objects that can be investigated, the types of questions that can be addressed, the sorts of propositions that may be either true or false, the sorts of distinctions that make sense." In the case of memory, the depth knowledge is the agreement that there are facts about memory. In the debate over the recall of repressed memories, both sides agree on the depth knowledge and fight over the surface knowledge.

The last thesis is that debates that prior to the late nineteenth century might have taken been about morality or spirituality now take place "at the level of factual knowledge." Hacking believes that people have given up on trying to hold absolute positions on good and evil. To raise the question whether incest is evil automatically, in his judgment, moves one into the subjective realm. To avoid that, "we . . . ask who remembers incest." This places the question within the realm of memory, about which one can obtain objective scientific knowledge.

Hacking then raises a moral question, introducing the concept of "false consciousness." This is the state of those "who have formed importantly false beliefs about their character and their past." Such individuals either no longer remember what did happen or remember incorrectly and use these "deceptive memories" as part of their self-image or sense of who they are. As an example, Hacking presents a patient suffering from emotional distress because of some sort of mental trauma. The physician uses hypnosis to make the patient forget the event—say, incest with her father—thus causing the distress to disappear. The patient is in a state of false consciousness but is able to function normally. What is the harm?

To Hacking, there is great harm in such a coping mechanism: "Self-knowledge is a virtue in its own right." To be a fully developed human being means being self-aware and autonomous. It is wrong for anyone to take away one's memories, even if such people mean well. He rejects any effort to defend the actions of such physicians on pragmatic grounds. They are morally wrong. No matter how difficult the consequences of autonomous self-awareness, it is a preferable state to false consciousness.

Hacking concludes by returning to the issue of multiple personality one last time. The generally accepted therapy for multiple personality syndrome is to identify the different personalities and work with each individually. The objective is to integrate them. Hacking worries that this therapy creates "a thoroughly crafted person," but not one with the autonomy and self-knowledge that define a human being. It results in false consciousness.

This is a challenging book. Hacking is presenting a single case study, but it is clear that he has been thinking about the larger context of memory and its implications for modern society. If any complaint might be raised, it would be that he has not fully developed some of his arguments and fully explained his terminology. For example, one might wish that he more closely argued and defended his four theses. Yet he raises some very uncomfortable and fundamental issues, especially for those who approach issues pragmatically rather than absolutely. Hacking will make his readers ponder.

Marc Rothenberg

Sources for Further Study

The Guardian. June 9, 1995, p. 5.
History of the Human Sciences. VIII, November, 1995, p. 107.
Nature. CCCLXXIV, April 27, 1995, p. 843.
New Scientist. CXLVI, June 10, 1995, p. 45.
New Statesman and Society . VIII, June 23, 1995, p. 39.
The Spectator. CCLXXV, August 12, 1995, p. 30.
The Washington Post Book World. XXV, July 16, 1995, p. 13.

THE RICHER, THE POORER
Stories, Sketches, and Reminiscences

Author: Dorothy West (1909-   )
Preface by Mary Helen Washington
Publisher: Doubleday (New York). 254 pp. $22.00
Type of work: Short stories and essays

Combining short stories with a variety of reminiscences and sketches, most of which were originally published in periodicals between 1926 and 1987, this collection reveals, through Dorothy West's accounts of her family history and of places and people she has known, many of the real-life sources for the themes and characters that appear in her fiction

This collection is a tour de force of short fiction written by an author who, despite a long career in journalism and early critical recognition for the fine craftsmanship of her short stories, has been primarily known as a novelist. *The Richer, the Poorer* is made up of seventeen stories, including West's first prize-winning work, "The Type-writer" (1926), and thirteen sketches, many of which first appeared in the *Vineyard Gazette.* The fiction and nonfiction segments of the book complement each other thematically, each section enlightening and embellishing a set of moral principles and life lessons presented in the other.

West writes self-consciously in the tradition of Fyodor Dostoevski and other Russian artists (whom, in the memoir about her trip to Moscow that appears among this book's sketches, West describes as her gods of good writing, for their works taught her that salvation lies in the soul) and with similarities to the work of O. Henry. She is a master of stories of psychological development that reveal moral character, twists of fate that revolve around a symbolic object, and parables of love or greed that involve either the giving or the withholding of material and spiritual gifts.

West's work, with its examination of race and class, has a significant place in the African American literary canon. One sketch, "Remembrance," tells how West, as a child, went to a motion-picture theater with her mother and saw displayed in celluloid a world where white people were rich and black people were poor. This entire collection plays on the many nuances of the dichotomy between wealth and poverty. A middle-class woman of education and privilege, West frequently uses storytelling to examine the lives of impoverished people. Desire in this world of have-nots is focused not merely on material pleasures—a penny candy, a lamb chop hidden at the back of a refrigerator, a winter coat bought at an August sale—but also on life ambitions tragically thwarted because of material poverty and racism, or because of poverty of character. In these stories of human longing, of choice and destiny—and often of humanity sadly constricted, falling far short of its potential—it is sometimes the richer in means who are the poorer in character, and the poor who are rich in family, loyalty, and love.

West's specific moral lessons are crafted against a larger thematic backdrop of age: Her child self (or that of her various child protagonists) is set up against the wisdom of her adult (middle-aged and then elderly) persona. Many pieces in the book have children or childhood at their center, so that the overarching theme of the collection has to do with identity-building and coming of age. This transformative process, with its childish state of innocence, self-centeredness, and incomplete perceptions, is juxtaposed to the double awarenesses and revelations—of self and of others—that come with maturity and hindsight. Given West's deep concern for African American experience, race and class are invariably addressed in her stories and sketches. Yet ultimately her themes are universal, penetrating and transcending boundaries of color and condition to ask fundamental questions about the formation of character and about fate and free will.

Many of the situations in West's stories emerge out of her personal experience—childhood, her work as a welfare investigator in Harlem, differences she experienced with her sisters. The sketches tell of the lives of her mother and father, her family's summer sojourns on Martha's Vineyard, her deep sense of place associated with Oak Bluffs, the town where she has long resided on that Massachusetts island. Missing from the fiction, with its focus on family and lower-class and bourgeois life, is the intellectual and bohemian world of journalists and writers, dancers and filmmakers that West encountered during the Harlem Renaissance of the 1920's, and the continued creativity of the Federal Writers Project of the Works Progress Administration, which formed the heart of her social network in the 1930's. These aspects of her life do emerge, however, in sketches such as "Elephant's Dance," a literary-biographical analysis of Wallace Thurman, a Harlem Renaissance writer, and "An Adventure in Moscow," an account of West's time in the Soviet Union in preproduction, in association with Langston Hughes and others, of a film on American race relations, *Black and White* (which because of the politics of the times was never completed). They are reflected also in the setting of "The Typewriter," a story of the thwarted ambitions of an African American man, for which West won second place (tying with Zora Neale Hurston) in a 1926 literary contest sponsored by *Opportunity* magazine. The award ceremony brought the nineteen-year-old West to Harlem from her native Boston and opened a new world to her.

Throughout stories and sketches there is a sociological awareness of class and social differences among African Americans that links these short works to West's better-known novel *The Living Is Easy* (first published in 1948 and reprinted in 1982 during the "feminist literary renaissance"). The analysis of class and color stratification within African American communities—which is perhaps the element for which West's fiction is best known—in turn connects the artistry of *The Richer, the Poorer* and *The Living Is Easy* with a long African American intellectual tradition harking back to W. E. B. Du Bois' classic study of black urban life, *The Philadelphia Negro* (1899).

West's treatment of racism themes ranges from the relative heavy-handedness of "The Typewriter" to the ironic subtleties of "Mammy" (1940), both first published in *Opportunity*. "The Typewriter" focuses on a middle-aged janitor who, through the serendipity of an object—his daughter's rented typewriter—develops a rich imaginary life in which he succeeds in a profession that in real life has been denied to him because of racism. He finds temporary fulfillment in the elaborate fantasy he creates in his mind; the characters in "Mammy," however, operate in a different kind of secrecy. West uses "Mammy" to contrast the racial slights that a privileged African American welfare investigator endures while visiting a high-class white apartment building with the much deeper story of a family in which a member has gained privilege by passing as white, disguising or disowning evidence of black relations in the process.

"The Five-Dollar Bill" and "Funeral" both feature a young central character named Judy, who in observing adult behavior sorts out lessons of parental duplicity and sexuality and becomes cognizant of the lesson that pervades many of the collection's stories—what West calls the tragedy of commonplace existence. Childhood is revealed in an unsentimental way here as a time of bewilderment, unrequited love, and fear.

The sensitivities of childhood consciousness also characterize "The Happiest Year, the Saddest Year" and "The Bird like No Other," as well as the book's longest story, "An Unimportant Man," and one of its shortest, "To Market, to Market." In the first, an eight-year-old struggles with hatred for a blond member of the family who is favored by fate over a darker member. In one of the few references in the book to the supernatural, it takes a ghost to heal the rift and restore love to the child's heart. In the second, a woman who has lost her own son helps a young boy to take a major step toward adulthood. Here the sociological underpinnings and communal values of African American extended family life are much in evidence as the African American woman plays an important role as a surrogate parent, or "other-mother" mentor, to the young people in her neighborhood.

"An Unimportant Man" and "To Market, to Market" both link the consciousness of a middle-aged man to that of a young daughter or son, weighing the respective need for discipline and the shaping of responsibility against the free will and emotionalism of youth. Upon reading West's sketch "Remembrance," which is about an incident when her mother took her to hear Billy Sunday preach, readers may suspect that Essie, the young and willful girl of "An Unimportant Man," who has a terrified reaction to the evangelicalism of her parents' church and wants, in defiance of her family's strict guidelines for success, to become an artist, is modeled on West herself. "Fond Memories of a Black Childhood," a nonfiction reminiscence about growing up in Boston, reveals that West's own family featured a range of skin tone from blond to (West's own) darkness, and like Deedee of "The Happiest Year," West faced various challenges relating to such family diversity.

Several of the stories focus on marriage and (mostly unhappy) comparisons of the actual course of one's life in middle age to one's youthful expectations. "The Envelope," "Fluff and Mr. Ripley," "The Roomer," and "An Unimportant Man" all feature marriages gone sour. In "Jack in the Pot," a middle-aged woman on relief is tortured by a choice she must make when she wins the pot in a lottery. As welfare recipients, she and her husband have been subject to investigation, while the janitor who maintains their building suffers an even greater burden of want and loss. At the same time, money has a corrupting influence—as it does in "The Penny," "The Roomer," and "Odyssey of an Egg," three other stories revolving around unexpected or secret acquisition of money.

Materialism and miserliness, spending and giving are themes of the sketches "The Sun Parlor" and "Love," as well as of stories such as "About a Woman Named Nancy," "Funeral," and "The Richer, the Poorer." "About a Woman Named Nancy," "Mammy," "Maple Tree," and "The Richer, the Poorer" all take up female relationships—between woman friends, mother and daughter, sisters, or women of different walks of life. The sisters of "The Richer, the Poorer," have lived opposite lives: One, a spinster, has worked, hoarded, and poured the energy of her life into her home, while the other married for love, traveled the world, and has been left penniless by the death of her jazz musician husband. The one is rich in experience, the other in things. The moral of "The Richer, the Poorer" is echoed in the sketch "The Sun Parlor," in which West explicitly explains—in detailing her own sin of ostracizing a young niece from the wonder of a newly painted sun room—that a child is more important than a house.

This is a lesson that West's mother, Rachel, knew well, and hers is a strong presence throughout the collection. From "Rachel" and "The Purse," sketches in which West wonders about the unrevealed breadth of her mother's private longings and her consciousness of responsibility to others, to "A Day Lost Is a Day Gone Forever," in which West remembers how a physical coldness invaded her own body as death came upon her mother in a hospital room on the other side of the city, West's mother emerges as the ultimate font of the wisdom that lies at the heart of all these stories and essays. In each of them, it is relationships between human beings that matter most of all.

Barbara Bair

Sources for Further Study

Booklist. XCI, July, 1995, p. 1854.
Boston Globe. July 23, 1995, p. 37.
Chicago Tribune. July 30, 1995, XIV, p. 3.
Los Angeles Sentinel. August 3, 1995, p. C4.
Los Angeles Times Book Review. August 3, 1995, p. 6.
Ms. V, May-June 1995, p. 73.
The New York Times Book Review. C, August 6, 1995, p. 12.
Publishers Weekly. CCXLII, May 22, 1995, p. 47.
Time. CXLVI, July 24, 1995, p. 67.
The Washington Post. July 6, 1995, p. C1.
Women's Review of Books. XIII, November, 1995, p. 20.

ROBERT E. LEE
A Biography

Author: Emory M. Thomas (1939-   )
Publisher: W. W. Norton (New York). Illustrated. 472 pp. $30.00
Type of work: Biography
Time: 1793-1870
Locale: The United States

A psychological biography of Robert E. Lee, commander of the Army of Northern Virginia in the American Civil War

> *Principal personages:*
> ROBERT EDWARD LEE, a military commander and son of a revolutionary war hero
> MARY CUSTIS LEE, his wife, a granddaughter of George Washington
> THOMAS "STONEWALL" JACKSON, his right arm and most trusted lieutenant
> JAMES LONGSTREET, his most capable lieutenant after Jackson

Robert E. Lee was the personification of the Confederacy at its best. He was the proof that good men could defend a cause that many considered evil, one that made God-fearing men—such as Lee himself—uncomfortable and that only few fanatics considered an absolute good; proof that courage and valor can triumph over greater numbers and superior material, and that eventual defeat is less painful when measured against the suffering and glory of the struggle; more than all that, proof that self-control and dignity—the preeminent southern virtues—had not died with the Lost Cause. Lee was the one prominent public figure not tarnished by the petty quarrels of the generals and politicians, not stained by postwar corruption and politics. Lee represented something more: a noble, selfless, quietly suffering figure to whom men and women of the North as well as the South could point and say, "There was a man!"

Such was the central myth of the Confederacy in the decades following Appomattox. No other Confederate came close to enjoying the adulation afforded this essentially modest, morally decent, politely restrained, yet straightforward aristocrat. "Stonewall" Jackson, though worshiped as God's chosen warrior and Lee's right arm, was too much a religious fanatic and too strange a personality to be imagined in any setting other than war. Jefferson Davis, the humorless, querulous president, failed even in fleeing the scene and was captured disguised in women's clothes. James Longstreet and John Singleton Mosby became Republicans. Others lent their names to efforts to keep former slaves "in their place."

Lee may not have been a perfect model—after all, he had made mistakes and must bear his share of the blame for the South's losing the war—but for Confederates eager to rescue honor from a miserably bungled effort to secede from the Union, Lee was the most perfectly balanced public figure to appear since the death of George Washington. Lee even had the advantage of being related to Washington through his marriage to Mary Custis.

In retrospect, it seems that Lee had spent a lifetime preparing to be a model for a southern nation and for an era that valued the martial arts, the leisure of wealth, and the credo of the aristocrat. Lee was the "marble model" at West Point—no demerits in his four years as a cadet; he had a successful career as military engineer; he was a hero of the Mexican War, superintendent of the Military Academy at West Point, and Winfield Scott's first choice for command of the U.S. Army in its task of restoring the Union after Fort Sumter.

Emory Thomas' beautifully written volume is, in its essence, a psychological study of the man who became this myth. Thomas, Regent's Professor of History at the University of Georgia, does not dispute the myth or change it in any of its essentials, but he does give it nuances and more polished facets than even his most skilled predecessors. Rather than detracting from Lee's fame, as is usually the case in an age of deconstruction, Thomas makes him an even more appealing personality.

Lee's most prominent personal characteristic, according to the author, was his lifelong obsession with balancing the demands of self-control and freedom. Self-control was paramount in his devotion to duty—to his family, state, soldiers, and students. Duty compelled him to remain in a marriage to a rather plain, basically dull, and increasingly arthritic woman. Freedom can be seen in his efforts to avoid unpleasant situations. A shy man, he did not enjoy public events; a modest man, he did not like dealing with men who were ambitious, scheming, conniving, and quarrelsome. Lee was not a man of words. A man who wrote much or orated memorably would not have remained an enigma long, nor could historians have used him as outrageously. Lee was a man of deeds.

The irony is that Lee was, ultimately, a failure in the most important task he undertook. The saving grace is that he undertook command in the Confederacy reluctantly—at least compared to the rest of the southern high command. His failure, nevertheless, was a heroic one, a failure of mythic proportions.

Thomas explains away Lee's military disasters as audacious gambles in desperate situations; not even the best gambler can win every hand, and Lee had to trust others to play the cards for him. Of the group known forevermore as "Lee's Lieutenants," only Jackson had the combination of daring, judgment, and good luck to carry out Lee's wishes instinctively, and even he had his lapses. Lee had to work with what he had, and when criticism arose, he could reply only that the Confederacy had made a fundamental error at its beginning, in assigning the worst generals to command the army and the best to be newspaper editors.

Thomas fundamentally revises the traditional view of the war's first year. He describes it as an almost uninterrupted series of Union victories—in Kentucky, West Virginia, the Atlantic coast, New Orleans—with the one Confederate victory, Manassas, being incomplete in every way. When Lee took command, he inherited an army that was outnumbered and poorly equipped, led by quarreling officers, and in a desperate strategic situation. Lee calmly pulled his forces together and went on the offensive. Thomas' description of the Peninsula campaign is the least satisfactory of his many capsule battlepieces, but he improves as he tries a variety of narrative forms to enliven what could have been a repetitious vocabulary and style.

Thomas relies more heavily on Lee's personal correspondence than on official records. Fortunately, Lee wrote lively, colorful letters to friends and family. Readers learn of Lee's irrepressible wit, his delight in the company of pretty, amusing women, and his deep love and respect for family and friends. His many frustrations are laid out: his wife's poor health, his children's inability to succeed on their own, the difficulty of managing the family estates, even the near impossibility of emancipating his father-in-law's slaves according to the terms of the will; the deteriorating military situation that caused Lee to gamble on a decisive battle at Gettysburg (another somewhat revisionist account); the loss of the family property; declining health; and the likelihood of being hanged ignominiously as a traitor.

Lee responded to frustration better than any of his peers. He made self-control and sacrifice into a high art. He could not be swayed by public opinion or his peers' censure; adulated by the public after the war, he could not be tempted to exploit the opportunity for personal gain or prestige; threatened with northern retaliation, he refused to cower or curry favor with the victors. Steady, honest, dignified, Lee told a congressional committee that he did not believe the former slaves capable of voting intelligently. Nevertheless, when a black man came to the rail to be the first to take Communion in church, it was Lee who finally rose from among the stunned congregation to kneel next to the former slave and share the Communion cup.

Thomas explains these apparent contradictions as outward manifestations of the inner paradoxes of Lee's personality, contrasting ideals and drives that could be kept in order only by manly self-control. Lee was a soldier who never shrank from battle, but he disliked personal conflict; he was a man's man, yet his best friends were women; he was not happy in his marriage, but he never went beyond flirtation with any of his female admirers. He resolved many problems by ignoring them—his wife, his family, the problems of supply—and by concentrating on whatever important task was at hand. Yet once any important task was accomplished, at least to the degree he could do it at the moment, Lee had his pen in hand, discussing each correspondent's concerns as though they were the only care he had (though they were generally quite inconsequential). In his faithful reports to Davis, Lee was honest about the conditions of the army and his plans for upcoming operations; he was fortunate that his correspondence and its contents never found their way into Union hands, in the manner that Federal intelligence often ended up being reported in Richmond, because his solicitude for Davis' belief that he was still an expert in military affairs (as he had been at the time of the Mexican War) allowed him to avoid the personality conflicts with the Confederate president that bedeviled other commanders.

What most frustrated Lee in the second half of the war and at the end of his life was his inability to impose his will on his body as he had done before. Always he had been the most handsome man of any gathering he attended. Now he had put on weight, incurred injuries from minor mishaps, could not shake severe colds, and had aged noticeably.

In the closing campaigns of the war, with the Army of Northern Virginia being pressed to the earth by Grant's Army of the Potomac, Lee's men repeatedly cried, "Lee to the rear!" Lee's repeated risking of his life did not represent a death wish by a man who could see no hope of victory in the field, no plausible alternative strategy to digging in, marching on as the enemy moved around the flank, and digging in again—it was a desperate attempt to impose order personally on the chaos of battle. Previously, he had been able to rely on his "lieutenants" to implement his wishes. Once they had seemed to intuit what his wishes were, but as the war approached its end that was no longer so. Many had died; he was not able to find replacements among the lower ranks, and he was unwilling to risk bringing in experienced men from other armies, because their egos and their ambitions would be more trouble than their skills could offset. Lee had all the pride any one army needed.

Pride is a necessary virtue for a personality centered on the performance of duty. It can also become a vice. Pride caused less damage to Lee's command than to most of his contemporaries, but it came to the fore very strongly in his last days of command— at Appomattox. Lee had to summon all of his formidable self-control to do what was best for his men and his nation: to surrender in a manner that would bring an honorable end to the conflict, to accept the outcome as final, and to make the best of life in the reunited republic.

Lee seemingly had no prospects for making a living. His home at Arlington had been confiscated for nonpayment of taxes, his investments in Confederate bonds were worthless, his pension was forfeit, and it was unlikely that he would be able to resume his career as an engineer or become a gentleman farmer. His wife was an invalid; his children were still dependent on his aid and advice. The invitation to become president of Washington College in Lexington, Virginia, was the most welcome surprise that an August day in 1865 could have brought. Lee, as always cautious, did not answer for two weeks while he pondered and consulted with friends and family; his answer was modestly stated but positive.

Lee's reputation transformed Washington College from a traditional, classically oriented, financially strapped small school into a vibrant, forward-looking institution with a national reputation. Enrollment quadrupled; the faculty tripled in size; the curriculum was modernized; the buildings and grounds were improved. Lee did more than simply preside: He took the same diligent care of every aspect of the college operation that he had given to every enterprise he had ever undertaken. He knew every boy by name, participated in oral examinations, traveled widely to raise money, lobbied in Richmond and Washington, D.C., and in such little spare time as he had, produced a new edition of his father's memoirs and sought in vain to collect sufficient materials to write his own.

Lee the university president was perhaps Lee at his very best. There was but one rule at the school, he said: to be a gentleman. From that came everything else— devotion to family, respect for one's fellow men, courtesy and gallantry toward women, and duty toward country. Becoming a gentleman was not a product of birth, unless one luckily came into a family that lived the virtues that society at it best preached. Lee was not a vocally religious man, but he valued very highly the

Christianity of his time. He saw in it all the attributes that went toward making men into gentlemen, women into ladies, and society into a community where individuals could flourish and everyone received love and care. This was the essence of that enduring South that southerners believed Lee personified and justified.

William Urban

Sources for Further Study

Booklist. XCI, April 1, 1995, p. 1375.
The Economist. CCCXXXVI, September 2, 1995, p. 80.
Kirkus Reviews. LXIII, March 1, 1995, p. 312.
Library Journal. CXX, April 1, 1995, p. 104.
Los Angeles Times Book Review. August 13, 1995, p. 4.
National Review. XLVII, May 15, 1995, p. 73.
The New York Review of Books. XXV, December 21, 1995, p. 10.
The New York Times Book Review. C, August 6, 1995, p. 25.
The New Yorker. LXXI, July 10, 1995, p. 78.
Publishers Weekly. CCXLII, March 27, 1995, p. 66.
The Washington Post Book World. XXV, June 11, 1995, p. 10.

ROBERT GRAVES
Life on the Edge

Author: Miranda Seymour (1948-   )
Publisher: Henry Holt (New York). Illustrated. 524 pp. $37.50
Type of work: Literary biography
Time: 1895-1985
Locale: England; Wales; Mallorca, Spain

A study that relates Robert Graves's experiences in World War I and his relationships with women to his theory of inspiration

> *Principal personages:*
> ROBERT GRAVES, a British poet, novelist, critic, and essayist
> AMALIE (AMY) VON RANKE GRAVES, his German-born mother
> ALFRED PERCEVAL GRAVES, his father, an inspector of schools
> NANCY NICHOLSON, his first wife, an artist and designer
> LAURA RIDING (NÉE REICHENTHAL), an American-born poet, his literary
>   collaborator and mistress
> BERYL PRITCHARD GRAVES, his second wife

In the introduction to this biography of Robert Graves, Miranda Seymour suggests that her subject is the greatest writer of amatory verse that the twentieth century has produced. Despite the sweeping generalization, she is absolutely correct—but only by default. Traditional love themes simply do not appear in the work of twentieth century poets. T. S. Eliot set the tone for loveless love poetry early in the century, and only the homoerotic poets of its latter decades have departed from the pattern. It is, therefore, not very surprising that Robert Frost, not Eliot, was Graves's own favorite.

Both Graves and Frost created and lived their own mythos. They considered themselves poets of the country rather than the city, and both are identifiable with their places of residence, Graves with the island of Mallorca off the coast of Spain and Frost with his New Hampshire farm. Both privileged plain language, though they often used words suggestively and enigmatically. Less familiarly, Frost loved England and began his career there. His persona as farmer-poet was one that he adopted only in midlife. His retirement to rural New England corresponds to Graves's withdrawal to what in the late 1920's was little more than a primitive, isolated island. Both poets could be irascible and arrogant, and more to the theme of Seymour's study, both lived amid domestic chaos.

Seymour argues cogently that the continually unstable associations Graves had with the women in his life were essential to his work. Almost all of her substantial study deals with these personal influences, and almost no critical interpretation of Graves's works appears. Seymour discusses successively Graves's strict upbringing in a large bourgeois family; his experience in World War I and his acquaintance with Siegfried Sassoon and Wilfred Owen; and the long series of women in his life, from his mother, Amalie (Amy) von Ranke Graves, to his wives, Nancy Nicholson (who never used the Graves name) and Beryl Pritchard Graves, to his formidable mistress Laura Riding and the series of "muses" identifiable with his later years. All these women inspired him, and his wives and mistresses clearly led him to become an amatory rather than a war poet.

General readers likely have a very different conception of Graves; for these he remains a writer of prose, the author of the popular classics *I, Claudius* (1934), *Claudius the God and His Wife Messalina* (1934), and *Goodbye to All That: An Autobiography* (1929; rev. 1957), his memoir of the Edwardian Age and World War I. In his own estimation, however, Graves was first of all a poet. He saw his popular prose as a means of raising substantial amounts of money quickly. In the first half of his life, with two wives, two families, and Riding to support, not to mention the continuing costs of his Mallorcan properties, large infusions of cash remained an ongoing necessity. To his credit, Graves tried hard never to shirk these responsibilities. This does not mean that his first children received from him the love they expected; it was not until Riding had ceased to be an active influence upon his life and after he began his second family that he saw his first children regularly. Even so, Graves bore all the difficult periods in his life (most of which were of his own making) like a good soldier, his own simile for his personal code derived from his wartime experience.

Seymour does an admirable job of presenting her subject positively, a task that is especially difficult given his irregular way of life and his capacity for arrogant behavior. In part, Seymour's positive slant follows from having had the complete cooperation of the Graves estate and access to nearly all of Graves's personal papers. Graves's second wife, Beryl, and their son William read Seymour's manuscript in its final state. Still, other sources support Seymour's positive assessment, and her coherent view of Graves's life is quite plausible, even if her repeated characterization of Graves as having a Puritan's personality seems paradoxical.

Graves's puritanism, as Seymour interprets the word, is synonymous with his willingness to endure hardship and his generally nonmaterialistic outlook. These qualities and a desire to achieve excellence came from his family. His German-born mother Amy moved to England permanently only after her marriage to Alfred Perceval Graves, a widower with children and by profession a school inspector, like the Victorian poet Matthew Arnold. The elder Graves was a poet by avocation with a slight acquaintance of several major Victorian poets: Alfred, Lord Tennyson, Thomas Hardy, and Dante Gabriel Rossetti. Initially, it was his interest in Welsh poetry and love of Wales that prompted their move from Wimbledon, then a sleepy village outside London, to Erinfa, their isolated estate on the Welsh coast. The Graves family's connection to Wales thus predates the beginning of World War I by only a few years. Their son grew intensely proud of this Welsh connection and elected to join the Royal Welsh Fusiliers at the outbreak of the war. Had Graves's marriage to Nicholson succeeded, he might well have remained in Wales for the rest of his life.

The Graves family had never seen the like of Nicholson. She was a strong feminist who affected what was for her a becoming, but for the period eccentric, manner of dress in military-style clothing of her own design. She was an artist and designer by profession, and she had drawn a cover for *Vogue* magazine when she was only fourteen.

Graves admired her strength and independence, but his family could never understand her firm refusal to accept her husband's name after marriage. Moreover, by mutual agreement, their daughters were christened with their mother's rather than their father's surname. By contemporary standards, Nicholson merely seems to have been ahead of her time, but she was clearly more than this in her initial acceptance of Riding.

Riding, when Graves first invited her to live with him and Nicholson, was a promising and ambitious American poet whose work he had admired. The original arrangement was to be platonic, with Riding serving as collaborator with Graves and companion to Nicholson. The platonic arrangement soon become a sexual involvement with Graves, which Nicholson ultimately could not tolerate. Having separated Graves and Nicholson, Riding persuaded Graves to leave Wales and return with her to London, at which time she convinced him to propose a ménage à trois with Geoffrey Taylor (born Geoffrey Phibbs), a young Irish poet who for a time at least agreed to leave his own wife to do this. As if this were not bizarre enough, Riding then withheld all sexual favors from Graves, ostensibly because sexuality demeans art and she wished their collaboration to be pure. When Taylor suddenly withdrew from the ménage, Riding calmly sat on the window ledge of their London flat, offhandedly said to Graves and the others in the room, "Goodbye, chaps," and jumped from the third floor to the courtyard below. Taylor then did not return to his own wife but briefly lived with Nicholson.

Riding was severely injured but not killed in the suicide attempt. Since she could have faced prosecution for the attempt and in order to escape notoriety, she and Graves emigrated to Mallorca. At the time of their departure, Graves was essentially little more than a Georgian war poet of modest reputation. It was to pay Riding's hospitalization costs that he wrote *Goodbye to All That*. Ironically, this was the work that brought his first popular success. He and Riding would live together on Mallorca, in a largely nonsexual relationship, from 1929 to 1936, when the Spanish Civil War threatened the island.

If there are any villains in Seymour's book, Riding would clearly take the prize. Seymour paints a vivid portrait of Riding's jealousy at Graves's success as well as Graves's attempts to serve the woman he thought more than a muse. She makes a good case that the Riding period catalyzed the theory of inspiration that Graves would ultimately propose in *The White Goddess: A Historical Grammar of Poetic Myth* (1948, rev. 1952). Increasingly, Graves would use this theory to justify his way of life as essential to his art.

Essentially, Graves believed that poetic inspiration came through a woman, a muse who during her time of service to the poet was herself an instrument of the White Goddess. The muse's service could not last beyond a period of several years. At this time, the woman ceased to be a muse; the poet had to look beyond her toward the terrifying Black Goddess, the more powerful sister of the White Goddess, who represented ultimate truth. If the poet could survive this experience, his work advanced in quality and the cycle would begin again, each successful encounter with the Black Goddess producing growth in the poet's work. Graves used this theory to explain his need for the series of women who played a sexual role in his life, even after his relatively happy second marriage. He believed that his work required instability rather than tranquillity. To her death in 1993, Riding claimed that Graves had plundered his theory of the White Goddess from her. Deborah Baker's biography of Riding, *In Extremis: The Life of Laura Riding* (1993), provides further insights into the erratic behavior of this thwarted and unhappy woman.

Clearly, Riding bewitched Graves. He finally broke her ten-year spell in rural New Hope, Pennsylvania, where he and Riding along with Alan and Beryl Hodge were guests of Schuyler and Katherine (Kit) Jackson. Riding openly seduced Jackson and saw to it that his wife was placed in a mental institution. Graves then left Riding, returned to England with Hodge, and calmly negotiated with him concerning his intention to marry Hodge's wife. Riding remained in the United States with Jackson and pursued a number of visionary schemes, including a political dictionary and a Florida farm-commune for artists. Graves would return to Mallorca with Beryl after the war, though he was unable to marry her until Nicholson agreed to a divorce.

The postwar years brought Graves greater fame, primarily because of the Claudius novels, and with this lucrative commissions, such as his two-volume work, *The Greek Myths* (1955), published by Penguin. This work contains not mere retellings of the myths but highly subjective interpretations of their origin and significance. It was only the first of several works that would provoke heavy criticism from the academic community. Traditional Christian theologians objected to Graves's anti-Pauline conception of Jesus Christ as presented in *The Nazarene Gospel Restored* (1953) and *Jesus in Rome: A Historical Conjecture* (1957), both of which were collaborations with the Sephardic Jewish scholar Joshua Podro. In these works, Graves presents Christ as well within the Jewish tradition, a reformer working within the Jewish community rather than the founder of a new religion.

Graves thoroughly enjoyed the furor that such works provoked. He took it as assurance that his artistic powers had not left him, that he had not lost the favor of the Goddess. Perhaps the fear of such a possibility explains the series of young women who became part of his life during the 1960's and early 1970's. He often lavished expensive presents upon them, gave one a house on Mallorca, built a house for another in Puerta Vallarta, Mexico, and gave them the copyrights to poems that he wrote in their honor. Beryl, his second wife, tolerated these involvements to an amazing degree, even though she was aware that at one point Graves had considered leaving her. He, and she for the most part, seemed to believe that such relationships were necessary for his art. It is true that he wrote some of his finest love poems at this time, though he was in his middle seventies.

From dangerous volunteer missions and a near-fatal wound in World War I to shell shock in the years that followed, from one tension-filled romance to the next throughout his life, Graves lived on the edge, as the subtitle of Seymour's book indicates. Such regrets as Graves may have had concerned his children: one, David Graves, was killed during World War II, and another, Jenny Nicholson Cross Clifford (who, like her mother, never used the Graves name), was the victim of a brain hemorrhage in 1964.

Yet Graves spoke little of these misfortunes. For Graves, life required undiminishing experience and use to its end; his own life remained consistent with that credo.

Robert J. Forman

Sources for Further Study

Booklist. XCII, September 15, 1995, p. 129.
Boston Globe. December 3, 1995, p. 72.
The Economist. CCCXXXVI, July 8, 1995, p. 83.
London Review of Books. XVII, September 7, 1995, p. 26.
The Nation. CCLXI, November 20, 1995, p. 634.
The New York Times Book Review. C, November 5, 1995, p. 10.
The Observer. July 2, 1995, p. 15.
Publishers Weekly. CCXLII, September 11, 1995, p. 69.
The Wall Street Journal. October 24, 1995, p. A20.
The Washington Post. October 6, 1995, p. B2.

ROBERT LOUIS STEVENSON
A Biography

Author: Frank McLynn
First published: 1993, in Great Britain
Publisher: Random House (New York). Illustrated. 567 pp. $30.00
Type of work: Literary biography
Time: 1850-1894
Locale: Scotland, England, France, the United States, and Samoa

The author traces Robert Louis Stevenson's career, noting the malignant influence of his wife and stepson and concluding that Stevenson "is Scotland's greatest writer of English prose"

Principal personages:
ROBERT LOUIS STEVENSON, the Scottish novelist and poet
THOMAS STEVENSON, his father, a renowned engineer
MARGARET "MAGGIE" BALFOUR STEVENSON, his mother
ALISON "CUMMY" CUNNINGHAM, his childhood nurse
FRANCES "FANNY" OSBOURNE STEVENSON, his wife
LLOYD OSBOURNE, his stepson
WILLIAM ERNEST HENLEY, an English poet, his friend
SIDNEY COLVIN, his literary agent and friend

Robert Louis Stevenson has remained an enigma because of the exaggerations of two sides in an acrimonious feud that erupted shortly following his death in 1894. Critics such as Arthur Quiller-Couch placed him in the company of William Shakespeare, John Milton, and John Keats: "Put away books and paper and pen. . . . Stevenson is dead, and now there is nobody to write for." Fanny Stevenson and Lloyd Osbourne fostered this image of Stevenson as literary giant, adding the enhancement of martyrdom, a genius struggling against debilitating congestive diseases that called for Fanny's constant care and Lloyd's creative assistance. Fanny forced Sidney Colvin, who had been Stevenson's own choice for biographer, to turn over the official project to the more malleable Graham Balfour, who finally produced *The Life of Robert Louis Stevenson* in two volumes (1901).

From the first, however, there were plenty of people able and willing to recall that Stevenson had feet of clay. In 1898 his old adversary Eve Simpson revealed the mild debauchery of his young manhood. William Ernest Henley used the pretext of a review of the official biography three years later to blast his old friend's vanity and narcissism and to note the debilitating influence of a domineering older wife who had ruined an author of great promise. Even admirers such as G. K. Chesterton unwittingly undermined Stevenson's reputation by tracing his inspiration to Skelt's juvenile theater. With debunking critical studies by Frank Swinnerton (1924), E. F. Benson (1925), and Thomas Beer (1926), the literary demolition was nearly complete.

Frank McLynn, after a thorough reading of the refinements in Stevenson scholarship, has in *Robert Louis Stevenson: A Biography* fashioned a unified articulation of two trends that have been emerging since that time. First, he clearly and persuasively destroys the image of Fanny as ministering angel, demonstrating that she was instead a constant drain on Stevenson's limited strength and an ever-present hindrance to his literary integrity. This had been clearly recognized by Henley and others, but in their mouths had been suspect on grounds of personal bias. Second, McLynn argues that Stevenson was a novelist of the first rank, treated "with great respect and sensitivity" by the "great figures of late Victorian literature," including Henry James, George Meredith, Rudyard Kipling, J. M. Barrie, and Arthur Conan Doyle. Although McLynn does not go to the critical extremes of Quiller-Couch, in the end his Stevenson is even larger than Fanny's, for he had to overcome the twin peaks of debilitating disease and neurotic wife.

McLynn emphasizes the significance of youthful experience to Stevenson's later life, particularly the psychological influence of two people. First in importance was his father, Thomas, a successful engineer and stern Calvinist, followed closely by his childhood nurse, Alison Cunningham, the devoted "Cummy" of legend. According to McLynn, Cummy was a "religious maniac" who stuffed Stevenson with the "more unacceptable excesses of Calvinism and the Old Testament." With Thomas, she planted in Stevenson a "deep sense of guilt that would never leave him." This combined with frequent sickness, harrowing nightmares, and the atmospheric gloom of Scotland to make Stevenson a lonely child who yearned for a broader, brighter world.

There is undeniable truth in the broad outlines of this picture of Stevenson's youth, yet much to suggest that the harshness has been exaggerated. As McLynn himself notes, Stevenson "appeared to bear Cummy no grudge" and in fact praised her for inspiring the "musicality" of his prose. Both Cummy and Thomas loved him (as did his invalid mother) and encouraged his interest in drama. Thomas early on treated his son as an adult and encouraged his literary ambitions. Too, McLynn recognizes that as early as 1863, Stevenson was able to poke gentle fun at the excesses of Cummy's personality.

Without Stevenson's categorical testimony to the terror of childhood, McLynn resorts to questionable interpretations of later phrases in letters and novels. It is hard to imagine, however, that Stevenson's wishful observation that in "a better state of things . . . every mother will nurse her own offspring" is a "sign of anger and resentment" against his own nurse. Nor need a phrase about unnoticed "only sons," from Stevenson's posthumously published *Weir of Hermiston* (1896), indicate more than a straightforward recollection of childhood circumstance. Stevenson undoubtedly was lonely on occasion, as were most boys when sent off to boarding school, was frequently ill, and did suffer from nightmares that were perhaps exacerbated by tales of hell from the nursery. On the other hand, this seems to have been more than compensated for by loving parents, comfortable surroundings, the company of vivacious cousins, and frequent opportunities for travel. By his thirteenth birthday, Stevenson had seen much of Scotland and the Lake District; had visited London, Salisbury, and Stonehenge; and had traveled twice to the Continent. Whether it was the terror or the bourgeois creature comforts that were responsible, he had already embarked on his career in writing, having produced numerous stories for his family and the South Grove school magazine.

Stevenson was always more influenced by his personal experience, rich in both suffering and joy, than by his formal education, which was patchy at best. Brief attendance at Edinburgh University gave opportunity for publication and for entranc-ing elders such as Fleeming Jenkin, the professor of engineering. This too was a gift with Stevenson, given his combination of worldly knowledge and youthful relish. In McLynn's fulsome record of his life, one cannot help but contemplate the greater opportunities that an Oxbridge education might have afforded the young author. As it was, Stevenson left Edinburgh in 1873 with the educational rewards of his poor attendance, a bohemian pose, and a small literary following.

McLynn takes Stevenson into his mid-twenties paying scarcely any attention to his writing, so that the reader is mildly jolted by Leslie Stephen's encomium of the author as the "young Heine." In part this a reflection of Stevenson's own perception that he was publishing nothing but obscure essays and reviews. Certainly McLynn's interest is in promoting Stevenson as master novelist rather than critical parasite. But his decision also has a solid biographical base, ensuring that Stevenson's early and inferior literary efforts do not distract the reader from the circumstances that contributed to his development as a novelist.

During the 1870's Stevenson was struggling to find his literary niche but was also wrestling with two fundamental moral issues that would largely be resolved by decade's end, with enormous implications for his life and career. First, what was he to do about his spiritual agnosticism? His dilemma was not the decision to renounce the orthodox Christianity of his youth but the way he should thereafter relate to his parents. In 1873, Thomas Stevenson began to question his son about his beliefs, and after some temporizing, Stevenson finally told him that he no longer believed in "the faith of his fathers." Over time, however, he softened and mellowed, as did his father. Though their relationship was never easy, the love of clan transcended the effects of the honesty that Stevenson felt bound to express in order to gain intellectual inde-pendence. This worthy motivation was mixed, however, with Stevenson's willingness to remain, until his father's death in 1887, the patriarch's pensioner. Stevenson was seldom extravagant in his spending, but he knew that the safety net was in place. It was this financial arrangement, based on the emotional compromises necessary to obtain it, that led Henley to attack vigorously the legend of "a martyr to consumption" struggling heroically for the good of humankind.

The second moral dilemma that Stevenson faced in the 1870's involved his attitude toward women. He had a strong sexual impulse that he had satisfied in a variety of carnal and utopian relationships. Yet he also had a profound respect for women and a keen sense of the injustice they suffered at the hands of society; he worried that he was sometimes contributing to the patriarchal system that was responsible for their plight. It is not necessary to go the whole way with McLynn in saying that his relationships suffered from "'oedipal confusion'—resulting from his mother's 'deser-tion' when she sided with his father in the family turmoil," but it is clear that the two great moral debates were filtered through the emotional bonds that tied him to his family.

A casual 1876 meeting in France with an American woman blossomed into the central relationship of Stevenson's adult life. Fanny Osbourne was ten years his senior and unhappily tied to an irresponsible husband. Short and dark-skinned, she had "an all-round aura of sensuality" that Stevenson could not resist and a whimsical sense of fantasy that appealed to his childlike sensibilities. Though far from the refined ideal of the Scottish middle class, after their marriage in 1880 she gradually won the affection of Stevenson's parents, and with it the ability to extract more money when she and her husband failed—as they usually did—to live within their means.

McLynn goes to great lengths to show that Stevenson's love for Fanny was both psychologically necessary and artistically destructive. He welcomed the mothering he had missed in his youth, but only gradually realized that it would end in a kind of maternal tyranny. Fanny excluded Stevenson's friends, censored his literary treatments of sexuality, promoted her deadbeat son, and fell into hypochondria the moment she seemed to be losing control. Far from an angelic helpmeet, she was a grasping and narrow wife who demanded material security but was jealous of a husband who intellectually outstripped her in providing it.

One of the strongest features of McLynn's biography is its unequivocating portrait of Fanny, which is necessary to any sound understanding of Stevenson's own character. The evidence suggests that the emotional and sexual dimension was most important to Stevenson early their relationship. Stevenson was *not* seeking an intellectual companion but a questing soulmate with whom he could share the vicissitudes of life. The nearer Stevenson came to that magic, settled place that would enable him to develop as a novelist, the less important Fanny became.

An unclouded view of Fanny's personality also enhances one's respect for Stevenson's work ethic. McLynn's portrait of Stevenson as a young man, though friendly, is by no means flattering. Set against a budding literary talent and an honest bonhomie is a constant and sometimes shameful reliance on his father's wealth. During the last years of his life, however, Stevenson's position altogether changed. By 1890 his father had died, he and his extended family had moved to Samoa, and he could support them all only by dint of sustained literary work. As his relationship with Fanny deteriorated and he came to realize how selfish and pathetic his stepson had become, he might well have been overwhelmed and refused to exert himself on behalf of those who hindered rather than helped him. Instead Stevenson shouldered his burden in love, and perhaps in gratitude for the lesser ministrations of his wife before he had hit his literary stride.

Though McLynn clearly focuses on Stevenson's life, his biography is informed by a desire to redress the prevailing criticisms of Stevenson as a serious writer. It has often been argued that his slick style concealed a poverty of insight. This criticism is closely related to the contention that Stevenson was primarily a writer of "boys' literature." McLynn counters by observing that the "disturbing darkness" of such early works as *Treasure Island* (1883) has been "absurdly glossed over" by critics.

A related criticism has been that adventure stories are not well suited to morally serious problems. McLynn invokes such works as *The Odyssey* (c. 800 B.C.) and *Moby Dick* (1851) to undermine this argument, enhancing it with careful critical readings of *Treasure Island*, *Kidnapped* (1886), *The Black Arrow* (1888), and *The Master of Ballantrae* (1889). More subtly, McLynn deflects attention from Stevenson's substantial but technical narrative gift by highlighting the psychological shadows in works such as *Dr. Jekyll and Mr. Hyde* (1886), *The Beach of Falesa* (1891), and *The Ebb Tide* (1894).

McLynn argues that Stevenson's globetrotting may ultimately have prompted the subsequent belittling of his literature, which could never compete with the adventure of his life. By demonstrating how ordinary were the everyday challenges Stevenson faced, whether in Silverado or in Samoa, he frees the reader from the implicit but traditional assumption that the artist was being driven by the peripatetic adventurer.

John Powell

Sources for Further Study

American Scholar. LXIII, Autumn, 1994, p. 619.
The Christian Science Monitor. January 5, 1995, p. 13.
Commonweal. CXXII, May 5, 1995, p. 22.
English Literature in Transition. XXXVII, March, 1994, p. 363.
New Statesman and Society. VI, May 21, 1993, p. 34.
The New York Review of Books. XLII, June 8, 1995, p. 14.
The New York Times Book Review. XCIX, December 25, 1994, p. 1.
The Observer. April 17, 1994, p. 21.
Publishers Weekly. CCXLI, October 31, 1994, p. 48.
Time. CXLV, February 27, 1995, p. 70.
The Times Educational Supplement. April 29, 1994, p. 16.
The Times Literary Supplement. June 4, 1993, p. 13.
The Wall Street Journal. January 3, 1995, p. A6.
The Washington Post Book World. XXV, January 8, 1995, p. 1.

ROBERTSON DAVIES
Man of Myth

Author: Judith Skelton Grant (1941-   )
First published: 1994, in Canada
Publisher: Viking (New York). 787 pp. $35.00
Type of work: Literary biography
Time: 1913-1993
Locale: Ontario, Canada (notably Thamesville, Renfrew, Kingston, Peterborough, and Toronto); London, Oxford, and Wales

This sprawling biography of Canada's most celebrated contemporary playwright, novelist, and editor, Robertson Davies, published shortly before Davies' death on December 2, 1995, details his life and writing

> *Principal personages:*
> ROBERTSON DAVIES, the Canadian playwright, novelist, editor, and
>   teacher
> FLORENCE MCKAY DAVIES, his mother
> RUPERT DAVIES, his father, an editor and newspaper owner
> FRED DAVIES, his brother, eleven years his senior
> ARTHUR DAVIES, his brother, ten years his senior
> BRENDA NEWBOLD MATTHEWS DAVIES, his wife
> MIRANDA DAVIES,
> JENNIFER DAVIES SURRIDGE, and
> ROSAMOND CUNNINGTON, their daughters

Readers of *Robertson Davies: Man of Myth* will quickly conclude that its author, Judith Skelton Grant, is the sort of person who never throws anything away. This characteristic accounts for both this biography's greatest strengths and its most significant shortcomings.

On the one hand, Grant has collected, organized, preserved, and presented remarkable quantities of primary material about her subject, clearly Canada's most prolific and probably most widely recognized contemporary author. Grant's research on Davies has already resulted in the three useful collections that she has edited and published: her two editions of Davies' journalism, *The Enthusiasms of Robertson Davies* (1979) and *Robertson Davies: The Well-Tempered Critic: One Man's View of Theatre and Letters in Canada* (1981), as well as *Robertson Davies: A Consideration of His Writing* (1978).

On the other hand, in her biography of Davies, which runs to nearly eight hundred pages, Grant apparently found it difficult to discard the bits of irrelevant information that most biographers acquire in the course of their research and jettison during the composing process. At times, she pursues in too much detail tangents that relate little to Davies and his work. She sets scenes competently, as when she describes the various places where Davies lived during his lifetime, but she often tells much more than is necessary to set the scene, thereby adding greatly yet unproductively to her book's prodigious length.

Despite such caveats, one must recognize that this biography, whose comprehensiveness equals that of Margaret Brenman-Gibson's *Clifford Odets, American Playwright: The Years from 1906 to 1940* (1981) or Jeffrey Meyers' *Hemingway: A Biography* (1985), will likely prove useful to future Davies scholars. One may hope that the factual information it provides in profuse detail will, in the long term, far outweigh Grant's sometimes plodding prose and the frequent presentation of facts almost totally lacking in thematic connection to Davies' work.

Grant frequently points out episodes in Davies' life that found their way into his subsequent novels or plays, but she generally settles for merely noting such occurrences without pursuing the deeper questions to which close reading and the application of the tools provided by recent critical theory would lead her.

Such readings of Davies' work—particularly psychoanalytical readings of it—will nevertheless be aided by the fundamental groundwork that has occupied Grant for almost three decades. She has tirelessly sought out and interviewed hundreds of people whom Davies knew through the years, much as Barbara and Arthur Gelb interviewed a staggering gallery of Eugene O'Neill's family and acquaintances for their monumental biography *O'Neill* (1962).

Unlike the Gelbs' subject, Grant's subject was alive during all of her research prior to the publication of this book. Her more than seventy interviews with Robertson Davies, therefore, have provided her with a wealth of information that will inform future scholars and that inform this biography uniquely. Grant, over an extended period, knew Davies and his family well and unquestionably demonstrates a comprehensive familiarity with her subject's life and writing.

Robertson Davies as Grant portrays him is far from appealing, although Grant's approach to him is positive, at times even fawning. Contemporary readers, particularly those from the United States, will likely come away from this book thinking of Davies as a man remarkably insensitive to many of the major social and political currents of his time, a man who insulated himself from events that he found painful or unpleasant. Grant never points this out directly. She does, however, offer information from which readers will inevitably draw their own conclusions.

For example, when World War II was raging, Davies, newly employed as a columnist and editorial writer for the *Whig*, a newspaper his father owned, wrote editorials about the Oxford twang, taking too many baths, and steam calliopes—this at a time when Adolf Hitler was running rough-shod over much of Europe and was consigning Jews, Gypsies, homosexuals, and dissidents to concentration camps where they would be summarily slaughtered. Davies' isolationist readers liked his well-written, light editorials, much as an uncritical public currently venerates Rush Limbaugh, who reinforces their most deplorable prejudices. The question one must ask is whether a man of Davies' standing and abilities should not have felt conscience-bound to do more than entertain his readership during such critical times.

If Davies is remembered a century from now, he will probably be remembered as a curious anachronism, a gifted curmudgeon who lived in a dynamic age but chose to detach himself from it. As late as 1963, when racial and ethnic consciousness was being raised rapidly worldwide, Davies returned from a visit to the Shetland Islands, his ancestral lands, and, according to Grant,

> reflected "how glad one is that one's stock was from clean, decent, wind-swept places, & not from the slums of Naples or Cracow. The strong strains which unite our children are country strains, with the physique—& alas the Calvinist strenuosity—that such an inheritance brings."

Grant, as she does elsewhere in the book, presents without comment this outrageous statement that contains sentiments to offend any thinking reader, following it merely with a genealogical chart of Brenda Davies' family. Grant loves genealogical charts, devoting endless irrelevant pages to them and to tracing the pedigrees of various principals in the Davies story when a brief paragraph would have sufficed.

Robertson Davies essentially was a nonconfrontational person, one who venerated authority and revered the status quo, although Grant does not pursue the interesting tack that this proclivity suggests. She does note the complex and strained relationship Davies had with his mother, a neurotic woman whose hypochondria virtually disabled her. In this biography, however, she never really brings the mother (or any of the other characters who surround Davies) to life. Rather than presenting information from which readers might draw valuable conclusions about a well-developed character, Grant usually merely reports, sans illustrations or examples, that a character is neurotic or emotional or vengeful.

One exception to this tendency is in Grant's revelation that from an early age, when Davies elicited his mother's anger, bringing her to the point of rage, he was forced to gain her forgiveness by kneeling before her and kissing her shoes. Grant relates this bizarre ritual, which continued into Davies' teens, without comment, although it is obvious that much of Davies' development as an adult was influenced by the sadistic demands of an irrational, neurotic mother.

The Robertson Davies whom Grant portrays was a talented writer. Despite his having received honorary doctorates and three times having made the short list for the Nobel Prize in Literature, however, he cannot legitimately be considered to have had a first-rate, analytical mind. Yet he was solidly intellectual within the narrow compass of the humanities. His early inability to comprehend even the most rudimentary mathematics is a clear indication of the kind of intellectual imbalance that marked his life. Whereas he was a keen observer and could record well the events and occurrences he observed—a skill that he honed as a journalist in his early days—he had neither a penetrating nor an analytical mind.

Grant, alas, appears to be of a similar stripe. She records but usually fails to analyze with any penetration the meaning of what she has recorded. She continually demonstrates a virtual absence of any well-developed ability to discriminate between the important and the trivial, which accounts for the unwieldy length of her biography.

Readers will come away from Grant's biography with no clear-cut picture of Davies' development as a writer, nor will they glean from the book a flesh-and-blood image of the writer, his family, and his associates. Any comprehensive conclusions that readers might draw from this book will be necessarily drawn on their own as they cull bits and pieces from the mountain of factual information that Grant presents virtually undigested. In order to reach this point, however, they will have had to finish reading a book that becomes heavier and heavier as one proceeds through it.

Nagging spelling errors and one glaring factual error suggest that proofreaders at Viking Press and Grant herself ran out of steam as they plodded through the manuscript, the galley proofs, and the page proofs. On page 490, Grant reproduces Rupert Davies' headstone, which is said to read "Born Welshpool Mont., N. Wales 1979, died Toronto 1967." Clearly the date of birth should have been 1879; it is surprising that no one caught this error during the book's various stages of production.

One cannot deny Robertson's place in Canadian letters. The sheer volume and variety of his work as well as the countless honors bestowed upon him have made secure his position in the pantheon of Canadian novelists and playwrights. In time, scholars will apply some of the principles of critical theory that have emerged during the second half of the twentieth century to an evaluation of his writing. The full body of Davies' work cries out for evaluation by psychoanalytic and Marxist critics as well as by deconstructionists and neohistoricists. Rhetorical analysis of his writing will also reveal much to explain Davies' popularity as a writer whose intellectual attainments were significantly limited.

Future scholars will perhaps pursue fruitfully the impact that being the youngest child in the Davies family had on him. His brother Fred, with whom he never got along, was eleven years his senior, and his brother Arthur was only a year younger than Fred. In this family dominated by an opinionated father, the young Davies had four older people to answer to: his father, his mother, and two siblings.

This complex, authoritarian family structure produced an adolescent and young adult who consistently knuckled under to authority and, subsequently, a mature, married newspaper writer who, while his father was still alive, could not bring himself to publish anything that might distress the elder Davies. All these raw data are presented in Grant's biography. Unfortunately, however, the author never focuses her critical attention upon them.

Although it is impossible to dismiss this book, which is important and should be made available to the reading public in a broad range of libraries, readers will soon become aware of its significant limitations. It is hard to imagine that Robertson Davies was not more scintillating in actuality than the character who emerges from this seriously flawed biography. Only occasionally, particularly in the final chapter, are there glimmerings of Davies' wit and humor.

R. Baird Shuman

Sources for Further Study

Publishers Weekly. CCXLII, October 2, 1995, p. 60.
San Francisco Chronicle. December 3, 1995, p. REV3.
The Washington Post Book World. XXVI, January 7, 1996, p. 3.

ROLAND BARTHES
A Biography

Author: Louis-Jean Calvet (1942-   )
First published: 1990, in France
Translated from the French by Sarah Wykes
Publisher: Indiana University Press (Bloomington). Illustrated. 291 pp. $35.00
Type of work: Biography
Time: 1915-1980
Locale: France

An overview of the life of a major twentieth century literary theorist and cultural critic

> *Principal personages:*
> ROLAND BARTHES, a writer, teacher, and scholar
> HENRIETTE BARTHES, his mother, a bookbinder
> PHILIPPE REBEYROL, his lifelong friend, a diplomat
> ALGIRDAS JULIEN GREIMAS, his mentor, a linguist
> JULIA KRISTEVA, a Bulgarian-born writer and feminist philosopher

Roland Barthes lived a life that provides ample material for a riveting biography and wrote fascinating, highly complex works that decades later still cry out for careful analysis. He was born in poverty but rose to international fame as a cultural critic and theoretician; his brilliant explorations of the "semiotics" of advertising, fashion, literature, and popular culture continue to influence scholars and attract numerous academic and nonacademic devotees. Yet *Roland Barthes: A Biography* only scratches the surface of what should be a compelling life story. While significant because it is the first biography of Barthes, it will surely be surpassed by later works that can easily build upon its plodding overview of data and thin, elementary analysis.

To be sure, Louis-Jean Calvet provides all the factual material that a reader might desire in a biography. One learns that Roland Barthes was born on November 12, 1915, to Henriette Barthes, an upper-class young woman married to a young seaman, Louis Barthes. Because of her financially unfavorable marriage and later romantic entanglements, Barthes's mother was forever estranged from her wealthy relatives, who continued to snub her even after the death of her husband in 1916; Henriette eventually had to take up bookbinding to provide for Roland and her second child, Michel Salzedo, who was born out of wedlock in 1927. The family's personal trials and financial problems were witnessed firsthand by Philippe Rebeyrol, who was Roland Barthes's classmate in the early 1930's and remained his close friend. From Rebeyrol, scholars know that Barthes's early years were marked by intense poverty and continuing familial upheaval, soon made far worse by serious illness.

Certainly Calvet is a competent biographer, carefully relating the facts surrounding the early onset of Barthes's lung disease, which began in 1934 and led to several very long stays in sanatoriums lasting through the mid-1940's. Calvet draws on Barthes's own letters, his published reminiscences, and interviews with numerous friends and acquaintances to provide an overview of the lonely life of a frustrated, gifted young student whose desire to continue his education remained unfulfilled because of uncertain health. Calvet also carefully details Barthes's ambitious and successful plan of self-study, which encompassed works by Walt Whitman, Charles-Pierre Baudelaire, and Karl Marx, tells of Barthes's interactions with fellow hospital patients and local townspeople, and surveys Barthes's first experiments in writing for student publications. Yet throughout Calvet seems highly reticent to probe beyond the surface; he rarely relates Barthes's severe bouts of depression to his sense of isolation as a young homosexual and never really explores the social and psychological implications of Barthes's highly uncertain class status (while Barthes had contact with his wealthy relatives, he could never look to them for financial support). Going similarly unexplored is the full impact of World War II upon the young Barthes, who in a sanatorium was isolated from major battles but whose work was profoundly influenced by the political turmoil that surrounded him. Skimming over these issues, Calvet seems intent solely on relating hard facts, and doing so in the most concise fashion possible.

Equally thin, and at times even mechanical, is Calvet's overview of the four years that Barthes spent as a teacher and cultural attaché in Bucharest, Romania, and Alexandria, Egypt, after he was finally pronounced cured and released from health facilities in 1946. Readers do learn a few details about Barthes's active social life and the beginnings of his writing career as a correspondent for the periodical *Combat* during the late 1940's, but nothing concerning the relationship between what he was writing and the life that he was living at the time. Even highly significant events are hastily reported and then dropped, such as Barthes's developing relationship with A. J. Greimas, whom he first met in 1949. Greimas is one of the most important linguists of the twentieth century; his work on language had clear and profound impact on the development of Barthes's own theories of cultural "signs" and systems of meaning. Yet again, Calvet seems unwilling to explore these connections, perhaps leaving to more analytically inclined writers the responsibility for probing and critiquing Barthes's work and the genesis of his ideas.

With Barthes's return to Paris in 1950, readers enter the era of his most prolific production as a writer and a time of immense intellectual dynamism. Barthes was a contemporary and acquaintance of Albert Camus, Jean-Paul Sartre, Michel Foucault, and other leading French intellectuals of the postwar period. With the publication of *Le Degré zéro de l'écriture* (1953; *Writing Degree Zero*, 1984) and *Michelet par lui-même* (1954; *Michelet*, 1987), Barthes was soon recognized as the progenitor of a new form of cultural criticism, one that encompassed both textual and extratextual material. Filled with idiosyncratic commentary and speculation, Barthes's writings are designed to provoke the reader and lead her or him to new levels of awareness concerning the interrelationships among writers, readers, and the contexts that produce them. Yet this is not readily apparent in Calvet's minimal commentary on Barthes's many books. Indeed, the reader who is unfamiliar with Barthes will come away from *Roland Barthes: A Biography* with little understanding of and probably no piqued interest in the work of its subject. Calvet rushes forward to tell about Barthes's financial problems, covering highly complex texts in a few sentences or brief paragraphs. Beyond his commendable reliance on factual material, Calvet simply does not do justice to his fascinating subject.

This is not to say that *Roland Barthes: A Biography* holds no interest for the general or academic reader; Barthes's life was too complex and incident-filled for even the most mechanical of writers to drain it of all power. Anecdotes concerning the production of Barthes's monumental work *Mythologies* (1957; English translation, 1972), his continuing but somewhat stormy relationship with Foucault, and his lifelong struggles with depression and insecurity, even at times of great public acclaim, are interesting enough in themselves to sustain the reader's attention, even when Calvet presents them only in their barest outlines. The Barthes enthusiast will find recountings of typical days in the writer's life quite fascinating; at times Calvet manages to capture successfully the work habits and internal reflections of a tortured, overly meticulous man. Through information provided by Julia Kristeva, Barthes's student as well as a superb writer and theorist in her own right, Calvet is also able to provide a portrait of Barthes the teacher, examining his work at the École Pratique des Hautes Études during the 1960's and early 1970's, up to and past his election to the Collège de France in 1976, one of the highest honors possible for a French intellectual.

Indeed, Kristeva seems responsible for many of the most significant insights of *Roland Barthes: A Biography*. Her relationship with Barthes, dating from 1965, was one of the most enduring and important of their lives. She remembers him as an engaging instructor who worked tirelessly to nurture original thought in his students rather than expecting them to repeat back to him his own ideas. After his participation in her successful M.A. thesis defense in 1968, they became fast friends as well as intellectual compatriots. She commiserated with him when he was depressed and offered support when his insecurity threatened to vanquish him. Calvet reports that Barthes repeatedly expressed his great love for Kristeva and even joked that she was the only woman for whom he might change his sexual orientation. Certainly she knew him very well, and Calvet draws liberally on her *roman à clef* titled *The Samurai* (1980), which gives numerous details concerning her rich and enduring friendship with Barthes; indeed, hers is the book to which many readers will still turn for insight.

Both Kristeva and Barthes are great stylists; their prose is fluid, at times baroque, and always filled with imagery and metaphor. Unfortunately, Calvet's prose suffers greatly in comparison, for it is often dry and unappealing. Even so, Barthes's life story does build to a natural climax of sorts, with his grotesque death in 1980 after being struck by a van while he was crossing a Paris street. Tragically, this occurred at a time of unqualified success for him and final relief from the financial worries that had plagued him throughout his life. His election to the Collège de France had cemented his stature as one of the premiere intellectuals of the mid- to late twentieth century. His indispensable contributions to the development of "semiotics" as a field of critical inquiry encompassing diverse fields had been heralded worldwide. His work continued to metamorphose. In *Le Plaisir du texte* (1973; *The Pleasure of the Text*, 1990), perhaps his greatest book, Barthes had turned his considerable skills at analysis toward the fascinating interconnections between writing, reading, and erotic desire. At the time of his death, he was even hoping to move into fiction writing. Certainly Barthes's talents were diverse; his many accomplishments even included an appearance in film, as William Makepeace Thackeray in Andre Techine's *Les Soeurs Brontë* (1978).

Barthes's was a memorable life; Calvet's commentary upon it is far less so, as he seems reticent or unable to investigate or speculate beyond the surface. Barthes's intense relationship with his mother, with whom he lived until her death in 1977, is here reduced simply to a case of her being overprotective. One learns little about her influence upon him and practically nothing about Barthes's relationship with his half brother, with whom he also lived for much of his life. Furthermore, Barthes's very active homosexual life, seemingly a significant component of his daily existence as well as a key to understanding his self-image and relationship with his cultural milieu, is mentioned several times in passing but is never the subject of sustained commentary. Granted, Calvet did not have copious primary materials with which to work, since Barthes was by nature a closed, even secretive, individual. Yet readers of biographies ask more from a biographer than simply an overview of data; they seek insight into a subject, and unfortunately Calvet provides little here.

Nevertheless, this biography can hardly be termed an abject failure. The scenes surrounding Barthes's death and the testimonials provided by his many friends and admirers are highly moving. The book's concluding chapter is perhaps its best, as Calvet struggles to assess finally the importance of Barthes's life and the impact of his work. Indeed, the generally conservative nature of this biography may be perceived as a significant attribute by some, making it highly attractive to those readers who desire factual material alone, a concise portrait of a complex man. Certainly the information that Calvet provides is highly credible, and he should be commended for his solid presentation of bibliographical data, his generous quotations from secondary sources, and his inclusion of numerous photographs that help the reader visualize a life unfolding. *Roland Barthes: A Biography* is well indexed, relatively jargon-free, and certainly timely. It is a solid base upon which future biographers can build.

One can only hope that such moves toward elaboration and critical engagement will occur in the near future, for Calvet's will not be the last word on the subject of Barthes's life and lifework. From the grimy halls of urban poverty to the exotic markets of North Africa, from public pronouncements as a renowned intellectual to private moments of erotic adventure-seeking, there is another story to be told about Roland Barthes.

Donald E. Hall

Sources for Further Study

ARTforum. XXXIII, Summer, 1995, p. B16.
Insight on the News. XI, April 3, 1995, p. 40.
London Review of Books. XVI, December 22, 1994, p. 6.
New Statesman and Society. VII, November 18, 1994, p. 56.
The Times Literary Supplement. October 6, 1995, p. 10.

RULE OF THE BONE

Author: Russell Banks (1940-   )
Publisher: HarperCollins (New York). 390 pp. $22.00
Type of work: Novel
Time: 1994
Locale: Au Sable, New York, and environs; Burlington, Vermont; and Jamaica

A coming-of-age novel about a fourteen-year-old homeless boy from upstate New York who seeks his father—and finds himself

> *Principal characters:*
> CHAPMAN "CHAPPIE" DORSET (A.K.A. BONE), a fourteen-year-old runaway
> MOM, his mother
> KEN, his sexually abusive stepfather
> I-MAN, a middle-aged Rastafarian migrant worker from Jamaica
> RUSS, a homeless boy and close friend of Chappie
> BRUCE, a motorcycle gang member
> BUSTER BROWN, an itinerant child pornographer
> SISTER ROSE (A.K.A. FROGGY), Buster Brown's young sex slave
> DOC, Chappie's biological father
> EVENING STAR, Doc's girlfriend

Russell Banks began his literary career in the late 1960's as a writer of experimental fiction. Over the years, Banks has steadily moved away from aesthetically self-conscious avant-garde forms in order to embrace a relatively straightforward realist idiom. At the same time, Banks has chosen to focus ever more intensively on the lives of working-class people. Both of these moves indicate a deliberate ideological agenda that happens to be at variance with that of most mainstream writers, who tend to make a fetish of their "art" or confine their subject matter to more politically neutral topics. Banks is a man with a mission—or several missions: to be true to a wide range of contemporary life, to write serious social critique, and to suggest to the American middle class how the other half lives. Implicit in all Banks's later work is the conviction that the United States is a class society that denies the very existence of social class as an everyday reality.

Rule of the Bone marks another step in Banks's evolution as a political writer who understands that politics is not really about government, voting, and the like; politics in the deepest sense actually plays out in terms of lifestyles, in modes of thought and emotional attitudes, in the myriad ways that marginal groups are ignored, condemned, or warred upon by the hegemonic powers that be. Fittingly, given his sociopolitical outlook, Banks builds *Rule of the Bone* around the severely damaged life of a fourteen-year-old "mall rat" from a broken home in upstate New York. Creating such a story in the third person would be a singularly ambitious imaginative endeavor for a successful writer in his mid-fifties, but Banks attempts the even riskier gambit of telling Chappie's story from the first-person point of view.

Yet Banks's choice of narrative approach is astute; half boy, half man, with one foot in society and one foot outside it, Chappie is well positioned to see the naked workings of "the system" in ways that more respectable folk never dare to imagine. Furthermore, Banks wisely refuses to condescend to his subject; he makes Chappie intelligent and aware, with a sardonic view of the state of things. The result of these narrative decisions is a generally gripping story that falters only in its last stages.

When readers first meet him, narrator Chappie Dorset sports earrings, a nose ring, a mohawk hairstyle, and a massive marijuana habit. Yet Chappie is not a social degenerate but simply the contemporary version of a lost, lonely, and alienated teenager. Ten years earlier, his father abandoned the family and was eventually replaced by Ken, an alcoholic pederast who makes lewd demands on his stepson.

Driven to the end of his endurance by Ken's abuse and his mother's indifference, Chappie leaves home in the middle of an angry confrontation with his stepfather over some stolen coins. He and another homeless friend, Russ, soon find themselves living with members of a biker gang (who call themselves "Adirondack Iron") in a slum apartment above a video store. This dubious situation sours when the bikers discover that Russ has been stealing their stolen loot. Fearing for their lives, the boys flee in the night, but not before inadvertently starting a fire that kills Bruce, a biker who dies in a mistaken attempt to save Chappie.

All connections with family and surrogate family broken, Russ and Chappie steal a Ford Ranger pickup, take a joyride, abandon the vehicle, and end up at a wrecked school bus occupied by the "Bong Brothers," a pair of drug-addled college dropouts. In trouble with bikers and with the police, Russ and Chappie decide to slough off their old identities and assume new ones. They develop aliases ("Buck" and "Bone," respectively) and acquire tattoos before moving to their next temporary haven: an unoccupied summer house nestled in the woods of Adirondack State Park in Keene, New York. Holed up in the house for a number of weeks, the boys eat what food is available, break up the furniture for firewood, and generally make a shambles of the premises. Eventually abandoned by Russ, Bone has no choice but to set out on the road before the owners arrive on the scene.

In a Dickensian coincidence, Bone is picked up while hitchhiking by Buster Brown, an itinerant child molester and purveyor of child pornography with whom he has already had a run-in at the local mall some weeks before. Although he fears this unpredictable, predatory adult, Bone dares to steal several hundred dollars from Buster Brown. He also manages to liberate Sister Rose, also known as "Froggy," a nine-year-old girl whose own mother "gave" her to Buster Brown to be his sex slave.

Bone takes Froggy back to the abandoned school bus in Au Sable. The Bong Brothers have departed, to be replaced by I-Man, a migrant worker from Jamaica with outsized Rastafarian dreadlocks. Kind, patient, and openhearted, I-Man becomes Bone's friend and mentor, schooling the boy in Rastafarian ways. Under this gentle tutelage, Bone begins to grow, spiritually and emotionally, for the first time in his life. The beginning of Bone's moral transformation is evident when he decides to take responsibility for Rose by sending her back home to Milwaukee. When I-Man decides to return to Jamaica, Bone opts to go with him, using Buster Brown's cash to finance the trip.

The final chapters of the novel take place in Jamaica and feature the rather far-fetched coincidence of Bone finding his real father, Doc, who turns out to be a mean-spirited narcissist. Equally obnoxious is Doc's girlfriend, Evening Star, a wealthy dilettante obsessed with sex, drugs, astrology, and all things fashionably hip. Life at their elegant compound, known as Starport, is a decadent free-for-all, awash in food, liquor, drugs, and faux Rastas who provide stud service to affluent whites avid for exotic sexual experiences.

Although Bone grows dreadlocks and comes to consider himself a full-fledged Rastafarian, he is not immune to the corrupting influences of life at Starport. Discovering I-Man having sex with Evening Star, Bone opts to tell his father about it out of some craven sense of familial obligation. In a jealous rage, Doc has I-Man and a cohort murdered. Bone stumbles on the bloody scene just as the hit men are leaving and is spared only because he is Doc's *white* son.

Although undeniably tragic, I-Man's death is Bone's redemptive moment; it grants him the resolve he needs to repudiate fully his amoral parents, their lovers, and everything they represent. In the end, Bone is free of his most cherished illusions regarding the sanctity of blood ties over chosen loyalties. As Bone puts it, "Stealing is only a crime but betrayal of a friend is a sin." Through I-Man's death, Bone also comes to the equally important realization that he is merely a make-believe Rasta, ultimately and always white, with all the attendant privileges of his race. Yet far from being a cause for discouragement, this realization is liberating: "Even though I was a white kid I could still become a true heavy Rasta myself someday as long as I didn't ever forget I was a white kid, just like black people could never forget they were black people."

In the end, Bone exacts his revenge on his father by eschewing the man's violent ways. Instead of killing his father, Bone seduces Evening Star: an act of Oedipal rebellion that ritualizes a moral shift back toward I-Man's Otherness. Although he embraces the biological fact of his whiteness, Bone succeeds in turning his back on the oppressive self-absorption of the First World. He comes to know who his friends really are—and were.

If all of this sounds vaguely familiar, it should. On one level, at least, *Rule of the Bone* is a masterful retelling of Mark Twain's *The Adventures of Huckleberry Finn* (1884). Both works are novels of moral education that feature a homeless white youth on the run from the bourgeois world. Both books introduce evil biological fathers counterpoised by black father-surrogates who act as spiritual and moral mentors. Through deed more than word, Twain's Jim and Banks's I-Man teach their charges the importance of acceptance, love, and loyalty over prejudice, convention, and fear. Where the books really differ is in their respective endings. In the final chapters of Twain's novel, Jim is toyed with by Huck and Tom Sawyer but finally freed from slavery. In Banks's novel, I-Man is brutally murdered—surely a comment on the increasingly violent and unforgiving nature of life in the late twentieth century.

In the final analysis, *Rule of the Bone* is a well-written novel, fast-paced and engrossing. Banks's rendition of the inner life, perceptions, and diction of a homeless fourteen-year-old is carefully realized and almost wholly convincing. Tough, stoical, and nobody's fool, Chappie is an extremely likable character, though sometimes, understandably, a less than reliable narrator.

Unfortunately, Banks's brilliant handling of character and narrative point of view is not matched by his management of plot. The novel loses credibility when Banks transports Bone to Jamaica in chapters 15 through 22. In real life, homeless children seldom make it out of the country, and those who do are not likely to find their long-lost fathers in a foreign land. Furthermore, the unambiguous villainy of Ken, the bikers, Buster Brown, Froggy's mother, and Doc—contrasted with the forlorn goodness of Chappie, Froggy, and I-Man—make for a black-and-white moral universe that seems too pat to be true. Similarly, the murder of I-Man adds a sensational element that suggests the triumph of melodrama over verisimilitude.

Yet despite these flaws, *Rule of the Bone* is an important and serious novel that presents a scathing critique of adult selfishness and irresponsibility while it pays homage to the everlasting resilience of youth.

Robert Niemi

Sources for Further Study

Booklist. XCI, March 1, 1995, p. 1139.
Hungry Mind Review. Summer, 1995, p. 22.
Los Angeles Times Book Review. May 21, 1995, p. 3.
The Nation. CCLX, June 12, 1995, p. 826.
The New Republic. CCXII, May 29, 1995, p. 40.
New Statesman and Society. VIII, July 7, 1995, p. 37.
The New York Times Book Review. C, May 7, 1995, p. 13.
Publishers Weekly. CCXLII, February 20, 1995, p. 193.
Time. CXLV, June 5, 1995, p. 65.
The Washington Post Book World. XXV, June 4, 1995, p. 9.

SABBATH'S THEATER

Author: Philip Roth (1933-   )
Publisher: Houghton Mifflin (Boston). 451 pp. $24.95
Type of work: Novel
Time of work: 1994, with flashbacks over sixty-four years
Locale: The United States

An aging former puppeteer and full-time philanderer recalls the excessive range of his sexual theatrics during the course of choosing whether to end his own life

Principal characters:
MORRIS "MICKEY" SABBATH, a puppeteer, con man, thief, and
    erotomaniac
DRENKA BALICH, his Croatian-born mistress
NIKKI, his first wife, who disappears
ROSEANNA, his second wife, a recovering alcoholic
MORTY SABBATH, his older brother, who is killed in World War II
KATHY, a student whom Mickey seduces
NORMAN COWAN, a friend and host whom he betrays

Toward the end of *Sabbath's Theater*, the novel's sixty-four-year-old protagonist, having chosen and paid (with stolen money) for his burial site, orders a monument over his grave and composes an epitaph for it which reads:

> Morris Sabbath
> "Mickey"
> Beloved Whoremonger, Seducer,
> Sodomist, Abuser of Women,
> Destroyer of Morals, Ensnarer of Youth,
> Uxoricide,
> Suicide
> 1929-1994

The self-portrait is accurate except for the last two lines, since Sabbath decides, at the end of Roth's longest work, that he is not yet ready to die, since "everything he hated was here," and he has an endless supply of loathing for the world.

Sabbath's Theater, which was awarded the 1995 National Book Award for fiction, is Philip Roth's most controversial text, making his notorious *Portnoy's Complaint* (1968) a liberating salute to conscience by comparison. Mickey Sabbath is Roth's most outrageous creation, deserving not only his tombstone's description but such labels as satyr, racist, pagan, nihilist, misanthrope, and all-around, over-the-top transgressor. He is an ideologue of the id, the personification of disorderly conduct and Dionysian excess. Yet he may well be Roth's greatest character, dominating his most ambitious and richest book.

While the novel begins with Mickey already in his sixties and considering suicide, he recalls in vivid scenes his past as youth, sailor, actor, puppeteer, sometime husband, and full-time philanderer. He grew up, like his author, on the New Jersey shore with his beloved older brother, Morty, who joined the Air Corps and was shot down by the Japanese in 1944, and his broken-down parents. His father was a poor, defeated butter-and-egg man, while his mother, driven into catatonic depression by her favorite son's death, took to her bed for two years before dying. (Her ghost haunts Mickey when he is in his sixties.) At seventeen, Mickey Sabbath shipped out as a merchant seaman and, encountering a worldwide field of whoredom, came to prefer what was mockingly known as the Romance Run of South American ports.

By 1953, at twenty-four, Sabbath was a street performer in charge of his Indecent Theater near Columbia University, using his fingers suggestively to perform penile exercises and, when the opportunity arose, unbutton the blouses of young women. That is how he met the six-foot-tall, exotic Nikki, a gifted actress who, enthralled by his cockiness and menacing charm, became his first wife. She was to fascinate him all his life by reminding him of a fairy-tale princess by her beauty and innocence. After she vanished, ten years later, he would increasingly hallucinate about having murdered her—hence the epithet "uxoricide" on his tombstone.

Marriage to Nikki did not keep Sabbath from having an intense, love-hate relationship with Roseanna, an alcoholic artist who was drawn to him because his domineering narcissism reminded her of her sexually abusive, violent father. They married to revile each other, with Roseanna hating his womanizing, self-absorption, and economic dependence on her after he was fired from a local college.

They had moved to a remote Massachusetts town after Nikki's disappearance and after arthritis in his hands had ended his career as puppeteer. Sabbath became an adjunct professor at the college, only to be disgracefully dismissed at age sixty after a tape of his sexually graphic telephone conversations with twenty-year-old Kathy had been "accidentally" left by her in the college library, then acquired by the college dean. Perhaps too obligingly, Roth provides readers with an "uncensored transcription" of the raunchy conversation in a twenty-page footnote. Explicitly stepping into his novel, Roth also advises his public not to be too hard on either Sabbath or Kathy: "Many farcical, illogical, incomprehensible transactions are subsumed by the mania of lust."

Sex, for Sabbath, is the only consolation for a life otherwise shorn of meaningful attachments except for one grand love: his Croatian-born mistress Drenka, wife of the local innkeeper, with whom he played out all of his erotic fantasies for twelve years before she died of ovarian cancer. Drenka was his "genital mate," his female counterpart in lechery, whom he taught to be joyously and voraciously promiscuous. Sabbath was delighted to hear of her lustiest feat: She managed to have sex with three lovers on a one-day trip to Boston, then, back at home, just before midnight, accommodated her husband to achieve a twenty-four-hour quartet. This made her, for the saluting Sabbath, "*a woman of serious importance.*" Their only disagreement occurred when Drenka astounded him by asking him to take a pledge of mutual sexual fidelity with her. He was offended: She self-righteously wished to suppress the satanic side of sex, thereby deforming his nature. After her death, he frequently visited her grave at night to masturbate there, and sometimes observed her other bereaved lovers paying her the same tribute.

The immediate action of the novel occurs after Drenka's death, with Sabbath a desperate, derelict sixty-four-year-old. Sober Roseanna is now a faithful member of Alcoholics Anonymous and preparing to throw him out of their house and marriage; he beats her to the act by leaving her, driving to New York City to attend the funeral of an old friend, a suicide, and to confront his self-destructive past. Roth half-mockingly pushes a Lear parallel for Sabbath: He is "wifeless, mistressless, penniless, vocationless, homeless . . . and now, to top things off, on the run." Both Lear and Sabbath are foolish, outcast, and battered old men, but while Lear rages against his wicked daughters in particular and justice in general, Sabbath can only rage against himself and compose a self-satirizing obituary that concludes, "Mr. Sabbath did nothing for Israel." Roaming the subways of Manhattan on his way to the funeral, he recites passages from *King Lear* while panhandling, imagining Nikki as his abused Cordelia and a sweet young woman on the Lexington IRT as Nikki's daughter. Sabbath now hates everyone, especially himself, and wants to die.

Not so fast. His old friend and former coproducer Norman Cowan, tanned from a tennis vacation—a saint of benevolence, both wealthy and generous—takes Sabbath into his humane Manhattan home. Such compassion is too much for Sabbath: All he knows is how to profane it. He masturbates while holding Norman's daughter's underwear and photograph, terrorizes the Hispanic cleaning woman while the Cowans are at work, and that night, at dinner, plays footsie with what he thinks are the unshod toes of Norman's wife Michelle, a periodontist. It turns out that the foot belonged to Norman, but Sabbath is not to be dissuaded from seeking to seduce Michelle, declaring, "A world without adultery is unthinkable." The next morning an outraged Norman evicts Sabbath after the daughter's underpants are found in his pants pocket. While Norman tries to arrange hospitalization for Sabbath after he has fainted, Sabbath steals ten thousand-dollar bills from Michelle's bedroom and drives away to New Jersey to buy himself a plot in the ravaged Jewish cemetery where his family is buried.

So begin the book's final one hundred pages, and they are brilliantly sustained as Sabbath leaves Lear's world for Hamlet's. He strolls among the graves, greeting the tombstones of his parents, his aunts, and the heroic brother, Lieutenant Morton Sabbath. Roth devotes an entire page to the names of all the buried "beloveds." Having made his funeral arrangements, Sabbath then visits the nearby home of his father's surviving cousin Fish, one hundred years old, "a mere mist of a man," a living death who recalls almost no one and nothing. Sabbath steals from the befuddled centenarian's house a cardboard carton containing his brother's personal belongings, which include a folded-up American flag. He takes the flag to the beach, unfurls it, wraps himself in it, and weeps for hours.

Partially redeemed but as unhappy as ever, Sabbath returns to Massachusetts to say farewell to the memory of Drenka and to kill himself. He composes a mock will, establishing a prize of five hundred dollars to be awarded annually to the college senior who has had sex with more male faculty members than her peers. Wrapped in his brother's flag, he urinates a farewell on Drenka's grave and is apprehended by her policeman son Matthew, who has read the scandalous diary his mother left behind.

Expecting Matthew to murder him, Sabbath is disappointed to be released—and to find that he still wants to live.

What are readers to make of this complex, energetic, disturbing, and provocative novel? Some readers will find it scandalous. Mickey Sabbath is not only sexually compulsive but also nasty, foul-mouthed, self-deluded, and willfully selfish. His narcissism can be considered loathsome, his racism and misanthropy repellent. Norman calls him a "walking panegyric for obscenity" and an "inverted saint whose message is desecration." Many will call him *Homo invectus*.

Nevertheless, *Sabbath's Theater* is also splendidly written and rascally fun to read. Roth gives Sabbath a clowning, perversely confessional, and reckless flow of language in a narrative that moves from phallic exuberance to flashing, slashing wit to a doleful account of suffering and loss. Roth knows how to build a novel, from flashbacks to vivid fantasies, from wild humor to desperate defiance of the world.

Can such a text be tamed into a generic classification? That of the picaresque novel may fit, though not entirely well. Like Reynard the Fox, Lazarillo de Tormes, Falstaff, Moll Flanders, and Felix Krull, Mickey Sabbath is a rogue, a con man and thief who lives by his wits, plays roles guilefully, and is remarkably loquacious, at times eloquent. Also roguish is his sharp insight into responses that he can manipulate to his own advantage, and his shameless indifference to established ethical standards.

Yet the picaresque mode proves too shallow and conventional to contain so devilish a person as Sabbath. He is socially subversive beyond the edge of criminality, ruthlessly willing to violate the well-being of others. His intensity of commitment to sex above all else, his passion for anarchic disruption, makes him one of the most dangerous and excessive protagonists in contemporary fiction. Roth's novel is also a profound account of the infidelity inherent in all flesh. When Norman tells Mickey that he is pathetically outmoded in his parade of his penis, an isolated relic of the 1950's, Sabbath responds defiantly that isolation is preferable to civilization and its discontents. Never will he rest in peace.

Gerhard Brand

Sources for Further Study

Commentary. C, December, 1995, p. 61.
London Review of Books. XVII, October 19, 1995, p. 10.
The New Republic. CCXIII, October 23, 1995, p. 33.
New Statesman and Society. VIII, October 20, 1995, p. 40.
The New York Review of Books. XLII, November 16, 1995, p. 20.
The New York Times Book Review. C, September 10, 1995, p. 7.
Newsweek. CXXVI, August 21, 1995, p. 53.
Partisan Review. LXII, Fall, 1995, p. 699.
Time. CXLVI, September 11, 1995, p. 82.
The Wall Street Journal. August 23, 1995, p. A10.

A SCATTERING OF SALTS

Author: James Merrill (1926-1995)
Publisher: Alfred A. Knopf (New York). 96 pp. $20.00
Type of work: Poetry

The last collection of poems, written between 1988 and 1995 and published shortly after his death, by one of the finest contemporary American poets

James Merrill died on February 6, 1995. *A Scattering of Salts* was the fifteenth and last in a series of collections of poems that began in 1951, when his *First Poems* was published. It brings to an end a career and body of work that became increasingly original with the passage of time.

From the beginning, Merrill was recognized as a master of verse forms and a prodigious technician. He always seemed to be at home with the most demanding requirements of poetry. Even as a young man, Merrill wrote with an almost Augustan control and intricacy. When he was twenty-one—an undergraduate at Amherst—he was worried that his voice was "clogged/ By an upheaval of the intellect." Instead of revolting against form, like the Beats in the mid-1950's and other poets he described as "dishevelled," he was able to use form—and a great variety of forms—for his own ends. In his hands, forms became new and capable of surprise. With some early exceptions, he did not use formal virtuosity for its own sake but as a vehicle in a deliberate search for meaning and exploration of experience.

One of the main themes in Merrill's poetry is autobiography and his own past. He has been criticized for emphasizing autobiography and for self-absorption. The criticism has some merit, and the fact that he was the son of the financier Charles E. Merrill is probably not of outstanding interest. It is the other themes that provide the excitement of this book: love, the passage of time, memory, openness to contemporary experience—a trait amply demonstrated in many poems in *A Scattering of Salts*—and the ability to communicate with the dead.

In "Nine Lives," for example, the narrator of the poem and his friend David Jones sit down at a Ouija board, and promptly receive a message from Bombay. In a brief explanation, Merrill writes:

> I hate to say it, but the neophyte
> Must take the full amazement of this news
> (At least till he can purchase and peruse
> A heavy volume called *The Changing Light*
> *At Sandover*) on faith.

This "heavy" collection of poems, published in 1982 and reissued in 1992, can be easily consulted by a reader interested in learning more about Merrill's ideas concerning the different forms taken by "spirit" and the return of souls. An acquaintance with *The Changing Light at Sandover* helps the reader to appreciate the poems in Merrill's last collection, although it is not a prerequisite. "Nine Lives" deals with cats, humans, and the many lives they both have. Numerous other passages in the collection evoke Merrill's ideas about spiritual communication, for example these lines about the inhabitants and "shades" of a volcanic island in the Pacific ("Volcanic Holiday"):

> Crested like palms, like waves, they too subsist
> On one idea—returning.
> Generation after generation
> The spirit grapples, tattered butterfly,
> A flower in sexual costume.

Merrill has always been a poet of the conceit and the pun, and these are much in evidence in *A Scattering of Salts*. The conceit has an ancient lineage in English literature; it is not eccentric, as some have claimed, and it goes back not only to the metaphysicals but indeed to William Shakespeare, sometimes in and sometimes out of fashion. *A Scattering of Salts* is filled with Merrill's trademark puns and conceits. In "The Great Emigration," his bus in Scotland passes some grazing sheep: "Sheep or stones?/ As we whiz by/ A local rock group/ Begins to bleat." In another poem ("The Ponchielli Complex"), nineteenth century entrepreneurs "tamed the wild/ Horses of steam, made fiction of the trees." Here "fiction" has two senses, a play on a word characteristic of Merrill. "Fat Venetian street/ Singers driven to verismo's brink/ Got their deserts"—that is, they aged. In "A Look Askance," Merrill catches sight of his own poem as it emerges above the carriage of the electric typewriter:

> see how their concrete poem
>
> Keeps towering higher and higher. See also at dusk
> Meaning's quick lineman climb from floor to floor
> Inlaying gloom with beads of hot red ore
>
> That hiss in the ferry's backwash.

A mirror that has been left outdoors reflects the approaching autumn: "Nature grows strong in you. Again last night/ Rustling forth in all her jewelry/ She faced the glacial croupier: Double or nothing!" ("Big Mirror Outdoors").

These are not merely isolated puns or plays on words to catch the reader's attention, but parts of a larger, rich matrix of analogies and correspondences that proves to be almost endless. They form Merrill's representation of the world, his version of mimesis.

These analogies and puns lead naturally to a vision of much larger units: The poem itself becomes a single, dramatized metaphor. The mirror left outdoors registers the globe's four-season cycle, but an analogous cycle is represented by the life of the individual person. If this were only a self-regarding artifice or display of invention, it would be easily forgettable, but the landscape, the narrator, and all people face this same "glacial croupier." On the psychological level it is a recurrent nightmare, "horrifying and harmless," an occurrence lethal and ordinary at the same time, seen through a household mirror.

Another poem on the act of writing, "To the Reader," begins:

Each day, hot off the press from Moon & Son,
"Knowing of your continued interest,"
Here's a new book—well, actually the updated
Edition of their one all-time best seller—
To find last night's place in, and forge ahead.
If certain scenes and situations ("work,"
As the jacket has it, "of a blazingly
Original voice") make you look up from your page
—*But this is life, is truth, is me!*—too many
Smack of self-plagiarism.

The meaning of this playful introductory passage is less elusive than it may seem. A "press"—small, commercial, and needing to advertise—writes of the daily round led by the sun and moon. The "one all-time best seller" is probably the present, and the acute interest that all people take in it. The "blazingly original voice" is each individual voice, original and unique, and universal.

The humor in this passage is typical of Merrill and reflects no strain. Merrill's "work"—writing—is an everyday occurrence and is equivalent to the present; it is "*life*," "*truth*," and "*me*." The humor is to be shared: It points away from isolation or preciosity and toward everyday encounters. "To the Reader" reflects the efforts of the small press known as "Moon & Son," and Merrill's style reflects the fabric of the everyday world.

Humor is central to Merrill's work, and he asks the reader to enjoy it just as he enjoys jokes or stories. Helen Vendler has observed (in "Chronicles of Love and Loss," *The New York Review of Books*, May 11, 1995) that Merrill is basically a comic poet, as were W. H. Auden and George Gordon, Lord Byron. Throughout his life, Merrill had a highly developed sense of comedy and play, and this "play" was both serious and not serious at the same time. Merrill played—often ironically—with the most serious themes; because they were everyday occurrences, it was fitting to treat them with the lightness and gracefulness of play.

Whole poems become metaphors in *A Scattering of Salts*; with Merrill, anything can be compared to anything or everything. No comparison is rejected for conventional or superficial reasons; Merrill's comparisons often cause both surprise and recognition. "Volcanic Holiday," which describes a real volcano, begins:

Our helicopter shaking like a fist
Hovers above the churning
Cauldron of red lead in what a passion!
None but the junior cherubim ask why.
We bank and bolt.

A series of seven seven-line stanzas builds up a concrete setting in the Pacific, a volcano with lava and underground magma. This leads to the history of the islands with their geology, flora, fauna, natives and tribal warfare, missionaries and tourists. As Merrill evokes the themes of instinct, expansion, and compulsion, the poem imperceptibly becomes an exploration of the nature of human sexuality (with the "obstacle course" of adolescence) and human love. After questioning the nature of words and emotion, the poem concludes:

> Meanwhile let green-to-midnight shifts of sky
> Fill sliding mirrors in our room
> —No more eruptions, they entreat—
> With Earth's repose and Heaven's masquerades.

Other poems chart similar long-distance comparisons, and these are among the most original features of this collection of poems, representing its most satisfying artistic achievement and delight. The lengthy and intricate operations of these forms cannot be illustrated by brief quotation; they are conducive to reading for pleasure as well as lengthy analysis and exegesis. The poem "Alabaster," like "Volcanic Holiday," compares a geological process to a human process, in this case aging. "Home Fires" is an extended meditation on the human house or home: the hearth, love, and domesticity. "Self Portrait in Tyvek (TM) Windbreaker" is perhaps the most amusing poem in the collection. It begins with a description of a parka that the narrator has bought that depicts a map of the world; through descriptions of amusing encounters with strangers, the poem becomes an exploration of the nature of the clothes and stores "catering to the collective unconscious/ Of our time and place." One of the longest poems in the book, "Family Week at Oracle Ranch," is set in a New Age rehabilitation center in "our brave new dried-out world"—Arizona. The poem turns into a series of hilarious encounters with social fads ("Pinned to your chest,/ A sign: *Confront Me if I Take Control*") and examines patterns of change and changelessness. It is an excellent example of how satire in Merrill's poetry can gradually build up into cosmology.

A Scattering of Salts contains poems that are formally dazzling, that make the reader burst into laughter, and that at the same time achieve a high level of meaning.

John R. Carpenter

Sources for Further Study

Booklist. XCI, March 15, 1995, p. 1303.
Library Journal. CXX, April 1, 1995, p. 98.
The New Leader. LXXVIII, June 5, 1995, p. 20.
The New Republic. CCXII, June 5, 1995, p. 38.
The New York Review of Books. XLII, May 11, 1995, p. 46.
The New York Times Book Review. C, March 26, 1995, p. 3.
Poetry. CLXVI, September, 1995, p. 354.
Publishers Weekly. CCXLII, February 27, 1995, p. 98.
The Virginia Quarterly Review. LXXI, Autumn, 1995, p. SS137.
The Yale Review. LXXXIII, October, 1995, p. 144.

THE SEARCH FOR THE PERFECT LANGUAGE

Author: Umberto Eco (1932-　　)
First published: Ricerca della lingua perfetta nella cultura europea, 1993, in Italy
Translated from the Italian by James Fentress
Publisher: Blackwell (Cambridge, Massachusetts). 385 pp. $24.95
Type of work: Literary history

This history of attempts to achieve an unattainable linguistic goal proves fascinating in itself, instructive and fruitful in unexpected ways

What is a "perfect language"? To Umberto Eco it might be one regarded as an original or mother tongue of humankind, an artificial one constructed to express ideas more precisely or to achieve universality or practical perfection, or a magical language meant for initiates only. Perfection being a relative concept whose achievement in fulfillment of one linguistic purpose, as in the case of a language intended for general communication worldwide, precludes fulfillment in another, as in that of a truly philosophical language, Eco has had to make a broad survey of notable attempts throughout the centuries, though limiting himself to those by Europeans.

Even measured by a relativistic standard, linguistic perfection is an elusive, not to say illusive, goal. Why, then, does a renowned professor of semiotics such as Eco devote a book to the history of this futile chase? For one thing, it is an activity that has engaged intellectuals of the caliber of Dante Alighieri, René Descartes, and Gottfried Leibniz. For another, it has usually been undertaken with the high-minded goal of overcoming political, religious, or ethnic conflicts and thus promoting universal harmony. Again, its unintended side effects have benefited humanity or at least foreshadowed beneficial achievements. Perhaps most of all, the subject fascinates its author. As to whether Eco succeeds in communicating his fascination to the reader, much depends on the reader. His accounts of the intricacies of these varied linguistic proposals and his criticisms thereof demand close attention and a degree of familiarity with linguistic and philosophical terminology. Any serious reader, however, will be stimulated by Eco's intellectual framework for *The Search for the Perfect Language*.

In his first chapter, "From Adam to *Confusio Linguarum*," as might be expected, Eco cites the profoundly influential eleventh chapter of Genesis, which begins with "the whole earth . . . of one language" and continues with the story of the Tower of Babel and the "confounding" of the builders' language. Then, however, he steps back to the less dramatic, less often noticed, and even less often explained references to the different "tongues" of Noah's sons in Genesis 10. Thus early in Judeo-Christian tradition linguistic confusion—and confusion about that confusion—emerges. Some subsequent pursuers of a perfect language, he alleges, "will oppose Genesis 10 to Genesis 11" with "devastating" results.

An early candidate for perfect language, needless to say, was ancient Hebrew, though its adherents did not agree on the reason. Hebrew was often thought to be the original language, that is, the one God presumably spoke to Adam and Eve; the medieval Jewish cabalistic tradition, on the other hand, favored it for its mystical symbolic density. It remained for Christian Europe a lost language, however, until the Protestant Reformers' insistence on recovering the text of Holy Writ created the necessity of a new biblical scholarship.

Dante, whose *Divina commedia*, or *Divine Comedy* (composed c. 1308-1321), is generally judged the greatest literary work of the Middle Ages, had already (probably between 1303 and 1305) composed the first scheme for a perfect language by a medieval Christian writer, *De vulgari eloquentia* (*On Vernacular Expression*). For Dante the closest approximation to a perfect language was the Italian in which he would compose his great poem. His vote for his own language can be more easily forgiven than the similar partialities of later seekers of the perfect language, none of whom composed the literary masterpiece of his tongue. Yet his preference for the vernacular, despite its enormous implications for subsequent Western literature, clearly did not satisfy the seekers of a perfect language then or later.

At about the same time, a Franciscan friar, Raymond Lull, devised a system for a perfect language as a better way of converting infidels than the use of force. Lull sought to convey a system of universally held ideas by means of a universal mathematics of combination. He drew up a table of nine absolute principles (such as goodness and wisdom), nine relative principles, nine types of question, nine subjects, nine virtues, and nine vices and projected a series of figures to perform operations such as the construction of predications ("Goodness is great") and syllogisms. His most famous figure took the form of a mechanism consisting of three concentric circles which could generate 1,680 answers to an established set of questions. Eco explains and criticizes this way of producing a vast quantity of philosophical content from fifty-four concepts (whose preestablished definitions were assumed). Lull's perfect language, relying on mathematics and deductive logic, inspired a plethora of similar attempts in the centuries to follow, and it is easy to see that his was the type of mind that in the electronic age would require, and inevitably produce, the computer.

After a series of chapters tracing developments in the camps of the monogeneticists (those who assumed that all languages descended from one mother tongue), the cabalists, and the Lullists, Eco turns to the pursuit of a perfect hieroglyphic language by those entranced by the idea of promoting communication by a language of images, ideograms, and phonograms after the model of languages like Egyptian or Chinese. Egyptian hieroglyphs could not be understood at all until the discovery of the Rosetta Stone in 1799, but Chinese, used daily by millions of people, suggested the possibility of a universal visual alphabet. Attempts along this line ran into great difficulties in developing an adequate grammatical structure and overcoming the lack of connotative flexibility in an artificial imagistic language and its inability to express new ideas. Ambitious claims for imagistic systems of communication nevertheless have persisted into the age of television. Eco compares exclusive visual communication by television to Jonathan Swift's wise men with their bags of things as referents, except that today one relying on such a visual language might need to go about carrying a camcorder, a portable television set, and a quantity of tapes.

Even the problem of radioactive waste disposal has inspired attempts at a universal language of images. Burial of such waste raises the question of how, ten thousand years from now when perhaps humans have lapsed into barbarism, people can be adequately warned about danger zones of still radioactive material. Supposing there were an influx of visitors from other planets, how would *they* be warned? A reliable imagistic language of at least rudimentary proportions might be the only way.

The great age of the pursuit of perfect languages seems to have been the seventeenth century. It is striking that three of the most influential English thinkers of the century—Francis Bacon, Thomas Hobbes, and John Locke—all dilated on the imprecision of natural languages and the confusion arising when a word signifies one thing to its user and another to its recipient. While not himself an inventor of an artificial language, Bacon, especially in that section of his *Novum Organum* (1620) which discusses his famous Four Idols, focused attention on the deficiencies of natural language. His most troublesome Idols, those of the "Market-place," consist of words that stand for nothing real (his examples being "Fortune," "Prime Mover," "Planetary Orbits," and "Element of Fire") as well as those "confusedly applied." For Bacon "humid" is an example of the latter, as is "earth," though he finds "mud" acceptable. When the Royal Society of London was formally instituted in the 1660's, one of its preeminent concerns became, in the words of its historian Thomas Sprat, "this vicious abundance of Phrase, this trick of Metaphors, this volubility of Tongue." In short, he laid the blame for linguistic confusion on poets.

The men whose labors Eco describes, however, were not going to waste their time rescuing the various vernaculars from the poets, and even the dead language (Latin) in which Bacon composed the *Novum Organum* no longer answered the need for an international language of science and philosophy. Linguistic criticisms such as Bacon's confirmed in their minds the need for an a priori language that would bind expression and content together indissolubly.

Some of the efforts in that direction were arcane indeed. Joachim Becher, for example, devised an "atrociously complicated" graphic language involving figures with a network of lines and dots whose number and position signified lexical and grammatical categories; Gaspar Schott later simplified it somewhat, but as a mode of communication it proved a failure, although it did anticipate computer translation in certain ways. To Eco, Becher's system suggests instructions like those that retrieve items from a computer's memory. Meanwhile, both the seekers of a polygraphy (a language intended for international communication, presumably available to all) and pursuers of a steganography (a secret or encoded language for insiders) remained busy. A Jesuit named Athanasius Kircher even produced one of each.

Paradoxically, the efforts of Leibniz, one of the most distinguished of the men attempting to construct a truly philosophical language, in effect turned the tide against this sort of endeavor by demonstrating the severe limitations of the a priori philosophical language. Thought and language were at length perceived as too tightly linked: The stubbornly recurrent lexical and grammatical changes of natural languages guaranteed that any perfect language of thought would soon be left behind—the last place an advanced thinker wanted to be. Leibniz's language is one of "pure syntax," incapable of what Eco calls "truths of fact," though sufficient for "truths of reason." Thus his calculus anticipated, more profoundly than any previous system of communication, the computer languages of today.

In addition, Leibniz's persistent but fruitless attempt to identify the primitives of language—that is, the basic but indefinable terms—pointed in the direction of an alternative, the eighteenth century encyclopedic movement, by which the available knowledge of the world would be organized and indexed so that a seeker could study a subject or subjects from varying points of view. This form of presenting knowledge incorporates at least the germ of the notion of "hypertext," a term that, familiar as it is to millions of computer users now, had in 1992 not made its way into the tenth edition of *Merriam Webster's Collegiate Dictionary.*

The eighteenth century also became interested in the possibility of a "deep" grammar common to all human languages, but Western linguistic thinkers tended to assume the universality of the grammatical structure underlying the family of languages that in the next century would be called Indo-European. Modern generative and transformational grammars clearly owe much to this trend.

Growing recognition that perfect languages could not escape dependence on existing natural languages or families of such languages discouraged the more utopian linguistic schemes thereafter, and in the late nineteenth century attention turned increasingly to artificial languages of the sort called "international auxiliary languages" (IALs), the best known of which is undoubtedly Esperanto, proposed in 1887. Like many earlier aspirers to universal languages, Ledger Ludwik Zamenhof, a Jew who had experienced much anti-Semitism in his homeland of Lithuania, offered Esperanto as part of a program for promoting peace and harmony in the world. Not surprisingly, Russia's czarist government banned it early in the century, and later the Nazis persecuted its speakers in nations under their control. Nevertheless, Esperanto survived and even prospered, probably because Zamenhof aimed not at perfection but at flexibility and grammatical simplicity, with the result that Esperanto has won plaudits from such linguists and philosophers as Otto Jespersen, Bertrand Russell, and Rudolf Carnap. Eco notes that more than one hundred periodicals and "most of world literature" can be read in Esperanto.

Esperanto and other a posteriori languages fall far short of the dream of the perfectly philosophical language capable of expressing all human ideas unambiguously, and there is always the danger of their breaking, like natural languages, into a variety of dialects, but their very status as auxiliary languages minimizes this latter difficulty. Eco closes his chapter on IALs by speculating on their prospects in an international community characterized by linguistic fragmentation.

Eco ends his book with another seeming biblical contradiction. In Acts 2, after a descent of Pentecostal fire, the apostles "began to speak with other tongues"; 1 Corinthians, on the other hand, seems to describe a "gift of tongues" that is an ecstatic but understandable language. Does the achievement of human concord involve a restoration of the conditions before Babel or a consecration of the ensuing polyglotism? Eco does not venture an interpretation of these conflicting passages but suggests that we must balance the need of humans for a common language with the need to maintain particular linguistic heritages. Aware of the Western linguistic limitations of his book, he closes by citing a myth found in the work of the Arab writer Ibn Hazm that holds the original linguistic gift to be a complex of all languages, but Adam sinned before he had mastered it, and thus its achievement was left to his descendants.

Robert P. Ellis

Sources for Further Study

Boston Globe. November 5, 1995, p. 70.
Library Journal. CXX, September 15, 1995, p. 66.
London Review of Books. XVII, November 16, 1995, p. 13.
New Statesman and Society . VIII, October 6, 1995, p. 39.
The New York Times. November 28, 1995, p. C13.
Publishers Weekly. CCXLII, August 14, 1995, p. 68.
The Times Literary Supplement. November 3, 1995, p. 27.

THE SECRET WORLD OF AMERICAN COMMUNISM

Editors: Harvey Klehr, John Earl Haynes, and Fridrikh Igorevich Firsov
Publisher: Yale University Press (New Haven, Connecticut). 348 pp. $25.00
Type of work: Political history
Time: 1919-1945
Locale: The United States and the Soviet Union

A carefully edited volume in a series, the Annals of Communism, *exposing the internal workings of the American Communist Party and demonstrating the great extent to which it was a clandestine and criminal conspiratorial organization, intent on the subversion of American institutions and beholden to the Soviet Union*

The key question for historians of the American Communist Party has always been whether it was a political party like any other operating within the laws of the United States. As the editors of this volume note in their introduction, many historians have given a qualified yes to the question, admitting that there may have been some Communist spies but contending that the overwhelming majority of party members were loyal, if dissenting, Americans. The editors call these historians revisionists, and throughout this volume they conduct an argument against what they consider to be an excessively charitable view of the American Communist Party's activities.

Yet what have the revisionist historians been revising? They developed their views during the Cold War (1945-1992), when the Soviet Union and the United States were the two great superpowers engaged in a tense rivalry. Revisionists argue that this competition stimulated a fanatical anti-Communism, skewing U.S. government policy into hostile interpretations of every Soviet move and polluting the American political atmosphere (with politicians such as Senator Joseph McCarthy accusing government employees, some in high positions, of treason). Revisionists point out that few employees were actually convicted of disloyalty, and in the celebrated case of Alger Hiss, who was found guilty of conspiracy to commit espionage, these historians have doubted the soundness of the government's evidence and even suspected the Justice Department or the Federal Bureau of Intelligence (FBI) of contriving to incriminate Hiss. Similar doubts have been expressed about the executions of Julius and Ethel Rosenberg for spying. Revisionists have also attacked the testimony of former Communists, often treating figures such as Elizabeth Bentley, Whittaker Chambers, and Louis Budenz as mentally unbalanced witnesses who enjoyed the spotlight and sensationalized their meager evidence.

Other historians—they might be called the traditionalists—have offered proofs of the Communist conspiracy to refute the revisionists. Yet traditionalists have not been entirely convincing, because they have not had access to classified U.S. government information or to the records of the American Communist Party. This situation has now changed in one significant respect. The archives of the American Communist Party, housed in the former Soviet Union, have been opened to American scholars. *The Secret World of American Communism* is only the first volume in the presentation and analysis of that archive, but it goes a long way, as the editors suggest, toward corroborating traditionalists' interpretations.

Document after document in this volume demonstrates that the American Communist Party slavishly followed the Soviet line. American party members who did express independence were punished and expelled from the organization. They were considered deviationists, undermining the struggles of the working class and the discipline of the party. When a wife of a party member was suspected of disloyalty, her husband was expected to abandon her. When the American party developed factions, the Comintern (established by Vladimir Ilich Lenin as the directing body for all Communist parties) decided which faction would triumph. All matters, great and small, were submitted to Soviet bureaucrats for approval.

Indeed, many of the documents in this volume make for tedious reading because American party members minutely recorded and justified the simplest activities and the most trivial disputes. Everything took on world-shaking importance for them, because they were beholden to the Soviet Union and worried about what their Soviet comrades would think of their work.

In total numbers, American Communist Party membership never exceeded one hundred thousand members. It never represented a direct threat to the stability of the U.S. government. As the editors of this volume show, however, the party's influence far exceeded its small size. Communists infiltrated labor unions and influenced their policies. Among the documents presented in this volume there are government documents, obviously copied by U.S. government employees, which gave the Soviet Union an inside view of how U.S. policy was shaped. Even intelligence services such as the Office of Strategic Services (the forerunner of the Central Intelligence Agency) harbored Communists.

Revisionists have contended that the presence of Communists did not necessarily mean that agencies were being subverted. Yet documents in this volume destroy the claims of several Communists who proclaimed their loyalty to the United States in public; actually these Communists took their cues from their Soviet masters. For example, Milton Wolff, who commanded Americans fighting for the Spanish Republic, still denies his ties to the Communist Party, although the editors produce documents of his party membership and trace the record of his lifelong fidelity to the Communist line.

This volume also goes a long way toward corroborating the testimony of former Communists Bentley, Chambers, and Budenz. Some of their allegations, which could not be proved in the 1950's, are given significant support in these documents. The editors are careful to say that not all charges of these anti-Communists have been substantiated, but the damage to the revisionist case is massive.

There can be no question now that Communists did infiltrate government agencies in the 1930's and 1940's and that the culmination of Communist underground work was the theft of crucial data about the atom bomb developed at Los Alamos, New Mexico. The American Communist Party worked closely with Soviet intelligence, sometimes suggesting likely spies even as U.S. government officials were slow to realize that a cadre of treasonous employees had infiltrated the bureaucracy.

It is this record of deception that most disturbs the editors of this volume. Communists lied to their government employers, many of them liberal democrats who had joined ranks with the Communist Party in the "Popular Front" period (1934-1939), when the party suddenly stopped attacking Franklin Delano Roosevelt and called for a united crusade against Fascism. Some liberals were inclined to reject and even attack the charges of anti-Communists (liberals and conservatives) who complained of clandestine Communist activity. In turn, certain anti-Communists branded pro-Communist liberals untrustworthy. In this way, Communists divided the American political landscape. As the editors conclude, Communist duplicity prepared the conditions in which Senator Joseph McCarthy could thrive, because American politics had been manipulated and factionalized by an American Communist Party that did not reveal its secret agenda.

Yet the agenda was apparent to certain anti-Communists—even those who had never been party members or sympathizers. The public record showed the American Communists' slavish following of the Soviet line. For example, before 1934 the party was anti-Roosevelt, calling him the worst kind of capitalist and imperialist. After Roosevelt's administration recognized the Soviet Union and established an embassy in Moscow, the Soviet line changed and that of the American party along with it, so that Roosevelt became an ally in the anti-Fascist cause. Then when Joseph Stalin signed a nonaggression pact with Germany, Communists once again, at Stalin's bidding, attacked Roosevelt and his support for an "imperialist war" with Germany. Wolff, the brave anti-Fascist fighter in Spain, himself took this line, even though as late as 1992 he claimed to the editors of this volume that he always supported anti-Fascists.

The earliest declarations of the American Communist Party (1919-1922) emphasized the need for world revolution and the violent overthrow of the U.S. government. This policy was printed in a party newspaper, and internally the party never abandoned it, although in its heyday (1934-1945) it presented itself to the public as merely a political party on the Left fighting for equal rights for blacks, decent wages for workers, and other democratic causes.

The documents in this volume prove beyond doubt that there was never a period when the party did not function as a criminal conspiracy. It always had an illegal branch and recruited spies. Certainly many party members never knew of this branch, or chose not to examine too closely the possibility that one existed. Yet other party members volunteered for service as underground agents, and many lived their entire lives with this separate, compartmentalized, secret career revealed for the first time in this volume.

It is often said that the facts or the documents speak for themselves. The editors of this volume do not believe this cliché and point out a specific case of a document that is seriously misleading. Earl Browder, head of the Communist Party from 1934 to 1945, claimed to have a direct line to President Roosevelt. In one document he even refers to a conversation he had with the president. In fact, he believed that he was working through an intermediary, Josephine Truslow Adams. Through Adams,

Browder supposed that he had access to important government information at the highest level and that he could influence American policy. Adams had some credibility because she did know Eleanor Roosevelt, although she made the most of a slight acquaintance. In fact, Adams was mentally unbalanced and was later institutionalized. When she tried to write a book on her role as intermediary between Browder and Roosevelt, her editor had to abandon the project, realizing that she had fabricated letters from Roosevelt, filling them with her own phraseology and fantasies.

On the face of it, Browder's claims are shocking, especially because he confidently refers in his reports to the Soviet to his conversations with the president. The editors of this volume point out that Browder wanted to believe that he had influence, that he was part of a world revolution, and that he merited special consideration from the Soviets. In short, he was bragging. Rumors circulated among party members and their friends that Earl Browder had a line into the White House. Party prestige was enhanced, and its apocalyptic fantasies were furthered.

As the editors note, historical context is essential in reading the documents in their book, and they provide as much not only in introductions and footnotes but also in a carefully worded introduction, a glossary of individuals and organizations, a chronology of American Communism, a description of the archival record, and an appendix on the organization of the American Communist Party. Thus readers are exposed to both the documents themselves (often reproduced in facsimile) and the editors' interpretations.

It is clear that the editors believe that the main points of the traditional school of historians have been vindicated. Yet the editors do not merely dismiss the revisionists; rather, they show where the revisionist argument is weakest and where more evidence is still needed to analyze both revisionist and traditionalist arguments.

Additional volumes in this series will perhaps support what in this volume remain the editors' hypotheses. For example, they suggest that if Soviet spies, aided by the American Communist Party, had not stolen vital information about the atomic bomb, perhaps Stalin (in possession then of his own bomb) would not have supported the North Korean Communist invasion of South Korea and perhaps the Chinese Communists would have refrained from entering the war. In general, Communist aggression might not have been so virulent had the United States kept its nuclear monopoly, the editors speculate.

This "what if" line of reasoning is precarious. Even though Stalin had a bomb, he did not have the missile delivery system to attack the United States, and he probably would have sustained nearly total annihilation from the vastly greater American arsenal. What effect an American nuclear monopoly might have had on Stalin and his successors is not really subject to historical interpretation, since it is a condition that did not exist. Yet subsequent volumes in this series may reveal Soviet perceptions of American nuclear might, if the documents provide insight not only into the American party but into their Soviet masters' minds.

Carl Rollyson

Sources for Further Study

Library Journal. CXX, June 1, 1995, p. 136.
The Nation. CCLX, June 12, 1995, p. 846.
National Review. XLVII, June 12, 1995, p. 63.
The New Leader. LXXVIII, June 5, 1995, p. 3.
The New Republic. CCXII, May 29, 1995, p. 36.
The New York Review of Books. XLII, July 13, 1995, p. 29.
The New York Times Book Review. C, May 14, 1995, p. 21.
The Times Literary Supplement. June 2, 1995, p. 5.
The Wall Street Journal. April 20, 1995, p. A10.
The Washington Post Book World. XXV, May 21, 1995, p. 1.

A SELECTED PROSE

Author: Robert Duncan (1919-1988)
Edited, with an introduction, by Robert J. Bertholf
Publisher: New Directions (New York). 230 pp. $24.95
Type of work: Essays

In a posthumous collection of representative essays by poet Robert Duncan, editor Robert Bertholf presents the reader with Duncan's views on subjects great and small, ranging from poetry and homosexuality to cosmology and bees

At some as yet unknown point after the beginning of the twentieth century, North American transcendentalism moved from the East to the West Coast. Influenced equally by German and English Romanticism and Chinese and Indian religions, American individualist philosophy flowered in the nineteenth century writings of Ralph Waldo Emerson, Henry David Thoreau, Margaret Fuller, and Walt Whitman. While the essays of Emerson found an immediate ear in the international literary world, many other transcendentalist writers waited outside institutional doors for years before receiving their literary canonization. East Coast optimism and idealism eventually paled before the advance of a mercantile realism; as Thoreau once wryly remarked, even in the 1840's one could determine the true worth of Boston by counting the number of barrels being unloaded at the harbor. The late San Francisco Bay Area poet Robert Duncan, an admitted poetic descendant of the bard of Brooklyn, Walt Whitman, argues for human potentiality and human freedom in the essays found in *A Selected Prose*, often with the deliberation of a twentieth century Emerson, though occasionally with the circumlocution of a Fuller. Duncan also shares the transcendentalists' wide interests in science, religion, and cosmology, all the while maintaining the necessary cutting humor of a Thoreau. As Duncan writes in "Pages from a Notebook," one of the essays included in *A Selected Prose*, "What I lack in pretension I make up in wit."

While the majority of the selections included in the text by editor Robert J. Bertholf concern themselves with poetry and the graphic arts, some of the most important deal with Duncan's views on politics and sexuality. For Duncan, the two issues were related: As (apparently) the first North American writer to present openly his homosexuality in the context of public debate, he knew well the political and practical consequences of honest statements concerning sexuality. The French critic Roland Barthes once remarked that in America, sex is everywhere but in the act itself. Duncan was equally unhappy with American attitudes about sexual identity and activity. His 1944 essay "The Homosexual in Society," which appeared in the journal *Politics*, was, as he notes, "the first discussion of homosexuality which included the frank avowal that the author was himself involved." Such an occurrence should have guaranteed Duncan a place in the pantheon of the gay rights movement. Duncan, however, as a good dialectician, places considerable fault on the actions of homosexuals, saying that their adoption of a narrow sexual identity could be just as limiting as a narrow adoption of heterosexuality. The expanded version of the essay presented in the text was finished in 1959; notably, it was not printed during Duncan's lifetime.

The revised version of the essay begins with a lengthy introduction that constitutes as much a statement on sexual politics as sexuality. Duncan begins, "My view was that minority associations and identifications were an evil wherever they supersede allegiance to and share in the creation of a human community good—the recognition of fellow-manhood." This statement fits into his poet-persona as a representative man. Notably, Duncan maintains the possibility of minority identification as a means to community, as long as it does not impinge on or exclude the creation of a larger human society. His ideas on the body politic, he writes in 1959, came through, among others, his "Socialist and Anarchist associations." Duncan sees, in retrospect, that his idealistic political views were about as likely to draw approval as his admission of his homosexuality.

Beginning with this idealistic position, Duncan criticizes the hypocrisy and narrow-mindedness of both the straight and the gay communities. Both, he argues, base their identity on principles of exclusion rather than inclusion. In particular, he notes the specialized vocabulary of gay circles and the derogatory names given to those who are not among the initiated (just as homosexual "camp" has gained a following among the hip on college campuses and society at large). While once a member of the "camp," Duncan rejects it as an obstacle to human freedom. He concludes, in a section added in 1959, with an idealistic Blakean statement regarding sexuality: "Love is dishonored where sexual love between those of the same sex is despised; and where love is dishonored there is no public trust." Sexual identity, according to Duncan, should be a way of creating connections among people and not used as a principle of exclusion.

Duncan's appeal to a universal sexuality parallels his poetics. He subscribes to the poetic principles of Charles Olson, who wrote in the 1950 polemical essay "Projective Verse" that poems must connect "the HEART, by way of the BREATH, to the LINE." By insisting on the importance of the body as well as the mind in the construction of a poem, Olson provided Duncan with a needed antidote to the academic orientation and theories of a poet such as T. S. Eliot. Instead, Duncan became a student of the vernacular, admiring poets as diverse as Dante, Whitman, and William Carlos Williams. The poems of Whitman's *Leaves of Grass* (1855-1892) and Williams' *Paterson* (1946-1958) became his benchmarks.

Duncan displays his poetic predilections most thoroughly in his 1970 essay on the poetry of Whitman, titled "Changing Perspectives in Reading Whitman." Just as Duncan was aware of the contradictions implicit in identification with the gay community, he recognized the problems inherent in Whitman's poetic persona. He begins his examination with a comparison of Whitman's and Dante's views on the use of the vernacular. Whitman, like Dante and William Wordsworth, found the spirit of humankind in the language of everyday life, though Whitman democratically extended the idea of pure language to children and illiterates. Whitman, Duncan argues, is best seen as a questioner and unsettler, taking his cue from the writings of Thomas Carlyle and Emerson. This brings about one of the first contradictions that Duncan finds in

Whitman's writing, the belief in the wisdom of the common person versus the grim realities of everyday life in the United States, including slavery and other forms of exploitation.

Duncan attempts to explain the contradiction by reference to one of Whitman's models in old age, the writer that Duncan finds Whitman closest to, the German philosopher G. W. F. Hegel. In Whitman's version of the Hegelian dialectic, explains Duncan, democracy is not the end of a process, a fulfillment of a dialectic, but a continual unfolding that allows human freedom to exist. Whitman finds in all the contradictions of society one eternal purpose, just as Emerson found the "eternal generator" in his otherwise decentering essay "Circles." Duncan, with the advantage of hindsight, sees the downside of Whitman's Americanism, imperialism and intolerance. Yet, Duncan argues, Whitman's consideration of the multiple layers of Democracy gives force to his poetry; his internalization of contradiction brings forth the contradictions within the reader. By recognizing the multivocalic nature of Whitman's poetry, Duncan anticipates much of the literary criticism of the 1990's.

Duncan also uses Whitman's writing, both prose and poetry, to elaborate on two of his favorite topics, sexuality and literary criticism. While the two may not seem related on the surface, Duncan provides a persuasive argument that goes to the root of his theory of poetics. Poetry, argues Duncan, following Olson, is a matter of the body, the line coming from the breath or, as in Whitman's case, the line coming from the breath of the vernacular. Because of this linkage, the poet needs the freedom to choose his or her particular form to help express individual experience. Whitman's free verse, Duncan writes, expresses his contradictory experience: individual freedom against the commodification and alienation of capitalism, homosexual desires versus officially puritanical culture. Whitman's great innovation became his adaptation of a vocal musical form to poetry, translating his love of Italian opera, and even bird song, into verse. His ability to use this new medium allowed Whitman to create a body of words that communicate an experience beyond the self.

Duncan then contrasts Whitman's practice of poetics with the reigning literary ideas of his own time, the New Criticism of the 1940's and 1950's. Duncan, like the New England Transcendentalists, considered himself an outsider when it came to institutional correctness. The New Criticism promoted strict, regular form and irony above other literary values. Duncan lambastes the New Critics as the functionaries of consumer capitalism, reducing the sublime art of poetry to packaging, with literary critics becoming the equivalent of consumer researchers. Having given in to the social realities of the marketplace, Duncan argues, the New Criticism effectively made poetry merely another product in the marketplace of ideas, and a rather marginal one at that. By celebrating Whitman as a model, Duncan hopes to liberate poetry from this stranglehold of form and economy.

In addition to his writing on poetry, some of Duncan's best writing deals with the graphic arts; here he shows the same anti-institutional and nonconforming spirit exhibited in his other writing. Duncan was personally acquainted with many artists who lived in the Bay Area and writes persuasively and knowledgeably on their behalf.

Jess, the artist who happened to be Duncan's longtime companion, receives the most extended commentary included in the collection, in an essay intended to serve as an introduction to his Translation series. Also included in the text are brief notes on the works of Henry Jacobus and George Herms. A significant piece of cultural history is contained in Duncan's essay titled "Wallace Berman: The Fashioning Spirit." Berman's artistic talents lay in the direction of the collage, or assemblage of images. He was also an advocate and participant of the West Coast and Beat drug culture and was found guilty of displaying pornographic material in 1957. Berman's belief in the importance of collage was central to his work, argues Duncan, who considers Berman the artist of context. Duncan, who avoided the drug culture, still managed to offer an kind of justification of Berman's drug use. Following the work of the French writer Antonin Artaud, Berman needed to return to the dark period that functions as the initial stage of individuation. Duncan even dedicated a poem to Wallace and Shirley Berman, celebrating their art as a means of the survival of spirit even as it was being trashed in the modern world. This celebration eventually led to the art of trash and the "found object" among artists in the Bay Area, Berman included. As Duncan writes, "The word 'junk' that in the 1950's would have meant the trashing of the drug heroin, in the 1960's came to mean the redemption of trash in the recognition of devotional objects, emblems and signs rescued from the bottom in the art of a new context."

Duncan's collection of essays as a whole reveals a mind firmly involved in the workings of art and politics. As a firm believer in the unfolding of the thought and the appropriateness of form to content, Duncan occasionally writes in an exceptionally dense and hyperbolic fashion. His strengths also tend to be his weaknesses: The fascination that is created in "[The Matter of the Bees]" is counterbalanced by the ramblings in the overly lengthy selection "Rites of Participation," where he goes walkabout with Australian mythology.

Duncan's current place in the canon of poetry and poetics may lie in the hands of his despised university and institutional critics, but his writing also remains a property of the culture at large. In it he has maintained a great idealistic tradition, though, like many of his transcendentalist predecessors, he may have written for an audience of the future.

Jeff Cupp

Sources for Further Study

Booklist. XCI, April 1, 1995, p. 1373.
Publishers Weekly. CCXLII, January 9, 1995, p. 52.

THE SELECTED WRITINGS OF JAMES WELDON JOHNSON
Volume I: The *New York Age* Editorials (1914-1923)
Volume II: Social, Political, and Literary Essays

Author: James Weldon Johnson (1871-1938)
Edited, with an introduction, by Sondra Kathryn Wilson
Publisher: Oxford University Press (New York). Volume I, 305 pp. $45.00; Volume II, 457 pp., $49.95
Type of work: Selected writings

A two-volume collection of selected editorials, articles, poetry, and fiction by the author of "Lift Every Voice and Sing" and The Autobiography of an Ex-Coloured Man

James Weldon Johnson is best known as the author of the words of what is still sometimes called the Negro national anthem, "Lift Every Voice and Sing," as well as the oft-neglected but never forgotten novel *The Autobiography of an Ex-Coloured Man* (1912), which is included in volume 2 of *The Selected Writings of James Weldon Johnson.* Editor Sondra Kathryn Wilson is interested in excavating the writings of a complete public intellectual, a man who, apart from his literary accomplishments, had much to say about politics, religion, American imperialism, literature, and race matters. Though the words and ideas on these pages are not of uniformly high quality, they certainly deserve to be preserved and disseminated. Whether these writings will convince readers to share Wilson's view that "his [Johnson's] influence must be subsumed into mainstream twenty-first century American thought" is another matter, but they succeed in her more modest goal of showing Johnson as a mass educator of black and white Americans who had special insights into the race issues of his day.

Johnson (born in 1871) was an activist high school principal of the Stanton School in Jacksonville, Florida (the largest black high school in the state), and the first African American member of the Florida bar when, in 1900, he wrote the words to "Lift Every Voice and Sing" (his brother, John Rosamond Johnson, wrote the music). It would come to serve as an uplifting anthem for black schools and organizations for years to come. The following year he was nearly lynched, an event that convinced him to leave the South for New York City. In his thirties, he became a songwriter, musician, and political activist, writing songs for the Teddy Roosevelt campaign. Roosevelt appointed him consul first to Venezuela, in 1906, and later to Nicaragua, in 1909. In 1912, Johnson published the work that remains his best argument for literary permanence, *The Autobiography of an Ex-Coloured Man.* After resigning from the consular service, in part because of the racial prejudice he encountered, he was appointed contributing editor of *New York Age,* one of the most important black newspapers of the day, and two years later he joined the staff of the National Association for the Advancement of Colored People (NAACP), the organization he was eventually to lead. Volume 1 focuses on this period of his life, 1914-1923, reprinting and organizing by theme selected editorials from the pages of *New York Age.*

Casual readers who may or may not have read other African American works from this period, such as W. E. B. Du Bois' *The Souls of Black Folk* (1903) or Booker T. Washington's *Up from Slavery: An Autobiography* (1901), will find these editorials pithy, intelligent, diverting, and occasionally eerie. Some of Johnson's concerns about violence, police treatment of black men, and the equality and privileges of women could as easily have been written in 1995 as in 1922. Readers who consider themselves serious students of African American literature, political journalism, or American race relations will find these editorials to be absorbing, necessary reading, a lens carefully ground to reveal a small portion of the past in sharp detail.

As a commentator, Johnson was fairly conservative. Letters to the editor would have their grammar, logic, and rhetoric analyzed and corrected before getting a response, regardless of what Johnson thought of the merits of their position. In another vein, he repeatedly criticized Marcus Garvey, ridiculing his plans to arrange a mass exodus of African Americans to Africa and his publicity stunts designed to support this scheme. Johnson did, however, acknowledge Garvey's ability to stir the imagination of the black population, and his harshest words were reserved for white leaders, not black ones.

Wilson has arranged the reprinted editorials into fourteen thematically grouped sections. The first section, "Race Prejudice and Discrimination," begins with an editorial attacking Henry Ford for comments on the supposed inferiority of the Negro skull, though Johnson commends Ford for hiring at least a limited number of black men in his factories. In later editorials he attacks D. W. Griffith for his film *The Birth of a Nation* (1915) and Thomas Dixon for his book *The Clansman: A Historical Romance of the Ku Klux Klan* (1905), on which the film was based. The onset of World War I finds him publicly rebutting any insinuation that American Negroes are in sympathy with the pro-German fringe, while urging his black readership to take advantage of the possibilities that military service offers to prove their value and patriotism. After the war, he fought in the court of public opinion for the respect that black soldiers had earned but were not receiving.

Of black churches, Johnson shows himself to be both a strong supporter and a firm, if loving, critic. In the editorials collected under the topic "religion," he urges young African Americans to consider the ministry as a profession and urges the church to be entirely worthy of the leadership position it held within the black community. "Union," he urges church leaders, "is what we need."

The short, pointed form of the editorial serves Johnson well when he is discussing specific social wrongs and accomplishments, but more unevenly when he turns his attention to literature and music. A July 20, 1918, editorial finds him agreeing with a comment by H. L. Mencken that the South had given birth to only one outstanding writer in its history; Johnson suggests the reason may have been that much of the South's energy was wasted trying to keep black people down. The desire to defend slavery and Jim Crow separation certainly did degrade much of the southern literature of the time. Mencken's judgment, however, is ridiculous. The closing decades of the nineteenth century had produced Joel Chandler Harris, Mark Twain, George Washington Cable, and Kate Chopin, among other southern writers; of these, the first three were active, vocal opponents to segregation. Mencken could get away with making outlandish statements; for Johnson to try to build a serious argument around such a statement, however, unwise.

Volume 2 includes much material Johnson wrote while he was active with the NAACP, first as field secretary and later as acting secretary. Subtitled *Social, Political, and Literary Essays* (somewhat deceptively, as the volume also includes fiction and poetry), volume 2 has a broader focus than the first volume, reprinting as it does material from books, magazines, newspapers, and even Johnson's college days. The tone and content are far more varied than is the case in the first volume, yet the portrait that emerges is not at all that of a dilettante, but of a man who was passionately interested in debating truth and ideas.

As in the first volume, the organization in volume 2 is thematic. Part 1 reprints articles on social issues from a variety of sources; most are from *The Crisis*, the official NAACP newspaper. One, titled "Negro Americans, What Now?" was originally published as a pamphlet. Written toward the end of his life, "Negro Americans, What Now?" is a defense of NAACP policies by a man who had been the organization's director for many years. It was written in the aftermath of the collapse of the Harlem Renaissance and, more specifically, Du Bois' call for black separatism. Johnson traces the development of various suggested solutions to the problem of race discrimination and rejects most of them. The possibility of mass exodus, he notes, had long been suggested, but he dismisses the suggestion that an exodus of twelve or more million people could peacefully resettle any place on earth. Noting that communism had recently captured the attention of many black people (particularly Richard Wright), Johnson argues that it represents another false promise. According to Johnson, the United States would be far more likely to convert to fascism than to communism. Similarly, he believes that blacks would be foolish to accept any sort of political self-segregation, such as Du Bois had suggested. The only answer is full integration of African Americans into the mainstream political process. To answer his own "what now?" question, he remarks that the days ahead will demand that blacks be willing to both fight and work for their rights, and he offers a pledge that he has tried to keep, which says in part:

I WILL NOT ALLOW ONE PREJUDICED PERSON OR ONE MILLION OR ONE HUNDRED MILLION TO BLIGHT MY LIFE. . . . MY INNER LIFE IS MINE, AND I SHALL DEFEND AND MAINTAIN ITS INTEGRITY AGAINST ALL THE POWERS OF HELL.

Johnson does not expect such a pledge to answer all the complex social and racial problems that he has noted; rather, it is a statement of personal direction that he hopes will help his readers find their way to answers throughout their lives.

Johnson's novel, *The Autobiography of an Ex-Coloured Man*, the longest single work in either of these volumes, was originally published anonymously in 1912. Although Johnson's friends, and quite a few other people, knew that he had written it as a novel, it was frequently read and reviewed as an autobiography. This genre confusion is an entirely appropriate reflection of the race confusion that the main character experiences. Born believing himself to be socially as white as his skin, the main character discovers as a boy that both he and his mother have black ancestry and thus, in the world of the South, are considered black. After an initial shock, he embraces this new self-definition. He travels around the country and, thanks to a wealthy sponsor, around the world, learning what it means to be black and becoming a pianist whose forte is translating themes from a ragtime to a classical idiom.

When he returns to the United States, it is with the intention of becoming a professional musician. After he witnesses a brutal lynching, however, he determines never again to present himself as a black man. He marries a white woman and successfully "passes" as white. At the time of the novel's close, he is filled with regret at what he has missed by not being black but has no determination to pass back over the color line.

The Autobiography of an Ex-Coloured Man is seen by scholars as a work that anticipated both the Harlem Renaissance—especially with its emphasis on jazz music, the street life of New York, and the migration of African Americans out of the South—and, more specifically, Ralph Ellison's *Invisible Man* (1952). Johnson's narrator is, like Ellison's, a man whose identity is obscured by race. He decides to be a black man, and he is received one way; he decides not to be, and he is received differently. While Ellison ends with his nameless character living literally underground, Johnson's similarly unnamed character has gone underground in another way, in his retreat from a public self-identification as black. More important, Johnson's novel (also like Ellison's) serves as a series of snapshots of the forces and trends that were shaping black life during the time he wrote it. However briefly, the reader gets glimpses of railroad men, black university life, migrations North and back South, ragtime music, the freedom of Europe, and, not least of all, the spiritual cost of "passing."

Somewhat less successful overall is the poetry included from *Fifty Years and Other Poems* (1917). The majority of the poems in that original volume were republished in *St. Peter Relates an Incident: Selected Poems* (1925). Wilson has published only the unselected poems—the leftovers—in volume 2. The overall quality is, not surprisingly, unequal to Johnson's best poetry. Even so, the folklore-inspired poetry of "The Temptress" and "The Ghost of Deacon Brown" stand out as poetic successes, and some of his dialect poetry, such as "The Seasons," "'Possum Song," and "Nobody's Lookin' But de Owl and de Moon," show that he did more than slavishly imitate his friend Paul Laurence Dunbar when he wrote in this vein.

It is to be hoped that much of Johnson's best poetic work—his songs and his poetic rendering of well-known black sermons in *God's Trombones: Seven Negro Sermons in Verse* (1927), not to mention the selection of material included in *St. Peter Relates an Incident*—will be included in later volumes. The author's note tells readers that Wilson is preparing another volume of writings by Johnson from his NAACP years. There is no way of knowing what gems she will unearth, but what she has included in these first two volumes indicates that it will be full of wisdom and analysis well worth preserving. The work Wilson is doing can have the effect of bringing James Weldon Johnson's voice into the twenty-first century. It seems evident that a one-volume collection that includes the very best of Johnson's prodigious output—and that would be more easily used in classrooms—would be an excellent way to complete her project.

Thomas Cassidy

Sources for Further Study

Ebony. L, October, 1995, p. 18.
The Washington Post Book World. XXV, July 23, 1995, p. 13.

SELF-RULE
A Cultural History of American Democracy

Author: Robert H. Wiebe (1930-   )
Publisher: University of Chicago Press (Chicago). 321 pp. $25.95
Type of work: History
Time: 1820 to the 1990's

A thought-provoking study of the history of American democracy

Robert H. Wiebe's *Self-Rule: A Cultural History of American Democracy* is an intensely ambitious work. In it, Wiebe tackles one of the most enduring questions in American history—the nature of American democracy. Wiebe is admirably fitted for the task; he is a master historian. Earlier books such as *The Opening of American Society: From the Adoption of the Constitution to the Eve of Disunion* (1984) and the classic *The Search for Order, 1877-1920* (1967) established Wiebe's ability to analyze and synthesize materials on a grand scale. He brings his matured powers to bear in *Self-Rule*. The result is a fascinating study, which, while not definitively settling the issue of American democracy, will contribute to debate for many years to come.

The issue of American democracy has been central to discussions of the United States since the 1820's. During that decade, in a torrent of electoral liberalization, the vote was extended from the propertied classes to virtually every white man. Rallying around the totemic figure of Andrew Jackson, the enthusiastic proponents of "Jacksonian Democracy" engendered a political and social revolution that would make the United States the most egalitarian state in the known world. European visitors swiftly publicized the new society taking shape in what was to them a wilderness. As early as 1835, the brilliant French nobleman Alexis de Tocqueville printed the first volume of his masterwork *Democracy in America*, which argued that the democratic polity emerging in the United States was the vanguard of a democratic wave that would sweep Western civilization.

Just as important, Americans themselves began to see democracy as their defining national characteristic. In a development that would have shocked the Founding Fathers, for whom "democracy" was a bad word, Americans began to understand even their inherited institutions in democratic terms. During and after the Civil War, the constitutional issue of states' rights paled in comparison with the democratic dilemma of slavery and freedmen's rights. By 1917, so firmly entrenched was the democratic ideal in the American imagination that President Woodrow Wilson, calling the nation to war, rejected justifications involving calculations of the international balance of power or American national interests and instead urged his compatriots to make the world safe for democracy. It was in the name of democracy, rather than capitalism or republican propriety, that the American people later resisted the pretensions of fascism and communism. The collapse of the Soviet Union and of the communist regimes in its satellite states was seen by most Americans as a triumph of democracy. The Goddess of Democracy raised by Chinese students during their 1989 occupation of Tiananmen Square, which resembled the Statue of Liberty, seemed to symbolize the association of democracy with the United States pioneered by Tocqueville 150 years earlier.

Yet at the moment when democracy appeared to be sweeping all before it abroad, doubts were being raised about its health in the United States. Critics pointed to such phenomena as a decline in voter participation, the egregiousness of television politics, and the none too subtle power of money and interest groups to argue that U.S. democracy was in need of repair. Suggested solutions varied widely, ranging from a revival of the traditional party system to extending the list of constitutionally guaranteed rights.

While preparing his work, Wiebe read books by more than sixty critics of modern American democracy, from publicists to social scientists to philosophers. While admitting the brilliance of much of what he read, Wiebe was struck more forcibly by the dissonant quality of this literature, with differences often boiling down to special pleading for one or another cherished reform. What was lacking was a useful historical perspective. Few of these works were grounded in an understanding of the growth of American democracy that went beyond clichés.

Here is where Wiebe believes that he makes his greatest contribution to the debate: He has constructed an elaborate account of the evolution of democracy in the United States. He uses this to buttress a concluding chapter in which he offers his own proposals for the future of American democracy.

The nature of Wiebe's historical narrative is of interest for the insights it offers into the nature of the American debate over democracy. He calls his study a "cultural history," meaning a history of the ways people's values informed their actions. He deliberately takes aim at the joining point between popular attitudes and their concrete expression in laws and institutions. As Wiebe is careful to make clear, his work is not a history of ideas, nor is it a traditional account of political behavior. His history records Americans' evolving understanding of their civic standing—their sense of obligation and entitlement to one another and the state. In short, Wiebe has written something very close to an existential history of American citizenship.

Notable for its absence from Wiebe's account is a treatment of constitutional history. Focusing tightly on the ongoing effects of democratic ideology, Wiebe virtually ignores the framework within which these democratic tendencies unfold. This is all the more interesting given the truism familiar to most schoolchildren, that the United States is a republic and not a democracy. The distinction between a republic and a democracy is not a hollow semanticism, as the Founding Fathers well knew. The Founders believed a free people to be the sovereign basis of the Constitution, but their definition of "people" was elastic, and they never intended the people to rule directly. Their ingenuity in simultaneously establishing popular sovereignty and limiting the popular voice is embedded in American institutions as diverse as the Supreme Court, the Senate, and the Electoral College. From time to time, especially in election years, undemocratic legacies such as the Electoral College are pilloried as anachronisms. Still, they continue to exist, preserved by inertia and perhaps a fleeting appreciation for the wisdom of the Founders' work. They remain enduring and real bounds on the democratic drama.

What this means is that Wiebe's work, and the literature to which he is responding, is on its most profound level not really concerned with the shape and structure of American government. Instead, in its preoccupation with the role of the individual citizen in the civic ritual and its hortatory prescriptions for democratic renewal, it reveals itself as a secular sermon. Notwithstanding the sophistication of his historical method, here Wiebe is first and foremost a moralist.

His historical narrative of the development of American democracy, brilliant on its own terms, takes on immense emotional force when cast as a cautionary tale of the rise and corruption of an ideal. Fortunately, like any good preacher, Wiebe at the conclusion of his description of the fall holds out the hope of redemption.

Wiebe begins his tale in the 1820's with the arrival of democracy. Surprisingly, he does not trace this development to the ideals of the American Revolution. Eighteenth century America was still governed by social and political hierarchies. These hierarchies of local worthies were not as entrenched and impermeable as the aristocratic elites of Europe, but they did demonstrate considerable flexibility in adapting to the tumultuous events of the revolutionary era. The hierarchical model, with its traditional patterns of deference, characterized politics during the early years of the republic. The first political parties were interstate associations of gentlemen that congealed around such prominent figures as George Washington and Thomas Jefferson.

Things began to change, however, with the dawn of the nineteenth century. The hold of the old elites began to slip. Taking a page from Frederick Jackson Turner, Wiebe attributes the rise of democracy to the opening of the frontier. A vast expanse of inexpensive land and an endemic shortage of labor destabilized the hierarchical order. A new ideology emerged, emphasizing individual self-determination. Economic self-sufficiency, whether through ownership of land or a more sturdily independent approach to wage labor, quickly led to a more egalitarian political ethos. Born of the forces remaking America, the new democracy celebrated decentralization. With political power largely concentrated locally, and even that used sparingly, the autonomy and equality of the individual voter stood out in high relief.

Indeed, Wiebe highlights the fraternal dimension of democratic politics for the white men who took part in it. As the duties of government were strictly limited by universal consensus, the chief purpose of the vigorous political campaigns of the day was dramatizing the sovereignty, and ultimately the solidarity, of the electorate. For the democratic culture of the nineteenth century, there was no contradiction between a fiercely held individualism and a clubbishness that Wiebe terms "lodge politics." American democracy was an association dedicated to maintaining the essential equality of its white male members.

Wiebe tolerantly describes the crudities in manners and mores of nineteenth century American society. Habits that appalled European visitors were, at least in part, manifestations of a genuine idealism. Yet Wiebe is careful to point out the limits of the democratic impulse. A private if vastly extended club, American democracy explicitly excluded women and African Americans. The equality of white men was all the more precious because of the oppression of groups outside their fraternity.

The egalitarian white man's democracy of the nineteenth century was the creation of the frontier. As long as land was cheap and jobs plentiful, it prospered. In the 1890's, however, the frontier disappeared. The future lay in America's rapidly expanding cities. At the same time, the Industrial Revolution was transforming the workplace, turning skilled laborers into cogs in mechanized factories. The politics of solidarity died as new hierarchies arose. Wiebe describes the division of American society into three classes—the increasingly marginalized poor, the localized middle-class elites of small-town America, and a new national middle class of educated experts, masters of the urban and industrial regime.

In contrast to the democrats of the nineteenth century, the new national middle class embraced political centralization. It made sense to these professionals that government should imitate the model set by the vast corporations reshaping the American economy. The members of the national middle class were offended by the noisy, and occasionally corrupt, rough-and-tumble of politics. They recognized that serious problems were not being addressed and believed that democratic electioneering was not the most efficient means of meeting the challenges facing the nation.

Thus in the Progressive movement of the early twentieth century, the new elite sponsored a series of reforms that recast political life in America. The powers of the political parties were undermined. Voter registration was made more stringent. Whole areas of public life were withdrawn from electoral politics and made the realm of appointed bureaucrats.

From the standpoint of their authors, the Progressive reforms were a complete success. American government ran more smoothly and, for the most part, more honestly. American government, however, was also much less democratic. A great mass of lower-class voters had been directly excluded from the polls. Many other voters became alienated from a political system that seemed forbiddingly complicated and unresponsive. Consequently, voter participation in the twentieth century declined precipitously from nineteenth century highs. The Progressive reformers also succeeded in fashioning the modern American administrative state, tended by hordes of functionaries, who over time interposed governmental authority into more and more regions of activity once thought private.

Wiebe believes that the current democratic malaise in the United States stems from the long-term effects of the Progressive assault on popular politics. Decades of centralization and class-based authority have atomized the American electorate, making it increasingly difficult for leaders to reconcile the claims of disparate interests. Denied the satisfactions of political engagement, many Americans have fallen back on the meretricious pleasures of consumerism. Political discourse today is dominated by the contradictory appeals of a strident individualism and a powerful yearning for a reborn sense of community.

In Wiebe's opinion, the only way to revitalize the democratic tradition is to reverse the trend toward political centralization and unseat the hierarchical power structure.

In his concluding chapter he argues eloquently for a "guerrilla politics" in which Americans organize outside established channels. In effect, he exhorts his readers to reclaim the nineteenth century heritage of democracy as individual self-assertion wed with civic solidarity. Only this new democracy would be a purer species, shorn of sexism and racism. The happy product of a rebirth of democracy in America would be a citizen fully conscious of his or her power and responsibility, for whom politics would be a sacrament as well as a duty.

This is a compelling vision. One does not have to believe in it to respect the force of Wiebe's argument or the fervency of the moral concern underlying it. *Self-Rule* is a strikingly original contribution to a necessary debate.

Daniel P. Murphy

Sources for Further Study

Booklist. XCI, April 1, 1995, p. 1364.
The Christian Science Monitor. April 27, 1995, p. B2.
Commonweal. CXXII, July 14, 1995, p. 19.
In These Times. XIX, September 18, 1995, p. 51.
The Nation. CCLX, June 12, 1995, p. 860.
The New Republic. CCXIII, October 23, 1995, p. 39.
New Statesman and Society . VIII, June 9, 1995, p. 37.
Publishers Weekly. CCXLII, March 13, 1995, p. 56.
The Wall Street Journal. June 20, 1995, p. A16.
The Washington Post Book World. XXV, April 16, 1995, p. 4.

SHAKESPEARE
A Life in Drama

Author: Stanley Wells (1930-　　)
Publisher: W. W. Norton (New York). 392 pp. $28.50
Type of work: Literary criticism

Wells offers a critical introduction to William Shakespeare's life and works

Although its title suggests a biography, Stanley Wells's *Shakespeare: A Life in Drama* is in reality a critical survey of the dramatist's literary achievement, encompassing all the dramas and poems. While the first chapter does summarize the essential facts of William Shakespeare's life and additional biographical details are scattered throughout the text, Wells devotes himself primarily to critical explorations. The book stands in the tradition of similar critical introductions such as E. K. Chambers' *Shakespeare: A Survey* (1959) and Mark Van Doren's *Shakespeare* (1939). A major difference, however, arises from the organization that Wells adopts.

Like the two books cited and numerous other works of their type, Wells examines the Shakespeare canon chronologically. Yet instead of devoting a chapter to each of the thirty-eight plays, he limits the number of chapters by assigning most dramas to groups. Among the plays, only *Othello* (pr. 1604) and *Macbeth* (pr. 1606) receive chapter-length analysis. *King Lear* (pr. 1605-1606) is logically paired with *Timon of Athens* (pr. 1607-1608), not only because of their proximity of composition dates but also because of their comparable themes and characters. Similar factors serve to link each of the two English history tetralogies in two separate chapters, with a similar single chapter dealing with five of the ten history plays. As many as five comedies are grouped in a single chapter, largely on the basis of settings and general chronology. Although Wells makes frequent comparisons among the plays that are considered within a single chapter, his analysis normally proceeds from play to play, and so discrete are the sections on single plays that he might well have used subheadings within the chapters.

Among Wells's previous scholarly achievements are numerous books on Shakespeare and work as general editor of the *Complete Works of Shakespeare* (Oxford University Press). Not surprisingly, his positions on textual and authorial problems reflect his scholarly experience and his long-standing interest in Shakespeare productions. An indication of Wells's interest in the theater is his long experience as a reviewer of live Shakespeare performances. In textual and other matters, Wells views Shakespeare less as a literary figure than as a man of the theater, a dramatist rather than a poet.

Impressions gleaned from his reviewing represent another factor that sets his critical introductions apart from others. Wells views Shakespeare the writer as one who functioned as part of a team including actors, directors, and revisers and who regarded stage production, not publication, as the final objective of his writing. The life in drama indicated by the subtitle really means not Shakespeare's life as a creative writer but rather the life of his dramas on stage and their potential for creating meaningful experiences for their audiences. Wells goes so far as to show how some of the dramas can be staged so that they become more relevant to contemporary issues.

To understand the significance of this, one must grasp fundamental differences between Shakespearean productions in England and in other English-speaking nations such as the United States. Worldwide, especially in English-speaking nations, countless live productions of Shakespeare are presented year round. Shakespeare festivals, summer programs, and academic as well as commercial productions are almost too numerous to record. Yet there is a qualitative difference between England and, for example, the United States. In England, it is not unusual to find Shakespeare plays produced in the commercial theater, whereas in the United States, commercial productions are infrequent. Those that do occur are likely to be modernized versions and or highly creative adaptations. At any one time in and around London, it is not uncommon to find several live productions on stage during the same week, and among them are traditional stage interpretations. The cast often features one or more of the most famous names of the English stage, and quality of production is universally high. English actors and actresses learn their skills through acting Shakespeare. After they have achieved fame in modern and more popular roles, they are often more than willing to return to Shakespearean parts. To find screen and television stars such as Jeremy Irons, Derek Jacobi, and Anthony Hopkins appearing on stage in traditional productions of Shakespearean plays is not unusual.

Steeped as he is in the theater, Wells finds the creations of actors and directors relevant to an understanding of the dramas. Drawing on live productions he has seen, and probably reviewed, he comments on the interpretive powers of performers largely of his own time, from Laurence Olivier and Peggy Ashcroft to Kenneth Branagh and Imogen Stubbs. In addition, he occasionally refers to film and televised versions. Further emphasizing dramatic criticism, he discusses performances of legendary actors of the past—such as David Garrick, Edmund Booth, and Edmund Kean—basing his commentary on his extensive knowledge of theater history.

For the dramas that ordinarily receive more scholarly attention than interpretive criticism, Wells sometimes makes live productions the major portion of his analysis. For example, his account of *Titus Andronicus* (pr. 1594), the early revenge tragedy, begins with details about its early stage history, including description of an extant drawing by a Shakespeare contemporary. After identifying the play's sources and clarifying its sensational plot, Wells explores critical responses to the tragedy and then describes three modern productions in detail, devoting more than a page to effects achieved by a rare uncut stage production at the Swan Theater, Stratford, in 1987.

Even works that saw no stage production—the poems, for example—are assessed within in a dramatic context. Writing of the two long poems *Venus and Adonis* (1593) and *The Rape of Lucrece* (1594), Wells suggests that one reason for their obscurity is that they have not been accorded the advantage of performance and adds that both are more moving when read aloud.

Although he normally includes a settled scholarly evaluation of the issues posed by the plays, Wells sometimes accepts the alternative interpretations that are introduced by directors to adapt Shakespeare to a more modern setting. He is sympathetic toward modernized adaptations that feature the music of Cole Porter and George Gershwin and actors in modern dress, and he welcomes new interpretations on the part of directors. Among these, he cites a production of *Measure for Measure* (pr. 1604) that exploited an ambiguity in the text to provide a feminist interpretation. In the final act of Shakespeare's most problematic comedy, the duke attempts to test all the wrong-doers in the plot and to assign a just penalty—one much more remarkable for its mercy than for its justice. In the end, quite unexpectedly, publicly, and almost abruptly, he asks for the hand of the heroine Isabella in marriage. In the remaining few lines, although the duke alludes to the upcoming wedding, Isabella never replies, leaving the director to convey her response solely through the action. John Barton's interpretation at Stratford in 1970 portrayed an anguished Isabella, who, after everyone else had gone offstage, made it clear to the duke that she would not marry him.

Although the interpretation is warranted by the text, Wells neglects to point out that Shakespeare's contemporaries would have had no doubts about Isabella's response. Her previous respectful tone toward the duke and Elizabethan assumptions about rank and degree mean that she could not have refused the proposal and indeed would have regarded it as an honor. Wells finds value in a less traditional interpretation of the episode because, it would seem, it better connects with the attitudes and assumptions of modern audiences.

In contrast, when he deals with *Julius Caesar* (pr. 1599-1600), Wells permits texts and original intent to weigh more heavily. During times of tyranny and dictatorship, the World War II period being a example, directors are inclined to cast Brutus as the hero and treat the assassination of Caesar as a blow for liberty, as if the play were making a serious statement about human rights. Even major Shakespearean critics such as Thomas M. Parrott have named Brutus the protagonist. Mark Van Doren, who acknowledges that Brutus' nobility muffles his intelligence, also considered Brutus the hero. Yet Wells follows a more conservative and traditional interpretation, convinced that Caesar was the hero Shakespeare intended.

Wells's inclination to emphasize live production does not generally undermine his sense of traditional critical approaches that one normally finds in scholarly introductions. Typically, his account of the plot provides sufficient information about the play that the reader acquires a genuine sense of the story. As his interest in productions might imply, he accords generous treatment to character analysis, though he is inclined to limit discussion to a few major characters. In *Julius Caesar*, for example, he explores the characters of Caesar, Brutus, Cassius, and Antony in some detail but does not mention Cicero, Calpurnia, or Portia. In his treatment of theme, he clarifies the major conflicts and thematic emphasis of each drama, usually succinctly. Like other books of this type, Wells's provides a generous sampling of quotations to illustrate character, theme, and poetic qualities of each drama.

In addition, Wells often discusses sources, texts, the dramatic genre of the drama, and the relationship of some plays to others. He is inclined to prefer those texts that are closest to what he regards as acting versions and clearly prefers to interpret the plays as dramatic rather than literary texts. Thus he comes close to accepting the view that the authoritative text is really the one that was acted, often one that was cut to meet the realities of the theater. This represents a bold if not heretical view to traditional literary scholars and editors, but one that seems obvious enough.

The analysis is uneven, as all critical surveys of Shakespeare must be, in part because of the diversity of the Shakespeare canon. At its weakest, Wells's work appears to incorporate numerous quotations stitched together with bare-bones critical commentary, as one discovers in the treatment of *Henry IV, Part II* (pr. 1597-1598). On the other hand, Wells gives a much fuller treatment to an often-neglected drama, *The Comedy of Errors* (pr. 1592-1594). The introduction stands as an important critical essay explaining why he considers the classical comedy Shakespeare's first dramatic masterpiece.

Although the extensive emphasis on productions sets this book apart from others of its kind, Wells updates scholarship and literary criticism in such a way that readers will at least become more familiar with modern issues and controversies. Questions concerning authorship will illustrate the point. Wells explores the grounds for thinking that Shakespeare wrote a lost drama entitled *Loves Labours Won*. Although he suggests that the manuscript may yet be discovered, he also hints that the reference to the play might well have been to *The Taming of the Shrew* (pr. 1593-1594). Another drama, *Cardenio*, attributed to Shakespeare and John Fletcher, is known to have been performed, but no copy of the work has surfaced; Wells treats it as an example of Shakespeare's inclination toward collaboration as his career approached its end. He follows other scholars in his analysis of *The Two Noble Kinsmen* (pr. 1612-1613) as a collaboration between Shakespeare and Fletcher. He accords brief attention to the question of authorship of the poem "Shall I Die?" attributed to Shakespeare in a seventeenth century manuscript; after exploring the slender evidence of authorship, Wells reaches no final decision.

For readers desiring an introduction to Shakespeare's achievement, Wells provides a gracefully written combination of dramatic and literary criticism. The book reflects his extensive knowledge of primary and secondary sources and achieves a concise but comprehensive survey of contemporary scholarly and critical issues. The work will also reward those who wish to refresh and update their previous knowledge of the Shakespeare canon.

Stanley Archer

Sources for Further Study

Houston Chronicle. August 27, 1995, p. Z23.
The Observer. April 17, 1994, p. 19.
The Times Literary Supplement. August 5, 1995, p. 20.
The Washington Post Book World. XXV, August 6, 1995, p. 13.

SHELLEY'S HEART

Author: Charles McCarry (1930-   )
Publisher: Random House (New York). 576 pp. $23.00
Type of work: Novel
Time: 2001
Locale: Washington, D.C.; New York City; Chile; Utah; Wyoming; Tibet; the Grenadines; Stamford, Connecticut; Camp David, Maryland; Manassas, Virginia; Pittsfield, Massachusetts; Bethesda, Maryland

The discovery of the theft of a presidential election leads to even more sinister revelations involving terrorists and the chief justice of the United States

> *Principal characters:*
> BEDFORD FORREST "FROSTY" LOCKWOOD, the president of the United States
> FRANKLIN MALLORY, his predecessor and opponent for reelection
> ZARAH CHRISTOPHER, a young woman befriended by Lockwood and Mallory
> ARCHIMEDES HAMMETT, chief justice of the United States
> R. TUCKER ATTENBOROUGH, JR., speaker of the House of Representatives
> SUSAN GRANT, Mallory's lover and chief of staff
> JULIAN HUBBARD, Lockwood's chief of staff
> HORACE HUBBARD, Hubbard's half-brother, a former intelligence officer
> ROSS MACALASTER, a journalist
> ALFONSO OLMEDO C., a lawyer hired by Lockwood
> JOHN L. S. McGRAW, Olmedo's investigator
> SLIM AND STURDI EVE, lawyer friends of Hammett
> JACK PHILANDROS, director of the Foreign Intelligence Service
> SAMUEL REES CLARK, majority leader of the U.S. Senate

Charles McCarry's previous novel *Second Sight* (1991) was, according to the author, the final volume in his seven-novel series about the Christopher family and their exploits in spying. *Shelley's Heart*, however, prominently features Zarah Christopher, introduced in the previous book in the series. While *Shelley's Heart* deals less overtly with espionage than his earlier efforts, it offers similar elements of treachery and romance. Set in the near future, *Shelley's Heart*, while continuing McCarry's concern with terrorism and the alleged betrayal of American ideals and institutions by radical liberalism, concentrates primarily on the process of determining who may inhabit the White House. Despite awkwardly grinding some partisan axes, *Shelley's Heart* is a well-written, enthralling entertainment, almost a right-wing version of Fletcher Knebel's *Seven Days in May* (1962).

Bedford Forrest Lockwood's first term as president of the United States is besmirched by terrorist attacks resulting from his apparently sanctioning the assassination of Ibn Awad, an oil sheik, to stop him from arming the Eye of Gaza, a terrorist group, with nuclear weapons. (The Lockwood-Mallory campaign and the killing of Awad are recounted in McCarry's *The Better Angels*, 1979.) Lockwood's second term is challenged on inaugural eve by allegations that his reelection has been stolen by altered results from several precincts in California, Michigan, and New York. The challenge comes from Franklin Mallory, his opponent and a previous holder of the office, who has proof that the election was stolen by Horace Hubbard, a former senior intelligence officer and half-brother of Julian Hubbard, Lockwood's chief of staff.

Mallory wants Lockwood to take the oath of office, swear him in as vice president (as the Twenty-fifth Amendment to the Constitution allows), and resign in Mallory's favor until Congress certifies his legal election. At a press conference to announce Mallory's intention to challenge the election results, Susan Grant, his lover and chief of staff, is killed when she steps in front of him and is shot by a terrorist assassin, who escapes.

After Lockwood announces that he will abide by the decision of Congress after it investigates the election, Julian Hubbard begins planning to save the presidency. The chief justice of the Supreme Court has recently died, and Hubbard persuades Lockwood to nominate his friend Archimedes Hammett for the post as a means of slowing down the likely impeachment process. Hubbard and Hammett both belong to the Shelley Society, a secret organization founded by World War I veterans at Yale in 1919 and devoted "to make the world a better place, no matter by what methods." The members follow the ideals of Percy Bysshe Shelley as expressed primarily in his political essays. McCarry's novel takes its title from the actions of Shelley's friend Edward John Trelawny, who, following the poet's request, burned his body, only to reach into the fire to tear out the heart.

Hammett becomes suspicious of Zarah Christopher, Hubbard's mysterious cousin, after she is drafted as go-between for Lockwood and Mallory and as it becomes clear that Mallory is romantically interested in her. Mallory asks Ross Macalaster, the only Washington journalist he can trust, to write the complete account of the events surrounding the contested election and the assassination of Grant. Mallory is convinced that a plot is under way to make Hammett president.

To prevent his impeachment, Lockwood hires Alfonso Olmedo C., the most famous trial attorney in America. Olmedo's investigator, John L. S. McGraw, a former New York City police detective, employs electronic bulletin boards to track down Horace Hubbard in Chile. Lockwood's situation is made more difficult by a tape recording of the president's giving Jack Philandros, head of the Foreign Intelligence Service, permission to kill Awad.

The situation is complicated even further when the vice president dies. Speaker of the House of Representatives R. Tucker Attenborough, Jr., decides to manipulate events to prevent Hammett from seizing the presidency. With the help of Sam Clark, the Senate majority leader, Attenborough hopes to head off Hammett. Slim Eve, one of the chief justice's two lesbian disciplines, discovers a way of using the Constitution to make him president.

Hammett's plot begins unraveling when McGraw discovers the existence of the Shelleyans. The Lockwood-Philandros tape is proved to have been electronically altered to cast blame on the president and protect the Foreign Intelligence Service. Grant is revealed to have been murdered because she was pregnant by Mallory. Then

Horace Hubbard, who has been motivated by the fear that Mallory would dismantle American intelligence, recognizes Slim as a member of the Eye of Gaza. A violent showdown ensues, and democracy is saved.

Shelley's Heart is an entertaining thriller by a writer knowledgeable about espionage, terrorism, and politics. McCarry is particularly adept at showing how members of Congress attempt to outmaneuver one another. Since Mallory has been illegally kept out of office, it is obvious that he will become president by the novel's end. The suspense comes from the process, and McCarry makes the efforts of Olmedo and McGraw fascinating. Also interesting are the constitutional loopholes involving who may inhabit the Oval Office under what circumstances. This seems to be a popular topic for conservative novelists, since John Calvin Batchelor's *Father's Day* (1994) deals with a similar crisis brought on by the Twenty-fifth Amendment.

Unlike many American spy novelists, McCarry knows how to create believable characters. His primary characters, with the notable exceptions of Hammett, Slim, and Zarah—the latter being too good to be true—have clearly defined positive and negative characteristics. While Attenborough may be a drunken lecher, he has enough strength of character to recognize the dangers inherent in an extremely complicated situation and how to use his political savvy to combat them. Mallory usually has the capacity to understand others' points of view and the ability to enlist them in his cause by showing them how seemingly opposed interests can be served at the same time.

McCarry, however, weakens his narrative too often with diatribes against the political left. Since these often-petulant outbursts rarely have anything directly to do with his plot, they come across as gratuitous. According to McCarry, liberals are snobbish, puritanical, and humorless. They would rather risk civil war than have someone like Mallory in the White House. Liberals in position of power, especially in the media, lie to and manipulate the public, though to what ends it is not clear. The Shelleyans are devoted to what they call "the Cause," but McCarry leaves its meaning open. Similarly, Lockwood's "progressive social programs" are mentioned but not defined. The Watergate period is referred to as "the last time the radicals tried to take over the world," apparently that meaning leftists deposed Richard M. Nixon—an unusual interpretation of recent American history.

McCarry envisions a world where film stars have terrorist boyfriends, where deer are destroying the flora of major American cities because of the interference of animal rights activists, where the most famous U.S. television news anchorman will say, "Archimedes Hammett's nomination is an appeal to the conscience of every decent American. Nothing in our lifetime has been more important to the future of justice in America than this nomination," and where Attenborough makes his first public impact in Texas in the 1960's by convincing a jury that when a "hippie from Cambridge, Massachusetts," is rude, it is acceptable to kill him.

If liberals are weak, deceitful, and muddle-headed, conservative heroes such as Mallory are their opposites. His solution to the original Eye of Gaza dilemma would have been to tell Awad that if the terrorists used the bombs, "the United States would strike every strategic target in his own country with neutron weapons that would kill every living thing but leave all its wealth intact and in our possession." If he had been president during the Cold War and the Soviets had launched their missiles, he would have "launched the counterstrike, then taken someone he loved by the hand and waited in the Rose Garden, ground zero, to be vaporized."

While McCarry has seemed in his earlier books to endorse a world best governed by white males from privileged backgrounds, in *Shelley's Heart* he goes to the other extreme. Mallory, Lockwood, Attenborough, Clark, Olmedo, and McGraw are essentially good men because they were born poor and have improved themselves through hard work and tough intellect. In contrast is the type represented by Julian Hubbard:

> the product of a system—the prosperous family, the Church Genteel, St. Grottlesex and the Ivy League, the creed of good works, the seal of secret societies—that was designed, like its model, the British public school system, to produce a class of competent, hardworking, unshakably self-satisfied clerks.

McCarry idealizes the past as a time when

> the two great political parties wanted to do the same things in slightly different ways and always found a way to make things happen. Now everybody behaved like a bunch of damn Frenchmen, each and every one of them wanting to have his own way and to hell with the Constitution, the country, the party, and most of all the idea of civilized behavior.

McCarry does approve of some aspects of the present, especially computers. One of the highlights of *Shelley's Heart* is his description of the use of virtual reality to solve Grant's murder. The novel's usual veracity is stretched when Lockwood cancels the inauguration luncheon and parade but the balls, the most significant part of the day for the president's loyal supporters, are not even mentioned. Credibility is also stretched when Mallory recalls that during his presidency, a few years earlier, he frequently slipped out of the White House "to roam the city on foot." When Slim is posing as a male Arab terrorist, she does not wear gloves and thus exposes her painted fingernails. Finally, McCarry's gratuitous comments are not limited to politics, as when Zarah claims that no one can tell the difference between Charlotte Brontë's *Jane Eyre* (1847) and Emily Brontë's *Wuthering Heights* (1847).

Michael Adams

Sources for Further Study

Boston Globe. July 4, 1995, p. 24.
The Christian Science Monitor. July 27, 1995, p. B1.
Los Angeles Times. June 21, 1995, p. E4.
The New York Review of Books. XLII, July 13, 1995, p. 42.
The New York Times Book Review. C, June 25, 1995, p. 9.
The Washington Post Book World. XXV, June 4, 1995, p. 3.

SIGHTS UNSEEN

Author: Kaye Gibbons (1960-   )
Publisher: G. P. Putnam's Sons (New York). 209 pp. $19.95
Type of work: Novel
Time: The early 1990's, with flashbacks to the 1960's
Locale: Bend of the River, a small community in eastern North Carolina

A young woman recounts her childhood with a manic-depressive mother

Principal characters:
   HARRIET BARNES, the narrator, whose life is shaped by her childhood
      experiences with a family scarred by mental illness
   MAGGIE BARNES, her mother, whose manic experiences make up the
      bulk of the narrator's remembrances
   MR. BARNES, Maggie's father-in-law, who coddles Maggie but damages
      the rest of the family with his patriarchal demands
   PEARL WIGGINS, the housekeeper, who is Harriet's surrogate mother as
      well as Maggie's nurse

   When Kaye Gibbons' *Ellen Foster* (1987) was published, critics hailed her protagonist's youthful, abrasive voice as a new addition to southern literature. Since then,
Gibbons' novels have offered her readers glimpses into other haunting interiors,
primarily showing psychological tensions between southern women.
   In *Sights Unseen*, her fifth novel, Gibbons continues to explore familial terrain using
first-person narration, this time in an attempt to uncover the memories of Harriet
Barnes, only daughter of a manic-depressive mother. Told from Harriet's perspective
as an adult, the novel explores the relationship between the emotionally neglected
Harriet and her manic mother, Maggie. Though the novel conveys the social stigma
of mental illness, in a larger sense the novel fails to illustrate the fragile mother-
daughter relationship. Furthermore, the use of first-person narration, so effective in
Gibbons' earlier novels, seems largely problematic rather than useful in this novel.
   Sights Unseen opens in the early 1990's, some time after Maggie has died in a freak
accident. Most of the action of the piece, however, occurs in flashbacks from around
and before 1967, the year Maggie was hospitalized and diagnosed with manic
depression. Harriet's retelling of her life with a manic-depressive mother and the often
freakish childhood events that shaped her adult life is reminiscent of Gibbons' earlier
narrators, particularly Ellen of *Ellen Foster*, who, like Harriet, had to adapt to often
horrific circumstances. Yet unlike Ellen, who so masterfully takes control of that novel,
Harriet Barnes seems to be merely a pawn in her mother's game. Consequently, her
reflections often define her mother's character while diminishing her own. Though
Harriet's plight should be at the center of the text, Maggie's manic episodes are so
dramatic that she becomes the main character of the novel; the narrator seems a mere
observer rather than someone intimately connected with the story's events.
   One of the problems Gibbons encounters in using mental illness as the centerpiece
for this novel is in the sheer liveliness and "fun" of manic activity. Had she chosen a

more dire mental illness such as schizophrenia or clinical depression, the reader might have found Maggie's plight more heart-rending. Under the spell of mania, Maggie resembles a lovable drunk—someone who must be protected and coddled by her family. Because of her lively presence, Maggie is far from the villain of the piece. As with John Milton's Satan in *Paradise Lost* (1667, 1674), readers know that they should despise Maggie, but they cannot, because she is so beautifully drawn and her mania is almost a pleasure to behold.

For example, Maggie becomes convinced that she has connections to several political, literary, and cultural figures of the day. Eventually she fixates on Robert Kennedy, who she believes will one day leave his wife for her. Acting on her expectations, she telephones several neighbors in an attempt to ascertain what a Catholic might like to eat for dinner. Even the event that concludes a six-week manic episode remains mostly comic in its ludicrousness. In this episode, Maggie drives downtown and runs over a woman because she thinks that the woman is dressing like her, wearing the coat, and adopting her mannerisms. Maggie fears that the woman is trying to steal her soul.

Maggie's assertiveness and assuredness in her manic moments, particularly the way she forces others to listen to her and play along, make her likable and knowable, despite her insanity. Though Gibbons tries to undercut Maggie's attractiveness, she fails at conveying the horror of a woman whose moods and ideas change hourly. The main problem is that Harriet never seems to be as affected by these occurrences as the reader thinks she could, and perhaps should, be.

Harriet has little to say about the significance of the events she relates. Though she is theoretically recalling her childhood from the vantage point of an adult who has learned from her experiences, she often presents remembered events as pristine artifacts, allowing the reader to decide how they would affect a twelve-year-old girl. While this technique saves the novel from becoming too maudlin, it also takes away Harriet's narrative presence in the recounting, allowing Maggie to take over the text. Harriet's detachment presents problems when juxtaposed to what appears to be Gibbons' purpose in the narration—to illustrate the nurturing needs of an essentially motherless young woman.

Because Gibbons largely refrains from editorializing, she seems to struggle to make sense of the events Harriet recounts. Offhandedly, Harriet discusses her mother's initial rejection of her as an infant, then later as a young adult. In one telling anecdote, Harriet becomes physically ill, but because her mother is having a manic attack, she is forced by circumstance to take care of her mother. Harriet points out this reversal in a rather cavalier manner. Her stoicism in the face of her mother's tempests seems less poignant than dull-witted, particularly since Harriet is speaking as an adult. If Gibbons expects her readers to care about Harriet's plight, Harriet needs to be less a youthful narrator and more an adult character.

The flashbacks seem to take the bite out of Harriet. Though she appears to tell the stories of rampage and insanity from the viewpoint of a child, she fails to appear believably bewildered. Eventually, the reader becomes unsure who is narrating—the child or the woman. Consequently, there is little of the immediacy one might expect from first-person narration except when Harriet discusses her manic mother. This shift in emphasis further undercuts Gibbons' ability to keep Harriet at the center of the text.

The novel seems further blighted by Gibbons' attempts to find a moral in the story; Harriet, in her retelling, hints at such a moral, but Gibbons never fully develops it. Harriet struggles to find her mother in the many masks of Maggie's mania. Within the first pages of the novel, Harriet claims that she "never abandoned the ideal of a mother" and that she and her mother "caught each other just in time"; thus the reader is deprived of most of the suspense of the novel—the two are reconciled. Readers learn from another flashback that Harriet's mother has died in a freak accident after being "sane" for fifteen years and that Harriet is deeply upset by her mother's death and fears she will not be able to rear her daughter without her mother's presence. These clues suggest a novel of reconciliation or, at the very least, a novel dealing with a difficult relationship and showing how the difficultly is resolved. Gibbons' suggestions at the outset of the novel, however, work against her. Because Harriet does not give voice to the actual reconciliation, the novel seems oddly off center, as if most of the important action occurs after it is over.

The reader does see the feeble beginnings of reconciliation, after Maggie undergoes eight electroconvulsive shock treatments and begins taking a wonder drug called Miltown. When she gets home, she asks Harriet to read with her in her room (tellingly, Harriet reads *Frankenstein* [1818]; Maggie is deep into a copy of *East of Eden* [1952] that she has stolen from the mental hospital). Later, Maggie begins to attend school functions and act more as a healthy mother might act. Still, the difficulties of the real reconciliation that Harriet hints at during the course of the novel, the years of trust building and anger, occur outside the novel's scope. *Sights Unseen* records the most dramatic part of the relationship, the easiest part to tell, and the most titillating. A sane Maggie would not offer as much dramatic flair as a mad Maggie. Maggie gets pushed into the background after she is healed, as if her strength of character rested in her mania—a dangerous assumption about the mentally ill that Gibbons perpetuates through this authorial decision.

Despite these criticisms, *Sights Unseen* does succeed as a sort of case history of a family caught up in the mysteries of mental illness in the 1950's and 1960's. Despite the fact that Maggie Barnes begins acting strange in 1948, Frederick Barnes, Hattie's father, does not take her in for treatment until 1967, and then only after Maggie hits the woman with her car and the family needs medical proof that she is insane. Until that point Maggie is coddled by her husband and father-in-law, allowed long days in bed when she is depressed and shopping sprees when she is manic. Indeed, her father-in-law seems to take great pleasure in squiring her around town as she buys clothing, furniture, and jewels, all in excess of her needs. To keep her contained in the house when she is not feeling well, her husband hires housekeepers, all of whom quit until Pearl Wiggins appears. Pearl takes on the task of nurse, keeping Maggie from hurting herself and others and, most important, keeping her away from the rest of the world when she is ill.

The family's willingness to hide Maggie away and medicate her mania with Sominex and alcohol seems ludicrous to modern readers, but Maggie's relatives seem to believe that they are doing the best they can under the circumstances. As Harriet points out in the novel, the Barneses are lucky because they can afford the illness—the housekeeper-cum-nurse, the spending sprees, the expensive treatment at Duke University Hospital. Yet the concealment of the patient and the denial of the illness that self-medication suggests indicate that the Barneses also simply do not want to be publicly seen as harboring mental illness. Led by its stalwart patriarch, Mr. Barnes, a man so fierce that no one except Maggie ever stands up to him, the family seems content to let him "handle" Maggie. He seems content to spend what must be thousands of dollars on Maggie in order to keep her illness from becoming apparent to the townspeople. He even offers to pay off police officers and the media in order to keep her car incident a secret. Because of the social stigma of the disease, the family follows Mr. Barnes's lead and develops strict internal codes and structures to protect itself from the intrusion of outsiders.

This rallying around Maggie, however, does her very little good except as a stopgap maneuver. Instead, she becomes a victim of her family's inability to admit she needs professional help. Maggie's family literally traps her in her mania.

Gibbons seems to have a much too ambitious agenda for *Sights Unseen*. Although the novel does make insightful points on the ways that families respond to mental illness, *Sights Unseen* fails to touch more than the surface of the tumultuous relationship between Harriet and Maggie. By limiting Harriet's voice to flashbacks, Gibbons loses the immediacy of her youthful experience and limits the reader's involvement in her problems with her mother. The mother rather than the daughter becomes the focal point of the novel, undermining the self-proclaimed significance of the narrator's need to be reconciled. Had Gibbons attempted to show only the effects of mental illness or only the relationship between mother and daughter, she might have been successful, but the narrative structure that she has chosen for *Sights Unseen* prevents her from fulfilling her ambitious agenda.

Rebecca Hendrick Flannagan

Sources for Further Study

Atlanta Journal Constitution. September 10, 1995, p. M3.
Los Angeles Times. October 9, 1995, p. E5.
The New York Times Book Review. C, September 24, 1995, p. 30.
The New Yorker. LXXI, August 21, 1995, p. 115.
Publishers Weekly. CCXLII, June 5, 1995, p. 48.
Southern Living. XXX, December, 1995, p. 88.
Times-Picayune. October 1, 1995, p. E6.
USA Today. November 2, 1995, p. D4.

A SISTERMONY

Author: Richard Stern (1928-   )
Publisher: Donald I. Fine (New York). 121 pp. $17.50
Type of work: Memoir
Time: 1990-1991
Locale: New York and Chicago

A brief memoir that deals with Richard Stern's life during the period of his sister's death

> *Principal personages:*
> RICHARD STERN, the novelist and professor
> RUTH LEVITON, his sister, who died in 1991
> CHRISTOPHER STERN, his troubled son
> PHILIP ROTH, the novelist, Richard Stern's friend
> RALPH LEVITON, Ruth's husband

In *A Sistermony*, Richard Stern counterpoints his sister's death to a number of historical events as well as to his own personal and professional activities. These activities included Stern's meetings with fellow writers and friends Saul Bellow and Philip Roth. Stern's troubled interactions with his own children, especially his son, Christopher, also constitute an important part of this memoir.

The book is loosely organized, sometimes almost randomly. Late in the book, Stern mentions consulting his journal for a note or fact. The book, then, is a restructuring of entries from a journal. At the end of the book, Stern reproduces his journal entries and goes back over the material he has already addressed. The structure is a dual one; readers are given a text and, later, the sources of that text.

The title, *A Sistermony*, uses a word that Stern was forced to invent to come to terms with his relationship with and loss of his sister. The relationship between sister and brother, especially when the sister is older, is very important in the lives of innumerable people, and Stern is to be praised for calling attention to the significant place a sister can have in one's life. There is, moreover, another context for the term and book. Stern is using Philip Roth's book about his father, *Patrimony* (1991), as a model, so he takes over the suffix and applies it to his relationship with his sister, Ruth. The term suggests not only a relationship but also an influence and inheritance from an older figure. The word Stern has coined is resonant with implications, but it is unlikely that it will ever find its way into the language.

Stern's sister, Ruth Leviton, was not famous or distinguished but was an ordinary wife, mother, and housewife. She held a number of jobs, including one with the publishing firm Simon and Schuster. Stern stresses her ordinariness, but he shows her to be extraordinary as she underwent the experience of dying. The account of how she deals with her condition is the most important part of the book.

In order to create a full portrait of Ruth, however, Stern must go back to their early years. Ruth was four years older than Richard, and her reaction to his birth was amusing and revealing. She saw him as an invader into her established world. As they grew up, they experienced the usual rivalry of two siblings in a household. The relationship between brother and sister was not always close; it was marked, instead, by competition and distance. He saw her as "pesty," while she saw him as arrogant and insensitive. In adulthood he considered her boring and ignorant and believed that her world was encompassed by her roles as wife and mother; in contrast, he was a well-known novelist and professor at the prestigious University of Chicago. The closest she came to any distinction was her work at a publishing firm. Thus from their early years through their middle years, their relationship was distant if not hostile. They did, however, become closer after the death of their parents.

The brother-sister relationship changed dramatically when Stern received news of his sister's illness. He was then forced to reassess his relationship to Ruth and come to terms with her life and her place in his life.

Stern makes some interesting remarks about the relationship between poet Howard Nemerov and his sister, the photographer Diane Arbus. Stern states that their relationship was "as divided by rivalry as fused by love." The rivalry between Richard Stern and Ruth Stern Leviton was not that intense, but divisions as well as love were clearly present.

After flying to New York to be with his sister, Stern was shocked at her physical diminishment. He spent most of his time reminiscing with her about relatives and other people in their earlier years. Brother and sister found themselves tied closely together by their shared history of people and experiences. Stern realized that in a way they possessed a language common only to them. Ruth maintained her humor in the midst of her illness; this reassured Stern, showing him that Ruth was "still Ruth."

Yet in the midst of his sister's dying, Stern had other concerns to address. He discusses encounters with his new publisher and his son. The conversation with the publisher was marked by Stern's discussing his meeting with Thomas Mann, the great German writer, while he was teaching in Germany. Mann was surprisingly modest and accessible and provided Stern with a model of what a great writer should be. There are, however, no significant revelations about Mann's writing or views. The only interesting detail is the revelation that Mann denied using very much biblical research in the writing of the tetralogy *Joseph und seine Brüder* (1933-1943; *Joseph and His Brothers*, 1933-1944) and other novels.

Arrangements for the meeting between Stern and his son, Christopher, was strained; it becomes clear that the two found themselves divided by rivalry and tension. Christopher at first refused to meet with his father, because he was engaged in a writing project and believed that his father would set him back and block his writing. (In Stern's earlier "A Father's Story," which uses Christopher as a character, the son is resentful and uncertain about his famous father.) After a number of tortured telephone conversations, however, father and son did meet and had a pleasant lunch unmarred by expressions of conflict or rivalry.

Soon afterward, Stern learned that his sister was far more ill than he had realized. Her doctor revealed that her cancer had spread and there was little that he could do for her. Stern and Ruth's husband, Ralph Leviton, kept the news from her, but she was momentarily frightened by an inept psychiatrist who wanted her to sign a document declaring a wish to be subjected to no life-saving devices. Stern, angry at this tactlessness, did his best to keep the offending psychiatrist from seeing Ruth again. Together with Ralph, he managed to calm her, and Stern and Ruth continued their reminiscing about the family. He writes movingly about her courage and dignity "in the midst of unhappiness and weakness."

Leaving his sister, Stern visited his daughter and later Philip Roth and then returned to Chicago. He continued to think about his sister, but he had his own life to pursue. Soon after his return to Chicago, he heard from Ralph that Ruth's condition had declined and she was expected to die soon. Stern flew to New York, but Ruth died before his arrival. Surprisingly, there is no discussion of any guilt feelings at being absent when his sister died.

Stern tries to enhance the significance of his sister's death by linking it to the destruction of the Soviet Union. During his account of the critical period of Ruth's illness, he cites the "resignation" of Mikhail Gorbachev and the presence of tanks in Red Square. Ruth's illness and death were not noted in the press, but to Stern they are no less momentous.

The business of the burial and funeral are described with sardonic wit. Stern notes, for example, the selection and pricing of a coffin and the curious billing procedure of the funeral home, which overcharged Ralph Leviton two thousand dollars. The funeral took place on a scorching New York day, and the air-conditioned limousine was late; Stern was forced to ride in an old car with no air conditioning. The grave was not properly prepared, and a clump of a tree stood nearby forlornly. In this part of his story, Stern seems to forget his mourning and concentrates on his rage at the incompetence of the funeral director. He did give an brief elegy for his sister at graveside. Having searched the Bible but "found few appropriate words," he quoted from Ecclesiastes. Yet he had little to say about Ruth's life other than to bid her good-bye.

After the funeral, Stern visited Roth again. This meeting was more interesting than the earlier one. Stern talked about a meeting with Ezra Pound in Italy and his own novel *Stitch* (1965), which uses Pound as the main character. He concentrates on Pound's anti-Semitism, links it to that of Mircea Eliade, and concludes that he cannot condone their works because the viciousness they endorsed had an effect on others, even though his experience with both was significant.

Stern did come to some realizations about his sister after he had lost her. He notes that he had been "blind" to her worth and value. So while Ruth remains at the heart of the book, Stern admits his failure to see her closely enough. He feels guilt and an absence in his life that cannot be repaired or replaced.

The rest of the book is taken up by Stern's journal entries, which return to the events dealt with at the beginning of the book. Some of the entries deal with writers. Stern records some wickedly amusing remarks by Saul Bellow on other writers; there is a section dealing with a visit to John Updike, but it is not especially interesting or revealing. Updike did mention that Bellow does not like Updike's fiction, and the reader notes that there seems to be a distance between Stern and Updike.

Stern also records his dreams in the journal section. In the most important of these, he dreams of meeting his mother, Ruth, and another sister, "Ruth's twin." The absence of his sister clearly weighs upon Stern's mind, and the dream is a way of restoring, even duplicating, that lost presence.

The most important journal entry has to do with his sister. "Why is love withheld—suppressed, unexpressed. It is like electricity, too powerful to release without insulation." This is a lament over Stern's inability to express the love that he felt—as well as a justification for not doing so. Love is the most powerful emotion, and to protect the recipient and giver there must be some "insulation." Yet the "insulation" seems to be stronger than the expression of love, which is, in this case, "withheld." The last entries speak of his own fears of death, but he puts them aside and looks forward to a new book.

The book ends with a "coda," which tries to come to terms with the events the book records. The death of Stern's sister still weighs on him as he thinks about her absence, but the claims of life remain strong. It is his birthday, and his children and friends call to congratulate him. Nevertheless, the death of his sister continues to darken his pleasure in his own accomplishments.

A Sistermony is a provocative book on a subject that has not been fully explored before. Stern has difficulty, however, in coming fully to terms with his relationship with his sister. The book does not give readers a full enough portrait of Ruth Leviton. Everything is seen through the eyes of Richard Stern, and the focus is on his life and experiences. Furthermore, the accounts of meetings with and discussions of writers tend to overwhelm the passages on Ruth. The relationship of this particular brother and sister is a fascinating one, but it is filled with unrealized potential. *A Sistermony* is an excellent and consistently interesting book, but it is not the definitive analysis of a relationship between a brother and a sister.

James Sullivan

Sources for Further Study

The Antioch Review. LIII, Fall, 1995, p. 454.
Booklist. XCI, February 15, 1995, p. 1054.
Chicago Tribune. March 19, 1995, XIV, p. 3.
Kirkus Reviews. LXIII, January 1, 1995, p. 68.
Los Angeles Times Book Review. April 2, 1995, p. 6.
Publishers Weekly. CCXLII, January 2, 1995, p. 64.

SKINNED ALIVE

Author: Edmund White (1940-   )
Publisher: Alfred A. Knopf (New York). 254 pp. $23.00
Type of work: Short stories

A collection of eight sensitive stories about the joys, sorrows, terrors, perplexities, and bittersweet memories of male homosexuals by the leading American chronicler of gay life

Edmund White, who is widely regarded as the late twentieth century's leading writer about gay life, won the National Book Critics Circle Award and the Lambda Literary Award for his book *Genet: A Biography* (1993). He has published five novels and several works of nonfiction, including *States of Desire: Travels in Gay America* (1980) and *The Joy of Gay Sex: An Intimate Guide for Gay Men to the Pleasures of a Gay Lifestyle* (1977). *Skinned Alive* is his first collection of stories.

One common theme echoes throughout this collection of stories about the international gay subculture: the contrast between the appearance and the reality of being gay. On the outside White's characters appear to be enjoying the sense of being elite, refined, sophisticated, liberated insiders who have stepped out of the closet into a world of cultural, intellectual, and sexual excitement. On the inside, however, his characters are suffering the torments that have traditionally gone with their ambiguous social and psychological physical condition, plus a new one worse than any of the others. White usually avoids mentioning acquired immunodeficiency syndrome (AIDS) or HIV by name, but the disease haunts his stories like an avenging demon. Most of his protagonists have gotten it, are afraid of getting it, are living with someone who has it, or are grieving the loss of a loved one who has just died of it.

"Pyrography" is one of three stories in which White, who has been diagnosed as HIV-positive, looks back at days before the epidemic he refers to as "the disease," "the plague," "*die Pest*," and "the scourge." A teenage homosexual goes on a camping trip with two "butch" acquaintances and has to conceal his sexual attraction to them for fear of being scorned and rejected. "Reprise" is another story about the days of irresponsible youth, told from the sadder but wiser perspective of an aging, lonely homosexual. It suggests that the gay lifestyle is far more appropriate to young men full of illusions about the intriguing possibilities of mysterious strangers. The same is true of "Watermarked," in which the narrator tells about his first lover and his introduction to the theatrical world. White intimates that he was happily homosexual as early as junior high school, when he "learned to camp outrageously" (as in "You vicious quane, I saw you makin' goo-goo eyes at mah man").

Gay men are often attracted to males who themselves are attracted only to women. In "Running on Empty," a man who has returned from gay Paris to the Bible Belt to die of AIDS reflects that "he'd never really gotten the guys he'd wanted, the big high school jocks, the blonds with loud tenor voices, beer breath, cruel smiles, lean hips, steady, insolent eyes, the guys impossible to befriend if you weren't exactly like them."

"Palace Days" is the story of two homosexuals who love each other and have lived together for years but are not really sexually attracted to each other. Ironically, the advent of AIDS has forced many gay men into monogamous relationships at just the time when the gay liberation movement was taking the legal danger out of promiscuity. The absence of a sexual bonding makes both of the story's characters feel insecure in an otherwise comfortable domestic relationship. Inevitably one gets infected with the unnameable disease because they have continued to "cruise" for furtive sexual encounters with virile strangers.

White, who is in his late fifties, writes with feeling about the subject that novelist Christopher Isherwood introduced so effectively in *A Single Man* (1964): the loneliness of the aging homosexual whose chances of finding another long-term lover are rapidly approaching zero. The young homosexual who comes out of the closet finds the gay world a source of exciting liaisons and social mobility; the aging homosexual finds himself without home, family, or friends (many of the latter have died prematurely). He often finds it impossible to fit in with the younger crowd because styles change in the gay world and few young homosexuals are interested in older ones unless, like Marcel Proust's Monsieur Charlus, the aging queens are willing to pay for the illusion of love.

In "An Oracle," a lonely man facing middle age is trying to recover from grief over his long-term lover who died of a series of diseases to which he had lost immunity through the unnameable scourge of homosexuals. The survivor's way of recovering is through picking up tough male prostitutes on the streets of a town in Crete. (Being a typical White character, he diligently adds to his Greek vocabulary in the process.) Like many gay men, he is attracted to heterosexual men who despise him—another way in which being gay is synonymous with being skinned alive.

"An Oracle" contains highly graphic descriptions of gay sexual behavior and does nothing to make it seem attractive, at least to the heterosexual reader. Commercial transactions for sex take place at night in a deserted schoolyard toilet. It seems as if the masochistic protagonist enjoys nothing so much as humiliation, pain, and physical danger. Here again there is a sharp contrast between the pretense of gaiety and the brutal reality of being gay. The illustration on the dust jacket of White's book shows what has become almost the trademark of gay fiction: a naked young man bowed in a posture suggesting complete submission, humiliation, and loss of manhood.

In "Skinned Alive," the title story of the volume, White incorporates a gruesome myth about a musical duel between the god Apollo and a satyr named Marsyas, who lost and was flayed alive, to symbolize the notion that homosexuals are challenging the gods each time they engage in sodomy or fellatio.

Under the influence of Proust, many writers have tried to flavor their prose with unusual similes. Most have failed because the comparisons are too *cherché*, or fail to clarify the author's meaning, or only partially fit, like pieces of a jigsaw puzzle forced into the wrong spaces. White is one writer who can actually play on the same court with Proust, at least in this matter of creating strange but strikingly appropriate figures of speech, which Aristotle identified as an unmistakable sign of genius. Here is an example from "Skinned Alive": "Sometimes his shyness brought all the laughter and words to a queasy halt, and it made me think of that becalmed moment when a sailboat comes around and the mainsail luffs before it catches the wind again." In "An Oracle," White writes: "The town had been badly bombed during the war, and empty lots and grass-growing ruins pocked even the most crowded blocks like shocking lapses in an otherwise good memory." White incorporates another example in that same story: "He thought it very likely that he was carrying death inside him, that it was ticking inside him like a time bomb but one he couldn't find because it had been secreted by an unknown terrorist." And here is a final Proustian simile from "Watermarked": "That night I drank lots of Drambuie and wandered through the Arboretum past lovers, homosexual and heterosexual, writhing beneath old trees like exposed root systems come to life."

White, who has been described as a "mandarin esthete," does not rely on dramatic devices to hold the reader's interest in his rambling autobiographical stories. Like many modern short-story writers, he has turned his back on such tricks of the trade as plots, narrative hooks, black moments, "ticking clocks," and MacGuffins. Edgar Allan Poe set the standards for the modern short story when he wrote that all the story's elements should go to create a "single effect." White's stories usually do create a single effect but are full of superfluities and digressions; he is the opposite of a minimalist. He relies on poetic language, stylistic legerdemain, his insider's knowledge of the still clandestine gay subculture, his unique life experiences, and his obvious—sometimes too obvious—erudition to hold the reader's attention. His writing is full of brilliant aperçus, which show that he deserves the critical acclaim he has received since publication of his first novel, *Forgetting Elena*, in 1973. White has often been compared to Vladimir Nabokov in reminiscing simply for the sake of reminiscing and being his own most interesting fictional character. Like Nabokov, he decorates his fiction with exotic trivia, so that the reader often has the illusion of having been lured into a world of wanton indulgence with illustrations by Aubrey Beardsley.

Unfortunately, White, like the elitist, cosmopolitan Gore Vidal, another homosexual writer whom he resembles, is sometimes guilty of too much brilliance, as in the following example:

> This was the Paul who had explained what Derrida had said of Heidegger's interpretation of Trakl's last poems, who claimed that literature could be studied only through rhetoric, grammar and genre and who considered Ronsard a greater poet than Shakespeare (because of Ronsard's combination of passion and logic, satyr and god, in place of the mere conversational fluency which Paul regarded as the flaw and genius of English).

If this sort of triple reverse handoff does not provoke the reader to slam the covers, then White can count on holding him to the end. Even the earnest reader who is trying to pick up a little culture may sometimes sense that he is being more dazzled than edified. White, like Nabokov, does not write for people who move their lips when they read. His method of holding attention seems to consist largely of challenging the reader to measure up to a high standard of literacy.

White's characters are obsessed with sex. Judging from these stories, it would seem that gay men, even in their fifties, spend far more time thinking about sex, talking about sex, cruising for sex, or bemoaning its loss or unattainability than heterosexual males, who are happy to compartmentalize the provocative nuisance through marriage so that they can devote their time to more profitable pursuits. Fortunately—or perhaps unfortunately—White's characters seldom need to do any work. They are elitists in incomes as well as in manners, tastes, and social connections. They either inherited money or are on seemingly perpetual sabbaticals, like characters in an Agatha Christie novel. Like Christie's characters, they all seem a bit suspect. They have plenty of time for pursuing their favorite sport down whatever dark alleys it might lead them. White makes it seem as if sex for gay men is a form of enslavement like alcoholism, drug addiction, or compulsive gambling.

His elite characters are better than "straight" men and worse, happier and more miserable, liberated and totally enslaved to their vice, proud of their emancipation and ashamed of their behavior, longing for love while unable to love men who are their own mirror images, intelligent, cultured, traveled, affluent, yet worshiping the most sweat-stained, muscle-bound troglodytes they can find in the world's public toilets. It seems a pity that White, like many other gay writers, including the talented David Leavitt, can interest himself only in facets of a single subject. Although White resembles Proust and Nabokov, his limited scope may prevent him from attaining their literary stature.

Being "gay" would seem to mean having "grace under pressure," in the old Hemingway sense. The pressure may be social ostracism, fear of disease, fear of a lonely old age, the feeling of biological failure, the disappointment of one's parents, rootlessness, self-loathing, the enigma of one's own self, or various combinations. No doubt the heterosexual reader of these stories—who will likely be in a minority—will gain more understanding of that other world and with it more compassion.

Bill Delaney

Sources for Further Study

Boston Globe. July 30, 1995, p. 35.
Library Journal. CXX, June 15, 1995, p. 97.
London Review of Books. XVII, August 24, 1995, p. 12.
Los Angeles Times Book Review. July 16, 1995, p. 4.
The Nation. CCLXI, August 28, 1995, p. 214.
The New York Times Book Review. C, July 23, 1995, p. 6.
The Observer. May 14, 1995, p. 14.
Publishers Weekly. CCXLII, May 22, 1995, p. 46.
San Francisco Chronicle. June 18, 1995, p. REV7.
The Times Literary Supplement. March 17, 1995, p. 20.
The Washington Post Book World. XXV, September 24, 1995, p. 13.

THE STORIES OF VLADIMIR NABOKOV

Author: Vladimir Nabokov (1899-1977)
Edited, with a preface, by Dmitri Nabokov
Publisher: Alfred A. Knopf (New York). 659 pp. $35.00
Type of work: Short stories

A comprehensive collection of sixty-five stories, written from 1921 to 1951, by one of the most accomplished writers of the twentieth century

The publication of this extensive collection of short stories by Vladimir Nabokov represents a singular pleasure for the admirer of Nabokov's work. Not only does the collection gather together fifty-two stories that were published in four separate volumes long out of print, but it also contains several stories (primarily from Nabokov's earliest years as a prose writer) that have not been readily accessible to Nabokov's readers. With the collection in hand, one can clearly see the many ways in which Nabokov's artistic talent grew and evolved over the first half of his career, before he attained widespread fame with the publication of *Lolita* in 1955. Critics have often noted that Nabokov was fond of reworking favorite themes and images, finding ever-new combinations and patterns to present to his readers. This collection offers a fresh view of the unique "combinational delight" to be found in Nabokov's fiction.

Nabokov entered literature as a poet, and some of his early stories reflect what he later identified in *Poems and Problems* (1970) as "Byzantine imagery"—the presence of angels, spirits, and the like in his work. Indeed, one is struck by how many supernatural beings populate the pages of Nabokov's earliest stories: a wood sprite expresses his dismay over the loss of Russia to the narrator of the first work in the collection ("The Wood-Sprite"); a strange, shaggy angel of the Alps takes cruel revenge on a woman in "Wingstroke"; the majestic "Thunder-god" Elijah descends to earth to retrieve a lost chariot wheel in "The Thunderstorm;" and the devil, incarnated as a tall, heavy, middle-aged woman, tries unsuccessfully to help a timid German collect a fabulous harem in fulfillment of his erotic aspirations ("A Nursery Tale").

In later years, such beings disappear from Nabokov's work, but not because he had lost all interest in the supernatural. On the contrary, he merely discarded its conventional trappings. In his mature work, beginning with the novel *The Defense* (1964) to *Transparent Things* (1972), the spirits of those no longer alive can be felt behind the scenes. His work suggests that such spirits retain an interest in the affairs of the persons they have left behind and perhaps can even have a subtle influence on their fate. In one of the last stories of this collection, "The Vane Sisters," Nabokov demonstrates the power of the departed to affect the living by having his narrator unwittingly encode an acrostic message from two dead sisters in the last paragraph of his tale.

This concern with the power of the dead to affect the living reflects a more profound preoccupation on Nabokov's part—his awareness of the cruel reality of loss, parting, and death in human experience. Throughout the collection, but particularly in the works written in the 1920's, one finds Nabokov returning to the theme of sudden death and untimely parting. One recalls that after losing his beloved Russia in the aftermath of the Bolshevik Revolution of 1917, Nabokov was faced with an even more devastating loss in 1922—the murder of his father by a man seeking revenge for the end of the Russian imperial dynasty. Transmuting his grief into his fiction, Nabokov presents a gallery of individuals who struggle desperately to overcome the pain of their personal losses.

Some, such as protagonists of "Wingstroke," "A Matter of Chance," and "Christmas," are so overwhelmed by tragedies that they contemplate or commit suicide, while others, such as the title character of "The Return of Chorb," strive for imaginative defenses against the specter of isolation and oblivion. After the sudden death of his wife by electrocution, Chorb retraces the path of their honeymoon, trying to "gather all the little things they had noticed together" in the hope that through this process "her image would grow immortal and replace her forever." The success of Chorb's quest, however, remains questionable at the end of the tale, and the intense self-absorption he displays throughout the work casts doubt on the validity of his method of reanimating the past.

A more stunning articulation of the human potential for survival and transcendence occurs in the brief sketch "Christmas." Sleptsov, the protagonist, is devastated by the sudden death of his son, and he decides to kill himself on Christmas Day. As he contemplates some of his dead child's most cherished belongings, however, he is startled by a strange sound—the cracking of a cocoon that his son, an amateur lepidopterist, had bought some months earlier but that was assumed merely to contain a dead chrysalid. Out of the cocoon comes a great moth. As its wings "miraculously" expand, they seem to take "a full breath under the impulse of tender, ravishing, almost human happiness." All is not lost; the spirit of Sleptsov's child lives on in the astonishing emergence of this fabulous moth.

Nabokov's fiction also looks to more mundane moments to assert a belief in the basic goodness and beauty of life. Writing to a former love in Russia, the narrator of "A Letter That Never Reached Russia" avidly records his impressions of a Berlin nightscape, and he declares that even though he himself will someday die, his happiness will remain "in everything with which God so generously surrounds human loneliness." The narrator of the sketch "Beneficence" makes a similar discovery. Although the woman he loves has jilted him and will not appear for an expected rendezvous, he takes comfort in the sight of an old woman receiving and reciprocating an act of kindness. In one of the most optimistic declarations to be found in Nabokov's fiction, he proclaims:

> Here I became aware of the world's tenderness, the profound beneficence of all that surrounded me, the blissful bond between me and all of creation. . . . I realized that the world does not represent a struggle at all, or a predaceous sequence of chance events, but shimmering bliss, beneficent trepidation, a gift bestowed on us and unappreciated.

Nabokov populated his stories with a memorable cast of characters, from modest dreamers to callous egotists. Particularly distinctive are those who see the world around them transformed, whether this transforming vision arises from trauma ("Details of a Sunset"), illness ("Terra Incognita"), or more enigmatic, even fantastic causes. The narrator of "The Visit to the Museum," for example, enters a museum in France, only to exit it onto the streets of Leningrad. Even more intriguing is the story "Ultima Thule," which features a character who claims to have "accidentally solved 'the riddle of the universe.'" Nabokov's suggestive prose indicates that this claim might just be true, at least for this fictional denizen of a fictional universe.

Several of these visionary characters share an important feature with their creator: They are artists or writers. The theme of art, and particularly of the self-conscious intentionality that goes into the fiction-making process, became increasingly prominent over the course of Nabokov's career. In "A Guide to Berlin," the narrator explains that "the sense of literary creation" is "to portray ordinary objects as they will be reflected in the kindly mirrors of future times." In "The Passenger," a writer and a critic contrast the inventive genius of a writer's plots with those of life itself. Finally, in "Recruiting," Nabokov's narrator reveals the secret of his creative conjury: After spinning out a touching tale about the lonely life of an elderly man, he discloses in the end that the entire story is a fiction projected onto the figure of an unknown person sitting on a park bench. These stories serve as something like a preliminary sketchbook for the complex novels Nabokov fashioned as he matured as a novelist, novels such as *The Gift* and *The Real Life of Sebastian Knight*.

When one surveys the entire span of Nabokov's short fiction, a palpable development can be discerned in the writer's art. Some of the earliest stories (such as "Revenge") are reminiscent of the work of O. Henry, Théophile Gautier, or Edgar Allan Poe; they are built around a central suspenseful anecdote, with a sudden plot twist (often macabre) coming at the end of the tale. Gradually, this type of work is supplemented by sketches with a more lyrical, poetic density which reminds one of the work of Anton Chekhov or Ivan Bunin ("Sounds" is a good example of this). These works testify to the writer's acute powers of observation and description. The texture of a young woman's skin, the complex play of light on the surface of someone's eye, the fresh way that everyday scenes and situations come alive when apprehended by the master's vision: All of these carry the unmistakable hallmarks of Nabokov's gifts.

It his mature works, however, that reveal a genius that is absolutely unique: They are multilayered, resonant, and cunningly rich. "Lips to Lips," for example, is on the surface a simple tale of an aging man's vain desire to win distinction as a writer. Yet while the story delicately evokes the lonely man's quest "not for fame, but simply for some warmth and heed on the part of readerdom," it manages both to satirize literary banality (in the trite formulas of the old man's writing) and to settle long-standing scores with some of Nabokov's adversaries from the ranks of contemporary Russian critics.

Examining Nabokov's finest achievements in the short-story form (such as "Signs and Symbols"), one can only be impressed by the way he elevates earlier themes and devices to an entirely new level of complexity. The suspense of a ringing bell in the sketch entitled "The Doorbell" reappears in "Signs and Symbols" as the excruciating tension of a series of telephone calls, but with much more powerful and disturbing implications. As the elderly parents of a suicidal boy anticipate in fear the possibility of a call from the hospital informing them that their son is dead, the telephone rings twice. In both cases, it is a wrong number. The telephone then rings for the third time, and before the old woman can answer it, the narrative comes to an end. Is it again a wrong number? Or is it the dreaded call from the hospital? Here Nabokov implicates the reader in the boy's affliction, which has been labeled "referential mania"—the delusion that everything happening around oneself is a veiled reference to one's own personality and existence. Trying to guess what the call will mean to the parents, the reader becomes caught up in the meaning-making process too. In fact, at this moment the reader becomes something akin to a coauthor: Depending on what meaning one assigns to the telephone call, the reader may either spare the parents the cruel certainty of the child's death or, on the contrary, confirm that very certainty. Ironically, Nabokov's description of the child's suffering may make the latter choice the more merciful one, for as the writer puts it, what the boy really wants to do is "to tear a hole in his world and escape."

The final blow never comes, however, and this suspension of likely death resonates with compassion on the part of the author. This work represents a high point of Nabokov's accomplishments as a short-story artist. While some of the later stories seem marred by a certain diffuseness or lack of focus, the subtle power and intensity of works such as "Signs and Symbols" earn for them a place next to Nabokov's more famous achievements in the novel form.

Julian Connolly

Sources for Further Study

Booklist. XCII, September 1, 1995, p. 6.
Library Journal. CXX, September 15, 1995, p. 96.
The New Republic. CCXIII, November 20, 1995, p. 42.
The New York Times. October 20, 1995, p. C35.
The New York Times Book Review. C, October 29, 1995, p. 7.
The New Yorker. LXXI, December 4, 1995, p. 108.
Newsweek. CXXVI, November 6, 1995, p. 90.
Publishers Weekly. CCXLII, September 4, 1995, p. 46.
Time. CXLVI, October 30, 1995, p. 40.

SUDDEN GLORY
Laughter as Subversive Activity

Author: Barry Sanders (1938-   )
Publisher: Beacon Press (Boston). 328 pp. $27.50
Type of work: Intellectual history

In a work ranging over several thousand years, historian Barry Sanders uses laughter and attitudes toward laughter to illuminate the complex relationships among language, literature, and society

Sudden Glory: Laughter as Subversive Activity surveys the history of human behavior—specifically, the history of laughter. In this history, Barry Sanders unlocks a number of other important stories: the relationship of humans to authority, for example, and the interconnections among joking, language, and literature. Most important, Sanders argues the subversive nature of laughter: that in the face of religious or political authority, laughter can become as powerful a force as war and break the stranglehold that civilized behavior often demands of people. As the ancients discovered long ago, "A single, sardonic laugh can devastate even the most powerful human being."

Laughter, Sanders contends, is the most natural of human expressions. It is what defines human beings, in fact, for humans are the only animals who have such a capability. (Aristotle actually referred to man as *animal ridens*, or "the beast who laughs.") Ironically, laughter also reminds people that they are animals at heart, and laughter at another person's stumbling or bumbling along only records the recognition of how close to animals all human beings really are. The billy goat butting the poor farmer on the comics page also links the two characters.

Laughter usually comes from surprise or the unexpected, and often at the expense of someone less fortunate (even in popular situation comedies). Turned against the authorities, however, as it often is in history, laughter also becomes a powerful weapon of derision and satire. Sanders is less interested in jokes or comedy themselves here than in the laughter that is produced by and that itself produces literature.

> The roots of literature, as I hope to demonstrate in the course of this book, lie buried not in hard work, revision, and serious description. That already smacks of high levels of literacy. Rather, like a sport, literature grew out of play and banter, joking and good times—out of humor and laughter, much of it, at least by the sixth century, the domain of women.

The most important parts of this story are the intricate and integral interconnections throughout history between laughter and language.

The story of laughter that Sanders has produced is an important new reading of both human and literary history. It is also a very scholarly study—by a professor of English and the history of ideas at Pitzer College, Claremont—complete with a long introduction, eight packed chapters, and an epilogue, all essentially divided into three parts. The first four chapters—and nearly half of Sanders' analysis—center on the earliest periods of human history and extend to the treatment of laughter in the Old Testament and among Greek philosophers such as the Stoics and the Rhetoricians. In the ancient world, Sanders contends, laughter and weeping were much closer than they were to become later, for both could express joy and pain. (Vestiges of this organic human unity can be found today in the expressions "he laughed until he cried" and "they wept for joy.") In a chapter titled "The Ancient World: Divine Origins of Laughter," Sanders retells the stories of Hephaistos and Prometheus to illustrate these ideas. Laughter in the Old Testament was either scornful or derisive, as Sanders shows, but the ancient Jews also became adept at irony—one of the first subversions of humor.

Human beings paid a high price for the privilege of society, however, and part of it was the loss of laughter as a natural expression of joyous feeling. Laughter was taken over by men and philosophers at an early stage of civilization, Sanders argues, and nearly every Greek philosopher felt compelled to say something about laughter as a category of human action. (Plato, for example, allows laughter in his *Republic* only under certain very limiting conditions.) Peasants and women must then find "a more subversive route to godlike power," Sanders postulates. This subversion story is one of the major underground streams running beneath the history Sanders traces in *Sudden Glory*.

> This is the punch line I am asking the reader to listen for, as the underground humor builds more force and finally collides with these ancient theories of wit and demeanor. . . . The explosion will be heard around the world and felt in every small village and town.

The first laugh in English is recorded in the seventh century epic *Beowulf*. Sanders anchors his entire study in the medieval world, for it was in the Middle Ages that laughter erupted as a powerful human voice railing against and trying to bring down authority. Condemned by church or state at various times (occasionally by both), laughter became a subversive weapon used by those without power, "the great swelling tide of laughter that buoyed the spirits of medieval peasants, what Mikhail Bakhtin calls in a brilliant phrase, 'the second revelation of the world in play and laughter.'" Students of medieval life mark it most noticeably in festivals, or in what Sanders refers to as the "carnivalization" of everyday affairs that becomes an essential part of life in the Middle Ages. Sanders poses an essential structural opposition in this part of his study between Carnival and Lent, the opposing forces of expansiveness and constriction, freedom and rule. This opposition will continue, his study reveals, throughout modern history.

The most extended literary analysis in *Sudden Glory*—developed in a chapter titled "Chaucer Punches the First Joke Home"—focuses on "The Miller's Tale" from *The Canterbury Tales* (1387-1400), for here is summed up much of the history that Sanders is attempting to describe. Geoffrey Chaucer represents what Sanders' favorite literary critic, the Russian Bakhtin, proposes as the "dialogic" (dialoguelike) struggles between the impulses of seriousness and playfulness. In "The Miller's Tale," the carnivalesque spirit clearly invades and invigorates the more sober fictions of Chaucer's tales.

Jokes and laughter, then, undermine not only social and religious authority but also, from Chaucer on, the authority of fiction, of storytelling, itself. As Bakhtin elsewhere argues, "Fictional discourse reaches meaning through the inherent joking nature of language itself, through its inclination to undercut itself." Thus in Chaucer the Miller's story—a kind of Abbott and Costello or Laurel and Hardy routine of cuckoldry and flatulence—marks the emergence of literature as it is now known, for the tale not only comically undercuts the other, more serious tales in *The Canterbury Tales* but breaks the rules of traditional storytelling as well. "The three pursuits, then—laughing, joking, and storytelling—reveal their interlocking connections right before our eyes, in Chaucer's extraordinary poetry."

In his two final chapters and a brief epilogue, Sanders conflates the rest of human ludic history, from the Renaissance through stand-up comics at the end of the twentieth century. While he makes a number of telling points (for example, "irony and satire in effect can be read as ridicule with class"), the history here unrolls too rapidly for the human eye or ear: from Rabelais, Shakespeare's Falstaff, and Jonathan Swift to Charlie Chaplin, Lenny Bruce, and Paula Poundstone. (Sanders's analysis of Chaplin's *The Great Dictator* is a model of understanding the intricate relationships between culture and society in the twentieth century.) In fact, a number of ideas in his final chapters become roadkills, run over at breakneck speed by Sanders' racing survey. Clearly a second book could be written out of the last seventy-five pages of this study, a book dealing with all the modern comic forms, from Renaissance comedy through late twentieth century television situation comedies. One hopes that Sanders will consider such a prospect in the near future.

Sanders' style throughout this book is almost as exuberant and playful as his subject. "Tremendous power resides in a single scornful laugh," Sanders writes early in the work. "Who in his or her right mind has not at one time or another fired off a well-aimed derisive shot at an unsuspecting target, and not experienced great joy in slowly squeezing the trigger?" Yet his prose can also be rich, dense, allusive, every paragraph packed with ideas and punch lines. The two styles at times work at cross purposes. *Sudden Glory* is a solid scholarly study—complete with footnotes on nearly every page and a forty-page bibliography listing virtually every major relevant work on humor and comedy. At the same time the book occasionally sounds like a stand-up routine. Sanders knew Lenny Bruce at an early and formative stage of his own intellectual development, and the influence of the comic on the scholar is obvious.

On its most interesting level, *Sudden Glory* has to do with language, with how it changes and grows through the centuries, for Sanders is always exploring the meanings of words and tracing their etymologies. The Old Testament Abraham does not have to cleave his son Isaac in two—and cleave means both "stick to" and "split apart," Sanders tells his readers in a footnote. Interestingly, the Hebrew words for laughter and sexual intercourse, he notes a few pages later, come from the same linguistic root. Cicero, he writes, divided humor into irony (*facetiae*, and hence the English word "facetious") and raillery (*dicacitas*), and Sanders goes on to record several pages of the linguistic consequences of such a division. Further on, he writes,

The Latin word for "story," *geste*, produces the modern English *jest*, a kinship that the English recognize as early as the time of King Aelfric. They use the word *racu* in some places to translate the Latin *historia*, and in other places to translate *commoedia*.

A few pages later Sanders devotes some time describing the weeks he spent as a freshman at the University of California at Los Angeles (UCLA) in 1956, attending nightly Lenny Bruce concerts at a Hollywood club: Future academic poststructuralist meets radical stand-up comic. The stories are not incompatible, however, for they come out of the same source: an intense interest in the interconnections between laughter and language. "So I ask you," Sanders writes on the first page of his preface,

> to listen in particular to those who have been denied access to writing—not only the peasants of every livery, but especially the women of every class—who have remained closely attuned to the heartbeat, the impulse, of vernacular speech. Every time someone like Plato advises against laughing to excess because it violates decorum or morality, imagine scores of common citizens cracking up for just those reasons. No sooner than the law tightens its rope, some smart alec will twist a noose into a loophole and make a clean getaway, laughing all the way to the border.

Lenny Bruce hardly escaped the nooses created both by society and by himself, but his career, and particularly the way his language shocked the authorities, fits Sanders' story perfectly in revealing the transformative power that laughter and language can have.

Sudden Glory explores these connections between play and language, between jokes and literature, and between laughter and social change. The book itself is written in a layered style that is three parts Halls of Ivy and one part Comedy Club. It is a brilliant performance, and a scholarly one that raises a number of intriguing ideas for readers—and not a few jokes, both ancient and current.

David Peck

Sources for Further Study

Library Journal. CXX, August, 1995, p. 75.
Publishers Weekly. CCXLII, July 3, 1995, p. 41.

SUI SIN FAR/EDITH MAUDE EATON
A Literary Biography

Author: Annette White-Parks
Publisher: University of Illinois Press (Urbana). Illustrated. 268 pp. $34.95
Type of work: Literary biography
Time: 1865-1914
Locale: Montreal, Canada; the American West Coast; and Boston

The first book-length study of the first Eurasian fiction writer to have her writings published in North America

> *Principal personage:*
> SUI SIN FAR (EDITH MAUDE EATON), an Asian American journalist and
> fiction writer

By putting the Asian name first in the title *Sui Sin Far/Edith Maude Eaton*, Annette White-Parks communicates not only her subject's Eurasian heritage but also Sui Sin Far's affirmation of her Asian identity in her mature writings. Born in England in 1865 to a Chinese mother and a British father, Sui Sin Far (Chinese for water lily) migrated with her family in 1873 to Montreal, where she lived in near poverty during a time of strong Sinophobia. At the age of ten she began working to help support her family. Later she traveled to the United States in search of work, living for a time on the West Coast and in Boston. She published both nonfiction and fiction in Canadian and American newspapers and magazines. She also published a novel, *Mrs. Spring Fragrance* (1914), shortly before her death in Montreal.

White-Parks' *Sui Sin Far/Edith Maude Eaton* is the third publication in the University of Illinois series The Asian American Experience, edited by Roger Daniels. The fourth volume in this series is a collection of Sui Sin Far's writings, *Mrs. Spring Fragrance and Other Writings* (1995), edited by Amy Ling and Annette White-Parks. Material on Sui Sin Far and later Asian American writers is included in Elaine Kim's *Asian American Literature: An Introduction to the Writings in Their Social Context* (1982), Amy Ling's *Between Worlds: Women Writers of Chinese Ancestry* (1990), and *Tricksterism in Turn-of-the-Century American Literature: A Multicultural Perspective* (1994), edited by Elizabeth Ammons and White-Parks.

White-Parks undertakes three tasks in her study of Sui Sin Far. First, she locates all of her subject's extant published literary works, journalism, and correspondence from the years 1888-1913; second, she presents the results of her extensive research into the biography and social context of the writer and her works; third, she analyzes and evaluates Sui Sin Far's writings, using both sociocultural and feminist critical approaches. By so doing, she gives contemporary Asian American women writers such as Amy Tan and Maxine Hong Kingston a literary foremother of distinction. Moreover, White-Parks breaks new ground in women's literary history.

In her biographical account in the first chapter, White-Parks traces her subject's choices to remain single and to pursue a writing career. Neither of these was the norm for women in the late nineteenth century, and in particular they were not the norm for women of Asian heritage. Still, by the mid-1880's, this oldest daughter in a large, impoverished family had published her first pieces in Canadian and American newspapers and magazines. At this time, the writer signed herself Edith Eaton.

In subsequent chapters White-Parks looks at the interrelationships of race, gender, and Sui Sin Far's writing. Thus the chapters are titled "Montreal: The Early Writings," "Pacific Coast Chinatown Stories," "Boston: The Mature Voice and Art," and, finally, "Mrs. Spring Fragrance." White-Parks concludes that although Sui Sin Far was never sustained by a community of writers or of women but sought instead to understand and write about the Chinese communities in North America, she succeeded in finding her unique voice. She did so by experimenting with and mastering strategies that would subtly confront Sinophobic and sexist views.

White-Parks includes extensive research on Sinophobia and sexism in Canada, America, and each city in which Sui Sin Far lived. At times, in fact, the reader might wish that there were fewer footnotes and citations. The background that White-Parks provides, however, is integral to an understanding of Sui Sin Far's struggles as an Asian American woman writer.

Sui Sin Far lived in a time when the need for cheap Chinese immigrant laborers for the Canadian and American transcontinental railroads had ended and both countries passed exclusionist acts against the Chinese. Negative stereotypes of Chinese people and their North American communities flourished in popular culture during this period of Social Darwinist theory and American imperialism. In the face of such national and local racism, Sui Sin Far's siblings all chose to deny their mother's heritage.

White-Parks points out that because the writer had the physical appearance of her European heritage, she could have remained Edith Eaton, a white woman and writer. Her earliest Montreal publications, as noted above, were signed Edith Eaton and did not deal with Chinese living in North America. In 1896, however, she began publishing stories with Asian American characters and signing herself Sui Sin Far. At this time Sui Sin Far had left Montreal and traveled to the American Midwest and to Jamaica in search of work. White-Parks gives evidence from a conversation recorded in a letter from this period that finding herself in a situation where Asian stereotypes were commonplace, Sui Sin Far stated aloud, after an inner struggle, that she was a Chinese American.

Thereafter Sui Sin Far lived in places where she could visit Chinese American communities and understand them better. At the same time, she developed writing techniques with which to express the truth about Asian Americans, especially women. White-Parks is careful to point out, however, that crossing over to her mother's Asian heritage and its community was not a change Sui Sin Far made all at once. Rather, throughout her life Sui Sin Far trod a wavering line between two selves, even as she leaned ever more toward the Chinese heritage and people. For example, when she was close to her family, Sui Sin Far visited them often. There were times, however, when because of the political climate she had to deny her Asian heritage to cross the border between the United States and Canada. White-Parks sees this experience of ambiguity as a key to understanding Sui Sin Far's fiction.

Making San Francisco her home, Sui Sin Far wrote what White-Parks calls the "Pacific Coast Chinatown Stories." In her analysis of these stories, White-Parks demonstrates that Sui Sin Far gains greater and greater skill in her craft as she experiments with similar characters, voices, and themes. In particular, Sui Sin Far's stories in this period examine exile, betrayal, disguise, and deceit; use Chinese and Chinese American characters; employ plots of marital and family issues; and explore themes of racism and sexism.

One story from this period, "The Sing Song Woman" (1898), tells of two young women about to marry husbands chosen by their families. One of the women, born in America, yearns to be Chinese but is about to marry an Asian American and will continue to live in the United States. The other woman, born in China, yearns to be American but is about to marry a Chinese man and return to China. The two meet and decide to disguise themselves and marry each other's intended husband. Thus exile, disguise, and deceit function in the story of marriage and family, and women manage to make their own life choices.

In analyzing one by one the Pacific Coast Chinatown stories, White-Parks demonstrates her thesis that Sui Sin Far counters stereotypes of Chinese women in North America as invisible, as silent, and as victims. Again and again Sui Sin Far's women characters assert themselves, bond with each other, break cultural rules, and trick other characters.

Most significantly, White-Parks points out, in these first Chinese American stories the writer begins her use of the literary figure of the trickster. The trickster figure is veiled in these stories, but in the later, more complex Boston stories the trickster is much more visible and integral. More important, the trickster is a key to Sui Sin Far's writing and publishing success. This device enabled her to present both antiromantic and antistereotypical ideas about her subjects in a way that deceived her mainstream editors and audiences but at the same time presented them with countercultural images and ideas.

In 1904 Sui Sin Far moved to the East Coast, settling in Boston. Between 1904 and 1909, she published nothing, but White-Parks believes that in her writings from 1909 to 1914, Sui Sin Far made her greatest achievement. In her publications from this period, including a book-length collection of her stories, the writer exhibits a mature style, extends the characterizations, plots, and themes of her earlier work, and achieves her most sophisticated use of the trickster motif. Sui Sin Far also explains herself as person and writer in several published essays. In "Leaves from the Mental Portfolio of a Eurasian" and "The Chinese in America," she both elucidates the oppression she and other Chinese Americans face and, using a light hand of irony, portrays herself and her chosen community as human beings of moral courage and dignity.

In this same Boston period Sui Sin Far published in a variety of national journals such as *Delineator* (edited by Theodore Dreiser), *Good Housekeeping*, and *New England Magazine*, as well as less-known smaller magazines. This publishing success also points to a superior achievement in her writing.

As in her earlier works, Sui Sin Far's fiction topics are marriage both within the Asian American community and across racial boundaries, rifts between generations of Asian Americans, and the Americanization of children. Conflicts over power abound, and it is in these conflicts, White-Parks argues, that the trickster becomes a key player not only in the struggles within the stories but also in the communication between the artist and her predominantly white audience.

While connecting Sui Sin Far's trickster devices to those of other folk cultures, such as the African American and Native American, White-Parks aligns Sui Sin Far's tricksterism with that of her oppressed female ancestors in China as well. *Nushu* was a secret code of storytelling used by women in China among themselves beginning in the tenth century. It was a language of rebellion and a means of female bonding and, in some instances, survival. White-Parks argues that just as *nushu* was a language of rebellion and a means of survival for women in China, so the writing of Sui Sin Far is a trick of resistance and a source of authority: Sui Sin Far is the author of herself and of her chosen community of North American Chinese people, particularly women.

Sui Sin Far's overall writing achievement, White-Parks argues persuasively, is that she creates fictions that break down cultural master texts and characterizations that are mischievous and manipulative toward those who supposedly exert power over them. At the same time, Sui Sin Far allows her audience to hear the Asian American voice, particularly the voice of Asian American women, and know the real-life experience of the Asian communities in North America in a time of severe racism and sexism.

Sui Sin Far/Edith Maude Eaton stands as an exemplary, vital contribution to American literary scholarship. So thoroughly does White-Parks the biographer detail Sui Sin Far's life that the connections she makes to the writing stand, and so well does White-Parks the literary critic analyze the stories that her conclusions about them stand also. Thus, as Sui Sin Far overcame great odds to preserve in her writings the voice and reality of Asian North Americans during the late nineteenth and early twentieth centuries, so White-Parks' literary biography brings to the canon of North American literature that voice and reality. Without the wealth of cultural material incorporated into White-Parks' scholarly text and without her analysis of more than fifty extant nonfiction and fiction publications by Sui Sin Far, a significant page in North American literary history would still be blank.

Francine Dempsey

Source for Further Study

Library Journal. CXX, August, 1995, p. 75.

TERRIBLE HONESTY
Mongrel Manhattan in the 1920's

Author: Ann Douglas (1942-   )
Publisher: Farrar Straus Giroux (New York). 606 pp. $25.00
Type of work: History
Time: The 1920's
Locale: New York City

A cultural history of New York City in the 1920's, looking specifically at the interaction between the black and white cultures

> *Principal personages:*
> LOUIS ARMSTRONG, the notable African American jazz trumpeter
> COUNTÉE CULLEN, a leading African American poet of the Harlem Renaissance
> T. S. ELIOT, the expatriate poet
> DUKE ELLINGTON, the famous African American bandleader and composer
> SIGMUND FREUD, the founder of psychoanalysis
> ERNEST HEMINGWAY, the expatriate American writer
> WILLIAM JAMES, the Harvard philosopher and psychologist
> PAUL ROBESON, a prominent African American actor
> GERTRUDE STEIN, the Paris-based experimental writer
> ETHEL WATERS, the celebrated African American singer and actress

The title and subtitle of Ann Douglas' massive study of New York City in the 1920's indicate the cultural context of this work. Alluding to the planned (though never written) autobiography of writer and wit Dorothy Parker, Douglas notes that the title of that book—"Mongrel"—could refer not only to Parker's mixed Jewish and white Anglo-Saxon Protestant heritage but also to the racially and ethnically mixed "mongrel" Manhattan. In another allusion, Douglas notes that detective writer Raymond Chandler said that "all writers are a little crazy but if they are any good they have a kind of terrible honesty." Thus Douglas' book explores a New York City in which artists of various kinds—from Louis Armstrong to Harry Houdini to Eugene O'Neill—exerted their influence to expose unpleasant truths, to focus on the facts, to speak and act and perform and create with a "terrible honesty."

The particular target of these New Yorkers was the generation that preceded it, the Victorian era. Channeling their energies toward the destruction of what Douglas calls "the Titaness, the Mother God of the Victorian era," the hundreds of creators dealt with in this book were united in an effort to design a new American culture, freed from the restrictions of their historical predecessors.

They were also united in their relationship to New York City, the world's most powerful city during this period. In the 1920's, the United States was for the first time in its history an urban nation, and New York was the largest city in that nation. Reading the stories of significant New Yorkers and the thousands of anecdotes about them, one sees the dual purpose of this book: to describe the larger American emancipation from

Europe and the nineteenth century and to examine the African American liberation movement within that larger context. As a sequel to Douglas' earlier study of Victorianism, *The Feminization of American Culture* (1977), this volume continues her exploration of the demise of nineteenth century culture, especially its idealized notion of the Victorian woman.

While the book is permeated with what appears to be an infinite number of facts, anecdotes, and allusions, the three-part organization provides a handy approach to this cornucopia of information. Part 1, entitled "Setting the Stage: The Players and the Script," does exactly that as it introduces the cast of characters and the major themes connecting their various dramas. The focus of part 2, "War and Murder," is the Great War and the ways in which that historical phenomenon accelerated modernism in America generally and in Manhattan specifically. The interaction of the black and white cultures in mongrel Manhattan is the heart of part 3, "Siblings and Mongrels." An epilogue, foreshadowing the legacy of the 1920's, provides the bookend to the introduction, thus suggesting a neatness that the profusion of information permeating the book sometimes conceals. With photographs, a bibliographic essay, and a selected discography, *Terrible Honesty: Mongrel Manhattan in the 1920's* plunges readers into the richness of life in the Big Apple during its halcyon days.

In the first part of the book, Douglas introduces the players in her script by race. The black men and women include performers such as Bessie Smith, Ethel Waters, Paul Robeson, and Josephine Baker; musicians and composer-lyricists Fats Waller, Louis Armstrong, Duke Ellington, and others; writers such as Countée Cullen, Jean Toomer, and Zora Neale Hurston; and intellectual leaders such as James Weldon Johnson and W. E. B. Du Bois. The white men and women are represented by those who lived in Manhattan and a quintet whom Douglas calls "outside insiders": Ernest Hemingway, T. S. Eliot, Gertrude Stein, William James, and Sigmund Freud. These five played out a debate that Douglas, with particular emphasis on James, Stein, and Freud, views as the dynamism of the 1920's—namely, a tension between the cultural pessimism of white culture and the cultural optimism of the African American culture. This contrast was complicated by the different religious heritages of the two cultures.

Different as these heritages and cultures were, the two worlds—black and white—were joined in the identity they shared as a lost generation, the phrase Stein used to describe the people of the 1920's. Douglas describes this predicament as follows: "If the white moderns thought of themselves as orphans, the black moderns, whose ancestors were kidnapped from their native land and sold into slavery in an alien country, were, in fact, America's only truly orphaned group." Douglas' book examines how these black and white orphans in New York City responded to their abandonment and interacted with one another in their response.

Part 2 of the book examines that response by focusing on World War I and showing how and why the United States emerged from that war as the most powerful nation in the world. A significant reason for the remarkable U.S. victory and Europe's tragic loss was the way in which the war enabled American productivity to accelerate in every way, from the steel interests to the film industries. Indeed, "acceleration" was the operative word for the postwar experience in America, exemplified most dramatically by the speed with which the assembly line could produce cars. In 1913, it had taken fourteen hours to assemble a car. By the end of 1914, it took ninety-five minutes. By October, 1925, it took a mere ten seconds. Douglas cites the study of American modernization, *Middletown* (1929), in which its authors reported that a boy in Muncie, Indiana, was asked by his Sunday school teacher to "think of any temptation we have today that Jesus didn't have." The boy's response was as quick as its message: "Speed." The United States—including Manhattan—were moving more quickly than its nineteenth century citizens could have imagined.

This movement was seen in all aspects of American life, but especially in its literary output. In addition to the speed with which Americans were producing great works of art, they were laboring intensively to forge an American declaration of literary independence. A number of American writers, including Van Wyck Brooks, William Carlos Williams, Lewis Mumford, and Columbia professor Raymond Weaver—almost all of them New York-based—were engaged in this process, which resulted in the rediscovery of classic American literature like *Moby Dick* (1851) and *The Adventures of Huckleberry Finn* (1884), as well as the production of new American literature such as that written by Hemingway. An unprecedented—and some would say unparalleled—flowering of American literature occurred during this remarkable decade, enriched by the interaction of blacks and whites in mongrel Manhattan.

Douglas begins the third part of her book, which examines this interaction, by noting that in the 1920's, for the first time in American history, many blacks and some whites recognized the separate evolution of the black tradition in the arts as having a powerful influence on white culture and as being a valuable, not inferior, culture. Just as nationalism was spreading abroad, so was Negro independence gaining prominence in America, and the two movements conjoined. By the early 1920's, about half the nation's population was first- or second-generation immigrant, with three-quarters of the immigrants in the late nineteenth century having arrived in New York. This influx of nonnative-born Americans precipitated a white nativist movement, which paradoxically intensified the status of the African American as an outsider while also heightening his and her sense of entitlement. African Americans in the United States in the 1920's were no longer alone: Italians, for example, were seen as only a few steps above the blacks, and Jews and Roman Catholics were fellow victims of the Ku Klux Klan.

While many of the newly arrived immigrant groups chose political means to establish their right to be considered full-fledged Americans, black New Yorkers chose culture rather than politics. Thus Ethel Waters, singer and actress, declared in many ways, including through her songs and performances, that she was an advocate of her own race, prompting Irving Berlin to write his protest song about lynching, "Suppertime," for her in 1933. Poet Countée Cullen, the central figure of Harlem's literary renaissance, admonished America to understand what he called "the double burden of being both Negro and American."

In addition to the many black writers of the decade who used their art to announce the complexities of a newly emerging black culture, the musicians of the 1920's used their medium as a means of declaring independence. This was dramatically evident in the outpouring of jazz, a music that "absorbed the national spirit, the tremendous spirit of go and nervousness, lack of conventionality and boisterous good-nature characteristic of the American, white or black, as compared with the more rigid, formal natures of the Englishman or German," according to black critic J. A. Rogers. Raising people as high as the skyscrapers and airplanes that also characterized this decade, jazz was invented by a generation that recognized its mongrel nature.

Yet the exuberance of this generation could not last forever—not even into the decade that followed it. The Depression ended the building spree that had created a skyscraper-dotted landscape. In fact, F. Scott Fitzgerald saw the 1929 Wall Street crash as a suicidal act: "As if reluctant to die outmoded in its bed [the decade] leaped to a spectacular death in October 1929." A country that had lived in an abundance of excess was quickly forced into abject deprivation, with economic hardships inflicted on the blacks in particular and psychological burdens on the whites. While blacks had been painfully accustomed, as whites were not, to reversals of fortune, whites were not prepared for the post-1920's reversals that befell them. The melancholia, depression, and alcoholism to which many white New Yorkers resorted symbolized their descent into their own darkness, a dark night of the soul that contrasted dramatically with the brightness of the 1920's.

Still, this darkness could not diminish the sunlight of the Jazz Age, an age that was unprecedented and unparalleled, an age committed to a terrible honesty that produced a wonderful legacy.

Marjorie Smelstor

Sources for Further Study

American Heritage. XLVI, April, 1995, p. 133.
Booklist. XCI, February 15, 1995, p. 1055.
Library Journal. CXX, February 15, 1995, p. 166.
The New York Review of Books. XLII, April 20, 1995, p. 50.
The New York Times Book Review. C, February 12, 1995, p. 1.
The New Yorker. LXXI, March 27, 1995, p. 102.
Newsweek. CXXV, March 13, 1995, p. 68.
Publishers Weekly. CCXLI, December 5, 1994, p. 59.
San Francisco Review of Books. XX, May, 1995, p. 42.
Time. CXLV, March 27, 1995, p. 76.
The Washington Post Book World. XXV, February 5, 1995, p. 3.

TESSERAE
Memories and Suppositions

Author: Denise Levertov (1923-   )
Publisher: New Directions (New York). 148 pp. $18.95
Type of work: Memoir
Time: 1887-1993
Locale: England (primarily London), Wales, Russia, Budapest, Provençal, Tonga

Denise Levertov's memoir is a collection of twenty-seven short prose pieces, chronologically arranged, presenting significant memories of her parents' lives, the poet's childhood and youth in England, and a few glimpses of her mature years

>   *Principal personages:*
>   DENISE LEVERTOV, the noted twentieth century American poet
>   PAUL LEVERTOV, her father
>   BEATRICE LEVERTOV, her mother
>   OLGA LEVERTOV, her sister

Tesserae are the individual fragments of glass, stone, or tile used to create a mosaic. In her memoir, Denise Levertov does not claim to have created a complete mosaic of her life but instead offers the reader a handful of fragments—"memories and suppositions"—written "from time to time . . . between poems." Each of the "tesserae" presented here reflects light at a different angle to illuminate a portion of the path the poet's life has followed.

Levertov has written elsewhere (in *The Poet in the World,* 1973) about her sense of life as pilgrimage and the importance of mythology, both universal and personal, in her poetry. *Tesserae* opens with a fragment of her personal mythology: her father's boyhood memory of a Russian street peddler whose bulging sack the boy believed held wings that would allow people to fly like birds. After her father's death more than half a century later, Levertov discovered that the painter Marc Chagall, who grew up in the same time and place as Paul Levertov, had also recognized the magic of the peddler's sack and had painted the old man in flight. This magical memory is connected with another piece of the poet's personal mythology, the story of her father's great-grandfather, the Rav of Northern White Russia, who in his youth declined to learn the language of the birds but nevertheless came to understand their speech in his old age. The Rav appears in Levertov's poem "Illustrious Ancestors" (*Overland to the Islands,* 1958); thus the one-page essay "The Sack Full of Wings" sheds a little light on the process that transmutes myth and memory into poetry.

The next three essays are more family stories, handed down over generations until they have acquired the soft patina of myth. "A Minor Role" tells the remarkable story of the conversion of Levertov's father, a scholarly Russian Jew, to Christianity. At the age of eight or nine, the boy, already a Talmud scholar, found trampled in the snow a scrap of printed paper that told of a boy like himself expounding Scripture to rabbis in the Temple. Not until he was a university student did he discover the source—the Gentiles' Gospel—of the fragment that had so captured his imagination. His fascination led him to conversion and, eventually, to lodgings in the home of an evangelical pastor; the marital designs of the pastor's elder daughter, however, led him to flee, first to Jerusalem and then to Constantinople, where he met the young Welsh woman whom he would marry. The poet recounts her father's story with a fine sense of the way human destiny works itself out in seemingly inconsequential, chance events.

"A Dumbshow" is a snapshotlike memory of her mother's own fateful journey to Constantinople. In the early-morning silence in Budapest, she happened to witness a little drama: "A maid, airing pillows on the balcony; the maid goes in; the pillow falls at the feet of a surprised little Hungarian girl, who seizes the prize in a flash and makes off with it; the maid comes out to search in vain for the vanished pillow." This charming vignette is capped with a few sentences of Levertov's evocative "supposing": What became of the child who took the pillow, and what events in her life followed inexorably from that single, chance, impulsive act?

The next dozen fragments of Levertov's mosaic, possibly the heart of the book, are memories and suppositions from the poet's own childhood, up to the age of about twelve, in and about London between 1923 and 1935. "Cordova" tells how the humdrum task of carrying freshly ironed handkerchiefs through the house to put them away was transformed by her imagination into a thrilling and dangerous journey through the mysterious lanes and alleys of a bustling "Arabian Nights" city crowded with Moorish architecture, and how the sounds or patterns of certain works of art can still elicit Levertov's imaginary memory of this place. Nearly everyone has dwelled in such mythic realms in childhood; Levertov's gift is to capture and evoke their magical essence, as she has done here in transparent prose, or, once again, to transform personal mythology into poetry as she did in the related poem "A Doorkey for Cordova" (*Breathing the Water*, 1987).

"Gypsies" provides another fragment of her parents' mythic history. En route by boat from Constantinople to Venice, they happened to do a favor for a fellow passenger who proved to be the king of the Romany Gypsies; they were rewarded with a solemn promise of help from Gypsies anywhere in the world for the rest of their lives. As a child, hiking with her family in Wales, Levertov witnessed how her mother's recounting the story to a Gypsy woman they met elicited powerful, frightening predictions concerning the poet's sister, Olga—predictions that were evidently borne out in essence if not in detail.

Two of Levertov's childhood memoirs treat another theme that runs through many of her poems—as suggested by the titles of two early volumes, *The Double Image* (1946) and *With Eyes at the Back of Our Heads* (1960). In "Janus," she expresses her sense of the doubleness of human experience: "how intimately opposites live, their mysterious simultaneity, their knife-edge union: the Janus face of human experience." The essay centers on her recollection of a small group of schoolgirls climbing the wall around an empty house and peering down into the garden. The exotic, waxy perfection of a blooming magnolia tree momentarily silences their giggles and whispers—but as soon as they regain their voices, a terrifying, hairy, purple-faced tramp bursts out of the house, shouting and waving a stick. This brief incident, held for decades in the poet's imagination and polished by a lifetime of mature, clear-eyed reflection on human experience—Levertov is too wise to reduce it to simplistic terms of sin and retribution—becomes the kernel of a beautiful little essay on the inherent intimacy of beauty and terror.

"The Gardener" also expresses Levertov's deep sense of the doubleness of existence, exploring her memory of the gardener Old Day, an ambivalent figure whom she treated poetically in "A Figure of Time" (*O Taste and See*, 1964). Capricious and earthy, tending and destroying, choosing in cryptic silence which orders he will and will not obey, armed with a scythe like Father Time or Death himself, the old man shambles forever through the fertile garden of the poet's imagination and is transmuted in the pages of her memoir into a powerful, mythic figure bringing both life and death and guided only by his own mysterious intentions.

Several of the memoirs of childhood and youth shed some light on Levertov's early development as an artist. "By the Seaside" describes how the seven-year-old Denise, dancing alone on the beach at sunset, transformed the discipline drilled into her by the fanatical ballet coaching of her much-older sister, Olga, into a glorious, free expression of her private ecstasy. "Meeting and Not Meeting Artists" describes her pursuit of painting lessons in early adolescence and later, at the age of twenty-two, the missed connection that ultimately helped her realize that her true passion and vocation was poetry, not visual art. Nevertheless, the study of both ballet and painting in her youth surely contributed to the rich visual element in her poetry and to the creation of the word pictures that grace her memoirs.

Two essays portray the future poet on the cusp between childhood and adolescence. "The Last of Childhood" tells of the abrupt end of a valued friendship, brought about in part by Levertov's own intransigence. "An Encounter—and a Re-encounter" describes how in 1935, as a naïve and passionate twelve-year-old filled with a confused jumble of notions about social issues, she came to spend her Saturday mornings peddling the Communist *Daily Worker* from door to door—until the face and words of a sad, shabby old man gave her her first inkling of the reality behind the rhetoric she had heard. Much later in life, the same ideals that had motivated her in childhood reemerged in her passionate antiwar poetry and social activism.

Of five essays that remember the poet's early adulthood, two stand out as exemplifying the theme of life as a pilgrimage or mythic journey, which runs throughout her work. "Oracles," like "Gypsies," mentioned above, deals with predictions about the future, this time concerning the poet herself rather than her sister. When she was only seven, Levertov overheard a hat-shop man telling her mother that she—Denise—was destined for something special in life.

Astonished and puzzled by the seemingly gratuitous prediction, the child was nevertheless left with a lasting sense of having a special destiny. This feeling was strengthened by a chance encounter, at the age of twenty, with a woman who read tea leaves. After making the usual silly, superficial predictions for the others present, the oracle manifested a startling change in tone and manner as she predicted, in complete seriousness, "great powers" for Levertov. Since the future poet was working as a nurse at the time, the tea-leaf reader cast her prediction in medical terms, predicting "healing powers." Levertov was left with a powerful sense that the woman had indeed glimpsed something deeply true about her—that she did indeed have some significant gift to give. Only time and the development of her poetic gift would reveal that her "healing power" was to be the power not of medicine but of words.

The sense of life as pilgrimage and of art as her chosen destiny was perhaps heightened by a visit she made to the studio of the painter Paul Cézanne, in Provençal, France, when she was twenty-eight. This treasured memory, here suitably labeled "Pilgrimage," tells of a sweltering, sleepy summer afternoon when the poet roused a sleeping caretaker to admit her to the painter's studio. Although Cézanne had been dead forty-five years, the studio looked as though he had just stepped out, carrying his hat and painting gear, to follow the irresistible demands of his art. A dreamy half-hour in this place, where the residue left by the painter's mind and eyes and hands lay thicker than the dust, served to strengthen in the young poet "the vision of art, the act of making paintings or poems, a life of doing that . . . awake when all else is sleeping."

The last six pieces are drawn from the poet's later adult life. The longest essay in the book, but one of the least satisfying, "Some Hours in the Late '70's," recounts the last hours of the poet's stay in Tonga. Amusing and perceptive in its description of her widely disparate fellow-travelers and their astonishing mutual unawareness, it nevertheless lacks the gemlike clarity of focus of many of the childhood memoirs.

The other five essays in this part of the book all deal with loss. "A Loss" mourns a luggage strap freighted with the memories of personal and family journeys; "Lost Books" remembers a treasured ancient cosmography, full of the tantalizing possibility of voyages to mysterious places; "Mildred" is a dream memory of an archetypal childhood dog; "What One Remembers" examines the curious selectivity of childhood memory itself.

The last fragment of Levertov's mosaic of her life is "A Lost Poem." The poem, its words and place of publication mislaid for many years, was based on a dream the poet had about a Cathedral of Pearls, its entire façade encrusted with a mosaic of pearls. What remains in her memory is the vision of the glimmering light of the pearls in the murky darkness of the city and the deep pleasure passersby drew from their beauty. So too may readers draw pleasure from these glimmering tesserae, polished fragments throwing a soft light on Denise Levertov's mythic journey through a life dedicated to the art of detecting and expressing the gleams of radiance that shine through everyday experience.

Jennifer Angyal

Sources for Further Study

Booklist. XCI, April 15, 1995, p. 1468.
Library Journal. CXX, April 15, 1995, p. 80.
Los Angeles Times Book Review. April 30, 1995, p. 6.

TESTAMENTS BETRAYED
An Essay in Nine Parts

Author: Milan Kundera (1929-　)
First published: Les Testaments trahis, 1993, in France
Translated from the French by Linda Asher
Publisher: HarperCollins (New York). 280 pp. $24.00
Type of work: Essays; literary criticism

Kundera's wide-ranging examination of the novel sheds much light on the nature of art, the views of artists, and the ways in which art is perceived, criticized, and condemned

In "Improvisation in Homage to Stravinsky," part 3 of his nine-part *Testaments Betrayed*, Milan Kundera writes about Igor Stravinsky's émigré status: "having understood that no country could replace it [his homeland], he finds his only homeland in music; this is not just a nice lyrical conceit of mine, I think it in an absolutely concrete way." Kundera's situation is similar to that of Stravinsky and to those of Joseph Conrad and Vladimir Nabokov, about whom Kundera also writes. Kundera, the most famous Czech writer, left Czechoslovakia in 1975 to live in Paris. He has continued to write fiction in Czech, but he has now written two works of nonfiction in French: *The Art of the Novel* (1986; English translation, 1988) and *Testaments Betrayed*. As Stravinsky inhabited the world of music and served as one of its most important citizens and statesmen, so does Kundera inhabit the world of the novel, communicate in its unique language, and serve as a spokesman for its worldview and its practitioners.

Kundera's area of interest is specifically the European novel, by which he means "not only novels created in Europe by Europeans but novels that belong to a history that began with the dawn of the Modern Era in Europe." He points out that the history of the European novel is transnational; he believes that it is a mistake to view the novel in terms of national literary traditions. At one point, Kundera mentions the reaction of the Austrian novelist Hermann Broch to his publisher's suggestion that Broch be compared to the Central European writers Hugo von Hofmannsthal and Italo Svevo. Broch proposed that he be compared instead to James Joyce and André Gide. Broch, like Kundera, believed that his realm was the macrocosm of the European novel, not the microcosm of Austrian fiction.

For Kundera, the novel is far more than a literary genre. It is a way of viewing the world which, when it is practiced by a great novelist, leads readers to think in fresh ways, to question some of their assumptions, to put aside their prejudices. In one interesting passage, Kundera speaks of the ways in which lyricism has been used in the service of totalitarianism. He mentions as an example the great Russian poet Vladimir Mayakovsky, a true artist who placed his verse at the service of the Russian Revolution. Kundera writes, "Lyricism, lyricization, lyrical talk, lyrical enthusiasm are an integrating part of what is called the totalitarian world; that world is not the gulag as such; it's a gulag that has poems plastering its outside walls and people dancing before them." In the world of the true novel, such lyricism is anathema, the enemy of clear thought. Repelled by the totalitarian lyricism he saw around him in the communist Czechoslovakia of his youth, Kundera turned to the novel. Kundera recalls:

> The only thing I deeply, avidly, wanted was a lucid, unillusioned eye. I finally found it in the art of the novel. This is why for me being a novelist was more than just working in one "literary genre" rather than another; it was an outlook, a wisdom, a position . . . a considered, stubborn, furious *nonidentification*.

Kundera wishes to be identified with no political position, no country, no rigid philosophical point of view; he wishes to view and to be viewed purely as a novelist.

Part of Kundera's passion for the novel derives from his belief that the novel is a "*realm where moral judgment is suspended.* Suspending moral judgment is not the immorality of the novel; it is its *morality*." True novels do not have an axe to grind. They do not simply promote ideas (Kundera loathes the so-called novel of ideas) or showcase the actions of characters who are intended to express particular positions. Kundera has no use for works such as George Orwell's *Animal Farm* (1945), which he views as a political work pretending to be a novel, and he disapproves of Fyodor Fyodor Dostoevsky's practice of creating characters who represent specific points of view. Such characters tend to be utterly predictable, to be led by an unfailing logic, whereas real people, no matter how strong their opinions, are typically less consistent. Leo Tolstoy's characters, as Kundera mentions, are more human and less predictable. They adopt different viewpoints at different times in their lives, and sometimes they change those viewpoints for what seem to be trivial reasons. They are fitting inhabitants of the true novel.

In part 1 of *Testaments Betrayed*, "The Day Panurge No Longer Makes People Laugh," Kundera speaks of the importance of humor in the novel. He loves the fact that the early novelists, such as François Rabelais and Miguel de Cervantes, reveled in humor and delighted in allowing their characters to make fools of themselves. He also writes that the history of humor is closely connected to the history of the novel. He quotes Octavio Paz, who said that humor "is the great invention of the modern spirit." Paz had pointed out that early non-novelistic writers such as Homer and Vergil were virtually devoid of humor; although the comic existed in early art, the variety of the comic that Kundera and Paz call humor did not. Humor, said Paz, did not take shape until Cervantes. Kundera writes, "A fundamental idea: humor is not an age-old human practice; it is an *invention* bound up with the birth of the novel." For Kundera, the key to humor is that, as Paz wrote, it "renders ambiguous everything it touches." In other words, humor is a nonjudgmental form of the comic. Without preaching, worshiping, admiring, or condemning, humor shows humans who they really are. Kundera warns his readers that humor "has not been with us forever, and it won't be with us forever either. With a heavy heart, I imagine the day when Panurge no longer makes people laugh."

Kundera makes the point that it is the nonjudgmental aspects of the novel that draw the most virulent attacks. For those who have a position to promote, the idea of a realm in which judgment does not exist is simply unacceptable. That is why the Ayatollah Khomeini issued the *fatwā* calling for the death of Salman Rushdie, whose novel *The Satanic Verses* (1989) certainly does not attack Islam, as Khomeini claimed it did. As Kundera points out, Rushdie's novel, like those of Cervantes and Rabelais, demonstrates clearly that it is not to be taken literally or too seriously. Like the works of the early masters of novelistic humor, *The Satanic Verses* delights in flouting the conventions of everyday reality. Khomeini's attack on Rushdie and his work, is, in effect, an attack on the worldview of the European novel, which is incompatible with the kind of rigid, judgmental, totalitarian thinking practiced by Khomeini and others of his ilk.

Throughout *Testaments Betrayed*, Kundera examines the ways in which critics, editors, and translators have misunderstood and misused great works of art. One of the best examples of this phenomenon can be found in the work of Max Brod, who befriended the great writer Franz Kafka and made it his mission to publish and promote Kafka's works. Brod meant well, and without his efforts, Kafka's works might have disappeared, but Brod had no true understanding of Kafka's art. Brod ignored Kafka's request that Brod destroy certain of his works after the writer's death. Instead, Brod made sure that virtually everything that Kafka had written was published. Furthermore, in his efforts to promote Kafka's work, Brod misinterpreted that work at every turn, portraying Kafka as a saint, a romantic and otherworldly figure. Brod even censored Kafka's comments about sex in his journals. Brod's concept of sex involved high-flown romantic dreams, whereas Kafka viewed sex as an everyday, unsentimental act, as his depictions of sex clearly demonstrate. In addition, Brod began the practice of interpreting Kafka's work on the basis of what is known of Kafka's life, thereby creating the questionable critical field the Kundera derisively calls Kafkology.

Some of Kundera's sharpest barbs are reserved for those who insist on interpreting works of fiction in the light of biographical information. At one point, he quotes a section of Ernest Hemingway's short story "Hills Like White Elephants," an unadorned scenario in which a man is apparently accompanying a woman who plans to have an abortion. In the story, Hemingway takes great pains to leave the situation ambiguous. Very few details are given, and the scene has a multitude of possible explanations. Kundera then quotes an analysis of the story by Jeffrey Meyers, a Hemingway scholar who interprets the story in the light of what he knows about Hemingway's life. The result is unquestionably a string of unwarranted assumptions and conclusions, all of them clichés, and all of them utterly opposed to what Hemingway was attempting to do in his work. "This," writes Kundera, "is how kitsch-making interpretation kills off works of art."

There are, of course, various ways to kill off works of art, and Kundera devotes one of his work's nine parts to one of them: mistranslation. In part 4, "A Sentence," Kundera takes a single sentence from Kafka's *The Castle* (1926; English translation, 1930) and demonstrates how three translators distorted Kafka's writing in their French translations. The versions are examined in detail, and Kundera provides both French and English translations. Ultimately, Kundera provides his own translation, which is not only undeniably effective but also serves Kafka better than the others do. Kundera explains part of the problem thus: "For a translator, the supreme authority should be the *author's personal style*. But most translators obey another authority: that of the *conventional version* of 'good French' (or good German, good English, etc.), namely, the French (the German, etc.) we learn in school." Good writers tend to avoid conventional expression, and when a translator alters the author's mode of expression, waters it down, smoothes what he or she perceives to be its rough edges, that translator betrays both the author and the reader.

Another of Kundera's concerns relates to the ways in which modern works of art are misunderstood and maligned. All too often, critics and consumers of modern art measure it against the tenets of romanticism, expecting it to adhere to standards and techniques that were developed during the eighteenth and nineteenth centuries. Kundera writes at length of the great Czech composer Leoš Janáček, who suffered greatly at the hands of critics because his works were more like those of the modernists Béla Bartók and Alban Berg than they were like those of romantics such as Bedřich Smetana, Czechoslovakia's best-loved composer. The romantics and the modernists, however, have entirely different goals and techniques, and it is a mistake to judge the works of one by the standards of the other. Kundera notes that various modern artists, such as Salman Rushdie, have begun to explore the techniques and styles of the early practitioners of their forms, finding in their work an attitude that serves as the perfect antidote for the poisonous effects of romanticism. Rushdie utilizes the kind of freedom and disdain for rigid rules displayed by his novelistic forebears Cervantes and Rabelais. In the world of music, Stravinsky did the same thing, conducting exhaustive studies of early music and incorporating what he learned into various compositions, only to be attacked by critics who had no idea what he was trying to do.

Testaments Betrayed is an examination and a defense of the European novel, and, at the same time, it is a defense of the concept of art for art's sake. For Kundera, a work that exists only to serve a purpose, to propose a view, to move minds in a specific direction—above all, to judge—is not truly art. For Kundera, the true novel grows out of a worldview in which moral judgment is suspended. The reader may judge, if he or she wishes to, but the novelist may not.

Shawn Woodyard

Sources for Further Study

America. CLXXIII, September 16, 1995, p. 33.
Boston Globe. September 27, 1995, p. 82.
Los Angeles Times Book Review. October 22, 1995, p. 2.
New Statesman and Society . VIII, October 13, 1995, p. 35.
The New York Times Book Review. C, October 22, 1995, p. 30.
The New Yorker. LXXI, December 11, 1995, p. 100.
The Washington Post Book World. XXV, October 8, 1995, p. 1.

THERAPY

Author: David Lodge (1935-   )
Publisher: Viking (New York). 321 pp. $22.95
Type of work: Novel
Time: The 1990's
Locale: London and Rummidge, a fictional city in the Midlands

A successful writer is required to keep a journal as part of his therapy for a midlife breakdown, yielding a rich mixture of crisis and comedy

> *Principal characters:*
> LAURENCE "TUBBY" PASSMORE, age fifty-eight, a successful television
>   script writer
> SALLY PASSMORE, his wife of thirty years
> AMY, a casting director and his platonic mistress
> MAUREEN KAVANAGH HARRINGTON, his first love
> BEDE HARRINGTON, Maureen's husband, a retired civil servant
> LOUISE, a Hollywood film producer
> SAMANTHA, a writer at Tubby's television studio

The protagonist and narrator of *Therapy*, Laurence Passmore or "Tubby," as he is known to his friends, would seem an unlikely candidate for an attack of late-middle-age angst. In fact, Tubby did not know the meaning of the word (literally; he had to look it up in a dictionary). At age fifty-eight, he is balding and a little overweight, but to all outward appearances he has achieved a successful life. He has been happily married for thirty years to his wife Sally, who stays youthful and trim; he has a lucrative job that he loves as writer of a British television situation comedy; he has an impressive home in Rummidge and an expensive car (the "Richmobile"); he has a flat in London, where he meets Amy, his platonic mistress, for theater and dinner dates. What could possibly be wrong?

Tubby does not know, and this is why he is immersed in therapies: cognitive behavior therapy, physical therapy, aromatherapy, athroscopic surgery on a knee. In fact, *Therapy* is a journal that Tubby is writing as part of his therapy, thus giving the reader a day-by-day account of his life. When his psychotherapist asks him to make up a list of the good and the bad things in his life, under "Good" he writes,

1. Professionally successful
2. Well-off.
3. Good health
4. Stable marriage
5. Kids successfully launched in adult life
6. Nice house
7. Great car
8. As many holidays as I want

Under the "Bad" column he writes,

1. Feel unhappy most of the time

Later he thinks to add another item:

2. Pain in knee

Gradually it becomes clear to the reader, but not to Tubby, that the pain in the knee is a physical manifestation of another kind of psychic or spiritual pain: his feeling that somehow he has lost "the knack of living." "How?" he asks himself. "I Don't Know," or IDK, also the acronym for Internal Derangement of the Knee, the unsatisfyingly vague diagnosis offered after surgery, has failed to help. Tubby's depression is intensified by a growing belief that more than his knee is deranged: The entire society seems to be deteriorating. Mournfully reflecting on the "Internal Derangement of the Monarchy," he feels sorry for "poor old Queen." He is concerned about "Internal Derangement" of property values, the "negative equity" of those unfortunate people whose mortgages exceed the value of their property. He worries about "Internal Derangement of the National Psyche," as indicated by Gallup polls that found 80 percent of British citizens dissatisfied with their government, almost 50 percent who would emigrate if they could, and 40 percent of all young people believing that Britain will become worse.

That Tubby is a worrier, a compassionate man who gives generously to a large number of charitable causes, endears him to the reader. Yet he is also an egotist who is so self-absorbed he cannot listen to others, does not communicate with his children, and does not even hear his wife when she says that she wants a separation. Self-centeredness is at the root of Tubby's problem, but it takes a series of disasters both comic and pathetic to jolt him into awareness.

When Sally wants not only a separation but also a divorce, his studio threatens to give his show to another writer, and his physical problems extend to insomnia and impotence ("Internal Derangement of the Gonads"), Tubby begins to know more than the dictionary definition of angst. Stumbling upon the writings of Danish existentialist philosopher Søren Kierkegaard, Tubby reads in the very titles a description of what he is feeling: *Fear and Trembling, The Sickness unto Death, The Concept of Dread, Either/Or,* "The Unhappiest Man." According to Kierkegaard, "The unhappy man is 'always absent to himself, never present to himself.'" Tubby writes,

> My first reaction was no, wrong, Søren old son—I never stop thinking about myself, that's the trouble. But then I thought, thinking about yourself isn't the same as being present to yourself. Sally is present to herself, because she takes herself for granted, she never doubts herself—or at least not for long. She *coincides* with herself. Whereas I'm like one of those cartoons in a cheap comic, the kind where the colour doesn't quite fit the outline of the drawing: there's a gap or overlap between the two, a kind of blur.

Forsaking his other therapies, Tubby plunges into desperate debauchery as the solution to his problems. Wrongly believing that Sally wants a divorce because she is involved with another man, he regrets his thirty years of marital fidelity and sets out to make up for lost opportunities—"for revenge, for compensation, for reassurance."

The result comes in some of the most comical scenes in the novel. Like many other British writers of comedy, David Lodge has a sure sense of the ludicrous and a gift for deftly conveying it. Tubby and Amy's holiday in Tenerife, where they go to consummate their erstwhile platonic affair, is a richly comic fiasco. Tubby's trip to Los Angeles, where he hopes to recoup an opportunity lost four years earlier with Louise, a television executive, becomes a double fiasco: Louise, whose biological clock is ticking, barely remembers Tubby, is intent on conceiving a baby with her current lover, and hands Tubby off to the available, experienced Stella. In fact, Stella is so experienced (talking about latex gloves and dental dams over dinner) that a panicked Tubby is soon on the next flight back to London: "If she was so concerned about safe sex . . . she must have reason to be." A trip to Copenhagen with his lovely young coworker Samantha, however, similarly degenerates into farce; instead of the hoped-for seduction in a luxury hotel, the highlight of the trip proves to be Tubby's visit to the grave of Kierkegaard.

After the failure of debauchery therapy, Tubby returns to his aromatherapist, who prescribes lavender. The scene evokes a Proust-like flood of remembrance of things past, particularly of Maureen, his first love. "Maureen: A Memoir" is a turning point in the novel. Laurence's (he was not Tubby then) adolescent passion for Maureen, her Catholic upbringing, which frustrated his desires for physical intimacy, his vengeful act of bad faith when he humiliated her in front of their peers—all of this adds dimension to the narrator's character and a nostalgic tone to *Therapy*. Convinced that he needs Maureen's forgiveness, he searches for her and finds that she is married to his teenage rival Bede (now a retired civil servant), but she is currently on a pilgrimage to Santiago de Compostela in Spain as an act of mourning for a son who has died. Tubby finds her and completes the last part of the pilgrimage with her, a kind of therapy for both: The pain in his knee miraculously disappears, they become lovers, and they return to their lives but are no longer the same. Tubby's wife Sally has by now found another man, thus ending any hope of reconciliation. Maureen is still Catholic, so she cannot think of divorce despite the fact that her marriage has become somewhat loveless; a mastectomy made her sexually repulsive to her husband. The three of them, Tubby, Maureen, and Bede, settle for an amiable relationship as good friends with mutual interests: All of them are "in recovery" from life's batterings and bruisings. All need therapy of one sort or another. Tubby and Maureen occasionally meet at his London flat ("I don't ask her how she squares it with her conscience. . . . My own conscience is quite clear"), but the three of them are planning a pilgrimage to Copenhagen. As Tubby observes, Kierkegaard "would make a good patron saint of neurotics."

Therapy's mixture of satire and seriousness, comedy and Kierkegaard, gives this novel an experimental quality, a term that has been used to characterize some of Lodge's other novels, particularly *The British Museum Is Falling Down* (1965). Unconstrained by the Either/Or of some critical theorists of the novel (a writer must choose either traditional realism or experimentalism), Lodge opts for Both/And, or what he refers to as the "aesthetic supermarket" of styles available to the modern novelist: "traditional as well as innovative styles, minimalism as well as excess, nostalgia as well as prophecy." Possibly some readers may be put off by his unorthodox mixtures, but Lodge is a fearless literary critic and novelist. He states,

> I have always regarded fiction as an essentially rhetorical art—that is to say, the novelist . . . *persuades* us to share a certain view of the world for the duration of the reading experience, effecting, when successful, [a] rapt immersion in an imagined reality.

Whether *Therapy*, his tenth novel, does persuade, whether the persona/mask of Tubby occasionally slips, giving a disconcerting glimpse of Professor David Lodge staging the whole show, each reader will decide, but the author must be given high marks for the creation of an engaging character set in what seems an all-too-real world. Lodge amusingly captures the whole dreck of contemporary life: Prozac, ubiquitous cellular phones and irritating Call Waiting, Hollywood, television soaps, conspicuous consumption, recreational sex and drugs, street people, social and cultural decline. By some standards Tubby appears to be innocence in a naughty world, but by others, Tubby in his "Richmobile" is culpable. He has become not only a fat person but also a fat soul. His life resembles the situation comedy that he scripts: "not real," as Grahame the streetperson says. It takes a brush with Kierkegaardian Dread and a trip into the past to shake Tubby out of his torpor and to decode Kierkegaard's ominous words: "Learning to know dread is an adventure which every man has to affront if he would not go to perdition either by not having known dread or by sinking under it. He therefore who has learned rightly to be in dread has learned the most important thing."

Rightly to be in dread yet not sinking under it is the difficult metaphysical balancing act required of those who would live in the real world despite the fact that there is truly much there to dread: not only the deaths of those one loves, but the death of love itself. David Lodge's ability to combine high seriousness and high comedy, to make us face up to the worst and therefore desire to live, laugh, and love all the more, is bracing, is therapy.

Karen A. Kildahl

Sources for Further Study

Los Angeles Times Book Review. July 23, 1995, p. 1.
National Review. XLVII, August 14, 1995, p. 54.
New Statesman and Society. VIII, May 12, 1995, p. 41.
The New York Review of Books. XLII, August 10, 1995, p. 24.
The New York Times Book Review. C, July 15, 1995, p. 9.
Publishers Weekly. CCXLII, May 1, 1995, p. 40.
San Francisco Chronicle. July 23, 1995, p. REV5.
Time. CXLVI, August 7, 1995, p. 71.
The Times Literary Supplement. April 28, 1995, p. 23.
The Wall Street Journal. July 14, 1995, p. A10.

TO THE WEDDING

Author: John Berger (1926-   )
Publisher: Pantheon Books (New York). 201 pp. $22.00
Type of work: Novel
Time: The early 1990's
Locale: Northern Italy and southern France

Ninon, a young Frenchwoman, discovers that she has the human immunodeficiency virus (HIV), but eventually agrees with her lover's demands that they marry anyway

Principal characters:
NINON, a twenty-four-year-old woman, native of France, tested positive for HIV
GINO, a young Italian salesman, her lover
JEAN FERRERO, a French railway signalman, her father
ZDENA SOLECEK, a Czech engineer and political activist, Jean's former lover and Ninon's mother
TSOBANAKOS, an Athenian peddler of tamata (a kind of metal good-luck charm), a blind seer who narrates much of the story

Ninon, an evidently healthy young woman who plans to marry her lover Gino, visits a doctor for treatment of a sore on her lip. After testing her, he informs her that she tests positive for the virus that causes acquired immunodeficiency syndrome (AIDS). Her intuition tells her that she caught the disease from a young apprentice cook with whom she made love only once. She visits him in prison to berate him and finds her suspicion confirmed by his moribund condition. Shattered by the news of her own mortal illness, Ninon tells Gino to have his blood tested, and when his results are negative she breaks off the relationship. Gino, however, insists that he still wants to marry her. Eventually Ninon agrees, although she insists on conditions that will protect Gino from infection.

The body of the novel is devoted to Ninon's narration of events in her earlier life and those leading up to the wedding and the day of the wedding itself, alternating with Tsobanakos' narrations of the preparations of Jean Ferrero and Zdena for their trips to Venice and the trips themselves. Jean travels from his home in southern France on his Honda motorbike, while Zdena takes the bus from Bratislava, Czechoslovakia, where she has lived since the fall of the Communist government in Czechoslovakia's Velvet Revolution.

Ninon receives strong support and sympathy not only from Gino but also from her parents, friends, and physicians. Her friend Marella convinces her that she should marry Gino. The rest of the world, however, views her with undisguised horror. She goes to Milano to investigate a new drug, and while there she visits the piazza to see the Duomo in the evening. A large dog, off its leash, paws her, and its owner, after assuring her that the dog will not harm her, begins to paw her himself, assuming that she is a whore. She tries to fight him off, but he persists, and finally in desperation she tells him that she is infected. He flings her to the ground and begins to shout curses, accusing her of trying to pick him up with the intention of infecting him. A woman passing by raises a heavy handbag to hit Ninon but is restrained by her husband, who says that the matter is none of their affair. The worst of the incident, says Ninon, is the hatred with which the woman and her husband regard her.

The single segment that is narrated by neither Ninon nor Tsobanakos is in the words of Gino's father when he learns that his son is about to marry Ninon. Horrified at the thought that his son will catch the disease from Ninon, he determines to kill her. Such an action, he rationalizes, will be a kindness, since it will save her months and perhaps years of suffering and will also spare his son similar suffering and death. Any jury, he reasons, would include fathers, and no father would vote to convict a man who had taken such an action to protect his son. When he comes face to face with Ninon, however, he cannot bring himself to shoot her.

While Ninon's segments of the story take her in time from her childhood to the history of her disease and the preparations for the wedding, Tsobanakos' narratives of Jean and Zdena take them from the final preparations for their separate trips to the wedding through the journeys themselves. Before setting out, Jean visits a mountain pool to which he had taken Ninon when she was a girl. He crosses the mountains on his bike, enjoys a pizza in a small workers' restaurant, and spends a night in a camp on the banks of the Po with three rebellious teenage boys before riding the final stage of his journey. Along the way he stops to buy a special perfume as a present for Ninon.

Zdena's preparations are more elaborate. She goes to a beauty shop to have her hair done for the first time in her life; the beautician misunderstands her words and thinks that Zdena herself is to be the bride. Zdena gives considerable thought to what she will take for a wedding present. Eventually, in a small shop, she buys two exquisitely hand-carved bird calls to take to her daughter. On the bus that is to take her from Bratislava to Venice, she sits next to a fellow Czech who had worked for the Communist government; now that his party is out of power, he keeps himself alive by driving a taxi. Despite their political differences, he and Zdena strike up a friendship, and at one point she bribes the bus driver to wait an extra couple of minutes so that her new companion will not be left behind. She is rewarded when the man surprises her with food and drink that he has bought.

Awareness of Ninon's illness is constantly beneath the surface of her parents' actions. She herself is able to keep her terror under control most of the time. At the wedding celebration she dances barefoot, seemingly lost in the moment. The account of the celebration, however, is the most harrowing part of the narrative. Tsobanakos is present at the wedding, at least in his imagination, and feels comfortable among Gino's friends, who are salesmen like himself. Yet his imagination projects the reader forward in passages that are interwoven with descriptions of the festivities. These interjections move to the stages of Ninon's disease when she first is ill with pneumonia and later must suffer through all the miseries of AIDS, while Gino tries to ease her pain and keep his own horror at bay. The novel ends as the wedding does, with the stark fact of a fatal disease and the counterbalance of Ninon's determination to live to the limit while she can.

John Berger is a British painter, social critic, art critic, poet and novelist who has lived much of his adult life in rural France. His most significant earlier fictions were *G* (1972), a novel that won Britain's prestigious Booker Prize, and a trilogy entitled *Into Their Labours* (1979-1990), a detailed naturalistic account of the decay of French peasant life over several generations. *To the Wedding* (the proceeds of which have been assigned to an AIDS clinic in New York City's Harlem section) is like those earlier works in focusing on a major social problem by studying its effects on a small group of characters. In almost every other way, however, the new novel is entirely different from its predecessors.

The layering of the stories through the voices of two different narrators causes some confusion in the early pages, but Ninon's longer-range account of her life soon becomes distinct from the shorter length of time occupied by Tsobanakos' accounts of her parents' journeys. The main threads of narrative play off one another, so that the matter of a ring Gino gives to Ninon is seen in the context of Zdena's pondering what sort of gift she can give to her daughter. The immediacy of Ninon's reaction to her illness is given a broader context by the Greek seer's comments on the other characters and their attempts to deal with their own dismay.

Berger makes much greater use of symbolism in *To the Wedding* than was the case in his earlier work. One major symbol of the novel is the ring Gino gives to Ninon, which she returns after her diagnosis and accepts again when she agrees to marry him. The ring is gold-colored, in the shape of a turtle. She can wear it pointing away so that the turtle swims out to see the world or pointing in so that the turtle is swimming home. After the wedding, when she prepares to dance, she wears it pointing in; her wedding ring she wears on another finger. The ring's pointing one way represents the courage to move out into the world; it is a reminder of the courage Ninon requires to face every day of her life. Pointing the other way, the turtle symbolizes the need for a safe haven, which Gino offers to Ninon, even as both recognize that it can last only a brief while.

The other major symbol in *To the Wedding* are the tamata that Tsobanakos sells in the marketplace. Drawings of examples of these small medallions decorate the beginning of each chapter in the novel. They are charms that people buy to ward off evil or to bring them good news about something that has been worrying them. Too often, Tsobanakos is aware, they are the last refuge of hope. In his only physical connection with one of the major characters, he sells a heart-shaped tama to Jean. On the novel's final page, Tsobanakos acknowledges, "The tama of the heart in tin was not sufficient." Only prayer is a final refuge.

The role of Tsobanakos remains an enduring mystery in *To the Wedding*, the clearest departure of Berger's technique from the conventions of formal realism. There is no indication in the novel of the source of the peddler's evidently unlimited abilities. Blind Tsobanakos sees into the hearts and minds of the other characters. His sympathies seem to be virtually unlimited, extending not only to Ninon and her family and friends but to Gino's father as well; he understands how a father would consider extreme measures to protect a beloved son against the threat of AIDS. It is only those who react to Ninon without pity who fail to receive Tsobanakos' sympathy.

His blindness, his Greek nationality, his role as omniscient narrator, and the breadth of his sympathies suggest a connection between Tsobanakos and Homer, the blind poet who is reputed to be the author of the great Greek epics *The Iliad* and *The Odyssey* (both c. 800 B.C.). While Homer's stories dealt with war and adventure, including the suffering and pain they involve, Tsobanakos is fated to tell of characters whose heroism is internal rather than external, shown in their determination to live lives as ordinary as possible under the most terribly extraordinary circumstances. The chief effect of this element in the novel is to raise Ninon to the level of a classical hero.

A story in which the central figure is a woman doomed to a terrifying illness and inevitable death is in danger of falling deep into sentimentality. In less skillful hands, Ninon's fate would be nothing more than a conventional tear-jerker. Berger, however, manages superbly to avoid the pitfalls of convention. The clear crispness and lyric power of his prose help to maintain a careful balance between vivid presentations of the emotions of the various characters and a detachment that permits the reader to admire them without tears. The account of the wedding and the feast that follows, intercut with projections of Ninon's eventual suffering, is one of the surpassing achievements of modern fiction. It is a threnody showing that humans, all of whom live in the shadow of death, can find cause for a joy that is enriched by the very shadows which darken it. *To the Wedding* is a short but powerful masterpiece.

John M. Muste

Sources for Further Study

Booklist. XCI, May 1, 1995, p. 1550.
Boston Globe. June 7, 1995, p. 86.
Kirkus Reviews. LXIII, March 1, 1995, p. 246.
Library Journal. CXX, May 1, 1995, p. 129.
Los Angeles Times Book Review. July 16, 1995, p. 6.
The New York Times Book Review. C, June 4, 1995, p. 11.
The New Yorker. LXXI, September 25, 1995, p. 106.
Publishers Weekly. CCXLII, March 6, 1995, p. 56.
The Times Literary Supplement. September 29, 1995, p. 24.
The Washington Post Book World. XXV, July 23, 1995, p. 6.

TOM
The Unknown Tennessee Williams

Author: Lyle Leverich (1920-   )
Publisher: Crown (New York). Illustrated. 644 pp. $35.00
Type of work: Literary biography
Time: 1911-1945
Locale: Chiefly Mississippi, Missouri, New York, New Orleans, and California

The opening volume of a projected two-volume authorized biography, tracing the beginning thirty-three years of the playwright's life as they are reflected and culminate in his first major Broadway success

Principal personages:
THOMAS LANIER (TENNESSEE) WILLIAMS III, one of the leading post-
    World War II American dramatists
EDWINA DAKIN WILLIAMS, his mother
CORNELIUS COFFIN (C. C.) WILLIAMS, his father
ROSE ISABEL WILLIAMS, his older sister
AUDREY WOOD, his literary and theatrical agent
JAMES LAUGHLIN, his publisher, the founder of New Directions

Authorized by the dramatist five years before his death in 1983, Lyle Leverich's *Tom: The Unknown Tennessee Williams* arrives as the first biographical study to draw extensively upon unpublished letters, as well as upon the journals and notebooks begun in 1936 that Williams termed the "emotional record" of his life. Yet even journals, like letters in which the writer can, chameleonlike, adopt a series of masks, may not necessarily present the naked truth. As Williams would admit, "These note-books despite their attempt at merciless candor . . . perhaps distort unfavorably for I seem inclined to note only the seedier things." As Leverich is at pains to emphasize, the young Tom deliberately assumed a persona that allowed the "inferno" inside to be externalized through his art.

Born on March 26, 1911—and related on his father's side to two minor American poets, Tristam Coffin and Sidney Lanier—Thomas Lanier Williams would one day subtract three years from his age to be eligible for a Group Theater playwriting contest that would net him a special award. He took the name Tennessee to signify his "fighting spirit" and his desired role as an avant-garde experimentalist in an American theater on the verge of a new era. Perhaps Leverich's inclusion of both "Tom" and "Tennessee" within his book's title is intended to intimate that there would always exist a tension, or at best an uneasy fusion, between the inner person and the outer persona, between the poet and the playwright, the lyricist and the realist, the artist and the theater practitioner and celebrity. Even Williams' chief literary influences, the poet Hart Crane (a volume of whose works he always carried with him) and the dramatist Anton Chekhov, and his earliest mentors while at Washington University in St. Louis, the poet Clark Mills McBurney and the theaterman Willard Holland, are indicative of this oppositional pull. He saw himself, in short, as suffering from a senseless division, an "enemy inside" that made him feel at times "half-mad."

After an introductory chapter that recounts how Leverich, a theater manager and director and, from the mid-1970's, a friend of Williams, unexpectedly found himself designated the authorized biographer, and a prologue that details the events surrounding Williams' death, *Tom* proceeds in straightforward, chronological fashion. It is structured like a scenario, narrating the tale of "the actual menagerie" that Williams the poet-playwright lived among and then recollected in his memory play *The Glass Menagerie* (1944). Leverich's unearthings of unknown aspects of the absent father—the play's "telephone man who fell in love with long distance"—and of the fearfully shy sister, renamed Laura in the play, take on new resonances as images of the playwright himself. The drama-rich story that Leverich painstakingly yet gracefully and with restraint tells is of Williams as son, as brother, as homosexual, and as artist.

Tom's parents were mismatched and sexually incompatible from the start. Edwina Dakin, daughter of a much-loved Episcopalian rector who, in turn, loved the "high drama" of the liturgy and of a music teacher whom Tom called "Grand" in real life and in fiction and thought of as God's embodiment on earth, was poetically nostalgic, garrulous, and full of Victorian inhibitions. Cornelius Coffin Williams was altogether crasser and more aggressive, though more cavalier, a traveling salesman who reveled in his drink, his poker, and his other women. Their children, especially the two older of the three, drove deeper the wedge between them. Leverich sees Cornelius as creating in Tom what he most feared, a bookish, withdrawn child, whom he referred to derisively as "Miss Nancy." Tom's unrequited love for his father resulted in a rage against him that helped fuel the son's artistic rebellion and passion to create; in Leverich's interpretation, the son's hate was actually sublimated love. Only after Williams underwent analysis following a bout of depression over his father's death in 1957 did he, according to Leverich, come to terms with and finally admit his long-repressed feelings of hatred for his mother.

If, in real life, Cornelius did not have the courage to leave his family as does the father in *The Glass Menagerie*, his son was always in flight. The physical dislocations early in life—from Columbus, Mississippi, where he was born, to Clarksdale, whose surroundings would become his mythical literary territory and where lived an actual Miss Wingfield with a collection of glass figurines in her front window, to a succession of residences on the west side of St. Louis—were enforced. Later moves—to New Orleans, to New York, to California, to Mexico, and even to Hollywood for an abortive screenwriting assignment at Metro-Goldwyn-Mayer for Lana Turner—were chosen, as if physical distance could help him escape his multitudinous phobias with their attendant symptoms: his dependency, vulnerability, and pathological shyness, his paranoia and fear of confinement, his psychosomatic illnesses and hypochondria, his mad cackle of a laugh, the "blue devils" of depression and madness. He always considered himself an outcast and a pariah and would adopt the motto "En Avant!" as a herald of his determination to endure.

If, in *The Glass Menagerie*, the narrator's need to assuage his guilt over having deserted his sister in order to pursue his own vocation compels him obsessively to remember the past, in real life the guilt resided in other acts of betrayal no less onerous. Although physically pure, the intense emotional attachment between Tom and his fragile, delusionary sister, Rose, was rooted, as even Williams would eventually come to recognize, in an incestuous desire, although initially unconscious and never acted upon. Earlier renditions of the life situate Williams' abiding guilt in his failure to take any action to prevent the prefrontal lobotomy intended to cure Rose's mental disorder; Leverich establishes, however, that the operation took place not in 1937, when Rose underwent insulin therapy to treat dementia praecox, but six years later, in 1943, when Williams was physically far away. Yet if Williams, whose own terror of loneliness contributed to his compassion for other misfits, would later condemn "deliberate cruelty" toward another as the greatest of sins, he himself fell prey to that unforgivable flaw at least twice in his taunts against Rose. Once he overheard her attempt to seduce a young man and recoiled angrily: "You disgusted me." Another time, out of pique that she reported one of his drunken parties to his parents, he berated her by saying "I hate the sight of your ugly old face!" The symbiosis between brother and sister was so close that, when dramatized, they almost seem like two sides of a single person—a male-female duality similar to that found in one of the writers Williams admired most, D. H. Lawrence, whose grave site and widow, Frieda, he visited in Taos, New Mexico.

A further motif in Lawrence that resonated on a very personal level for Williams was the desired fusion of the sensual with the spiritual, forces continually at war in the playwright himself. He only gradually became aware of (at first through male friends of his sister and various college roommates) and even more gradually acted upon (not until he was in his late twenties) his homoerotic impulses. He would remain, even after his brief though intense affair with the dancer Kip Kiernan, ambivalent and terribly conflicted about his homosexuality—to which he would allude only covertly and fleetingly in *The Glass Menagerie*, through mention of seeking out companions in bars. Essentially, Williams was terrified by aloneness and needed human contact if not love in order to prevent onslaughts of morbidity and to enable him to write. Although he accepted the fact of his homosexuality as natural and held to the ideal of a long-term mutual commitment, that did not prevent intense feelings of shame and "spiritual nausea." The lack of inhibitions, the cruising and promiscuity, may have been an overcompensation for an early life of puritanical repression. Yet the sense of revulsion and the need to feel clean and pure remained and could be satisfied only by absorption in work. Thus the act of artistic creation became its own obsession.

Although Leverich's exhaustively researched volume purports not to be a literary life, in that it refrains from extended critical analyses of the poems, stories, and plays, it makes no pretense of divorcing the life from the work. Indeed, it does just the opposite, partly through recounting the progress of that lifework, from Williams' very earliest publications when he was in his teens through his first produced plays dating from the late 1930's and the abortive pre-Broadway Boston tryout of *Battle of Angels* (1940), which sent its already shocked audiences running up the aisles from a smoke-filled theater, to *The Glass Menagerie*'s triumphant run in Chicago (where it was kept alive by the critics) and then New York. This latter play won for Williams his first New York Drama Critics Award and an uncontested niche in the pantheon of America's greatest dramatists.

If Leverich does not dwell at length on Williams' recurrent themes and the lyrical style and cinematic structure that made his works vastly different from the proletarian social realism that had characterized much American theater in the 1930's, he does give them ample notice. Thematically, Williams would consistently focus on the destructive impact that society exerts upon its more sensitive members; he would protest repeatedly the way in which the contemporary value system seeks to destroy a "romantic attitude" that would uphold beauty, gentility, poetry.

Perhaps of greatest significance was Williams' awareness of his attempt to alter the nature of dramatic art itself. Considering himself first a poet, he understood that to write well in that form would not necessarily produce technically good dramatic writing. To blend lyricism with realism, he knew that he must create a new form that would allow him to articulate his deepest feelings. Thus he developed what he would call a "sculptural drama" or a "new, plastic" theater, a nonrealistic form—often structured cumulatively by a succession of short scenes, with cinematic lighting and music effects—that would, paradoxically, serve to deepen and intensify the sense of reality.

The genesis of *The Glass Menagerie* was long and arduous, requiring that Williams reveal his own heart "without concealment or evasion and with a fearless unashamed frontal assault upon life that [would] leave no room for trepidation." That journey resulted, however, in a play by which the American theater would indisputably be forever changed and renewed. Leverich tells the story of that genesis in a quiet and understated biography, one that is content to supplement rather than attempt to supplant the dramatic work itself and its intensely troubled yet immensely gifted poet-playwright.

Thomas P. Adler

Sources for Further Study

Booklist. XCII, October 1, 1995, p. 210.
Library Journal. October 1, 1995, p. 82.
Los Angeles Times Book Review. November 19, 1995, p. 1.
The New York Times Book Review. C, November 19, 1995, p. 15.
The New Yorker. LXXI, December 18, 1995, p. 113.
Publishers Weekly. CCXLII, September 11, 1995, p. 68.
San Francisco Chronicle. October 22, 1995, p. REV1.
The Spectator. CCLXXV, November 18, 1995, p. 58.
Times-Picayune. November 19, 1995, p. E6.
The Washington Post Book World. XXV, November 12, 1995, p. 4.

TOM PAINE
A Political Life

Author: John Keane (1949-   )
Publisher: Little, Brown (New York). Illustrated. 617 pp. $27.95
Type of work: Biography
Time: 1737-1809
Locale: England, France, and the United States

Keane chronicles the life of Thomas Paine, an important eighteenth century thinker and revolutionary

> *Principal personages:*
> THOMAS PAINE, a revolutionary thinker and propagandist
> THOMAS JEFFERSON, an American revolutionary and third president of the United States
> GOUVERNEUR MORRIS, an American statesman, ambassador to France
> GEORGE WASHINGTON, the commander of the American Revolutionary Army and first president of the United States

Thomas Paine, who liked to view himself as a citizen of the world and who was in fact a citizen of three different nations, ran the risk of ending his life as a man without a country. A child of revolution, he played a major part in two important upheavals of the late eighteenth century, in the United States and France, and sought unsuccessfully to bring about another in England. In a carefully detailed, objective, and comprehensive biography, John Keane chronicles the life of this famous revolutionary, a man significant because of his role as a theorist and propagandist.

Because Paine lived through an age of revolution, his biographer is challenged by a complex, rapidly changing setting. As if to show how Paine coped with the shifting sands that he found under him, Keane concentrates on placing him within the historical setting and accounting for the works promoting revolutionary ideas that flowed from his pen. Although Keane has written numerous other books, he reveals more than a temporary interest in Paine, for he has also prepared a scholarly bibliography of Paine's writings consisting of more than six hundred titles. This work, when published, will serve as the foundation for a complete edition of Paine's writings.

For his strident deism and his partisanship as well as his occasional poor judgment in attacking others, Paine has been subjected to more negative attention than other leaders of early America. It was his fate to achieve greater success at arousing and guiding public opinion than at steering the course of a movement into practical, productive channels. Keane attempts a balanced assessment, portraying Paine as a talented writer and thinker who made no more mistakes than most other influential thinkers and who from modest beginnings played an important role in history. Largely leaving the personal life to speak for itself, Keane nevertheless provides a wealth of detail about Paine, both personal and professional.

Few men of prominence and significant achievement had origins more humble than Thomas Paine. Born in England into a lower-middle-class family, he was educated at

Thetford Grammar School and started his working life as an apprentice staymaker, his father's trade. Bored by the tedium of this menial work, he enlisted on a privateer and served briefly as a part of the "unofficial" English navy. During one voyage, he earned sufficient share of booty to move to London, where, at age twenty, he began to make friends among prominent intellectuals. His wit, pleasing demeanor, and generosity made him a congenial companion. From the London setting he began to absorb the democratic ideals rife at the time—such principles as popular sovereignty, consent of the governed, and inalienable human rights. Hired by the government as an excise collector, he was eventually dismissed for absenteeism and for agitating for changes in the tax system. The event reflects a handicap that Paine faced in practical affairs: a tendency to press his own solutions to problems to the point of exasperating others.

An optimist who believed in the idea of progress before it became popular, Paine served briefly as a Methodist minister, largely because of the humanitarian element in the Methodist movement, but increasingly he turned to writing pamphlets and articles promoting democratic ideals. This interest catapulted him into the major revolutionary movements of his time, where he achieved status as an important, though unlikely, player. In London he met Benjamin Franklin, who encouraged him to emigrate to America and offered him a letter of introduction. Paine arrived in Philadelphia in 1774, just in time to launch his career as a writer of revolutionary propaganda.

In America, his visionary zeal promptly led him beyond limits that many of his peers were willing to tolerate. During the American Revolution, he assailed what he believed to be dishonesty in another public figure, Silas Deane; in support of his claim, Paine revealed information that he was bound, as a matter of public trust, to keep confidential. Further, unlike many of his fellow revolutionaries, Paine attempted to apply his democratic principles to issues such as slavery and the treatment of Native Americans—an effort that made him persona non grata among the upper class. He appeared to assume that others would show the same selflessness and disinterested zeal for revolution and reform that he himself felt.

Throughout the biography, Keane not only portrays Paine as an untiring and energetic writer but also analyzes numerous individual books, pamphlets, and papers. He provides a rather full examination of the four major works that came from his subject's revolutionary pen and makes a serious effort to assess their success and influence. The most important, *Common Sense* (1776), stressed the timeliness of American independence and systematically explored the logical grounds for separation from England. This pamphlet, probably Paine's most influential work, enjoyed spectacular success in the colonies and abroad. During the Revolution, he followed with a series of sixteen pamphlets; jointly titled *The American Crisis* (1776-1783), they exhorted Americans to support the Revolution, primarily through exploring and pointing out the costs of defeat and advantages of victory. His next work, *The Rights of Man* (1791-1792), supported the French Revolution against an attack by Edmund Burke in his *Reflections on the Revolution in France* (1791). Paine upheld principles such as limits on governmental power, inalienable rights of the populace, and popular sovereignty. Finally, his most controversial major work, *The Age of Reason* (1794-

1795), represented a sustained assault on institutional religion and, though widely read, aroused a storm of opposition.

In treating Paine's personal life, Keane is faced with two problems: how to deal with the exaggerated and often partisan reports of his flaws and how to enliven the essentially colorless life of a revolutionary who lived a plain—in some senses almost austere—existence. Paine took little interest in his own welfare and seemed almost devoid of practical instincts. Having lost his first wife through her early death in childbirth and having failed in a second marriage, he had only himself to care for, and even that self suffered neglect. Never tidy in his personal habits, he slowly descended into a squalid old age, a condition exacerbated by the penury he largely brought upon himself. Perhaps the most successful author of his day in sales and popularity, he realized little income from his writings on behalf of revolutionary causes because he neglected to make appropriate arrangements with publishers to receive royalties.

Like many children of revolution, he was almost consumed by the cause for which he struggled. In France, mistaken for an aristocrat, he barely escaped hanging at the hands of a Jacobin mob and later avoided the guillotine only through the bungling of prison officials. Heedless of his own safety and security, he possessed in old age little money and few of life's necessities. A list of his personal belongings, compiled during his final years, suggests an impoverished existence. Yet as Keane's account shows, Paine was never broken in spirit. Even when assailed by fellow Americans whose cause he had eloquently supported, he maintained his principles and integrity.

When dealing with Paine's flaws, which early biographers made apparent, Keane attempts to put them in perspective and to write about them objectively. Paine normally lived within walking distance of a tavern, where he found conviviality a compensation for his lonely existence, and as Keane makes evident, he was too fond of rum and brandy. On the other hand, his drinking, frequently noted by his contemporaries, rarely impaired his wit or powers of expression. Even in his late sixties, he continued to support himself by writing regular newspaper articles. He died at age seventy-two and thus lived considerably beyond the normal life expectancy of his day.

Contemporaries also noted his vanity and self-importance, which emerged frequently in conversation. This quality alienated some but was accepted by other friends as an example of poor taste, for he *was* important. The tendency did, however, prompt him to make the preposterous claim that his *The Rights of Man* had been the blow that broke Burke's spirit, rather than the recent death of Burke's son. Even Keane, who normally finds Paine's flaws understandable, seems embarrassed by this example of vanity. Wounded vanity more than once prompted Paine to publish tactless and petty attacks on former friends. Believing that George Washington had forsaken him by allowing him to languish unaided in a French prison, Paine sent a diatribe against the president to an American newspaper, criticizing, among other things, Washington's role as a revolutionary general.

The attack on Washington foreshadowed Paine's attitudes in old age; he appeared to believe that he had claims on others that required them to spring to his aid. Related to this kind of indiscretion, he had a tendency to send "open" letters to his opponents, unfortunately published in newspapers before reaching the intended recipient. During his impoverished later years, he barraged Congress with pleas for assistance for his past services—appeals that aroused some sympathy but produced no action.

From his youth, Paine embraced revolution and the idea of progress wholeheartedly and thus found himself repeatedly grappling with new ideas. Believing and asserting that he lived to do good in the world, he did not limit himself to political affairs or theoretical philosophy but, like many intellectuals of his time, explored pragmatic matters as well. He acquired a passion for designing single-span iron bridges and made models in the hope that builders would be found. None appeared. He published papers proposing to stop the plague of yellow fever that swept over American ports in the summers; ironically, though his analysis of the cause was incorrect, his recommendation for placing a quarantine on shipping from the West Indies would have halted outbreaks of the disease. Further, he advocated a publicly sponsored pension plan for workers over fifty years old.

His participation in a wide range of important public debates produced mixed results as well. In a strange irony of history, Paine—who had opposed monarchy all of his life—found himself, as an elected member of the French Assembly, arguing strenuously but vainly that the life of Louis XVI should be spared. Convinced that England in the 1790's teetered on the brink of financial ruin and that disaffected citizens would support an invasion, he worked long and carefully on a plan for a French invasion across the English Channel; he continued to advocate his plan even after the British Navy under Horatio Lord Nelson had destroyed the French fleet at Trafalgar. Yet after Paine returned to the United States, knowledge of French affairs made him useful as an adviser to his friend Thomas Jefferson. For example, Paine's advice influenced Jefferson's decision to buy the entire Louisiana Territory instead of only a portion.

By treating his subject in an objective, scholarly manner, Keane enables the reader to grasp Thomas Paine's amazing achievements as well as his limitations. Painstaking examination of numerous sources has enabled Keane to present a lucid and thorough account of his subject. Yet beyond biography, Keane re-creates Paine's time and thus narrates the history of two important revolutions. For most readers, the book thus offers an expanded understanding of late eighteenth century history.

Stanley Archer

Sources for Further Study

The Economist. CCCXXXVI, July 22, 1995, p. 82.
National Review. XLVII, May 15, 1995, p. 65.
The New Republic. CXII, April 24, 1995, p. 34.
New Statesman and Society. VIII, March 31, 1995, p. 35.
The New York Review of Books. XLII, June 8, 1995, p. 19.
The New York Times Book Review. C, March 12, 1995, p. 1.
The Times Literary Supplement. May 19, 1995, p. 5.

THE TORTILLA CURTAIN

Author: T. Coraghessan Boyle (1948-   )
Publisher: Viking (New York). 355 pp. $23.95
Type of work: Novel
Time: The 1990's
Locale: Southern California and Mexico

The parallel lives of a homeless Mexican couple, illegal immigrants, and a white, middle-class couple are presented in ironic juxtaposition against a background of increasing intolerance of outsiders

> *Principal characters:*
> DELANEY MOSSBACHER, a nature writer
> KYRA MENAKER-MOSSBACHER, his wife, a real-estate agent
> CÁNDIDO RINCÓN, a Mexican immigrant
> AMÉRICA RINCÓN, his wife
> JACK JARDINE, the Mossbachers' neighbor

T. Coraghessan Boyle's novels present conflicts between cultures and values: Englishmen in Africa and an African in Victorian England in *Water Music* (1982), marijuana growers and Northern California rednecks in *Budding Prospects* (1984), Dutch settlers of New York and Native Americans in *World's End* (1987), a young Japanese and the American South in *East Is East* (1990), health crusaders and quick-buck artists in *The Road to Wellville* (1993). *The Tortilla Curtain* makes overt all that is implicit in these novels and several of Boyle's stories.

The antagonists this time are illegal immigrants from Mexico and well-to-do Southern California suburbanites, though the antagonism is mostly one-sided, with the middle-class whites fearing that the invasion from the south is growing out of control. Another conflict occurs with nature, much less easy to manipulate and rationalize than human endeavors. Here Boyle combines the plight of the impoverished, materialism, racism, and natural forces to construct a blatantly didactic message. Taking his epigraph from John Steinbeck's *The Grapes of Wrath* (1939), Boyle presents another desperate journey toward hoped-for prosperity. Such an approach is unusual for Boyle, who is essentially a comic satirist, but *World's End* was an even darker vision of human pettiness.

Boyle tells the story of two contrasting couples mostly in alternating chapters. The middle-aged Cándido Rincón had ventured into the United States before because of the lack of work in Mexico. This time he brings his pregnant seventeen-year-old wife, América. They plan to live in the open until Cándido earns enough money to find them a cheap apartment. Things fail to go according to this plan from the very beginning, when he is struck by a car and slightly injured.

The driver is Delaney Mossbacher, who lives in the posh Arroyo Blanco Estates with his second wife, Kyra, and her six-year-old son, Jordan. Delaney, a native New Yorker who writes a column for a nature magazine, loves where he lives because it is close to the wild. Kyra, a workaholic real-estate agent, loves Arroyo Blanco for its property values and will do anything to protect it. She is concerned that the Mexicans who gather nearby to look for work will drive down property values, and she turns against nature when a coyote leaps over a fence into her backyard to snatch one of her beloved Dandie Dinmont terriers. When Jack Jardine, president of the Arroyo Blanco Estates Property Owners' Association, wants to have a wall built around the development, Kyra supports the plan, but Delaney is appalled at being cut off from nature and by the implied racism of the residents' desire to live in a fortress.

While the Mossbachers worry about invaders, the Rincóns are concerned with surviving. They find some work—América cleans statues of Buddha—and see their meager savings grow, but América is assaulted, and Cándido is beaten and robbed. After they have accumulated another nest egg, Cándido is given a turkey for Thanksgiving, but when he begins cooking it, he sets Topanga Canyon on fire. The blaze, which almost reaches Arroyo Blanco, consumes the Rincóns' savings, which had been buried in the ground in a jar. On the run from the fire and the authorities, América gives birth to a daughter, Socorro. After Cándido steals the materials to make his family a crude hut, rains cause a mud slide that washes it—and the baby—away.

The Rincóns' misfortunes are presented in ironic juxtaposition to those of the Mossbachers. Delaney's Acura is stolen, Kyra's other dog is also taken by a coyote, and her cat goes missing in the fire. (It and other pets are eaten by the desperate Rincóns.) Delaney's liberalism erodes, and he comes to see the Mexicans as the cause of all of his troubles.

Boyle presents Cándido and América as noble sufferers but tries to make them believably less than perfect. América is intolerant of her husband's failures and longs for the same material comforts that the inhabitants of Arroyo Blanco desperately want to protect. When she and Cándido first lose their money, she experiences a nervous breakdown and does not speak to her husband for days. Even the Job-like Cándido once loses his temper and strikes his pregnant wife.

Cándido's quest is for more than work, money, food, and shelter. He needs to acquire an ordinary way of life to restore his sense of dignity, as well as América's respect for him. (His wife's ironic name works on several levels.) More than anything, he longs for América's admiration and is willing to endure anything for her. The money he earns through long hours of construction jobs becomes a symbol of his love.

Despite one setback after another, Cándido cannot give up:

> He couldn't go back to Mexico, a country with forty percent unemployment and a million people a year entering the labor force, a country that was corrupt and bankrupt and so pinched by inflation that the farmers were burning their crops and nobody but the rich had enough to eat.

He is outraged at in the injustice of a society that forces him to break the law simply to obtain work:

> They lived in their glass palaces, with their gates and fences and security systems, they left half-eaten lobsters and beefsteaks on their plates when the rest of the world was starving, spent enough to feed and clothe a whole country on their exercise equipment, their swimming pools and tennis courts and jogging shoes, and all of them, even the poorest, had two cars.

Boyle's didacticism is, unfortunately, this blunt throughout the novel.

América, who never wanted to leave her meager comforts in Mexico, blames herself for bringing all these troubles on her husband. She is less judgmental about El Norte than Cándido and is dazzled by all it holds tantalizingly before her, as when she passes by a furniture store: "If she could have done it, she would have moved right into the store and slept on a different couch every night and it wouldn't have bothered her a whit if the whole world was looking in at the window." (She is amazed that even in this world of plenty, white Americans such as a drug addict she encounters compete for lowly jobs with illegal immigrants.) Cándido is both repelled and attracted by the materialism that América craves:

> These people sanitized their groceries just as they sanitized their kitchens and toilets and drove the life from everything, imprisoning their produce in jars and cans and plastic pouches, wrapping their meat and even their fish in cellophane—and yet still the sight and proximity of all those comestibles made his knees go weak again.

Their economic conditions are made worse by the prejudices they encounter, narrow-mindedness embodied by the residents of Arroyo Blanco. When Delaney tries to defend the immigrants from what Jack Jardine calls the Tortilla Curtain, Jack argues that the manual labor that immigrants perform is becoming irrelevant because of automation and, besides, they cost too much: "The illegals in San Diego County contributed seventy million in tax revenues and at the same time they used up two hundred and forty million in services—welfare, emergency care, schooling and the like." Another of Boyle's representative racists makes even more blatant generalizations: "The more you give them the more they want, and the more of them there are."

Kyra's business is based on people's fear and resentment of what they consider invaders, not only from Latin America but from Asia and the former Communist Europe too. Her customers want "something out of the way, something rustic, rural, safe"—and ethnically pure. When Kyra's most prized property goes up in flames because of the fire that she knows Mexicans started, her resentment explodes: "They were like the barbarians outside the gates of Rome, only they were already inside, polluting the creek and crapping in the woods, threatening people and spraying graffiti all over everything, and where was it going to end?"

Boyle draws numerous parallels between these invaders and the natural order of things. Delaney compares the immigrants to migratory animals "and how one population responded to being displaced by another. It made for war, for violence and killing, until one group had decimated the other and reestablished its claim to the prime hunting, breeding or grazing grounds." When Delaney writes a column about how coyotes have killed his dogs, he tries to make clear—though many of his readers think otherwise—that the suburbanites, not the animals, are responsible for creating the conditions that drive coyotes onto their properties. Boyle intends to make a similar point regarding illegal immigrants.

Kyra and Delaney are depicted as the opposite of the Jack Jardines: intelligent, compassionate, reasonable people capable of seeing more than one side to an issue.

Kyra chastises herself for her grief after her first dog is killed: "There were people out there going through Dumpsters for a scrap to eat, people lined up on the streets begging for work, people who'd lost their homes, their children, their spouses, people with real problems, real grief. What was wrong with her?" What is wrong, according to Boyle, is that she is caring and liberal only in theory; when a crisis develops, she thinks only for herself and her kind.

Boyle portrays Delaney as an Everyman, enlightened but weak, who allows events to dictate his behavior. Labeled a "liberal humanist" at the beginning of the novel, Delaney is a nature writer seemingly because he is much more at ease in the wild, away from "the sad tarnished state of the world," than in the civilization he only thinks he comprehends. Like Kyra, his initial response is self-serving. When he hits Cándido, he worries about damage to the Acura before he thinks about the pedestrian. While Kyra hides from life's complexities in her work, Delaney retreats into a daily routine, feeling disoriented when it is disrupted, sensing security only in "the womb of language." He believes that he asserts his individuality by opposing the wall around Arroyo Blanco, yet he will not join a neighbor in actively fighting it. He resembles his more virulent neighbors in the intense desire that nothing intrude upon his privacy.

Boyle is usually an adept satirist, but his anger and compassion seem to blunt his wit in *The Tortilla Curtain*. The Mossbachers' neighbors are gross caricatures, mindless conformists playing with their expensive toys inside plastic cocoons. Boyle's vision of the American suburb is too obvious, not far removed from what less imaginative writers were producing in the 1950's. His technique of having parallel catastrophes befall his couples—relatively minor ones, naturally, for Delaney and Kyra—helps unify the novel but also makes it too predictable. Here Boyle keeps not only his humor but also his stylistic flourishes in check, writing more simply than in his previous novels. *The Tortilla Curtain* is also less literary, less allusive, than his earlier works, despite the fire and rain that evoke T. S. Eliot's *The Waste Land* (1922). The plethora of pain inflicted on the Rincóns—their baby is blind—almost becomes so excessive as to be laughable. Such defects show how anger and compassion can cloud a usually clear artistic vision.

Michael Adams

Sources for Further Study

Los Angeles Times Book Review. September 24, 1995, p. 4.
The Nation. CCLXI, September 25, 1995, p. 326.
New Statesman and Society . VIII, November 10, 1995, p. 39.
New York. XXVIII, October 9, 1995, p. 85.
The New York Times Book Review. C, September 3, 1995, p. 68.
San Francisco Chronicle. September 10, 1995, p. REV9.
The Times Literary Supplement. October 27, 1995, p. 25.
The Washington Post Book World. XXV, August 20, 1995, p. 3.

THE TRIAL OF ELIZABETH CREE
A Novel of the Limehouse Murders

Author: Peter Ackroyd (1949-   )
First published: Dan Leno and the Limehouse Golem, 1994, in Great Britain
Publisher: Nan A. Talese/Doubleday (New York). 261 pp. $22.00
Type of work: Novel
Time: The late nineteenth century
Locale: London

Set in Victorian London, this novel is arguably Ackroyd's most entertaining, erudite, and teasingly enigmatic foray into historical fiction, postmodern-style

> *Principal characters:*
> ELIZABETH CREE, an orphan, an actress, a gentleman's wife
> JOHN CREE, her husband
> THE LIMEHOUSE GOLEM, a serial killer
> DAN LENO, a comic actor
> KARL MARX, the socialist writer
> GEORGE GISSING, a British writer

"Yes, I have returned to the past," notes narrator Timothy Harcombe, son of a spiritual medium and healer, at the outset of Peter Ackroyd's 1992 novel, *English Music.* So, of course, has Ackroyd, in work after work—so much so that readers may well find themselves saying of *The Trial of Elizabeth Cree* what several characters say *in* it: "Here we are again." The surprise "here" is not that Ackroyd has returned to his old narrative haunts—temporal palimpsests, metaphysical mysteries, historical co-nundrums—but that in following the same basic modus operandi he continues to dazzle and delight, this time with his most inventive, inspired, and artfully contrived work to date (no mean feat given that his 1989 novel, *Chatterton,* was shortlisted for the Booker Prize).

The Trial of Elizabeth Cree invites the attention of scholarly readers because it is obviously a historical novel. Ultimately, however, Ackroyd's novel is "in fact" a historical novel in a postmodern key, closer in spirit and texture to Don DeLillo's *Libra* (1989) and Salman Rushdie's *Midnight's Children* (1981) than to the novels of John Jakes and James Michener. Erudite and entertaining, Ackroyd plays fast and loose with the historical record. He changes the real Dan Leno's year of birth from 1860 to 1850, a switch few readers will notice. He also fails to mention the murders committed by Jack the Ripper in 1888, upon which he has modeled the fictitious ones committed eight years earlier by the novel's equally mysterious Limehouse Golem. Yet what may at first seem a rather odd omission in a novel that drops literary and historical facts the way some people drop names turns out not to be so odd after all; most readers will make the connection without needing any additional prompting. What does all of this mean? Maybe, as one reviewer suggested, *The Trial of Elizabeth Cree* is a novel to be enjoyed but not to be trusted. Maybe Ackroyd is a version of the title character of his 1993 novel, *The House of Doctor Dee,* the sixteenth century mathematician and astrologer described in the *Oxford Companion to English Literature* as "a profoundly learned scholar and hermeticist, but also a sham."

Ackroyd shuttles between roles the way *The Trial of Elizabeth Cree* shuttles between its several main characters (real and imaginary) and various London settings (East End, the British Library, a prison, a courtroom, various music halls and residential areas). For all of its diversity, the novel creates a foggy atmosphere of odd coincidences, mysterious connections, and possible conspiracies. Sitting side by side in the British Library's Main Reading Room in the spring of 1880, for example, are Karl Marx nearing the end of his career, George Gissing at the beginning of his, and (the fictional) John Cree, the son of a wealthy manufacturer, a man with literary aspirations but little talent. His wife Elizabeth, later to be found guilty of poisoning him, formerly worked with Dan Leno, "the funniest man alive on earth," who has also spent time in the library reading about his hero, the eighteenth century pantomimist Grimaldi, in an essay by Thomas De Quincey. Another of De Quincey's extended essays, *Murder Considered as One of the Fine Arts* (1827), plays an important role in a novel that in many ways seems like something out of De Quincey's most famous work, *Confessions of an English Opium Eater* (1821), by way of Lewis Carroll's *Alice's Adventures in Wonderland*, published the year the fictional Elizabeth and the differently fictional Dan Leno meet (1865).

The novel also shuttles between titles (it was published as *Dan Leno and the Limehouse Golem* in Great Britain) and, more important, between narrative methods. Elizabeth Cree's story takes up twenty-six of the novel's fifty-one chapters: eleven in conventional first person, eight in the form of extracts of the trial "taken from the full report in the *Illustrated Police News Law Courts and Weekly Record*," and three more in conventional third person. Eleven chapters concern her husband, John: eight in the form of extracts from his diary and three others in third person. Of the remaining fourteen chapters, all in third person, three concern Dan Leno, four George Gissing, two Karl Marx, one Inspector Kildare, and three the Limehouse Golem, as the murderer comes to be called by the press. At times the change from one chapter to the next is abrupt. At other times one chapter segues into the next; a question posed at the end of a trial extract, for example, is "answered" by Elizabeth in the first person but not in her trial voice.

Elizabeth is a fascinating character. The illegitimate daughter of a prostitute who subsequently "got religion," she becomes an orphan at age fourteen, her mind as scarred as her large hands, the one through sexual abuse by a mother who wanted her to avoid the sinfulness of sex, the other through years spent helping her mother eke out a precarious living by sewing sails. She is fascinated by the theater and the possibilities for transformation it provides (not unlike her mother's religious conversion, and not without similar risks). After hearing her sanitized, melodramatized version of her past, Dan Leno hires her first as a prompter and copyist, later as a performer. Although she will never realize her ambition of rising from the low comedy of the music-hall stage to the high drama of legitimate theater, she will attain respectability playing (as it were) the role of legitimate wife of the wealthy gentleman whose diary exposes him (to the reader, at least) as the notorious Limehouse Golem. "The might-have-been is but boggy ground to build on," contends the narrator of Herman Melville's *Billy Budd* (1924). Yet "the might-have-been" is the very stuff of Ackroyd's mesmerizing yet strangely demystifying narrative with its intricately wrought "network of the most curious associations." Eleanor Marx's situation, for example, reflects Elizabeth's, only in reverse. Having inherited her father's "innate theatricality" but ever mindful of her family's desire to appear respectable, she limits herself to serious dramas and thus forgoes her dream of playing in the very music-hall comedies to which Elizabeth feels unjustly confined. Eleanor's credits include a part in an Oscar Wilde play and another in the tub-of-blood docudrama *The Crees of Misery Junction*, in which she plays the part of Elizabeth's maid, a former music-hall actress named Aveline Mortimer. In no less intriguing and comic a turn, Dan Leno is approached by a down-and-out actor who lives in the very rooms once occupied by Leno's idol, Grimaldi. Invited up, Leno sees that the man's infant son is gravely ill, offers to send his own physician to treat him, and essentially saves the child's life. The young actor is named Harry Chaplin, his child the famous Charlie, born here a bit premature—nine *years* premature. By a similar twist of fate, or fiction, Marx shares a carriage from Bloomsbury to Limehouse with John Cree (or perhaps Elizabeth impersonating him), on the way to visit Solomon Weil, a Jewish scholar, who both by design (Cree goes there the next day to murder "the Jew") and chance ("the Jew" he had in mind being Marx—a case of mistaken address) becomes Cree's next victim.

That the murderer becomes known as the Limehouse Golem is another accident masquerading as its opposite: The book Weil had been reading and on which the murderer placed his victim's severed penis happened to be open to an article on the golem. Things get curiouser and curiouser, more and more complicated and more and more comical. As Marx and Weil point out in a philosophical exchange that bears a striking similarity to music-hall repartee,

> "But, you know, when we look for hidden correspondences and signs,"
> "Yes, they are everywhere."

Marx might have explained this to Inspector Kildare had his friend's death not caused him to read the Limehouse murders in a more narrowly symbolic, less openly semiotic way, with the victims ("Jews and whores"—actually only one of each) deliberately chosen "symbols of the city" and scapegoats.

The novel is intellectually stimulating, but it is also a tease, every bit as contrived and artificial as the golem of Jewish legend and as full of doubts and doubles as music-hall songs and skits are of double-entendres. The ventriloquism, cross-dressing, and playing of multiple parts function as much off the music-hall stage as on, as Ackroyd examines the underside of Victorian London. Even as the novel looks back to the Ratcliffe Highway murders of 1811 (which the novel, following De Quincey, misdates one year later) and, more obliquely, to "the spectre stalking Europe" in *The Communist Manifesto* (1850), it looks ahead not only to Jack the Ripper but also to

Robert Louis Stevenson's *Dr. Jekyll and Mr. Hyde* (1886) and Oscar Wilde's *The Picture of Dorian Gray* (1891). Just as Sherlock Holmes has his Dr. Watson, Inspector Kildare has his roommate George Flood, a civil engineer with the London Underground. Yet it is Ackroyd's tunneling, not the policeman's, that reveals the Governor of Camberwell Prison, Mr. Stephens, in the privacy of his home clad only in the plain white gown Elizabeth Cree had worn when she was hanged.

Although there is not a dull moment in the book—an amazing feat given that Elizabeth is executed in the very first sentence and the little revelation concerning Mr. Stephens comes only a page later—the last fifty pages are especially good as Ackroyd, true to the "shocker" conventions of the time, pulls out one narrative surprise after another. Elizabeth, self-cast as the dutiful Victorian wife (she thinks of each of her several changes of identity as a change of role, a little murder, a rebirth), secretly completes her husband's play only to have it rejected. She then pays to have it performed, only to have her husband refuse to see it and the audience of out-of-work actors with which she fills the theater treat it as comedy. In a mood for revenge, she plots her husband's downfall, arranging his seduction of their maid, then feigning shock when she discovers them together, all so that she can assume mastery in their marriage. The reader already knows that Elizabeth has been found guilty of poisoning her husband (whether she actually poisoned him is another matter) and executed (though only now can the reader begin to understand what Elizabeth must have felt as she played her last role before so small an audience, Victorians having made hangings private rather than, as previously, public spectacles).

On the eve of her execution, Elizabeth tells the chaplain that she has nothing to confess, that she is in fact "the scourge of God." Then, however, she confesses to having committed the Limehouse murders dressed as John Cree, writing his diary in order to fix blame on him, and poisoning him because he had become suspicious. This is quite a revelation, or coup de théâtre, which the priest, a doubly captivated audience, may never reveal.

The novelist, his role less sacred, more secular, tells all—sort of. Corroborating evidence is provided almost as an afterthought in chapter 48 but is hardly conclusive and certainly does not close the novel's most teasing loophole, that Elizabeth is playing the part of murderer, life following art (as Wilde said), histrionics beating history every time. Even here, however, there is still more up Ackroyd's narrative sleeve, a grand finale too good to give away.

Robert A. Morace

Sources for Further Study

Booklist. XCI, May 1, 1995, p. 1550.
Boston Globe. June 4, 1995, p. 77.
Los Angeles Times Book Review. June 25, 1995, p. 12.

Necrofile. IX, Summer, 1995, p. 5.
New Statesman and Society. VII, September 9, 1994, p. 39.
The New York Review of Books. XLII, September 21, 1995, p. 49.
The New York Times Book Review. C, April 16, 1995, p. 7.
The New Yorker. LXXI, August 21, 1995, p. 129.
The Observer. September 11, 1994, p. 20.
Publishers Weekly. CCXLII, April 3, 1995, p. 44.
San Francisco Chronicle. May 21, 1995, p. REV3.
The Spectator. CCLXXIII, September 10, 1994, p. 33.
Time. CXLV, May 29, 1995, p. 72.
The Times Literary Supplement. September 9, 1994, p. 21.

THE TROUBLE WITH COMPUTERS
Usefulness, Usability, and Productivity

Author: Thomas K. Landauer
Publisher: MIT Press (Cambridge, Massachusetts). 425 pp. $27.50
Type of work: Science; current affairs

Thomas Landauer laments that information technology has not produced the business productivity gains it was expected to because of issues of usefulness and usability, and he points the way to a solution through user-centered design, development, and deployment

Thomas Landauer has written a book that very well could meet with two very different reactions. Those already critical of new forms of information technology ("IT," in Landauer's terms) may hail the book as proving that computers have been a huge waste of money and time. Others, mostly avid users of the new technology, may believe that they could never live without computers and that no amount of evidence to the contrary will convince them that they would be better off without them.

Yet either of these reactions would betray an incomplete reading of the book. Landauer is not inveighing against computers or their use in principle. He is, however, highly critical of how they have been used so far. As Landauer states in his preface, computers have not contributed nearly as much to personal and especially business productivity as expected. Nevertheless, they still could live up to their promise. His prescription for the IT industry is UCD: user-centered design, development, and deployment.

In the first part of the book, Landauer spends considerable time trying to show just how far short of expected productivity gains in business the use of computers has fallen. Even though many of the statistics he uses are "soft," because of the many variables of business cycles and the difficulty of assessing their relative impact, he approaches the issue of productivity from so many different angles and with so many different examples that eventually the sheer weight of his arguments forces one to admit that he is probably right. Landauer admits a major difficulty in economic analysis is that while correlation is relatively easy to establish, causation is notoriously difficult. Yet as he points out, the investment in IT has the "right economic size and shape" to explain the relatively meager gains in productivity in virtually all sectors of the economy where computers and related technologies have played a major role.

A determined IT user will probably find it counterintuitive to think of his or her work with computers as anything but greatly enhancing of productivity. After all, these machines help people do things that they surely could never have done nearly as efficiently before, whether typing a letter, balancing a checkbook, or searching for books in a library. Still, consideration of all the time invested in learning how to work the machines and making the machines actually do the desired work may lead some individuals to admit that perhaps computers have not been as efficient as users have allowed themselves to believe.

Landauer focuses on comparisons to the productivity gains made in earlier applications of automation to industry, including earlier deployment (phase one) of computer-related technologies. Here he makes one of the key observations in his book: While in various manufacturing processes there are obvious gains to be had in speeding up repetitive processes that were largely done by hand until the advent of automation, in information-based industries the kind of work involved makes the application of computer technology (phase two) more problematic. Information work is qualitatively different, requiring kinds of thinking that the computer is not yet even close to doing. Spell-checking is fine, as is being able to fix mistakes without correction fluid and giving texts a "desktop publishing" look, but these are not what really slow people down in their writing. Putting thoughts together into a coherent stream that individuals can then present to others as a finished product is the task that requires the most time, and computers and their software have not helped out very much as yet with such needs.

In part this situation is the result of the sheer complexity of the tasks humans routinely ask their brains to perform. Computers are extremely accurate and fast at simple math, and if users can break complex math into simple components, computers can be just as accurate and almost as fast at very complex math as well. Yet much of what humans use their brains for has not been broken down and mimicked by computer hardware and software, and it will likely still be some time before truly creative uses of computers come to fruition. Landauer points out a very important problem here, one that he unfortunately glosses over when presenting his own solutions.

Usefulness is diminished even further when people try to use computers for such tasks of which they are not optimally capable. Workers can actually lose time. For example, how many times do users of computers retype their documents as compared with typists in earlier days? Even if one does not lose time, in order to calculate productivity one has to factor in the cost of the equipment and software and the time spent making them work. There is also the cost differential involved in who is actually typing the letter now (the boss versus a secretary) and how much more per hour that person's time is reckoned to be worth. Yet Landauer is surprisingly optimistic on this point. He believes that a realignment of business uses of IT will virtually eliminate these problems of usefulness.

So much for usefulness. According to Landauer, usability is an even more important factor in the reasons that computers have not increased overall business productivity as anticipated. In a highly competitive industry, usability has not been as important as other market factors: features, performance (speed), and price. Landauer rightly laments this fact. Even the one bright spot in this area, the Macintosh interface, is only the partial exception that proves the rule.

At the heart of Landauer's argument is a criticism of the way organizations are run, a criticism that was already registered by Shoshanna Zuboff in *In the Age of the Smart Machine* (1988). He returns to her arguments about the proliferation of paper, excessive generation of reports, and the difficulty of sorting out truly useful and timely information in the sea of facts with which the machines are capable of presenting us. Like Zuboff, Landauer notes that too many organizations use the new technology to apply the principle of the division of labor to brainwork and in so doing turn interesting jobs into boring ones, damage employee morale, and miss myriad opportunities for productivity enhancement.

The point is rather simple: Happy workers are more productive workers. Thus rather than simply trying to use the machines to keep track of employee keystrokes (not a bad idea as a means to determine what employees are really doing from time to time), hardware and especially software engineers should observe what workers actually do and then, in active dialogue with them, should design their machines and software tools to help the workers with *their* work. Too often workers are hampered by systems designed by managers with higher-level reporting concerns or worse, by software designers with little idea of what the needed work really is.

In order to do the job right, IT specialists must stop trying to get the general user to think like a computer (something the IT specialist has already done without really thinking about it) and start getting the computer to act in ways that the general user would expect. Some would claim that there is really no such thing as an intuitive way of doing things and that people simply must be trained to do tasks that eventually will seem perfectly natural. Landauer draws on his years of experience at Bellcore to prove this idea wrong. It is not that everyone thinks alike, but there are indeed statistically more and less "user-friendly" ways of designing computers and programming them.

What is more, Landauer claims, it is not even a case of the commonly assumed tradeoff between designing for experts and designing for novice users. His many studies in this area lead him to believe that systems designed with inexperienced users in mind will not cost the power user time or cause him or her frustration, but that the expert user will be neither hurt nor helped, while huge gains will be made by the less experienced. These technologically disfranchised tend to be those not gifted in formal logic and spatial memory and, to a lesser degree, older people and people who are not good at mathematics.

So why do many people still love computers? They are fun, Landauer answers. Landauer considers the psychological addictive nature of computers, explaining how the repeated yet somewhat unpredictable successes that most regular computer users experience when debugging their equipment or software is exactly the right stimulus for psychological addiction, as proved in laboratory tests with animals.

Landauer does see some bright spots for usability—the Macintosh interface, automatic teller machines (ATMs), and a program he helped develop called Superbook among them. He is quite hopeful about the possible future, believing that six fairly simple usability tests at the development stage would remedy about 90 percent of the problems users have with computers. He thinks that similar investment at the design and deployment stages would virtually eliminate usability problems altogether. This is a fairly dramatic claim, even more surprising than his beginning premise that computers have not really done the job that people expected them to do.

Landauer ends his book with several fantasy system scenarios. The screens on these fantasy computers are four times as large as those on the best machines of the 1990's, with resolution ten times that of 1990's technology. The systems are networked in such a way as to produce true paperless transactions from start to finish, and they are designed such that at every stage it is not only easy to carry out each function (a sale, for example) but almost a delight. The model for Landauer in this regard is the design of computer games.

What is wrong with Landauer's analysis? There are several problems, but these should not lead readers to dismiss him entirely. First of all, he rightly claims that information work should not be subdivided into an assembly-line process that dehumanizes the worker, lowering morale to such an extent that productivity is likely to fall. The problem here is that he cites for comparison examples of huge productivity gains that have been made with the same division-of-labor and automation process in low-technology industries. This part of his argument thus turns out to be a moral, not an economic one, and it applies equally well to what has already transpired in many other industries. The history of that former battle has already largely been written, and the workers who lost it have been memorialized in folk song.

Also, though Landauer recognizes that one of the problems with computers is their high cost, his solutions require hardware not likely to be available for five to ten years nor affordable for another five to ten years after that. Predictions in this area are notoriously prone to be wrong, whether optimistic or pessimistic, so one should not press the point. Ultimately the market will decide issues that might well be better decided elsewhere. The problem with democracy (and the free market) is that people do not always know (or choose) what is good for them.

Finally, serious problems remain in the area of usefulness even if usability issues can be resolved. Have humans tried to get computers to do too much, or just the wrong things? Will computers ever really do serious thinking for humans? Landauer leaves the impression that all usefulness problems can be solved along with those of usability, and solved fairly easily. If only it were so.

In the end, Landauer is more convincing about what has gone wrong with computers than he is about how easy it will be to fix them. Perhaps he is hoping to convince business leaders and workers, hardware manufacturers and software developers to band together and call a halt to the crazy, wasteful ways in which computers are being designed, developed, and deployed. Unfortunately, in spite of what Landauer says about productivity, too much money is being made, particularly within the computer industry itself, for the process to be altered significantly anytime soon.

Robert Bascom

Sources for Further Study

BYTE. XX, July, 1995, p. 45.
Choice. XXXIII, November, 1995, p. 499.
Commentary. C, July, 1995, p. 34.
Datamation. XLI, July 1, 1995, p. 78.
The Washington Post Book World. XXV, September 10, 1995, p. 6.

TRUST
The Social Virtues and the Creation of Prosperity

Author: Francis Fukuyama (1952-   )
Publisher: Free Press (New York). 457 pp. $25.00
Type of work: Current affairs; economics

An intriguing and original argument that culture molds economics and that trust is the key to prosperity

Francis Fukuyama has never shrunk from controversy. In his 1992 book *The End of History and the Last Man*, he announced that humankind had come to the end of history. In doing so, Fukuyama was not arguing that the world had reached the end of wars, assassinations, and elections. Rather, he was trumpeting the advent of a consensus, hard won after seventy-five years of brutal ideological conflict, that democracy and capitalism provide the only viable path to development. Fukuyama was ridiculed by critics who misunderstood his book. Yet *The End of History and the Last Man* remains one of the most compelling documents to have emerged from the end of the Cold War. With his latest book, *Trust: The Social Virtues and the Creation of Prosperity*, Fukuyama confirms his place as one of America's boldest and most original social commentators.

Having laid the past to rest with his first book, in his second Fukuyama looks to the future. He addresses the issue of international economic competition, which has replaced the military balance of power as the leading concern of American foreign policy. Fukuyama observes that while people may look forward to a liberal and democratic dispensation, there are different kinds of liberalism and different kinds of democracies. Some nations will prosper more than others in the new world order. Fukuyama believes that the wealth of the successful will reflect more their cultural than their material resources.

In arguing for the importance of culture in a nation's productive life, Fukuyama is challenging an economic orthodoxy—one recently made all the stronger by the collapse of the Soviet Union. With Marxism consigned to the historical rubbish heap, neoclassical economists have come to cling all the more tightly to the twin pillars of the free market and economic individualism. Fukuyama suspects that this faith could ultimately prove as self-defeating as the Marxists' attachment to the Communist ideal.

Man does not live by bread alone. This homely truth from the Jewish and Christian Scriptures lies at the heart of Fukuyama's message in *Trust*. He is careful to point out that Adam Smith, the intellectual father of modern capitalism, had the same insight. Although Smith is most famous for his great tome *Inquiry into the Nature and Causes of the Wealth of Nations* (1776), he was also the author of *The Theory of Moral Sentiments* (1759), which argued that the economic motivations of people are highly complex and always involving concerns that transcend the desire for profit. In short, Smith realized that people create values as well as goods.

Fukuyama has long been preoccupied with the importance of "values" when calculating social policy. He wrestled with the threat of human desires to the capitalist order in *The End of History and the Last Man*. In that book, he predicted that the greatest challenge to the safe and comfortable world emerging in the developed nations would be the human drive for mastery and the taste for glory that accompanies it—what the German philosopher G. W. F. Hegel termed the desire for recognition. According to this view of human nature, people want respect just as much as material well-being. As many poets and moralists have observed, power is every bit as seductive as gold. Pride as well as greed runs before a fall. Hence humankind's long history of wars and oppression, with lust for supremacy clothed in the specious rhetoric of martial virtue and political necessity.

Like it or not, argued Fukuyama, the old warrior passions lie just beneath the surface in modern men and women. Liberalism, he said, faces the delicate task of redirecting these energies into constructive channels. One of his suggestions for doing this was to sublimate the struggle of the battlefield into the competitiveness of the boardroom—to let business become the moral equivalent of war. Such considerations make a mockery of the "rational man" model of conventional economic analysis.

Fukuyama believes that economics must grapple not only with unreconstructed man, full of tumultuous needs and emotions, but also with constructed man, the socialized product of a culture, programmed with the inherited habits and prejudices of generations of forebears. People betray both individual wants and collective ambitions. They operate within a web of meaning and intent shared with others. No individual can be fully understood outside the context of the culture within which he or she was reared. In *Trust*, Fukuyama takes these social facts of life and applies them to international economic rivalries.

He assumes that it is possible to discern national styles of economic enterprise, rooted in the idiosyncrasies of culture. Differences in choices made by societies reflect variations in these societies' understanding of the good. Some societies will value communal cohesion over individual self-expression. Others will celebrate the private at the expense of the public. All such cultural predilections will find concrete expression in a nation's economic organization and institutions.

Fukuyama's rejection of orthodox economics, and his reification of the economic importance of culture, makes *Trust* a book at once exciting and frustrating. His brave venture into an anthropology of the business world is refreshing in its iconoclasm. The insights he draws from this approach are remarkably evocative. At times, his sweeping and pungent generalizations read like the judgments of a latter-day Alexis de Tocqueville, skillfully dissecting the soul of democratic man. Yet Fukuyama's theoretical temerity comes at a price. His assertions are often stunning in their explanatory elegance but also essentially unprovable. He is vulnerable to charges that his thesis masks more mundane reasons for the phenomena he describes. Ultimately, any analysis of events predicated on social psychology must become as ambiguous as the wants of the human heart.

Fukuyama's path, for all of its inevitable imprecision, nevertheless remains well worth following. He reminds readers that all social constructs are in the end products of men's and women's aspirations and needs and are not the expression of abstract forces, divorced from the messiness of human reality.

The cultural trait that, in Fukuyama's eyes, most conditions economic activity is the quality of trust embedded in a society. The unsung virtue of trust is what makes the economic world go round. The level of trust in a society determines the degree to which people will cooperate to build and maintain businesses. Societies vary widely in levels of trust. For example, Fukuyama points to the rescues of Mazda Motors of Japan and Daimler-Benz of Germany during the Arab oil embargo of 1973-1974. Declining sales pushed both of these automakers to the brink of bankruptcy. In each case, however, a bank with a tradition of doing business with the company stepped in, extended credit, and preserved its future. Each bank swallowed short-term losses in order to maintain a working relationship with a business that, over time, had earned trust. The confidence of these banks would be rewarded handsomely a few years later, when prosperity returned to Mazda and Daimler-Benz.

On the other hand, Fukuyama cites a 1950's study of southern Italy, where it was found that the inhabitants of a small town were unwilling to cooperate to found such badly needed institutions as a school and a hospital. The townspeople possessed the necessary labor and money to build what they needed. Yet they believed that it was the task of the government, and not themselves or their neighbors, to undertake improvements. Lacking a tradition of communal solidarity, they did nothing and had to live without a school or a hospital.

Fukuyama divides the capitalistic world into high-trust and low-trust societies. High-trust societies are blessed with a high degree of spontaneous sociability, the capacity for individuals to build firm relationships, both within and without such traditional structures as the family. In a high-trust society people easily come together to form a variety of organizations, ranging from church congregations to trade associations. In the economic realm, people in high-trust societies are able to join in large, bureaucratically sophisticated corporations and, bound together by no other ties than loyalty to the organization, to work toward common goals.

Low-trust societies lack this capacity for unrelated people to cohere in associations, either formal or informal. In such societies, people's allegiances are tribal; they trust only kin or clan. Low-trust societies tend to produce small, family-run businesses. Because of the vagaries of demography, these are difficult to sustain for more than a generation or two.

Fukuyama terms the propensity for trust "social capital." The more social capital a society possesses, the more likely it is that its members will be able to create flourishing and enduring economic institutions.

Fukuyama uses this schema to classify current economic giants and in doing so subverts commonly held assumptions. He challenges notions of Asian communitarianism, and dispels fears of a monolithic Asian economic threat, by firmly classifying Japan as a high-trust society and China as a low-trust society. While accommodating time-worn stereotypes in describing France and Italy as low-trust societies and Germany as an exemplar of a high-trust society, Fukuyama defies expectations by including the United States in the high-trust camp. He counters the self-image of Americans as resolutely individualistic, arguing that traditionally Americans have been a remarkably gregarious people. A nation of joiners, satirized by foreigners for their love of committees, Americans have tempered their ideological celebration of individual independence with a remarkably elaborate network of voluntary associations. The lone riders of romance have their place in the history of the United States, but Fukuyama does well to remind readers that Americans pioneered modern corporate organization.

As a high-trust society, the United States stands to reap great benefits. Only high-trust societies can create the great corporations capable of producing such complex goods as automobiles, semiconductors, and aerospace equipment—the leading edge of industrial development. Such societies are financially and technologically better adjusted to adapt to innovations in products and shifts in markets. They also foster businesses sufficiently stable to establish widely known and accepted brand names. Kodak, Siemens, and Hitachi are American, German, and Japanese brand names recognized and respected around the world. It is much harder, Fukuyama notes, to identify a Chinese brand name. Chinese firms, usually family-run, are too small and volatile to distinguish themselves in this way.

There are some notable exceptions to Fukuyama's rule, which he forthrightly acknowledges. Korea, a cultural offshoot of China, and France both have built impressively large and famous corporations. Yet, Fukuyama insists, these nations reinforce rather than contradict his core insights. Heavy industry in both Korea and France was encouraged and subsidized by governmental fiat. Thus the cultural effects of a low-trust culture can be minimized through determined political action, but only at the cost of establishing less efficiently run state enterprises.

The hybrid success of Korea and France is the converse of a process Fukuyama addresses toward the end of his book. If social capital can be artificially stimulated, it can also be depleted. This, according to Fukuyama, is a danger facing the United States. America's rich endowment of social capital has rapidly dissipated in recent decades. Social scientists have measured a precipitous decline in voluntary associations. Community life has suffered with the rise in the divorce rate and single-parent households. The fear of crime has further chilled civic commitments. As broad-based coalitions have faded into the background, special-interest groups have proliferated and gained in influence.

Fukuyama attributes this unhappy state of affairs to a concatenation of social forces and corrosive ideals—most notably the cult of ever-expanding "rights." He firmly believes that this explosion of unchecked individualism poses a grave menace to the economic well-being of the United States. An atomized American society, increasingly devoid of trust, will be unable to sustain the industries and institutions that have fueled its economic progress.

Fukuyama ends his book on a high note, rounding out his conviction that culture conditions economics and that trust is the root of prosperity. The Founding Fathers, he says, recognized that the liberal order that they were establishing could exist only on a foundation of nonliberal, traditional values. George Washington, not a conventionally religious man himself, wrote eloquently of the necessity for religious belief to guarantee the rights promised in the Constitution. This paradox—the dependence of liberalism upon values, upon culture—points the way for future action. Fukuyama concludes as he began, as a moralist, exhorting his fellow citizens to reclaim the communal virtues that were once the glory of the American nation.

Daniel P. Murphy

Sources for Further Study

Commentary. C, October, 1995, p. 34.
The Economist. CCCXXXVI, September 2, 1995, p. 79.
Forbes. CLVI, September 25, 1995, p. 24.
Industry Week. CCXLIV, July 17, 1995, p. 27.
The Los Angeles Times Book Review. July 30, 1995, p. 3.
The Nation. CCLXI, September 25, 1995, p. 318.
The New Republic. CCXIII, September 11, 1995, p. 36.
New Statesman and Society. VIII, October 13, 1995, p. 30.
The New York Times Book Review. C, August 13, 1995, p. 1.
Publishers Weekly. CCXLII, July 10, 1995, p. 51.
The Wall Street Journal. August 11, 1995, p. A7.
The Washington Post Book World. XXV, August 27, 1995, p. 2.

THE TUNNEL

Author: William H. Gass (1924-   )
Publisher: Alfred A. Knopf (New York). 652 pp. $30.00
Type of work: Novel
Time: The 1960's
Locale: A Midwestern university

When a history professor begins writing an introduction to his magnum opus on Nazi Germany, it turns into an exploration of his own life

Principal characters:
WILLIAM FREDERICK KOHLER, a history professor in his fifties
MARTHA, his wife
HIS MOTHER AND FATHER
MAGUS TABOR, his former history professor
CARL, his son
ANOTHER SON, whose name is never mentioned
CHARLES CLARENCE CULP, a colleague
PLANMANTEE, a colleague
WALTER HENRY HERSCHEL, a colleague
TOMMASO GOVERNALI, a colleague
LOU, a lover
SUSU, another lover

The central figure and nonstop voice of *The Tunnel* is William Frederick Kohler, a history professor at a major Midwestern university. Of distant German ancestry, Kohler studied in Germany during the 1930's and was later a consultant during the famous Nuremberg Trials, after which he wrote a book that made many critics think that he was not completely unsympathetic to the Nazis. Yet William Gass has said that the subject of *The Tunnel* is not political fascism but that it uses Adolf Hitler's grand demonic plan for Germany and the world as a metaphoric backdrop for domestic life in America. The real subject of his long-awaited novel, says Gass, is the "fascism of the heart."

At the beginning of *The Tunnel*, Kohler has just completed a magnum opus entitled *Guilt and Innocence in Hitler's Germany.* When he tries to write a simple self-congratulatory preface, however, he finds himself blocked and begins to doodle idly and to write about his own life. Instead of the carefully controlled, highly structured historical writing for which he has an academic reputation, he writes a sprawling, seemingly shapeless personal exploration filled with bitterness, hatred, lies, self-pity, and self-indulgence. As Kohler "tunnels" metaphorically into his own psyche, he begins to tunnel literally in his basement, concealing both his personal manuscript and his earthly burrowing from his wife (whom he professes to despise), hiding the pages of his journal within the manuscript of his historical study (which he knows that his wife will never want to see), and hiding the dirt from the tunnel in his wife's bureau drawers (which, curiously, she does not discover until they are filled).

There is no physical action as such in this novel and no dramatized dialogue encounters. The entire book consists of Kohler's psychic digging into his past. In *The Tunnel*, everything that has happened to Kohler, everyone that he has encountered, is converted into the stuff of his mind. Kohler's mind is not one that many will find hospitable, for it is the closed-in, claustrophobic world of the narrow-minded bigot. Kohler does not seem to like anyone or to be happy about much of anything. Long passages reveal his resentment toward his unforgiving, hard-fisted father and his self-pitying, alcoholic mother, his loathing of his fat and slothful wife, his contempt for his nondescript adolescent sons (one whose name he refuses even to utter in the book), and his scorn for his pedantic colleagues and his superficial lovers.

Yet it is not this rambling, referential subject that makes *The Tunnel* Gass's most ambitious effort thus far; rather, it is the highly polished prose, wonderfully sustained for more than six hundred pages, and the philosophic exploration of the relationship between historical fascism and domestic solipsism that makes those who know and love Gass's work highly enthusiastic about the novel. Gass, a philosophy professor at a Midwestern university, has produced three previous works of fiction as well as three collections of theoretical literary criticism and a philosophical study of the color blue.

The Tunnel is most like Gass's last work of fiction, a relatively brief novella titled *Willie Master's Lonesome Wife* (1971), which, like the more ambitious *The Tunnel*, is a first-person autobiographical and philosophic exploration featuring a number of graphic inserts and typographical variations that serve to draw attention to the texture of the book as book, not simply the book as a depiction of the so-called real world. Gass has always been one of the best-known spokesmen of postmodernist self-reflexivity, having coined the term "metafiction" decades ago to refer to that brand of fiction that more frequently refers to its own fiction-making processes than to some "as if" reality outside itself. Gass has said that the primary tension taken on in *The Tunnel* is the tension between a work of fiction that is intensely referential and a work of fiction that does not depend on that reference. Gass's view has always been that the quality of a novel does not depend on its subject but on its linguistic style.

Indeed, the first thing one notices about *The Tunnel* is that Gass continually breaks up the naïve realist illusion that the subject of a novel—the territory it depicts—is identical to its maplike pattern or language. A professor through and through, Kohler produces a first-person text filled with references to previous texts, the great works of history, philosophy, and literature that he both honors and debunks in what seems like a rambling stream-of-consciousness free association but is really a carefully controlled aesthetic pattern so heavily loaded toward the metaphoric that readers cannot for a moment lose sight of the fact that it is language they are reading, not everyday physical life they are vicariously experiencing.

Kohler writes about his student years in Germany (when for a short time he became involved in the Hitler youth movement), his history professor, his marriage and its gradual self-destruction, his love affairs (both real and imagined), his alcoholic mother, his bigoted father, his unmarried aunt, and his four colleagues in the history department, whose theories about history correspond to their domestic situations. Kohler's examination of his own family and his observation of the domestic lives of others convinces him that a new political party should be developed—the Party of the Disappointed People (of which he imagines himself leader), brought into being by widespread resentment. Kohler says that it is not bad luck that makes people so resentful, but the realization that much of their disappointment has been caused by others:

> There is an enemy out there who has stolen our loaf, soured our wine, infected our book of splendid verse with filthy rhymes; then we are filled with resentment and would hang the villains from that bough we would have lounged in languorous love beneath had the tree not been cut down by greedy and dim-witted loggers in the pay of the lumber interests.

In a novel filled with poetic language, the most prominent and recurring metaphoric obsessions in *The Tunnel* are scatological and sexual. Although much of the novel's humor may appear to some to represent little more than adolescent fascination with the physical, Gass's intention in having Kohler constantly refer to bodily functions both excretory and sexual is to confront directly that area of human experience that is simultaneously most fraught with desire and most repressed. Gass's sexual and scatological references are in the tradition of Jonathan Swift, Mark Twain, and James Joyce; they focus on the imaginative nature of sex, with intercourse a poor substitute for masturbatory fantasy. One of the most common devices throughout the book is Kohler's use of sexual, sacrilegious limericks—a form that his colleague Culp defends as a postmodern form par excellence—"all surface . . . no inside however long or far you travel on it, no within, no deep."

Some skeptics may believe that this definition is a metaphor for Gass's own book. Indeed, *The Tunnel* does not presume to teach by example any great moral lesson, but aims rather to present the basic reality of human experience as being constantly complicated by forbidden desires, inherent fascination and repulsion with the lumpish body with which each person is saddled, and inescapable self-reflection that threatens to dissolve human beings into pure subjectivity. Like Fyodor Dostoevski's underground man, Kohler runs the risk of thinking too much and constantly undermining himself.

Gass's novel will not be widely welcome in an era of American literature in a state of reaction against postmodernist self-reflexivity. There is certainly nothing "minimalist" about this book, nor is it the kind of "moral fiction" that John Gardner advocated and that Raymond Carver began to write at the end of his career. No part of it will ever be reprinted in anything like William Bennett's best-selling *The Book of Virtues*, for there are no easy moral lessons here, only the very hard lessons of daring to face honestly what it means to be human.

The Tunnel is one of those great narcissistic novels in which the only real person in the book is the narrator himself; all others are merely grist for his mental mill. What it means to be human, the novel suggests, is to confront the hard truth that ultimately the self is the only consciousness one can hope to grasp. Kohler knows that if one does not become pure subjective consciousness, one runs the risk of being transformed into the consciousness of someone else. It is his solipsistic conviction that no one is quite as aware and real as the one who constitutes his inescapable fascism of the heart. Like the wizard of Oz, however, Kohler also knows that beneath the imposing rhetorical illusion that he creates, he is but a vulnerable lump of flesh subject to all the weaknesses that flesh is heir to. Gass suggests, as Dostoevski did a century before, that when one dares to burrow deep within, one always finds the same narcissistic egoism and the same shameful vulnerability. Gass presents the political fascism of the Nazis as a parallel to this uniquely human dilemma; Kohler's historical study—although no passages of it are presented—probably perceives both guilt and innocence in the Nazi endeavor.

Gass relishes the process of digging a tunnel as a perfect metaphor for his novel, for he sees it as having three basic elements: the hole, or nothing; the dirt that is taken out; and the supports that were stolen from somewhere to hold up the hole. The supports that hold up this work's hole—all the literary and historical allusions that buttress the work—Gass ransacks from all of Western culture. The hole itself is a void, a vacuum, an emptiness from which things have been removed. The very nature of the hole is existential paradox that seems a significant plentitude even as it is a pure process of hollowing out.

Gass's admirers will say that *The Tunnel* is a masterpiece, one of the great novels of the twentieth century, comparable to James Joyce's *Ulysses* (1922). Others—not such great fans of Gass's poetic and philosophic style—will say that it is a bloated monster of a book, a self-indulgent collection of all the most deplorable vices of self-conscious postmodernism centering on the verbose ramblings of a repugnant bigot. The paradoxical truth of the matter is that Gass's tunnel is an escape route out of the prison of the self and at the same time a gold mine in which the way to the treasure *is* the treasure. It is the entrance to the womb, the removal of all human restraints, and the reduction of the self to its most elemental. It is a book so honest and thus so hard to bear that it will probably be one of the most talked about, and largely unread, books of the late twentieth century.

Charles E. May

Sources for Further Study

The Christian Science Monitor. March 6, 1995, p. 13.
Esquire. CXXIII, March, 1995, p. 164.
Los Angeles Times Book Review. LXII, March 19, 1995, p. 1.
The Nation. CCLX, March 20, 1995, p. 388.
National Review. XLVII, May 1, 1995, p. 82.
The New Republic. CCXII, March 27, 1995, p. 29.
The New York Times Book Review. C, February 26, 1995, p. 1.
The Review of Contemporary Fiction. XV, Spring, 1995, p. 159.
The Washington Post Book World. XXV, March 12, 1995, p. 1.

THE UNCONSOLED

Author: Kazuo Ishiguro (1954-   )
Publisher: Alfred A. Knopf (New York). 535 pp. $25.00
Type of work: Novel
Time: The 1990's
Locale: An unnamed provincial city in central Europe

The immensely accomplished, haunting, long-awaited fourth novel by one of Great Britain's most talented writers, whose previous novel won the prestigious Booker Prize

Principal characters:
RYDER, a famous concert pianist
SOPHIE, a woman who seems to be at once the daughter of a porter at a
    local hotel and (perhaps) Ryder's wife
BORIS, Sophie's young son
MR. BRODSKY, a disgraced local conductor
MISS COLLINS, Brodsky's estranged wife

As of 1989, with three increasingly well-received novels under his belt, Kazuo Ishiguro had yet to take a false step in a career that had gone from strength to strength and showed every promise of developing into a major body of work. *A Pale View of Hills* (1982) and *An Artist of the Floating World* (1986) were exquisitely wrought, dialogue-driven and delicate, foreshadowing their young author's tour de force demonstration of his superb ear for social misunderstandings and things left unsaid in *The Remains of the Day* (1989). The first two novels were remarkable for being set in Ishiguro's native Japan, which he had not visited since his family emigrated to England in 1960. *The Remains of the Day* was even better crafted than its predecessors and remarkable for a complete absence in its ostensible subject matter (the late-career sadness and moral dilemmas of a thoroughly proper English butler) of anything whatsoever to do with Japan. *The Remains of the Day* brought its author sudden celebrity, winning Britain's prestigious Booker Prize and inspiring a popular film.

The Unconsoled, Ishiguro's fourth novel, deals with the elusiveness of identity, the treachery of memory, regret, and the hope of redemption. Anita Brookner's endorsement—"a novel of outstanding breadth and originality: almost certainly a masterpiece"—seems right. The narrator is a Mr. Ryder, a classical pianist of international renown who arrives to give a concert in an unnamed provincial city in central Europe, only to find himself puzzled by an inability to remember why exactly he is there or where he is supposed to be next, and under siege from the solicitous and demanding local burghers. The town is experiencing an unspecified civic or historical crisis as well, and as the story unfolds it becomes evident that in addition to exhibiting his musical prowess, Ryder is expected to bestow on the locals some equally unspecified but definitive wisdom in the form of a speech. As Thursday night—the scheduled date of the concert—approaches, Ryder's sense that he lacks control or even adequate awareness of what is unfolding intensifies; he experiences panic and confusion as he tries to meet his commitments and retain his poise and a modicum of control over his experience of the passage of time.

Early reviewers compared *The Unconsoled* to the work of Franz Kafka; the comparison, even if obvious, is apt. The setting itself is a tacit allusion to Kafka, and the atmosphere of controlled absurdity is reminiscent. There may be as well a sense in which the setting is meant as a deliberate metaphor. If Milan Kundera is right in his intriguing if sometimes shrill claim that the geographic heart of Europe is the heartland of European, hence Western, civilization (see his *The Art of the Novel*, 1988), then Ishiguro may be making a powerful point about the nature of human civilization itself. It may follow that scattered references to cultural and technological items that place the story in the late twentieth century are intentional. Is it fanciful to suppose that Ishiguro's point is that, even now, we live within history—that our plight, our world, is the same as that of which Kafka wrote?

The novel's atmosphere has been described as dreamlike, but in an important sense it is a work not of fantasy but of hyperrealism. "I was keen not to write the kind of thing where people actually grow wings and fly off or anything like that," Ishiguro told Katherine Knorr of the *International Herald Tribune* (April 28, 1995). Truth be told, odd things happen in "real" life as well, although in concrete, banal, unfantastic ways. To the extent that any work of literature is successful, it is an articulated metaphor for the "real" world or some aspect thereof. The greatest literature is paradoxically—(paradox being a fundamental trait of the universe humans inhabit) the most precisely enigmatic. If the "real" world were less thoroughly mysterious than it is, there would have existed no need for Ishiguro to articulate the metaphor that he has titled *The Unconsoled*, whose enigmatic precision is of a very high order.

True narrative is something beyond the pigeonholes labeled "fiction" and "nonfiction," and it always has a strong picaresque aspect. Narrative in truth is simply a synonym for history (another term usually used too loosely), which in turn is only another word for the fundamental enigma called the passage of time. The odd, implausible ways in which Ryder comes to know things, to eavesdrop inadvertently on other characters' private lives, to retrieve snatches of personal memory and local history, raise the profoundly intriguing question: How does anyone come to know anything? Are any so-called facts truly verifiable? One's only authorities are hearsay and experience. Even if "facts" are verifiable—or, equally, if they are not—what, if anything, do they mean? These all are terrifyingly unanswerable, perhaps literally maddening questions, and it is these and their like that Ishiguro has the audacity to address, making astonishingly agile use of conventions of narrative writing, verb tenses, and novelistic devices (such as subtly alternating first- and third-person narration) in ways that underscore rather than resist the apparent absurdity of life as it is actually lived.

If most novels take the stuff of "real" life and mold it, more or less consciously, into patterns designed to satisfy the author's felt need for sense and order, *The Unconsoled* seems instead to yield to history as it is truly, contingently experienced. Awareness transcends consciousness, and Ishiguro's is the awareness of a literary artist of somewhere very near the first rank, a writer who refuses to concede the presumptions of "reality" in any of the vulgar senses in which that term is customarily employed. As readers undertake the arduous work of trying to puzzle out the story's elusive meaning, they begin to realize that the elusiveness *is* the meaning, and snatches of phrasing and dialogue acquire a distilled, epigrammatic significance. They may find themselves underlining single sentences, as though these might be partial keys to which they might later need to refer. "I had assumed she was leading me either to a particular spot in the room or to a particular person," relates Ryder, "but after a while I got the distinct impression we were walking around in slow circles." Later he tells readers:

> Naturally, as I listened to Fiona, I sensed I should be feeling considerable remorse over what had happened the previous night. However, despite her vivid account of the scenes at her apartment, as much as I felt deeply sorry for her, I found I had only the vaguest recollection of such an event having been on my schedule.

Miss Collins, a major character, tells her former husband, the alcoholic conductor Mr. Brodsky, "Of course I forget. Why would I remember such things? There have been so many more vivid things to remember in the years since. . . . How much you live in the past, Mr. Brodsky!" A single clause in Ryder's tale, referring to a scene he witnesses at a funeral, expands to serve for his presence in the city itself, and beyond that to his (and the reader's) presence in the place the city symbolizes: "And I could see that in no time things would be as they had been prior to my arrival."

Perhaps these are the lessons readers are meant to absorb: that truth—certainly factual truth, probably even moral truth—is occasional and contingent; that memory and present experience are no more (or less) real than a dream; that responsibility is inevitable but indefinable; that after we, individually and as a species, are gone, in no time things will be as they were prior to our arrival. The more puzzled the reader becomes, the more powerful the metaphor grows, until truly universal truths seem to come just a bit clearer than they were before.

What may be the tale's central passage occurs less than halfway through, in a monologue on music Ryder's rival Christoff offers, uninvited, as they, inexplicably, climb down a steep hillside. "The modern forms, they're so complex now," says Christoff.

> Kazan, Mullery, Yoshimoto. Even for a trained musician such as myself, it's hard now, very hard. The likes of von Winterstein, the Countess, what chance do they have? They're completely out of their depth. To them it's just crashing noise, a whirl of strange rhythms. Perhaps they've convinced themselves over the years they can hear something there, certain emotions, meanings. But the truth is, they've found nothing at all. They're out of their depth, they'll never understand how modern music works. Once it was simply Mozart, Bach, Tchaikovsky. Even the man in the street could make a reasoned guess about that sort of music. But the modern forms! How can people like this, provincial people, how can they ever understand such things, however great a sense of duty they feel towards the community?

It is an incisive and, metaphorically, a universally important question for human beings—all of whom are provincial—at the end of the twentieth century. It is not the only question the book raises. Like all truly important literature, *The Unconsoled* raises more questions than it answers, beginning with: Who is Ryder? (Which is to say, who is "I"?) Where did he come from? Why is he here? Where is he going next? Is individual identity—whatever that is—fundamental, or is our inevitable involvement each with every other fellow human the bedrock of who we "really" are?

With respect to its author's career, the question *The Unconsoled* raises is the same as that posed by *The Remains of the Day*, raised to a much higher power: Where can he go next? What is left for him to accomplish? Ishiguro seems aware—in the sense in which all genuine writers are aware, within themselves—of his direction, if not of his eventual destination. Explaining to the *International Herald Tribune* why he never writes journalism, he said, "I guess I've always felt that as a novelist I'm on a long-term search for something, and I didn't want anything that was going to interfere with that." What is certain is that with his fourth novel, Ishiguro has both firmly established himself as a major novelist and considerably raised expectations in his admirers and the stakes for himself. If the trajectory of his achievement through 1995 is any indication, he probably will be up to the challenge.

Ethan Casey

Sources for Further Study

London Review of Books. XVII, June 8, 1995, p. 30.
The Nation. CCLXI, November 6, 1995, p. 546.
The New Republic. CCXIII, November 6, 1995, p. 42.
New Statesman and Society . VIII, May 12, 1995, p. 39.
The New York Times Book Review. C, October 15, 1995, p. 7.
The New Yorker. LXXI, October 23, 1995, p. 90.
Newsweek. CXXXVI, October 2, 1995, p. 92.
Publishers Weekly. CCXLII, September 18, 1995, p. 105.
Time. CXLVI, October 2, 1995, p. 82.
The Times Literary Supplement. April 28, 1995, p. 22.

VIEW WITH A GRAIN OF SAND
Selected Poems

Author: Wisława Szymborska (1923-   )
Translated from the Polish by Stanisław Barańczak and Clare Cavanagh
Publisher: Harcourt Brace (New York). 214 pp. $20.00
Type of work: Poetry

This selection of poems from six different collections by Wisława Szymborska, published between 1957 and 1993, gives ample confirmation that she is one of the finest living European poets

Many readers of contemporary poetry know that the poetry written in Poland after 1945 is particularly original and dynamic. American readers have become familiar with the work of Czesław Miłosz, Tadeusz Rozewicz, Zbigniew Herbert, and Miron Bialoszewski. Wisława Szymborska has been slower to reach the attention of the English-speaking public. Born in 1923, a member of the same generation as the last three names mentioned above, Szymborska crafts poetry that is on the same high level.

Some critics have claimed that each new volume by Szymborska has become better and better—and the observation contains some truth. Her 1993 volume *The End and the Beginning* (*Koniec i poczatek*) has a large proportion of superb poems; they consistently excite and dazzle, are genuinely meaningful, and are marked by high formal achievement. On the other hand, readers should be reminded that Szymborska has been writing fine poems for some time. "Conversation with a Stone" and "The Joy of Writing" were written in the 1960's and are as good as anything she has written subsequently. It can be argued that each volume after *Salt* (*Sol*, 1962) has had as high a proportion of successful poems as her latest collection.

Two reasons might be found for the tardy recognition of Szymborska. The first is that many of her earlier poems exhibited unfortunate and irritating mannerisms. Rereading poems from *Salt* that are included in the present selection of translations, one can see what Szymborska has successfully avoided in subsequent volumes: schematic approach, preciosity, and overfacile, disdainful irony. "O Muse," she exclaimed at the end of her poem "Poetry Reading," with evident fatigue. Her frequent self-referential glances were dangerous, and as a procedure they narrowed her perspective.

A second reason is that she was an antipolitical poet. For a generation steeped in the poetry of Miłosz and Herbert—even in the mid-1990's a controversy between the two poets was being kept alive in Polish periodicals—it is difficult to define Szymborska's place, and she defies political categorization. Her poems were not relevant to topical matters such as Solidarity, martial law, or censorship, at least on the level of narrow partisanship. They were entirely relevant, however, on a level of broader experience. Her poems address universal topics such as hatred, imperfection, utopia, death, and the body.

Szymborska's breadth of reference can be seen in many poems included in the present volume. A good example is the excellent "Utopia," originally included in Szymborska's 1976 collection *A Large Number* (*Wielka liczba*). The poem, typically, addresses not a single "issue" but a concept that underlies many issues. The poem is satirical and playfully compares utopia to an island. "Island where all becomes clear," the poem begins. The flora on the island is only too familiar—for example,

> The Tree of Understanding, dazzlingly straight and simple,
> sprouts by the spring called Now I Get It.

The description of valleys, caves, springs, and other topographical features proves to contain remarkable parallels to human intellectual and political history. The ending of the poem displays one of Szymborska's great strengths, her dynamism. The poem is not a static allegory but contains as many contradictions as human nature and history contain. Though the island is uninhabited, it has countless footprints that lead toward the sea. All one can do on the island, she writes, is leave it, "and plunge, never to return, into the depths./ Into unfathomable life." All along, it turns out, the poem was not describing a really isolated island, but an island set in the surrounding sea.

The mode of inquiry in these poems almost always begins from a point that is purely personal. On the other hand, they consistently reach a high degree of generality in their closure. Szymborska's forms are consistent. The first lines are usually relaxed, observational, and direct, proceeding into the rest of the poem in a listlike, incremental manner. From the first word the reader is persuaded that *this* is the world, hers but also mine, our common reality. She registers the world around her as it is, ordinary and without suspicion of bias. It is the endings of the poems that achieve great force, but the beginnings are important as foils. In the poem "Seen from Above," the first line reads simply, "A dead beetle lies on the path through the field." The poem "View with a Grain of Sand" begins, "We call it a grain of sand." From these relaxed starting points each poem proceeds gradually, effortlessly, toward unexpected realizations about the nature of death and the nature of time. This effortlessness conceals a prodigious amount of art and synthesis.

Much of the drama in a typical Szymborska poem comes from a tension between lightness on one hand and breadth on the other; this is as true of the texture of individual lines as of the larger structures. Her trick is to maintain the lightness and breadth at the same time. As she wrote at the end of the poem "Under One Small Star," "Don't bear me ill will, speech, that I borrow weighty words,/ then labor heavily so that they may seem light."

The translations of this collection are careful, and they always show a thorough knowledge of the original texts; at the same time, they display a resourceful use of English. These virtues are expected from Stanisław Barańczak a master translator from English to Polish and fine poet himself, and his cotranslator Clare Cavanagh, who is at home with the American idiom. The translations are invariably smooth, easy to read, and attractive. Richard Howard has called them "dapper." Some have a breezy quality; several might even be called jazzy.

One caveat might be registered, however, about the colloquialness of a few translations. Although successfully carried out in the great majority of these poems, colloquial speech or the translators' colloquial voice sometimes lacks modulation. This can be seen in the translation of the short poem "In Praise of Feeling Bad About Yourself":

> The buzzard never says it is to blame.
> The panther wouldn't know what scruples mean.
> When the piranha strikes, it feels no shame.
> If snakes had hands, they'd claim their hands were clean.
>
> A jackal doesn't understand remorse.
> Lions and lice don't waver in their course.
> Why should they, when they know they're right?
>
> Though hearts of killer whales may weigh a ton,
> in every other way they're light.
>
> On this third planet of the sun
> among the signs of bestiality
> a clear conscience is Number One.

The original poem is highly compressed and contains ironic contradictions. In paraphrase, it states that a variety of predatory animals have no conscience, or have at least a clear conscience; this is characteristic of our planet. Humans are omitted from the list, but the ironic final stanza suggests that humans are included after all: They too are characterized by a clear conscience, or more likely a lack of one. The poem's title, however, directly praises the opposite of this "clear conscience."

The following is a more literal translation of the same poem, which is titled "In Praise of Self-Deprecation":

> The buzzard has nothing to fault himself with.
> Scruples are alien to the black panther.
> Piranhas do not doubt the rightness of their actions.
> The rattlesnake approves of himself without reservations.
>
> The self-critical jackal does not exist.
> The locust, alligator, trichina, horsefly
> live as they live and are glad of it.
>
> A hundred kilograms weighs the killer-whale's heart,
> but in another respect it is light.
>
> There is nothing more animal-like
> than a clear conscience
> on the third planet of the Sun.

This second version, by Magnus Krynski and Robert Maguire, indicates some alternate interpretations of the poem. The translation lacks colloquialness entirely; it is literal, prosaic, often flat. Some lines are awkward and even archaic. Yet the more literal title and a few word choices render some meanings skirted or absent in the more graceful translation by Barańczak and Cavanagh, whose "feeling bad about yourself" is probably too talky. The English rhymes have a tone that is slightly childish. Szymborska's notion of "clear conscience" (really the opposite of conscience) begs for sharp irony.

The translation of this particular poem is exceptional, not typical of the others in the book, which are almost always distinguished by resourcefulness and care. The translators make use of a broad range of the tools available in the English language and writing skills, applying them creatively to Szymborska's poetry. Too often translations are impoverished by excessive literalness, and it is a pleasure to observe in this collection the resources of the writer joined to those of the translator. Barańczak and Cavanagh consistently carry out a double task: On the one hand, the original text and its meanings are carefully preserved and interpreted; on the other hand, attractive texts are built up in English. They have presented a great poet in English with admirable skill.

John R. Carpenter

Sources for Further Study

Library Journal. CXX, July, 1995, p. 85.
The New Republic. CCXIV, January 1, 1996, p. 36.
Salmagundi. Summer, 1994, p. 252.
The Washington Post Book World. XXV, July 30, 1995, p. 8.

VIRGINIA WOOLF

Author: James King (1942-   )
First published: 1994, in Great Britain
Publisher: W. W. Norton (New York). 699 pp. $35.00
Type of work: Literary biography
Time: 1882-1941
Locale: London, Cornwall, and Sussex

Drawing on the wealth of scholarship about Woolf, King presents a detailed account of her life, which he relates to her work

> *Principal personages:*
> VIRGINIA WOOLF, the British novelist, essayist, and biographer
> JULIA DUCKWORTH STEPHEN, her mother
> LESLIE STEPHEN, her father, a writer
> THOBY STEPHEN, her brother
> GEORGE DUCKWORTH and
> GERALD DUCKWORTH, her half-brothers
> LEONARD WOOLF, her husband, a political figure
> VANESSA BELL, her sister, an artist
> VITA SACKVILLE-WEST, the British author, her friend
> VIOLET DICKINSON, another friend
> LYTTON STRACHEY, the British biographer
> ROGER FRY, the British artist

"I think I shall prepare to be the Grand Old Woman of English letters," a young Virginia Stephen commented, and she has achieved that status. Though neglected at mid-century, she has become, according to a 1995 study by the Modern Language Association, the female author most written about and the only woman among the top ten subjects of literary scholarship. Her works have been translated into more than fifty languages; three journals are devoted to her; virtually every surviving scrap of her writing, even the reading notes she took for her book reviews, has been published.

Virginia Woolf became a writer by inheritance and inclination. Her father, Leslie Stephen, was a leading man of letters in the latter half of the nineteenth century, and his first wife was the daughter of the novelist William Makepeace Thackeray. Like most women of the late Victorian period, Woolf had little formal education, but she enjoyed free range of her father's extensive library, and she took classes in Greek and history at King's College, London. As Octavia Wilberforce, the doctor who saw Woolf the day before the writer killed herself, observed, Woolf was "nurtured on books. She never gets away from them."

James King demonstrates that writing came to Woolf early and easily, and she may have used her talent as a means of gaining her father's attention. Her mother had little time for her: Despite the family's many servants, Julia Stephen had to deal with a large number of children from her first and second marriages and with the archetypically demanding paterfamilias Leslie. Hence, the young Virginia turned for affection to her older sister, Vanessa, and to her writer father. By the time she was five, she was making up stories to tell him, and she later recalled "scribbling a story in the manner of Hawthorne on the green plush sofa at [the family's summer vacation home in] St. Ives while the grown ups dined." Her father recognized her talents, writing to his wife that Virginia "takes in a great deal and will really be an author in time; though I cannot make up my mind in what line."

Shortly after her ninth birthday, Virginia encouraged her siblings to produce the *Hyde Park Gate News* (named for the family residence), describing the activities of the Stephen children but also including fiction. Even the usually preoccupied Julia was amused. When she sent one of Virginia's stories to a relative, along with the comment that the piece was "imaginative," Virginia felt "like being a violin . . . being played upon." Virginia herself felt confident enough to send a story to *Tit-Bits*, a magazine for children. This story, now lost, was rejected, but apparently it contained the germ of *The Voyage Out* (1915), her first novel, and it illustrates her determination to write and to be read.

This resolution is evident in the way she later structured her days. Leonard Woolf wrote in his autobiography,

> We should have felt it to be not merely wrong but unpleasant not to work every morning for seven days a week and for about eleven months a year. Every morning, therefore, at about 9:30 after breakfast each of us . . . went off and "worked" until lunch at 1.
> Afterwards Virginia read for or wrote reviews, sent letters, pondered works in progress or planned future projects, and, after 1917, helped with the Woolfs' Hogarth Press. Virginia thus probably worked ten to twelve hours of every twenty-four.

Virginia Woolf's ability as well as her inclination manifested itself early. King quotes a passage from her diary for August 13, 1899, when she was seventeen: "By the faint glow we could see the huge moth—his wings open, as though in ecstasy, so that the splendid vision of the underwing could be seen—his eyes burning red, his proboscis plunged into a flowing stream of treacle." Woolf was not a faithful diarist until 1915, but her early jottings emphasize her determination to pursue a writer's life. In 1903 she began the Hyde Park Gate diary, which contains 157 entries, including thirty unpublished essays including "A Garden Dance," "Stonehenge," and "The Beginning of the Storm." This resolution to write also appears in her letter of September 30, 1904, to her close friend Violet Dickinson: "I am longing to begin work. I know I can write, and one of these days I mean to produce a good book. . . . Life interests me intensely, and writing is I know my natural means of expression."

Soon Woolf was reviewing for Mary Kathleen Lyttleton, editor of the Women's Supplement of the *Guardian*, a weekly published for the clergy. Woolf's first published works reflect lifelong concerns. Her first review for the *Guardian*, of William Dean Howells' *The Son of Royal Langbrith* (1904), commended the American novelist's focus on thought rather than action. A decade later, in the *Times Literary Supplement* for February 22, 1917, she praised Fyodor Dostoevski for probing his characters' psyches. In "Modern Novels" (*Times Literary Supplement*, April 10, 1919) she castigated H. G. Wells, Arnold Bennett, and John Galsworthy for concentrating on the externals of life rather than on interior states of mind. "Mr. Bennett and Mrs. Brown" (1923) repeats this criticism, and in the *Nation and Athenaeum* for November 12, 1927, she attacked E. M. Forster's recently published *Aspects of the Novel*:

> If the English critic were less domestic, less assiduous to protect the rights of what it pleases him to call life, the novelist might be bolder too. He might cut adrift from the eternal tea table and the plausible and preposterous formulas which are supposed to represent the whole of our human adventure.... The novel in short might become a work of art.

Woolf's fiction followed her creed.

Woolf's biographical impulse is evident in "On a Faithful Friend," an account of her family's Skye terrier, Shag. This piece anticipates not only *Flush* (1933), the life of Elizabeth Barrett Browning's dog, but also Woolf's other fictionalized and conventional biographies. Her feminism also surfaces in her writing for the *Guardian*. William Leonard Courtney's *The Feminine Note in Fiction* (1904) claimed that women's concern for detail interfered with "the proper artistic proportion of their work." In her *Guardian* review for January 25, 1905, Woolf cited Sappho and Jane Austen as proof to the contrary and argued, as she would a quarter of a century later in *A Room of One's Own* (1929) and again in *Three Guineas* (1938), that lack of education and opportunity explained the paucity of female writers.

King emphasizes Woolf's efforts "to eschew the masculine" in her writing, a stance that he attributes at least in part to early sexual abuse by George and Gerald Duckworth. A similar point has been made by Roger Poole's *The Unknown Virginia Woolf* (1978) and Louise DeSalvo's *Virginia Woolf: The Impact of Childhood Abuse on Her Life and Work* (1989). Woolf certainly championed women writers in the abstract, and in her essays she praised her female predecessors. In *The Speaker* for April 21, 1906, she wrote of Elizabeth Barrett Browning,

> The vigour with which she threw herself into the only life that was free to her and lived so steadily and strongly in her books that her days were full of purpose and character ... [impresses] us with the strength that underlay her ardent and sometimes febrile temperament. Indeed, there is no questioning her deliberate and reasonable love of literature and all that the word contains. Not only was she a very shrewd critic of others, but, pliant as she was in most matters, she could be almost obstinate when her literary independence was attacked.

In the *Times Literary Supplement* for November 12, 1908, Woolf praised Christina Rossetti. Eight years later she wrote admiringly of Charlotte Brontë, and the two *Common Reader* volumes (1925-1932) contain flattering essays on Jane Austen, George Eliot, and Dorothy Osborne.

Of living authors, male or female, she was less complimentary. Woolf's rivalry with other writers serves as a leitmotif running through King's biography. While recognizing the talent of Katherine Mansfield—her story "Prelude" was the second publication of the Hogarth Press—Woolf called *Bliss and Other Stories* (1920) "so brilliant,—so hard, and so shallow, and so sentimental" that she hoped that it would not win the Hawthornden Prize. Mansfield's *The Garden Party and Other Stories* (1922) earned reviewers' admiration and Woolf's acerbic diary entry, "The more she is praised, the more I am convinced she is bad." Even after Mansfield's death on January 9, 1923, Woolf gave her only grudging praise, though she continued to worry whether Mansfield would have liked the work Woolf was producing.

A similar pattern emerges in her relationships with other contemporaries. In *Jacob's Room* (1922), Woolf placed the name of the novelist Bertha Ruck on a tombstone. Vita Sackville-West was a close friend and briefly Virginia Woolf's lover; her writings did much to keep the Hogarth Press profitable. Yet Woolf criticized her for writing too easily, and in her diary entry of July 4, 1927, wrote of her, "She never breaks fresh ground. She picks up what the tide rolls to her feet."

While Woolf's feminism thus did not prompt her to support women writers, it may have sharpened her attacks on male authors, including Henry James, T. S. Eliot, John Galsworthy, Arnold Bennett, E. M. Forster, and James Joyce, whose *Ulysses* (1922) Woolf refused to publish when Hogarth was offered the manuscript. In confining *Mrs. Dalloway* (1925) to a single day (like *Ulysses*) Woolf may have been demonstrating another aspect of her struggle with her contemporaries.

King illustrates that whatever Woolf's literary borrowings may have been, the chief source of her writing was her experiences: her life, her family, her friends. She began *The Voyage Out* shortly after Vanessa's marriage, and her letter to Violet Dickinson on September 1, 1907, makes clear that the work was a response to that event: "Shall I ever bear a child I wonder?" meaning a book that would compensate for her lack of offspring. Woolf's April 22, 1918, letter to Vanessa comments, "I've been writing about you all the morning," referring to Katharine Hilbery in *Night and Day* (1919), though the literary dandy who pursues Katharine at the beginning of the work is a composite of Virginia's suitors. Woolf's third novel, *Jacob's Room*, is a tribute to Thoby Stephen, who died at the age of twenty-six; he appears again in *The Waves* (1931) as Percival. *To the Lighthouse* (1927) is her peace treaty with her parents and draws on her childhood experiences at St. Ives. *Orlando* (1928) was inspired by and is a tribute to Sackville-West, but its androgynous hero(ine) is also Woolf herself. King illustrates this point by quoting from Woolf's letter of July 23, 1927, to Vanessa: "Poor Billy [one of Woolf's pet names for herself] isn't one thing or the other, not a man nor a woman." *The Waves* is also autobiographical in the sense that each of the six major characters derives from some aspect of the author. *The Years* (1937) begins with the impending death of Mrs. Partiger, modeled on Julia Stephen.

King's discussion of Woolf's writing is excellent, making one wish that he had adhered more closely to the promise in the introduction to provide a literary biography. Too much space is devoted to the nonliterary aspects of Woolf's life, most of which have been well documented in her published letters and diaries and in Quentin Bell's definitive biography (1972). The familiar treatment of Woolf and her circle is also disconcerting. One may excuse "Virginia" and "Vanessa" as a means of distinguishing these women from their husbands, but "Roger" for Roger Fry, "Lytton" for Lytton Strachey, and "Morgan Forster" for E. M. Forster seem inappropriate, as well as confusing for those not intimately acquainted with the Bloomsbury circle.

Nevertheless, King's is a major contribution to Woolf scholarship, worthy of a place beside Bell's life and required reading for the serious or curious student. It also testifies to Woolf's success in making herself "the Grand Old Woman of English letters."

Joseph Rosenblum

Sources for Further Study

Booklist. XCI, March 15, 1995, p. 1302.
London Review of Books. XVII, April 6, 1995, p. 28.
Los Angeles Times Book Review. June 11, 1995, p. 12.
New Statesman and Society. VII, September 2, 1994, p. 38.
The New York Times. April 18, 1995, p. C17.
Publishers Weekly. CCXLII, February 27, 1995, p. 91.
San Francisco Review of Books. XX, July, 1995, p. 39.
The Spectator. CCLXXIII, September 3, 1994, p. 34.
The Washington Post Book World. XXV, April 2, 1995, p. 4.
Women's Review of Books. XIII, November, 1995, p. 5.

A VOID

Author: Georges Perec (1936-1982)
First published: La Disparition, 1969, in France
Translated from the French by Gilbert Adair
Publisher: Harvill (London). 284 pp. $24.00
Type of work: Novel
Time: Principally the 1960's
Locale: Primarily France

Devised as an extended lipogram, a linguistic stunt using only twenty-five letters of the alphabet, Perec's third novel, renewed by an innovative English translation, emerges as an entertaining, thought-provoking parody of the traditional detective novel, also an inquiry into the nature of reading, writing, and identity

>   *Principal characters:*
>   ANTON VOWL, a sleuth who disappears
>   AMAURY CONSON, his boon companion
>   OTTAVIO OTTAVIANI, a Corsican policeman
>   AUGUSTUS CLIFFORD, a British officer
>   DOUGLAS HAIG CLIFFORD, Augustus' son
>   SQUAW, the elder Clifford's maid
>   OLGA MAVROKHORDATOS, once married to Douglas
>   ARTHUR WILBURG SAVORGNAN, friend of Anton Vowl

Born in Paris in 1936 to Jewish émigrés from Poland, Georges Perec spoke several languages from childhood. Orphaned by World War II and the Holocaust, the young Perec was reared in the family of his father's sister and brother-in-law, the latter a remote figure more than forty years Perec's senior. David Bellos, author of the exhaustive *Georges Perec: A Life in Words* (1993), traces the origins of Perec's unique literary vocation to his solitary childhood in the aftermath of World War II, living in France while belonging, if at all, to a culture more European than French. Although obviously gifted as a student, respected by his classmates and teachers, the young Perec nevertheless failed to achieve the early distinctions that would lead toward success and visibility. Determined to become a writer, Perec developed during his adolescence and early adulthood an intricate system, or series of systems, for generating his material. Fascinated by mathematics, the sciences and game theory as much as by literature, Perec seems to have prepared his texts from an eccentric, bewildering inner program that was often misunderstood during his lifetime. His first published novel, *Les Choses: Une Histoire des années soixante* (1965; *Things: A History of the Sixties,* 1967), met with unexpected success and even a literary prize, in part because it was misinterpreted by its first readers and critics as an outgrowth of the new novel originated in the 1950's by such otherwise dissimilar authors as Michel Butor, Alain Robbe-Grillet, and Nathalie Sarraute.

As Bellos shows in his Perec biography and elsewhere, *Things* was mainly an outgrowth of Perec's singular preoccupations. Earlier completed novels, perhaps more typically Perecquian, had failed, meanwhile, to achieve publication. It thus happened that Perec's second novel to be published was *La Disparition*, (1969; the disappearance), an elaborate linguistic exercise conceived as a lipogram, using fewer than the twenty-six letters of the standard Roman alphabet. In the case of *La Disparition*, the object of omission is the letter *e*, all the more crucial to French than to English because it can represent no fewer than three vowel sounds, depending upon the accent mark. Unquestionably bizarre both in concept and in execution, *La Disparition* tended to keep a low profile in French literary circles, with one prominent reviewer completely missing the point by not missing the missing letter. Among literary insiders, however, the book would build and keep an intrigued, even devoted readership, a phenomenon that accounts in part, if not entirely, for Gilbert Adair's labor of true literary love in preparing *A Void*, an English version of Perec's work, of necessity less a translation than a rewriting, which appeared on British bookshelves a quarter-century after the French original and a dozen years after Perec's death of cancer at age forty-six. In the meantime, Perec's work, crowned by the masterful *La Vie mode d'emploi* (1978; *Life: A User's Manual*, 1987) had become the subject of considerable critical commentary and debate, in Great Britain as well as in France. David Bellos, Perec's eventual biographer, translated no fewer than four of Perec's novels into English during the decade following the author's death.

A Void, Adair's version of *La Disparition*, rigorously faithful to Perec's fondness for wordplay as well as to his self-imposed constraint in avoiding the letter *e*, is, like the original, a remarkable if idiosyncratic achievement, successfully testing the limits of readerly and writerly imaginations. Anton Vowl (Voyl in the original, from the French *voyelle*), somewhat plausible as a literary character, disappears early in the novel after pondering such clue-ridden mysteries as a shelf with twenty-five instead of twenty-six books. Vowl's supposed boon companions, most endowed with heavily allusive names, join the search for Anton, only to vanish themselves, each in his or her turn. Within the framework of such a basic plot, Perec and his translator/co-conspirator have managed to weave several intriguing subplots rich in irony, wordplay, literary in-jokes and historico-political commentary. Among the more entertaining, if admittedly juvenile-seeming, insertions are lipogrammatic translations or versions of famous canonical texts, such as "William Shakspar's 'Living or not living' soliloquy," rendered in its entirety, and "Black Bird, by Arthur Gordon Pym," with the refrain, "Quoth that Black Bird, 'Not Again.'" Thanks in part to such philological shenanigans, *A Void*, like the French original, risks being dismissed as something of a schoolboy prank, a showing-off of reading and research not always lightly worn. As elsewhere in his writing, Perec also incorporates tables, enumerations and equations of scientific rigor and accuracy. At a deeper level, however, both *La Disparition* and Adair's English text, although demanding of the reader, go beyond the merely ludic to displace many standing assumptions and expectations concerning literary art.

Both as exercise and as "fiction," *A Void* derives in part from the theoretical and aesthetic pursuits of the Paris-based Ouvroir de Littérature Potentielle (Workshop for Potential Literature), usually known by the acronym OuLiPo. Developed in 1960 under the general inspiration of the poet, polymath, and editor Raymond Queneau,

OuLiPo was, and is, a loose confederation of writers and mathematicians pledged to explore the creative possibilities of both disciplines working together. Thanks to friends acquainted with his various works-in-progress, Perec was tapped, or coopted, for membership in OuLiPo in March, 1967. For the first time, the compulsive writer who had felt somehow sidelined from the mainstream of French literary life (as had Queneau himself), found himself among friends and, more importantly, among co-conspirators. The lipogrammatic project of *La Disparition*, although consistent with Perec's general preoccupations and ambitions, owes much to his association with OuLiPo. As Bellos points out, the lipogram was already a pet project at OuLiPo, in part because it echoed the group's chosen name, and also because of its allusions to the Chinese poet Li Po, whose writings included similar linguistic tricks. When Perec, as if on a dare, undertook the construction of a book-length lipogram, he was assured of the moral support and collusion of his fellow Oulipians, several of whom, including Queneau himself, contributed sustained *e*-less passages incorporated in the published text.

As Bellos observes in his biography, the writing of *La Disparition* required, in effect, the invention of a parallel language, the lack of one major vowel imposing a monstrous constraint that, for Perec, proved immensely liberating, defeating any trace of the writer's block that he had feared. Comic scenes and social satire abound, shaped into memorable vignettes by the curiously stilted prose. Yet beneath the many antics lies, as Bellos observes, the darkened consciousness of the Holocaust orphan; *disparition*, or disappearance, a common enough bourgeois French euphemism for death, was also the term used in official documentation regarding those Jews who, like Georges Perec's mother, simply vanished without a trace during World War II. In the end, what seems at times a parlor-game parody of the detective novel tapers off into its own nothingness, all of its characters having dropped into the menacing void that provided Gilbert Adair with the title for his impressive English version of an otherwise baffling text.

David B. Parsell

Sources for Further Study

London Review of Books. XVI, November 10, 1994, p. 6.
Los Angeles Times Book Review. February 12, 1995, p. 3.
New Statesman and Society. VII, October 14, 1994, p. 46.
The New York Times Book Review. C, March 12, 1995, p. 3.
The New Yorker. LXX, February 6, 1995, p. 91.
Publishers Weekly. CCXLI, December 19, 1994, p. 45.
The Review of Contemporary Fiction. XV, Summer, 1995, p. 200.
Time. CXLV, February 6, 1995, p. 74.
The Times Literary Supplement. October 7, 1994, p. 28.
The Washington Post Book World. XXV, March 12, 1995, p. 11.

VOLCANO
A Memoir of Hawai'i

Author: Garrett Hongo (1951-   )
Publisher: Alfred A. Knopf (New York). 339 pp. $24.00
Type of work: Memoir
Time: The 1950's to the 1980's
Locale: Volcano, Hawai'i, and Gardena, California

The narrator traces his footsteps back and forth between his Hawaiian hometown and Gardena, California, interweaving descriptions of trips to his birthplace, studies of family history, and recollections of places that have helped him reclaim his sense of ontological and cultural identity

> *Principal personages:*
> GARRETT HONGO, the narrator
> TORAU HONGO, his paternal grandfather
> YUKIKO KIRIU, his biological grandmother
> KUBOTA, his maternal grandfather
> ALBERT HONGO, his father
> CHARLOTTE GOYA, his aunt

In the study of Asian American literature, autobiography is subject to controversy. In "Come All Ye Asian American Writers of the Real and the Fake" (*The Big AIIIEEEEE! An Anthology of Chinese and Japanese American Literature*, 1991), Chinese American scholar and critic Frank Chin posits that Chinese American writers such as Jade Snow Wong (*The Fifth Chinese Daughter*, 1945), Maxine Hong Kingston (*The Woman Warrior*, 1975; *China Men*, 1980; *Tripmaster Monkey: His Fake Book*, 1989), and Amy Tan (*The Joy Luck Club*, 1989; *The Kitchen God's Wife*, 1991) who use the "exclusively Christian form" of autobiography are the fake. These writers' portrayal of the "Christian yin/yang of the dual personality/identity crisis" not only misrepresents Chinese history, legends, and lore but also betrays their traditional values.

Chin's article raises a legitimate question over the issue of how to integrate Asian histories and cultures in Asian American literature. His rejection of autobiography as an inappropriate form for depicting the Asian American experience, however, is too judgmental and arbitrary. Chinese American scholar Kai-yu Hsu, while critical of autobiographies that "confirm rather than modify a stereotyped image of the Chinese and their culture," acknowledges that they are "the path of development of many writers." Indeed, while the merits and demerits of the so-called slave narratives are open to discussion, no one can deny the instrumentality of Frederick Douglass' three powerful autobiographies (*Narrative of the Life of Frederick Douglass, an American Slave*, 1845; *My Bondage and My Freedom*, 1855; *The Life and Times of Frederick Douglass*, 1881) to the development of African American literature and political movements. Similar to autobiographies that help democratize and diversify American literary voices, Garrett Hongo's *Volcano: A Memoir of Hawai'i* represents yet another attempt to delineate the cultural configuration of American society through the portrayal of personal experience.

Hongo's is one of the most exciting voices in the latest development of Asian American literature. He is a Sansei, a third-generation Japanese American. His previous two books of poetry have won critical acclaim: *Yellow Light* (1982) was nominated for the Pulitzer Prize in 1989, and *The River of Heaven* (1988) was the Lamont Poetry Selection of the Academy of American Poets. *Volcano* is Hongo's first prose work. As Maxine Hong Kingston says, the work successfully breaks out "of careful verse into the freedom of prose." She ranks Hongo with William Carlos Williams, Rainer Maria Rilke, Sylvia Plath, Raymond Carver, and Louise Erdrich.

In *Volcano*, Hongo traces his footsteps back and forth between Hawai'i and the mainland in search of his connection with the past, with the community, and with the land. He was born in Volcano, a small village in Hawai'i, twenty-nine miles from Hilo on the Big Island. When he was a child, his father lost the family business, the Hongo Store. The family had to uproot and move to the mainland, leaving behind painful memories and looking for new economic opportunities. Physical displacement was accompanied by cultural dislocation and disorientation. In the opening of the book, the narrator vividly describes the struggle he went through learning "Mainland English" while trying to lose the Hawaiian pidgin English: His mother

> teaches me fricatives, gives me exercises, shows me where to place my tongue against my teeth. I say there, there, there, constructing a calisthenic phalanx of enunciations. I say earth. I say with. She teaches me to flatten the melody of my speaking, taking the lilt of Portuguese from my sentences, the singsong of Canton Chinese.

Yet Hawai'i kept beckoning to him and invading his dreams. In his early thirties, Hongo decided to visit Hawai'i with his family. He realized that to know his roots, he would have to solve the "mystery" of the family's past; to know who he really was, he would have to reestablish the ontological connection with the place where he was born. The journey proved to be as much a visit of the family's past as an opportunity to develop a profound understanding and appreciation of both the inner and outer landscapes of Volcano. It helped him learn more about himself, bridge the gap between the past and the present, and redefine his connection with both the mainstream American culture and the one that gave Hawai'i and its Japanese American community their unique distinction and identity.

At Volcano, Hongo found out that his grandfather Torau was an Issei, a first-generation Japanese immigrant. He came from an impoverished samurai family. The "Gentlemen's Agreement" between the Japanese government and the U.S. government in the early part of the century stipulated that Japan send more members of the educated class to the United States. Torau was in that group. He was an artist and a shrewd businessman, popular with women.

Hongo learned that his biological grandmother Yukiko Katayama was a *sensei*, or teacher, of traditional Japanese dance. She devoted delicate and thorough attention to the "art of dress and gesture through part of childhood, a formal adolescent apprenticeship in Japan, and then the rude adulthood of life in the floating world of Honolulu's bar culture of the twenties." Yukiko was abused by Torau and eventually ran away with another man. Hongo also heard stories about Aunt Charlotte, his father's half-sister, who had to care for the three children after Yukiko left and who, despite all Torau's failings, had fond memories of her father.

The second half of the book includes descriptions of the narrator's experiences on the mainland and his ensuing trips to Volcano as well as recollections of persons and places that helped form his sense of identity. Bert Meyers, a passionate Jewish American poet, taught Hongo the importance of speaking the truth. During a trip to Japan, Hongo learned in a Buddhist temple that "the poet must learn to intone the song, which is music," must "learn the dance, which is the body's movement," must "learn the word, which is the speech of man in the universe," and "must learn to write them all in his own face." Wakako Yamauchi, an earthy Japanese American writer, explained to the narrator the difference between "shame," "silence," and "passivity" as they were experienced by Nisei—second-generation Japanese Americans—after they left the relocation camps in World War II: how they used detachment to protect their emotional integrity. C. K. Williams, a demanding Caucasian professor, taught the narrator how to get in touch with his true feelings and write about what was real.

What pushed Hongo into poetry, though, was his friendship with Regina, a "white girl," in high school. They studied together, they talked about literature, they discussed John Steinbeck, Ken Kesey, J. D. Salinger, and James Baldwin. Wanting to impress her, he started writing poetry. Later, however, the young Hongo learned that separated "societies police their own separations." Boundary crossing had earned him hatred from his Japanese American classmates. He was ostracized, taunted, and beaten by them. His initiation into a society of racial discrimination taught him that race was "an exclusion, a punishment, imposed by the group."

The narrative voice in *Volcano* resonates with that of French writer and philosopher Jean-Jacques Rousseau's *Confessions* (1781), German writer Johann Wolfgang von Goethe's *Faust* (1808-1832), and American essayist and poet Henry David Thoreau's *Walden: Or, Life in the Woods* (1854). Hongo notes that in his early years as a poet, he learned from Irish writer William Butler Yeats that "for a poet to write a lasting work, he must first find metaphors in the natural figures of his native landscape." That idea was "so romantic," he recalls in *Volcano*, that it "stuck with" him.

Volcano, indeed, is opulent with descriptions of "the natural figures" of the narrator's "native landscape." Hongo has a sharp eye for natural beauty and talent to evoke emotional responses from the reader with precise and powerful images. *Volcano* amalgamates prose and poetry. Its narrative is lyrical, rhythmic, and melodic. Its description invites and urges the reader to feel and experience. Mainland English, the narrator learned from his mother, was "*like the swaying breeze-through-the-trees of wandering* hula *danced to a wary melodic song,*" whereas Hawaiian English was "*like* kahiko, *the ancient dance, the* kanaka *dance of tradition, . . . harsh moves, slaps, and full of pounding force.*" Telling of being beaten by his schoolmates for going out with Regina, the narrator pictures

hand-sized reef fish, in a ritual of spawning, [that] leave their singular lairs, gathering in smallish,
excitable schools—a critical mass—and, electrified by their circling assembly, suddenly burst the
cluster apart with sequences of soloing, males alternating, pouncing above the finning group,
clouding the crystalline waters above the circle with a roil of milt.

As he sat in a coffee shop in Hollywood and stirred his coffee, "its surface jiggered
like the riffle on a mountain stream," and a "silver light shone on it"; a "streetlight,
like a mechanical palm, winked on" above him.

The description of Hongo's search for family history is as fascinating as his
depiction of Volcano's landscape is enrapturing. It is a landscape that displays both
the natural beauty and spiritual powers of earth: the mighty and majestic volcano
exhibiting its destructiveness and tectonic potential, the lush trees of the rain forest
surrounding the volcano like faithful guards, the immortal *hapu'u*, the fertile and tough
uluhe, and the adaptable *'ohi'a* demonstrating their tenacity and viability in the face
of adversity. They captivated the narrator, entrancing him and entreating him to touch
them, embrace them, claim them as his own.

It is true that the *ugetsu* (a place "of moonlight and rain," a "world of faery and
imagination where the dead might dance in the right light"), the *onsen* (Japanese
teahouse), and the Hongo Store at Volcano revived in the narrator a memory that the
experience of cultural estrangement was not strong enough to eradicate and recon-
nected him to a place too beautiful to forget. Together with the botanical history of
Volcano and its ecological and geological landscape, they demonstrated to the narrator
"a way to belong and a place to belong to." Yet *Volcano* is not only about solving the
mystery of the past but also about getting connected with the present, not only about
the importance and urgency of reattachment but also about how not to "live in a local's
identity" or to "live in the past, as the past was lived."

Similar to the landscape in Rousseau's *Confessions* and the gurgling springs and
majestic mountains in William Wordsworth's poems, the beauties of Volcano serve as
stimuli, as evocators. Indeed, at Volcano, Hongo is local, a native son, and yet he is
global, a prodigal. "If the ethnic past is to be transmitted, it will be through this
ungendered and interracial jumble like the dark core of vinegared vegetables and pink
shrimp powder at the center of a roll of sweetened rice." It is with this conviction that
the narrator proudly announces at the end of the book, "I belong nowhere. . . . *I belong
in Volcano.*"

Qun Wang

Sources for Further Study

Boston Globe. July 1, 1995, p. 30.
Los Angeles Times Book Review. July 23, 1995, p. 2.
The New York Times Book Review. C, July 15, 1995, p. 20.
The New Yorker. LXXI, August 21, 1995, p. 131.
San Francisco Chronicle. July 30, 1995, p. REV1.
The Washington Post Book World. XXV, June 25, 1995, p. 1.

WALT WHITMAN'S AMERICA
A Cultural Biography

Author: David S. Reynolds (1949-   )
Publisher: Alfred A. Knopf (New York). 671 pp. $35.00
Type of work: Literary biography
Time: 1819-1892
Locale: Long Island, Brooklyn, and Manhattan; New Orleans; and Camden, New Jersey

Award-winning literary critic David S. Reynolds examines the life and work of American poet Walt Whitman and the turbulent culture from which he sprang

Principal personages:
WALT WHITMAN, the poet, journalist, and essayist
LOUISA VAN VELSOR WHITMAN, his mother
WALTER WHITMAN, his father
ABRAHAM LINCOLN, the sixteenth president of the United States

Nearly everyone familiar with the field of American literary criticism would instantly recognize the name David S. Reynolds. His previous book *Beneath the American Renaissance* (1988) was widely praised and won the Christian Gauss Award. In that pioneering study, he explored the often piquant relationship between American antebellum writers and the sensationalism of the emerging mass media. Authors such as Herman Melville, Nathaniel Hawthorne, and Emily Dickinson seized upon the bizarre imagery and radical democracy of nineteenth century popular culture in order to create what Reynolds calls "subversive" literature. In the case of Walt Whitman, a fascination with the reform rhetoric of the period led to a rebellious poetic stance.

As this synopsis implies, Reynolds believes that a discussion of a poem should go beyond the poem itself. His approach emphasizes what some critics would call the intertextuality of a work. That is, any given piece of literature—no matter where or when it was written—is a kind of patchwork quilt of other texts that preceded it. Some of these influences (such as the Civil War in Whitman's case) are readily apparent and easily grasped by all. Other forces—say, cultural fads—are often missed by readers of later generations. As Reynolds himself states in the biography's introduction, "Literary texts are intricate tapestries whose threads can be followed backward into a tremendous body of submerged biographical and cultural materials." His work represents an attempt to recover the cultural matrix out of which Whitman and his poems were formed. It was the stance that he employed in *Beneath the American Renaissance*—with brilliant results—and it is the same tack that he adopts here.

Walt Whitman is the most self-consciously American of poets, and Reynolds sets out to reconstruct what the poet's America was like. Whitman, like most of his contemporaries, was raised in then-rural areas such as Long Island and Brooklyn. By the time he was twelve years old, he was already apprenticed to a publisher. Reynolds recognizes two facts here that would prove crucial to Whitman's career: He learned the craft of "artisan publishing," with its close attention to detail, and he began his work in journalism. It was during his years as a newspaperman that Whitman produced his most popular work—not the masterful book of poems *Leaves of Grass* (1855-1892) but rather the dark temperance novel *Franklin Evans* (1842). The antebellum period was noteworthy for its perceived societal evils and the reformers who attempted to purge them from the land. Reformers strived through rhetoric—the art of persuasion— to win over the public. Their descriptions of the so-called evils, however, were often so lewd as to undercut their intended message. Whitman, who immersed himself in the popular diversions of the time, made use of the sensationalized language of the reform movements. In *Franklin Evans*, a farmer becomes so debauched by alcohol that he abuses his family; the supposed moral message about the evils of drink is couched in a titillating tale designed to please the masses. Reynolds demonstrates that the same tendency is evident in *Leaves of Grass*. The first edition of that work (1855) was a kind of sensationalized reform book: Whitman sought to unite his highly fragmented antebellum society with themes that were both erotic and sensational.

One of Whitman's chief innovations in his poetry was his effective use of free verse, eschewing rhyme schemes and metronomic regularity in favor of more natural, proselike speech patterns. When compared with the bulk of the published verse of the time, Whitman's comes across as bold, even revolutionary. Indeed, the modern reader would be unable to account for it based only on the poetry of the period. Yet Reynolds proves that even though Whitman was ahead of his time in this realm, he was still a man very much of his time. Again, reformist zeal provided the basis for this develop- ment. In the antebellum era, especially in the 1840's and 1850's, the art of oratory reached its peak in the United States. Successful speakers spoke directly to the people, employed familiar imagery, and extemporized their performances—they did not write their speeches ahead of time. Although Whitman himself never became an accom- plished speaker, Reynolds cites numerous examples to show just how the poet absorbed popular oratorical devices and created a distinctive style by exploiting them in his poetry. In Reyholds' words, "Whitman changed the participatory lecture style into a new participatory poetics. This is Reynolds at his best, shedding new light on the poetry through historical research. Moreover, to Reynolds' credit, his own lucid style is perfectly matched to his subject, being free of scholarly jargon.

Even more fascinating is the relationship that Reynolds explores between the personality that the poet projected in his poetry and the street culture in which he immersed himself. In essence, the poetic persona in *Leaves of Grass* reflects the "b'hoys" of Manhattan's Bowery. These young, streetwise, working-class men wore distinctive clothes, employed slang expressions, and were often seen walking with their equally colorful "g'hals." This is essentially the persona that Whitman presents in *Leaves of Grass*—bold, familiar, and unconventional. Early reviewers recognized this, but it takes the persistent research of someone like Reynolds to remind modern readers of this connection. Interestingly, Whitman's identification with the "b'hoys" was reflected in the famous engraving of the author in the 1855 edition of *Leaves of Grass*. His saucy stance—one arm akimbo, shirt open—reveals the poet's identifica- tion with this urban culture.

This correlation between nineteenth century popular culture and Whitman's poetry is intriguing in its own right, and there are few who could surpass or even match Reynolds in making such correlations. Reynolds also manages, however, to unearth some new information that has escaped previous biographies of Whitman. Even the casual reader of *Leaves of Grass* cannot help being struck by its potent sexual imagery. "Song of Myself" and "I Sing the Body Electric" are rife with sexuality, and there has been much speculation about Whitman's own sexual preferences. Crucial to an understanding of this complicated man is an incident that apparently took place while Whitman was a schoolteacher in the fishing village of Southold, Long Island, on January 3, 1841. On that date, the Reverend Ralph Smith denounced Whitman because of his treatment of his students. It should be noted that it was common practice for teachers to board with families, often sleeping in the same room with the pupils. Sodomy was the charge, and there were reports of blood-stained bedding as well. Local tradition has it that Whitman was tarred and feathered by the irate townsfolk and run out of town.

This story is certainly the most riveting section in Reynolds' book (and ironically appropriate, considering Whitman's acquaintance with sensational literature), but one wonders why previous Whitman biographers failed to mention it. According to Reynolds, there is no documentation to support the story. Historical sources are sketchy from this period in the town's history, and church records have been altered. Oral testimony, however, provides a detailed account of the incident. One could easily dismiss the report as mean-spirited hearsay or debate the propriety of publishing this undocumented charge. Yet Reynolds gives a balanced presentation of the incident and ultimately leaves judgment regarding the veracity of the incident up to the reader. Perhaps most telling is the fact that the tale had currency in the Whitman family.

It is true that homoeroticism is featured in Whitman's works, but it would be a mistake to conclude that the poet was ahead of his time in this regard or even that he was criticized for it. Again, Reynolds' approach bears fruit: His study of nineteenth century American culture dispels a long-held misconception of the poet's work. Although antebellum America was torn by factionalism in many ways, it was surprisingly tolerant of same-sex passions. Phrenology and transcendentalism sanctioned such feelings, and even Abraham Lincoln—who would become an obsession for Whitman—felt free to express them.

More than merely close friendships, according to Reynolds, these romantic relationships often involved kissing and hugging. Although genital contact was unusual in such relationships, it was not condemned by society. Reynolds cites compelling evidence to show that consensual sodomy was not criminalized until 1882. Indeed, the modern concept of homosexuality would not arrive until the late nineteenth century, and then by way of Europe.

Some critics might fault Reynolds for taking up so much space on such a well-worn topic in regard to Whitman, but the attention is justified because he is taking a decidedly revisionist stance. It is worth noting that Reynolds is by no means the first biographer to discuss the romantic nature of nineteenth century same-sex relationships. Joan Hedrick described the same phenomenon in her superb biography *Harriet*

Beecher Stowe: A Life (1993). Moreover, it would be inaccurate to state that Whitman was entirely innocent of the opposite sex. The poet did have sexual relationships with a few women, but his preference was for men. All of this points to the complex nature of Whitman's personality, and Reynolds' discussion of the subject serves to illuminate such sexually charged pieces as the "Calamus" poems.

Another vital element of Whitman's career was the changing face that he presented to the public. Since he himself was closely allied to the persona he presented in his poems, Reynolds is able to trace the changing poetic "I" in the various editions of *Leaves of Grass*, his most significant body of poetry. As already mentioned, the "I" of the 1855 edition was close to working-class people, especially the "b'hoys" of the Bowery. Reynolds accurately describes it as being a dictatorial tone, since the Whitman of 1855 wants to command his fragmented antebellum society, to bring together the diverse threads through a kind of poetic decree. Again, Reynolds' method of correlating the poetry and the period bears fruit. The profoundly agrarian society of the 1850's was transformed by the Civil War into a thriving urban—and increasingly industrialized—culture. The era of the individual craftsman gave way to a world of mass production. In addition to the growing technology, Whitman's interest in Darwinism prompted him to retreat from his cherished democratic views. In short, the postwar world became too complex for an all-encompassing poetic "I."

Concomitant with this change in Whitman's poetic voice was the metamorphosis in his public image. Reynolds correctly observes that this "man of the people," who thoroughly understood popular culture and deftly manipulated it, ironically never became a public success. Indeed, one of the more tragic aspects of the poet's life in Reynolds' account is Whitman's continual scheming to gain public acceptance. He repeatedly reconstituted *Leaves of Grass* to find a wider audience and engineered controversies between his promoters and detractors to boost sales. He constantly—and falsely, it should be added—pleaded poverty while accepting the patronage of moneyed interests and sanitizing his public image. By the end of his life, Whitman had transformed himself from the Bowery rough into the "Good Gray Poet."

It is to Reynolds' credit that he can successfully interweave this remarkable life with the astonishingly vibrant society in which it was rooted. Critics of this caliber are rare.

Cliff Prewencki

Sources for Further Study

America. CLXXIII, October 21, 1995, p. 24.
Los Angeles Times Book Review. June 11, 1995, p. 1.
The New Republic. CCXII, June 19, 1995, p. 33.
The New York Review of Books. XLII, October 19, 1995, p. 23.
The New York Times Book Review. C, May 14, 1995, p. 3.
The New Yorker. LXXI, June 12,. 1995, p. 98.
The Washington Post Book World. XV, April 9, 1995, p. 7.

WALTER PATER
Lover of Strange Souls

Author: Denis Donoghue (1928-   )
Publisher: Alfred A. Knopf (New York). 364 pp. $27.50
Type of work: Literary biography
Time: 1839-1894
Locale: England

Distinguished literary critic Denis Donoghue outlines the life of the father of the Aesthetic movement in England, Walter Pater, and offers extended critical commentary on the writer's major and minor works

Principal personages:
WALTER PATER, the British critic and essayist
CLARA PATER and
HESTER PATER, his sisters
GERARD MANLEY HOPKINS, the British poet
OSCAR BROWNING, a British educator
SIMEON SOLOMON, a British artist
JOHN ADDINGTON SYMONDS, the British critic and historian
ARTHUR SYMONS, the British poet, critic, and biographer
GEORGE MOORE, the British novelist
LIONEL JOHNSON, a British poet
OSCAR WILDE, the British critic, dramatist, and social lion
MRS. HUMPHRY WARD, a British novelist

When a first-rate critic explores the life and work of an enigmatic and elusive writer, readers can expect a provocative treatise. Denis Donoghue's *Walter Pater: Lover of Strange Souls* is just such a work. The author or editor of more than twenty monographs on literary figures from the eighteenth through the twentieth century, Donoghue brings his exceptional knowledge and keen insights to his study of the writer he unabashedly calls the Father of Modernism in England. "The main justification for writing a book on Pater at this point," Donoghue remarks in his introductory chapter, "is to clarify the recognition one is claiming for him." Having written extensively about modern poets and critics, Donoghue is particularly well prepared to trace the influence of this nineteenth century figure on his successors in the following century.

Donoghue selects for his subtitle a phrase from Pater's essay on Leonardo da Vinci which is, in the biographer's view, the key to Pater's mission as a critic: "But a lover of strange souls may still analyse for himself the impression made on him" by the works of an artist "and try to reach through" that impression to a definition of genius. The "strange souls" Pater loves are not only his contemporaries but also the historical figures about whom he writes and the fictional ones he creates—though, as Donoghue points out, these are most often simply extensions of their creator himself. Throughout, great stress is placed on Pater's "antinomianism," the tendency (prevalent in modern writings) to see great literature as an antithesis to the predominant values of a society rather than as a reflection of those values. Donoghue considers Pater a leading figure in "a tradition of dissent," a spokesperson for a quiet counterculture. In fact, using Pater as his chief example, Donoghue defines modernism as "the art and literature of an adversary relation to the official purposes of late-nineteenth-century society."

Anyone expecting a standard biography will be disappointed. Carefully avoiding speculation, even when the temptation to engage in the practice might be overwhelming, Donoghue refuses to embellish even the sparse details available about his subject. Consequently, the "life" of Pater offered in this volume is little more than a sketch occupying a mere eighty pages—barely a quarter of the entire text. What information Donoghue does offer focuses primarily on the relationships Pater had with others, especially other creative figures, many of whom were influenced in some way by the critic's ideas and writings. In five succinct chapters, Donoghue reviews his subject's fleeting friendships with dozens of men and women of influence great and small in English letters, most notably among them the poets Gerard Manley Hopkins, Lionel Johnson, and Arthur Symons; educator Oscar Browning; artist Simeon Solomon; critic and historian John Addington Symonds; novelists George Moore and Mrs. Humphry Ward; and that most controversial and enigmatic literary luminary Oscar Wilde. With great sensitivity Donoghue discusses Pater's homosexuality, noting how in both published writings and correspondence with friends he introduces words and phrases that were part of the homosexual code of his day. Yet Donoghue does not dwell on this aspect of Pater's life; accepting it as fact, he simply admits that it affected Pater's dealings with others, causing him embarrassment and on occasion more serious difficulties in a century when homophobia was commonplace.

By far the bulk of Donoghue's study is given over to an examination of Pater's published writings. In these, rather than in the facts of his life, lie the clues to Pater's nature as a thinker and a critic; in them Donoghue finds his reasons for assigning the key role to Pater in the development of the modernist spirit. Donoghue's method is to show how Pater reacted to the works of other artists; by doing so, he claims, it is possible to come to some understanding of the critic himself.

Donoghue analyzes both major works and minor ones, giving many of them a sensitive reading that reveals something of Pater's method of composition and ideology. Interestingly, some of Donoghue's commentaries (for example, "Botticelli" and "Winckelmann") seem to be imitative of Pater's style; they are impressions rather than formal essays, revealing those elements of Pater's work that strike Donoghue as particularly illuminating or provocative.

Unfortunately, a few of Pater's essays are given short shrift; for example, Donoghue devotes only three pages to his writings on Shakespeare, and what he offers seems more like appreciation than analysis. Similarly, the chapter on Pater's unfinished novel *Gaston Latour* appears fragmentary, more summary than analysis. The chapter on *Marius the Epicurean* (1885), while offering some sensible commentary, seems dismissive.

On the other hand, in a number of short chapters Donoghue offers exceptional insight into Pater's mind. In the essay on William Wordsworth, he shows how Pater rescued the Romantic poet from the conventional Victorian version painted by

Matthew Arnold and others. His commentary on Pater's essay on Plato shows how Pater could take an unlikely hero and appreciate him—on the critic's terms, of course.

Not surprisingly, the bulk of Donoghue's commentary centers on the essays that make up Pater's most influential work, *Studies in the History of the Renaissance* (1873). With great perceptivity and an unusual sense of balance, Donoghue details ways that Pater dissociated himself from John Ruskin, the great critic of the Renaissance and moral arbiter of English art during the nineteenth century. Similar emphasis is placed on Pater's rejection of Arnoldian principles of criticism. Pater's clever reversal of Arnold's dictum that the role of the critic is "to see the object as in itself it really is" has become the touchstone for modernist criticism: "The first step towards seeing one's object as it really is, is to know one's own impression as it really is, to discriminate it, to realise it distinctly." Defining the role of the critic was of crucial importance to Pater, as it was to Arnold, for both recognized the significance of the critic in shaping values and attitudes. Pater, however, takes what for Arnold is a moral duty and removes it to the realm of aesthetics; for him, the critics' primary responsibility is to experience intensely the effect that a work of art may have on them.

As he does elsewhere in his writings, Pater saw himself as an adversary of the trend toward certitude, a dissembler in the temple of traditional rectitude. Comparing Pater to Arnold allows Donoghue to comment on larger issues, as he does in an observation on the dated nature of Arnold's pleading for literature as a means of reforming the world:

> Arnold's confidence in ideas as the social means of overcoming modern anxiety is strange to us. The excitement with which he sees ideas at large in France is an emotion we have difficulty appreciating. The loss of confidence in ideas, or the rejection of them because of the complacency the possession of them induces, is easily explained: ideas have not saved us.

Nevertheless, Donoghue is careful to point out that on many occasions Pater's critique of Arnold amounts to little more than special pleading.

Although Donoghue devotes attention to the contrasts between Pater's writings and those of Arnold and Ruskin, a major portion of his analysis is given over to discussing parallels between Pater and various nineteenth century French writers and between Pater and modern figures. In the final section of his study, Donoghue continues this method of comparison, using it to examine a number of issues that have become critical to an understanding of Pater and his place in the literary tradition: his notion of modernism, his insistence on "art for art's sake," and his style. Donoghue has praise for Pater's style and for his success in freeing art criticism from the demands of earlier critics that art must be moral to be great.

Fortunately, Donoghue is not so close to his subject that he cannot be critical when necessary. He describes Pater's epistemology as exhibited in *Studies in the History of the Renaissance* as "vulnerable," noting that it did not occur to the critic "to question the self-certainty from which idealism starts." He freely admits that Pater's "sense of the Renaissance wasn't historical" and that "what he saw was what he wanted to see" in the works he chose for analysis. He recognizes that for Pater, the "object" under discussion was valuable only insofar as it was of interest—or more specifically, as it made an impression—on the mind of the critic, Pater himself. With numerous references to the work of Pater's contemporaries, Donoghue explains how the writer drew from the works of others and in turn influenced the writings of the next generation.

Donoghue does not overstate his case or elevate his subject to heights on which he cannot stand. According to him, Pater "was not an original thinker"; rather, he was an aesthetic critic "working upon art, mythology, and literature," concerning himself not with the works themselves but "with the types of feeling they embodied." He tries to show whenever possible the sources of Pater's ideas; for example, he traces Pater's notions of Greek myth to the work of Edward Tylor, author of *Primitive Culture* (1871). More frequently, Donoghue observes, Pater wrote to refute the work of others— specifically, those who supported what he considered more traditional, rational notions of life and art.

In Donoghue's estimation, Pater achieved minimal success as a novelist because "he couldn't really believe in the existence of feelings other than his own, so his characters look as if they were seen through water." Pater's most serious defect as a writer of fiction stemmed from his belief that characters could be created and sustained merely by assigning to them a series of ideas, with no attempt to show them acting out their lives in a world peopled by others besides themselves. Though he acknowledges that Pater's chief contribution to letters was the creation of a distinctive style, Donoghue is not so enamored with his subject that he cannot accuse him of vagueness or even pedantry. Furthermore, Donoghue is full of refreshing admissions of his own perplexity. "Some parts of the theory are not clear to me," he admits regarding Pater's idea of myth. Such a balanced assessment is refreshing and makes Donoghue's judgments about this seminal figure in the modernist movement convincing and enlightening.

Laurence W. Mazzeno

Sources for Further Study

London Review of Books. XVII, August 24, 1995, p. 9.
Los Angeles Times Book Review. May 28, 1995, p. 3.
The New Republic. CCXII, May 22, 1995, p. 34.
The New York Review of Books. XLII, November 2, 1995, p. 48.
The New York Times Book Review. C, May 14, 1995, p. 15.
The New Yorker. LXXI, May 15, 1995, p. 87.
The Sewanee Review. CIII, April, 1995, p. 313.
The Wall Street Journal. May 12, 1995, p. A11.
The Washington Post Book World. XXV, June 11, 1995, p. 4.
The Wilson Quarterly. XIX, Spring, 1995, p. 88.

THE WINGED SEED
A Remembrance

Author: Li-Young Lee (1957-   )
Publisher: Simon & Schuster (New York). 205 pp. $20.00
Type of work: Memoir
Time: Circa 1900-1990
Locale: China, Indonesia, Hong Kong, and the United States

A Chinese American poet records his memories about his family and family history stretching back three generations, especially about his father's odyssey to America

> *Principal personages:*
> LI-YOUNG LEE, a Chinese American poet living in Chicago
> KUO YUAN "PERFECT COUNTRY," his father, a refugee and pastor
> JIAYING, his mother, a granddaughter of China's first president
> LAMMI, an Indonesian nanny

For readers not previously acquainted with Li-Young Lee, it needs be said that he is a highly accomplished Chinese American poet whose initial volume, *Rose* (1986), won the Delmore Schwartz Memorial Poetry Award given by New York University and whose second volume, *The City in Which I Love You* (1990), received the Lamont Poetry Prize of the Academy of American poets. Readers familiar with Lee's deeply moving and exquisitely crafted poems will recall his many haunting pieces that remember, evoke, and interrogate the almost mythic figure of the poet's deceased father, Kuo Yuan Lee. To a large extent, the autobiographical *The Winged Seed*, Lee's first prose work, is a lyrical and sometimes surrealistic memorializing of the author's father and the author's relationship with him. This memoir is also, as its title indicates, the saga of the Lee family's participation in the twentieth century diaspora of Asians fleeing from the political upheavals of Asia and seeking to take root in the promise of America. Thus the book is a complex fabric made up, on the one hand, of a highly subjective psychological history about the formation of dominant themes and images in a poetic imagination that is woven, on the other hand, with factual history of world events. Although names, dates, and places are mentioned, they are tucked into the text offhandedly as if to underplay the significance of such external "facts," and the reader who wants them must often work to unravel them. What matters most for the book are the internal truths of the psyche and the sensibility that are conveyed in Lee's hauntingly evocative poetic prose.

Immediately indicative of its fundamentally poetic character, the book begins with a waking from dream. The dream has to do with Lee's unquiet father, who has appeared to the author in his funerary clothes and the worn-out shoes in which he has tramped from his Pennsylvania grave to his son's Chicago dwelling, bearing a jar of blood and pockets full of seed. These oneiric images are presented starkly, without explanation; their possible significations evolve and accrue in the course of the book. Eventually the reader realizes that, among other things, blood and seed are both signifiers of life and death. Blood signifies life's genetic traits passed down through the generations of a family, and its spilling spells potential death; seed signifies the sowing of potential new life as well as the death of the blossom that produced it. That such powerful images emerge from the realm of dreams also adumbrates other motifs of the book—the question of what night is, what unconsciousness knows, how insomnia becomes creativity, and the driving force of the sun.

Although Lee's father is the dominant presence in the book, Lee also provides some fascinating glimpses of his mother, Jiaying, and her patrician lineage. Lee's maternal great-grandfather was Yuan Shih-K'ai, a name that Lee mentions with disarming casualness, without contextualization. Anyone acquainted with modern Asian history will recognize, however, that General Yuan (1859-1916) was a major player in Chinese politics at the turn of the century. He was the right-hand man of the empress dowager during the last years of the Manchu Empire, then became the first president of the Republic of China. Yuan later was a cause of civil war and made a serious though failed attempt at creating a new imperial dynasty with himself as its progenitor.

Jiaying was the granddaughter of Yuan's fifth wife. There are brilliantly recollected vignettes of her life growing up in the privileged class of China, munching on lychees (a reprise of the seed image), learning of the suicide of an unhappy servant, attending the funeral of the family matriarch, journeying to the ancestral burial ground, and discovering the pillage of these graves by revolutionaries. Jiaying was living in the French quarter of Tientsin when Lee's father joined her destiny with his.

In Lee's memoir, Jiaying emerges as a capable mother and fiercely loyal wife; she had to bring up four small children while her husband was a political prisoner—whom she tried to visit daily and attempt to free—and she was prostrated by grief and guilt when one of her children died of meningitis.

Gripping as Jiaying's story may be, she remains a comparatively minor personage in Lee's memoir and only an occasional presence in his poems. The defining image of Jiaying that settles in the reader's memory is the one that introduces her in the book. She and her immigrant family have just arrived in America with only what they can carry. On a train from Seattle to Chicago, they are seated by a poor American teenage mother with a hungry baby. The inexperienced mother does not know how to feed the infant with the only available food—cookies the Lees have given her. Jiaying finally takes the baby in her arms and chews a cookie in her mouth to form a pabulum that the child can accept—a way of preparing infants' food that is common in Asia. Here Jiaying emerges as a wise, strong, nurturing woman: As an immigrant and a refugee in a new world, she is teaching a native how to survive in it.

Lee's father was the scion of a family from the Peking (Beijing) environs. The generations-old family fortune was derived from the fishing industry. Apparently some dubious strains had developed in the blood lineage of the Lee family. Lee's grandfather, it seems, was a swindler, sensualist, and tyrant who starved his wife and children in order to gorge himself and was a pedophile not to be trusted with his own granddaughter. There was a strain of insanity, too. Lee's great-granduncle had been insane, and Lee's great grandfather had also died mad, chained to a four-poster, his mind ravaged by syphilis. It may be Lee's anxiety about this defect in his blood lineage as well as the reverence that he feels for his ancestors that supplies his dreams with his father's jar of blood and pockets of seeds.

Lee's relationship with his father, Kuo Yuan, has several facets, but the constant in them all is the awe and respect that Lee feels toward his forebear. Although his lyrical and highly subjective narrative provides only a few chronological markers, one makes out that by the time Lee was born, his father had already left China, which had been taken over by the Communist regime. He had migrated to Jakarta, Indonesia, losing his eldest son in the process, and had become a vice president at Gamaliel University in the late 1950's. Unfortunately, as most students of modern Asian history will realize, this coincided with the period when President Sukarno had instituted his "Guided Democracy" (with himself as "Guide") in Indonesia and was fanning flames of anti-Chinese sentiment by blaming his country's economic woes on its Chinese inhabitants (a tactic similar to Adolf Hitler's scapegoating of the Jews). Swept into the undertow of ethnic cleansing, Kuo Yuan was imprisoned in 1959. Physically abused in prison (his toenails were pulled out, and his kidneys failed), he bribed his way into less harsh incarceration in an insane asylum (an ironic note struck on the theme of insanity). There Kuo Yuan preached the gospel powerfully, first to inmates and then to their jailers as well.

By bribery and luck, the Lee family managed to escape to Hong Kong, where Kuo Yuan preached to throngs numbering in the thousands. Thence they migrated in 1964 to the United States, where, at the age of forty, he attended theological school. A changed and subdued man, he was appointed a minister in a Rust Belt Pennsylvania town whose congregation called him their "heathen minister"—an oxymoron that captures the small-mindedness of the community. Through these vicissitudes, Kuo Yuan emerges as an intelligent, gifted, tenacious survivor with traits of integrity and spiritual power that did not flourish on American soil.

This image of Kuo Yuan fits very well with the admirable figure that is to be found in Lee's poetry. Yet the memoir shows a dark side to the father-son relationship as well. Lee's memories do speak of a deep tenderness between father and son, but they also mention instances of paternal harshness. Curiously, both tenderness and harshness are bound up with images of language and of the hand. During Lee's infant years, he did not speak. His father would lay his hands tenderly around Lee's head and pray, seemingly for hours, for the gift of tongue; at the age of three, the boy suddenly began to speak in complete sentences. Yet Kuo Yuan could be a harsh taskmaster. Lee had to read the Bible aloud all day on Saturdays, and when he fell short of his father's expectations, he would be beaten harshly with his father's bare hands.

Tender or harsh, the bond between father and son was excruciatingly intimate, viscerally so. Lee had to nurse his father after the latter's fourth coronary; he had to bathe him and even help him to defecate by reaching into his colon with the fingers of his gloved hands.

Apart from these strong parental influences, one gathers that Lee's early childhood experiences in Indonesia played a formative role in shaping his imagination, even though there are few overt references to those experiences in his poetry. In Indonesia, with his father in jail and his mother distracted by family woes, Lee was largely cared for by his Javanese nanny, Lammi. Through her he became aware of family conflicts and love affairs; more important, Lammi used to take Lee to her village home, where he watched performances of *wayang* (the Indonesian folk theater) and imbibed the mythological tales they dramatized. Through Lammi and her friends, Lee was exposed to stories of spell-binding medicine men and women (*bomoh* is the Indonesian term), whose power was confirmed by the Lee family's experience of hailstorms bombarding their house until their mother agreed to sell it. Lee's early childhood exposure to the folk art and shamanistic tradition of Southeast Asia may have contributed to the qualities of mythic resonance and paraordinary sensation that mark some of his writing.

The ending of *The Winged Seed* contains an instance of this mythic-magical wordcrafting, which in this case is couched in prose. Here Lee pulls together the book's recurrent images of blood, seed, hands, and language as he invents the conclusion of a fable about seeking and finding:

> Children, I know you wonder how a hand may enter a place so narrow as a seed. The answer is the hand must die. So the hand lay down next to the seed, opened, and the three ravenous birds ripped up its flesh and gobbled up the blood, and put the bones in a sack.
>
> Once inside the seed, the thief, who had been blind, could see. He moved toward the heart of the seed, but found his way blocked by a book. Leafing through the book, he noticed many pages missing. . . . He sat down and began to read. . . . Reading first the odd-numbered pages, and then the even, he read out loud, while all one hundred rooms of the house of the seed echoed with the sound of a hand reading.

The Winged Seed, then, is a finely wrought memoir affording fascinating insights into the formation of a literary imagination and the origins of the most powerful images and themes that stir it. The book also provides revealing glimpses of some decisive political moments in twentieth century China and Indonesia. Often couched in highly poetic prose, Lee's memoir is crisscrossed by motifs and tropes that richly repay thoughtful and attentive reading.

C. L. Chua

Sources for Further Study

Booklist. XCI, January 1, 1995, p. 794.
Chicago Tribune. April 23, 1995, XIV, p. 6.
Hungry Mind Review. LXIX, Summer, 1995, p. 27.
Kirkus Reviews. LXII, December 1, 1994, p. 1592.
Library Journal. CXX, March 15, 1995, p. 70.
Los Angeles Times. July 3, 1995, p. E6.
Publishers Weekly. CCXLII, February 13, 1995, p. 71.
San Francisco Chronicle. March 5, 1995, p. REV8.

WITH MY TROUSERS ROLLED
Familiar Essays

Author: Joseph Epstein (1937-   )
Publisher: W. W. Norton (New York). 317 pp. $25.00
Type of work: Essays

The engaging but prickly fifth collection of personal essays from Joseph Epstein, whose reflections center chiefly on the complex pleasures of middle age

The personal or familiar essay is a distinguished if homely form, going back to Michel de Montaigne, whose *essais* (tests or trials) were occasions for him to indulge his curiosity and try out his judgment on the everyday features of his sixteenth century landscape. His now-famous question—"Que sais je?"—propelled him, as it has scores of other practitioners since, into endlessly fascinating reflections on himself and his world. "What do I think of that?" "Am I amused or distressed, moved or baffled by that?" "How do I make sense of that?" The "I" in such questions is as much the subject of scrutiny as the world of "thats" out there. The interior contours of the essayist's mind and sensibility, in other words, are as prominent as the exterior features of the culture, perhaps even more so.

As the essayist tries out his or her views, complains or celebrates, remembers or fantasizes, speculates or pontificates, readers feel like confidants entrusted with the writer's private store of opinions. The writer shares views and, along the way, confesses to vanity, pettiness, partiality, uncertainty—and readers reward this honesty with something close to absolution.

Still, readers need to encounter more than a genially frank presence if the familiar essay is to work. They need a new awareness, an insight about something already known but not thoroughly investigated, or a confirmation that their view of the world is not hopelessly idiosyncratic. No doubt one of the reasons readers respond generously to the essayist's self-exposure and quirks of personality is that it reaffirms common humanity. One recognizes one's own face in the mirror the essayist holds up to his or her own.

Epstein is no newcomer to the familiar essay. Editor of *The American Scholar*, professor of English at Northwestern University, literary reviewer, and sometime critic, he has written more than eighty familiar essays collected in four earlier volumes: *Familiar Territory* (1979), *The Middle of My Tether* (1983), *Once More Around the Block* (1990), and *A Line Out for a Walk* (1991). Many of the essays first appeared in *The American Scholar*, where, under the nom de plume Aristides, Epstein opens each quarterly issue with a set of leisurely reflections on fad diets, say, or book collecting or euphemisms or snobbery or the etiquette of power at professional conventions. To regular readers these essays have built up a fairly clear portrait of the man: Jewish, midwestern, urban and urbane, divorced and happily remarried, a traditionalist and Anglophile with clear and occasionally fussy tastes and with a merciless ear for solecisms and linguistic infelicities, an early riser, a nonjogger, a BMW owner, a onetime smoker, a clever and inveterate punster who is uneasy about feminism and dead set against rock music but who admits to an abiding love for shined shoes, good haircuts, seventy-dollar Charvet bow ties, and the novels of Henry James. Even without his likeness on the dust jacket, readers begin to get the picture.

Perhaps even more than Epstein's overt self-characterizations ("the least likely man in America to appear in a ponytail" or "one of the country's leading solipsists"), the tone of voice itself gives clear hints about the man behind the essays. Certainly Epstein has mastered the time-honored tone of the familiar essayist: conversational, self-deprecating, confessional (indeed, "I must confess" and "Truth to tell" are among his favorite sentence openers). Yet his writing voice is marked by something else: a recurrent smugness. For all the acuity of vision, the cleverness of language, the clear command of the form, Epstein is a pretty self-satisfied commentator on his life and times, a complacent "fella," as he would likely put it (he loves the common touch, especially when it is embedded in some very uncommon, Jamesian syntax).

This juxtaposition of tones, the calculated descent from the literary to the vernacular, is a regular feature of his prose. He revels in phrases such as "*au* bloomin' *contraire*": the cockney interrupting the French to produce a tangy offhandedness. In the same way, Epstein will frequently dredge up a cliché only to alter one word in the expected phrase ("You live and yearn" or "In for a penny, in for a pounding"). It is a strategy reminiscent of the deliciously artificial plays of Oscar Wilde, another writer more than half in love with his own cleverly mannered voice.

Epstein has a penchant, too, for the periodic sentence, the drama derived from parceling out only bits and pieces of the base clause, interrupted by parentheses, small digressions, smaller clauses—a practice that requires readers, if they want to reach closure, to stay riveted to the voice leading them through this syntactic maze. He takes a clear pleasure in controlling the reader and directing attention to the subtle linguistic play that, one senses, is Epstein's real concern. "See how witty I am? See how artfully I can craft a sentence, how cleverly I can sustain your interest?" Although he never actually asks these questions, readers feel again and again as if they are meant to answer them.

Now, it needs to be said that there is nothing fundamentally wrong with this kind of showing off; such self-conscious virtuosity can be, and occasionally is, charming—especially when Epstein candidly owns up to it. In "Merely Anecdotal" he admits to being fascinated by his own experience and compelled to make artful arrangements of it in print. "Live and tell" becomes his performer's motto, and indeed it admirably accounts for what is probably a personal essayist's necessary self-absorption. In "The Bonfire of My Vanities," Epstein confesses to being vain—about seeing his name in print, about the nattiness of his Brooks Brothers clothes, about the respectable amount of hair left on his head. In so gleefully disclosing his vanities, he largely disarms any criticism. Where the self-congratulatory note does seem like smugness is in the lovingly rendered catalog of his tastes, "Such Good Taste." There can be little objection to Maurice Ravel and Darius Milhaud, Edgar Degas and Henri Matisse, Cole Porter and George Gershwin; yet Epstein's tone in listing these touchstones suggests that veering from his personal standard consigns one to the ranks of the culturally benighted.

He seems to know too much and to be unable to conceal that fact, even beneath all the faux modesty and self-deprecation. Epstein likes presenting himself as an amateur, sloughing off his academic expertise for the more attractive mask of an enthusiast. This works acceptably in "An Ignorant Man's Guide to Serious Music," where he *is* largely an amateur, a man who came to classical music somewhat late in life and who thoroughly enjoys his unsystematic listening experiences. When it comes to literature, however, it does not matter how many casual phrases such as "swell books" he throws around: The reader does not buy his regular fella act. Readers know, and he knows, that this is simply a professional literary gentleman gone slumming, and there is something uncomfortably condescending or cute about the pretense.

This voice, this constructed persona—in Epstein's own apt phrase, "simple, if more than occasionally pretentious"—has been the consistent feature in all of his essays. Yet there are changes in *With My Trousers Rolled*. It is a far less varied collection than were the first four; it is more like a variation on a theme. As the title's nod to T. S. Eliot's "The Love Song of J. Alfred Prufrock" clearly suggests, that theme is the anxiety of middle age (though it also alludes to Epstein's lifelong preference for cuffed trousers). He is still responsive to issues of language, oddities of behavior, and the great mysteries of popular culture. Nevertheless, in this book, apart from an amusing piece on car ownership and a moving remembrance of his mother, all of his topics lead him back to reflections on what it means to be middle-aged, how that makes him relate (or more to the point, not relate) to what he finds on the terrain of the 1990's. He turns more regularly to time, mortality, death. It would be going too far to say that an autumnal atmosphere pervades the book—it is finally too witty for that predictable adjective to capture the spirit of the essays; yet it is fair to say that a feeling of resignation permeates these pages.

Epstein is now less interested in the questions, more interested in his answers. It is not simply that, being comfortably ensconced in middle age, he now knows what he thinks: He makes it clear that what he thinks is what all right-minded people should think. This is an understandable posture, except that for a familiar essayist it may be the kiss of death. Can one really imagine Montaigne ceasing to question himself and settling instead for complacent descriptions of how he has arrived at his answers? There is an important difference between self-scrutiny and self-regard, and Epstein is too frequently guilty of the latter. In these essays he risks detachment from his material and a too-great delight in being, in the title of one essay, "Nicely Out of It." He relishes the fact that he has never seen an Andrew Lloyd Webber musical or the television show *L.A. Law* and is delighted that one of his reviewers has called him "crankish." He seems all too ready to embrace a premature curmudgeonhood, enticed by the carte blanche it offers for ridiculing views and positions that oppose his own.

Several of the essays cluster around the theme of a decaying culture and his happy alienation from it. "Decline and Blumenthal" (a pun on "decline and bloomin' fall"—again the piquant collision of highbrow with street slang) traces the demoralization of contemporary American life and indicts the usual suspects: feminists, rock music ("unintelligible violence of primitive rhythms"), and "tony deconstructionist notions" within academia. Epstein has little patience with the contemporary university scene, cavalierly dismissing attempts to redress inequities in the traditional structures of power as signs of trendy political correctness gone amok. Holding aloft the banner of the *ancien régime*, he releases an Olympian sigh and moves on to think of more agreeable things: "of beautiful children in concentrated play, of Mozart's music for oboe and harp and flute, of Winesap apples and cold green grapes, of large-hearted men and women who refused to be daunted in much darker times than ours."

Such imagistic lists occur frequently (amounting to a kind of credo), as do staggering numbers of allusions, averaging more than twenty per essay. Like all practiced essayists, Epstein orchestrates this wide range of references to give depth and breadth to his treatment of a topic and to locate himself in a centuries-long conversation on such topics as privacy, vanity, or heroism. He makes it seem as natural as breathing, moving seamlessly from Montaigne, Guy de Maupassant, and Myra Hess to Michael Jordan, Robert Redford, and Groucho Marx. If it is true that "by their books ye shall know them," then by Epstein's books we know him to be a man whose view of the world is grounded in Arthur Schopenhauer's philosophy, Edward Gibbon's history, Philip Larkin's poetry, and Henry James's novels. He has placed himself in a tradition—at once stylish and skeptical—and given himself a pedigree. Like the figures he adduces, Epstein sees humans as irrational, unpredictable, hopelessly comical, yet eminently worthy of readers' most finely tuned attention.

In the opening essay, "Livestock," Epstein revealingly confesses to having spent more time in the previous year with his cat than with any human being and observes that like this four-legged companion, he is good at being left alone, withholding affection, and gaining attention when he needs it. Perhaps there is too much of the feline temperament in this collection for it to be entirely enjoyable. Yet as any cat lover knows, if one can take a cat on its own terms, it can be good company indeed.

Thomas J. Campbell

Sources for Further Study

The Hudson Review. XLVI, Autumn, 1995, p. 493.
Kirkus Reviews. LXIII, March 1, 1995, p. 287.
Library Journal. CXX, June 15, 1995, p. 69.
Los Angeles Times. May 17, 1995, p. E4.
The New York Times. May 18, 1995, p. B5.
The New York Times Book Review. C, May 7, 1995, p. 26.
Publishers Weekly. CCXLII, February 27, 1995, p. 93.
The Sewanee Review. CIII, January, 1995, p. R1.
The Wall Street Journal. May 2, 1995, p. A16.
The Washington Post Book World. XXV, July 23, 1995, p. 3.

THE WOMAN WHO FELL FROM THE SKY

Author: Joy Harjo (1951-   )
Publisher: W. W. Norton (New York). 96 pp. $19.95
Type of work: Poetry

In Harjo's prose poetry, metamorphosis is a constant state of the human condition, activated by events as diverse as the memory of a simple meal of potatoes and coffee and a vision of lightning as "a bag of white arrows"

Readers of contemporary poetry often have to struggle with how to categorize a work because of the absence of obvious external markers. For example, most people, if asked, would say that one of the key differences between "poetry" and "fiction" is that poetry is written in lines while fiction is written in paragraph form. Yet what of so-called prose poems or narrative poems written in prose format? When does a poem stop being a poem and become fiction? Joy Harjo's *The Woman Who Fell from the Sky* may well be puzzling and perhaps even irritating to those who expect a tight, formal definition of "poem" in order to believe that they are reading one.

Yet it seems unlikely that Harjo's primary objective in using the format she most frequently chooses throughout the book is to make a bold statement about poetic form. Rather, she seems mostly to be doing what she does best: defining the universe, and poetry along with it, on her own terms, in her own way, with no apologies or unnecessary bows to established protocol.

Two centuries ago, William Wordsworth wrote in his preface to *Lyrical Ballads* (1798) that poetry is "the spontaneous overflow of powerful emotion." He shocked the literary establishment by writing about field hands and orphans, flowers and clouds in a way considered "radical" at the time. While Harjo follows in general the broadly Romantic tradition first established by such poets as Wordsworth and Walt Whitman (with more than a nod to the unique mysticism of an Emily Dickinson), poetry seems for her to be a kind of incantation invoking truth. Her roots for such "truth-telling" lie not so much in the Western tradition of literature as in a generic tribal memory that she both invokes and reinvents. Rather than having Western white man's literature assimilate her and her work into its canon, she seems to be assimilating what is useful from white American culture into her own work, as if weaving a balance back into the universe out of the cosmic disruption caused by the virtual eradication of America's native peoples. Her manner of addressing readers is rhetorically similar to that of Malcolm X: The voice seems essentially indifferent to the largely white audience that might be reading it—they are welcomed incidentally into a world in which blacks or, in this case, native peoples speak directly to, about, for, or against one another.

Most of the poems in the collection follow a format in which stanzas become paragraphs and each poem is followed by a star serving as an asterisk or pause and then an italicized comment on the poem and the experiences that gave rise to it. Such an approach is formalistic heresy insofar as a poem is to be considered "complete" in itself; in such a theoretical framework, comments by the author about what the poem "means" to him or her or what originally prompted it are considered superfluous at best. Harjo seems unconcerned with such judgments, just as she seems unconcerned with making a postmodern or feminist statement by choosing certain formalistic disciplines over others. Her format seems to allow a recurring pattern to be woven more holistically through the collection itself. Metamorphosis is a constant state of being with an aim: to interconnect everything irreversibly until there is no separateness, no us and them, yours and mine, past and present.

Harjo describes this aim frankly in a paragraph/stanza from the title poem, "The Woman Who Fell from the Sky":

> This unnameable thing of beauty is what shapes a flock of birds who
> know exactly when to turn together in flight in the winds used to
> make words. Everyone turns together though we may not see each
> other stacked in the invisible dimensions.

Admittedly, this innovative combination of structural pattern and thematic generosity is hard to discern from merely reading the poems on the page, and "The Woman Who Fell from the Sky" is perhaps the most inscrutable in mere print. Reading these pieces silently can give rise to confusion about form, with looseness of technique being confused with looseness of message. The audiotape of Harjo reciting her work, sometimes with the assistance of her band, Poetic Justice, is thus an indispensable interpretive tool. The subdued, serious cadence of her voice allows the epic quality of cultural metamorphosis she is endeavoring to create in this collection to comes through almost as a matter of fact, instead of remaining enigmatic. Hearing Harjo's voice saying that "myth was as real as a scalp being scraped for lice" makes the statement stand out. Readers know from her recitation that it is a kind of legend with which to read the map of these poems, because she delivers such "un-Western" statements as if she were telling the reader to turn left at the next four-way stop sign. The sound of her voice makes the interpretation of and articulation between "poem" and italicized comment seem like business as usual, when it is actually quite unusual.

The main characters in "The Woman Who Fell from the Sky," Johnny (also known as Saint Coincidence) and Lila (also known as The Woman Who Fell from the Sky), are as different and as alike as the poem and the following comment are. Harjo would not see her narrative of Johnny and Lila at Indian Boarding School (contained inside Saint Coincidence's vision of Lila's vision through the power of memory) as a case of reality and the dream world colliding. For her—and for readers, as they learn to enter her world—the dream world is also reality. In such a world, wolves can approach the campfire of a solitary Indian man on their hind legs, be offered coffee, store meat, and fried potatoes, and then have a conversation with no words—which Harjo describes with words that evoke truth unfurling in layers of silence and memory ("Wolf Warrior"). Indeed, all the poems use this layering of experience inside memory inside experience, or memory inside experience inside memory. "Wolf Warrior" expresses the hope that "our children [are] empowered with the clothes of memory in which they are never hungry for love, or justice," and this image is made concrete by association later in the poem, when the hero in a remembered story for which the poem is a vehicle sees "a thousand white butterflies climbing toward the sun."

The terrain of the poems, although strongly evoking the natural world, ranges through the streets of Chicago in the backs of cabs and lingers in the privacy of a hotel in Washington, D.C. In each place, whether it be the land or the city, elements from each clash, connect, converge, and transform into one unbreakable web. Even taxicab drivers, in such poems as "Letter from the End of the Twentieth Century," survive by evoking their ancestral, tribal truths. In such a way a story of senseless, anonymous urban murder becomes an agent of forgiveness and surrender to transformation, and readers, along with Harjo, who crafts herself as a listener within the poem, learn that "the smallest talking drum is an insistent heart." It can beat out a story that "sustains [us] through these tough distances."

The "tough distances" alluded to at the end of this poem are the conditions of earth ravaged by the dishonorable empiricism of white colonialism, leaving alcoholics, veterans, nonwhite immigrants, women, children, and the land itself chained to an indentured physical reality. Yet while the poems point an accusing finger at the "death-wish" of Western culture, none of the heroes and heroines so crushed by it is a mere victim. Their spirits, inherent in the power of memory, keep them whole in the midst of their fragmentation and despair, lifting them through and beyond to a "mythical reality" in which they are inviolable. For such a journey "the complications of NASA" are unnecessary, even trivial. The storytellers who are the characters in these poems travel without need of technology beyond its dead end at empirical knowledge. The language of mythic and Native American cosmology cleverly subsumes "white science."

As readers listen carefully to Harjo read her work in the slow, sensually urgent delivery that is distinctively hers, they will discover words such as "vortex," "equation," and "molecular" most often in statements of loss, despair, or inadequacy, while the language that redeems chaos sounds more mythic, less quantitative, allowing such esoteric statements as the following passage from "Witness" to seem inevitable:

> We can walk through walls eventually by faith and could all along,
> as misty forms passing through myths no one would ever believe:
> the tragic heroine becomes the trickster caught in the circle of ob-
> scenity becomes the woman who after pulling in her laundry from a
> window adjusts her bra strap. It is the only gesture in the world.

Interestingly, such ambitious teleology is anchored by Harjo's use of active subject-verb-object combinations that gallop with the Anglo-Saxon rhythm of English. Perhaps the most startling example in "Witness," the poem just quoted, comes after this teleology has been set up. Harjo describes the death of a Navajo woman whose spirit is "on the run" with her as she walks the streets of an Italian town. She hammers out a sentence that rings, "She put her ear/ to the ground and ran shoulder first into the earth." Turns of phrase such as these, combining Native American vision with the cadence of English, make the puzzle pieces of each poem worth sorting through, since they sound the fierce tenor of uncompromising vision.

Harjo's lyricism and visionary generosity are at their height in her love poems. The two poems most obviously crafted in the conventional spirit of this genre are "The Myth of Blackbirds" and "Promise of Blue Horses." In "The Myth of Blackbirds," addressed openly to a lover, the lovers' encounters are juxtaposed to the treachery of Washington, D.C., which stands symbolically in all these poems for the broken promises and betrayals perpetuated by the U.S. government. Even though it is a "city of disturbed relativity" in which computers are "stealing names" and "spirits of the disappeared [drink] coffee at an all-night café," the lover is "thankful to the brutal city for the space which outlines [her lover's] limber beauty."

The poem opens with the beautifully lyrical statement "The hours we counted precious were blackbirds in the density of Washington." The blackbirds metamorphose throughout the poem in a "loop of mystery" woven by love, ancestral memory, and the natural world. Harjo's italicized comments begin with "I believe love is the strongest force in this world." One almost wishes she could let this poem stand alone, since its way of making that statement is much more startling and memorable than what comes after.

Toward the end of the book, "Promise of Blue Horses" brings back and evolves a familiar image from the famous Harjo poem "She Had Some Horses." It has one of the shortest and most noticeably "poemlike" structures in the book and is reminiscent of Harjo's earlier poems, while maintaining succinctly the complex storytelling themes of this collection. "Perhaps the World Ends Here," the last poem, also uses the repetitious structure of a chant in the same vein as "She Had Some Horses" and successfully and memorably grounds the complexities of the book at the kitchen table, at which "the world begins," making it simultaneously archetypal and mundane. The whirling, dynamic circle is complete, eternal, and somehow ordinary by the end of the poem, which doubles back on itself to muse, "Perhaps the world will end at the kitchen table, while we are laugh-/ ing and crying, eating of the last sweet bite." The kitchen table is a strong and credible image for making even the least visionary individuals feel the pull of the eternal in the most ordinary of human moments.

Maria Theresa Maggi

Sources for Further Study

Booklist. XCI, November 15, 1994, p. 573.
Library Journal. CXIX, November 15, 1994, p. 70.
Ms. VI, September, 1995, p. 70.
The Progressive. LIX, March, 1995, p. 44.
Publishers Weekly. CCXLI, November 28, 1994, p. 54.
Whole Earth Review. Summer, 1995, p. 43.

WOMEN ON THE MARGINS
Three Seventeenth-Century Lives

Author: Natalie Zemon Davis (1928-   )
Publisher: Harvard University Press (Cambridge, Massachusetts). Illustrated. 360 pp. $24.95
Type of work: Biography
Time: The seventeenth century
Locale: Europe, Canada, and Suriname

A study of three women—Jewish, Protestant, and Catholic—whose lives demonstrate the rich experiences of seventeenth century women far from the centers of economic, social, or political power

Principal personages:
GLIKL BAS JUDAH LEIB, a Jewish wife, merchant, and storyteller
MARIE DE L'INCARNATION, a nun who went to Canada to teach and became the first mother superior of the Ursuline order in the New World
MARIA SIBYLLA MERIAN, an artist and illustrator of insect metamorphosis, who did her most important work in Suriname

Natalie Zemon Davis has long been familiar with margins. Born into a wealthy Jewish family in Detroit, married young to a promising scholar who was barred from teaching in the United States during the McCarthy era, attending graduate school and establishing herself as a historian while busy rearing three children, Davis has often worked from the margins. It is from the margins that she has most often chosen the subjects of her historical inquiry. From the peasants and common people of sixteenth century French cities and countryside (*Society and Culture in Early Modern France,* 1975) to imposture and the imposed-upon in a small French village (*The Return of Martin Guerre,* 1983) to narratives of convicted felons hoping to win pardon from the king (*Fiction in the Archives: Pardon Tales and Their Tellers in Sixteenth Century France,* 1987), Davis, a historian of *mentalités,* has always been interested in the culture and identity of those who occupy the borderlands of historical inquiry. In *Women on the Margins: Three Seventeenth-Century Lives,* she has richly redefined the concept of marginality, demonstrating the interactions of many margins in the lives of three women, Glikl bas Judah Leib, Marie de l'Incarnation, and Maria Sibylla Merian.

The first thing that strikes one about the three subjects of *Women on the Margins* is their difference: Glikl bas Judah Leib, the wife and then widow of a busy gold trader, living in Hamburg and later Metz; Marie Guyart, who became the Ursuline nun Marie de l'Incarnation, cofounder of the first Catholic school for Amerindian women in North America; and Maria Sibylla Merian, German artist and naturalist who went to Suriname to continue her work of illustrating insect metamorphoses in the New World. In fact, the three women seem so different that Davis puts them in imaginary dialogue with one another in her prologue, where each notes the unsuitability of being linked with the others.

The most striking difference among the three is religion. Glikl was a Jew, Marie a cloistered Catholic, and Maria Sibylla, for a time, a member of a radical Protestant sect, the Labadists. Yet for all three women, religion placed them on the margins of seventeenth century society. This is obvious for the Jewish Glikl and the Protestant sectarian Maria Sibylla, but it was true even for the Catholic Marie de l'Incarnation, who participated in the revitalizing mysticism of the Counter-Reformation church. Like her spiritual model, the recently canonized St. Teresa of Ávila, Marie communicated directly with God through the "Divine Word." Yet the church hierarchy, particularly the Jesuits, were threatened by the experiences of women like Marie; thus her energies were channeled into the teaching mission of the new Ursuline order, which ultimately led her to Quebec, on the margins of the New World.

The occupations of these women served to marginalize them as well. Glikl, married at thirteen, with twelve children to rear, was active in her husband's gem-trading and money-lending business, continuing it even after his death:

> As for the family business, Haim [Glikl's husband] had felt no need to name executors or guardians ("My wife knows about everything," he said on his deathbed), and the widowed Glikl assumed the responsibility herself. . . . She set up a shop in Hamburg for manufacturing stockings and sold them near and far; she bought pearls from every Jew in town, sorted them, and sold them by size to appropriate buyers; she imported wares from Holland and traded them in her store along with local goods; she attended the fairs of Braunschweig, Leipzig, and other towns; she lent money and honored bills of exchange across Europe.

Glikl bas Judah Leib was certainly efficient, energetic, and confident, both as a partner in her husband's enterprises and as a widowed businesswoman, but as Davis often points out, "the situation of being a Jew gave Glikl bas Judah Leib a constrained and vulnerable status in Christian Europe." With many children to marry off, Glikl carried out the Jewish strategy that her husband Haim had begun before his death, of marrying some of her children to partners in distant cities: a daughter in Hannover, another in Amsterdam, one in Metz, other children in Berlin and Copenhagen, and finally a son as far away as London. Davis notes that "the wide dispersal of one's kin was an economic advantage and a safety measure. One never knew when the wheel of fortune might turn." Clearly, while Glikl prospered most of her life, it was always within the margins set by her status as a Jew in an overwhelmingly Christian political, economic, and social structure.

After the death of her beloved first husband, Glikl began to compose her autobiography in Yiddish. It was intended for her family and, by the time of her death, consisted of seven books. It was not a diary, for it shows many signs of revision and artistic rearrangement, and it does not gloss over troubles such as the financial reversals that plagued her second husband in Metz. It contains many stories, most traditional, but with many added motifs. Davis demonstrates the difference between Christian and Jewish autobiography: While Christians are concerned with the definitive conversion experience, Jewish autobiography often recapitulates the history of the chosen people, of sinning, suffering, and exile. Glikl bas Judah Leib and her people may have existed on the border of the European Christian world, but her autobiography makes her world, a world of Jewish tradition, the center of meaning.

Like Glikl bas Judah Leib, Marie Guyart and Maria Sibylla Merian came from the artisan-commercial classes. Marie Guyart was born in Tours in 1599, the daughter of a baker. At seventeen, she married a silkmaker, who died two years later, leaving her a widow with an infant son. Losing most of her inheritance to lawsuits, she and her son went to live with her sister Claude, and her brother-in-law Paul Buisson, a successful merchant wagoner. She performed a variety of tasks, from grooming horses to keeping books and writing letters for her brother-in-law, until, ten years later, she joined the Ursuline order, taking the name Marie de l'Incarnation and leaving her son in her sister's household. It was a wrenching separation, followed within a few years by her departure for Quebec to take up a teaching mission among the Hurons, Algonquins, and Iroquois.

Eventually, Marie de l'Incarnation became mother superior of the Ursuline convent in Quebec. In order to instruct Amerindian girls, she learned to speak and write the Amerindian tongues. She composed catechisms, prayer books, and dictionaries in Huron, Iroquois, and Algonquin. She wrote for the annual *Jesuit Relations* and carried on a large correspondence with people in France. Finally, in response to entreaties from her son, who had grown up to become a priest, she composed her autobiography, which he later edited as *La Vie de venerable Mere Marie de l'Incarnation* (1677). Examining this autobiography, filled with descriptions of the culture and habits of the Amerindians, Davis points out Marie de l'Incarnation's habit of universalizing the experiences she observed, so that Amerindian girls are given motives and aspirations much like those of French girls. No matter what the cultural distance, Marie thus brought the center to the margins.

Maria Sibylla Merian, born in Frankfurt in 1647, was the daughter, stepdaughter, and sister of well-known artists, engravers, painters and publishers. Being born into such a family allowed her to develop her own talents in the supportive atmosphere of a busy and prosperous atelier. In 1665, she married Johann Andreas Graff, a student of her stepfather. The couple moved to Graff's hometown of Nuremberg, where they had two daughters. There Maria Sibylla Merian Graff was exposed to Latin nature books and continued the study of insects, particularly silkworms, which she had begun when she was thirteen. In 1679, she published her *Raupen* (translated into English as *Wonderful Transformation and Singular Flower-Food of Caterpillars . . . Painted from Life and Engraved in Copper*), followed by a second volume in 1683. As Davis points out,

Merian was a pioneer, crossing boundaries of education and gender to acquire learning on insects and nurturing daughters as she observed, painted, and wrote. Her focus on breeding, habitat, and metamorphosis fits nicely with the domestic practice of a seventeenth century mother and housewife. We have here not a female mind uneasy with analysis or timelessly connected to the organic (images that have been thoroughly challenged in recent scholarship), but a woman perched for scientific enterprise on a creative margin—for her a buzzing ecosystem—between domestic workshop and learned academy.

Around 1685, Maria Sibylla Merian did a startling thing: She abandoned her marriage, gave up her worldly goods, including a recent inheritance, and retired to a Protestant religious community in Friesland founded by Jean de Labadie. Labadie taught that the reign of Christ was at hand and that believers must withdraw from the world in order to achieve full repentance and regeneration. Unlike Marie de l'Incarnation, Merian did not have to give up her family for her faith; her two daughters and her mother accompanied her to the Labadist community, but it is clear that she repudiated her husband.

Merian continued her observations and nature studies while at Wieuwerd, the Labadist community, though she was obliged to leave them in a far less finished state than her previously published watercolors and copperplates. Indeed, her work became a spiritual exercise: Her study book from the period opens with the preface "With God!" Within six years, however, Merian left the Labadist community with her daughters (her mother had died) and settled in Amsterdam.

Davis presents Maria Sibylla Merian as a woman who, unlike Glikl bas Judah Leib or Marie de l'Incarnation, was careful to keep her inner life to herself, so it is difficult to know the exact reasons for her departure from the sect. She never made any statements or denunciations concerning the Labadists. Explaining this period with a metaphor from the world of nature that Merian never abandoned, Davis says that the five years' retirement "turned out to be just that: a time of chrysalis, of hidden growth and learning for a woman who could not be pinned down."

Merian's scientific drawings of insects were always concerned with metamorphosis, but unlike many other naturalists of her day, she had little interest in classification, preferring to show the insects as they changed and the plants on which they fed. She even depicted the holes left in the plant leaves where the insects fed. Davis describes her approach as "ecological . . . centered on interactions in nature and on transformative organic processes." She was in frequent contact with the many naturalists and collectors in Amsterdam, but finding that their taxonomic approach neglected origins and transformations, she yearned to see the exotic New World insects for herself. Finally, in 1699, she and her daughter left for the recently acquired Dutch colony of Suriname, to collect specimens and create drawings for what was to become her fullest and best-known work, *Metamorphosis of the Insects of Suriname* (1705).

Unlike Glikl bas Judah Leib and Marie de l'Incarnation, Maria Sibylla Merian wrote very little beyond the necessary descriptions for her botanical prints. Davis compensates wonderfully for this lack of autobiographical texts by reading the prints and accompanying descriptions as texts. She does a particularly good job with the powerful and frightening plate 18, showing spiders and ants devouring a hummingbird and one another on a ravaged guava tree. Davis claims that Merian's ethnographic mind-set, unlike Marie de l'Incarnation's universalizing mind-set, brought news of the exotic margins back into the center of European scientific thought.

As in all of her other work, Davis' impressive scholarship informs *Women on the Margins*. Her archival research is unequaled, as more than one hundred pages of notes attest. Yet Davis always tells a story well, so that the book is a pleasure for the informed reader as well as the more specialized scholar. In writing of these "forgotten" women, Davis has not merely added to "herstory" in an accretive way. Instead, she gives readers details and comparisons that allow for placement in an enlarged cultural landscape. As she reminds readers, for these women, margins were not the devalued places of modern economic usage but the "borderland between cultural deposits that allowed new growth and surprising hybrids."

Kay Holston Smith

Sources for Further Study

The Christian Science Monitor. October 26, 1995, p. B1.
The Guardian. November 24, 1995, p. 20.
Library Journal. CXX, October 15, 1995, p. 72.
Los Angeles Times Book Review. January 7, 1996, p. 3.
The New York Times Book Review. C, December 10, 1995, p. 18.

WONDER BOYS

Author: Michael Chabon (1963-   )
Publisher: Villard Books (New York). 368 pp. $23.00
Type of work: Novel
Time: The mid-1990's
Locale: Western Pennsylvania

During a weekend writers' conference, Grady Tripp comes to grips with some of his problems and with his uncertainties about the nearly completed manuscript on which he has worked for seven years

> *Principal characters:*
> GRADY TRIPP, an overweight, thirty-five-year-old marijuana-smoking writer and university instructor of creative writing
> EMILY, his third wife
> IRVING and IRENE WARSHAW, Emily's Jewish parents
> SARA GASKELL, the university chancellor, Grady's forty-five-year-old mistress
> WALTER GASKELL, Sara's husband and the head of the English Department
> TERRY CRABTREE, Grady's old friend, an editor for a major book publisher
> ANTONIA (TONY) SLOVIAK, a transvestite
> JAMES LEER, Grady's student, an incipient writer
> HANNAH GREENE, Grady and Emily's tenant and Grady's student
> ALBERT VETCH (AUGUST VAN ZORN), a writer

Grady Tripp is talking with his father-in-law, Irv Warshaw, who has just reread Grady's early novel, *The Bottomlands*. Asked how he likes the book on second reading, Irv responds (not unkindly, the author is quick to note), "It's a young man's book. It got me remembering how it felt to be young." Asked how one likes *Wonder Boys*, one might answer (not unkindly) that it, too, is a young man's book.

Michael Chabon's second published novel, appearing seven years after his celebrated tour de force *The Mysteries of Pittsburgh* (1988) quickly draws readers into a rollicking world of interesting, zany people, quite talented, assembled on a college campus for WordFest, an annual event that brings writers and editors to town. Grady Tripp, overweight, just about over his third marriage, and overindulging in pot smoking, teaches creative writing at the host institution and is trying to complete the novel *Wonder Boys*, on which much of his academic future hangs. At it for seven years, he has a long manuscript that lacks the right ending. He should be able to finish it in two weeks or so, but he has been saying that for a long time.

It is interesting that after his first novel, Chabon went through a comparable dry spell. He took a hefty advance for his second novel, surrendered half of it to his former wife in a divorce, and finally presented an unwieldy manuscript, "Fountain City," to his publisher, who found it unsuitable. The book remains unpublished.

Over a seven-month period following that disappointment, Chabon, who regularly had been publishing short stories (including the 1991 collection *A Model World*), produced *Wonder Boys*. This second novel is not only an exhilarating read but also a model of crisp, convincing characterization and, most especially, of intricate presentation of detail. Chabon is a highly visual person, and what he sees he remembers and describes with remarkable acuity. His other senses well attuned, he is competent as well with smells, sounds, tastes, and textures, which enter continually into his narrative.

Grady Tripp, orphaned by age four, has his first exposure to writers at an early age. Reared by his grandmother in her western Pennsylvania hotel, The McClelland, Grady gets to know one of the regular guests, Albert Vetch, a William Blake specialist who teaches English at nearby Coxley College. Vetch, using the pseudonym August Van Zorn, writes horror stories to pay for his wife's confinement in a sanatorium near Erie, publishing them regularly in magazines and producing gothic novels in an unrelenting flow. Vetch's wife dies as Grady broaches puberty. One day shortly thereafter, Grady, taking Vetch his lunch, finds him sitting in his chair, still rocking, dead from a self-inflicted bullet wound to the head—a neat death, as Grady remembers it.

It is because of Vetch that Grady, while an undergraduate taking a creative writing course, comes to meet Terry Crabtree, who some twenty years later would remain his closest friend and would-be editor. Grady and Terry are both due to present a story in the creative writing class, but Grady, unable to come up with anything, swipes one of Vetch's stories and passes it off as his own. Ironically, Terry, having never intended to write an original story, swipes the same Vetch story. Because each of these literary thieves has the good sense to alter Vetch's story somewhat, they alone are aware of the purloining, and this awareness creates between them a bond that strengthens through the years.

When Terry arrives for WordFest, at which he is a presenter, he has in tow his seatmate from his flight, Antonia Sloviak, whom Grady instantly recognizes as a transvestite. This character, although colorful, adds only color to the story and seems superfluous. Chabon reveals Terry's homosexuality in other ways, so there is little artistic need for Antonia (Tony when she is not in drag). She departs before the real action begins.

Emily, Grady's third wife, has left him on the day WordFest begins. She has gone home to spend Passover with her family, the Warshaws, and has left a note indicating that she will not return. Through her sister Deborah, she has learned that Grady for five years has carried on an affair with Sara Gaskell, chancellor of the university (Sara's husband, Walter, is Grady's boss).

Grady has little moral stamina. He wears his heart on his sleeve, falls in love easily, and takes what he can. Chabon develops him cleverly through having him continually say one thing and think another, the thought always following the quoted material: "'You are looking so well.' Doesn't she look awful?"

Into the mix comes James Leer, Grady's student, depressed because his story has just been torn to shreds by the students in Grady's creative writing class. Grady and Terry are attending a party the Gaskells are hosting in their home for WordFest. Grady steals outside and finds James there in the moonlight, a small revolver in his hand, seemingly about to kill himself. James tells Grady that the revolver is only a toy, but it proves not to be, as Grady discovers when James shoots and kills the Gaskells' dog, Doctor Dee, a blind, mangy mutt that has attacked Grady. The attack occurs when Grady takes James, an inveterate film buff, to the Gaskells' bedroom to show him the black silk jacket with ermine trim that Marilyn Monroe wore when she married Joe DiMaggio. Walter Gaskell, a baseball buff, surrounds himself with such memorabilia.

Terrified by what has happened, Grady gets the dog's carcass into the car's trunk, where, in narration reminiscent of William Faulkner's *As I Lay Dying* (1930), it remains, rotting, through much of the remainder of the novel. James, in a moment of light-fingered enthusiasm, makes off with the black silk jacket—an act that eventually brings the police into the matter.

Meanwhile, Terry has been trying to put the make on the sexually confused James, whom Grady whisks away to Kinship, the rural retirement venue of his Warshaw in-laws. They will have Passover with the Warshaws, who are a curious lot: a Jewish couple whose own son drowned and who adopted Korean children, of whom Emily is one. These Koreans are now also Jews who celebrate the high holidays.

James turns out to be a pathological liar who has constructed a fictional family for himself that he tries to pass off as real, but even their town, Carvel near Scranton, exists only in his unpublished novel about a boy whose father is also his grandfather. Is Chabon suggesting that if one wants to write fiction, it helps to be a pathological liar? At any rate, before story's end, it is James Leer's book that is accepted for publication.

In the course of the Passover visit to the country, Grady accidentally runs over and kills Grossman, a boa constrictor as thick as transatlantic telephone cables once were, a creature the Warshaws have been tending for their foster son. Grady stuffs Grossman into the trunk of his old Galaxy, which already holds the dead Doctor Dee and Albert Vetch's tuba.

In a subplot, Chabon reveals that the Galaxy, given to Grady to satisfy a debt but never titled to him because of missing paperwork, really belongs to Vernon Hardapple, a punchy prizefighter whose real name proves to be Peterson Walker. Earlier in the novel, a drunken Vernon tries to reclaim the car and in one great leap lands on its hood with an impact sufficient to leave on it the unmistakable impression of his derriere.

After Grady and James return home following the Passover meal, Grady, high on pot, having left Doctor Dee for James's super-straight, country club parents (or grandparents, as James insists they are) to find, vows to return Marilyn Monroe's jacket to Gaskell with an explanation that will mollify both him and the police, but all of that must wait until morning. Grady parks his car, with the jacket neatly folded on the back seat, boa and tuba still in the trunk, in his driveway. The next morning (a Sunday), it is gone. The loss of the car is less of a problem than the loss of the jacket, because James has now been taken in for questioning by the police, to whom Grady had promised the return of the missing jacket.

In his pursuit of the car, Grady takes with him the only copy of his novel, which

Hannah Greene has just read and on whose ending she has commented negatively. Terry, who has also read parts of the novel and tells Grady that he cannot recommend publication because his own job is on the line, is driving. In the course of a nasty parking-lot encounter with Vernon Hardapple, the pages of the novel begin to blow away; Grady manages to save only seven of them, one for each year he has been working on it.

In the end, in a scene reminiscent of the final chapter of Evelyn Waugh's *A Handful of Dust* (1934), Walter is presiding over the closing session of WordFest. He announces that one outcome of this year's meeting is that Terry Crabtree has accepted James Leer's novel for publication. He does not know that Terry has finally gotten James into bed.

A great irony in the story is that Grady and Emily have been trying for years to conceive a child. Emily thought that Grady's pot smoking had reduced his sperm count, which accounted for their lack of success. It turns out, however, that Grady has impregnated Sara, now forty-five years old. She decides to have the baby, her first. She and Grady, once divorced, marry and go off to Coxley College, Vetch's old institution, where Sara becomes dean of students and Grady teaches creative writing part time.

Reading *Wonder Boys* is good fun. Chabon has an excellent sense of ironic juxtapositions. He gets away with outrageous improbabilities simply by making them too outrageous for his readers to contest. In James Leer he builds an alter ego, whereas in Grady Tripp he has constructed his superego. The balance he achieves works well.

The writing in this novel is deft and—save for a few seeming lapses such as the gratuitous introduction of the transvestite—extraordinarily well controlled. Chabon's satirical tone is light and well sustained throughout the novel, which contains a persistent undercurrent of critical commentary on the academic world. Whereas much contemporary satire ends in a suicide of overdone detail, the satire in this book remains sparkling, cogent, and appropriately light.

R. Baird Shuman

Sources for Further Study

Kirkus Reviews. LXII, December 1, 1994, p. 1557.
Los Angeles Times Book Review. March 26, 1995, p. 3.
The New Republic. CCXII, June 26, 1995, p. 40.
The New York Times Book Review. C, April 9, 1995, p. 7.
Newsweek. CXXV, April 10, 1995, p. 76.
San Francisco Review of Books. XX, March, 1995, p. 40.
Time. CXLV, April 10, 1995, p. 87.
The Times Literary Supplement. April 21, 1995, p. 20.
Vogue. CLXXXV, April, 1995, p. 236.
The Washington Post Book World. XXV, March 19, 1995, p. 3.

WORDS UNDER THE WORDS
Selected Poems

Author: Naomi Shihab Nye (1952-   )
Publisher: Far Corner Books/The Eighth Mountain Press (Portland, Oregon). 176 pp. $22.95; paperback $13.95
Type of work: Poetry

Nye's poetry is multicultural yet individual, realistic yet encouraging

The current poetry scene is fragmented, with the postmodernists, the followers of Ezra Pound and Charles Olsen, on one side and the neoformalists on the other. In the middle stand those who practice a free verse that is accessible to general readers of literature. The middle group often catches flak from both sides, from the postmodernists for insufficient intellectual density and from the neoformalists for not being controlled by rhyme and rhythm, the factors they believe make poetry. Yet with these "mainstream" poets lies the main hope of demarginalizing poetry. The middle voice has a strong champion in the appealing yet nuance-filled poetry of Naomi Shihab Nye.

If anyone's poetry can open its audience out to a wider group of readers and listeners than other poets, it is Nye's. Her appearance on the Bill Moyers series was more convincing than those of some of the later poets, as she has found a voice that is not self-indulgent although it is personal, and she has found a way to explore her ethnic identity in a way that includes the readers who do not share it.

A popular guest on campuses all over the United States, Nye has a way of pulling the listener into her poetry, not only by the poetry itself but also by her genuine interest into all that passes through her purview. Each of Nye's readings is different, because the circumstance and audience are allowed to affect the selection and presentation. Nye has done much to bring contemporary poetry back to life, and life back to contemporary poetry. From her first chapbook in 1977 to her book of selected poems published in 1995, Nye has been the poet of the daily, the casual, the overlooked, and she has written of those things in such a way as to tap into their unexplored life. Her work has not gone unhonored: Her honors include two Voertman Poetry prizes, three Pushcart prizes, and the I. B. Lavan Award, as well as having her books twice designated "notable books" by the American Library Association.

Words Under the Words: Selected Poems is a selection of poems from three earlier collections: *Different Ways to Pray* (1980), *Hugging the Jukebox* (1982), and *Yellow Glove* (1986). In this vibrant collection, readers hear Nye's voice in several different keys. A joyous naturism is balanced by a darker social criticism that describes the difficulties of the oppressed without the slightest trace of condescension, and then, especially in the later poems, there is an exploration of ethnicity—Nye's Palestinian American background—in such a way as to make awareness of cultural heritage a value to be shared.

The themes of family and culture merge and reemerge in this collection, as the speaker is always aware of what it means to belong to a family or a culture. Identification with one's heritage can be binding as well as liberating. The positive and negative valences of the cultural bond are explored in one of Nye's earlier poems, "Biography of an Armenian Schoolgirl," which comes from her first full-length collection, *Different Ways to Pray*. The schoolgirl has "lived in the room of stone," where "you could dig/ for centuries uncovering the same sweet dust." She looks at her future with a husband chosen for her: "Yesterday my father met with the widower, the man with no hair." She thinks of the irony of her education and of other possibilities for her future besides the one that has been set out for her. At the end of the poem, she appears to have another schoolgirl as her double. The girl whose future is determined shares a bench with the girl whose future is open:

> They teach physics, chemistry. I throw my book out the window,
> watch the pages scatter like wings.
> I stitch the professor's jacket to the back of my chair.
> There is something else we were born for.
> I almost remember it. While I write, a ghost writes on the same tablet,
> achieves a different sum.

The first section of *Words Under the Words* is a bright phantasmagoria of cultures, snapshots of California, Mexico, South America, and elsewhere. Yet these are not "travel poems"; they show a real sense of identification and participation, as is exemplified in "Biography of an Armenian Schoolgirl." The collection from which "Biography of an Armenian Schoolgirl" comes was recognized for its craft and for its sensitive response to different cultures; it was awarded the Voertman Prize by the Texas Institute of Letters in 1980.

The middle section of *Words Under the Words* does contain a number of "travel poems"—that is, poems more concerned with the physicality of traveling, with passports and stolen cameras and the sights one sees as a tourist. The collection *Hugging the Jukebox*, which first included these poems, is perhaps less intense than *Different Ways to Pray*; nevertheless, these poems too are successful in their attempt to show the meaning in ordinary actions and the value in things, and sometimes in people, that are generally overlooked. Nye describes trashpickers in "The Trashpickers, Madison Street" as "poking inside with bent hanger and stick" while they "murmur in a language soft as rags." The things they find are renewed and celebrated: "The crooked skillet finds its first kingdom/ on a shelf where nothing is new." Thus the found items are like the finders. Only within the group of the outcasts are finders and found important, but there they have significance and stature.

There is a strong narrative element in Nye's work, and many of the poems have the aura of familiar essays about singular or ordinary experiences. "The Passport Photo" reflects on the details of this mundane experience and on what it means to prepare to cross borders and to enter the unfamiliar. "The Flying Cat" describes preparing to send a trusting household animal off in an airplane. The friendly feel of these poems is easily experienced in "Where Children Live," which begins,

> Homes where children live exude a pleasant rumpledness,
> like a bed made by a child, or a yard littered with balloons.

Through description of these homes, the poet reinvents childhood:

> To be a child again one would need to shed details
> till the heart found itself dressed with a coat with a hood.
> Now the heart has taken on gloves and mufflers,
> the heart never goes outside to find something "to do."

The conclusion fancifully suggests that the homes of children communicate the spirit of childhood, even when the children are away: "the yards glow/ with the leftovers of their affection,/ the roots of the tiniest grasses curl toward one another/ like secret smiles." With a few exceptions, such as the chilling "The Mother Writes to the Murderer: A Letter," these are poems of light and warmth. *Hugging the Jukebox* also won the Voertman Prize.

The poems in the last third of *Words Under the Words* have the same straightforwardness and honesty, but their tone is sometimes darker. "The Yellow Glove," the title poem of the collection that held these poems, is a poem of affirmation narrating the tale of a child's loss and later recovery of a glove and reflecting on loss and restoration. Yet many of these poems show an awareness of aging and death, of human misery in remote places, of losses that are irretrievable. The mask of the tourist is gone, although a wide variety of cultures are still alluded to in these poems. The speaker now becomes more of a citizen of the world and visits such diverse scenes as the Palestinian-Israeli conflict, Mother Teresa's orphanage, and Beirut. This work reflects an awareness of subtle differences in culture and the variety of responses to life's major events, as well as of how all the various peoples Nye evokes are similar. Her own mixed heritage becomes a part of this wide screen.

Many of the poems describe the tremendous effort required to survive in situations where love or even affection is a barely imaginable luxury. Yet even in the midst of death, life and the blind urge toward life are celebrated, so that the message is anything but nihilistic. Even in the most barren of surroundings, love and friendship manage to take root and grow.

As always in Nye's work, there is a gentle humor, which in the more negative poems turns into a wry irony. How can it be, they seem to ask, that those who have so much in common cannot see the beauty of their differentness? Is not the shared humanity the important factor, to dwarf all tiny divergences? This is the question suggested by the title of Nye's anthology of poets around the world, *This Same Sky: A Collection of Poems from Around the World* (1992).

The poems about America and American things toward the end of *Words Under the Words* import the mystery of other places, and often they describe cultures within the larger one. "Where the Soft Air Lives" is an unusually long poem for Nye, the vast majority of whose poems are a page or less. It takes Jack Kerouac's description of Mexican San Antonio as having "the softest air I'd ever known" as a starting point for a series of brief, vivid sketches of those who breathe "the softest air," ending with a sympathetic portrait of the priest at the Mission Espada who "keeps a little goat/ tied to a stump" and who serves as his people's historian and guide.

"Catalogue Army" imports the foreign into the familiar in another way. The speaker receives catalogs in the mail "for towels and hiking equipment,/ dresses spun in India,/ hand-colored prints of parrots and eggs." She is fascinated by the fact that these catalogs keep arriving at her home in her name, and she "secretly applauds" their arrival. Why, she wonders, does she welcome the arrival of catalogs although she has never been much of a consumer? It would seem that they seem to promise her continued existence by assuming it. She asks them to

> Be my companion on this journey between dusts,
> between vacancy and that smiling stare
> that is citizen of every climate
> but customer to nothing,
> even air.

Air is indeed Nye's element; all the possible textures and shadings of air sparkle through these poems.

Naomi Shihab Nye is in the vanguard of a movement to return contemporary poetry to where many believe it belongs—that is, with the people who read for enrichment and enlightenment. She credits William Stafford, another poet who wrote for a wide audience, for part of the direction of her poetics. In an interview for *Contemporary Authors* she commented, "I believe everything poet William Stafford ever said. (He would tip his head and look skeptical to hear that.) I believe poetry is as basic to our lives (as in 'getting back to basics') and to education as anything else there could possibly be." Nye's work is familiar and comfortable, a poetry of affection and sudden sweetnesses. It serves to educate her readers about the meaning of cultural identity and to make them want to know other cultures as well as to explore their own ethnic identity. Even her less optimistic messages are conveyed with a warmth and humor that project an irrepressible joy. Contemporary poetry with the strong appeal of *Words Under the Words* is rare.

Janet McCann

Sources for Further Study

Booklist. XCI, March 1, 1995, p. 1175.
Library Journal. CXX, February 1, 1995, p. 77.
The Progressive. LX, January, 1996, p. 43.

WRITING AND BEING

Author: Nadine Gordimer (1923-   )
Publisher: Harvard University Press (Cambridge, Massachusetts). 145 pp. $18.95
Type of work: Essays

Explorations in the art of literature and the art of life by a South African Nobel laureate

The title of this collection of six essays, first delivered as the 1994 Charles Eliot Norton Lectures at Harvard University, reflects Nadine Gordimer's belief that the morality of living and the morality of writing are one. Reading her books (she has written nine collections of short fiction and eleven novels and was awarded the Nobel Prize for Literature in 1991), one likes to think that passionately committed writers such as Gordimer, some of whose books were banned in her native land of South Africa, played an essential role in the collapse of the white racist government and the end of apartheid there. Clearly, Gordimer believes that in countries where oppression and absence of basic freedoms are facts, the writer has a responsibility to speak for the oppressed and act against the oppressors, whoever they may be. What has most engaged her imagination is the perilous journey toward tomorrow, the slow stumbling toward human freedom, the fumbling efforts to throw off the shackles (racial and religious hatreds, censorship, injustice) now occurring on a global scale. Four of the essays here are directly concerned with this phenomenon, while the other two deal with more writerly issues.

"Adam's Rib: Fictions and Realities" is an inquiry into the sources and processes of fiction, particularly in fiction's relationship to life. Gordimer discusses the vexing problems of what she calls "predatory realism," readers' tendency to read fiction as biography or autobiography. She holds that this "prying game" played by readers reveals a naïve attitude toward fiction and the complex, mysterious processes of the writer's imagination. She acknowledges that fiction has a connection with real life, real persons, but it is not the kind of connection that allows a writer simply to create a clone from Adam's rib. The writer draws upon fragments, fleeting impressions, shifting intimations and intuitions stored in the unconscious; through imaginative transformation and shaping, a fictional character is created that is both imagined and drawn from life. In fact, in order to seem lifelike, "a character always must be *larger than life*, more intense, compounded and condensed in essence of personality."

The complex relationship between fiction and reality is mysterious even to writers themselves—for example, Gordimer's own experience in writing *Burger's Daughter* (1979). Although she had personally known the man (a white hero who died in prison for his anti-apartheid activities) and his daughter who were the inspiration for this story, she had deliberately cut herself off from them during the four years she wrote the novel, partly to avoid any impression that she was "studying" them and partly as a "test of creation." Because she knew that readers would inevitably connect her fiction with their well-known case, she sent the unpublished manuscript to the daughter to read and apprehensively awaited a response. After several weeks of silence, it came:

All the daughter said was, "This was our life." She meant not that the book was factually true, but that it had a truth of vision, that Gordimer had somehow guessed, intuited, and imagined rightly. For Gordimer, the daughter's few simple words were the best response, the highest tribute, she could hope for: "No critic's laudation could match it; no critic's damning could destroy it."

"Hanging on a Sunrise: Testimony and Imagination in Revolutionary Writings" records Gordimer's changing attitude toward the merits of testimonial writings. In the 1970's, she had believed that in order to avoid debasing the very concept of literature, the same standards and value judgments that apply to imaginative literature must be applied to testimony; she questioned whether testimony should be regarded as literature. Now, in post-apartheid South Africa, reading the memoirs of African National Congress members that bring home the horrifying realities of the struggle against apartheid, she finds such writing a vital record of a past that is missing because of government censorship and terrorism. Such writing is needed to help "reconstruct our country and our lives in unfamiliar freedom." She is convinced, however, that poetry (and she might have added fiction and drama) has more durability, for after testimony is out of date, poetry can continue "to carry the experience from which the narrative has fallen away."

Three essays focus on contemporary writers, Naguib Mahfouz from Egypt, Chinua Achebe from Nigeria, and Amos Oz from Israel, whose novels of the postcolonial world all seem to her to be asking, "Where is the way to tomorrow?" Significantly, these writers do not belong to Euro-American literature, nor are they engaged in the search for personal identity commonly found in that literature. Gordimer stresses that these authors know who they are; it is their place that does not know them. In fact they have been censored, branded as traitors, or exiled by their countries for "going too far," for defying accepted political ideas and norms. Gordimer believes writers must "not be afraid to go too far, for the truth lies beyond" (in the words of Marcel Proust). She is generous in her praise of these three writers whose quest for "home" may be our best hope: "The truth is the real definition of 'home': it is the final destination of the human spirit beyond national boundaries."

Reading Naguib Mahfouz's *The Cairo Trilogy* (1956-1957; English translations as *Palace Walk*, 1990; *Palace of Desire*, 1991; *Sugar Street*, 1992), which reflects the social and political realities of Egypt from 1918 to 1944, Gordimer is interested in the ways in which political, social, and sexual freedoms are linked. Revolutionary politics enter into familial life, for example, bringing demands for freedom from the oppression of a tyrannical father or husband, or separating two brothers into opposing camps of Muslim Brotherhood and Communist Party. Ironically, they end up in the same prison. Gordimer finds the Muslim fundamentalists the most chilling, since they stone people who disagree with them and pronounce the *fatwā* of death on writers they consider blasphemous (Salman Rushdie being a well-known case). Although communism has failed terribly, Gordimer believes that it offers, "as no other ideology does, the iconoclastic right and will-power to plough down palaces" and will therefore continue to have appeal for people who suffer under unjust systems. Yet for Egypt, after generations of foreign occupations, after the restoration and overthrow of the monarchy, after terrorism, assassination, revolution, where is the path to tomorrow? In her essay "Zaabalawi: The Concealed Side," what Gordimer particularly admires about Mahfouz's epic work is its courage in posing the hard questions, rather than embracing accepted ideologies of either the Right or the Left. As Mahfouz puts it in *Sugar Street*, "The issue is how we are to mold for ourselves a belief system that is worthy of life. . . . The choice of a faith has still not been resolved."

The Nigerian novelist Chinua Achebe's *Anthills of the Savannah* (1987) is the subject of Gordimer's essay "To Hold the Yam and the Knife" and the next example of a text that "goes too far" in pursuing unpalatable truths. British imperialism has ended, but the civilian government that replaced it has been overthrown by a military coup. The corruption of this military regime shows the indigenous people behaving worse than their hated foreign masters. When the noble characters are killed off by the villainous in charge, when the people are so brutal that they are able to enjoy public hangings, questions are raised about whether such people are worthy of freedom. Yet Achebe finds a saving remnant of strength and sanity in African traditional culture and people, particularly in their storytelling: The "anthills of the savannah survive to tell the new grass of last year's bush fires," a metaphor that conveys endurance and continuity but does not evade or romanticize the violent realities on the perilous path to tomorrow.

A third novel discussed by Gordimer, in "Forgotten Promised Land," is the Israeli author Amos Oz's *Fima* (1993), set in Israel in 1989. The protagonist Efraim Nisan, or Fima, a shabby Jewish poet, pursues the concealed side of truth in a moral wilderness. The blind self-righteousness of his government, its refusal to acknowledge the rights of the Palestinian Arabs whose land the Israelis occupy, the paranoid reaction to any talk of peace as a Nazi plot aimed at Jewish genocide—all of this gives Fima a bad case of "existential heartburn." Fima sees the irony of his persecuted race's becoming the oppressors, but his father believes that it is fine if the Jews are the Cossacks for a change. Fima wonders, "Is there no way for the Jews to get back onto the stage of history except by becoming scum?" How can it be that pursuing the good can cause enormous evil and pain? Is Zionism itself the sickness? Where is the path to tomorrow? The only thing Fima knows is that we must grasp "as much as we can, or at least . . . grasp our inability to grasp." Again, what Gordimer admires is the novelist's courage in posing difficult questions, his honesty in pursuing the concealed side of truth.

The final and most personal essay in the collection, "That Other World That Was the World," records Gordimer's own search for home. As an English-speaking South African of European descent, she was unable to feel that either England or South Africa was her country. Although educated in the culture of Europe, "that other world" which she believed to be the real world, she felt excluded, too far removed from London or the English countryside. Yet because of apartheid, the vast majority of the people of South Africa were even more remote from her than Europeans. Through her childhood and adolescence, blacks were not part of her consciousness, but in the 1950's she for the first time began to meet black writers and artists in association with a bohemian circle in Johannesburg. This experience marked the beginning of a transformation of consciousness and led to her determination to fight apartheid as writer and as citizen.

Gordimer states that after South Africa left the British Commonwealth in the 1960's, she considered it possible to speak of South Africa as "my country," but she could still not refer to its people as "my people." Despite the fact that she wrote fearlessly, transgressed taboos of color, and risked charges of treason to hide people and help them escape over the borders, it was not enough; it would never be enough until freedom and justice for blacks became a reality under the law. Gordimer was not alone in believing that such a thing could never happen in her lifetime, but in April of 1994, South Africans of all colors elected their first democratic, nonracist government. "It came to pass." Thus did South Africa become for Gordimer "the world, whole, a synthesis," and after years of alienation, she could finally say "my country, my people." She knows her country, and by now it is clear that her country knows her.

Karen A. Kildahl

Sources for Further Study

Booklist. XCII, September 15, 1995, p. 129.
Boston Globe. November 5, 1995, p. 71.
Chicago Tribune. November 5, 1995, XIV, p. 6.
Library Journal. CXX, September 1, 1995, p. 176.
Los Angeles Times Book Review. September 17, 1995, p. 6.
The Nation. CCLXI, October 16, 1995, p. 431.
Publishers Weekly. CCXLII, August 14, 1995, p. 63.
The Spectator. CCLXXV, November 18, 1995, p. 55.
The Times Literary Supplement. December 1, 1995, p. 7.
The Wilson Quarterly. XIX, Autumn, 1995, p. 89.

WRITING WAS EVERYTHING

Author: Alfred Kazin (1915-   )
Publisher: Harvard University Press (Cambridge, Massachusetts). 152 pp. $17.95
Type of work: Memoir; literary criticism

In this memoir, originally presented as the Massey Lectures at Harvard University, Alfred Kazin surveys his literary career and discusses many leading writers of the twentieth century

> *Principal personages:*
> ALFRED KAZIN, an American author and critic
> SAUL BELLOW, a Canadian-born novelist
> HART CRANE, an American poet
> CZESŁAW MIŁOSZ, a Czech poet and Nobel laureate
> EDWIN MUIR, a Scottish poet and translator of Franz Kafka
> FLANNERY O'CONNOR, an American novelist and short-story writer
> GEORGE ORWELL, the British author
> MARK ROTHKO, an American artist
> EDMUND WILSON, an American literary critic

Oscar Wilde observed that criticism is the only civilized form of autobiography, a truth exemplified by Alfred Kazin's work, particularly his first and best book of literary analysis, *On Native Grounds* (1942). Begun when Kazin was only twenty-three and published when he was twenty-seven, the volume discusses American novelists and critics from 1890 to 1940. Yet in a variety of ways *On Native Grounds* is as much about Kazin as it is about William Dean Howells, Hamlin Garland, Ernest Hemingway, Sherwood Anderson, and F. Scott Fitzgerald.

Kazin's choice of American literature as a field of study was itself an expression of his desire, as the son of Jewish immigrants, to belong to the New World. Working in room 315 of the New York Public Library gave him a sense of "a world of power in which my own people had moved about as strangers." In *Writing Was Everything*, Kazin describes reading as Herman Melville did whaling: "my Yale College and my Harvard," not only as places of education but also as institutions offering and signaling membership in the American elite. With equal justice Kazin might have said that reading for him was the equivalent of seafaring for Melville's character Ishmael, who went to sea as Kazin took to books, "whenever it is a damp, drizzly November in my soul. . . . This is my substitute for pistol and ball." As Kazin wrote in *A Walker in the City* (1951), "I read as if books would fill my every gap, legitimize my strange quest for the American past."

A literary radical and, at least in the 1930's, a political radical as well, Kazin harmonized philosophically with many of the figures he described in the opening section of *On Native Grounds*. *Starting Out in the Thirties* (1965) noted that like these American writers, Kazin believed "in the ideal freedom and power of the self, in the political and social vision of radical democracy. It was as if I started from the same human base and was accompanying them to the same imaginative goal." That goal, traced in *On Native Grounds*, expressed Kazin's guarded optimism for the future of

American life and letters. His was, he said, "the immigrants' sense of America—of American history as a process by which the good society might at last be realized." Unlike Irving Kristol and Lionel Trilling, Kazin never abandoned his left-liberal leanings, though the past tense of the verb in *Writing Was Everything* reflects his view that ideologues now threaten literature. He ends *Writing Was Everything* by asking, "But where—how—is the writer to be found who will have the inner certainty to see our life with the eyes of faith, and so make the world shine again?"

Kazin in the 1930's resembled his favorite authors not only in their confidence but also in their sense of alienation. In "The Critic as Creator," he observed that the most important ingredient in his work was "the fact that I was a Jew who grew up in the immigrant world of Brooklyn." In *A Walker in the City*, Kazin contrasted his world of Brooklyn's Brownsville with Manhattan, his Jewish immigrant experience with secular America. Brooklyn Bridge linked not only two boroughs but also two worlds; it is Kazin's central metaphor in his longer autobiographical works, and the image appears in *Writing Was Everything*. Kazin's love of Hart Crane's celebration of the bridge and his appreciation of Walt Whitman—also from Brooklyn and a walker in the city who sang of crossing from Brooklyn to Manhattan—derive from a shared vision of the bridge as a link between self and community, self and other.

While Kazin's criticism thus is autobiographical, his autobiographies, including the present volume, have been exercises in civilized criticism. Ralph Waldo Emerson observed that "an autobiography should be a book of answers from one individual to the many questions of the time"; Kazin's has met that requirement. The autobiographical impulse struck Kazin almost as soon as he had published *On Native Grounds*. In *Harper's* of January, 1971, he recalled stepping out onto a street in Greenwich Village after playing the violin with Isaac Rosenfeld and thinking that he wanted "to write something not in the name of history, but to gratify myself alone. . . . I had written a book but did not yet feel like a writer." The result of this desire was an autobiographical trilogy, *A Walker in the City*, *Starting Out in the Thirties*, and *New York Jew* (1978), covering, respectively, the periods 1915 to 1934, 1934 to 1945, and 1945 to the 1970's. *Writing Was Everything* traverses much the same ground in its three chapters: "Before the War," "During the War," and "After the War." While these chapters may be familiar to previous Kazin readers, even they will welcome these twice-told tales. Newcomers will find Kazin's short book a splendid introduction to the man and his thoughts.

Kazin here begins his narrative in 1934, when he was a junior at City College of New York. In that year he started reviewing books for *The New York Times*, the *New York Herald Tribune*, and *The New Republic*. John Chamberlain gave Kazin a letter of introduction to the literary editor of *The New Republic*, Malcolm Cowley, but Kazin excises Chamberlain from this memoir—a reflection of Kazin's view that Chamberlain lived on ideas but missed "the color and emotion of the human crisis behind them." Kazin describes himself as sitting on the "hungry bench" in the offices of *The New Republic* with other would-be writers and intellectuals waiting to be asked to write 150-word book reviews for the magazine. The original "hungry bench" was the Friday-night gathering place for poor Jews, especially students, in the synagogues of

European shtetls. Kazin's choice of the phrase, like much else in his work, reflects the tension between his desire to join the larger world of American culture and his appreciation for, his sense of need of, his Jewish heritage.

This latter attitude came to Kazin in 1945, perhaps because by then the critical acclaim accorded to *On Native Grounds* allowed him to afford the feeling. Kazin noted that "the war made many of us Jews again." In *Starting Out in the Thirties* and again in *Writing Was Everything*, he tells of sitting in a motion-picture theater in London in the spring of 1945 and seeing the first newsreels from Bergen-Belsen, one of the newly liberated German concentration camps. As Kazin wrote in the earlier book:

> On the screen sticks in black-and-white prison garb leaned on a wire, staring dreamily at the camera; other sticks shuffled about, or sat vaguely on the ground, next to an enormous pile of bodies, piled up like cordwood, from which protruded legs, arms, heads.

This film casts its long shadow onto all of Kazin's subsequent writing, affecting the memories of his childhood as much as it influenced his later work.

The hungry bench provided Kazin with his first connection to the world of American letters. By 1934, Edmund Wilson no longer was literary editor of *The New Republic*, but Wilson influenced Kazin, and Kazin's 1962 volume of literary criticism, *Contemporaries*, is dedicated to this mentor. Kazin is not blind to Wilson's faults. *Writing Was Everything* denies that Wilson was an original thinker and claims that the man could be obstinate, especially in repudiating opinions that he had once espoused. Yet Wilson had the ability to put "a writer into historical perspective, inserting the writer with his book into some great historical drama"—the aim of Kazin's criticism as well.

Another writer whom Kazin met on the hungry bench was the young John Cheever, who had published his first story in *The New Republic* at the age of eighteen. Kazin's skill with the epigram, evident in his first book, remains keen. In *On Native Grounds* Kazin had described Ernest Hemingway as "one of the great half-triumphs of literature"—a phrase that was prescient in 1940 as well as pithy. With similar deftness in *Writing Was Everything* he praises Cheever's ability to create "polite hopelessness."

Kazin's chapter on the war years—mainly 1945, when he visited England and Paris—begins with a discussion of George Orwell, whom Kazin never met. Though Kazin reserves his highest praise not for Orwell's fiction but for the four-volume *The Collected Essays, Journalism and Letters of George Orwell* (1968), he offers illuminating observations about the novels. For example, he notes that descriptions of life in *Nineteen Eighty-four* (1949) derive much of their horrific power from scenes Orwell witnessed in London during World War II: falling bombs, destroyed houses, poverty.

Kazin did meet the Scottish poet Edwin Muir, whose translation of Franz Kafka leads Kazin to reflect on that author. Kazin comments that Kafka's surrealistic world, comic in the 1920's, became the terrible reality of the later twentieth century. In Paris in 1945 Kazin bought a copy of Albert Camus' *L'Etranger* (1942; *The Stranger*, 1946). Kazin admires Camus' philosophical absolutism, a quality he also found in the work of Simone Weil and Jean-Paul Sartre. Kazin suggests that such an attitude is peculiarly European, though Flannery O'Connor and Saul Bellow exhibit a similar trait.

Back in America after the war, Kazin encountered many of the leading literati and artists of the period: Delmore Schwartz, gifted but depressed; the painter Mark Rothko, also talented and unhappy; Robert Lowell. Kazin provides insights into the lives and works of these and other figures whom he knew. He claims, correctly, that Randall Jarrell was a better critic than poet; that Hannah Arendt could never escape the influence of Martin Heidegger despite the latter's acceptance of the Nazism that drove Arendt to America; that Norman Mailer is so fascinated by the corruption and violence of America "that he seems propelled to imitate its every appetite and to ride its roller coaster."

The prologue to the book, "All Critics Are Mortal," assaults the vogue for theory and the overweening pride of scholars such as Jonathan Culler of Cornell University, who claimed in *Framing the Sign* (1988), "Formerly the history of criticism was part of the history of literature (the story of changing conceptions of literature advanced by great writers), but . . . now the history of literature is part of the history of criticism." Despite Kazin's volumes of criticism, he asserted in an interview in *Horizon* (July 4, 1962) that he is a writer, not "a professional scholar or formal academic critic." *Writing Was Everything* insists on the primacy of literature. Kazin quotes Rainer Maria Rilke, who maintained, "Works of art are of an infinite loneliness, and nothing so little as criticism can reach them."

Like all Kazin's other works, *Writing Was Everything* is a work of art. It reveals to the reader the intellectual debates of the 1930's, not unlike those of the 1980's and 1990's; Kazin has no more sympathy with the New Critics of the earlier era than he has with deconstructionists and other theorists who have succeeded them. *Writing Was Everything* presents a panorama of American writers from the 1930's to the 1990's. More important, the book places the reader within the mind of one of America's greatest men of letters. Kazin's "Autobiography as Narrative" (1964) provides an apt epigraph for this book:

> In a society where so many values have been overturned without our admitting it, where there is an obvious gap between the culture we profess and the dangers among which we really live, the autobiographical mode can be an authentic way of establishing the truth of our experience. The individual is real even when the culture around him is not.

Joseph Rosenblum

Sources for Further Study

Boston Globe. August 20, 1995, p. 34.
Los Angeles Times Book Review. August 27, 1995, p. 6.
The New Republic. CCXIII, October 9, 1995, p. 37.
The New York Review of Books. XLII, October 5, 1995, p. 23.
The New York Times Book Review. C, September 3, 1995, p. 6.
The Sewanee Review. CIII, Fall, 1995, p. 661.
The Wilson Quarterly. XIX, Autumn, 1995, p. 89.

ZOLA
A Life

Author: Frederick Brown (1934-   )
Publisher: Farrar Straus Giroux (New York). Illustrated. 888 pp. $37.50
Type of work: Literary biography
Time: 1840-1902
Locale: Paris and Aix-en-Provence, France

A comprehensive biography and literary discussion of the founder of naturalism, who became one of the nineteenth century's most influential literary figures

> *Principal personages:*
> ÉMILE (ÉDOUARD CHARLES ANTOINE) ZOLA, the French novelist whose works helped inspire the naturalist movement in literature
> FRANÇOIS ZOLA, his father, a civil engineer whose untimely death had a profound effect upon Émile's childhood
> PAUL CÉZANNE, the French painter, who was Zola's boyhood companion during their years in Aix-en-Provence
> GUSTAVE FLAUBERT, a French novelist who was one of Zola's early mentors
> ÉDOUARD MANET, the pre-Impressionist painter whose works were championed by Zola
> IVAN SERGEYEVICH TURGENEV, the Russian author, who was an important member of Zola's literary circle in Paris
> (LOUIS MARIE) ALPHONSE DAUDET, an author of humorous sketches of Provençal life who became one of Zola's lifelong friends
> EDMOND LOUIS ANTOINE DE GONCOURT, a French author who praised Zola to his face while angrily accusing him of plagiarism behind his back
> ALFRED DREYFUS, a French army officer who was falsely convicted of treason

Frederick Brown's *Zola: A Life* is a massive work. The product of almost two decades of research, it discusses each of the author's novels in some detail and provides a vivid account of intellectual life in France from the Second Empire through the Third Republic. Where Brown proves to be especially informative is in his account of Zola's relationships with other major authors of his day, including Gustave Flaubert, Alphonse Daudet, Ivan Turgenev, Joris Karl Huysmans, and the Goncourt brothers, Edmond and Jules. The public support and mutual criticism that these authors provided to one another (not infrequently accompanied by private jealousies and secret contempt) gave rise to a burst of creative activity that forever altered the shape of the modern novel.

Brown's approach consists of both historical analysis and traditional literary criticism. He avoids the temptation to practice Zola's own "naturalism" upon his subject, dissecting the author in terms of heredity and psychological peculiarities. Nevertheless, Brown does occasionally speculate about psychological factors that may have affected Zola's idiosyncrasies or his writing. Invariably when this happens, the result is less than convincing and seems somehow incongruous in this otherwise well documented biography. Brown wonders, for example, whether the death of Zola's father may have brought about the novelist's compulsive work habits: perhaps, he continues, Zola harbored an unconscious fear that his talent might vanish as suddenly and inexplicably as his father. Elsewhere, Brown speculates that Zola became involved in the Dreyfus affair—writing an angry newspaper piece accusing the government of conspiracy—in a belated attempt to seek revenge against the same social class that had robbed his mother of her annuity. Fortunately, these arguments, while relatively weak, are also relatively rare. For the most part, Brown presents his readers with a portrait of Zola that is neither tendentious nor simplistic. Brown's Zola is an individual who earns his reputation as a great author but who is also recognizable as a flawed human being.

One of the most useful features of Brown's biography is his summary of nearly every one of Zola's novels. Brown provides an outline of the Rougon-Macquart cycle—much of which was planned by Zola before he even began writing the series—with great attention to detail. The twenty volumes of the Rougon-Macquart novels remained surprisingly faithful to the novelist's initial vision while still permitting his perspective to develop over time. Zola was not above making use of fortuitous situations that had piqued his audience's interest in particular professions or social classes. From these he adapted the subjects for several of his novels. Brown also traces the origin of each of the Rougon-Macquart novels and untangles the complex relationships of Zola's fictitious family. Readers who know this cycle only from selected works in the series will find these portions of Brown's biography to be invaluable.

Brown presents Zola's development of literary "naturalism" as influenced by three major factors. First of all, there were the political upheavals of the mid-nineteenth century, which set republicans and supporters of universal human rights at odds with those who defended religious and social conservatism. The rise of "new ideas" among the political left suggested to Zola that the world needed a new type of fiction, a style of writing that would embody modern, "scientific" views of the human condition. Zola thus placed himself in opposition both to Alexandre Dumas *père*, whose romanticized novels about the aristocracy seemed to champion social conservatism, and to Victor Hugo, who idealized the poor and created sentimental novels about human suffering that ended up doing little to relieve it. In contrast to these authors, Zola envisioned a literature that would embody gritty realism, depicting even human depravity with unflinching candor. If the frothy operettas of Jacques Offenbach represented "gay Paris" at one extreme, Zola chose to reflect the other side of Parisian life, creating in the process a literature that was sober, realistic, and utterly nonjudgmental.

In painting as in literature, Zola preferred truth over beauty. He was among the first supporters of the Impressionistic school, whose focus upon ordinary scenes and everyday people stood in sharp contrast to the academic school of Jean Léon Gérôme, Jean (Louis Ernest) Meissonier, and Adolphe William Bouguereau.

The second factor that Brown presents as contributing to Zola's literary style was his journalistic background. Zola began writing by working for newspapers, supplying them with stories, essays, and social commentaries. Gradually, his contributions began to include satirical character sketches, attempting to capture the personality of an individual in a few succinct phrases. Even in these early works, Zola maintained a preference for stories that dealt with *la bête humaine* (the human beast), a phrase that would become both the title of one of his most famous novels and the theme of the Rougon-Macquart series as a whole. His journalistic training also encouraged Zola to present himself throughout his life as a mere reporter of human activity. Just as he rejected the fanciful novels of Dumas *père*, he also condemned the moralizing fiction of Dumas *fils*, who, he believed, had criticized modern life without ever attempting to understand it fully.

Finally, Brown traces aspects of Zola's literary philosophy to the novelist's compulsive need to write. Zola adopted the Latin phrase *nulla dies sine linea* (no day without a line) as both his personal motto and his fixation. In the twenty-four years that he devoted to the Rougon-Macquart cycle, he produced twenty massive novels, numerous essays, a host of articles, and lengthy letters to his friends. He filled notebook after notebook with studies for future works, detailed descriptions of possible settings, and analyses of the family relations and hereditary factors that would influence all the potential characters of his novels. The attention to exact detail that characterizes Zola's novels resulted, in no small part, from the author's obsessive concern with minutiae and his tendency to catalog nearly everything that he encountered in his reading and in his life.

The irony of Zola's naturalism is, then, that it was not really "natural." It was a studied approach to the world and, in its own way, a highly artificial one. All the information that Zola's novels contain about railroads, department stores, courtesans, Parliament, the mining industry, the Catholic church, the stock exchange, and the like came not from the author's own experiences but from his reading or, even more frequently, from the recollections of his friends and acquaintances. On those occasions when Zola actually visited the locations that would be featured prominently in his novels, he toured them in a day or two, absorbing only the flavor of the sites without taking the time to understand their true character or importance. Zola's novels, Brown concludes, did not embody the life that their author had led but the information that he had taken pains to gather.

The theoretical basis for Zola's naturalism was inspired, at least in part, by a series of lectures titled "Conférences de la rue de la Paix," which were organized by Émile Deschanel during the late 1850's and early 1860's. In these lectures, Deschanel called for the creation of new critical and literary techniques that would parallel the objectivity of the natural sciences. Articulated when Zola had already begun his realistic articles and character sketches, Deschanel's theories encouraged the novelist to continue an approach that had by that time attracted his sympathies. Moreover, the rise of photography (an art that would become one of Zola's passions) inspired the author to create a form of literature that would exactly reproduce the world as he saw it—though only in shades of black and white.

The portrait of Émile Zola that emerges from Brown's biography is of an author who rationally sought to chronicle his times but also of a complex and troubled individual. Brown reveals that Zola was subject to superstitions and compulsive behavior. Believing that even numbers were more perfect and "complete" than odd numbers, Zola would blink precisely seven times each night before falling asleep; with this ritual he hoped to ward off death. As Brown demonstrates, the numerical obsessions that Zola attributes to Lazare Chanteau in *La Joie de vivre* (1884; *Life's Joys*, 1884) were actually derived from the author's own life.

In many of his peculiarities, Zola was very much a man of his time. Like a number of his contemporaries, he was obsessed with his health and filled letters to his friends with details of the complaints that afflicted him. Late in life, he took a mistress, establishing a second household and rearing a secret family. His terror of public speaking, perhaps stemming from a childhood speech defect, made him reluctant to read his works before large groups of people even after his fame had been well established.

Surprisingly, Brown treats Zola's role in the Dreyfus affair in a rather cursory fashion. To some extent, this may be attributable to the biographer's interest in Zola as an author rather than as an historical figure; also Brown may have chosen not to dwell on an episode that has been thoroughly treated by other authors. Nevertheless, in the light of the painstaking detail that Brown devotes to nearly every other aspect of Zola's life, his brief treatment of the Dreyfus affair gives the ending of this biography a feeling of haste, even of anticlimax.

One other criticism of Brown's biography has to do with the author's occasional idiosyncrasy of style. At times, he creates images that are so strained that they divert attention from their subject. Brown describes Zola, for example, as "licking up detail like an aardvark feasting in a termitarium" and compares Henri, count of Chambord, to "a Pirandellian solipsist." The eccentricity and awkwardness of such imagery obscures the central arguments—valid in both cases—that the author is trying to make. Similarly, Brown has a tendency to use unfamiliar words where simple expressions would have served his purposes better. His repeated use of such terms as "tergiversations" (which appears four times in the book!), "gallimaufry," "heresiarch," "kermis," and "causeries" may cause even well-educated readers to scurry for their dictionaries when they should be spending their time enjoying Brown's text.

These few lapses are unfortunate because, for the most part, Brown has created a biography fully worthy of its subject. The Émile Zola whom one encounters in this work is an individual who embodied several of the most important social and artistic forces of the early modern age. His fiction, though it shocked his contemporaries, inspired direct imitations such as Frank Norris' *McTeague* (1899) and also the social realism that pervades twentieth century literature and film.

Jeffrey L. Buller

Sources for Further Study

Booklist. XCI, May 1, 1995, p. 1547.
Commentary. C, November, 1995, p. 124.
Journal of the History of Ideas. LVI, July, 1995, p. 523.
Library Journal. CXX, June 15, 1995, p. 69.
The New Republic. CCXIII, July 31, 1995, p. 36.
The New York Times Book Review. C, June 4, 1995, p. 10.
The New Yorker. LXXI, June 19, 1995, p. 96.
Publishers Weekly. CCXLII, March 13, 1995, p. 52.
The Wall Street Journal. May 9, 1995, p. A18.
The Washington Post Book World. XXV, June 11, 1995, p. 5.

ZORA NEALE HURSTON
Volume I: Novels and Stories
Volume II: Folklore, Memoirs, and Other Writings

Author: Zora Neale Hurston (1891-1960)
Edited, with notes, by Cheryl A. Wall
Publisher: Library of America (New York). 2 volumes. Volume I: 1041 pp., $35.00; Volume II:
1001 pp., $35.00
Type of work: Prose collection

*The Library of America's two-volume collection of all of Zora Neale Hurston's published
books and a selection of her stories and essays solidly establishes her reputation as one of the
twentieth century's most original and influential writers*

It is clear as one reads through these two volumes of Zola Neale Hurston's works
that above all else she valued a good story told in vivid language. The Library of
America's choice of Hurston as the first African American woman to include in its
canon of "America's greatest writers" not only acknowledges the influential position
her work has come to have in the last quarter of the twentieth century but also provides
access to a broad spectrum of her writings, including some that were not always easily
accessible.

Since the late 1970's, Hurston's best-known novel, *Their Eyes Were Watching God*
(1937), has delighted countless readers, been analyzed and deconstructed by numerous
critics, and become a staple of American literature courses. Even the redoubtable
Harold Bloom included the novel as part of his *The Western Canon: The Books and
School of the Ages* (1994). Hurston's other novels and her nonfiction works are much
less celebrated and sometimes puzzled over, especially by critics or champions who
have a particular political or literary point to make. The Library of America's edition
serves to allow the reader to experience a substantial bulk of Hurston's writings and
to understand them in relation to one another. Editor Cheryl Wall's thorough biographical chronology supplements and corrects the "lies" (Hurston's own word for stories)
sometimes found in her autobiography, *Dust Tracks on a Road* (1942). The complexity
of Hurston's experiences and ideas enriches the reader's experience of the individual
works, while definite themes and authorial preoccupations begin to emerge.

Zora Neale Hurston was a self-made woman who probably could not have created
herself had she not grown up in one proud and vibrant community and later been
adopted into another creative and intellectual community. The old African proverb
that it takes a village to raise a child is particularly illustrated in the nurturing of young
Zora in Eatonville, Florida, the first incorporated African American town in the state.
Despite her claim to have been born in Florida in 1901 or 1903, she was actually born
in Georgia, the fifth of seven children of Lucy Ann Potts and John Hurston, who moved
to Eatonville when Zora was three. It was Eatonville, entirely owned and governed by
its citizens, that instilled in Zora her joy in her African American culture and reinforced
the self-confidence that her mother encouraged when she told her daughter to "jump

at de sun." It was to the front porch of Joe Clarke's general store in Eatonville that the Barnard College graduate returned to collect the "lies" that she would publish in *Mules and Men* (1935), her groundbreaking collection of African American folklore, and that she would continue to scatter through her novels and short stories. Eatonville has celebrated its daughter since 1990 with an annual festival in her honor.

Yet it was by leaving Eatonville that Hurston managed to enter a wider world and gain the distance and education that would allow her to become its voice. When Zora was thirteen, her mother died, and she was sent to a secondary school in Jacksonville along with her elder sister. This education abruptly ended when her father remarried and stopped supporting his children. Zora and her younger siblings lived with various relatives until 1915, when she joined a traveling Gilbert and Sullivan troupe as maid to one of the singers. Landing in Baltimore, she attended Morgan Academy and then Howard University, earning an associate degree. After she published a story, "Drenched in Light" (1924), in the literary journal *Opportunity*, its editor, Charles S. Johnson, a leading proponent of the "New Negro" movement, encouraged her to move to New York. In 1925 she followed his advice and moved into the Roaring Twenties, the Jazz Age, and the Harlem Renaissance.

The artists and intellectuals, both black and white, who created and supported the Harlem Renaissance welcomed the audacious Zora Hurston into their community. She became friends with such luminaries as poets Langston Hughes and Countée Cullen, author Carl Van Vechten, and novelist Fannie Hurst, for whom she served as chauffeur for a time. Under the sponsorship of Annie Nathan Meyer, one of the founders of Barnard College, she integrated the college and began to study under and work for Columbia University anthropologist Franz Boas.

The contradictions and correlations between her anthropological training and her artistic sensibilities run through much of her work. Like most significant artists, she is both observer and performer. Hurston's impulse to perform was well noted by her New York associates; Hughes, remarking on the circle of Harlem artists with whom they socialized and worked, said, "Zora Neale Hurston was certainly the most amusing. Only to reach a wider audience, need she ever write books—because she is a perfect book of entertainment in herself." Robert Hemenway, her biographer, has pointed out that her inspiration came from the oral sources of storytelling in Eatonville and that she was the only member of the Harlem Renaissance literati less than a full generation removed from the actual folk traditions they cherished. She understood that the creation of folklore was not a one-time act but a process changing from generation to generation and necessarily involving performance.

Throughout the 1930's, she was involved in the writing and presentation of revues and plays both in New York and in Florida under the auspices of Rollins College in Winter Park. Unfortunately, her ill-fated collaboration with Hughes on a play entitled *Mule Bone* led to the end of their friendship. Although this collection does not include any of Hurston's dramatic pieces, the performance aspect of her art is apparent in her best work.

John Pearson, the protagonist of *Jonah's Gourd Vine* (1934), wears "a cloak of a cloud about his shoulders" when he stands preaching in the pulpit. In *Moses, Man of the Mountain* (1939), Moses succeeds in leading the Hebrews out of Egypt because he can outconjure the magic of Pharaoh's priests. The storytellers on Joe Clarke's porch and in the turpentine camps and "jook joints" of central Florida spun out their tales to the listening anthropologist who remained one of them. The same anthropologist charmed voodoo priests in Haiti and New Orleans into initiating her into their cults, where she participated in magical rituals later recorded in *Tell My Horse* (1938).

Janie, Hurston's beloved protagonist of *Their Eyes Were Watching God*, is celebrated for finding her voice and telling her own life story. The story of Janie Mae Crawford Killicks Starks Woods is that of a woman finding love and self-awareness by daring follow her heart in defiance of social expectations. After two frustrating marriages in which her spirit is "squinched" in patriarchally dominated rituals, she marries Verigible "Tea Cake" Woods, a young gambler fifteen years her junior, who takes her to the Everglades to cut sugar, dance, and make love.

The balance of power in marriage is a central issue in Hurston's four novels and many of her short stories and her essay "Love." In a very significant way it is an issue that Hurston never seems to have satisfactorily resolved either in her fiction or in her life. Even in Janie's happy marriage to Tea Cake, it is Tea Cake who determines how and where they will live. Hurston can visualize Janie's final achievement of independence only by killing off her husband.

The earlier *Jonah's Gourd Vine* fictionalizes the marriage of Hurston's parents, in which a strong woman continued to stand by and support her charismatic but philandering husband until she died, undoubtedly worn out by childbearing and heartbreak. In *Moses, Man of the Mountain*, Moses must leave two marriages behind as he becomes the leader of the Hebrews in their exodus. Although he has no regrets about abandoning a wife chosen for him in Pharaoh's court, he resists leaving the domestic tranquillity he has found with Zipporah. Nevertheless, his ascent to the mountain is a lonely one that cannot encompass a marital partnership.

Seraph on the Suwannee (1948) tells of the troubled marriage between Arvay Henson, a poor white "cracker," and Jim Meserve, an impoverished descendant of southern aristocracy who succeeds in the New South. Jim declares to Arvay when he courts her, "Lady folks were just made to laugh and act loving and kind and have a good man to do for them all he's like to have, and make him so happy that he's willing to work and fetch in every dad-blamed thing that his wife thinks she would like to have. That's what women are made for." Arvay tries to fulfill his expectations but finally realizes that Jim wants something more—praise and appreciation for all that he has done for her. The novel ends with her realization that her job is mothering—she has mothered her children to success, and now "Jim was hers and it was her privilege to serve him. To keep on like that in happiness and peace until they died together, giving Jim the hovering that he needed."

Hurston's last novel has been most problematic for critics, first because she leaves her customary milieu of African American experience, and second because of the highly traditional resolution reached by Arvay in the novel. Yet when one takes *Seraph on the Suwannee* in the context of the rest of her fiction, it becomes clear that Hurston could not visualize a marriage in which a woman could remain independent *and* find happiness beyond the first romantic flush. Her own experience gave her no models—her two marriages to men whom by all accounts she loved and delighted in were very brief—ending because she could not give up her field work and take on the role of wife. Hurston described what she knew, what she observed from the life around her—she did not create idealistic or ideological models to be followed. She shaped her own life and perhaps left Janie Crawford at the end of *Their Eyes Were Watching God* to shape hers as well, but such a life required self-empowerment and independence.

Hurston explored power in a variety of venues. Her conservative political views are revealed in her depiction of those who achieve power in leadership, creativity, or even generosity as targets of jealousy and belittlement from those who do not have the courage to take the same risks. Power also resides in cunning and cleverness; thus her favorite slave hero, High John de Conqueror, who traveled from Africa to keep his people's hope and spirit alive, inevitably makes a fool of Ole Massa and even manages to trick the Devil himself.

The power of spirituality was another of Hurston's major interests. Her folklore studies led her into the religious beliefs practiced in African American churches and rituals. Her belief that the rituals of African pagan religions were embedded in Christianity led her to the West Indies, where she studied Haitian voodoo and the Pocomania cult in Jamaica. *Tell My Horse* (the title refers to the spirits who possess believers by "riding" their hosts) pioneered studies in African Caribbean American cross-cultural institutions. Although her life and work were drenched with religious experience, Hurston in the chapter titled "Religion" in *Dust Tracks on a Road* declares her allegiance to no particular church or divinity:

> So I do not pray. I accept the means at my disposal for working out my destiny. It seems to me that I have been given a mind and will-power for that very purpose. . . . I accept the challenge of responsibility. Life as it is, does not frighten me, since I have made my peace with the universe as I find it, and bow to its laws. . . . Why fear? The stuff of my being is matter, ever changing, ever moving, but never lost; so what need of denominations and creeds to deny myself the comfort of all my fellow men? The wide belt of the universe has no need for finger-rings. I am one with the infinite and need no other assurance.

Finally, at the core of Hurston's work is a recognition of a universal existential loneliness beyond racial or gender distinctions and assumptions—a realization that the choices one makes to become great or to exercise one's creativity, or even to find some kind of knowledge of oneself, will necessarily make one an outsider simply because of one's own awareness.

Jane Anderson Jones

Sources for Further Study

Booklist. XCI, February 15, 1995, p. 1034.
Chicago Tribune. February 26, 1995, XIV, p. 1.
Houston Post. March 19, 1995, p. G11.
Library Journal. CXX, February 1, 1995, p. 104.
National Review. XLVII, April 3, 1995, p. 58.
The New Republic. CCXIII, July 3, 1995, p. 30.
Newsweek. CXXV, February 13, 1995, p. 81.
San Francisco Chronicle. March 19, 1995, p. REV9.
U.S. News and World Report. CLXXXVIII, February 20, 1995, p. 75.
The Washington Post Book World. XXV, March 5, 1995, p. 4.
Women's Review of Books. XIII, November, 1995, p. 28.

MAGILL'S
LITERARY ANNUAL
1996

BIOGRAPHICAL WORKS BY SUBJECT
1977-1996

859

BIOGRAPHICAL WORKS BY SUBJECT

867

BIOGRAPHICAL WORKS BY SUBJECT

SARRAUTE, NATHALIE
Childhood (Sarraute) (85) 89
SARTON, MAY
World of Light, A (Sarton) (77) 941
SARTRE, JEAN-PAUL
Adieux (Beauvoir) (85) 1
Hearts and Minds (Madsen) (78) 379
Letters to Sartre (Beauvoir) (93) 449
Life/Situations (Sartre) (78) 529
Sartre (Cohen-Solal) (88) 795
War Diaries (Sartre) (86) 932
SAVAGE, RICHARD
Dr. Johnson and Mr. Savage (Holmes) (95) 176
SCHAPIRO, MIRIAM
Working It Out (Ruddick and Daniels, eds.) (78) 937
SCHIESLER, M. ANTOINETTE
I've Known Rivers (Lawrence-Lightfoot) (95) 384
SCHOENBRUN, DAVID
America Inside Out (Schoenbrun) (H-85) 22
SCHOPENHAUER, ARTHUR
Schopenhauer and the Wild Years of Philosophy (Safranski) (91) 711
SCHORER, MARK
Pieces of Life (Schorer) (78) 657
SCHWARTZ, DELMORE
Delmore Schwartz (Atlas) (78) 249
Letters of Delmore Schwartz (Schwartz) (85) 548
Poets in Their Youth (Simpson) (83) 608
SCOTT, WALTER
Walter Scott (Millgate) (85) 989
SEARS, CYNTHIA LOVELACE
Working It Out (Ruddick and Daniels, eds.) (78) 937
SEE, CAROLYN LAWS
On Gold Mountain (See) (96) 523
SEE, EDDY (MING QUAN)
On Gold Mountain (See) (96) 523
SEE, FONG
On Gold Mountain (See) (96) 523
SEE, LETTICIE (TICIE) PRUETT
On Gold Mountain (See) (96) 523
SEE, LISA
On Gold Mountain (See) (96) 523
SEE, RICHARD
On Gold Mountain (See) (96) 523
SELZER, RICHARD
Down from Troy (Selzer) (93) 244
SENGHOR, LÉOPOLD SÉDAR
Black, French, and African (Vaillant) (91) 80
SÉVIGNÉ, MADAME DE
Madame de Sévigné (Mossiker) (85) 595
SEXTON, ANNE
Anne Sexton (Middlebrook) (92) 21
Anne Sexton (Sexton) (78) 54
SHACKLETON, ERNEST
Shackleton (Huntford) (87) 765
SHAKESPEAR, DOROTHY
Ezra Pound and Dorothy Shakespear, Their Letters, 1909-1914 (Pound and Shakespear) (85) 243
SHAKESPEARE, WILLIAM
Real Shakespeare, The (Sams) (96) 619
Shakespeare (Fraser) (93) 723

Shakespeare's Professional Career (Thomson) (93) 728
Young Shakespeare (Fraser) (89) 933
SHAW, GEORGE BERNARD
Bernard Shaw, 1856-1898 (Holroyd) (89) 89
Bernard Shaw, 1898-1918 (Holroyd) (90) 63
Bernard Shaw, 1918-1950 (Holroyd) (92) 34
Bernard Shaw, 1950-1991 (Holroyd) (94) 80
Bernard Shaw (Shaw) (89) 84
SHAW, ROBERT GOULD
Blue-Eyed Child of Fortune (Shaw) (93) 91
SHEED, WILFRID
Frank and Maisie (Sheed) (86) 313
SHELLEY, MARY WOLLSTONECRAFT
Claire Clairmont and the Shelleys, 1798-1879 (Gittings and Manton) (93) 157
Footsteps (Holmes) (86) 297
Letters of Mary Wollstonecraft Shelley, Vol. I, The (Shelley) (81) 501
SHELLEY, PERCY BYSSHE
Claire Clairmont and the Shelleys, 1798-1879 (Gittings and Manton) (93) 157
Footsteps (Holmes) (86) 297
SHOSTAKOVICH, DMITRI
Testimony (Shostakovich) (80) 808
SIDNEY, SIR PHILIP
Sir Philip Sidney (Duncan-Jones) (92) 761
SIMON, HERBERT
Models of My Life (Simon) (92) 519
SIMON, KATE
Bronx Primitive (Simon) (83) 80
Wider World, The (Simon) (87) 985
SIMPSON, EILEEN
Poets in Their Youth (Simpson) (83) 608
SINGER, ISAAC BASHEVIS
Lost in America (Singer) (82) 485
SIRICA, JOHN J.
To Set the Record Straight (Sirica) (80) 822
SITWELL, EDITH
Edith Sitwell (Glendinning) (82) 190
SITWELLS, THE
Sitwells, The (Pearson) (80) 763
SMITH, DAVID
World Unsuspected, A (Harris, ed.) (88) 984
SMITH, FLORENCE MARGARET "STEVIE"
Stevie (Barbera and McBrien) (88) 860
SOCRATES
Socrates (Vlastos) (92) 766
SOLZHENITSYN, ALEXANDER
Solzhenitsyn (Scammell) (85) 839
Solzhenitsyn and the Modern World (Ericson) (94) 751
Solzhenitsyn in Exile (Dunlop, Haugh, and Nicholson, eds.) (86) 843
SOONG, CHARLIE
Soong Dynasty, The (Seagrave) (86) 852
SOREL, GEORGES
Cult of Violence, The (Roth) (81) 215
SOTO, GARY
Summer Life, A (Soto) (91) 782
SOUTHERLAND, ELLEASE
World Unsuspected, A (Harris, ed.) (88) 984
SOYINKA, WOLE
Aké (Soyinka) (83) 10
SPARK, MURIEL
Curriculum Vitae (Spark) (94) 196

CATEGORY INDEX

1977-1996

ANTHROPOLOGY. *See* SOCIOLOGY,
ARCHAEOLOGY, and ANTHROPOLOGY

ARCHAEOLOGY. *See* SOCIOLOGY,
ARCHAEOLOGY, and ANTHROPOLOGY

AUTOBIOGRAPHY, MEMOIRS, DIARIES, and
LETTERS
Abba Eban (Eban) (78) 1
Adieux (Beauvoir) (85) 1
Aké (Soyinka) (83) 10
Akhmatova Journals, 1938-41, The (Chukovskaya)
(95) 19
Albert Einstein (Einstein) (80) 19
All God's Children Need Traveling Shoes (Angelou)
(87) 25
All Rivers Run to the Sea (Wiesel) (96) 18
Always Straight Ahead (Neuman) (94) 11
America Inside Out (Schoenbrun) (H-85) 22
American Childhood, An (Dillard) (88) 25
American Life, An (Reagan) (91) 24
And the Walls Came Tumbling Down (Abernathy)
(90) 39
Anne Sexton (Sexton) (78) 54
Another World, 1897-1917 (Eden) (78) 59
Answer to History (Mohammad Reza Pahlavi) (81) 47
Antonin Artaud (Artaud) (77) 52
Arna Bontemps-Langston Hughes Letters, 1925-1927
(Bontemps and Hughes) (81) 57
Around the Day in Eighty Worlds (Cortázar) (87) 45
Arrivals and Departures (Rovere) (77) 62
As I Saw It (Rusk) (91) 56
Asking for Trouble (Woods) (82) 28
Assault on Mount Helicon (Barnard) (85) 27
Atlantic High (Buckley) (83) 29
Autobiography of a Face (Grealy) (95) 56
Autobiography of Values (Lindbergh) (79) 43
Becoming a Doctor (Konner) (88) 77
Becoming a Man (Monette) (93) 62
Berlin Diaries, 1940-1945 (Vassiltchikov) (88) 95
Bernard Shaw, 1856-1898 (Holroyd) (89) 89
Bernard Shaw, Collected Letters, 1926-1950 (Shaw)
(89) 84

Better Class of Person, A (Osborne) (82) 45
Between Friends (Arendt and McCarthy) (96) 73
Beyond the Dragon's Mouth (Naipaul) (86) 56
Blessings in Disguise (Guinness) (87) 71
Blind Ambition (Dean) (77) 96
Bloods (Terry) (H-85) 48
Blooming (Toth) (82) 55
Blue-Eyed Child of Fortune (Duncan, ed.) (93) 91
Born on the Fourth of July (Kovic) (77) 115
Borrowed Time (Monette) (89) 112
Boston Boy (Hentoff) (87) 84
Boswell (Boswell) (78) 140
Breaking Ranks (Podhoretz) (80) 101
Breaking with Moscow (Shevchenko) (86) 81
Broken Cord, The (Dorris) (90) 76
Bronx Primitive (Simon) (83) 80
Brothers and Keepers (Wideman) (85) 57
Byron's Letters and Journals, 1822-1823 (Byron)
(81) 108
Cassandra (Wolf) (85) 74
Chance Meetings (Saroyan) (79) 92
Chief, The (Morrow) (86) 121
Childhood (Sarraute) (85) 89
China Men (Kingston) (81) 137
Chinabound (Fairbank) (H-83) 61
Christopher and His Kind (Isherwood) (77) 158
Clear Pictures (Price) (90) 104
Clinging to the Wreckage (Mortimer) (83) 127
Cloak of Light, A (Morris) (86) 140
Collected Letters, 1911-1925 (Shaw) (86) 145
Collected Letters of Dylan Thomas, The (Thomas)
(87) 132
Collected Letters of Joseph Conrad, 1861-1897, The
(Conrad) (84) 178
Collected Letters of Joseph Conrad, 1898-1902, The
(Conrad) (87) 138
Collected Letters of Joseph Conrad, 1903-1907, The
(Conrad) (89) 175
Collected Letters of Katherine Mansfield, 1903-1917,
The (Mansfield) (85) 106
Collected Letters of Katherine Mansfield, 1918-1919,
The (Mansfield) (88) 165
Collected Letters of W. B. Yeats, 1865-1895, The
(Yeats) (87) 142

CATEGORY INDEX

CATEGORY INDEX

CATEGORY INDEX

CURRENT AFFAIRS and SOCIAL ISSUES

CATEGORY INDEX

CATEGORY INDEX

CATEGORY INDEX

CATEGORY INDEX

CATEGORY INDEX

CATEGORY INDEX

CATEGORY INDEX

903

CATEGORY INDEX

905

CATEGORY INDEX

CATEGORY INDEX

CATEGORY INDEX

PSYCHOLOGY

RELIGION. *See* PHILOSOPHY and RELIGION

SCIENCE, HISTORY OF SCIENCE, and TECHNOLOGY

CATEGORY INDEX

TITLE INDEX
1977-1996

921

TITLE INDEX

TITLE INDEX

TITLE INDEX

TITLE INDEX

TITLE INDEX

Joe (Brown) (92) 384
Joe Papp (Epstein) (95) 396
John Adams (Ferling) (93) 413
John Calvin (Bouwsma) (88) 433
John Cheever (Donaldson) (89) 422
John Cheever (Hunt) (84) 389
John D. (Hawke) (81) 459
John Dewey and American Democracy (Westbrook) (92) 388
John Dewey and the High Tide of American Liberalism (Ryan) (96) 393
John Dickinson (Flower) (H-84) 248
John Dollar (Wiggins) (90) 454
John Dos Passos (Ludington) (81) 464
John Dryden and His World (Winn) (88) 438
John Foster Dulles (Pruessen) (H-83) 229
John Henry Newman (Ker) (90) 459
John L. Lewis (Dubofsky and Van Tine) (78) 478
John Maynard Keynes (Hession) (H-85) 250
John Maynard Keynes (Skidelsky) (95) 400
John Ruskin, 1819-1859 (Hilton) (86) 487
John Steinbeck (Parini) (96) 398
Joke, The (Kundera) (83) 363
Jorge Luis Borges (Monegal) (80) 444
Joseph Brodsky and the Creation of Exile (Bethea) (95) 404
Joseph Conrad (Karl) (80) 449
Joseph Conrad (Najder) (84) 395
Joseph Conrad (Tennant) (82) 412
Joseph Cornell's Theater of the Mind (Cornell) (95) 408
Josephine Herbst (Langer) (85) 499
Journals (Ginsberg) (78) 483
Journals, 1939-1983 (Spender) (87) 446
Journals of Denton Welch, The (Welch) (85) 504
Journals of John Cheever, The (Cheever) (92) 393
Journals of Sylvia Plath, The (Plath) (83) 367
Journals of Thornton Wilder, 1939-1961, The (Wilder) (86) 491
Journey for Our Times, A (Salisbury) (H-84) 252
Journey into Space (Murray) (90) 464
Journey to the Sky (Highwater) (79) 335
Journey to the West, Vol. IV, The (Wu Ch'êng-ên) (84) 401
Joy Luck Club, The (Tan) (90) 468
Joyce's Book of the Dark (Bishop) (88) 443
Joyce's Dislocutions (Senn) (85) 509
Joyce's Voices (Kenner) (79) 340
J. P. Morgan (Jackson) (H-84) 257
Jubal Sackett (L'Amour) (86) 496
Jubilation (Tomlinson) (96) 403
Julip (Harrison) (95) 413
Julius Streicher (Bytwerk) (H-83) 234
July's People (Gordimer) (82) 417
Jump (Gordimer) (92) 398
Just Above My Head (Baldwin) (80) 456
Just Representations (Cozzens) (79) 343
Justice at Nuremberg (Conot) (H-84) 261
Justice Crucified (Feuerlicht) (78) 487
Justice Oliver Wendell Holmes (White) (94) 431

Kafka (Hayman) (83) 372
Karl Marx (Padover) (79) 349
Kate Chopin (Toth) (91) 475
Kate Vaiden (Price) (87) 451
Katerina (Appelfeld) (93) 418
Katherine Anne Porter (Givner) (83) 376
Katherine Mansfield (Tomalin) (89) 427
Kay Boyle (Mellen) (95) 417
Keep the Change (McGuane) (90) 473
Keeping Faith (Carter) (H-83) 239
Kennedy and Roosevelt (Beschloss) (81) 467
Kennedy Imprisonment, The (Wills) (H-83) 244
Kenneth Burke (Henderson) (90) 478
Kentucky Straight (Offutt) (93) 422
Keywords (Williams) (77) 388
Khodasevich (Bethea) (84) 408
Khrushchev (Medvedev) (H-84) 266
Khubilai Khan (Rossabi) (89) 432
Killing Ground, The (Settle) (83) 381
Killing Mister Watson (Matthiessen) (91) 480
Killshot (Leonard) (90) 482
Kindly Inquisitors (Rauch) (94) 436
Kindness of Strangers, The (Boswell) (90) 486
Kinflicks (Alther) (77) 391
King, The (Barthelme) (91) 485
King Edward VIII (Ziegler) (92) 403
King of Children, The (Lifton) (89) 436
King of Inventors, The (Peters) (94) 440
King of Ragtime (Berlin) (95) 422
King of the Fields, The (Singer) (89) 441
King of the Jews (Epstein) (80) 458
King of the World (Gerber) (91) 489
Kingfisher, The (Clampitt) (84) 413
Kings of Cocaine (Gugliotta and Leen) (90) 490
King's Way, The (Chandernagor) (85) 515
Kissinger (Isaacson) (93) 426
Kitchen (Yoshimoto) (94) 445
Kitchen God's Wife, The (Tan) (92) 408
Kith (Newby) (78) 491
Kleist (Maass) (84) 418
Knight, Death, and the Devil, The (Leffland) (91) 493
Knocking on the Door (Paton) (77) 396
Knowing When to Stop (Rorem) (95) 427
Kolyma (Conquest) (79) 354
Korean War, The (Hastings) (88) 447
Krazy Kat (Cantor) (89) 445
Krik? Krak! (Danticat) (96) 406
Krippendorf's Tribe (Parkin) (87) 456
Kronstadt, 1917-1921 (Getzler) (H-84) 271

Labors of Love (Cassill) (81) 471
Labyrinth of Exile, The (Pawel) (90) 495
Ladder of Years (Tyler) (96) 410
Lady from Dubuque, The (Albee) (81) 475
Lady of Situations, The (Auchincloss) (91) 498
Lady Oracle (Atwood) (77) 400
Lafayette (Buckman) (78) 495
Lake Wobegon Days (Keillor) (86) 500
Lamplit Answer, The (Schnackenberg) (86) 505

939

TITLE INDEX

Miss Herbert (Stead) (77) 509
Missed Connections (Ford) (84) 552
Missing Measures (Steele) (91) 601
Missing Persons and Other Essays (Böll) (78) 577
Mr. Bedford and the Muses (Godwin) (84) 556
Mr. Cogito (Herbert) (94) 530
Mr. Happiness *and* The Water Engine (Mamet) (79) 828
Mr. Ives' Christmas (Hijuelos) (96) 461
Mr. Madison's War (Stagg) (H-84) 303
Mr. Mani (Yehoshua) (93) 527
Mr Noon (Lawrence) (85) 619
Mr. Palomar (Calvino) (86) 620
Mr. Summer's Story (Süskind) (94) 535
Mistress Anne (Erickson) (H-85) 319
Mrs. Jordan's Profession (Tomalin) (96) 465
Mrs. Ted Bliss (Elkin) (96) 469
Mists of Avalon, The (Bradley) (84) 561
Model World, A (Chabon) (92) 514
Models of My Life (Simon) (92) 519
Modern American Religion, 1919-1941 (Marty) (92) 524
Modern European Thought (Baumer) (78) 581
Modern Greek Poetry (Keeley) (85) 624
Modern Ireland (Foster) (90) 573
Modern Irish Literature (Mercier) (95) 495
Modern Japanese Poets and the Nature of Literature (Ueda) (84) 566
Modern Poetic Sequence, The (Rosenthal and Gall) (84) 570
Modern Times (Johnson) (H-84) 306
Modernist Quartet (Lentricchia) (95) 499
Moksha (Huxley) (79) 451
Mom Kills Kids and Self (Saperstein) (80) 541
Moment of True Feeling, A (Handke) (78) 585
Momo (Ajar) (79) 454
Money (Amis) (86) 624
Mongoose, R.I.P. (Buckley) (88) 574
Monkeys (Minot) (87) 557
Monkey's Wrench, The (Levi) (87) 564
Monolithos (Gilbert) (83) 484
Monsignor Quixote (Greene) (83) 489
Montgomery Clift (Bosworth) (79) 457
Montgomery's Children (Perry) (85) 629
Monty (Hamilton) (82) 531
Moo (Smiley) (96) 473
Moon Crossing Bridge (Gallagher) (93) 532
Moon Deluxe (Barthelme) (84) 576
Moon Pinnace, The (Williams) (87) 568
Moon Tiger (Lively) (89) 558
Moonrise, Moonset (Konwicki) (88) 579
Moons of Jupiter, The (Munro) (84) 580
Moor's Last Sigh, The (Rushdie) (96) 478
Moortown (Hughes) (81) 569
Moral Animal, The (Wright) (95) 504
Moral Life of Children, The (Coles) (87) 573
Moral Sense, The (Wilson) (94) 539
Morality, Reason, and Power (Smith) (87) 577
More Collected Stories (Pritchett) (84) 584
More Die of Heartbreak (Bellow) (88) 583

More Perfect Union, A (Peters) (88) 589
More than Cool Reason (Lakoff and Turner) (90) 578
Morgan's Passing (Tyler) (81) 573
Morning of the Poem, The (Schuyler) (81) 578
Mornings Like This (Dillard) (96) 482
Mornings on Horseback (McCullough) (82) 537
Mortal Acts, Mortal Words (Kinnell) (81) 582
Mortal Friends (Carroll) (79) 462
Mortal Hero, The (Schein) (85) 635
Moshe Dayan (Dayan) (77) 513
Mosquito Coast, The (Theroux) (83) 496
Mosquitoes, Malaria and Man (Harrison) (79) 466
Most Beautiful House in the World, The (Rybczynski) (90) 582
Mostly Morgenthaus (Morgenthau) (92) 529
Mother and Two Daughters, A (Godwin) (83) 501
Mother Country (Robinson) (90) 586
Mother Love (Dove) (96) 486
Mount Eagle (Montague) (90) 591
Mountain of Fame (Wills) (95) 509
Mountbatten (Hough) (82) 542
Mountbatten (Ziegler) (86) 629
Mousetrap and Other Plays, The (Christie) (79) 470
Move Your Shadow (Lelyveld) (86) 635
Moving Target, A (Golding) (83) 506
Mozart (Solomon) (96) 490
Mozart in Vienna, 1781-1791 (Braunbehrens) (91) 606
M31 (Wright) (89) 562
Mulligan Stew (Sorrentino) (80) 544
Mungo Park the African Traveler (Lupton) (80) 550
Munich (Taylor) (80) 555
Munich 1923 (Dornberg) (H-83) 298
Murrow (Sperber) (87) 582
Murther and Walking Spirits (Davies) (92) 535
Muse Learns to Write, The (Havelock) (87) 590
Museum of Clear Ideas, The (Hall) (94) 543
Music of What Happens, The (Vendler) (89) 566
Music Room, The (McFarland) (91) 610
Muslim Discovery of Europe, The (Lewis) (H-83) 303
Mussolini (Mack Smith) (H-83) 308
Mussolini's Roman Empire (Mack Smith) (77) 520
My Alexandria (Doty) (94) 547
My American Journey (Powell, with Persico) (96) 494
My Century (Wat) (89) 571
My Father's Island (Angermeyer) (91) 614
My Name Is Saroyan (Saroyan) (84) 588
My Own Country (Verghese) (95) 515
My Son's Story (Gordimer) (91) 619
My Traitor's Heart (Malan) (91) 624
Myself with Others (Fuentes) (89) 577
Mysteries of Motion (Calisher) (84) 593
Mysteries of Pittsburgh, The (Chabon) (89) 581
Mysteries of Winterthurn (Oates) (85) 640
Mysterious History of Columbus, The (Wilford) (92) 540
Mystery to a Solution, The (Irwin) (95) 519
Mystic Chords of Memory (Kammen) (92) 545
Myth Makers, The (Pritchett) (80) 560

TITLE INDEX

TITLE INDEX

AUTHOR INDEX

1977-1996

AUTHOR INDEX

AUTHOR INDEX

967

CHANG, JUNG
  Wild Swans (92) 894
CHAPPELL, FRED
  Bloodfire (79) 60
  Earthsleep (81) 264
  Wind Mountain (80) 877
CHARTIER, ROGER
  History of Private Life, Passions of the
    Renaissance, A (90) 386
  Order of Books, The (95) 582
CHASE, JOAN
  During the Reign of the Queen of Persia (84) 252
CHATWIN, BRUCE
  On the Black Hill (84) 638
  Songlines, The (88) 840
  Utz (90) 835
  What Am I Doing Here (90) 874
CHEEVER, JOHN
  Falconer (78) 309
  Journals of John Cheever, The (92) 393
  Letters of John Cheever, The (89) 480
  Oh What a Paradise It Seems (83) 558
  Stories of John Cheever, The (79) 713
CHEEVER, SUSAN
  Home Before Dark (85) 405
CHERNOW, RON
  House of Morgan, The (91) 432
CHERRY, KELLY
  Relativity (78) 700
CHIAROMONTE, NICOLA
  Worm of Consciousness and Other Essays, The
    (77) 956
CHICKERING, ROGER
  We Men Who Feel Most German (H-85) 479
CHING, FRANK
  Ancestors (89) 19
CHISHOLM, ANNE, and MICHAEL DAVIE
  Lord Beaverbrook (94) 488
CHOMSKY, NOAM
  Reflections on Language (77) 668
CHRISTIAN, SHIRLEY
  Nicaragua (86) 655
CHRISTIANSON, GALE E.
  In the Presence of the Creator (H-85) 236
CHRISTIE, AGATHA
  Mousetrap and Other Plays, The (79) 470
CHUKOVSKAYA, LYDIA
  Akhmatova Journals, 1938-41, The (95) 19
CHURCHLAND, PAUL M.
  Engine of Reason, the Seat of the Soul, The
    (96) 232
CHUTE, CAROLYN
  Letourneau's Used Auto Parts (89) 460
CISNEROS, SANDRA
  Woman Hollering Creek (92) 909
CLAMPITT, AMY
  Kingfisher, The (84) 413
  Silence Opens, A (95) 713
CLARK, KATERINA, and MICHAEL HOLQUIST
  Mikhail Bakhtin (86) 608
CLARK, RONALD W.
  Benjamin Franklin (H-84) 54
  Edison (78) 284
  Freud (81) 357
  Greatest Power on Earth, The (82) 343
  Life of Bertrand Russell, The (77) 423

CLARK, TOM
  Charles Olson (92) 88
CLARKE, ARTHUR C.
  2010 (83) 844
CLARKE, AUSTIN
  Selected Poems (77) 715
CLARKE, GERALD
  Capote (89) 135
CLARKE, JAMES W.
  American Assassins (H-83) 37
CLARY, KILLARNEY
  Who Whispered Near Me (90) 889
CLECAK, PETER
  America's Quest for the Ideal Self (H-84) 16
CLEMENS, SAMUEL LANGHORNE. See TWAIN,
  MARK
CLENDINNEN, INGA
  Aztecs (92) 30
CLIFFORD, CLARK, with RICHARD HOLBROOKE
  Counsel to the President (92) 123
CLIFTON, LUCILLE
  Generations (77) 318
COCHRAN, THOMAS C.
  Frontiers of Change (82) 301
COETZEE, J. M.
  Age of Iron (91) 5
  Foe (88) 334
  Life & Times of Michael K (84) 455
  Master of Petersburg, The (95) 469
COFER, JUDITH ORTIZ
  Latin Deli, The (94) 454
COGGINS, JACK
  Campaign for North Africa, The (81) 113
COHEN, LEONARD
  Stranger Music (94) 764
COHEN, MORTON N.
  Lewis Carroll (96) 422
COHEN, STEPHEN S., and JOHN ZYSMAN
  Manufacturing Matters (88) 529
COHEN-SOLAL, ANNIE
  Sartre (88) 795
COLE, WAYNE S.
  Roosevelt and the Isolationists (H-84) 382
COLEBROOK, JOAN
  House of Trees, A (88) 403
COLES, ROBERT
  Call of Stories, The (90) 81
  Dorothy Day (88) 252
  Flannery O'Connor's South (81) 350
  Moral Life of Children, The (87) 573
  Political Life of Children, The (87) 665
COLETTE
  Collected Stories of Colette, The (84) 194
COLIN, AMY
  Paul Celan (92) 619
COLINVAUX, PAUL
  Why Big Fierce Animals Are Rare (79) 857
COLLEY, LINDA
  Britons (93) 105
COLLIER, PETER, and DAVID HOROWITZ
  Destructive Generation (90) 168
  Roosevelts, The (95) 664
COLLINS, MICHAEL
  Liftoff (89) 506

AUTHOR INDEX

AUTHOR INDEX

DURANT, WILL, and ARIEL DURANT
Age of Napoleon, The (77) 33
Dual Autobiography, A (78) 280
DURAS, MARGUERITE
Lover, The (86) 547
War, The (87) 941
DURRELL, LAWRENCE
Sicilian Carousel (78) 771
DYBEK, STUART
Coast of Chicago, The (91) 142
DYSON, FREEMAN J.
Infinite in All Directions (89) 381

EAGLETON, TERRY
Literary Theory (84) 464
EARLY, GERALD
One Nation Under a Groove (96) 537
EATON, CLEMENT
Jefferson Davis (78) 464
EBAN, ABBA
Abba Eban (78) 1
New Diplomacy, The (H-84) 317
EBERHART, RICHARD
Of Poetry and Poets (80) 610
EBERSTADT, FERNANDA
Isaac and His Devils (92) 359
Low Tide (86) 551
ECKHOLM, ERIK P.
Losing Ground (77) 450
ECO, UMBERTO
Foucault's Pendulum (90) 277
Interpretation and Overinterpretation (93) 390
Island of the Day Before, The (96) 385
Name of the Rose, The (84) 598
Postscript to *The Name of the Rose* (85) 697
Search for the Perfect Language, The (96) 680
Semiotics and the Philosophy of Language
(85) 807
EDEL, LEON
Bloomsbury (80) 88
Stuff of Sleep and Dreams (83) 765
EDEN, ANTHONY
Another World, 1897-1917 (78) 59
EDEY, MAITLAND A., and DONALD C.
JOHANSON
Lucy (82) 514
EDMUNDS, R. DAVID
Shawnee Prophet, The (H-84) 409
EDWARDS, G. B.
Book of Ebenezer Le Page, The (82) 59
EDWARDS, MARK W.
Homer (88) 398
EGERTON, DOUGLAS R.
Gabriel's Rebellion (94) 325
EHRENPREIS, IRVIN
Swift, the Man, His Works, and the Age, Vol. III
(84) 849
EHRLICH, GRETEL
Islands, the Universe, Home (92) 364
Solace of Open Spaces, The (86) 840
EHRLICHMAN, JOHN
Witness to Power (H-83) 473
EIKENBAUM, BORIS
Tolstoi in the Seventies (83) 821
Tolstoi in the Sixties (83) 816

EINSTEIN, ALBERT
Albert Einstein (80) 19
EISENBERG, DEBORAH
Transactions in a Foreign Currency (87) 881
Under the 82nd Airborne (93) 829
EISENHOWER, DAVID
Eisenhower, at War (87) 226
EISENHOWER, DWIGHT DAVID
Eisenhower Diaries, The (82) 199
EISENHOWER, JOHN S. D.
Allies (H-83) 20
ELDREDGE, NILES
Dominion (96) 198
ELEY, GEOFF
Reshaping the German Right (81) 682
ELIADE, MIRCEA
Ordeal by Labyrinth (83) 572
ELIOT, T. S.
Letters of T. S. Eliot, The (89) 488
ELKIN, STANLEY
George Mills (83) 273
MacGuffin, The (92) 465
Mrs. Ted Bliss (96) 469
Pieces of Soap (93) 629
Rabbi of Lud, The (88) 715
Van Gogh's Room at Arles (94) 831
ELKINS, STANLEY, and ERIC McKITRICK
Age of Federalism, The (94) 5
ELLEDGE, SCOTT
E. B. White (85) 209
ELLISON, RALPH
Collected Essays of Ralph Ellison, The (96) 128
Going to the Territory (87) 331
ELLMANN, RICHARD
a long the riverrun (90) 1
Oscar Wilde (89) 630
EMERSON, CARYL, and GARY SAUL MORSON
Mikhail Bakhtin (92) 500
EMERSON, RALPH WALDO
Emerson in His Journals (83) 224
EMERY, JANE
Rose Macaulay (93) 693
EMMERSON, JAMES THOMAS
Rhineland Crisis, The (78) 712
EMPSON, WILLIAM
Argufying (89) 46
ENCHI, FUMIKO
Masks (84) 514
ENDŌ, SHŪSAKU
Deep River (96) 160
Final Martyrs, The (95) 235
Samurai, The (83) 674
Scandal (89) 752
Stained Glass Elegies (86) 856
Wonderful Fool (84) 967
ENGELS, FRIEDRICH, and KARL MARX
Selected Letters (83) 722
ENGELS, JOHN
Blood Mountain (78) 117
ENRIGHT, D. J.
Alluring Problem, The (88) 11
Old Men and Comets (94) 577
ENZENSBERGER, HANS MAGNUS
Europe, Europe (90) 227
EPSTEIN, HELEN
Joe Papp (95) 396

AUTHOR INDEX

JOHANNSEN, ROBERT W.
To the Halls of the Montezumas (86) 887
JOHANSON, DONALD C., and MAITLAND A. EDEY
Lucy (82) 514
JOHNS, RICHARD, and DAVID HOLDEN
House of Saud, The (H-83) 195
JOHNSON, CHARLES
Being and Race (89) 80
Middle Passage (91) 591
Sorcerer's Apprentice, The (87) 795
JOHNSON, DAVID ALAN
Founding the Far West (93) 293
JOHNSON, DENIS
Fiskadoro (86) 279
Jesus' Son (94) 427
Resuscitation of a Hanged Man (92) 679
JOHNSON, DIANE
Dashiell Hammett (84) 212
Persian Nights (88) 683
Terrorists and Novelists (83) 783
JOHNSON, GEORGE
In the Palaces of Memory (92) 342
JOHNSON, JAMES WELDON
Selected Writings of James Weldon Johnson, Vol.
I and Vol. II, The (96) 694
JOHNSON, PAUL
Birth of the Modern, The (92) 52
History of the Jews, A (88) 392
Modern Times (H-84) 306
JOHNSON, SAMUEL
Letters of Samuel Johnson, The (93) 444
JOHNSTONE, ROBERT M., JR.
Jefferson and the Presidency (79) 331
JOLLEY, ELIZABETH
Foxybaby (86) 306
Well, The (87) 958
JONES, ARCHER
Civil War Command and Strategy (93) 153
JONES, ARCHER, RICHARD E. BERINGER,
HERMAN HATTAWAY, and WILLIAM N. STILL,
JR.
Why the South Lost the Civil War (87) 980
JONES, DAVID RICHARD
Great Directors at Work (87) 362
JONES, DOUGLAS C.
Arrest Sitting Bull (78) 72
JONES, EDWARD P.
Lost in the City (93) 491
JONES, J. SYDNEY
Hitler in Vienna, 1907-1913 (H-84) 207
JONES, JAMES
Whistle (79) 843
JONES, LOUIS B.
Ordinary Money (91) 647
Particles and Luck (94) 611
JONES, MADISON
Last Things (91) 503
JONES, PRESTON
Texas Trilogy, A (77) 812
JONES, R. V.
Wizard War, The (79) 888
JONES, STANLEY
Hazlitt (91) 381
JONES, THOM
Cold Snap (96) 124
Pugilist at Rest, The (94) 676

JONG, ERICA
Fanny (81) 309
How to Save Your Own Life (78) 413
JORDAN, HAMILTON
Crisis (H-83) 93
JORDAN, JUNE
Technical Difficulties (93) 779
Things That I Do in the Dark (78) 826
JOWITT, KEN
New World Disorder (93) 559
JUDD, ALAN
Ford Madox Ford (92) 218
JUDIS, JOHN B.
William F. Buckley, Jr. (89) 908
JUDSON, HORACE FREELAND
Eighth Day of Creation, The (80) 273
JÜNGER, ERNST
Aladdin's Problem (93) 6
JUNGK, PETER STEPHAN
Franz Werfel (91) 313
JUST, WARD
American Ambassador, The (88) 20
Jack Gance (90) 445

KADARE, ISMAIL
General of the Dead Army, The (92) 242
KADOHATA, CYNTHIA
Floating World, The (90) 273
In the Heart of the Valley of Love (93) 374
KAEL, PAULINE
Reeling (77) 662
KAFKA, FRANZ
Letters to Friends, Family, and Editors (78) 526
Letters to Ottla and the Family (83) 401
KAGAN, DONALD
On the Origins of War and the Preservation of
Peace (96) 528
KAHLO, FRIDA
Diary of Frida Kahlo, The (96) 182
KAHN, DAVID
Hitler's Spies (79) 281
KAHN, HERMAN, WILLIAM BROWN, and LEON
MARTEL
Next 200 Years, The (77) 559
KALB, MADELEINE G.
Congo Cables, The (H-83) 80
KAMIN, LEON J., R. C. LEWONTIN, and STEVEN
ROSE
Not in Our Genes (H-85) 329
KAMINER, WENDY
Women Volunteering (H-85) 516
KAMMEN, MICHAEL
Machine That Would Go of Itself, A (87) 503
Mystic Chords of Memory (92) 545
KAPLAN, BARRY JAY, and NICHOLAS MEYER
Black Orchid (78) 100
KAPLAN, FRED
Dickens (89) 241
Henry James (93) 330
Thomas Carlyle (84) 869
KAPLAN, JUSTIN
Walt Whitman (81) 883
KAPLAN, ROBERT D.
Arabists, The (94) 42
Balkan Ghosts (94) 66

987

AUTHOR INDEX

AUTHOR INDEX

AUTHOR INDEX

AUTHOR INDEX

AUTHOR INDEX

1007

AUTHOR INDEX

STEWART, JAMES B.
Den of Thieves (92) 162

STIGLER, STEPHEN
History of Statistics, The (87) 397

STILL, WILLIAM N., JR., RICHARD E.
BERINGER, HERMAN HATTAWAY, and
ARCHER JONES
Why the South Lost the Civil War (87) 980

STINCHCOMBE, WILLIAM
XYZ Affair, The (82) 972

STOCK, R. D.
Flutes of Dionysus, The (91) 304

STOCKING, GEORGE W., JR.
Victorian Anthropology (88) 928

STOCKMAN, DAVID A.
Triumph of Politics, The (87) 886

STONE, I(SIDOR) F.
Trial of Socrates, The (89) 855

STONE, NORMAN
Hitler (81) 434

STONE, ROBERT
Children of Light (87) 112
Flag for Sunrise, A (82) 284
Outerbridge Reach (93) 593

STOPPARD, TOM
Dirty Linen *and* New-Found-Land (78) 268
Night and Day (80) 586

STOREY, DAVID
Prodigal Child, A (84) 711

STOUTENBURG, ADRIEN
Land of Superior Mirages (87) 461

STOWE, REBECCA
Not the End of the World (93) 575

STRAIGHT, SUSAN
Blacker than a Thousand Midnights (95) 85

STRAND, MARK
Dark Harbor (94) 209
Selected Poems (81) 723

STRATTON, JOANNA L.
Pioneer Women (82) 642

STRAUB, PETER
Ghost Story (80) 349

STRAUSS, WILLIAM A., and LAWRENCE M.
BASKIR
Chance and Circumstance (79) 88

STROUSE, JEAN
Alice James (81) 21

STUECK, WILLIAM WHITNEY, JR.
Road to Confrontation, The (82) 690

STYRON, WILLIAM
Darkness Visible (91) 184
Sophie's Choice (80) 774
This Quiet Dust and Other Writings (83) 796

SUGDEN, JOHN
Sir Francis Drake (92) 757

SULLEROT, EVELYNE
Women on Love (81) 947

SULLIVAN, WILLIAM M., et al., editors
Habits of the Heart (86) 380

SULZBERGER, C. L.
Such a Peace (H-83) 411

SUNDQUIST, ERIC J.
To Wake the Nations (94) 806

SÜSKIND, PATRICK
Mr. Summer's Story (94) 535

SUTCH, RICHARD, and ROGER L. RANSOM
One Kind of Freedom (78) 622

SUTTER, ROBERT G.
Chinese Foreign Policy After the Cultural
Revolution, 1966-1977 (79) 108

SWANBERG, W. A.
Norman Thomas (77) 570
Whitney Father, Whitney Heiress (81) 921

SWANN, BRIAN, and ARNOLD KRUPAT, editors
I Tell You Now (88) 413

SWEET, PAUL ROBINSON
Wilhelm von Humboldt, 1767-1808 (79) 868

SWEETMAN, DAVID
Mary Renault (94) 521
Van Gogh (91) 843

SWENSON, MAY
New & Selected Things Taking Place (79) 472

SWIDLER, ANN, et al., editors
Habits of the Heart (86) 380

SWIFT, GRAHAM
Waterland (85) 1000

SWIR, ANNA
Happy as a Dog's Tail (86) 391

SYMONS, JULIAN
Critical Observations (82) 156

SZATMARY, DAVID P.
Shays' Rebellion (81) 732

SZULC, TAD
Fidel (87) 282
Illusion of Peace (79) 300

SZYMBORSKA, WISŁAWA
View with a Grain of Sand (96) 790

TAKAKI, RONALD
Different Mirror, A (94) 230
Hiroshima (96) 334
Strangers from a Different Shore (90) 772

TAKAMURA, KOTARO
Chieko's Sky (79) 105

TALBOTT, JOHN E.
War Without a Name, The (81) 896

TALBOTT, STROBE
Deadly Gambits (H-85) 110
Master of the Game, The (89) 544

TALBOTT, STROBE, and MICHAEL R.
BESCHLOSS
At the Highest Levels (94) 62

TALESE, GAY
Unto the Sons (93) 842

TAN, AMY
Hundred Secret Senses, The (96) 351
Joy Luck Club, The (90) 468
Kitchen God's Wife, The (92) 408

TANIZAKI, JUN'ICHIRŌ
Naomi (86) 640

TANNER, TONY
Jane Austen (87) 435

TARTT, DONNA
Secret History, The (93) 711

TATE, JAMES
Collected Poems, 1919-1976 (78) 188
Constant Defender (84) 202
Viper Jazz (77) 888
Worshipful Company of Fletchers (95) 895

TAUBMAN, WILLIAM
Stalin's American Policy (H-83) 400

AUTHOR INDEX

TOLAND, JOHN
  Adolf Hitler (77) 17
  Infamy (H-83) 210
  No Man's Land (81) 624
TOLKIEN, J. R. R.
  Letters of J. R. R. Tolkien, The (82) 448
  Silmarillion, The (78) 780
TOLSON, JAY
  Pilgrim in the Ruins (93) 633
TOLSTAYA, TATYANA
  On the Golden Porch (90) 637
  Sleepwalker in a Fog (93) 740
TOLSTOY, LEV
  Tolstoy's Letters, Vol. I and Vol. II (79) 754
TOMALIN, CLAIRE
  Katherine Mansfield (89) 427
  Mrs. Jordan's Profession (96) 465
TOMALIN, RUTH
  W. H. Hudson (84) 935
TOMLINSON, CHARLES
  Annunciations (91) 43
  Collected Poems (87) 151
  Door in the Wall, The (94) 244
  Jubilation (96) 403
  Return, The (88) 753
TOOLE, JOHN KENNEDY
  Confederacy of Dunces, A (81) 188
  Neon Bible, The (90) 596
TOOMER, JEAN
  Wayward and the Seeking, The (81) 904
TORREY, E. FULLER
  Roots of Treason, The (84) 751
TOTH, EMILY
  Kate Chopin (91) 475
TOTH, SUSAN ALLEN
  Blooming (82) 55
  Ivy Days (85) 466
TOTMAN, CONRAD
  Japan Before Perry (82) 408
TOURNIER, MICHEL
  Fetishist, The (85) 272
  Four Wise Men, The (83) 267
TOUVAL, SAADIA
  Peace Brokers, The (H-83) 335
TOWNSEND, KIM
  Sherwood Anderson (88) 817
TRANSTRÖMER, TOMAS
  For the Living and the Dead (96) 283
TRASK, DAVID F.
  War with Spain in 1898, The (82) 908
TREFIL, JAMES S.
  Unexpected Vista, The (H-84) 462
TREGLOWN, JEREMY
  Roald Dahl (95) 660
TREVELYAN, RALEIGH
  Rome '44 (H-83) 372
TREVOR, WILLIAM
  Beyond the Pale and Other Stories (83) 57
  Excursions in the Real World (95) 214
  Stories of William Trevor, The (84) 829
TRILLIN, CALVIN
  Remembering Denny (94) 692
  Uncivil Liberties (83) 849
  With All Disrespect (86) 950

TRILLING, LIONEL
  Last Decade, The (81) 480
  Speaking of Literature and Society (81) 764
TRISTAN, FLORA
  Flora Tristan's London Journal, 1840 (82) 288
TROGDON, WILLIAM. See HEAT-MOON,
  WILLIAM LEAST
TROYAT, HENRI
  Catherine the Great (81) 117
  Chekhov (87) 105
TRUMAN, HARRY S.
  Dear Bess (H-84) 117
TSVETAEVA, MARINA
  Art in the Light of Conscience (93) 36
TSVETAEVA, MARINA, RAINER MARIA RILKE,
  and BORIS PASTERNAK
  Letters (86) 514
TUCHMAN, BARBARA W.
  Distant Mirror, A (79) 151
  First Salute, The (89) 302
  March of Folly, The (H-85) 277
  Practicing History (82) 647
TUCKER, PAUL HAYES
  Claude Monet (96) 120
TUCKER, ROBERT W., and DAVID C.
  HENDRICKSON
  Empire of Liberty (91) 253
TUCKER, WILLIAM
  Progress and Privilege (H-83) 352
TUOHY, FRANK
  Collected Stories, The (85) 126
TURGENEV, IVAN
  Turgenev Letters (84) 879
TURNER, FREDERICK
  Beyond Geography (81) 82
TURNER, HENRY ASHBY, JR.
  German Big Business and the Rise of Hitler
  (86) 338
TURNER, MARK, and GEORGE LAKOFF
  More than Cool Reason (90) 578
TUROW, SCOTT
  Burden of Proof, The (91) 115
  Pleading Guilty (94) 636
TWAIN, MARK
  Mark Twain's Letters (89) 535
TWOMBLY, ROBERT
  Louis Sullivan (87) 499
TYLER, ANNE
  Accidental Tourist, The (86) 1
  Breathing Lessons (89) 116
  Dinner at the Homesick Restaurant (83) 194
  Ladder of Years (96) 410
  Morgan's Passing (81) 573
  Saint Maybe (92) 703
TYLER, W. T.
  Rogue's March (83) 659
TYLER-WHITTLE, MICHAEL
  Last Kaiser, The (78) 509
TYNAN, KATHLEEN
  Life of Kenneth Tynan, The (88) 482

UBALDO RIBEIRO, JOÃO
  Sergeant Getúlio (79) 672
UEDA, MAKOTO
  Bashō and His Interpreters (93) 53

AUTHOR INDEX

WAITE, ROBERT G. L.
  Psychopathic God, The (78) 677
WAKOSKI, DIANE
  Emerald City of Las Vegas, The (96) 218
  Jason the Sailor (94) 422
  Man Who Shook Hands, The (79) 414
WALCOTT, DEREK
  Arkansas Testament, The (88) 52
  Fortunate Traveller, The (82) 293
  Midsummer (85) 609
  Omeros (91) 643
  Star-Apple Kingdom, The (80) 777
WALDRON, ARTHUR
  Great Wall of China, The (91) 368
WALKER, ALICE
  Color Purple, The (83) 139
  In Search of Our Mothers' Gardens (84) 368
  Meridian (77) 501
  Possessing the Secret of Joy (93) 651
  You Can't Keep a Good Woman Down (82) 976
WALKER, MARGARET
  Richard Wright, Daemonic Genius (89) 722
WALL, STEPHEN
  Trollope (90) 827
WALLACE, ANTHONY F. C.
  St. Clair (88) 790
WALLACE, DAVID FOSTER
  Girl with Curious Hair (90) 299
WALSER, MARTIN
  No Man's Land (90) 619
WALSER, ROBERT
  Selected Stories (83) 734
WALSH, JOHN EVANGELIST
  Into My Own (89) 390
WAMBAUGH, JOSEPH
  Glitter Dome, The (82) 325
WANGERIN, WALTER, JR.
  Book of Sorrows, The (86) 77
WARD, GEOFFREY C.
  First-Class Temperament, A (90) 258
WARD, GEOFFREY C., et al.
  Civil War, The (91) 137
WARNER, MARINA
  From the Beast to the Blonde (96) 290
WARNER, ROGER, with HAING NGOR
  Haing Ngor (89) 335
WARNER, SAM BASS, JR.
  Province of Reason (H-85) 368
WARNER, SYLVIA TOWNSEND
  Letters (84) 432
  One Thing Leading to Another (85) 658
  Scenes of Childhood and Other Stories (83) 679
WARREN, EARL
  Memoirs of Earl Warren, The (78) 567
WARREN, ROBERT PENN
  Being Here (81) 76
  Now and Then (79) 501
  Rumor Verified (82) 704
  Selected Poems, 1923-1975 (78) 753
WARREN, ROSANNA
  Each Leaf Shines Separate (85) 204
WASHINGTON, GEORGE, and DAVID
  HUMPHREYS
  David Humphreys' "Life of General Washington"
    (92) 147

WASSERSTEIN, BERNARD
  Secret Lives of Trebitsch Lincoln, The (89) 762
WAT, ALEKSANDER
  Lucifer Unemployed (91) 545
  My Century (89) 571
WATKINS, PAUL
  Promise of Light, The (94) 667
  Stand Before Your God (95) 752
WATSON, RICHARD
  Philosopher's Demise, The (96) 581
WATT, IAN
  Conrad (81) 193
WAUGH, EVELYN
  Charles Ryder's Schooldays and Other Stories
    (83) 105
  Diaries of Evelyn Waugh, The (78) 258
  Essays, Articles and Reviews of Evelyn Waugh,
    The (85) 238
  Letters of Evelyn Waugh, The (81) 489
  Little Order, A (81) 517
WEART, SPENCER R.
  Nuclear Fear (89) 610
WEBB, SIDNEY, and BEATRICE POTTER WEBB
  Letters of Sidney and Beatrice Webb, The
    (79) 378
WEBER, DAVID J.
  Spanish Frontier in North America, The (93) 749
WEBER, RONALD
  Hemingway's Art of Non-Fiction (91) 386
WEBSTER, GRANT
  Republic of Letters, The (80) 705
WEEKS, EDWARD
  Writers and Friends (83) 928
WEESNER, THEODORE
  Winning the City (91) 905
WEIGL, BRUCE
  Song of Napalm (89) 803
WEIGLEY, RUSSELL F.
  Eisenhower's Lieutenants (82) 210
WEIL, JIŘÍ
  Life with a Star (90) 531
WEINBERG, ARTHUR, and LILA WEINBERG
  Clarence Darrow (81) 152
WEINBERG, GERHARD L.
  World at Arms, A (95) 885
WEINER, JONATHAN
  Beak of the Finch, The (95) 65
WEINGARTNER, JAMES J.
  Crossroads of Death (80) 162
WEINSTEIN, ALLEN
  Perjury (79) 540
WEINSTEIN, FRED
  Dynamics of Nazism, The (81) 254
WEINTRAUB, STANLEY
  Disraeli (94) 239
  London Yankees, The (80) 508
WEISS, THEODORE
  Views & Spectacles (80) 846
WELCH, DENTON
  Journals of Denton Welch, The (85) 504
WELCHMAN, GORDON
  Hut Six Story, The (H-83) 201
WELDON, FAY
  Puffball (81) 670

1015